HANDLING
YOUR OWN DOG

HANDLING
YOUR OWN
DOG
FOR SHOW, OBEDIENCE,
AND FIELD TRIALS

MARTHA COVINGTON THORNE

DOUBLEDAY & COMPANY, INC.

GARDEN CITY, NEW YORK

1979

Library of Congress Catalog Card Number: 73–81451

Library of Congress Cataloging in Publication Data

Thorne, Martha Covington.
  Handling your own dog for show, obedience, and field
trials.

  Includes index.
  1. Dogs—Showing. 2. Dog shows. 3. Dogs—
Obedience trials. 4. Field trials. 5. Dogs—Training.
I. Title.
SF425.T43   636.7'08'88

To "Pooka,"
for fifteen years best friend and perfect lady,
this book is dedicated.

She was so tiny when I first met her that she didn't cover the palm of my hand. She stayed just small enough to be able to travel around with me, wherever I went, in my handbag. She grew to be just big enough to fill my heart with love and all my hours with the sunshine and strength of her devotion.

Her many admirers in the field trial world visited her faithfully on the top of the van where she held court beneath her own little umbrella. At dog shows her devoted fans brought gifts of liver and leftovers to her red wicker basket.

By some extremely fortunate twist of fate, it was decreed that she should love me best in all the world. She was not my dog; I was her people.

It was a relationship of which I shall be proud and for which I shall be grateful all the days of my life.

Contents

PART TWO · HANDLING FOR SHOW

HANDLING
YOUR OWN DOG

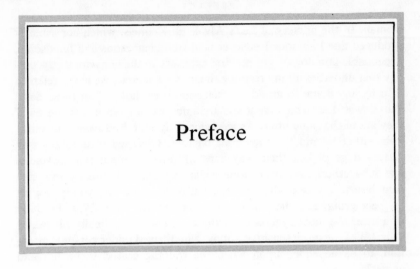

Preface

Periodically, while I was writing *Handling Your Own Dog,* I daydreamed about the time when I would have an opportunity to thank publicly those who helped me in so many different ways during the years I was putting it together.

Now that the moment of truth is here, I seem frozen as hundreds of names swirl around in my brain like a flock of sparrows who have forgotten the way back to Capistrano!

The "What if's" are nagging at me. What if I forget someone who was important? What if I thank somebody who doesn't want to be thanked? What if I inadvertently give credit for something to the wrong somebody? Then, too, where should I begin?

I guess perhaps the first thing to do is to apologize to all the people there isn't space to mention, people who helped along the way and to whom I will always be indebted. You know who you are; rest assured you are loved and appreciated.

And the second thing, I guess, is to start at the beginning.

THE MEN IN MY LIFE

Once upon a time there was a wild and beautiful three hundred acres following the shoreline of the Chesapeake Bay on the eastern shore of Maryland. The black letters on the weathered white posts at the head of the long, winding drive, said *Bolton.* And it was there at Bolton Farm, under the tutelage of J. H. Lee Fisher, that I got my first real start as a professional retriever trainer and bona fide dog woman. In the nursery of Lee's Alvaleigh Kennels, which consistently produced fine Labrador Retriever field trial champions and handsome, dependable gun dogs, I got my first exposure to the behavioral psychology that underlies all my training theories. Of course, we never referred to it by any name so grand as "behavioral psychology" in those days! But it was Lee who taught me that no two dogs are alike, even if they are of the same litter. As we twice daily exercised twenty to thirty Labs either behind the tractor or on foot, I learned to question why certain dogs picked their way carefully around unfamiliar obstacles and why others flew over stone walls and plunged directly into rip-shin briers. I was challenged constantly to study the young dog in his peer group and then on his own for the first time. Was the bully of a litter the most aggressive of the bunch when he finally hit center stage? Was the more sensitive puppy, who thrived under personal attention, to be depended upon when the training ceased to be fun and games?

It was at Alvaleigh Kennels I came to believe that while cleanliness was important, perhaps there were things more significant in the raising of good dogs than stainless-steel feed dishes, cement runs, and chain-link fencing. I learned that breeding could be easy and natural, as was whelping. We rarely used a veterinarian and so I gave injections, cut cords when necessary, removed dewclaws, poked hundreds of worm pills down hundreds of throats. And for many, many years, until he encouraged me to go off on my own, I was privileged to be a part of the realization of this man's dream—a dual-purpose Labrador who was successful both in the show ring and in the field.

Lee Fisher was the first one to believe I might someday be good enough to train and handle other people's dogs. He whistled up my first two paying dogs, Joe and Scooter, and for a long, long time all Alvaleigh puppies with field potential were sold with the understanding they had to take their Derby training with me.

Oh, the wonderful hours spent hip-deep in the Chesapeake Bay throwing bumpers for Lee's puppies; it was here I learned early on that in retriever training, when anything goes wrong, it's the bird boy's fault! There were exciting years during which I handled his Labs to derby honors in the field and championships in the ring. I was standing in the driveway at Bolton when the mailman brought me confirmation of my A.K.C. handlers license.

During those years at Bolton Farm, Lee and his wife Carol encouraged me to write the training articles which were the forerunners of the regular dog columns soon carried by all the papers on the Eastern Shore. They were behind me when I began teaching obedience classes and training clinics and handling classes, activities that added to my knowledge and led to my being instrumental in starting the James River

Retriever Club in Richmond, Virginia, and the Talbot Kennel Club in Easton, Maryland. Certainly I would never have been able to learn so much on such good dogs had it not been for J. H. Lee Fisher. So, Lee, I want you to know how deeply and truly I appreciate the uplifting memories, funny and sad alike, and the time-tested standards you insisted I set for myself. Dear, good friend, I am beholden.

On the obedience front I owe a debt of gratitude to Colonel Wilson Davis of Baltimore, Maryland, in whose advanced class I turned up one night many years ago. I had just left Boston, where I had trained with the New England Dog Training Club. My Irish Setter, "Monster," and I had done a great deal of winning in licensed obedience trials, and I considered myself quite an authority in this field. It came as a jolting shock to realize that Colonel Davis was unimpressed with me and my trophies!

Oh, I grew to hate him mightily before he made me stop parroting and start thinking for myself. I thought many times that if he asked "Why?" just once more, in response to some statement of mine about obedience training, I would walk out and never return. But I didn't, and Wilson kept heckling and nagging until I was forced to realize how little I knew.

He did his best to show me the difference between obedience training and retriever training. In those days I could never have been considered an easy pupil. I knew he had collaborated on much of the A.K.C. obedience rule book, so I stuck it out, often gracelessly, I'm afraid.

But looking back now, I know how much I learned from Wilson Davis; and I want him to know that I appreciate all he did and undid to make me a better trainer.

I was thrice blessed, you might say, for my introduction into the dog-show world came on the arm of the first professional handler I ever met, who turned out to be Arther Baines. Art and Audry steered me away from the shoals of the "hot shot" handler and into the calmer waters of the more relaxed, informal type of operation. The Baineses took time off to get away from dogs; they also took time to laugh at themselves and to enjoy their animals as individuals. If they gave their word to man or dog, it was not easily broken. They did not try to "special" dogs just because they had titles in front of their names. As devoted Irish Setter breeders they brought much to their breed that will live after them.

Until I felt qualified to evaluate dogs on my own, I sent people seeking such counsel to Art, and he always began the same way: "Do you want me to tell you what you want to hear, or do you want me to tell you the truth?" When Art realized I was determined to show dogs, he pushed me into obedience. "Learn," he said, "until you get yourself a good dog someday." When he thought I was mellowed enough, he sold me my first pup; it turned out to be a disappointment. We cried together and he replaced it. The second dog just missed greatness by a hair; also, he was utterly terrified of thunderstorms. Art made me find him a good home. Shortly after that, he began letting me handle here and there when he had conflicts.

In all the time I knew him, I never heard Art raise his voice to a client or a dog. All his dogs worshiped him in spite of the fact that he rarely remembered their names. And I have never heard anyone speak anything but good of Art Baines—a rarity in the highly competitive world of dog showing.

These, then, were the men in my life. They supported me, pushed me, advised me, corrected me—and never once suggested that I must recognize certain professional limitations because I was a woman. So much for male chauvinism in the dog world!

THE ORGANIZATIONS IN MY LIFE

Dog clubs with all their good and bad facets are a part of every doggy person's life. Over the years I have been a member of so many of these organizations that I am inclined to go along with the advice of some anonymous wag on how to belong to such clubs and still remain sane and sans ulcers: "Join, pay your dues, support the newsletter, and never under any circumstances attend a meeting if you can possibly avoid it!"

There have been groups, however, to which I have belonged and belong now that have enriched my life, expanded my knowledge of people as well as dogs, and contributed far more to me than I ever contributed to them.

Shortly after moving to Vermont, I got together a handful of retriever people and we called ourselves The Northern New England Retriever Club. We dedicated ourselves to remaining a teaching organization. Licensed trial clubs around us predicted we'd never last unless we held A.K.C.-sanctioned and -licensed trials. We stuck to our guns. We concentrated on teaching sound fundamentals of retriever training to handlers and dogs alike. The others held their licensed trials and we held training trials and competitive work trials. We invented stakes which allowed the local gun dogs nobody ever heard of to show off once a year, and so the interest in gun dogs properly trained and under control grew steadily. And for every three or four gun-dog men, one would get hooked on the idea of field trials.

We opened our trials and training sessions to all breeds of dogs that retrieved naturally. Our first puppy trial was won by a Newfoundland; one of our best graduates was a German Wire-haired Pointer.

I am proud of my association with this group of wonderful men, women, and children, and I would like to thank them all for the years they permitted me to work with them and their dogs, trying out new teaching techniques, studying hundreds of different dogs, and learning how the needs and motivations of the handler are reflected in the dog.

THE KIDS IN MY LIFE

For many years I ran my business almost entirely with the help of junior handlers who studied with me to learn how to bathe, groom, medicate, leash-break, field-train, show-handle, clean up after, discipline, soothe, and feed the dogs traveling with me. Until they grew up and went their separate ways, I depended on them as they depended upon me; neither one of us let the other down very often! Some of them lived with me for long periods of time; some joined me only on weekends and in the summers. They ranged in age from ten to twenty. They cried when I won; I cried when they lost; we all cried when it came time to say so long—we were a very wet group!

With few exceptions I enjoyed working with my kids. I loved watching them develop poise, a sense of responsibility, self-confidence. I particularly love five who will always be special to me because of the good things they did in my behalf and because of the good things they are doing with their lives now.

Gary Gerthoffer lived at Quickstep for almost three years while he became an excellent show handler and a top-drawer retriever trainer. He is now a professional handler breeding Lhasas and Labs. Duncan Stitt was my second in command for almost two years until he decided to go back to school and major in forestry. He now handles dogs in Canada and has many Best in Shows on the fine German Short Haired Pointers he breeds.

For many, many years my weekends and summers were spent shoulder to shoulder with Eileen Hackett. More daughter than student, Eileen was one of the finest handlers I ever graduated—she still is, as she wins regularly in the ring with her English Setters and Golden Retrievers when she is not studying to be a veterinarian.

Connie Holt came to me with a winning record in junior showmanship competitions and a lot of experience handling her family's Newfoundlands. It took me about five minutes to realize the great potential in this outstanding youngster. Equally at home with the bully or the pussycat, nothing ever flapped her, and her sunny disposition and willingness to work stand her in good stead today as she breeds her own Newfies, finishes them in the ring, and trains them in obedience. In her spare time she judges junior showmanship competitions all over the United States.

Sue Saddler, suitcase in one hand and Basset Hound in the other, was the oldest of my "kids." An excellent groomer of all breeds, her sweet disposition and ladylike manner were great assets to me professionally; in addition, she possesses one of the finest pair of hands I have ever watched. It was a rare thing when she didn't win with a dog I gave her; at the very least, she always made the animal look better than he was. Today she is grooming and handling professionally in Canada when she is not breeding or showing her Best-in-Show Bassets.

It is important to me that those reading this book realize how much I owe this group of young people for the years of running and lugging, the weekends of little sleep and poor food, the indoor shows when the cement floors crippled us, and the outdoor shows when we either fried in the sun or drowned in the rain. "Greater love hath . . ." etc., etc.

THE TROOPS IN MY LIFE

Early in my career as a handler I realized there were many fine dogs which deserved to be shown, whose owners weren't proficient enough to win with these animals themselves, and not wellenough endowed, financially, to hire a handler. However, they wanted to learn and were willing to work, so I began trading my services in the ring for their services at ringside. The idea was that they would work for me until they got their sea legs, then they would take over their own dogs and be on their way. But like The Man Who Came to Dinner, our relationship was so pleasant, so beneficial to us all, that they stayed on—and on, and on. Soon they were calling me "Mother," just as my kids did; not long after that they became known as "The Troops." They drove my vans, groomed and fed the dogs, took dogs from me at one ring and covered for me in another until I got there. They soothed over-anxious clients, dispensed Band-Aids and constructive criticism. They mucked out crates as cheerfully as they went to the trophy table to collect our winnings.

Over the years they have been with me, many new clients have come to me initially because they thought I was a capable handler; they stayed because, as they often remarked, "The Troops" made my setup such a pleasant, fun place to be, a completely efficient but still relaxed and friendly oasis in the confusion of the dog-show scene. And when they weren't at shows with me, they wrote or wired or called to nag about the book: How is it coming? When will it be finished?

For the past years of good-fellowship and those to come, I owe much to Joanne Martin, Maida Puterman, Geri Thompson, Pat Krause, and Giancarlo Sgarbossa.

THE COMPETITORS IN MY LIFE

Thank you, every one of you who beat me in the ring or in the field. You enabled me to keep my head screwed on straight and taught me I wasn't always 100 percent right and didn't always do a good job. You taught me early in life that the best dog doesn't always win and that purity of purpose rarely moves judges!

Those of you who were poor sports and behaved badly in public contributed in "living color" the kind of picture I never want to be a part of. When you outhandled me, however, you left me frustrated enough to experiment with different techniques. The handful of you who stood in the No. 1 spot and jumped up and down chanting, "I beat a pro! I beat a pro!" caused me to wonder if I and my buddies could possibly be responsible for such an attitude. You forced me to look at the whole picture, and I was often depressed because I didn't like what I saw.

But those of you who took the time to say something pleasant, win or lose, made me proud to be part of the competitive world of dogs and more determined than ever to do my part to give that world a good name.

THE EDITOR IN MY LIFE

As nearly as I recall, I was sidestepping my way through a crowd at a Rhodesian Ridgeback Specialty when I spied a bottle on the floor. I picked it up, inadvertently rubbing it in the process, and "Poof!"— there she was, proving that Aladdin hadn't lied about genies! I looked down at this neat little woman. She peered up at me through horn-rimmed glasses and said, "I'm Ellin Roberts. I've enjoyed your articles in the *Ridgeback News.* I'm an editor with Doubleday and I think you ought to write a book."

In the years that followed, Ellin and her husband, Dick, housed me, fed me, poked and prodded me, and never once let me entertain the thought that perhaps I might not be equal to the task ahead. When things got too hectic at the kennels, I would hitch up my little trailer, load the cats, the house plants, and my two mixed-breed pets, and take off for Woodstock, New York, where I knew I could hide away and write steadily eight hours a day, surrounded by wall-to-wall Ridgebacks.

I shall never forget the evenings we spent in the kitchen while the patient "Gus," Ellin's best friend and No. 1 Ridgeback, played guinea pig as we strove to find the best words to describe how to put a training collar on a dog. Then there was the wet, stormy night the black snake decided to curl up between me and my trailer—I don't think Dick will ever forgive me for making him move the critter! But whether the problem was book-oriented or an extraneous crisis such as my trailer jackknifed across their road, somehow we battered our way through until we finished "our" book. It is, you know, "our" book, Ellin. You make the words "thank you" seem very, very inadequate.

THE EQUALIZERS IN MY LIFE

I was showing a Staffordshire Bull Terrier and had dressed particularly carefully for the occasion. Hardly any judge ever looks at a Staffordshire, because these plain, chunky little dogs are simply not flashy enough to win against the colorful Wires, the Cairns with their personality-plus, or the artistically sculpted Kerries. Mine was a particularly fine example of the Staff breed and I was bound and determined to "get a piece" of this Terrier Group! Accordingly I had cloaked my frame in a hot-pink pantsuit with matching jewelry—even the dog's leash was color-coordinated in my effort to make canine history.

Well, I managed to get the judge's eye and keep it; "Zerox" showed like a bandit, and I avoided overhandling. Wonder of wonders, we placed fourth, which, for a Staff, is equivalent to a Group first for any other dog.

I left the ring after the pictures were taken, feeling smug as could be that my superior handling had obviously triumphed over prejudice. Suddenly a fat little lady came running up to me.

"Oh," she panted, "you handled the funny little dog that placed fourth, and I just have to tell you something!"

"The Staffordshire Bull Terrier, yes," I agreed amiably. Obviously I was now going to hear how great I was.

"I watched you all through the judging, and do you know what?" she raved on.

"No. What?" I replied in a kindly tone. The poor dear was obviously overcome by a case of hero worship. I must be patient.

"Did you know," she blurted out, "that your slacks are exactly the color of your dog's tongue?"

Then there was the retriever demonstration I was participating in at the Syracuse, New York, fairgrounds one year. We had set up a duck-hunting, husband-wife skit, and for the third time that day I had fallen overboard and allowed my dog to tow me to the edge of the pool. As I reached land, the resounding applause of the crowd encouraged me in my belief that perhaps only Helen Hayes was more talented than Martha Thorne!

My high opinion of myself was mirrored in the eyes of the twelve-year-old son of the trainer I was working with at the fair. He came running up shouting, "Oh, Mrs. Thorne, you were just great. You're the best lady dog trainer in the whole world!"

"Thank you, dear!" I purred to this obviously highly perceptive child as I squeezed the water out of my socks and emptied my boots. Just then I happened to look up and see him scratching his dear little head.

"Of course," he finished, "you're the *only* lady dog trainer I've ever seen. . . ."

These are the kinds of experiences all of us laugh over for years and years; they are also the very necessary balloon busters which keep our feet firmly on the ground. How grateful I am for the humor and the lesson in each such happening!

THE BUSY FINGERS IN MY LIFE

Every writer needs at least one typist; I had a veritable platoon of typists!

In Canada, Heather Higson spent months ignoring the impatient, unsympathetic, prodding noses of her Borzoi, who obviously had better plans for her than typing all day long. As she finished each chapter, she sealed it in germproof plastic and stacked it in her increasingly crowded freezer—mine is probably the only completely freeze-dried, antiseptic manuscript on record! As Heather typed away in her living room, not far away Diana Scanlon sat in her business office, where she sacrificed lunch hours and coffee breaks to grind out page after sparkling page.

In the United States, at the same time, Ruth Christopher was hard at work sandwiching in typing chores between a full-time job, dog-show weekends, a house full of cats, Deerhounds, and Rhodesian Ridgebacks.

Without these unselfish ladies who refused to accept a cent in exchange for their services and even brushed aside my frantic efforts to put my appreciation in words, the book you are holding would still be in grocery cartons on the floor. I can't thank them enough!

THE PHOTOGRAPHER IN MY LIFE

A number of fine amateur and professional photographers have been kind enough to contribute photos to this book.

However, most of the photo work was done by my very dear friend Pierre Wibaut of Nicolet, Quebec, Canada. Famous for his lifelike dog portraits, which resemble fine paintings more than photographs, Pierre has gone out of his way to make sure we ended up with just the photo I had in mind, whether in the field with the retrievers or in the ring with the show dogs. As one of Canada's top dog-show photographers, Pierre has never been too busy when I asked for special favors concerning photographs we needed in a hurry.

Unless another photographer's name appears with a particular photo, all pictures in this book were taken by Pierre Wibaut.

So now, as Art Baines would say, "Do you want me to tell you what you want to hear, or do you want me to tell you the truth?"

If you opt for the latter, read on.

PART ONE

THE BASICS

1

Nine Basic Principles
for Successful Handling

When the idea was first presented to me that I should write a single book encompassing my ideas on breed handling, obedience training, and field work for retrievers, I had some misgivings about my ability to tie together three such diversified fields.

I have believed for years that field, obedience, and breed were not half as far apart as most people would have you believe. I have argued with the show buff who insisted the field trainer was ruining sporting dogs by teaching them to kill, and that obedience trainers took all the spirit out of dogs so you couldn't show them. I have debated with the obedience handler who believed that show folks don't care a whit if a dog has a mind or uses it. And I have locked horns with retriever folks who leap with joy at the opportunity to ridicule show dogs as universally useless in the field. But it wasn't until I plonked myself in front of my typewriter that I truly realized how similar these three fields are when looked at from the angles of motivation and result.

Whether we are talking about a meticulously groomed Poodle sailing around the breed ring, or a burdocked, mud-spattered retriever plunging through a swamp after a crippled Mallard, or a sleek German Shepherd strutting along at heel in Novice competition, it is 100 per cent safe to assume that each handler wants his dog to work with alertness and bounce. Each would readily agree that his dog's wagging tail should proclaim to the world, "Hey, look at me! Ain't I sump'n else?"

You can call it style, flash, fire—whatever tag you put to it, we are all talking about the same thing, that elusive ingredient in any dog which, in any situation, makes the beholders' hearts beat faster. This special something which nobody has ever been able to put a name to is the elusive ingredient that gives the animal in competition the edge over his rivals who simply do what they are supposed to do, period.

Certainly a good deal of this is hereditary; but all too often the congenital "wiggle and giggle" can be quashed by foolish training and handling practices. On the other side of the coin, many dogs who start out biddable but quite wishy-washy about the whole idea of learning can be helped to develop more bounce through the application of intelligent training techniques.

Way back when I decided that I could be really happy only by "going to the dogs," I was determined to approach dog training in a businesslike manner. To that end, when I acquired my first paying client—a Chesapeake who was eating his birds—I purchased an inexpensive notebook. In it I listed in careful order the wondrous things I did, reasoning that once I sent this dog home as a useful addition to any duck blind, my training record would make it a snap to train all future retrievers by simply opening my little black book.

Well, Somebody Up There had the presence to bless my endeavors, and in time I did send the Chessie home well-trained and obedient, delivering to hand, happily convinced that kibble and hamburger were for dogs while fresh caught goose was for people. Because this dog was a success, his owner kindly recommended me for another job of training—again a retriever. I forget just what *his* problem was, but I do distinctly remember opening my notebook and proceeding to train dog No. 2 according to my laboriously recorded notes on dog No. 1. Can you guess what happened? Evidently this new pupil was uninformed as to the powers of my "system," for he simply didn't respond to my methods *at all!* Well, then, reasoned I, there must be not one but *two* ways to train a retriever. So I started a nice fresh page in my notebook and once more carefully wrote down "the other way" to train a gun dog. This job was a success also.

To make a long story short, it took this greenhorn about four dogs before it actually began to dawn on her that no notebook on earth, no published tome of sacred authorship, could ever list *the* way to train *all* dogs! Lo and behold, it seemed that, like people, dogs are individuals. No two are alike: any one can be the exception to any or every rule.

Not long ago a dear old friend was out with me when I started a green Springer puppy on his novice obedience. After watching me awhile she said quite sincerely, "Oh, my, how wonderful it must be to know just exactly what to do with each dog!" I'll never forget the look on the poor soul's face when I burst out laughing and replied, "I haven't the vaguest idea what to do with this puppy, not the vaguest. Except that I know enough to do absolutely nothing with him until I have learned what makes him tick and he learns what turns me on. We've been introduced; now we have to get to know each other."

For many years I have instantly and instinctively distrusted the "trainer" who sees a dog walk onto the training floor and proclaims immediately to all within earshot what is the matter with the animal and how to cure it. This "trainer" would never put his hands on a dog of mine—nor would his cousin, the idiot who firmly believes "all" Chesapeakes are sullen, "all" German Shepherds are one-man dogs, "all" terriers are fighters, "all" toy breeds must be handled with great delicacy, "all" giant breeds must be "settled down" immediately.

Obviously, then, the first plank in my training platform is:

1. EVERY DOG IS AN INDIVIDUAL. Take time to get to know his habits and his needs and let him learn yours before you take off in high gear toward perfection in whatever field you are training for. Approach every new beastie with an open mind. "Learn" him as you teach him. You have just as much to learn from every new dog you put your hands on as he has to learn from you. And when you get to the point where you honestly believe there is nothing more you *can* learn from your pupils, then you are useless as a trainer of any type.

2. The second training principle I believe in applies equally to all three fields: NEVER LIE TO A DOG. To put it more simply, never give a command you are not prepared to enforce; don't get him to the point where he can count on your responding to him in a reliable manner and then change your pattern so that, while he has done his part as you have taught him to do it, he is still wrong, because you *lied* to him by not being able to be depended upon.

The Show Dog

If I had a nickel for every dog brought to me because "he just won't show any animation for me in the ring!" I could retire. The moment an amateur says to me that Prince Igor of the Tundra won't bait, I become suspicious that perhaps somebody has lied to His Majesty and that is the reason "Igor isn't eager any more." This isn't always the case, of course, but more often than not what has happened is very simple. The amateur handler sees the professionals teasing dogs in the ring with bits of whatever, and they mimic what they see, but nobody bothers to explain that even the most ravenous dog isn't going to beg forever if nothing is forthcoming. Tease him, play games of hiding the bait in your hands, pretend to throw it, but frequently, in order for him to continue to enjoy the game he *must* be rewarded with a tidbit so that he is constantly reminded how yummy the reward is going to be when he finally gets it. *Dont lie to him*—it didn't work for the little boy who cried "Wolf!", and it won't work for you.

The Retriever

Perhaps the worst kind of lie is that perpetrated on an eager retriever whose handler, intentionally or unintentionally, sends him for something that is not there. At the core of the entire retrieving mystique is the psychology that the dog always goes forth when sent, *first* because his instincts make it impossible for him *not* to go and *second* because he has been conditioned to believe that at the end of his "line" will be something to retrieve—duck, goose, pheasant, evening newspaper, baby's squeaky toy, even baby. It doesn't matter *what,* but *there must be something there for him to bring back if he is sent.* This is an even more sacred precept on blind retrieves than on marks. If you doubt me, I suggest you attend a retriever trial and taste the atmosphere when, as does happen occasionally in spite of the best laid efforts of marshals and judges, the bird boy neglects to plant the blind. At the end of a tortuous course over land and through water, the dog arrives to discover there is nothing to retrieve, and *then* you will hear such screaming as you wouldn't believe. The handler is almost rabid because he has been unwittingly put in the position of lying to his dog; the bird boy is scurrying about trying to correct his mistake; judges and marshals are yelling instructions to correct the error, for they all have dogs and they all know that this one lie could see hours, weeks, months of training built on trust and truth washed down the drain. Oh, verily, this is not a happy time!

Obedience

In obedience, lack of progress is the middle name of the trainer who means what he says on Monday, Tuesday, and Wednesday, but lets it slide on Thursday because he's late to his bridge game, or his favorite television show is about to begin. As an example, take the command to come. I have always maintained that if I ever die of a coronary, it will be because I called a dog and he didn't respond. I am meticulous about this command, for to me it is one of the most important any dog should learn and lays the foundation for a mutual faith which can make training an enjoyable and far easier process for both dog and handler. To me, except in the very rare instance we will talk about later on, the word "Come!" must be synonymous with good things if it is obeyed and bad things if it is not—a simple rule which clearly defines for the dog the difference between right and wrong in a manner that even the slowest learner can easily understand. In the case of my own dogs, from infancy I never call a dog to me to punish it, to give it a pill, to cut its nails, to throw it immediately into a crate or a kennel. My dogs usually come running at my call because they have always been able to count on my being glad to see them. In my world, the word doesn't signify *the end of anything*—a romp, a retrieve, a potty break, a swim; instead, it signifies *the beginning of something else,* and they know when they hear that word, or the come whistle in the field, that when they respond I will be glad to see them.

So, as a stickler for this training premise, if a dog does *not* come when called, I would not see red, I would see scarlet! To my way of thinking, to insist on obedience to any one given command anything less than *always,* denotes the lazy teaching practices of a liar, not a trainer.

3. All of which leads us easily into the third plank in my training platform: WHENEVER POSSIBLE USE THE POSITIVE INSTEAD OF A NEGATIVE APPROACH.

Scientific research into animal behavior has proven irrefutably that dogs learn much better and faster by succeeding than by failing.

In the Field

The field dog will learn his long singles much more quickly if you start with short falls for which you can praise him honestly. Each time you run the test make sure your bird boy, or thrower, puts his bumpers in the same area, but as the dog is returning each time, *you* back up several yards so that he isn't conscious of going long distances. To him, he's simply returning to a place he's familiar with—and lo and behold, you have a 100-yard retrieve with no unsureness, no quitting, no hollering and screaming. It's like giving a child his castor oil in orange juice!

In Obedience Training

The obedience dog learning his stays will look forward to them if, in the beginning, you leave him for only thirty seconds, after which you return to him and praise him as if he had stayed a full hour while the Concorde flew over. If you leave him for unnecessarily long periods and then repeatedly jump him when he breaks a stay, you soon get more training problems than you had bargained for.

With the Show Dog

The show dog who is the happiest in the ring is the one who has been conditioned to believe that show rings are fun places. Take him to sanction matches and training classes from infancy by all means— but not to "train" him or to expect great wins; rather, your whole purpose of bringing him along as a youngster should be to make him look forward to jumping in the car and going to a building full of other noisy dogs. Leash-break him easily, taking plenty of time to laugh with him so that while his lead may not be the greatest thing he ever experienced at the outset, at least it is an exciting, fun time. If he soils the training floor or sanction ring, smooches the judge instead of posing like a statue, or jumps up on the training instructor instead of lying down, take it all with a grain of salt. Sure, this method takes longer and will be the cause of pursed lips and raised eyebrows, but when the time comes to settle down the puppy, he won't even notice it—you can take my word for it!

4. One of the most important points in using the positive approach, IS NEVER FINISH A TRAINING LESSON WITH A FAILURE. Failures are negatives, and a negative memory on Tuesday of the last thing he can remember happening on Monday is dangerous.

Show Dog

So it was only to be a fifteen-minute show training session—and then something went wrong. If you have to stay there an hour, make sure you and the dog quit with success and a succulent piece of liver.

Field Dog

After a long, especially exciting day in the field, before you load up for home, throw three or four "fun" bumpers. No sits, no stays, just "Wheeeeee!" and heave it as far as you can for him a few times— no sitting or return, no delivering, just puppy throws, and make sure the last thing you put into his crate is his *wagging* tail!

Obedience Dog

If the obedience session you thought would be a cinch proves to be frustrating, don't be afraid to back up. If he simply doesn't get "Hold it!" and you are getting tense, go back to something he does enjoy for a few minutes, something he is particularly good at. Then return to the bottleneck only long enough to make your point: *a single time for a single second.* Then forget it until tomorrow.

5. One of the easiest ways to practice the power of success instead of the discouragement of failure is to STRESS THE FUNDAMENTALS. No matter what the sport is, champions in any field are those that have a firm foundation in basics. For figure skaters, it is compulsory figures; pianists learn scales before attempting sonatas; swimmers, per-

fect breath control before attempting the English Channel. Things are no different for dogs in training.

In obedience, a dog who does not heel well off leash obviously was not ready and should be back *on* leash; the retriever who turns out to be a fabulous marker was allowed to develop this talent at short distances in easy cover before moving to triples in a corn field at two hundred yards; and the show dog who gallops around the ring stopping occasionally to wave his forelegs in the air obviously hasn't the foggiest notion of what leash-breaking involves.

There is a very real danger, however, when you start stressing fundamentals. Many trainers pound away at them so constantly that they become a bore, not a training aid, and sometimes such overemphasis can greatly alter a dog's natural enthusiasms. But when taught intelligently, fundamentals can forever be used as a training aid for the teacher and a source of renewed confidence for the dog.

6. While you are laying a firm foundation in fundamentals for the show ring, obedience competition, or field trials, it is wise to remember this equally important rule: TEACH ONLY ONE THING AT A TIME: Now before somebody starts screaming at me, I freely acknowledge that many commands are taught as a single unit—heel and sit in obedience; to go out and return fast in the field; standing still and being examined in the show ring. But these exercises are presented to the dog as one. The retriever who learns that the quicker he goes out after a bumper and gets it back to his handler, the quicker the handler will throw it for him again, isn't aware he is learning two exercises. Therefore he thrives. But try steadying a retriever at the same time you teach him to mark and see what happens . . . *chaos!* Or ask a green obedience dog to learn sit at heel and stand for examination at the same time . . . *bedlam!* And the poor show dog who is offered bait while he is being trained to move on a loose leash . . . *disaster!* One thing at a time, please, and progress will be your immediate reward.

7. Solutions to the problems that naturally arise in any type of training aren't all to be found in books, my friend (not even in *my* book!). So DON'T BE AFRAID TO EXPERIMENT with solutions that sort of pop out at you unexpectedly. Some of the little tricks I now use as naturally as breathing, occurred to me in the middle of a training session or in a sticky situation "under fire" when *nothing* seemed to be going right. Necessity is indeed the mother of invention—as long as your brainstorm works, it doesn't matter how silly you sound, look, or feel. If the dog "digs it," you've got it made. You may never use that particular ploy again; or you may incorporate it into your training routine as a regular exercise; but never sell short the ideas that "just happen."

I spent several years teaching my dogs to jump into their cages at the word "Kennel!" by thrusting them bodily into the contraption—not much to it with a Papillon, granted, but it gets right wearing with a St. Bernard! Then, by mistake one day, I threw a cookie into a crate to reward the occupant for something—and two other beasties dived in too. From that point on, I taught "Kennel!" by throwing a biscuit into the crate with the same hand and in the same motion as I issued the command. It was my sixty-year-old mother who stumbled on how to get a young Golden more excited about the pigeons he picked up with a complete lack of enthusiasm. Instead of forcing the birds on the dog as we had been doing unsuccessfully for days, she suggested making it more difficult for him to get them. We tied a dead pigeon to a length of line and hid Mother around the corner of the garage. She threw the pigeon and I sent the dog, but each time he got up to it, she would jerk the line and pull it away from him. A few lessons with Mother's reverse psychology and we had the problem licked! But the following story is one of my favorites when it comes to experimenting through necessity.

I was showing a very young St. Bernard named Hanna who had been defensive, shy, and insecure when we first met but was now taking to dog shows like the proverbial duck to water. We had shown in three indoor shows and taken the points with ease. She trotted around the ring with great glee and plenty of style, lapping up the applause which accompanied her wins. At the fourth show, since the rings inside were small and it was a lovely day in early summer, the judge decided we would move outside. That suited me perfectly, as the bigger ring would allow me to move my gallumphing charmer more freely. *But I completely forgot that Hanna had never been shown outside up to this point*—and, friend, when she hit that lovely, smelly grass, it was all over! Instead of a St. Bernard, I had an enormous, shaggy Bloodhound. I am a strong female, but I was physically unable to get her massive, stubborn head off the ground. Oh, she moved beautifully as always, but somehow a Saint Bernard digging a trench in the soft turf of a show ring with her nose leaves a lot to be desired. In spite of the U-shaped profile she presented, the judge was smitten with her and kept after me to try and get something more resembling a working breed's behavior out of my entry. "Move her again," he said, as he came back to her time after time, but nothing worked. She wouldn't trade her green grass for liver; she couldn't be threatened or cajoled; it was impossible to reason with her, as she had suddenly gone deaf. If I slowed down, she sat; if I speeded up, she galloped. My professional cool was fading and I was yearning for a two-by-four and three minutes of total darkness.

Suddenly, a little bird sailed through the ring with a shrill "Tweeeeet! Tweeeeet!" Hanna threw up her head and I didn't need further encouragement. "Tweeeeet! Tweeeeet!" I mimicked in a trembling falsetto—and it worked! "That's more like it!" the judge said. My adrenalin started to flow and, against a background of numerous spectators all of whom were literally doubled over with hysterics, Hanna and I circled the ring, her big head high in the air, and me "Tweeeeeting!" for all I was worth until, with a wave of his hand, the judge gave us the coveted points which made Hanna a Champion.

To this day, there are still people who tease me with remarks like, "Oh, there goes the 'tweeeeetest' handler we know!" So what? Look who wound up with the win!

8. Praise (reward for a job well done) and punishment (discipline for conscious, deliberate infractions of the rules) are two parts of training we will go into at great length later on. The point I would like to make now is that whether it's a field exercise, an obedience routine, or a show-handling problem, remember always to BALANCE PUNISHMENT WITH PRAISE.

These two training aids are quite useless without each other. Together, they form the patform for an intelligent training regimen which will take you far in the least possible time; each one, used only by itself, can be extremely damaging and confusing to any dog, and can waste valuable time.

The average amateur in any field of training seems to find it quite natural to correct when correction is called for. I find it amazing that green handlers seem to have this instinct almost from the beginning. But the one phrase I find myself repeating most often to training classes and field clinics alike is: "OK—the dog did it right that time, *now praise him!*" Just as correcting a dog for goofing up an exercise or a test teaches him that "wrong" is "bad," it is equally important to convince him when he performs as directed that "right" is "good." If he consistently gets jumped on when he's wrong and nothing happens when he does it correctly, you are cheating him and yourself; you are upsetting the balance that makes training logical to a dog's way of thinking. He quickly begins to hate his work, loses his edge, and winds up a confused bundle of nerves.

Housebreaking is where we most often see the error of too much punishment and not enough praise. I had a little German Shepherd brought in to me whose family insisted she could not be housebroken. After I finished quizzing them, I knew why. They spanked her and put her outside when she initialed the carpet. But nobody told her why she was outside or went with her to watch her do her thing so she could be told "Good girl!" when she did it right.

Never forget the old song that contained these wonderful lines: "When no one cares, and no one shares, what's the good of a job well done?"

Nobody—not even you, I'll bet—likes to be *always* taken for granted except when you make a mistake. Right?

9. And finally, the last but far from the least important plank in my training platform goes like this: THERE IS NOTHING QUITE SO VALUABLE AS A DAY OFF.

This rule is a sleeper. It seems almost superfluous even to bother to mention a holiday from training. But a day off can often be the best training aid in the world. Like so many other things in life, it is such a simple thing, it's difficult to take it seriously. And yet as simple as it is—perhaps *because* it is so simple—it is the hardest rule to get an inexperienced trainer to pay any attention to whatsoever. The key here is to remember Rule No. 1—*know your dog!*

When I was a beginner regularly running derby dogs at field trials, I soon learned that some of my charges needed a holiday in the middle of the week after which they should then be trained right up until I took them to line. Others, I found, worked best when drilled all week, then put "up" the day before the trial. All of us have seen the tragedy of the bright show dog steadily going downhill as he is overshown and overpushed. And how sad the obedience dog that is so overtrained he has all the style of a wet teabag.

All dogs, no matter what their needs, get a day off each week at Quickstep. They need to get away from me and I know I return to them a *much* better trainer if I can get away from them for twenty-four hours.

So, no matter what field of endeavor you are particularly interested in, these are the precepts I happen to believe in, starting with No. 2:

2. Never lie to your dog.

3. Use a positive, not a negative approach.

4. Never finish on a failure.

5. Build a firm foundation in fundamentals.

6. Teach just one thing at a time.

7. Don't be afraid to experiment.

8. Balance punishment and praise.

9. Give time off for good—or bad—behavior.

But before you apply any of the above rules, first get to know your dog and let him know what kind of a person you are. Throughout all kinds of training at any level, never lose sight of the most important precept of all:

1. Every dog is an individual.

Now, I cannot and will not promise you three five-point majors in a row on your future show champion, any more than I would be caught dead guaranteeing obedience scores of 200 every time out, or that your retriever will win his field title overnight if you read my book.

But I give you my word that if you will follow the ideas expressed above and those to follow, *using your common sense in interpreting them as you go along,* if you will use what I have learned as an aid while you train yourself to think and question and wonder every step of the way, I promise that you will wind up with a new awareness of your own mental and emotional limits as a direct result of your relationship to the stylish, happy, enthusiastic dog working beside you. Training, like the game of bridge, requires that you *play partners.*

That wonderful day when the judge's moving finger points at you for your first, precious championship point; that deep feeling of accomplishment when your obedience score sheet finally puts you in the 190s; that crisp, frosty morning when your first retriever charges back to your side with a big cock pheasant in his mouth—in each setting that magical moment can never be replaced or relived, either with that dog or with dogs to follow. Because this is the moment you realize that by working as a team, you and your dog did what you set out to do—*together.* Believe me, it's the only way to go.

2

Tools of the Trade:
Basic Equipment for All Three Fields

COLLARS AND LEADS

While dogs in obedience, field, or shows all use pretty much the same type of equipment, each classification uses that equipment a bit differently. For instance, when it comes to educating the dog to the basic commands essential to any animal, whatever his role in life will be, I prefer, as do many trainers, to use a slip (choke) collar and a six-foot training leash made of webbing or leather. If I am teaching a show dog to adapt his gait to the speed I think is best for him, I will put his collar on immediately before the training session and remove it immediately upon completion of the lesson, for a chain collar wears into the neck hair, and can leave an unsightly "chewed"—looking place even on smooth-coated dogs. The obedience dog wears his collar, usually a nylon or chain slip collar, most of his life, and most all of his commands will require the trainer to use the leash and collar simultaneously. The field dog starts out with the same "tack" and learning the same basic commands, but his trainer will get him out of his collar as soon as possible because he will be required to work most of his life with no restraint of any kind.

During many years of training all breeds of dogs, I have found that for me, at least, the chain choke collar is the best starting tool. To the many people who feel this is "cruel," I would point out that *any* kind of collar can become an instrument of torture in the hands of the wrong person. But slip collars of webbing, nylon, or chain are actually the most humane of training devices, for when properly used they apply pressure to the neck *only* when the dog needs to be corrected. In the beginning I use a chain of rather heavy links, as this does less coat damage. Once the dog is under control, I graduate to a finer chain—again for different reasons.

Never underestimate the importance of correctly fitted collars for field dogs, show dogs in training, and obedience dogs. Leather, chain, or nylon choke collars that are too large will swing back and forth against the dog's chest and could easily prove a distraction. For dogs the size of retrievers and up, take a tape measure and, going under the neck and up over the occiput (the bump on top of the dog's head), tally the number of inches you come up with, and add three. Collars that are too snug can cause problems also, for there is too little give and the animal feels he is *always* being corrected. A collar that hangs, when not in use, at just about the level of the hollow at the base of a dog's throat, is probably the right size for that dog. Those that dangle between the front legs are dangerous.

In selecting a leather, webbing, or nylon leash, make sure it is light-weight and supple. A toy breed would not only need a very slender, light leash, but you wouldn't want a great big heavy snap on it either—more than one initially eager heeler, regardless of size, has been ruined by clumsy snaps swinging in his face as he went along!

Which brings us to the subject of fasteners on the end of leashes. There are many different types and weights—all the way from the fool-proof "Seeing Eye Bolt," which is suitable only for medium-to-large breeds, to the very dangerous snap clip type, which wouldn't hold a cantankerous field mouse. Strangely, some of the most expensive leashes have snaps or bolts that could release at some unsuspecting moment, leaving you in the middle of a dandy dogfight—and nobody, for obvious reasons, wants to have a partially trained dog suddenly loose in city traffic. Even toys can wax exceedingly strong if they want to! So make certain the bolt on the end of your leash is strong, reliable, and tailored to the dog's size.

How to Put on the Training Collar

Putting a slip collar together properly, whatever material it's made of, and then getting it on the dog so that it hangs correctly, is one of life's most baffling mysteries to the amateur. So let's get this problem out of the way first. Before we even begin, put your trained dog at heel at your left side and give him the command to stay. If the dog, like you, is untrained, get a friend or helper to hold the animal in a sitting or standing position beside your left leg.

1. Holding the ring at one end of your slip collar parallel to the floor between the thumb and index finger of your left hand, allow the chain or nylon cord to hang down perpendicularly to the floor. The ring in your left hand—keep it parallel now!—is called the "dead"

ring, and the rest of the collar should hang freely from that side of it which is closest to the palm of your left hand.

2. With your right hand take hold of the chain or nylon cord close up to the "dead" ring and start pushing the chain up through the "dead" ring, which must still be kept parallel to the floor.

3. Keep threading the surplus collar up through the "dead ring" with your right hand, letting the surplus flop over the side until the ring on the far end of the chain comes up against the "dead" ring and you can "thread" no more. This second ring is the "live" ring.

4. Now with your right-hand palm toward you, take hold of the end of the loop of chain opposite the rings so that the loop rests across the inside of your fingers. Release your left hand so that both the live and dead rings, lying against each other, are hanging down toward the floor from the collar, suspended in your right hand. *Keep your right palm toward you at all times.*

5. Being very careful not to turn your hand either in or out—palm toward you, remember—bend down and slide the collar over the dog's head so that the live and dead rings are under his chin. Now let go of the collar, get your leash and attach it to the live ring.

6. Adjust the collar so that the rings lie against the right side of the dog's neck between him and your left leg. If you pull up on the "live ring" you will notice that the dead ring will slide away from you across the dog's neck. A slip (choke) collar will not tighten and release easily or automatically unless it is worn in this manner.

Now for a warning on the use of slip collars: *Never, under any circumstances,* should any dog be allowed to run free, unsupervised, wearing a slip collar. Should the loose ring get snared by something, the dog could easily choke himself to death while attempting to get free. And *never, under any circumstances,* should any dog be left alone in car or crate with a choke collar on, especially with his lead still attached. One loop around the steering column and it's all over.

There is a way to lock chain collars so that if you must leave the chain on your dog when you are not around, he is perfectly safe; should he become caught on something, his struggles would simply allow him to pull it over his head and he would be free.

To "lock" a chain collar is a simple matter. Stretch it out so it is hanging free of knots or tangles. Now take both rings and hold them together as one. Take the doubled end of the chain and drop it through both rings at the same time, pulling it tight. When you slip the collar over the dog's head you will find it will not slide an inch in either direction, no matter which of the two rings you tug on.

There is a collar being manufactured that combines the usefulness of a buckle-type collar when the dog is running free and the control of a slip or choke collar when the dog is in training. This is a chain collar with a ring in one end, a small, strong, harness-type leash snap fastened to the other, and a free ring loose along the chain between the two ends. When the dog is unsupervised, he wears the collar safely if the snap at one end is fastened to the ring at the other. When in training, the collar may be converted without removing it from the dog by fastening the snap into the free ring, which then becomes the dead ring, and the ring at the end of the collar, fastened to your leash, becomes the live ring. Make sure when you pull up on your leash that the dead ring slides away from you across the dog's neck.

These convenient dual-purpose collars can be found in some hardware stores, once in a while the pet section of grocery stores, and can be ordered from any of the supply sources listed in dog publications and outdoor magazines such as *Field and Stream* or *Sports Afield.*

In the Show Ring

Once a dog is trained for the show ring, once you can count on him to gait and stand reliably, his leash and collar assume a mostly cosmetic role. Nothing would look worse on a sleek Doberman Pinscher, for instance, than a heavy clunky collar marring the lines of his proud, slender neck. You will find that most of the smooth, sharp-looking breeds—Dobes, Boxers, Danes, Weimaraners, Rhodesian Ridgebacks— are exhibited on a very fine chain choke collar attached to a standard fiber, grosgrain, or nylon leash. This is particularly true of dogs that move on a loose leash, heads carrred high. This type of unobtrusive equipment says to the judge, "See, my dog doesn't need my assistance to move—he flies on his own." I personally don't like heavy leashes and collars on *any* animal in the ring, and I use the light chain with very fine leash combination on everything from Miniature Pinschers to Irish Wolfhounds.

For heavier breeds, which often require that they be moved on a tight or semitight leash because of a disinclination to carry their heads as high as we humans feel they should, the handler may turn to the popular "french choke," which also comes in chain, grosgrain, or nylon. Again, we are discussing what the well-dressed canine wears in the ring only, and again I like to see the equipment as lightweight and "refined looking" as possible.

The "french choke" is really two chains. The first goes under the neck and about halfway up the side of the throat on both sides. A small ring is attached to either end of this first chain. The second chain is fed through these small rings and is brought up over the head where both ends meet in one slightly larger ring to which your leash is attached. This kind of collar gives excellent support to heavy-headed dogs without cutting off the dog's wind supply. You will find this type of collar a boon in presenting properly those breeds whose standards call for very "wet" heads (i.e., heads having a great deal of loose skin)— Basset Hounds and Bloodhounds, for instance. Because it does not rub on itself, it does little damage to full coats. It is also helpful on hairy breeds which favor a massive top skull, such as St. Bernards and Newfoundlands, for the skin of the backskull can be pulled forward, the collar then tightened, and you can maintain the illusion of a more impressively headed dog than perhaps you actually have on the end of the leash.

Many handlers and owners prefer to show all their dogs on a one-piece noose-type lead. The well-known Resco show leash (a trade name which has become a descriptive word) is the most popular and comes in two widths and a variety of colors. Constructed of a stiffish lightweight tube webbing, it limbers up with frequent use. These leashes have a loop at one end for the human (a loop which should *never* be slipped over the hand or wrist) and a larger loop at the other end to accommodate the dog. It is secured by a tiny brass clip which can be easily slipped back and forth, so that one Resco fits all breeds and sizes of dogs. The nylon duplicates of the Resco come in even more widths and colors, as do the grosgrain slips, and all three are washable by machine or by hand, though the nylon will eventually get fuzzy and unsightly. Many people prefer to combine a fine choke collar with a resco slipped through the live ring.

One of the prime advantages in using this kind of leash is that, once it is in place, it stays put. Undesirable extra skin in the throat area can be neatly and easily hidden from sight with this kind of leash, and it rarely tangles in the longer hair of breeds such as Lhasa Apsos or Old English Sheepdogs.

The use of a leash that is a different color from your dog has a great effect on how he appears to those looking at him from a distance. It makes little difference what color leash and/or collar you use with a fuzzy dog on which the lead appears to rise suddenly from the back of his neck—the rest of it is invisible, of course, buried in the coat. But when showing a black Labrador Retriever it would be wise to study the dog's head and neck before using a white leash. For the white, slashing across the black, will cut the neck in two. If the dog is short in neck, he will look even shorter in that area if you use a white leash. Black would be best in this instance. If, on the other hand, he has a lovely neck and a handsome head, then use a white leash, by all means—it will frame that head and draw it to everyone's attention. Again, if the neck is too long, a leash and/or collar of a different color will help give the illusion of shortness. It's much the same thing as smart overweight ladies who know enough to look for dresses with vertical rather than circular stripes.

It is also possible to obtain a one-piece nylon or grosgrain leash which is a french choke in a single unit with a leash of the same material. Again, all these are washable and available in various widths and lengths. Pet stores sometimes carry all the above-described leashes and collars, although the average pet-store clerks have no real knowledge of their correct use or fitting. If you can attend a licensed dog show, you are most likely to be able to fill your needs there, and you will enjoy a wide variety to choose from and assistance from concessionaires who specialize in dog-show and obedience equipment and know what they are talking about. Or you can secure such show equipment by sending away to mail-order houses, as suggested earlier.

GROOMING TOOLS AND GEAR FOR THE SHOW DOG

Grooming the show dog requires tools perhaps unnecessary to retrievers or the Obedience dog. In fact, these tools vary from breed to breed, as different dogs require different grooming devices. If you are buying a Poodle, for instance, you will have to invest in electric clippers and take lessons from a professional groomer, your breeder, or some experienced amateur; you might even want to attend classes at a grooming

Short leads, long leads, slip leads, snap leashes, plain choke (or chain) collars, and the so-called "french choke" (third chain collar from the right, which is also available in nylon)—the variety of tack for the show dog is endless. But whatever you choose as comfortable for you to handle and flattering to your dog, note that they are all fine, narrow leashes and collars. Heavy or coarse leashes and collars make the show dog look exactly the same way—heavy and coarse!

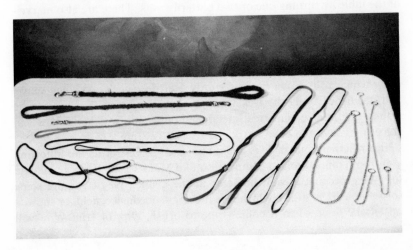

school, many of which advertise in dog magazines and telephone books. There are also excellent charts and how-to grooming books available.

Electric clippers would not be essential to the owner of a Pekingese. In fact, the mere sound of electric clippers at any range closer than three miles has been known to cause even the bravest Peke-person to fall over in a dead faint! Setters need towels and blanket pins. Maltese equipment includes tiny hair bows and a long bone knitting needle.

Whatever your breed of dog or the field of endeavor you are most interested in, all dogs must be groomed and bathed sometime in their lives. Because the show dogs of the world involve more complicated techniques and tools than their obedient or retrieving brothers, we ask that our trainers pick from the following list of "equipment" the items that fit their needs and use them as directed.

Nail clippers, of either the guillotine or pincher type, are high on the list. These days some people file nails; if this procedure appeals to you, you'll need a large dog nail file or a special toenail attachment which fits onto the motor unit of your electric clippers.

Spray bottles may be purchased, or you can use your old Fantastik or Windex containers.

You'll need a crate, about which we'll go into detail later, and a grooming table. A piece of heavy plywood covered with rubber matting and cut to fit the top of your crate makes an inexpensive unit, easily transportable. Or, you may purchase a professional-sized standard table with restraining arm. The latter is a removable length of metal tubing with an adjustable noose affixed to one end which, when clamped onto or screwed into your grooming table or top, permits you to anchor your dog during grooming, leaving both your hands free and your mind at peace. Clever home carpenters can make these tables themselves. Commercially, you have your choice of inexpensive, lightweight models or fancy tables with extra legs which allow you to regulate the height of the table by turning one or two butterfly nuts. There are also marvelous creations that, while not readily portable, operate on the principle of a barber's chair; you may move them from side to side, raise or lower them with a touch of your toe. For my money, the best buy in grooming tables is the one that, when folded flat, becomes a convenient dolly which rolls along on four sturdy built-in wheels. At some shows and obedience trials the trek from the parking lot to the ring can be a long one, and commerical metal or homemade wooden dollies can sometimes save the day.

But whether your table is going to spend the rest of its life following you from competition to competition like Mary's little lamb, or remain in your grooming area at home or in the kennel, please acquire some sort of nonslip platform which gets the dog—obedience, field, or show—up off the floor when it comes time to brush, clip, or trim. You will avoid backaches as you bend over dogs on the floor, and precious minutes are foolishly wasted crawling around on your hands and knees teaching bad habits to any animal. The floor is Fido's realm; he's at home in it and you can rarely stump him in his own backyard, so to speak. Get him up on your level and he's in your world. You can see him more realistically as he's at eye level, and he remains quieter because he's the least little bit unsure of himself; that's the kind of edge no intelligent person should dismiss lightly!

You will also need a small-sized medium-fine comb which can be used for touch-ups in the ring and can be carried in a pocket. As you get more experienced, you will probably require different kinds and lengths of combs. Brushes are varied in size and shape too, and experience is invaluable here, as they range from wire to rubber to fiber, and all have specific uses. Invaluable to the short-coated dog's owner is the mitt or grooming glove. On one side are fiber or metal bristles; on the other is corduroy or some soft material. These mitts slip over either hand, and some buckle securely so that, whether you are brushing with one side or buffing with the other, your hand fits the contours of the dog's body.

A "must" is some commerical powdered coagulant in case you "nick" a toenail just prior to ring time, as well as scissors and thinning shears—the latter being scissors with little teeth in either one or both blades, allowing you to trim without leaving hack marks in the coat. Most people keep their own dog's teeth tartar-free by using a tool similar to a small file, also available from mail-order houses. Eventually, you will have to purchase or make a benching chain and collar, for benched shows are not quite a thing of the past, as we'll see anon. To restrain a dog on the bench your best bet is a sturdy rolled-leather buckle collar and a length of smooth chain with leash snaps on either end. Most exhibitors these days use their crates on their bench area at dog shows, but in the topsy-turvy world of dog shows it's best to be prepared.

By now it should have become abundantly clear that you will need some sort of container in which to carry all these impedimenta. Zippered flight bags such as those given out by commercial airlines are excellent. To save time and endless hassle, your kit bag, of whatever kind you choose, can be packed with whatever you might need at shows (as opposed to the equipment you'll want at home), and then stashed in the closet ready for the weekends. If you need more room than is afforded by the zipper bag, try a medium-sized tool or bait box; those with the divided, swing-up trays are especially easy to keep organized. Or you can hold out for a "genuine, real live" tack box, of wood or metal, with rods for storing leashes and trays for scissors and combs. Again, these may be homemade, or procured through dog-show concessionaires or mail-order houses.

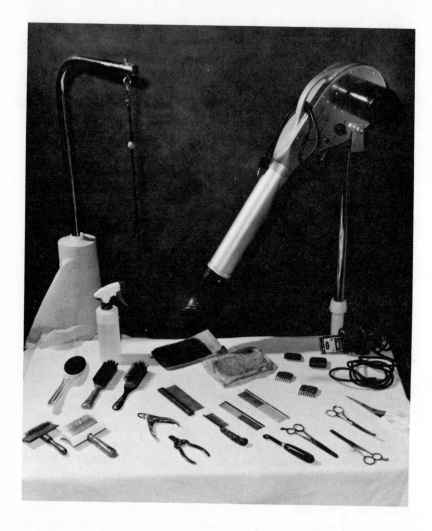

Whether your dog is in obedience, breed classes, field trials or a beloved family pet, there is a wide variety of tools available to help you keep him well-groomed.

The floor model blow drier in the background can be a great help, but a hand drier such as you use yourself is often more than adequate. Electric clippers are a must for breeds such as Poodles, but hand clippers like a barber uses on the back of your neck may be all your particular breed needs. You can see the different kinds of brushes, grooming mitts, combs, toenail clippers, and scissors it is possible to obtain through pet supply stores or concessionnaires at dog shows. The spray bottle can be purchased also—or you can use the one you bought at the market full of cleaning detergent.

Dog-show people are good folks who will lend you just about anything you need at a dog show—except their dog, their grooming equipment, or their P.H.A. pins. In order to protect the investment you have made in equipment, mark your combs and brushes with colored plastic tape or nail polish, or buy an inexpensive printing tape machine and put your name on everything. To your tack box or kit bag affix your name, address, telephone number, and those two golden words which usually insure return of lost things: REWARD OFFERED. Being a "self-contained unit" at a dog show will, I assure you, have great bearing on your peace of mind and the state of your nerves. So here is a list of what *else* to include in your tack box and/or the back of the family wagon. I'm fairly sure it's complete, as I drew it up by sitting down beside my own adored, battered tack box and removing things one at a time while making a list as I went along. Many of these things will not be completely explained until later, so have faith! This list is composed of items carried *in addition* to the grooming tools your particular breed needs.

Glycerine suppositories.   Aspirin.
Book matches.   Rubbing alcohol and cotton.
Heavy-duty, wide rubber bands. Tweezers.
Thumbtacks.

Copy of A.K.C. and/or C.K.C. rules and regulations for dog shows.

Copy or photostat of your dog's registration, inoculation for distemper, hepatitis, leptospirosis and rabies; duplicate of the entries you made out for the weekend.

Pens and/or pencils.   Business cards.

"Mad Money"—a secret cache of about five dollars which you never remove from the tack box and can therefore count on in emergencies. (A note to Canadians: U.S. coins will work in Canadian pay phones, but Canadian change is no good in U.S. phones, so keep some change in your tack box.

Bait—be it a squeaky mouse, a rubber ball, or liver. (Liver or uncanned dog meat should always travel in an ice chest.)

Can opener and dog food, food and water dishes, mixing spoon.

Water from home. (Nothing causes loose staols in dogs faster than changes of water; carry your own whenever possible.)

Dog-show ticket, judging schedule. (Your dog-show ticket and/or exhibitor's pass should travel in your purse or pocket.)

Kleenex.   Paper towels.   Needle and thread.

Vaseline (for last-minute shine to toenails and nose).

Rug, mattress, or blanket for crate or benching stall. Never use newspaper in a clean show-dog's crate, as the newsprint comes off all over the dog—a spotless white dog can be ruined in just a few minutes of lying on newspaper.

Wipe-ettes (tradename)—commercially treated cleaning cloths for people.

Magic Brush (tradename)—takes hairs off trousers and skirts, and dandruff off dry coats; available in dime and drug stores.

Identification label for your crate so that if, in your absence, your dog should need help of some kind, people will know to whom he belongs.

Kaopectate or Pepto-Bismol for upset tummies of people or dogs— tablet form makes dosing easy for dogs *or* people.

Alka-Seltzer—for the morning after your Best-in-Show party the night before.

Grooming sprays, designed specifically for coat control, conditioning, and extra luster. These go into your spray bottle if they are not already in spray containers. But see recent A.K.C. rules regarding use at shows.

Insecticide sprays—such as flea sprays (those that will not interfere with the appearance of the show dog in the ring) and sprays to disinfect or to deter flies and mosquitoes on people and dogs.

First-aid kit—this can contain, in the main, items that would be useful in the treatment of either dog or handler, and might include in addition to the regular tape, bandages, and Band-Aids, ammonia capsules, hydrogen peroxide (excellent for painlessly disinfecting and bubbling-out impurities in open wounds), cotton, gauze pads, antihistamine (which is useful to man for colds and may be used by both man and dog against systemic reactions to wasp or bee stings), and whatever preparation you "swear by" when hot spots (or eczema) rears its ugly head.

Exercise pen—when traveling, many people prefer portable pens to walking dogs for miles on a leash, over very suspect ground, while the dog locates just the right place to relieve himself. These pens can also double as deluxe "apartments," as we will see later on.

Small portable cooler—this important piece of equipment can preserve your bait for several days, as well as dog meat, ice water, soft drinks or juice for you (the latter may sometimes be available only *miles* away at the other end of the show grounds, and at prohibitive prices.

Towels—wet and dry. In the summer, never leave the garage without at least two wet towels buried under the ice in your cooler. If you don't wet the towels first, the ice will stick to them. Heat kills fast, and more than one dog has been saved by using wet towels. (In a later chapter we will go into the problems presented by hot weather, discussing in detail the dangers confronting your dog in the heat and how to prepare yourself against them and prevent disaster.) Throw in a couple of old sheets or an old blanket that can be turned into shade-makers, wet or dry.

Newspapers—to be used as flooring for indoor exercise pens. If you have dogs with white on them, use plain newsprint which can usually be purchased from your local paper in sheets or on rollers.

Foul-weather gear—you have finally "arrived" when you have figured out that the only safe way to handle the problem of weather is to keep two extra sweaters, a pair of high black "muck'n" boots, two pairs of heavy socks, a pair of cotton work pants, a pair of gloves, and a rain slicker or cape with hood all rolled neatly together in a storage space in the car. Raincoats can cut a cold wind as capably as they turn the rain. I have been at summer shows where it actually snowed, while bone-chilling sleet is not unusual at early-spring or late-fall outdoor shows.

NECESSARIES FOR THE OBEDIENCE DOG

Putting together a tack box full of equipment for the obedience hopeful is not quite as complicated as packing for his brother who is going to be shown for conformation. Since the obedience dog is going to be judged on how he works, not on how he looks, your cosmetology can be done at home the day before or the morning prior to the obedience trial. If you want to give him a quick, last-minute slick-up, one brush won't take up much room.

Of course he will wear his training collar and leash to and from the trial, and most of the time during. I do not in any way mean to imply that because he is going "just in obedience" (I hate that phrase! It sounds so demeaning!), your dog shouldn't look neat and clean. He most certainly should. But carrying a lot of grooming equipment around is not necessary.

Your obedience kit should contain the items from the foregoing list which obviously would be of use to you or the dog at shows. Once you get to the Open work, you'll have to make room for your dumbbell; if you climb as high as Utility, then you'll need scent articles. Many trainers who must travel long distances and stay overnight to compete in obedience favor two sets of articles—one to practice with at the motel the night before the competition, and one to use when the big moment arrives.

The wooden dumbbell that dogs are required to retrieve in Open A and B can be purchased or homemade. When picking or designing one, remember to tailor it to the size of your dog's muzzle. The bar by which he picks it up should be high enough off the ground so that he does not stub the end of his nose when retrieving, and it should be wide enough so that he can comfortably hold and carry it without it pinching the outside of his lips or flews. Weight is important too— three or four pounds might not throw a Mastiff, but I'd hate to see a Chihuahua try to return it to hand! Proper weight has a lot to do

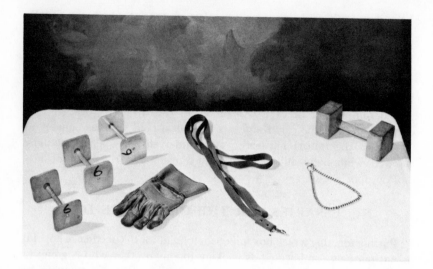

The obedience dog needs less equipment than either the show dog or retriever. From left to right are scent-discrimination articles (leather, metal, and wood), gloves for directional retrieving, six-foot training leash, chain collar, and wooden dumbbell—that's all there is.

Solid, broad, and bar practice jumps are handy when you get into more advanced training such as Open and Utility. Directions for making these are in both the Canadian and American Obedience Rule Books. Add a basket or kit bag to carry your training equipment and you're ready to travel.

with your ability to place it fairly when you throw it also, so pay a lot of attention to the "heft" of that dumbbell.

In securing scent-discrimination articles for Utility work, you can spend a small fortune on made-to-order sets complete with well-ventilated carrying cases and individualized tongs for picking up and spacing articles. Or you can make them at home for next to nothing. You'll *need* five leather, five wood, and five metal; but while you're at it, make six of each just to be safe. Again, the size of the mouth of the dog has a lot to do with your creativity. My first Utility dog was an Irish Setter. I used small frozen orange juice cans with both ends removed for the metal articles, and to keep them from rolling, I flattened one side of each can with my trusty hammer. For wood, I "liberated" five blocks from my niece's alphabet blocks—she had lost all but eight anyway. For leather, I chopped up a perfectly good leather belt of my first husband's into six pieces about five inches long. I then stapled the two ends of each together to make six tear-shaped articles. I used a wicker mending basket to carry them.

You will also need three plain white cotton work gloves for the directed retrieving exercise. These may be purchased very inexpensively at any hardware, dime, or paint store. I suggest you purchase three sets, so that you have extras in case of loss.

If you can afford a custom-made set of jumps for Open work, fine— bar, high, and broad jumps are included and painted white, just like the ones you'll be using at the trials. If you want to build your own, the A.K.C. rule book gives plans for a complete set. If you are even poorer than that, use white adhesive to wrap a four-foot length of broomstick doweling and balance it on two chairs for the bar jump; leave it where it is and drape a white sheet over it for the high jump. For the broad jump, hunt up a length of broken snow fencing (try the local dump) and support it on Coke cans. It won't be white, but you could tape or paint the slats for very little money. Your A.K.C. rule book will tell you the heights and distances your dog will ultimately be called upon to negotiate.

One of the nicest things about obedience is that it is one phase of dog training which can be kept within the reach of most pocketbooks from start to finish, because the necessary equipment is sensible and easily made by hand in most cases.

FIELD EQUIPMENT

Unfortunately, this is not true of equipment necessary to put a retriever in the field. Oh, you can keep costs down with a firm do-it-yourself approach, especially up through the Derby stage (i.e., until a dog is two years of age). This early part of a pup's training requires largely marking work, and while shotguns, live shackled game, and freshly shot birds must of course be included, corners can be cut by using training pistols or shotguns with blank "popper" loads and substituting dead, frozen birds much of the time. But as the dog gets more advanced, so does the equipment needed, and costs are admittedly higher than in either of the other two fields with which we are dealing here. Moreover, the equipment is the most uniquely specialized that can be imagined.

At the kindergarten level we need puppy bumpers; then we graduate to regular-sized bumpers, and sooner or later to enormous, heavy ones. Bumpers are in reality boat fenders, also referred to as dummies. They come in canvas-covered down or kapok; some are even stuffed with bits of foam rubber. Whatever the innards, they have to float, and they are the object a dog learns to look for in his retrieving from the cradle to the grave. Nowadays your best buy in training dummies is hard molded plastic, which doesn't rot with repeated dunkings, and is difficult for even an aggressive dog to put holes in when he gets overly excited. Since few dogs really like the feel of plastic in their mouths, I have a habit of covering the center area with strips cut from old burlap grain sacks and binding these in place with electrician's tape. This used to be in the interests of economy as well as making the bumpers more palatable, and I liberated old "granny sack bags" from farmers who left them lying around to mildew in the cow shed. Today, my friend, those same bags are worth sixty cents apiece to the farmer and he isn't about to let them go for less than that! With a short length of rope fastened into the grommet on one end of the bumper, you have a long-lasting, easily thrown training tool which, because of its addional heft, is somewhat easier to place than the canvas ones.

The average trainer with one young dog would need at least twelve bumpers in his bag. Any less and he'd be spending valuable training time running bumpers back and forth to the bird boys instead of setting up tests.

Which brings us to the most important piece of a field trainer's "equipment"—his bird boy. Bird boys may be young or old, male or female, skinny or fat, black or white or any other hue—but they are truly the one piece of equipment the field trainer cannot get along without. There are substitutes for just about any other training aid, but even the "Retriever Trainer" device, which permits the isolated trainer to "throw" several hundred yards and gives a shot to boot, is no substitute for the long-suffering bird boy. You can start a puppy by throwing for him yourself, but as soon as possible he must stop looking to you for his birds and start focusing straight ahead, the direction from whence come all birds at trials and in the shooting field. Because bird boys are going to be a great part of the rest of his life, he must see them constantly and get used to them.

The six-foot training leash and properly fitted chain choke collar are the basis of a dog's life as a retriever. You will also need a thirty-foot check line, blank pistols, and blank ammunition; shotguns and popper loads (blank loads in 12-gauge shell casings), boats, oars, decoys, training blinds, handling boards, sending lines, and the feathers from the birds your neighbor kills, feathers you allow to dry and then tape to bumpers as a "training bridge" between retrieving only bumpers and retrieving birds.

The minute a person gets into retrievers his entire dentition changes, for from that moment on he spends a large part of his life with an orange (Roy Gonia) or black (Acme) plastic whistle stuck in his mouth. The Gonia is a more fluid whistle which travels far and which I prefer because I can say more with it. But *no* whistle can sound as low-down dirty as an Acme. For this reason you will usually see at least one of each strung around a trainer's neck. Several whistles are usually necessary as irate, frustrated retrieverites have been known to blow out the side of one in a heated moment.

A short traffic lead, which is little more than a leash handle with a snap at one end, can be fastened to a belt loop when not in use, and doubles nicely as a field whip when corporal punishment becomes necessary.

But if your dog has any fire at all, face up to it, sooner or later you will need to "get in on him," and nothing beats a standard field-trainer's whip. At a distance you might possibly want to use a CO^2 cartridge pistol to slow a dog down or get his attention when he thinks he is physically and mentally beyond your reach.

Birds—that is, live pigeons, ducks, geese, and pheasants—are extremely costly and difficult to come by. But to produce a well-rounded field trial dog or shooting companion, they are a must. Pigeons and ducks, if properly handled, can be shackled and used over and over again. This cuts costs somewhat. But pheasants don't keep well and their nervous systems are so delicate that I have seen them drop dead of fright at the mere approach of a dog. They must be thrown and shot for the dog to retrieve, but after a shoot-to-kill session birds still in good condition can be wrapped in plastic and put in the freezer to be thawed and reused several times. Again, this represents a saving to the retriever trainer.

Clothes for the obedience and the show-dog handler are quite simple and inexpensive. But reliably waterproof rain gear comes high, and the field trainer has to have it. Insulated boots are a necessity, again waterproof. White handling jackets or rain suits are also a must for "blinds" in all weather *except* snow. When directing a dog against a snowy background, the white handling jacket is useless, so a second jacket of some dark color is vital, as are gloves to protect against freezing rain. To facilitate the handling of slippery, wet birds at fall and winter training sessions or trials, I like to think I "invented" one solution. I experimented for some time before I settled on a combination of Playtex rubber gloves (the kind recommended to housewives for protecting delicate skin from harsh detergents) over thin cotton liners, those light-weight brown woven cotton gloves you can purchase at hardware stores to "line" the heavier ones linemen and construction workers use. I found they kept my hands reasonably warm, absolutely dry, and gave me a safe, nonskid grip when getting cold, slippery, live or dead game out of a dog's mouth without dropping it, thereby costing precious points.

Much of the equipment listed above as training tools will be carried

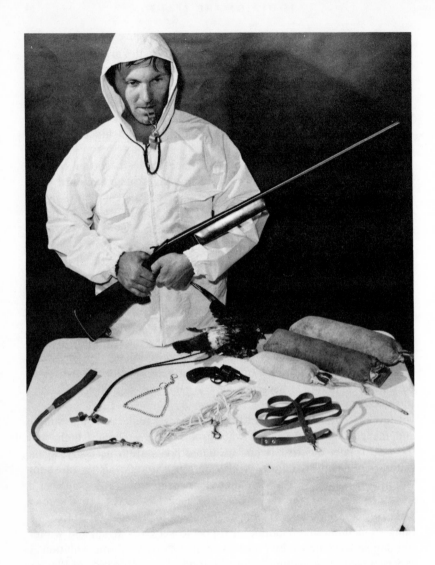

If we had added the live game, burlap bags, training boats, and decoys to this picture we'd have lost the table! Field dogs require lots of equipment. You'll invent a number of training aids yourself as you go along. But these we have lined up on the table are the basics. They include a short "traffic" leash which can double as a field whip, lanyard and two whistles, chain training collars, sending line, six-foot check leash, thirty-foot check line, different sizes and weights of training bumpers of canvas or plastic, training (or blank) pistol, dead game, white jacket or shirt for handling from a distance, and the ever-present shotgun.

right along with you when attending work trials or licensed field trials. We'll go into just what you take and why in our field-trial chapter, but the final piece of field equipment I want to include right here goes whither thou goest *at all times,* especially during the fall, winter, and early-spring months. Many years ago, Lady Conners who had Goldens, (in England) and was one of the world's most devoted breeders and handlers of field trial dogs, was asked by what standards she judged fellow trainers, amateur and professional alike. She is purported to have answered promptly and decisively, "Dry bedding! I cannot imagine how the owner or the handler of a dog who has worked his heart out all day through skim ice or freezing water, or has run a trial in sleet or rain, can take to his own bed without first making sure his dog has been supplied with a warm meal and fresh, dry bedding." Me either, Lady Conners! Arthritis of some sort or another comes early, sometimes, to these hard-going, great-hearted animals. The least we can do is provide them with a warm, dry place to sleep after a day's work. So-called "brite straw" is excellent; so are cedar *curls,* which do not pack down like shavings. For one whole season I swore by poultry bedding—a powdered substance comprised of the dried stalks of sugar cane; its advantage is that for some reason the top layer always stays dry. But whatever you use, carry it with you even if you have to lash it to the roof of the car. *And don't forget your own water!*

THE SECRET INGREDIENT

It is quite obvious, I'm sure, that each of the three fields we are exploring demands it's own set of tools to get the job done. In recent years ultrasonic radio transmitters have been pressed into use in all three fields, as have electric collars, CO^2 cartridge pistols, and electric leashes. I have used all these devices, both in the field and in the home, and with a particular case boasting unique requirements, *any training aid is justified if it is used in an intelligent manner.*

The tragedy is, I think, that as our equipment gets better and better, more and more refined, there are those who try to *substitute* mechanized training aids for sound training in fundamentals. When this happens, a dog is lost. When you get to the place in life where you forget that a man's best piece of training equipment in the field, in the ring, or in obedience, is the invisible cord that ties the man and his dog together with the privileges of love and the dignity of respect, then you have ceased to be a trainer or a handler. You have lost the "secret indgredient" of training, and with it the joy and enormous pride that a man and his dog should always be able to share together, as with no one else on earth, at the conclusion of tough job well done.

CRATES, CAGES, AND BARRIERS

Very few of us forget that dogs are carnivores, lovers of meat. But when it comes to using crates (or cages, if you prefer), many dog lovers throw up their hands in horror, forgetting that, like their antecedents the fox and the wolf, dogs are den creatures. Far from being cruel to the dog, providing him with his own crate is in reality a kindness, as it gives him a portable "den" in which he can, as he has done for hundreds of years, hide his treasures, turn his back on the world, and just plain claim a corner all his own for a midday snooze.

I can imagine going through the rest of my life without indoor plumbing, using margarine instead of butter and safety pins instead of buttons. I don't cherish the thought, but I could probably survive without lipstick or instant coffee. But *never,* in my *wildest* dreams, could I envision my future existence in dogs without at least one crate. The mere suggestion would proabably throw me into a state of shock from which I might never recover!

Already I can hear the "uninitiated" reader mumbling in his beard, "Oh Lord, she's one of those!" Of *course* I am—you would be too if you had seen as many examples as I have of the worthiness of crates— or kennels, or cages, if you prefer.

In my early days I too was hesitant to sing their praises. The first instance I can remember when their purpose was clearly brought home to me involved a black Lab belonging to a friend of mine, Nelson Sills. After a day of field training in Maryland, Nelson bid me a fond adieu and put his dog in its crate on the back seat of his convertible and drove home to Delaware. I later learned that in trying to avoid an oncoming car which was clearly out of control, Nelson swerved across the median and rolled his convertible over three times. They took *him* off to the hospital. But while the cloth top of the automobile was completely demolished, the crate with the dog still in it wasn't even dented, and the *animal* sustained, at worst, a few days of stiffness. Now, of course, even if this dog had only been somebody's beloved little mixed breed, this was still an occasion for rejoicing. I think, however, it's rather interesting to note that this particular "pet" later went by the title "Fld. and Amateur Fld. Ch. Dutchmoor's Black Mood," winner of the Amateur National Retriever trials.

A story with a less happy outcome involves a fellow handler who once celebrated finishing the title on his very own Gordon Setter bitch by letting her ride home on the seat between him and his wife. The granting of such "special permission" resulted in his beloved new champion flying full force into the windshield when the driver was forced to slam on his brakes without warning. The setter broke her neck and died in her owners' arms!

Horrible tales? Horrible, indeed! Yet at every show I see cars arriving with clusters of dog heads sticking out of the windows, leashes snaggled every which way around feet and legs. These drivers are obviously exponents of the "crates are cruel" school of thought. If you are at all faint of heart, please do not try to imagine what would happen if those cars should have to stop suddenly, or if other vehicles sideswiped them in traffic. Even if nothing at all went wrong, most dogs have sensitive ears, and a constant rush of air into the ear canal could cause serious problems. In emergency situations the dog uses his crate to brace himself much as you and I use our seat belts.

It's almost impossible to give you an idea of what you should pay for a crate. Sometimes you can get plastic shipping crates from airlines for a very small outlay. In most cases you'll pay more for a crate from the average dog-show concessionaire than you would by dealing directly with the company. Sometimes you can pick up secondhand ones from handlers or by keeping a close eye on the classified section of your local newspaper. If you have a "kennel account" with some mail-order houses, you get a discount on such things. You can often save money by making your own dog container—sometimes it works just the opposite.

I feel that crates are so important to your dog's well-being and your peace of mind, that what should be taken into consideration here is not what it would cost you *to have one,* but what it might cost you because you *didn't have one!*

For about two years I handled a handsome Mastiff whose owner went into a purple tirade at the mere thought the dog might be mentioned in the same breath as the word "crate." He purchased a lavish mobile home with air conditioning so the animal would be cool until he had to go into the ring—except that every moment the dog was in the mobile home, the owner was holding court, inviting endless streams of friends to come and see his marvelous dog—and, "Sit up for the people, doggy," and, "Move over here so they can see you better, doggy," etc., etc. The dog was a reluctant showman to begin with, but no amount of lectures or explanations would convince the gentleman that his dog was worn out from socializing, that he needed time to have a nice, long snooze in the shade. At one particularly torrid show, the owner left the dog with me while I worked on him on the grooming table, and when he came back he was immediately upset because he couldn't find his pride and joy. "I'm done with him," I explained, "so he went where he could find some peace and quiet." The owner's face fell when he saw the dog in the large wire grooming crate, only his tail hanging

out the open door, proving *I* hadn't put him there, but that the dog
had sought this refuge himself. Furthermore, no amount of coaxing
would get him out. He was having a lovely nap and he stayed put. I
don't think the owner ever forgave me because his dog and I knew
more about the animal's needs than *he* did!

Quite aside from their safety factor is the utilitarian function that
crates fulfill. From the beginning of a puppy's life, his crate can mean
the difference between adjustment and maladjustment in a strange new
world. Since most kennels use crates with puppies, moving a puppy
to another kennel makes the change only a small one if he goes from
one familiar enclosure to another. If he is to go from a kennel to a
home, the security of the same type of place he has known since his
eyes opened can make those hectic first days less traumatic. Small children love new puppies, but their judgment about leaving them alone
is questionable, and every puppy needs time to himself. So when you
put the puppy in his "house" two or three times a day, you are not
locking him away from the children—you are keeping the little darlings
from driving *him* bananas, and honestly now, doesn't he have some
rights, too?

Dogs trained to eat in their crates seldom produce feeding problems
for their owners. There is little distraction in a crate, the food is in
close proximity, and you can see exactly what each is or is not eating.

Dogs housebroken from a crate are subjected to less confusion and
trauma—and their owners ditto. The average dog hates to soil his place
of rest—his "den." Given half a chance, he'll keep his crate clean,
and if he is never allowed to mess in the house, he will never *learn*
to mess in the house. The trick is to make sure he is taken out of his
crate *often* to where it is fine and good for him to relieve himself.

In all the instances listed above you may notice that we have applied
Ye Olde Positive Approach, for *every single instance in which a dog
is confined to a crate is a pleasant one!* He can see better and is safer
riding in a crate. Since most dogs quickly learn to love to travel, his
crate means that exciting old "bye-bye" time. He gets fed in his crate,
and to eat is to be happy. He has a safe, warm, dry, *private* place of
his own for napping and sleeping, where undisturbed he has his dreams
of cats he can chase forever and knuckle bones that never go sour.

The point I am trying to make is that the only reason a dog should
be unhappy in a crate is that some idiot human made the crate a *bad*
thing, sometimes *dirty,* or *lonely,* or *unpleasant.*

New "victims" coming to slave at Quickstep start out as cleaner-
upper people, and they are usually amazed at how little time we spend
cleaning crates and cages—with rare exceptions, *we don't have dirty
crates.* Just a few minutes' effort first thing in the morning to get every-

body out bright and early and *clean* saves hours on your knees and elbows.

A good way to spoil a dog's appreciation of a crate is to squash him into one that is too small. On the other hand, a crate too large for him can be just as dangerous while traveling as no crate at all. The average St. Bernard or Newfoundland is too cramped in the ordinary, large-sized, slant-fronted wire crate. I want a dog this size to be able to lie down without having to double anything under him if he doesn't want to. If he can't quite sit up straight, that's OK, because I want him to lie down in transit most of the time. And he'll probably elect to curl up like a kitten in one corner of the thing anyway. But if he *wants* to stretch out, I happen to think it's necessary for his proper movement later on that he be able to do so.

Very few wagons are big enough to accommodate the larger-sized wire crates needed by the giant breeds, so wire barriers in the back of the car are the best bet until you get to a show where you can set up your collapsible wire crate.

Certain breeds such as Borzoi and Deerhounds, with their particular spring over the loin, will eventually also be happy in these large wire crates. But getting that arched back through a small doorway in the beginning is often nigh impossible. Since the wire crates that are big enough for these breeds come with rather small doors, I "doctor" a few of these cages myself so that the entire end opens until the dog gets used to the fact that his crate is his castle. Then I secure that end once more and use the regular entrance.

At indoor or outdoor shows where the exhibitor may set up at leisure wherever it seems convenient, a standard exercise pen telescoped to the size needed for particularly large dogs is an excellent solution. Most of the giant breeds are not eager jumpers to begin with, and even the more agile can be taught that beautiful word "No!" A rug or blanket spread on the ground or floor inside the pen transforms it quickly into a luxurious enclosure which keeps Ch. Fitasafiddle out of the deviled eggs at lunchtime. Exercise pens come in many different heights, and their circumferences are easily altered by adding or removing a panel with screwdriver and pliers. Some pens come knocked down into single sections you connect with metal rods threaded through eyes at the end of each panel, or with leash snaps more easily hooked and unhooked. It is even possible to get tops for some models and tie-down stakes which may be driven into the ground like tent pegs for added security.

In fact, these pens are so easily portable that they are used for a variety of purposes I'm sure the manufacturer never thought of; it's not at all unusual to see such a structure turned into a ringside playpen for junior, who lies on his blanket and plays with his teething ring while a canine buddy or two does the baby-sitting!

Which brings us to the introduction of an older dog to the joys and beauty of crates and cages after he has spent years never knowing such things existed. Here is where most of your "See, my dog just *hates* crates!" refrains begin. The poor animal whose family is going away for a while delivers him to a strange kennel to be locked away from them for—who knows how long? Perhaps forever, as far as he is concerned. He disapproves of the entire procedure to begin with, he doesn't like the noise, the kids are crying, some strange creature is trying to be nice by shoving a dog cookie in his face—and then they expect him to duck his head and happily flump through a tiny opening into a wire box from which there is obviously no escape. You gotta be kidding! Again, it isn't the crate, it's the people.

That's why we put newcomers of this caliber right out into the big back yard at Quickstep until their family is gone, things are quieted down a bit, and the dog has his feet under him. Then when crate time comes, we put him down in front of it quietly with a nice new bone in front of him. A *pleasant* experience. We let him gnaw on it awhile and then throw it into the crate. Usually he trots in after it. If this does *not* work, whoever is in charge calls an assistant and together they gently *back the dog into the box.* It is absolutely amazing how many dogs that tend to throw tantrums at going in headfirst (some widdle, some defecate, some scream, some bite) will permit themselves to be gently but firmly inched into a crate *backwards* with little or no resistance. In fact, a Deerhound friend of mine who was especially leery of cages, now happily inhabits his own—but he enters all by himself, *hind end first!*

Crates serve an almost endless variety of purposes and are found in a wide variety of circumstances wherever you go. Many years ago when I was doing a great deal of professional retriever training on the eastern shore of Maryland, a friend from Baltimore brought me an interesting problem. He had a young dog rar'n to go; duck season was coming on and he was anxious to use the pup; the animal was the precocious type that could use the experience. On the other hand, I didn't want to steady him yet, as it would have to be a rush job and I was against this. The owner had shooting rights on a small island just offshore adjacent to the south end of the Bay Bridge, a small piece of land with nothing and no one else near, so he felt it was an ideal place to start the puppy off; still, neither of us wanted him dashing about the island out of control. We put our craniums together and took the man's wire crate which he used in the automobile, and removed the back end panel. We then made a wooden frame for the panel so it could be slid up and down guillotine fashion. Then we collapsed the crate, tied it to the back of our motorboat, and floated it out to the island. In just a few hours we had erected a very informal brush blind out of swamp grass, cattails and stovepipe wire. We planted the crate smack dab in the middle of our shooting man's Hilton, with the open backside facing the water. With wire we laced our guillotine door in place, brushing the whole thing over except for the small wire panel in the front of the wooden frame. Then we ran a piece of clothesline back into the blind so all we had to do was pull it to release the dog. The front of the crate was in the blind, and when the youngster brought his birds into his "hideout" we dropped the sliding door to keep him in place and simply took the bird from him by opening the regular front, and praising him highly. At the risk of ruining the gun-dog profession of any number of us trainers, may I say that it took no time at all for the dog to catch on, and soon we never used the drop door at all—the dog would lie in his nest, warm and dry and hidden from the wildfowl, dashing out to bring us our booty as they hit the water; after bringing it in his "den" he would turn around, lie down, and wait for the next flight. We never got soaked, he was never out of control, and the only birds we missed were the ones we didn't lead enough. By the time the season was over, we had a steady, well-adjusted gun dog of which any man would be proud, and nobody ever laid a hand on him!

In quite another atmosphere I learned of the architectural advantages of crates when a very wealthy client of mine asked me to tea in her ancestral home, again on Maryland's eastern shore. A waterfront mansion, it was full of small-sized champions gamboling thither and yon. We laughed and played with the dogs awhile, but finally enough was enough. My hostess clapped her hands and said, "OK, kids, naptime!" Whereupon they all dived for different end tables or occasional stands, all of which I suddenly saw had been turned into crates by the addition of charming ornamental radiator grills. She snapped shut small doors behind them, and peace and quiet reigned in the only French-provincial "kennel" I have entered to this day!

Young, precocious dogs which must be left alone in homes and apartments for several hours at a time learn positive patterns of good behavior when they are left in crates with toys and a bowl of water instead of being turned loose to chew on the sofa legs or demolish Aunt Agatha's needlepoint sewing basket.

In the early days of breeding inexperienced dogs or bitches, placing the bride and bridegroom side by side in wire crates for a while each day does wonders for the attitudes of both.

And poor eaters are a cinch to hoodwink by placing the skinny-minny in the center one of three wire crates, flanking him with two dogs which eat as if it were going out of style, not nasty, growly eaters, now, just positive, cheerful chewers. After placing the reluctant model in the center, I put the marvelous munchers on either side of him and feed them about a quarter of what they usually get, ignoring the middleman entirely. After I have fed the rest of the kennel, I come back and give my end men the rest of their food, also slipping in a small plate of nummies to the poor eater immediately after the other two are working on their victuals again. Generally it works beautifully, and we keep the problem dog in this kind of a setup until he is attacking his food with relish. Poorly started eaters, I have sometimes found, must be fed this way all their lives.

Immediately after worming any group of dogs, I put each one in a crate alone for about twenty minutes to make sure they retain their pills. Nothing is more maddening than to carefully pop those slippery footballs down the throats of six puppies—and then return to the pen a half hour later to discover a single lone, squashed capsule. Who up-chucked? The puppies, you can bet, are *not* talking! So one poor little guy still has a tummy full of enemies.

We could go on for pages and pages about when and where to use a crate, but the list of uses is limited only by your own imagination! Let's talk for a moment about what kind of crates to use. Any dog owner, professional or amateur, has a wide variety to choose from.

Shipping crates come in wood, aluminum, and plastic. When choosing one, be sure it is lightweight but sturdy, and is big enough, has sides constructed in such a way that nothing can be pushed tight against it rendering the air holes useless and the dog airless; and the more air holes the better. Fancy, expensive models have removable floors and feed and water dishes which can be put in without opening the crate door. But at the risk of upsetting your conviction that your pet is going to be watered, fed, and changed in transit, I must assure you that ninety-nine and forty-four one hundredths per cent of the time, it just isn't true, Magee. So why pay for useless extras? In fact, the shipping of precious, valuable dogs is, in my humble estimation, so slipshod that I will do almost anything rather than ship! But when I *have* to, I prefer a wood or plastic crate, well-ventilated, with a safety-proof lock. Open wire cages for shipping are dangerous, drafty, and invite bitten fingers and crushed paws and toes.

For everyday use, I personally do not favor closed crates, though the vast majority of professional handlers do. The dogs cannot see and are therefore quieter; the handlers have to worry less about drafts and inquisitive fingers, and fussy coats which tangle and bruise easily are maintained more readily in wooden or plastic boxes. I, too, have several crates of this type for dogs that I feel do better in them. But on the whole, I like my dogs to be able to look around at the world both while they are moving and when they are waiting to be shown. I do not like to leave dogs benched on chains, because I cannot check on them often enough to insure my peace of mind that they are not tangled or choking, so wire crates are vital for benched shows. I worry much more about heat prostration in closed crates in the summer, particulary with the giant breeds, than I do about draft on the wee ones in the winter—it's very simple to buy or make plastic or canvas covers for any model of wire cage. Certainly, in many instances wooden closed crates are necessary, and most of the time they are easier on the handler—but I've never been a real believer that the "easier" way is always the "best" way, and I'm afraid that I'm eternally more concerned about the comfort of my dogs, mentally and physically, than about myself or my help. I have found that dogs which are at all inclined to be nervous or shy do much better in open wire crates when they can see that all the noise, the hustle and bustle, is not going to harm them. Sensitive dogs have a great inclination to run and hide, and nice dark "dens" are great to hide in. But the longer they hide, the more they get used to hiding, and, my oh my, what problems this presents!

The field trainer set has long known the value of crating dogs—to keep them under control, to help them save their nervous energy for the field, and to protect the inside of station wagons whose beading and upholstery are among the young retriever's favorite fare. Why spank or whip the puppy for chewing on the inside of your van when he hears the guns go off? He's excited, he wants to go. Isn't that what you paid your money for? Why penalize him for having the spirit you coveted when you picked him out? And why let him get hysterical, hot, and worn out in an almost closed vehicle when he could stay cool and be saving all that drive for the "line"? Frankly, I get nervous every time I see a young retriever snoozing quietly in the front seat of a car while the birds are flying and the guns are blasting. If he's calm and bored now, what's going to happen when I cast him off in the field?

Also, there is a rhythm to running field dogs: frankly, I feel that if more obedience people would recognize and use the same rhythm, their dogs could benefit too. First the dog exercises (goes to the bathroom) and is watered; then he jumps into his crate, the door is shut, and he is alone; then the door is opened, he is exercised, he goes to the line, does his thing, is exercised, watered, returned to his box. He is alone. Now I'm out and I work; now I'm in and I rest. It is a pattern retrievers start when, as baby puppies, they are lifted into crates to travel and to sleep. When the handler opens the door of the crate, good things happen. When that cage door is closed, there is nothing to think about until it is opened again.

When using open wire crates for field trial dogs, either buy or make covers for them, or don't park your wagon anywhere near the line if you have an average, anxious dog to run. You may have to walk a little further, but get him away from the excitement and the confusion where he *can* rest, unless he is the exception who needs to be psyched up. Remember that even in the winter his sporting blood keeps him hotter, physically, than house pets, so don't be afraid to leave the windows down a bit even in cold weather.

Obedience dogs do much better in the ring if they are not dragged around all day before they compete. It discourages me that so many obedience-o-philes don't understand the difference between leaving their dogs on the "down-stay" and leaving them to relax and forget all tensions. Over and over I get the argument: "I never use a crate—my dog is trained to stay." Tell me, gentle reader, how would you like to have to be a perfect lady or gentleman twenty-four hours of the day, seven days a week! No wonder some obedience dogs wind up behaving like poorly oiled toys! *Purchase a crate.* When you get to the show, find your ring, set up your crate in a quiet corner, put the dog inside and *go away.* You will be absolutely *amazed* at how glad he is to see you upon your return, and at what a spirited performance you get in the ring. You will be delighted at the improvement and sharpness of your own handling too. I have puzzled for years over why most lady obedience handlers drag their dogs to the ladies room with them. I made the mistake of asking once and was haughtily informed, "I wouldn't leave my dog alone anywhere!" This kind of answer always tempts me to say, "Then, what's the point of training him, lady?" But I have no desire to die young. What people like this mean, I'm convinced, is that this is the way *they* want to do things. Never mind the fact that just once, for ten beautiful minutes, the *poor dog* might like to get *away from everybody!*

In discussing the types of crates, let's not forget the homemade job. Some of the most gorgeous crates I ever gazed upon were turned out by do-it-yourself-ers. If you are not handy with tools and find the cost of most crates does not lie within the boundaries of your budget, I can heartily recommend a certain model of back-yard incinerator available at most hardware stores. Depending on the size you want, they range in price from about six to twelve dollars. They are rectangular in shape and made of sturdy wire in squares a little larger than so-called hardware cloth or rat wire. The whole top end opens and may be easily secured with a couple of harness snaps. Lay the incinerator on its side, put in a rug or pad, and you are all set!

Speaking of harness snaps brings us to one more important point which should not be overlooked: the fact that your dog might turn out to be a canine Houdini. Take it from a gal who has chased too many liberty-bound doggies any number of miles on the dead run: no matter what the advertisements say, there is no such thing as a one hundred per cent escape-proof animal container! Wooden crates with twist latches through which you may thread a safety catch are probably the "fool-proofest." But dogs have been known to chew out of wooden, wire, metal, and plastic à la the busy beaver. Long-suffering dedicated inventors have, no doubt, gone to their graves crushed in body and spirit by the knowledge that no matter how clever a fastener they dreamed up, *somewhere, sometime, sooner or later* along would come a dog who was just a little more clever!

So be like the farmer who held his pants up with a belt and suspenders—don't take any chances. Purchase a couple of heavy-duty harness snaps (leash snaps, if you prefer to call them that) and position them so that they fasten the top and bottom outer corners of the door to the door edging on any crate you build or buy. To make sure these don't get lost, attach them to the crate with short lengths of plumber's chain.

Then you're all set. The day there comes along a dog that can reach around from the *inside* and unsnap a harness catch on the *outside,* is the day I am going out of dogs into breeding that particular brand of tropical fish one of which eats the other whenever two of them meet. At least you don't have to chase them!

What should you put in a crate under a dog? Oh boy, what *not* to put in a crate under a dog!

We have discussed bedding for field trial dogs earlier; I will add here that in the hottest months they are better off, and far cooler, with nothing under them except the metal crate pans or pieces of fiberboard or plywood. Because of their great desire to work, except in rare, rare instances, I have found it was a total waste of money to put foam-rubber pads or special mattresses under working retrievers. A shredding machine has nothing on what one of these dogs can do to such!

Obedience and show dogs do very well on a nice cotton throw rug or a foam-rubber pad. Ordinary human-type mattress pads come in all sizes and can easily be folded or cut down, wash well and are comfy, as are the mats professional movers use to protect fine furniture. Some dogs set great store by their individual blankets, especially the tinier breeds; but I have known Wolfhounds and Boxers which also craved their "security blankets" when the lights were turned out. Clean newspaper is absorbent and cheap, but newsprint comes off and you'll save yourself lots of work by not using it where white or light coats are concerned.

I have found that large, white disposable shower mats, such as those supplied to hotels and hospitals, can be purchased in wholesale lots and work beautifully. More cheaply and sometimes more conveniently procured is plain blank newsprint which comes in heavy rolls before it is used; or your local paper sometimes will sell those sheets spit out by the printing machine. White shelf paper does well for toy breeds, as do those soft, disposable crib liners. Old sheets and bedspreads are naturals, and commercial cushions made to fit the crates are available, as are washable crate covers.

By trial and error, you can determine what is best for your dog's comfort, but please don't turn into one of those creatures who put the dog in his crate with nothing between him and the wire! How would you like to sleep in your bed if somebody put a length of two-by-two galvanized fencing over the bottom sheet?

The main thing is to pick a sturdy wire crate, if that is the type you decide upon, collapsible, with not too much space between the wire and with no wide opening under the door sill.

Finally, just as it is truly said that "guns don't kill, people do," so it is wise to remember that crates aren't bad, only some of the ways some of the people use them are. There is nothing sadder than a big dog squished in a small crate—unless it is an ashamed, lonesome puppy huddled in the back of a filthy, wet cage.

There is nothing nicer to see than clean, well-ventilated dogs riding safely in their family's cars, protected by their crates just as their family is protected by safety belts.

And please don't misunderstand me—I don't for a minute believe that any dog that isn't crate-trained is miserable, and any owner who doesn't believe in crates is an unmitigated brute. There are dogs that board in my home that have never seen the inside of a crate and probably never will—not that they would have shriveled up and blown away if exposed to one, but simply because they are that especially nice kind of dog who melts into your home and your heart leaving few waves or ripples.

My host, while I was writing this chapter, was asked to give me suggestions and ideas after he had read it. "Well," he grumbled good-naturedly, "it's very informative and I learned a lot, but you aren't gonna convert *me* to crates!" Fine and dandy—he is absolutely and totally convinced that Deerhounds *have* to sleep in the bedroom with their masters or they will ultimately perish. It's *his* bedroom! He has four Deerhounds in there now and is determined that the female he is going to breed will have her puppies in his bedroom and that her puppies will all sleep in his bedroom. Well, as I said earlier, it's *his* bedroom!

I just feel, very strongly, that no matter what you are discussing in the world of dogs, it is vital to get the facts straight! I have given you the facts—now it's up to you to make your *own* decision.

What you do with your own dogs is your business, of course. But when you are taking care of other people's animals, then you have an even deeper responsibility to take *no chances whatsoever.* The few handlers who still go to shows with a car full of loose dogs and who tie them to fences and picnic tables and then go off and show other dogs, are asking for trouble—and usually get it. Most tied dogs become belligerent, and if a wandering bully comes along and his foolish, irresponsible owner isn't paying attention, fights occur and valuable dogs are sometimes permanently injured. I have clients who insist on bringing their dogs to the shows, on staying with them, and then taking them home when finished. Fine—as long as you plan to be responsible for that animal, we'll live happily ever after. To paraphrase Voltaire—I don't agree with what you feel, but I will defend to the death your right to have those feelings.

FOR YOU

Finally, unless you are of the Amazon ilk, sooner or later you'll want to sit down. Whoever first invented the chair must have been a lovely person. Maybe his progeny did lean to obese derrières, but I'll bet their inner souls were at peace!

At field trials chairs are never provided. Literature on dog shows and obedience trials which instructs you not to bring chairs because they will be provided is not quite accurate. Oh yes, the club did indeed rent chairs—and the first one hundred people who got there are sitting on them by the time you arrive. You and the other eight hundred exhibitors are left to lean on a loved one, fall exhausted on ground rarely covered with anything softer than broken glass or peastone, or you can balance like storks, first on your left pedal extremity, then on your right.

Folding chairs are so very popular and so often forgotten that you are wise to print your name and address on them in large colorful letters. In the field, chairs with slender legs have a tendency to disappear from sight the moment you sit on them if the ground is at all wet. Shooting sticks have a guard to prevent you from slipping completely from view, but they can get a bit tippy when you get a bit the same way. And they are no good on blacktop, wood, or cement. The best folding chair in the field is the kind that rests on lengths of tubing, not legs.

One of the best bets all around are campstools, which are stowed easily and are good indoors or out. Some come with compartments for carrying dog-show catalogues and/or field glasses.

Whatever you choose, bring something along to allow you to get off your feet for a few moments whenever a precious break comes your way!

PART TWO

HANDLING FOR SHOW

1
Picking a Show Puppy

Picking a puppy as a potential show dog is probably one of the most difficult tasks in the world. As carefully as it is done, with great attention to the breed standard, conformation, movement, coat, type, intelligence, and personality; as diligently as we study sire and dam and their parents and their parents; as much advice as we ask for and get from experienced handlers, breeders, and other owners—it is still a gamble at best. But I do *not* think the solution is, as one prominent dog authority suggests, to locate a well-bred litter, close your eyes, and grab!

When it comes to acquiring a dog for show purposes, I personally happen to be against purchasing *very* young puppies. The most reputable breeder in the world can give you a pup which, at eight weeks, he highly recommends as being a potential titlist in at least four countries—and at six months he'll be the first to say those awful words, "Sell it as a pet!"

It just didn't turn out, and this is nobody's fault. In our human world many beautiful babies mature into plain Janes, and many ugly ducklings "down the block" turn into raving beauties. Certainly a pedigree peppered with champion ancestors is important, but unfortunately, good pedigrees, proper diet, social exposure during puppyhood, and plenty of intelligently supervised exercise guarantee absolutely nothing. These things are simply the sum and substance of the best ammunition we have to work with.

WHAT'S IN A HUNCH?

One of the greatest mistakes people make, I believe, is in not trusting their hunches. Not long ago, a friend who became quite an experienced breeder of Rhodesian Ridgebacks saw a puppy she had sold as a pet from one of the earliest litters. I was with her and considered the dog absolutely gorgeous. "Oh, damn!" she said, "I had a hunch about that pup from the moment she was born. She was the smartest, the quickest, the easiest to get weaned. But the books tell you that's not how to pick a puppy, so I went by the book. The pup I picked to keep isn't half as good as this one. Oh, double damn!"

There are all sorts of good rules to follow when picking a puppy, but never forget that for every rule in the world there is at *least* one exception. In fact, those "exceptions" go Best in Show every month of the year, which is why I, for one, am violently opposed to breeders who stoutly maintain they can tell the good puppies in a litter while they are still crawling out of the sack and who therefore "put down" everything that doesn't look like a future champion at birth. But first things first. Before we can pick our *pup,* we must first decide on a *breed.*

WHAT IS BEST FOR YOU?

In selecting just the right breed from which to pick your show puppy, there are many factors to consider, factors that are *much* more important than the fact that you simply adore the Poodle down the street.

First of all is cost. Rare indeed is the show prospect you can purchase for less than three hundred dollars at eight weeks. But breeds enjoying a current popularity may cost twice that much.

How much land do you control? How big is your home or lot? Large breeds such as St. Bernards and Irish Wolfhounds cannot develop correctly in small, confining setups, no matter what some breeders will tell you. They also take a lot of time because they must be exercised "by hand," and if you are not a physically active person, this would present a real hardship to both you and this kind of dog.

Small and medium-sized dogs are hardy, don't take an abnormal amount of exercise and time (although every dog requires some), and generally fit in well in a normal family situation. But *toy breeds* are not generally a good idea if you have very small children, who do not always understand about gentle handling. Young, poorly disciplined children can cause a toy breed to become quite nasty and defensive because the whole world is bigger than he is.

How much time do you spend on your own toilette? Do you like fooling with your hair or your children's? If the answer is no, you probably wouldn't be happy for very long with any of the breeds that demand constant, complicated grooming. The Old English Sheepdog, for instance, from puppyhood to the grave, needs daily brushing, which starts at about fifteen minutes with the puppy coat and ends up demanding as much as three hours each day if the adult dog develops the kind of coat he simply must have to win in top competition. Afghans require a lot of time-consuming personal attention. Poodles that are going to be shown must be kept in one of two show clips once they are out of puppy coat; you could do it yourself, in which case you will need electric clippers, or you could have it done by a professional handler or poodle groomer. This costs quite a bit of money. A word of warning: veterinarians and their assistants do not know how to groom show dogs! It is doubtful if your friendly neighborhood pet shop does, either. Such dogs cannot be turned out a few days before a show— they must spend their entire lives, *as long as they are going to be showing,* in the same condition as when you take them into the ring. So before you decide on a breed, be sure you are fully aware of what you are getting into. It could boil down to "a nice place to visit but I wouldn't want to live there!"

White dogs are nice—have you the time to keep them clean and to use special preparations which prevent the permanent staining of that white coat from tears or the processes of elimination?

Breeds that have their ears cut at various ages—Boxers, Doberman Pinschers, Great Danes—often require hours and hours of taping and massaging to make sure the ears stand properly by the time they are ready to show. Also, there is some degree of gamble here, as every so often the ears *don't* do what they are supposed to in spite of taping and care, and you wind up not being able to show your show dog.

You might also wish to consider the advantages of an older puppy. Your family or job responsibilities might make puppy schooling or prolonged housebreaking very inconvenient. Then, too, you might want to get into the show ring without waiting months for a puppy to be eligible. As we said earlier, wee puppies are a gamble. The risk of failure is greatly reduced when you purchase a slightly older puppy, say between eight and eleven months. He isn't mature either, by a long shot, but he's mature *enough* for you to be able to see now exactly what he will be later. He may need filling out and road work but there will be fewer surprises of a kind no one really needs in life. You'll spend a little more initially, but in the long run you could conceivably save a whole lot of money.

The time you will have to spend in housebreaking, socializing, and training is greatly reduced in a dog that is already "halfway there," and the extra moments you gain could be invested in puppy shows, sanction matches, and breed classes.

It is equally wise to consider the number of dogs being shown in the breed you are considering. It is exceedingly difficult for a novice to finish a German Shepherd in the show ring, because while a Shepherd is easy to care for and a delight to groom, in order to get the points you'll need to finish her championship, she will have to defeat almost forty other bitches at least twice, in contrast with the ten females a Basenji must defeat for title.

Rare breeds are interesting. It's thrilling to be in on the "birth" of a new kind of dog. But will you have to travel hundreds of miles to find points in order to finish this animal?

Should you select a male or a female? Males can sometimes be quite aggressive to handle, but if you achieve a champion, you might want to show extensively. Generally speaking, males will win oftener than females. Females, in addition to this drawback, come in season and must be carefully supervised during this period so that no "accidents" occur. Sometimes they are gentler than males, sometimes *not.* Since spayed females cannot be shown, this could present a needless problem if you are not interested in breeding later on. Bear in mind that if you are planning to breed your show dog, the bitches will be brought *to* the stud dog. Females must sometimes be flown half the country away to pick just the right sire, and stud fees can range into the hundreds of dollars.

And what about the noise factor? If you live fifty miles out in the country on the top of a deserted mountain, it won't make any difference how much barking goes on. But if you have neighbors you'll simply *have* to take into consideration the fact that not everybody enjoys a constant serenade of "bow-bow-bow!" Some toy breeds and some terriers can be very, very noisy! While this can be controlled to an extent with discipline at an early age, nevertheless the sound of yapping animals is going to have to be considered. Even the Basenji, which is touted as being "barkless," has what I call a charming "yodel." This sound can be spine-chilling if you are not used to it.

Temperament must certainly be taken into account. Certain breeds that are devoted to their families and are easy to show from a grooming standpoint are very often quite aggressive toward other dogs. In the hands of an experienced person, a Chesapeake Bay Retriever or a Bull Terrier in a ring full of other dogs presents no real problem. But if you are a gentle soul whose idea of stringent discipline boils down to a waggled forefinger and the words "Bad Dog!" then I would suggest you turn to one of the other two retriever breeds—Goldens and Labradors—or perhaps a Basset Hound.

Finally, I don't think you can afford to overlook what kind of a person you are yourself.

Are you the active, athletic type? Do you like to sit a lot and daydream, or perhaps lose yourself in the pages of a good book? Are you basically a fuss-budget who can't stand disorder or discord? Are you calm and serene, rarely getting emotionally up-tight about things? Are you

you perhaps high-strung, given to impulses and moods? This aspect must be taken into consideration when deciding what kind of a show dog you should have—if you should have a dog of any kind!

Remember, show dogs may be more expensive and flossier than that enchanting nonregistered pet next door, but just like the next-door dog, they are animals.

If this show-dog project of yours is going to be a pleasant one, give a great deal of thought to what you want to get out of it, as well as what you feel you can give to it.

Before we go any further, let me clearly emphasize that I adore all the breeds mentioned above and wouldn't hesitate to recommend any one of them—*but not to just anybody!* What we're doing here is trying to make sure the show dog you get is something you can afford, in time, in effort, and in money, so that the resulting experience will be a pleasant one for you and your entire family as well as for the dog.

LEADING A DOUBLE LIFE

Every once in a while the show-dog dream is most cherished by Mother, while Father wonders what's in it for him. Can they find a breed he can work with in the field, for instance, and at the same time come up with a show dog for Madam? Yes, indeed! There are several breeds that can be hunted or field-trained at the same time they are being shown. In fact, having done exactly that for many years, I can assure you this is a most rewarding experience and often gives a man and his wife a chance to be real partners in developing something very special. The retriever breeds lend themselves beautifully to a dual existence, as their coats are easily handled and thick cover doesn't unduly disturb them. The Irish or English Setter can rarely be expected to compete in the bird field and in the ring at the same time, for his feathering is essential to his winning. Weimaraners, Vizslas, and Pointers do well living a double life, and so do Basenjis, who hunt like bandits! Coonhounds, Bassets, Bloodhounds, Foxhounds, Harriers, and Beagles—any of the smooth-coated working hounds—can be shown and hunted at the same time if intelligence and care are used. Because of weight and coat problems, Huskies and Malamutes that are going to be shown can also work in harness provided you take certain precautions. I find that show Newfoundlands thrive on water work. If settling on just the right breed for you sounds complicated, believe me, it is! Picking a pet for the family requires a lot of prior planning, but picking a puppy with show potential draws many more conditions into the matter.

RESEARCHING YOUR DOG

The first thing you want to do, then, is to narrow the field to no more than ten breeds. Start going to dog shows. Find the nearest obedience class through ads in the paper or a call to your Chamber of Commerce, then watch dogs at work. If you are interested in a sporting or working breed or in a hunting hound, look into the possibility of attending local field trials or dog-sled races, water trials for Newfoundlands; there are lure coursing and racing meets for "sight" hounds and even working certificate trials for terriers, if that is your "dish" of tea. Your veterinarian can usually tell you about these events. Also watch your local paper and listen for radio and television bulletins.

By all means, attend the functions of your local kennel club if such exists. Look for the address and location in the newspaper, and your veterinarian will certainly be able to help you here. Most clubs maintain breeder directory services. Use them. Any nearby reputable kennel can steer you. By joining before you get *your* dog, you'll have a chance to listen and observe all kinds of dogs and form opinions which may "jell" your thoughts.

A letter to the American Kennel Club in New York or the Canadian Kennel Club in Toronto can bring you a list of the names and addresses of the secretaries of breed clubs of the breeds you are interested in. When you write, request the breed standards for each breed you are considering.

WHAT'S IN A STANDARD?

A breed standard is a set of qualifications and detailed descriptions of the points of an ideal example of that breed. It is assembled through the efforts of a breed club with the sanction of the American or Canadian Kennel Club and calls for a type of movement, conformation, intelligence, coat, and personality that distinguishes a certain breed from all other breeds. This standard is usually based on the purpose for which the breed was originally intended. While it is essential that the German Shepherd breed has sound running gear for its work as shepherd, guard, and attack dog, a Papillon, created mainly as a companion animal, would not necessarily have to have such sturdy underpinnings.

Your public library might have a copy of the latest edition of The American Kennel Club's *The Complete Dog Book,* which contains the standards for all recognized breeds; if not, write to the American Kennel Club or ask your book store to get it for you. It's a valuable addition to any doggy library. Then read those standards you are interested in

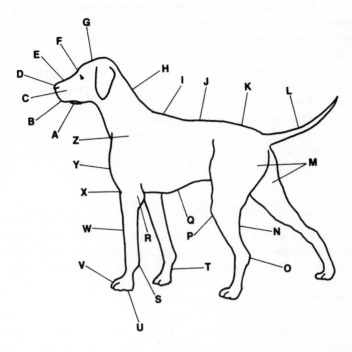

DOG

A, Jaw; B, Flews; C, Cheek; D, Nose; E, Muzzle; F, Stop; G, Forehead; H, Neck; I, Withers; J, Back; K, Croup or rump; L, Tail; M, Thigh; N, Breech; O, Hock; P, Stifle; Q, Chest; R, Elbow; S, Knee; T, Pastern; U, Pad; V, Paw; W, Forearm; X, Upper arm; Y, Brisket; Z, Shoulder

until you understand them perfectly, and while you're at it, read anything else you can get your hands on pertaining to purebred dogs.

In the process of reading the standards of breeds that interest you, and in talking to people who own, train, or breed these dogs, you may discover that what you read and what you hear would lead you to believe that all purebred dogs, regardless of type or size:

1. Are excellent with children
2. Are easily housebroken
3. Eat next to nothing
4. Are not biters or fighters
5. Are not noisy
6. Are not expensive
7. Have no drawbacks whatsoever and are, in other words, not *only* perfect for *you* but perfect, *period.*

I urge you to use the intelligence God gave you to sort out such misleading snarls of information: The perfect dog has yet to be invented—if he were wandering the face of the earth today we wouldn't need handlers, trainers, or books either. We might not even need owners! All dogs are sometimes dirty, annoying, cross with the kiddies, fussy about food, grumpy with other dogs, noisy, and costly. Much of this depends, of course, on how you raise, train, and condition them. But just remember, no matter how much time you spend "dog shopping," a dog has problems just as any other animal, two- or four-footed, has. If he can afford to forgive you for *your* occasional transgressions, you'd better be ready, able, and willing to forgive him *his!*

TIME TO GO VISITING

Having done your homework and narrowed the field, make appointments in advance at local kennels which breed your choice. Never be afraid to ask "stupid" questions—one does not learn through osmosis. Continue going to dog shows so that you can see the breed you've chosen in relation to other breeds.

If you have selected, say, a Weimaraner, don't be afraid to stop that man over there walking his "Y-Mar" to ask him politely what he thinks of his breed. Remember, you don't have to agree, but it doesn't cost a penny to listen, and you might even learn something! Ask your veterinarian what his experiences have been with that breed. Breed or show handling classes are sometimes held in conjunction with obedience classes, sometimes independently. These are taught by professional show handlers or very experienced amateur exhibitors, both of whom make excellent sounding boards.

Pet shops and casual breeders

You will spare yourself endless heartache and disappointment if you steer clear of pet chain stores, which are often supplied by breeding factories.

Before we go any further, let me make myself clear. I think pet shops have a perfect right to sell pets, provided the same health and sanitation standards are maintained that I would expect from a private kennel or breeder. The Jones family down the street has twelve Beagle puppies for sale at twenty dollars each, papers included, because they wanted their children to witness the miracle of birth and don't care about "making money." While this makes it a bit harder for me to sell my puppies at the standard one hundred and fifty dollars, this, in my opinion, is hardly a hanging offense, provided the pups are well cared for and loved. And while I would never go to either of these sources to find a show dog, there have been some very famous dogs from time to time in the history of shows that came from just such backgrounds.

In your travels, stick to those outlets that have the same ideas you have—famous, well-known kennels which produce top dogs year after year after year; and/or the owners of a champion bitch who have bred her correctly and can usually be counted on to do everything possible to see that the puppies are placed where they can do the breed the most good.

What is a good kennel?

This is a hard one to answer because there are so many different ingredients that go into making a good kennel. While you are visiting all sorts of doggy places and meeting all sorts of doggy people, it is to be hoped you would settle on the places that are the cleanest and that contain the happiest, noisiest dogs.

Fancy establishments with miles of expensive, made-to-order runs are impressive, but such a showplace cannot guarantee you anything more than the shabby but comfortable smaller place a few miles up the road can.

Guarantee—there's a word to be wary of! Glad-handing proprietors who "guarantee" everything from soup to nuts make me nervous; as a breeder myself, I know just what the vagaries of puppyhood can do to the most sincere "guarantee."

And brace yourself against the sly fox who insists, "Well, if you're not sure, take it home for two weeks; if you don't like it, bring it back." Ha! Did you ever know a puppy that couldn't worm its way into the heart of Attila the Hun in two weeks!? That's the oldest "come-on" in the books!

The people who have dogs for sale should be just as interested in your finding exactly the right dog as you are. But if they are not as overjoyed to welcome you as the puppies seem to be, don't be alarmed. Conscientious breeders aren't about to turn over something warm and dear they've fed and loved and cleaned and snuggled for eight weeks just because you have a fat roll of bills in your hot little fist. If you come as strangers to them and their breed, you can be prepared for quite a cross-examination. Be frank and answer all questions honestly. They are as interested in sizing you up as you should be in doing the same to them. I would be far more wary if they fell over their feet to welcome you.

Sometimes you will visit a litter which is all sold. But if you make your sincerity and your determination clear, you could get your name on a waiting list for the litter expected next week, or next month—or next year.

Sometimes the litter may be too young to go, and you will get a chance to watch the puppies in various stages of development; reputable breeders favor people who are interested enough to come back again and again. And sometimes, ready to go or not, you may have to "endure" several interviews before being accepted as a proper buyer and owner.

Breeders who do care where their puppies are going and to whom, and kennels that investigate prospective buyers first and hold their palms out later, are to be treasured rather than despised.

Be sure you "see" when you look

If you are going to put time and effort into finding the right dog for you—and to do any less is penny wise and pound foolish.—it's a smashing idea to have some idea of what you are looking *for,* apart from and beyond the requirements of a breed standard.

Disposition and intelligence are paramount, to my way of thinking. A stupid dog drives me up the wall, just as a stupid person does. Smart puppies are curious puppies. They come running out to meet you, wanting to see what you're up to, why you are there, what kind of knots you use on your shoelaces. One of the tests the Seeing Eye uses in picking its future guide dogs is retrieving. A puppy that will chase a ball is a puppy with a questing mind. I agree. No matter what I'm picking a puppy for, I eventually throw something for it so that I can watch its attitude. I don't care if it picks up or returns the object; I just want the puppy to be alert and to be interested enough to check and see *what* was thrown.

The puppy that functions well as part of its peer group is one thing; to separate the sheep from the goats, so to speak, find out what happens when you *remove* that puppy from the nest. Is he interested in being alone and outside, curious about why you singled him out? Or does he immediately turn and try and get back with his sisters and brothers? Of course, a lot of his reaction when you single him out has to do with his raising prior to your arrival. If he's been stuck in a room somewhere with nobody to see him, you can't expect him to blossom just because *you* come along. But a normally raised puppy that has been handled a lot and is familiar with strange noises, different places, and play periods with people-type creatures, should be interested in what you have in mind, in or out of the whelping area.

Soundness is important too, of course. Watch the puppies as they move in a group, as they jump each other, roll each other over, climb on top of one another. Do they have good push in the hind quarters, strength in the forequarters? Do they use their legs well? If they have been leash-broken, have someone else trot the ones you are interested in up and down for you, and watch them coming and going. Allow, of course, for the fact that these are children whose bones and muscles and sinew haven't really "jelled" yet, but at the same time remember that what they possess *now* in the way of running gear, they will *always* possess. If they are cow-hocked at eight weeks there is a possibility that this condition can be improved with proper conditioning over the growing months, but if they have little rear angulation as puppies they are not suddenly going to develop it in maturity. You can allow for looseness in the shoulder or pasterns, but puppies that toe out or in drastically at eight weeks rarely do anything else when they grow up. Soft backs, slab-sidedness, flat, elongated feet in breeds calling for pussy-cat rounded feet—these can be helped by proper vitamin supplements and by putting the dog on a crushed-stone surface for exercise, but the tendency is there and always will be.

Beware of the breeder who won't let you into the puppy area for any reason, no matter how sensible it sounds. While every once in a while we are all forced by extenuating circumstances to purchase a puppy sight unseen, try to avoid this situation as if it were the plague, and if the prospect does rear its ugly head it should only be because of great distances between you and the litter. During your visiting around, it may be that you will *not* get to see an entire litter for reasons we'll explain later, but try to see all the puppies whenever possible.

It is entirely possible to discover, when meeting a litter of young puppies for the first time, that the lack of personal attention or some congenital throwback has ruined them, just as can be the case with an older dog. No matter how your heart bleeds, take the advice of old "Softie" here, who has done it too many times herself and should *know* better: *don't* pay any attention to that pathetic, forlorn, limpid-eyed, adorable, trembling creature who huddles in the back of the box! *No,* he is *not* waiting just for you to save him! Half price, huh? I don't care if the lady *gives* him to you, *don't take him* if you are hunting for a show dog! Yes, it will *so* make a difference if you hold him just a minute because he's so lonesome! Yes, I *know* he looks miserable; that's because he *is* miserable, poor darling, and chances are, exceptions aside, he will continue to feel more or less miserable the rest of his life. Cheer up—some nice family will come along and take him as a pet and love him to death. But you are not that family. You are after a show dog, remember, and show dogs that slink, no matter how pathetic, are incredibly difficult to finish in the show ring! One final word on behalf of the ladies: the men do it too; no matter how those tough, masculine creatures protest, they do it too! To you both let me say that love, my friends, does *not* make *all* things right!

Two words of warning about purchasing an older dog: first, make sure that he hasn't been shut away in a kennel situation, no matter how clean and spacious, from the time he was eight weeks of age.

Since some of our smaller breeders, who have no excuse for such carelessness with a dog, are often the worst offenders, and some of the larger kennels which you wouldn't think had time to give to a gnat do the best job in keeping an older kennel animal people-ized and socialized, it is sometimes difficult to determine whether an older dog *will* adjust.

If he is nervous when he meets you, tends to hang back, wags his tail between his legs and looks uncertainly from person to person, you could be asking for real trouble. There are exceptions, as I have said earlier, and I have known "kennel shy" older dogs to blossom almost immediately when put in a warm, friendly, secure, happy situation where they can wallow in being the center of attention for the first time in their lives. But I have known many more that bore the emotional scars of lack of attention from the cradle to the grave.

Second, make very sure the older puppy hasn't been bounced around from one foster home to another so that in addition to being uncivilized, as most young dogs are, he has lots of bad habits to *un*teach.

If that older beastie fairly bowls you down as he is introduced, squeaks with delight, chews on your nose, has a seemingly endless supply of sloppy smooches, chances are that while you may collect some rather ingenious black-and-blue marks in the weeks to come, you will nevertheless come out of it with a high-stepping extrovert who was born for center stage and knows it.

The rights of visitors

As you have gone around visiting this litter and that, if the puppies were too young to go home with you when you first met them, the chances are that mother dog was either still supervising or was nearby and available for you to see. Her condition during motherhood gives you an excellent indication not only of the kind of people you are contemplating dealing with, but of how their puppies may look at maturity.

Some dams (mother dogs) are more possessive about their children than others, and it's not unusual for a dam to growl low in her throat if you approach her "nest" or to look you over with a very jaundiced eye. But if you are introduced to her as a friend by her owner and she settles down, quite content to have you share her pride in her family, this is quite normal.

Personally, I never buy from litters whose mothers hurl themselves at strangers, snarling and barking, tossing and tumbling puppies in all directions. I have great respect for the motherhood syndrome, but in my humble opinion, bitches that carry on in this exaggerated manner are insecure about themselves as well as their puppies. I cannot help but wonder what insecurities I would be buying if I selected from such a litter.

Make sure you see Daddy (the sire) too, if at all possible, but as often as not, many bitches are sent away to distant places to be bred. Pictures will suffice in this case (usually it's a matter of getting breeders *not* to hold you for hours with their living-color photo album!).

And if some dear soul hands you a puppy and says brightly, "This one is for sale," refusing to show you anything more of the litter or the parents, make your excuses promptly and get out of there! All is not well somewhere along the line.

There seems to be a great difference of opinion among breeders on whether or not to let prospective buyers see litters of very young puppies. Certainly there is a health risk: strangers might bring in viral infections on their clothing. Ill-mannered children, accompanied by parents who obviously cannot or will not control them in their desire to maul and poke and pet, often ruin visiting privileges for everyone. But this behavior is rarely seen when show dogs, as opposed to pets, are the aim.

Fortunately, there are still old-fashioned creatures like me who *want* people to visit their puppies and whose dams are conditioned to this. I happen to feel that the most normal outgoing puppies are those who learn that hands are good things even before the eyes are opened.

Not so incidentally, your reception as you go researching will be greatly enhanced by dressing neatly and simply, speaking in a low voice around puppies, permitting only the older, more reliable children to accompany you in the earliest stages, and keeping your hands to yourself until given permission to do otherwise.

BREEDERS AND BUYERS

In fairness to breeders everywhere, I must confess that most of the bad puppies I have had brought to me over the years were not by any means exclusively the fault of the breeder, who certainly has a serious obligation to the buyer. All too often, bad dogs were acquired through the sheer gullibility and absolute stupidity of the buyer. Often the seller who is *not* a breeder is the culprit.

A casual friend once called to tell me about a lovely year-old Springer he had just purchased from a previous owner, who was not the breeder of record. As he introduced the dog to me later, he explained he had gotten a good buy because "the people were moving and couldn't keep her." (Warning: people who love their dogs take them with them even if they are moving to Glocca Morra!) "Look," I pointed out, "she has a dandy case of roundworm." "Oh?" he said. "It was so dark down there I guess I didn't see it." "Down where?" I inquired. "In the basement—they didn't believe in letting dogs in the house." "Did you ask to see her in the light?" I asked, not believing my ears. "I didn't want to embarrass her," came the answer.

Well, let me tell you, he deserved what he got and I told him so— a knock-kneed, sway-backed, cow-hocked roundworm-infested fear-biter who had lived out her entire twelve months in a hole in the ground by the light of a 60-watt bulb. He "stole" her for a mere one hundred dollars and brought her home in the dark. As far as I know, this gentleman is *still* in the dark and always will be.

Then there was the lady who waited months for a pick-of-the-litter Coonhound. As the breeder placed the pup in her arms she told her, "You will notice the puppy is undershot, but this will change with age." The buyer actually paid five hundred dollars for an undershot dog, guaranteed to be show quality! I must confess, the mouth did indeed change with age—it got so bad the poor animal could hardly eat its food.

In the first case the breeder wasn't even involved, and the seller, obviously overanxious to dump a dog he didn't want and should never have bought in the first place, took advantage of a buyer who deserved everything he got (or didn't get!).

In the second example, the breeder and the buyer both acted foolishly. But the breeder, I feel, was mostly to blame, for she was presumed to be the educated party in the deal and it's part of the breeder's job to make sure the buyer knows what he is getting. It is also the buyer's duty to educate himself as fully as possible before wandering into the marketplace.

It never ceases to amaze me that perfectly intelligent people who wouldn't dream of purchasing a car without a test ride, a dress without trying it on, or a TV set without a written guarantee, will blithely hand over hundreds of dollars for a breed of dog they know absolutely nothing about on the word of a complete stranger they have known for about fifteen minutes! But it's done every day. Most of us agree that the only solution that makes any sense is education, education, education. And today, because lots of concerned people want to stop these things from happening, there are marvelous books to guide your neophyte eyes, pet columns in almost every newspaper in the world, radio programs about the care of purebred animals, and TV shows that emphasize the responsibilities of breeders and professional kennels. Your veterinarian's office is lopsided with free pamphlets on every phase of owning a dog. Kennel clubs sponsor seminars, maintain breeder referral services and adoption agencies. The A.K.C. and C.K.C. publish reams of information, as do the Humane Societies and S.P.C.A.'s of the world—and still people buy dogs that are sick, lame, congenitally nasty, inferior examples of a breed, and very often not even members of the breed in which they are registered. You'd almost think the wealth of information available at everybody's fingertips was presented in a foreign language! Some people look and do not see; some listen and do not hear. To others a high price tag guarantees perfection, while a low price tag stands for second-best.

As I write this, I am still "shook" about an experience I had recently. A young woman, dedicated to a rather unique breed of dog, came to me at one of the larger American dog shows and asked if I had time to take a look at her brand-new brood bitch. This girl had spent about four years in her breed. I had handled dogs for her from time to time and we both agreed she needed new blood, particularly foundation stock with A-1 dispositions, as the breed has a temperament problem. I had shared her tears as we decided to put not one but several dogs to sleep because they were either in acute pain from hip dysplasia or so congenitally shy nothing could cure them. I was delighted she had taken my advice and gone "out" of her own blood lines to secure new ones to strengthen her breeding program. I could tell she was excited over the new dog, for which, she confided, "I spent an awful lot of money, Martha, but it was worth it."

There are absolutely no accurate words to describe my inner feelings when she returned with the dog. It slunk toward me on the floor, the end of its tucked-under tail vibrating, "Please like me, please like me." Its coat was speckled with dandruff, denoting dry skin, and both eyes were weeping in a way that strongly suggested inverted eyelids. I squatted down and, in spite of the fact that I held my hand under her chin, not over her head, she flared from the sight of my hand and the sound of my voice. Over and over in my head, like the words of some horrible song, I kept hearing, "I spent an awful lot of money, Martha, but it was worth it!"

In order to get a grip on myself, I asked her to move the dog for me. From what I was able to tell when she got it halfway up off its belly, it was severely out at the shoulders and absolutely flat-footed. The new owner herself apologized for the left-rear leg, which, she confided, I might think was a bit stiff but "It's a hundred per cent better since I've been road-working her."

As she stood waiting for my opinion she offered, "I remembered what you always said about an older dog being a safer bet." I wanted to scream, "Is that *all* you remember I said in four long years?"

Perhaps you think I'm overemotional—I don't agree. For four years I had worked with this girl. For four years she had had the benefit of not only my professional counsel but also that of countless others to whom I had introduced her. I had showered her with books, dragged her to films on dog movement and symposiums on every other conceivable subject she might need to know about. Either I and about fifty other people were bad teachers, or this girl was totally blind and stone-deaf. I was upset then, and as I think back on the incident I get more and more upset.

"Toby" (that is not her real name), I asked quietly, "Where did you get this animal?"

"From a breeder in the West. She chose it for me herself; it was her pick of the litter!" (So much for never buying a puppy sight unseen!) "You don't like her, do you?"

I just kept shaking my head in disbelief. "Toby, I'm sorry, but . . ."

"That's OK, that's OK, I wanted your frank opinion."

"She is just *awful!* There isn't anything good about her. If this is pick of the litter, I shudder to even think what the rest were like. You couldn't hire me for any amount of money to take her in the ring, and as a dedicated, ethical breeder, you simply *cannot* breed to her! Can you send her back? Can you get your money back?"

"Oh, I couldn't send her back, Martha. I've spent so much money now, and besides she loves me."

End of serious dog person, end of show career, end of story. Of course I feel sorry for shy dogs, of course I love all animals, but we're talking now about showing and eventually perhaps breeding, and shy dogs, substandard dogs are heartbreakers, time consumers, money wasters. No matter how hard you work with them, how much you love them and spend on them, that's what they will always be, basically, and so will their puppies. They'll never make it in the ring, and neither will their offspring. And the only people who would breed a dog like this to their stud are disreputable breeders whose stud dog cannot get good bitches because he's nothing to write home about. Do you see the awful circle within a circle within a circle?

Here we have a sad case of a truly educated buyer who acted very foolishly. But we also have an example of an unscrupulous (or perhaps just stupid) breeder who did herself and her kennel name irreparable harm in her transaction. Someone placed trust in her; she betrayed that trust. However, thanks to our "circle system," our buyer will not suffer half as much as the seller. For when this bitch is bred, as I'm unhappily sure she will be, the name of the dam's breeder plus the name of the kennel from whence she came will go on the pedigree. And after seeing what awful stock will, in all probability, result from using this dog as a brood bitch, no one will exactly beat a path to her door for more of the same.

FOOLISH CHANCES

In reading those standards you are interested in, pay particular attention to any disqualifications, for a disqualifying fault prevents a dog from being shown. Moreover, in the case of all male puppies you are looking at, make very sure that both testicles are present and located in the scrotum or sac which houses them between the hind legs. *No breed of male dog can be exhibited in licensed dog shows in the United States or Canada if he does not have two normally descended testicles.*

Since the beginning of time, a male animal's testicles have been closely aligned with his nervous reactions; puppies which have two perfectly normal testicles at time of purchase can later draw them up when they are cold, or sometimes when they are frightened. The presence of these two vital pieces of masculine equipment are usually easily determined by very gentle examination with your fingers. But should you have any doubt at all that the puppy you are buying is perfect in this department, either refuse to purchase it or hold up your payment until after a competent, independent veterinarian has examined the dog in your presence and assured you that all is well, after you have made it clear to him that this pup is being purchased as a potential show dog.

Sometimes puppies will have been examined by a veterinarian prior to your arrival and the breeder will assure you in all good faith that both testicles are present but one has not "dropped" yet (i.e., slipped down into the scrotum). As author of this book I cannot follow you around forcing you to do what I suggest. But in this instance *please,* no matter *how much* you like the puppy or trust the breeder, wait to take him home until both testicles are in position, or hold out for a different puppy, perhaps from another litter.

Reputable breeders replace such puppies when they don't turn out, of course, but you can waste a lot of time and money and face the possibility of great heartbreak when you finally have to "give up" and realize you will not be able to show your dog. Life is traumatic enough; who needs this?

When it comes to mouths, the decision to buy or not to buy can be more complicated. Crooked mouths appear so often in some breeds that one rarely sees a good one; undershot puppies (those whose lower teeth extend out beyond the upper teeth at the front of the mouth) can correct with maturity and sometimes do, but I would be particularly wary here, as the lower jaw is the moving jaw, and generally the more it moves the more it grows. I would be less concerned about overshot puppies (those whose upper teeth extend beyond the lower teeth at the front of the mouth), because the lower jaw will often grow out to meet the upper.

Nevertheless, when purchasing a show dog, I wouldn't, myself, hand over the amount of money it takes to buy a show dog if there were anything about him that indicated at time of sale that he might not conform to standard at maturity. Again, if you are torn with indecision or just plain nervous about any such condition, check it out with a veterinarian before accepting the pup at any price.

THE MATTER OF MONEY

As you near the end of your research, don't forget to inquire about costs and methods of payment. This should never be left until the last moment.

If you are interested in a litter yet unborn which on paper promises much, the breeder may require you to put down a deposit to hold your puppy for you. This is a very common practice. Since you do not in most cases get your deposit back if you change your mind, it protects breeders from "window shoppers" who ask to have a puppy saved for them and then, when the pup is ready, refuse to take it. More and more breeders are requiring deposits on all puppies spoken for prior to time of departure from the kennel, so don't be alarmed if you are asked for a portion of the purchase price in advance.

Also, make sure just *which* puppy you are getting. If pick-of-the-litter is available when you decide to buy from a specific breeder (sometimes it is the breeder's pick, sometimes yours or your professional handler's choice), that means the breeder cannot sell *any* of the litter until you have first removed what you want. Such a pup would probably cost you more than his sisters or brothers, who could turn out to be just as good.

Make sure the breeder knows whether you want a bitch, a dog, or just a good puppy, either sex.

Some kennels accept credit cards most do not; some have time-payment plans of their own; some will take a deposit in advance, then the balance in two payments; some demand cash, some will take checks.

Whatever the financial details, make sure you and the breeder settle them early.

SPECIAL CONTRACTS

This, I think, is the time to point out that sometimes dogs or puppies—particularly those purchased with an eye to showing—are not always sold outright.

This means that because the seller and/or breeder thinks a great deal of a certain prospect, he wants to maintain some sort of control over the animal until he is sure the buyer can be trusted to keep his promises. A breeder, for instance, may sell a male, specifying that he wants to keep stud rights (i.e., he wishes to be able to use that dog at maturity to breed to his bitches). Or because a female is a good breeding prospect, he may sell her and retain rights to choose the stud dog when it comes time to breed. Or a dog or bitch may be sold for a lower figure, with the seller getting back one or more puppies from the first litter or one or more stud services. Co-ownerships are quite common also; this means that two people together control the ownership of one dog, sharing expenses and responsibilities.

There are any number of possible arrangements. Just make sure that if you agree to this type of sale, you understand *every single* facet of the arrangement and that you *want* to go along with it. Such contracts can help you immeasurably by insuring you the support and advice of an experienced breeder; but such contracts can boomerang just as easily. Therefore, make certain you take *nothing* for granted, that neither buyer nor seller *assumes* one thing. Write down in duplicate exactly what the special arrangement is to be, *from soup to nuts.*

Here's a prime example of a type of conditional sale which can lead to trouble if everything isn't taken into consideration: A female is sold with the understanding that the seller will get back first and third pick of her first litter bred to a stud of the seller's choice. The two parties sign a statement and each goes merrily on his way. The time arrives for the first breeding and, oh boy, are we in trouble! You see, the stud the seller wants is located 6,000 miles away. The bitch is to be shipped—well, who pays for *that?* The stud fee is enormous—who pays for *that?* In due time the bitch whelps just one puppy—to whom does that puppy belong? See what I mean?

THE BIG DAY

So today's the day you are picking out your show puppy. Whatever breed you decide upon, it is hoped you will select a sound, alert, adventurous pup with healthy coat, clear eyes, pink gums, and a wagging tail (or bottom, in case of the tail-less breeds). And it is also hoped that you have made it very, very clear to the breeder exactly what you want this dog for—that you want eventually to show it with the idea of getting its championship.

This last point is most important. Reputable breeders with a background in show animals want their good dogs in competition. Since few of us have money enough to keep, raise, train, and exhibit all the promising puppies we produce, it behooves us to place them in the hands of those who will do all this *for* us; as breeders, we will get publicity in direct proportion to the good dogs—or bad dogs—we send into the show rings of the world. Our puppies are our best—or worst— advertisement, so most breeders, knowing you are intending to show, will make every effort to give you a dog they can be proud to have bred.

And don't forget, as we have intimated several times before, it is rarely a case of going to see, picking out, paying money, and bringing the pup home all in one visit. While you may have seen the entire litter as it developed over the preceding weeks, you can expect to see only the bitches, if you are interested in a female, when it comes time to make the big decision. Unless you have specified pick-of-the-litter for yourself, this and any other puppy spoken for previously will not be on hand when you arrive to select yours. But never accept a single puppy as "the pup you're buying," unless of course you *asked* the breeder to select *for* you. Otherwise, it's your money and you have a right to pick what you buy from what is available.

Don't feel insulted if you, comparative stranger that you are, tried to purchase the pick and were turned down. Too many sincere breeders have been "badly bitten" by purchasers who swore all sorts of marvelous things, even put their good intentions in writing, and then were never heard from again. Many's the dog I myself have let people talk me out of because they just *had* to have that dog to show, only to discover months later that they "loved" it so much they couldn't bear to let it go away weekends. There sits a Best in Show animal in some jerk's living room—and you can't do a darned thing about it in most cases.

Anyway, the time has come to stop talking and start signing things.

PAPER WORK

Dogs purchased in Canada or the United States that are eligible for registration with C.K.C. or A.K.C., or both, are the only kinds of dogs that may compete in dog shows. So make very sure that the registration certificate you get with your puppy says clearly that it was issued by one of these two organizations. Don't let anybody "con" you into a pup registered with the International Kennel Club or the Sporting Dog Show Registry or some such fly-by-night organization.

Purebred American dogs usually come either with white individual registration certificates or with so-called "blue slips" attesting to the registration of the litter. Canadian dogs are registered in a somewhat different manner.

When purchasing a registered dog accompanied by A.K.C. papers in the United States, the buyer takes home the registration certificate which has been correctly filled in by the seller and signed by the buyer in the seller's presence. Then the buyer fills in another section asking for such information as his address, etc., signs it again and sends it to A.K.C. with the necessary fee (given on the certificate). In time the individual registration will be returned to the buyer.

In Canada, when purchasing a registered dog, the importer, breeder, or seller must be the one to apply for registration of the individual dog, *and must also pay all fees involved.* This is in accordance with the by-laws of the C.K.C. and with the provisions of the Livestock Pedigree Act, which is a federal statute.

It is entirely possible that the American dog's blue slip or registration certificate is still with A.K.C. at the time you purchase your dog; and in the case of Canadian dogs it is highly improbable that you will receive your pup's papers at time of sale, due to a great backlog of registrations at C.K.C. in Toronto. Most "how to" articles on dogs warn you time and time again never, under any circumstances, to accepting a purebred dog or puppy without papers "attached." This is a fair and proper warning, but, unfortunately, due to the number of litters being registered in Canada and the United States these days, compared with five years ago, it isn't always possible to do these things as they should be done.

If you have done the proper homework and have visited and talked to enough kennel owners and breeders, you'll have a darned good idea of whom you can and cannot trust. If the papers for some perfectly logical reason are not available at time of purchase, you can protect yourself in the following manner:

1. Insist upon a dated bill of sale with or without registration papers.

2. Included in that bill of sale should be the vital statistics about the puppy you are buying—date of birth, litter number, if available, A.K.C. or C.K.C. registered name and number of sire and dam, breeder of record, any identifying marks on the puppy, its color, the purpose for which it was purchased, the amount charged and method of payment.

3. Also include a statement, if applicable, that the reason the papers have not been issued at time of purchase is such and such and that they are to be forwarded to you by a mutually agreed-upon date or the seller will refund full purchase price and you may return the puppy without obligation of any kind.

To save time, you might type up in advance a first copy and a duplicate of this "contract," filling in your part before going to pick up the puppy. The rest you and the breeder can fill out together. Then both of you sign it, with a witness signing both copies. I cannot think why any reputable breeder would object to this. Chances are the agreement will never be used, but it is a businesslike way of handling things and it protects you both. A sample form for your convenience is included here; it may be changed or altered to suit your particular needs, of course.

Most reputable breeders have forms similar to this which they ask *you* to sign. Also, while there is no law forcing them to do so, most breeders supply with each puppy sold a three-generation (at least) pedigree of the animal, showing his parents, grandparents, and great-grand-parents, with due note of their titles, if any.

If you are purchasing with any sort of "agreement" involved, spell it out, word by word, for both your sakes, and make sure you each keep a copy.

In addition to the litter form or individual registration (if available), the bill of sale, and the statement of special purchase agreements, the breeder should supply you with a certificate stating that the puppy or older dog is free of internal and external parasites, is a healthy animal, and has been inoculated against distemper and hepatitis. It seems that veterinarians prefer to inoculate in slightly different manners at slightly different times. Some veterinarians include a leptospirosis inoculation with the distemper and hepatitis, some give it later, some don't recommend it at all. Some breeders give their own inoculations, do their own worming, and supply their own "health" certificates. Whatever the arrangement, make it clear that you intend to take the animal you have just purchased to your own veterinarian within twenty-four hours to get his OK. There should be no objection to this from a reputable breeder. It should be noted that a healthy, roly-poly puppy can be correctly inoculated, be recently wormed, look clean, and act spirited—but when you get to your veterinarian you are told it still has a flea or two and there is evidence of roundworm in the stool. This is hardly an occasion for hysteria on your part. As diligent as kennels are, fleas do creep in, but they are reasonably easy to dispatch permanently with little inconvenience to the dog. And a mild case of worms is entirely possible even if the dog has indeed been wormed once or twice. I think it is fair to say such problems do not constitute a reason either to return the pup and demand a refund or to cease all contact with the seller who "lied."

I realize there are owners who swear their dogs and puppies have never been wormed because they have never had worms—well, I quit believing such fairy tales *years* ago! Many stool samples from dogs known to be wormy read "negative" simply because that particular sample of stool contained no worms or worm eggs.

While we are discussing the health of the new dog, since this animal is probably going to be bred as well as shown, it is important that you ask for *written proof* at the time of selecting for purchase that the animal's parents were clear of hip dysplasia and that they were both certified negative for retinal atrophy. These two dog problems and lots of others are being slowly but surely gotten under control by means of diligent breeding practices and periodic testing. The puppy himself cannot be tested until he is older. I caution you that because the parents were clear does not guarantee that the puppy will be fine. Dysplastic puppies result from the breeding of clear parents, and dys-

SAMPLE FORM FOR BILL OF SALE WHEN REGISTRATION
PAPERS ARE OR ARE NOT IMMEDIATELY AVAILABLE

On this date _____ I _____
              date   name of purchaser(s) *

residing at _____

in the City or Township of _____

telephone _____ purchased for the sum of _____
                                                      buying price

or down payment of _____ the balance of which is due
                              down payment

before _____ 19_____, one (1) _____ _____.
                                         sex of dog   breed of
                                                         dog

Sire of puppy purchased is _____.
                             titles, name & registered number

Dam of puppy purchased is _____.
                             titles, name & registered number

The puppy was whelped on _____ 19_____. The litter

registration and number _____, individual registration and

number _____ (check one) which is not available at this time,

because _____

is to be forwarded to me before _____.
                        (date by which seller safely feels papers can be guaranteed)

If this is not the case, I am to be refunded all monies heretofore paid and the puppy may
be returned to the person from whom I purchased said puppy and who owned at time of
sale said puppy or litter containing said puppy, or was acting as duly authorized agent of
legal owner; that person being _____
                                name of seller

residing at _____ in the City or

Township of _____ telephone _____.

Signed this date _____ 19_____, in good faith by

_____

                        name of buyer*

_____

                        name of seller

and witnessed by _____

* in the case of a married woman purchasing a dog, she should sign herself Mary Whitney Black,
not Mrs. John Black. If husband and wife are both buying the dog, they would sign Mary Whitney
Black and John Elliot Black, not Mr. and Mrs. John Black. If a minor child is purchasing a dog it
should be co-owned with one parent, or other adult, in case of legal problems. And no matter who
is buying the dog, the name on the bill of sale should be *exactly* the same as you wish it to be
recorded on your registration form. Also, the seller's name should be written exactly as he or she
is recorded as owner of the litter on the litter registration form or individual registration form.

plastic parents have been known to produce "clear" progeny for several generations. No breeder worth her salt will "guarantee" anything at all in this department except that she will replace the puppy, *under certain conditions,* if it should test negative. Since breeders' arrangements concerning these problems differ from individual to individual, again, *get in writing* in exactly what respect your breeder stands behind her dogs.

A MATTER OF RECORD

From the moment you scoop that puppy into your arms and your heart, *start keeping records.* Purchase a manila file or envelope, label his call name across the front, and make sure everything pertaining to that puppy goes into it.

Keep a photostat or exact copy of your registration form, or, if it is not available, keep a complete record of all information you *do* have so that if you wish to show the puppy at a match before his registration is returned, you will have adequate information to do so. Please don't forget to include in that record your bill of sale *and* the way you signed your name on the bill of sale. You may sign your checks Mary W. Black, but if you purchased the puppy as Mary Whitney Black you must enter him, always, as belonging to Mary Whitney Black. Failure to remember this could cost you wins, points, or result in disciplinary action by the registering organization.

Pictures showing him at time of purchase and as he grows and matures, particularly color pictures, are invaluable should he become lost, strayed, or stolen. His health record is important (many veterinary clinics supply booklets with places to record the dates of shots, wormings, etc.). And there should be a record of matches and shows entered and his wins, with particular attention given to his points.

Each time he gets points make a note of the name of the show, the date, the class he was in, the judge who awarded them, the awards he won, how many class animals were entered, and how many points were earned. Keeping your catalogue pages and all first, winners, and best of winners ribbons stapled together, show by show, is a foolproof way to prove your figures are right if need arises.

As depressing as the thought may be, let's face it: something could happen to you without warning. Then what becomes of the dog you have purchased?

Since none of us knows what tomorrow may bring, your show dog's personal file is the place to make note of what you wish done in the event of your demise. This in no way serves as a will, but it gives those left behind who have your best interests at heart some idea of what you would like to have done with the dog you have left behind you.

YOUR FACILITIES

As you come nearer and nearer to bringing your show puppy home, don't get so involved with breed standards and kennel hopping that you forget to make some provision for containing this "wunderhund" once he becomes part of your family.

Later we'll discuss raising pups indoors as well as outdoors, but whatever you decide, you will have to make some decision about a yard or run, unless you have kennels already.

When I was a little girl growing up with all sorts of dogs, nobody kenneled their animals. Traffic wasn't a problem then, and if the neighbor's Husky and my Cocker Spaniel ran merrily around the block visiting the gas station on the corner, the grocery store, and the bicycle shop until we kids got home from school, so what?

Today with superhighways a stone's throw from that "country" ranch house, this arrangement *cannot* be considered! Even if you live on a mountaintop with miles of your own posted land don't let your dogs run free or you will be inviting disaster. Wild animals don't enjoy being hassled by dogs and will tear and rip in self-defense. It's against the law in some states (and should be in all) for dogs to chase deer; animals caught doing so may be shot on the spot. Dognappers are everywhere these days, and even a tattoo listed with the National Dog Registry isn't one hundred percent effective. The farmer next door is within his rights, as far as I'm concerned, in destroying dogs that constantly hassle his livestock.

Oh, I know the argument—"a dog has to be able to run; it's cruel to confine him." Of *course* he has to run and will do so—*supervised!* But what is "crueler"—confining him where he is safe, or turning him loose to die from food poisoning contracted by eating rotten garbage? A leg broken by being snapped in somebody's long-discarded roll of barbed wire can be set; but chances are the dog can never be shown. So, please don't talk to me about "cruel"—not unless you want to face facts dead on!

Every dog deserves a yard of his own, and show dogs especially need a place to play and exercise safely, particularly when you cannot always be with them. To save steps and money, a roll or two of snow fencing painted to match the house and attached to the house, so that you simply open the door and let the dog out for a romp, is a marvelous solution. Commercial portable kennels are available from Montgomery Ward and Sears Roebuck; they vary in height and length and can be used with confidence, handled with ease, and removed when not needed. As they can be purchased by the panel, you can spend just as much or as little as your budget allows.

I do not approve of tying dogs, but there are situations in which a pen isn't feasible. In this case a running line can be purchased in kit form, including a strong steel cable which can be stretched between two trees. To this cable is fixed a chain or chew-proof line which works on a pully arrangement so the dog can move freely in a wide area without becoming tangled. You would use a flat, buckle-type leather collar if this kind of arrangement was the best you could manage, *never* a choke collar!

Whatever solution is best for you, now is the time to set it up and make sure it is ready for use *before* the new arrival moves into your life and heart.

Before we go into early training for the show puppy, let's stop a moment to scatter some crumbs of advice in another corner.

EXCEPTION TO THE RULE

Every once in a while someone will purchase a purebred, registered dog or puppy as a pet, never intending to show. But as the animal grows *up* it begins to grow *on* you and on everyone else who sees him; friends begin suggesting he should be shown and you tend to agree, although you are the first to admit that neither you nor your friends know anything about show dogs. Now is the time to start reading, watching, studying, just as we advised the person who is planning to purchase a show dog. Above all, procure a copy of your breed standard and read it carefully—not once, but many times.

Still, in spite of the number of shows you attend, unless you are *exceedingly* experienced, when it comes to determining whether or not to show the erstwhile "pet," it will be necessary, probably, for you to seek the advice of your breeder or of a breeder in your area, who will usually be happy to evaluate the animal for you providing you make an appointment and make it clear you are willing to pay for his or her services.

Whether or not you are able to do this, here is a good "test" you can take at home. Get out that breed standard and a plain white sheet of paper. Draw a line down the middle of the paper, heading one side YES and the other side NO. Then, with the dog in front of you and your heart in your hip pocket, *as objectively as possible* read the first requirement of the standard; if your pup, *in your objective opinion,* fits that paragraph pretty well, put a check in the YES column. If the next paragraph finds him a bit wanting, put a check in the NO column. When you are all done, count up and see whether you have more YES's than NO's. If the YES's have it, consider giving it a whirl. If the NO's are preponderant, it might be wise to wait a bit and see if maturity improves the picture.

IN SICKNESS AND IN HEALTH

All the way through this chapter we have constantly advised you to "consult your veterinarian." If this show dog happens to be your first dog, then you haven't ever used a veterinarian and it becomes quite clear that you are going to need a few words on the subject of dog doctors, "yours" or anybody else's.

Picking a veterinarian does not mean zeroing in on the one nearest you because he lives across the street. If you can find a conveniently located veterinarian who is also *show*-dog oriented, who is up on the latest developments in veterinary medicine, who doesn't treat you as if you had the intelligence of a lobotomized ant, truly thou art blessed! But it is rarely that simple.

Talk to your kennel club friends about which veterinarian they use. Question the breeders and the kennel people you visit. You might ask your local humane society or S.P.C.A. who does their work. If one name keeps cropping up more than others, it's probably a safe bet that this man is worthy of the trust being placed in him by all these other people. But this doesn't mean that the man or woman used by the majority of people in town is going to be the one for you and your dog.

Picking a veterinarian is a very personal thing, like picking a doctor for the family. The person, male or female, who gives you confidence, who keeps a record on your dog so he can remind you of boosters and immunizations coming due, whose handling of your dog pleases you and the animal, who is anxious for you to see his facilities and is obviously concerned about the animals in his care—this is the vet for you.

Since dogs cannot tell a doctor "where it hurts," veterinarians have to do an awful lot of their diagnostic work "by guess and by golly." So the veterinarian who always says he knows what the matter is, *instantly,* no matter how your dog is acting, should make you a bit suspicious. On the other hand, the man who examines your sick dog and says, "Mrs. Brown, I think he's got thus-and-such but I'm not sure and I want to call in Dr. Smith for consultation" is a man who honestly wants to get to the bottom of things. I have no objection to any veterinarian saying to me, "I just don't know what it is, but we're going to find out." I'm soothed by the fact that he admits he hasn't the answer and then prepares to go about getting the answer by every means at his disposal.

Respect begets respect. Demand at all times to know exactly what is being given or done to your dog. I have nothing but disgust for the owner who relates, "Oh, he told me what it was for, but I didn't want to sound like a fool by asking him to explain." Make it clear that *nothing* is to be done or given to your dog without your knowledge or consent, unless it is an emergency and it is impossible to reach you.

Do not insult your veterinarian by insisting he waste time doing jobs you should be doing, like cutting your dog's nails. In my opinion, dogs should not be boarded in veterinary clinics or even be taken into examining rooms unless they are deathly ill or bleeding to death, and that young puppies should never be in these areas, where infection is everywhere, no matter how careful and clean the veterinarian and his staff keep the premises.

With your veterinarian's aid, learn to do your own worming at home when it is necessary. Don't call him up during or after hours to chat with him idly about some article you've read which you are sure applies to the sneeze Fifi had last week.

Make very sure he isn't a faddist who believes, for instance, that meat is bad for dogs. Be certain that he understands the special needs of show dogs: more weight than the average pet; no shaving when it can possibly be avoided in cases of surface lacerations; no tattooing or vaccinating where it can be seen or where it might interfere with a show dog's gait or coat.

Don't hesitate to question him if you think he's wrong. You're paying the bills and you have a right to be consulted. And don't be slow to change veterinarians if the two of you are obviously not of the same mind on most things. When it comes to show dogs, you can't afford to "let Jack do it."

And speaking of bills, pay your veterinarian's on time, but always ask that they be itemized.

2

Early and
Intermediate Training

So, having decided that your puppy is going to be treated as a show prospect, or having determined that your older dog shows promise, what's the next step?

EARLY TRAINING

If you have bought the puppy from a reliable breeder, he or she will be eager to light your way, and you should follow his or her instructions. This is a relationship to be cultivated at all costs for many reasons you will discover as the friendship ripens. Having attended meetings of the local kennel club, now is the time to join it, and your breeder can be instrumental in getting you accepted for membership in this or various national breed clubs. Belonging to these organizations which provide you with much written material pertaining to your kind of dog is, to my way of thinking, the most intelligent way to become established, oriented, exposed, instructed, and protected as you learn the in's and out's of dog shows and purebred dogs.

But no matter how many helping hands are available to you, there is still much to be done on your own, so let's get started!

Bringing the Puppy Home

Bringing home a puppy is always an exciting time for everybody, and show puppies are no different than Heinz Fifty-Seven Varieties dogs—they want to investigate everything, chew almost everything, eat anything they can get in their mouths, and they usually drink a great deal of water. This is because your home, no matter how dedicated you are to preserving energy, is usually warmer than any kennel. While most authorities prattle, "Make sure a bowl of fresh, clean water is always available to the puppy," you'll have less cleaning up to do if you give him his water in small amounts frequently until he settles in. The charm of puppies doing the breast stroke in their water bowls fades a bit after mother has mopped the entire kitchen floor seventy-seven times!

Make sure he knows where his crate is. Pop him in it for a moment immediately upon arrival with a luscious dog biscuit or a scrap of meat you've saved for the occasion. In that way, the first thing he'll remember about his new home is the nice experience he had in his crate. During the days that follow, pause every now and then to toss a tidbit or a toy into his crate, which is *always left open* where he can get to it. In no time he'll be retiring there, quite on his own, for naps and nibbles.

Toilet Training

Having gone into the kind of papers that come *with* a dog, let's discuss the kind of papers you put *under* him. Housebreaking is a subject about which one could probably write an entire book. Everyone has his own theories on this subject and I am no exception. I beseech you to remember that we are dealing here with a *puppy!* Even if you selected an older animal of nine to ten months, as "grown up" as he looks to you, you must still in all fairness to him approach this problem exactly as you would approach an eight- or nine-week-old model, for the older "child" has been raised largely in the kennel. Like his infant brothers and sisters, going to the bathroom is very natural and quite clean as far as he's concerned.

Please, *don't scream* at any dog you are attempting to housebreak—you'll only frighten him into such a state of insecurity that he'll "go" more and more often because he's a nervous wreck.

There are certain toy breeds that, because of their lack of coat or sometimes because of their abundance of it, go outside only on very rare occasions. These are exceptions to our housebreaking rules, for to them paper always means potty time. Some tiny dogs are seriously susceptible to changes in temperature; some unusual types of coats break off and never reach desirable length if the wearer romps on anything harsher than white paper—even rugs are fatal. These dogs are not, repeat *not,* miserable! But theirs is a very special world, and if you have purchased this kind of animal, your breeder, experienced owners, and professional handlers will guide you through the intricate mazes surrounding the raising of this species of dog.

Don't attempt to leash-break and toilet-train a new dog at the same time! Remember our initial rule which stated, "Teach one thing at a time"? Well, this is a perfect example. Later on we'll discuss leash-breaking and getting the dog to "exercise" on leash. But in the beginning the two things that the new dog will be doing most often are eating and evacuating. So we have to get these under control first.

Any change of food or water from what he received at his original home may produce loose stools. If the animal's tummy is out of whack, you can't expect him to control himself all the time. And until he settles into his new routine and his stools are firm, he doesn't need a leash around his neck to further upset him emotionally.

We warned you earlier about some sort of outside enclosure for your pending house guest—use this if you are going to exercise him outside. Just don't start off with both feet in your mouth by overwhelming him with a list of house rules he can't possibly assimilate.

If you don't have a kennel and this dog is going to be in your home much of the time, we can go about the problem of housebreaking in one of two ways.

Providing you or some *responsible, willing* member of the family is going to be on hand with the dog almost constantly, we can get it quickly trained to go out of doors even in the winter, although it cannot be left out without proper shelter. This first method is the tried-and-true system of outside opportunities being offered fifteen minutes after each meal, and regularly at other times *throughout the day and night.* The secret is that while most dogs can perfectly well figure out they have "goofed" as you show *quiet* disapproval at their "performing" indoors, they are not psychic. If you don't go outside with the dog and praise him when he does his business *there,* he has no real way of knowing why he's being tossed out on his ear, particularly if the crime is already a matter of record. This method is dandy *only* if you can accompany the dog outside and *only* if most of the time you get him out *before* the urge overtakes him. We went into this system a bit earlier, showing how crates can be an aid in housebreaking. Remember, in the case of a very young puppy, he *can't* control his bowels and bladder for very long periods any more than you could when you were a child. Crate him when not supervised and at night; and no water after 5 P.M., please.

If it isn't convenient for you to always be "on duty," we have another idea, thanks to modern equipment and notions of psychology, that might fit better into your scheme of things.

Confine the pup to one room, the kitchen probably being your best bet. Kitchens are where the family spends much of its time, and kitchen floors are more puppy-proof than deep pile carpeting. Also, kitchens are busy, noisy places where a puppy can see and hear all sorts of things while spending most of his time with his new family. Place his crate in an out-of-the-way area which can be "roped off" with a home-made barrier or a commercially available wire pen suitable for indoor or outdoor use. Around his crate, plaster the floor with newspapers. Place a big garbage container lined with a strong plastic bag nearby and relax and enjoy the puppy. He'll be clean all in good time; meanwhile if he soils, pick it up without undue commotion, commit to the garbage, spray a bit of disinfectant around, and put down more clean paper.

This sort of paper-lined pen has another advantage. Accommodations at dog shows may require that the dog use a paper-lined exercise pen for the bathroom. If he gets used to this early in life, there is one less problem to hassle with later. Once he is paper-trained, he can be quickly encouraged to use the out-of-doors by moving a soiled piece of paper nearer and nearer the door until he is going outside entirely.

I would charge you to remember that the old-fashioned method of rubbing a dog's nose in his error probably caused more dogs to be filthy than it ever cured, and sensitive puppies often have severe psycho-logical reactions to such "training."

Feeding

Feeding puppies can lead you down some nerve-wracking paths, but you can avoid most of them by using your noodle. Most breeders send you home with a long list of items to buy, vitamins to get, a sample of their kibble or meal, and reams of advice both they—and I—know in our hearts you aren't going to follow. What's easy for a kennel person feeding twenty dogs is often ridiculously complicated for the owner of a single beastie.

When I sell a puppy I take the people into the kennel room and show them how I mix meat with whatever dry food I have on hand. I give them some idea of how much they should expect a single puppy to consume and caution that in the beginning they should *underfeed* rather than *overfeed* to establish positive eating habits. Puppies, you will find, are usually so enamored of the new surroundings, new noises, sights, people, and smells, not to mention the surplus of personal atten-tion, that while they are addicted to chair legs, the contents of wastebas-kets, squeaky toys, and that green glove you thought you'd lost, food-type food sometimes doesn't overly enthrall them for several days. I suggest the new parents feed a very young baby three times a day and an older pup twice. But for the first week it might be wise to cut the baby down to two and the older dog to one—*they will not die, nor will they starve to death*. They *will* learn to look forward to and *consume promptly* that which they are given at as regular intervals as possible, especially if food is not left with them, which is an awful thing to do, in my eyes!

Incidentally, I do not happen to believe that the regimen of an entire family must be reversed overnight in order to establish a good diet or a good routine for any puppy, show or otherwise. Rather, it is my contention that a puppy who learns from the beginning to fit into the rather casual lifestyle of most families today, grows up to be a healthy, happy relaxed dog.

All the special stress and so-called "science" diets touted by the manufacturers can, indeed, be useful with the pup that proves the exception to the rule. But in my opinion, dogs are carnivores. They need meat daily, raw or cooked, a sensible broad-spectrum vitamin supplement, and some sort of dry food—meal, kibble, crumbs, or buds. Ninety-nine per cent of these dry feeds are excellent as long as they are fed with intelligent attention to protein and vitamin-mineral supplements.

On the back of my stove I keep an old-fashioned "stock pot" into which goes everything left over from human meals—everything except bones and vegetables with seeds in them. When I mix my food the dogs get a ladle full of this yummy concoction, or more if I think it's warranted. Milk, according to some people, is supposed to cause loose stools. I have fed every kind of milk, from whole-dry as in calf-starters to skim as in diet, ever since I started in dogs with no such effect. Another theory holds that chocolate will cause worms, but all my dogs have snitched from my occasional candy bars with no ill results. And while uncooked whites of eggs are supposed to be undigestible to dogs, I've been giving mine raw eggs for twenty years without so much as a burp!

The point I'm trying to make is that there is no *one* correct method of feeding dogs. If you get your puppy going on something well-balanced which he loves and which makes him look splendid, than what difference does it make if my dogs, which also look splendid, are fed differently? Whatever we both are doing, we both must be doing something right. So don't yell for the stomach pump if you catch him chewing on an eggshell from the sink—it's pure calcium!

If you use frozen raw meat in your feeding plan, you can hasten the thawing process by submerging the meat in a pan of boiling water and covering it for a short while. Try never to feed meats, cooked or raw, that are colder than room temperature.

There are people who feed something different every day of the week on the theory that dogs get bored with eating the same thing over and over again. I've never found any basis for this. What they are saying is that *they* get bored feeding the same thing to the dog over and over again. Most experienced dog people feed more or less the same type of food year in and year out. They may supplement it with such goodies as a dollop of bacon grease twice a week because they believe it improves the coat (so do I!), or a portion of my "stock pot," or even a spoon of cottage cheese or a cup or two of noodles or spaghetti for the dog that needs more weight, but the basic ingredients are always the same.

Feeding dogs—be it one dog or twenty—can be just as expensive and complicated as you want to make it. Or you can use the same intelligence you use when preparing budget meals for your entire family. Occasional treats are one thing, but roast hummingbird wings are never a true necessity. For many years I was fortunate in having regular servings of fresh asparagus tips and white meat of chicken carried in lovingly by hand and entrusted to my care for the ultimate delight of a toy Poodle who boarded with me. "Herkimer will eat absolutely nothing else!" the lady explained, "and I know you are too busy to cook for him." Right on! Herkimer bloomed on cooked meat and kibble and I bloomed on chicken and asparagus. It was a divine arrangement which unfortunately ended all too soon when Herkimer, every pudgy, rotten-spoiled inch of him, moved to another state.

Exercise

Dogs started in the house can't spend their entire lives there. They must get out in the yard or in a run where they can get ground and gravel under their feet and wind and rain in their hair. Mother Nature grows coats better than anything that ever came out of a bottle, and for the average hardy breeds (most sporting, hound, working breeds, and a few of the other three groups), exposure to the elements and regular brushing are a foolproof combination. If this type of dog is kept constantly inside and scrupulously clean, it won't develop much coat, muscle tone, or strong feet, I can guarantee you.

So don't hesitate to put a hardy dog out if it is raining or snowing. He won't shrink, get pneumonia, or freeze to death—and above all, *don't* knit or buy him a doggy coat or blanket. His coat will never develop unless it gets a chance to do what it was put there for—protect the dog.

Again, we have exceptions. If you have ever had to dry and groom a sopping-wet Afghan or Poodle, you'll do all you can to avoid a second experience, though running in all other sorts of weather is a necessity. Then, too, there are breed standards that do not call for thick coats— Dalmations and Whippets are sometimes seen wearing blankets because we don't want Mother Nature to get her busy fingers into these coats! But again, these dogs, like all dogs, must get a chance to develop their underpinnings. Standing around whining to come back inside does no earthly good. So unless you can get out there yourself and play all sorts of games with Rover to stir his blood and stretch his legs, you'll have to solve the problem in other ways. Sometimes there is a friendly neighborhood dog whose owner would not be averse to his playing with your baby once a day (make sure he's up on all his shots!). Young puppies particularly, regardless of size at maturity, have got to have a chance to run and tear, "fromp and frolic," gallop and gallumph. If this is going to be an impossibility for you, there's no one else in the family to help, it doesn't cost much to hire a teen-ager to come by after school and take the pup for a romp. Keep close tabs on the relationship until you can count on the boy or girl not to overdo or to be too rough. Once high-school youngsters have had it explained to them *why* the dog is "different," what the *purpose* of his daily exercise is, how *important* their handling of the animal can be, I have found them to be extremely reliable and very proud of the part they are playing in developing a star of tomorrow.

The Outside Dog

Just as the inside dog, regardless of size, must get out of doors, so the outside-housed dog must be brought inside at regular intervals. Dogs used to spending most of their time indoors sometimes find their introduction to exercise pens or the back yard a traumatic thing; even more traumatic can be that first trip of any puppy *into* the house. Houses, to the kennel-oriented, inexperienced puppy, are great boxes filled with all sorts of "enemies"—slippery floors, sliding rugs, heavy things that go "boom!" when they are bumped. So if you want your show dog to handle unusual ring situations and confusion, give him a chance, in puppyhood, to learn about all kinds of environments.

Good Grooming Habits

Here we go with exceptions again—grooming for some breeds is so highly specialized that to go into each and its incipient problems would take forever. You don't brush a Labrador the same way you brush a Bearded Collie; you may use a comb on a Cairn Terrier but rarely on an Old English Sheepdog. The basic practices and habits of good grooming, however, are the same for dogs the world over, so here are some general rules for all dogs concerning daily attention to their persons.

BRUSHING

No matter what breed you have to work on, smooth-coated or long, there is a right and a wrong way to use your brush.

Place your hand on your dog's back, pressing down gently. Now, if you move your hand back and forth you will notice that the skin moves back and forth with your hand. If you understand this, it is simple to see why standing back and brushing the coat with one hand does little or no good. All you'll do is smooth the top layer of hair, because the skin will move to some extent with your movements of the brush and you'll never really touch the undercoat at all.

Dogs are brushed in single "areas" at a time. If you are right-handed and working on the left rear leg, for instance, take your left hand and starting at the dog's foot, pull the hair up the leg as far as the skin will move. Now use your brush to gently but firmly pull the hair back down out from under your left hand so it falls properly. Now move up the leg a few more inches and do that area.

In the case of smooth-coated breeds, use a mitt or medium-bristled brush to stimulate the hair and the skin. Again, brush by areas, not pulling the coat up but holding the skin taut so you get down to the "roots" of the matter.

TABLE TIME

Once a day it's up on that crate or grooming table for a quick once-over with mitt, brush, or comb. While up there, the greenhorn learns there is nothing to fear from the grooming loop (or restrainer) and that standing still pleases the boss. Never mind *how* he stands right now, even if he crosses his legs. Just get him to stand still by soothing words and soothing motions of your hands. And in the beginning, very short periods on the table, please, topped off with a special tidbit of some kind *before* you lift him down. Notice I said "lift him down"— letting him jump encourages him to do so when your back is turned, and he could hang himself or be seriously frightened if he turned the table or crate over on top of himself. Also, at maturity, many large breeds can hurt themselves leaping off tables even on command. Don't *start* this bad habit with your pup, and you'll save a lot of time, worry, and disappointment.

MANICURE SESSION

Once a week it's Toenail Time in the Teepee. Yep, I said toenails; and, nope, you are *not* going to let the vet do it—remember, we discussed this earlier? There is absolutely nothing to be gained by getting in a swivet over toenails. They are to be found at the end of the dog's toes, just like yours are found at the end of your toes, and you cut your pup's nails just as regularly and as matter-of-factly as you do your own. In fact, in early puppyhood, you can use the same clippers. But sooner or later you'll have to have one of those manufactured for this purpose. There are three or four different kinds, and choosing one is a matter of which looks easiest for you to use. The only word of caution I would issue here is that the guillotine type (those with a hole in the blade which cannot be changed in size) are soon outgrown by the giant breeds, so the pincher models are best for all-around use.

One of the "secrets" to successful nail cutting is to determine just how far you can safely cut without nicking the quick. This is done by getting the foot in a position where you can clearly see the area of

Sometimes the first time on the table doesn't bring giggles and smiles. Take a moment to reassure the puppy by hugging and patting. You'll be surprised at how quickly he becomes used to the procedure.

dead nail. This calls, first of all, for a good, strong light over your grooming table.

Instead of standing in front of the dog and facing him, stand at one side. Take hold of his pastern, or ankle, and tip the foot up and back the way it naturally goes, so that you are looking at the foot upside down. If you approach your task from this position—much the same position, incidentally, as that used by the blacksmith when he shoes a horse—the underneath part of the toenails will be facing you and you will be able to see, quite easily, just what is dead nail and what is not. Dead nail on all but black toenails is white, as opposed to the pink part of the nail which begins right where the end of the quick lies. In the case of solid black nails, you can usually tell the dead portions becaues they are full of dirt and form a small hook on the end of the nail.

It is unlikely that the nails of your young puppy have grown to such a serious length that you will have to cut beyond the quick. So simply take the paw in one hand, clippers in the other, and to build your confidence as well as the pup's, snip off a ridiculously teensy bit of the end of the nail in the beginning. Do one foot, then put the clippers down and brush a bit. Progress like this until all toes are tackled, including dewclaws if still attached. When not removed at birth, the dew claws are located a few inches up the front leg and sometimes also on the hind leg.

If you approach this project in a matter-of-fact way, chances are the pup will too. But from the very beginning of this particular phase of grooming *I warn you to tolerate absolutely no nonsense.* If he starts to scream, don't look at him—you might try humming loudly or even singing. The words, "I am not hurting you!" sung over and over to the tune of "Ta-ra-ra-boom-tee-aye" constitute counter-noise and at the same time bolster your morale. If, though securely anchored in the grooming noose, he twists and fidgets, reach over and swat him on the back of the lap and *keep on going,* do not pause an instant. If he is still struggling so you can't get a good grip on the paw or are afraid it will break off in your hand, move around behind the pup so that his bottom is firmly braced against your tummy and *keep on going.*

Puppy or no puppy, some of them, not getting your attention any other way, will bite. This does not mean the puppy is vicious, and anybody who says he is afraid of a puppy shouldn't own a dog. "My dog won't let me cut his nails," spoken within hearing distance of this author, has been known to cause a reaction which shook steeples miles away. Your animal is your child, and to admit, even to yourself, that you can't manage your child, or worse yet, that he manages you, is absolutely unbelievable to me!

Slapping dogs in the face is not a good idea to practice on a regular basis unless you want a hand-shy animal ducking every time you say "Boo!" Dogs or puppies that try to bite—I say *try* because if you nip it in the bud now you'll never have to worry about it later—are the exception to this rule. The very second those little teeth settle on your hand or wrist, swat firmly and accurately and—stop me if you've heard this before—*keep on going!*

Do not sympathize under any circumstances! If you inadevertently nick a puppy nail and it bleeds, continue; it will stop in a moment or two. If you nick a nail on an older dog or puppy, you may need a commercial coagulant to stop the bleeding, but don't bother with that until you are through with the foot you are presently working on. If the bleeding is severe, don't panic—nails bleed as though they would never stop, but they do stop in all but the most unusual cases of "bleeders." Even in these rare cases, the nail has to bleed for *hours* before the dog will even become slightly weak from loss of blood. Gory it may get; fatal it isn't likely to be!

In the absence of powdered or liquid coagulants manufactured for use on dogs' nails, use talcum powder, ordinary baking flour, cornstarch, cold water, or alum. Fill a container (such as a paper cup ripped down to half-depth) with the powder and plunge the whole foot into it, pressing firmly into the powder.

In the event of such a "happening," I can guarantee you the dog will not hate you the rest of your life, nor will he never "permit" you near his feet again—that decision is up to you. Remember, *you* are *his* owner, not vice versa.

With older dogs whose nails have grown too long, you may have to deliberately cut them back. The nails are a proper length on any dog when you cannot hear them tick-ticking on the floor as he walks. This is a most unpleasant session and will require professional or experienced help. Do it *now;* then regular toenail care will guarantee against having to repeat the procedure.

Contrary to popular opinion, cement runs or city sidewalks or gravel do not always take care of toenails. Some dogs have to be clipped twice a week; some do fine with a once-a-month trimming. They are like people in that some of us grow more nails than others, due in part to the amount of calcium in the system. If your pup does not require weekly nail jobs, fool regularly with his feet anyway so it becomes a part of his lifestyle.

With older dogs that have not been introduced to toenail drill or with particularly rambunctious puppies, you might try doing the rear feet first. If they don't see what you're doing, you sometimes get a head start.

I can just hear particularly sensitive readers moaning, "Lordie, if it's going to be such a battle, why bother?" You "bother" because you'll absolutely ruin the feet if you don't keep nails under control. Dogs are never comfortable walking on their nails (would you be?), and as the nails press more and more against the ground, the toes are shoved further and further apart.

It was once my lot to "operate" on an eleven-year-old mixed breed of the spaniel type. Her very elderly lady owner brought her to the kennel because the little dog was growling whenever anyone touched her feet or legs, and she had never acted this way in her life before. The owner was almost blind and asked for help. That poor animal's nails had grown all the way around and back up into her pads! The ends had pierced the feet wherever they touched the skin, and each nail had forced its own "socket" of discharge and infection. No wonder she was growling! I had to send out to the local garage for insulation cutters which opened wide on the end, because I could not get at the ends of the nails to slide either type of standard dog nail clipper into position. I had considered muzzling the dog, but I looked in her eyes as she lay on the table and I knew that in her awful misery she realized we were trying to help. I cut every single nail almost back to the toe and there wasn't a drop of blood, that is how long they were. And not once did she move, bless her heart, except to follow with her eyes every movement of my hands.

We soaked her feet, packed the holes with antiseptic ointment, and gave her a shot of antibiotic. She healed beautifully. I kept those nails in a jar in the kennel for years—as a lesson.

As we mentioned in an earlier chapter, you may prefer to do your pup's nails with the attachment that can be purchased for use on the end of electric clippers, in which case you'll want to spend time getting him used to the clipper motor. You may prefer to file nails. Whatever solution seems best to you, approach the process with the same advice given for cutting nails. I really don't care how you do them, just *do* and *keep doing* on a regular basis.

OTHER COSMETIC CHORES

That new pup must also get used to having his ears cleaned, his teeth scraped if necessary, his whiskers trimmed in many breeds, and his tail brushed. All of these things may meet with resistance in the beginning, but once again, *keep on going* is the best advice.

For the average-sized ear I use rubbing alcohol, which breaks up wax deposits. I put a piece of cotton over my index finger, soak it in alcohol, and squeeze out the surplus. Then I use my finger to swab out the ear canal—no, there is no danger of puncturing the eardrum, believe me. With smaller breeds, use Q-tips, but I usually add extra cotton to be doubly sure of not scratching. Be certain ears are dry

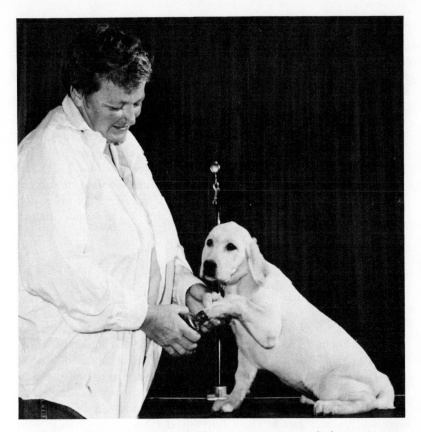

Starting early is a big help, whether you are cutting whiskers, trimming nails, or just brushing out dead hair. Keep the sessions short and always end them on a happy note.

when you finish by using a dry cotton swab. Alcohol will sometimes make a dog drool, so don't worry if he does. Never use it in sick ears—ears that are pink or red with irritation call for warm baby oil or a veterinary's product. Again, use your head. Teeth that collect tartar are unsightly; it is easily removed with a tool made for this purpose. When the dog is up on the table, any work you can do around his mouth to teach him to permit his mouth and teeth to be examined is "money in the bank." It's foolish to keep whiskers cut all the time— but regular snipping noises made with scissors around the dog's muzzle become an excellent dress rehearsal for the real thing.

If your dog is one of the breeds that must lie down to be groomed, teach him early. With the dog standing broadside to you on the grooming surface, remove his head from the grooming loop, surround him with both arms, pull him *to* your chest, then bend forward over him to put him on his side. *Under no circumstances lie on him, pinning him to the table to hold him in position*—this is absolutely the most terrifying experience any dog can have, and if he bites you during such a "lesson" I hope he gets you good! Once you have him on his side, stand up and croon, "Stay, Stay," petting him for a few seconds as he lies there mystified at how he got where he is so suddenly. Then issue a command which, from that point on, will always mean release to the dog— "Okay!"—and when he gets on his feet put your arms around his neck and smooch him as you praise him.

All these things take time for any pup or inexperienced dog to get used to. But they will settle into a routine if you do. Your show dog will grow up to be nervous and neurotic only if you behave around him in a nervous and neurotic manner.

BATHING

Now wake up that older dog and start paying attention, because baths are next on the agenda. The older dog is going to be hardest to handle here, for obvious reasons. If he has learned to stay in tub or shower without turning the whole thing into a six-round, no-holds-barred wrestling match, fine and dandy; if not, treat him as if he were eight weeks or six months old and start all over again, one step at a time, as we are about to explain. Obviously, it's much easier to teach a wee pup that baths are neither anything to be afraid of nor an opportunity for fun and games. Dogs can slip and hurt themselves in tubs and showers just as people can, and a show dog isn't much good at any age with a bruised shoulder.

The first thing to tackle is that tubs and showers are not to be feared. From time to time, plonk your show pup in the tub and feed it a biscuit, then plop it out. Or walk it into the shower stall using the same techniques.

Just as you are working on standing (or stacking) on the table, use the same technique in the bath. I mention the use of showers because some people don't have tubs in their homes. If you have a very small breed or puppy, a metal lawn-type end table with a folded towel on it is a good idea in a shower so that the pup is up and not likely to be as frightened as he would be way down *"there"* with tons of water pelting him from way up *"here."* In any case, when using a shower to wash a dog, strip down yourself and go on in with him. There's no point in trying to stay dry while showering a dog—it's virtually impossible!

To get puppies used to sprays of water, start by just using a plain warm spray for a moment or two. Then turn it off, towel-dry your victim, and take him to the grooming table where you can use your hand dryer or table model carefully and briefly while he gets used to the sound of the motor. Breeds that are groomed with electric clippers can be gradually introduced to that sound by leaving the clippers running near them while they are in their crates, loose in the kitchen, or when they are getting brushed on the grooming table.

We'll go into the fine points of shampoos and rinses later on; for now, all we're interested in is getting the puppy, old or young, and the more mature but inexperienced dog familiar with the practices, sights, and sounds he will encounter the rest of his life as a show dog.

The bottoms of tubs and showers are slick. To avoid slipping, use old towels to help the dog keep his footing.

Leash-breaking

Once the puppy feels at home, he must learn to walk on a leash if he is to safely negotiate the world beyond the front door. Leash-break-ing—a perfectly horrible term—more often than not means that the dog gets broken while the leash stays whole! If this pup of yours, not to mention the older dog, is to look and act happy in the show ring, he must look and act happy on his leash. This is accomplished by associating his leash with pleasant things.

I would hardly recommend the cruel solution of one "dog lover" I knew who simply tied her terrified charges by their leashes to trees and let them flip-flop themselves into submissiveness born of absolute terror! Little breeds can sometimes be tougher to leash-break than giant breeds, but whatever the size of the animal, I urge extreme caution and a liberal application of common sense.

Let your infant or greenhorn drag his leash around the home for a while until he gets used to having something attached to him. When it comes time for him to move along with someone holding said leash, apply reverse psychology. Most dogs when sitting on the end of unfamil-iar leashes instinctively want to go the other way when you entice them to "come." So do things their way.

Get someone else the pup loves and knows to hold him on leash while you run away, encouraging him to catch you. Use a tidbit if you feel it's called for. Instruct your helper to scoot right along with the puppy as he comes, putting little or no restraint on the leash but always holding it. When the pup reaches you, get right down on the floor and wrestle with him until he is almost drunk with delight. Now you hold the leash while his other friend plays the same game. After a few times the game gets to be more "fun than anything," and in his efforts to reach either one of you to be rewarded with love or a choice tidbit he forgets all about the "attachment," and little by little you can increase pressure.

Or, you can pick up the dog and, with leash attached, remove him from the house or kennel area. Because strange surroundings don't "send" him, he'll usually dive back from whence he came, with you running along and encouraging him as you hold onto the leash. Whatever method you choose, use it wisely and very sparingly. Use only a straight-slip show leash to begin with; you are not interested in control now, only in self-confidence.

Teaching puppies to got to the bathroom on leash is vitally important, and puppyhood is the time to start. Once your pup is leash-broken you can use it during housebreaking drill. Make sure you don't use areas where you can be accused of lack of consideration for other people or of abusing the property of others. If accidents should happen (and they will), show your sense of responsibility by removing the evidence with the trusty wads of Kleenex or plastic bag you carry in your purse or pocket at all times.

Always praise when success is achieved. We'll give you more advanced techniques for effective "on demand" toilet training as we go along.

The Car-sick Dog

Now it is time to start traveling; it is also time to face the fact that now is the time you will probably be confronted with the problem of the car-sick dog. And believe me, even with a *little* dog this can be a *big* problem.

Early automobile rides and plenty of them for the young puppy usually do the trick, and take my word for it, puppyhood is the time to tackle this problem. Whether dealing with a puppy or an older dog, I don't believe you should try to solve it with the so-called motion-sickness pills. I'll admit I have met people who used them with satisfactory results; I have met many more who ran into such problems as no-car-sickness in exchange for dogs so dopey when they got to where they were going it was impossible to move them, let alone train or exhibit them.

From the moment I discover I have a puppy or a dog with this problem, that animal goes everywhere I go—along with *mountains* of newspaper! He is put in his crate in the car where I can watch him carefully. The moment I notice he is starting to pant or drool I pull over to the side of the road, snap on his leash and take him for a short walk, praising him lavishly. Then back in the car. If the poor thing should "woops" before I can get him out, I simply lift him over the mess, walk him, roll up the soiled paper, put fresh down, and we start out again. I never scold—he doesn't do it on purpose, for heaven's sake!—but I never praise unless I get him out of the crate *prior* to disaster. The "mistake" I treat as a matter of course. Usually after two or three "barfings" he gives up and is quiet. Sometimes it takes lots more messes. And each time we start out I know I'm going to have to expect the situation to rear its head all over again. But usually, sooner or later, *he will get over it!* Some dogs go through their whole lives throwing up within the first five miles or so of any trip, and then they are fine until they get home. Some do better in closed crates, some in wire ones; the company of other dogs in a car sometimes helps; many people believe that it is *how* the dog rides that causes his upset—never crossways or backwards, for instance.

Other suggestions: position your dog's crate forward in station wagons so it is not located over the rear axle but between the front and rear axles; there is less vibration this way. Talk to your dog pleasantly as you drive. It matters not what you say—you can recite the alphabet if you can't think of anything better, but the sound of your unruffled voice sometimes helps. Or turn on the radio, but bear in mind that hard-rock blaring in the animal's ear is liable to frighten him or make him even more tense. How you drive is important too. Take it easy on roller-coaster roads and swing into turns vvvveeeerrrryyyy gradually. Don't forget to check the air intake and exhaust on your car when carrying *any* kind of dog. It might be necessary to get a flap to direct the flow from the exhaust pipe, especially when driving during the summer months with rear windows open; such fumes do little to soothe ruffled stomachs in man or beast, and can be deadly.

Whatever causes it, car sickness is a problem no dog or his owner really needs. Withholding food or water for several hours before the start of a car trip certainly helps. But I have known dogs with nothing in their tummies to drool and hiccup so badly that their papers had to be changed as regularly as if they were actually vomiting.

I do *not* happen to believe that the solution is to let the dog lie in his mess to teach him that it's "bad" and "nasty" to get car-sick. Such reasoning is sloppy, lazy, and stupid.

In pleasant weather I will often crate a car-sick pup in the stationary car for the night with perhaps a good traveling buddy for company. I have found that sometimes the realization that the car isn't always moving helps.

Until triumph is yours, think positively. I can assure you, from years of experience, that sooner or later *most* dogs that travel regularly and have happy associations with a car do get over or outgrow this problem.

Whither Thou Goest

In the beginning, take that puppy or green older dog absolutely everywhere you go, barring jail and Sunday-morning services. And I don't mean to take him in a box in the back of the car. I mean carry him in his crate or cage in the car and remove him whenever you stop to window-shop. Laundromats are neat places to bring your dog—while the clothes whirl around in washer or dryer, you and he can whirl around the block and amble back and forth in the parking lot of the crowded shopping center.

You will find that by concentrating on your pup, and looking neither right nor left, you will never see the signs saying "No Dogs Allowed" or, "Health Regulations Prohibit etc., etc.," so you cannot be accused of knowingly breaking the rules. I have spent my life "exposing" puppies to areas so marked and only three times have I been asked to leave, which, of course, I did promptly and politely. But by then I had gotten what I came for!

At the same time you are getting the pup used to the big, wide world (and be sure that *all* his inoculations are completed before you start early training anywhere but on your own property), try to locate nearby handling classes. If you have joined a kennel club, it probably sponsors them and will give you the details. If not, check with ye-olde-breeder again, or the newspaper or your veterinarian. Handling classes or breed classes are the ideal place for any pup to learn what fun it is to be in a ring and attend dog shows. While he's having a good time becoming an extrovert, you will be learning about gaiting patterns, stacking and grooming techniques, what is meant by "baiting," and getting your little monster agreeable to having strangers look at his teeth and fondle his private parts.

I realize that lots of people feel that a twelve-to-fourteen-week-old puppy is too young to bring to class, but I don't agree. The thing to remember here is that a young puppy's span of concentration is *extremely* limited. While you want him to develop without hang-ups, don't forget that too much exposure can be just as foolhardy and danger-ous as too little. If the handling classes last an hour, go ahead and take part—but work your baby just a few minutes at a time. Tote his crate along and, for part of the class, allow him to sit in it, watch the other dogs, and get used to the confusion and noise.

If the only class near enough to you to be considered is an obedience class, all is not lost. Contact the trainer and explain that you have a show puppy which needs exposure and that you are perfectly willing to pay the fee for the course, but that all you want is to get the puppy walking on a leash and standing. Explain that you will do your own handling at your own speed and that the pup is too young to be con-stantly on the floor. Most obedience trainers are perfectly wonderful, dedicated men and women who will understand and wecome you to their group, provided you in no way hold up their classes or interfere with the dogs that are there to learn training exercises.

Now comes the query, "Well, as long as I'm attending, why *not* take the obedience course?" The answer is this—whether you take the obedience class or not depends on your dog's age, his disposition, and most of all, on who is in charge of the training class you are planning to attend.

Because most professionals blanch visibly when they hear that a dog they may be handling has had obedience training, people sometimes believe handlers are against obedience. Nothing could be further from the truth! What we are against is that *minority* of trainers who do *not* know what they are doing and who take the spirit and style out of every dog they get their hands on by demanding exacting work too soon.

While there are show puppies that should have serious obedience work when they are four months old, and others whose mental make-up decries formal obedience work of any kind at any age, these are exceptions. The main thing, whether you train formally or informally, is that you keep and channel the wiggle and giggle if you ever hope to win at point shows. Once you've taken the enthusiasm out of most puppies, *nothing on earth can ever put it back.*

The main problem most show folks find with obedience dogs is that they are conditioned to sit every time the handler stops; the show dog, when not gaiting, is supposed to stand in the show ring. Since I have shown a lot of C.D.X.ers and working retrievers to their show titles, this doesn't bother me in the least. No one is going to arrest you if your dog sits in the show ring, and since part of obedience is learning to stand on command as well as sit, I can't see any real problem. As long as you can get the dog to stand when it is his turn to be examined, I don't care what he's doing with his "bod" during the time the judge is looking elsewhere. Position in life, I have learned, is not necessarily everything!

INTERMEDIATE TRAINING

Baiting

It now behooves us to learn about the preparation and use of bait in getting our standing show dog to look alert and alive in that position.

Having used bait of one kind or another in the ring for years and years, with all breeds of dogs, it always comes as a shock to me to hear "You don't bait Wolfhounds!" or, "You are not supposed to bait sporting dogs, you know!" or, "I don't use bait—that's cheating!" or even, "My dog won't bait."

There was a time in life when I listened to such claptrap because I was trying to learn and I naïvely supposed that anyone who would volunteer a bold statement like this must know what he was talking about. Once upon a time I lost the breed in Welsh Springers at Madison Square Garden because I believed a perfectly sincere owner who swore his dog wouldn't bait in the ring; by the time I discovered he didn't know what he was talking about, it was all over but the weeping.

The reason for using bait is to keep the dog on his toes when the going gets hot and dreary; to prevent boredom in long classes; and to pull from that dog the most engaging attitude and expression it is possible to get out of him.

As a handler, professional or amateur, it's your job to make the dog you have in the ring look as sharp as he possibly can. If this requires a squeaky mouse, then you enlist the aid of the nearest squeaky mouse. If the sound of a dime-store clicker hidden in your pocket does the trick, invest a quarter. A practical joker may have one of those buzzers you can palm for "startling" handshakes—borrow it, and if it works without causing the judge to leap through his skin, fine and dandy. I have baited Chesapeakes with the feather from a Mallard's tail, and a Basset Hound named Eloise reacted splendidly to somebody's "lucky" rabbit's foot. I have known a Keeshond to go "ape" for chocolate-covered mints, and I finished a Schipperke who did handsprings for peanuts.

But over the years I have become convinced that the one bait more dogs take to than anything else is liver, pork or beef, whatever happens to be cheapest. Before we discuss how to use it, let's take a moment to find out how to prepare it.

After purchasing a pound or two of liver, bring it home, put it in a saucepan full of water, and boil it until the squishy raw stuff becomes firm. Remove from the water and rinse off any residue by holding it under the cold-water tap. Now place the clean, firm pieces of liver in exactly the same-sized pieces it came from the market on a cookie sheet or a piece of foil in a 200-300-degree oven. Sprinkle it lightly with ordinary table salt and bake until the top side is dry. Flip the pieces over and repeat the process. When both sides are done—dry— take it out and let it cool. Then freeze it and take out what you need when you need it. Liver prepared this way, when thawed at the show and dried with paper towels to eliminate the sweat that might have accumulated between freezer and cooler, can be used in the pockets of your finest trousers or dresses without fear of stain.

And pockets, ladies and gentlemen, are where bait is kept when you are in the ring, not in plastic bags clutched in your hand and then securely snarled in your leash when you need it. What if you don't have pockets? Then tuck it behind your arm band or in your belt. Since male attire is eminently more sensible than that of the female, men rarely have pocket troubles.

But men and women alike can have trouble with liver if they don't harken to these two warnings:

1. Don't salt your liver before cooking with garlic salt. Sure it preserves, and sure, dogs love the smell; many people do not, however, and since every now and then you are reduced to holding a chunk of liver in your mouth, forget the garlic unless you want the judge to flee in self defense when you breathe in his direction!

2. Do not dice up the liver until the pieces are practically microscopic. Sometimes it is necessary to throw liver to get the dog's ears up, and he'll never see the bait if you slice it until it resembles peastone gravel. Even with toy breeds, leave the pieces large and chunky. You can break off smaller pieces from that chunk, or he can tear pieces from it with his teeth, but make sure there's enough of it, in a single hunk, for him to see plainly and clearly.

It's wise to start using bait early in the dog's show training, and it's also wise for you to get used to carrying it and using it. While you should always let him know you have tucked it in your pocket, use it only at classes, matches, and shows so he learns to look forward to these places early in life. Small puppies learn to stack easily if they first learn to stand free and bait.

Any dog's first experience with bait generally sets the tone of his baiting habits. When training the show puppy or the older dog, don't feed before training and then expect him to go crazy for liver or any other food. When it comes to classes, matches, and shows, feed him after you get home as a sort of reward; it may interrupt his feeding schedule, but it won't cause dwarfism, nor will he starve. Puppies are usually curious about nibbles of any kind, so they learn to bait sweetly and delightfully. Don't overdo it; teasing will turn them off faster than overfeeding, but tempting them before rewarding their attention should bring the desired results in dogs of any age. With the dog on a loose leash in front of you, facing you, hold your bait in both hands at the level of his muzzle. Extend it so he can see what it is and start talking to him quietly and excitedly. "Well now, what's that? Oh boy, doesn't that smell good? It *is* good—try some." Rip off a little piece and let him eat it to prove your point. "There—isn't that yummy? Well, want some more? You do? (in a low tone from the pit of your tummy) "You do?" (in a squeaky high voice from the top of your head). The change in voice, if exaggerated enough, should cause him to tilt his head engagingly in his curiosity and start his tail wagging. Give him another piece—and keep up the monologue. And as you tempt, reward, and coo, hold your hands steady with that muzzle; don't bring them up too high, or as Confucius (he was an old Chinese dog handler!)

used to say: "When head goes up, bottom goes down!"

If any dog, puppy or adult, is the type who sees food and then launches himself at you full tilt, you'd best break it up fast before you land flat on your back with the dog sitting on your tummy licking your face and asking for more. This super enthusiasm can be channeled without losing the spirit behind it in one easy lesson, provided you do it right the first time.

Bracing yourself carefully, stand up bravely and show him the bait. As he hurtles through the air at you, bring one knee up and bump him sharply so that he falls back off balance. Immediately snap your leash to make him stand and give him a big piece of liver. Done correctly, the dog has no idea "wot hoppened" and approaches the bait with more respect in the future. As I said, timing is all important here, and if you get this lesson out of the way the first time his taste buds overcome his good manners, you'll never have any more trouble. On the rare occasion when you can sense he might be about to forget himself, just raise that knee and watch him settle down!

Many amateurs are deeply confused about *when* to bait. Except in rare instances, never bait while moving your dog, for you ruin his true gait and make it impossible for a judge to evaluate his ability to move. Dogs leaping up and down trying to get liver from an outstretched hand as they gallop along generally do not delight the hearts of judges. So even when you are practicing alone in the back yard or cellar, when you get ready to execute any ring pattern, show him your free hand to make it clear to him there's nothing in it.

The occasions when the art of baiting is best employed, in training or in actual practice, are numerous. Bait in the ring during that boring period after you have been examined and before you are individually moved. As you complete your pattern and are returning to the judge, stop about two feet away and swing around in front of the dog to allow him to stand on a loose leash and bait as the judge appraises him standing free. Of course your dog must learn to stand in a posed show position. But if he is particularly good front and rear, stack him as little as possible. Pose him free, at the end of your leash, whenever possible, at training classes, sanctioned matches, or licensed shows. What if you are the only one handling this way? you ask. Well, what if you *are?* What's the matter with standing out in a crowd? Bait also when you first enter the ring and the judge is not quite ready or the steward is still checking armbands. I find this is the period that causes many novices to go to pieces. Not knowing what to do while waiting, they start pushing and pulling at the dog. By the time the judge arrives, the dog is ready to go home. Whenever you don't know what to do, whenever you are particularly nervous, haul out the goodies and bait.

Show dog or obedience dog, family pet or working retriever, muddy paw prints decorating your clean clothes are never funny. The time to discourage such behavior is during puppyhood; but a carefully aimed, well-placed knee will discourage the most mature delinquent. Done right the first time, once is enough to convince most dogs that the best place to collect love and kisses is when a dog is sitting or standing firmly on all four feet. *Photo by Glenn Easton*

It generally delights the dog so much that you gain confidence in his attitude and both of you settle down.

Except in very unusual instances, don't punish severely by slapping or screaming threats when the dog is so sharp for the bait that he gets your fingers by mistake. This is the spirit you want in the ring, so early training is the place to encourage it. Some dogs are born with it, some are not, but "them wot does" are jewels to show and you will thank your lucky stars for that desire before you are through. You will soon learn how to offer the nether end of a large piece of liver and survive without bloodshed; the trick is *not* to pull your hand away but to push it at the dog as he munches. (Also, nipped knuckles stop bleeding almost immediately if you suck on them.) Years ago I showed a marvelous little bandit of a Corgi, and today the third finger of my right hand is still a network of very tiny scars. Whenever I'd let my mind wander in the ring he would bring me back to reality in short order with a lightning swipe at the liver that usually left tears in my eyes. But nowadays when I look at that battle-scarred pinkie, it brings back only the good memories of the exciting wins he gave me!

Every now and then you run across the dog that doesn't immediately take to liver. The reasons for this range from his being too busy looking around at everything else in the ring to have time to nibble on request, to a plain and simple dislike for liver. It is often possible to change his mind if you make a real project of it.

Instead of "bisqies" by way of reward at home, start tossing him little pieces of liver. If he's going to be alone in his crate for a while, drop a few bits into his cage and leave him alone; with nothing to distract him he just might try it and discover he likes it. Skip a meal and about an hour after he should have been fed, give him some liver. When you do feed, top off his bowl with a hunk of liver used as a garnish like a maraschino cherry. Sometimes you can slip a piece of liver into a dog's mouth, hold the mouth loosely shut until he starts chewing and discovers he enjoys what he's eating.

Under no circumstances force or pressure the dog until baiting becomes ugly and unpleasant. Try everything you can think of and if everything fails, start looking for something other than liver to turn on your dog.

One more quick story about baiting, and then we'll go on to other things to teach the intermediate dog. Several years ago I was starting a rather sullen bitch. She was structurally lovely but hated dog shows, crates, people—anything I liked, actually. So I showed her the first time, and it was a disaster. She wouldn't bait and she urinated all over the judge's hand—oh, it was splendid, just splendid! I put her back in the car and took her out in the late afternoon to try to win some kind of positive response. She was hungry now and snapped wolfishly at the bait.

All of a sudden I had a stylish, wagging-tailed dog to show. My kennel girl was watching this session in the show's parking lot. A stranger wandered by and stopped to observe. I praised the dog lavishly and handed her back to the girl, saying, "That's the secret, then, keep her hungry." (Meaning, of course, that we would feed the dog *after* she was shown from this point on.) The poor observer completely misunderstood and said with some alarm, "Is that the way you do it—if they don't win, you don't feed 'em?"

Open Wide

When a judge examines a dog's mouth he can be doing so for several reasons.

Certain breed standards call for a dog not to be undershot (like a bulldog) or overshot (like Mortimer Snerd). If this is the case, the judge will ask to see the "bite" (i.e., how the teeth come together in the front of the mouth). To show your dog's bite, support the lower jaw with the right hand by holding a flap of loose skin under the jaw with your fingers. With your thumb, push down gently on the lower lip at the front of the muzzle, baring the lower teeth. At the same time, using your left thumb and index finger, slide up the soft, loose skin of the upper muzzle on either side of the nose, exposing the upper teeth. *The mouth must be firmly closed as you show the bite.*

I know my directions seem to call for more than two hands and at least twenty fingers. But it works out very easily, actually. If the dog tends to back away, take the smallest of those eleven fingers (on the right hand) and hook it through his collar or leash. Above all, keep your own head up and out of the way; the judge is supposed to look— you don't have to! And tilt the dog's head up slightly in the process so the judge doesn't have to crouch down to see what he is looking for.

Other standards call for "complete dentition," such as required in Doberman Pinschers and German Shepherds. In this case you must also be able to pull the lips all the way back toward the ears on either side of the mouth, turning the dog's head from side to side to make things easier for the judge.

Some breeds, such as the Chow Chow, which must have a blue-black tongue with black mouth tissues, must get used to permitting you to open their mouths wide while strangers peer into the depths. Never cover a dog's nose with hand or fingers as you handle his mouth, because interrupting his breathing processes frightens him.

It is wise in early and intermediate training to get a pup used to having every inch of his mouth made available for inspection. Be firm and quiet in your demands, but insist on obedience. Nothing turns off a judge more than to ask to see the mouth and wind up ten minutes later still waiting while the handler wrestles with an inexperienced dog. There is nothing painful in this process and no reason for disobedience except inexperience. This is best taught alone on a table in the beginning, particularly with toy breeds, who tend to show great disapproval at

Showing a dog's teeth, or bite, to the judge needn't be a traumatic experience if you will expend a little time practicing. Some judges are more patient than others, but the most understanding in the world is not likely to be terribly "turned on" by having to wait to see a dog's mouth until the handler has steer-wrestled the dog to the ground! Teach the dog to think nothing of having his mouth and muzzle handled. Keep your own head out of the way and see to it that your hands function lightly and quietly.

the arrival from above of strange, enormous, prying fingers, each one of which is probably bigger than the dog!

A Private Matter

Male dogs must get used to having judges touch them in very private areas to determine whether they indeed have two testicles. In the beginning, especially (doubly especially with toys!), "cold hands, warm heart" may be OK in couplet form, but such poetic niceties are wasted on Mr. Dog. You can lick this problem as you groom in puppyhood by stroking the male dog in the area under his tail. He will probably react by sitting down and glaring at you the first time you try it, "Well of all the nerve!" dripping from his injured countenance. *Do not get rough about it!* Pull his head down with one hand and scratch his tummy with the other and he will stand again. Continue your examination. If sitting persists with large breeds, hold one hand under the tummy while you gently "examine" with the other. Make the lessons short and happy. If you have a Dachshund, you will have discovered by now, as we all do sooner or later, that it is sometimes difficult to *tell* whether the animal is sitting or standing. In training the Dachshund to stand while his testicles are examined or while the rest of him is being handled, a frozen orange juice can which is thawed enough so that it won't stick to things which come in contact with it, can be placed on its side under the dog's tummy. If the dog tries to sit, his tummy gets cold, and that usually does the trick.

As soon as the dog is used to being handled "there," ask friends to examine your male dog while you hold him. Make sure no one is ever rough or sudden about it and that, as you hold the dog, your hands stay quiet, untense and soothing.

Mirror, Mirror

One of the most valuable investments you can make is a very inexpensive closet-door mirror purchased from the local dime store. Once the dog is standing quietly on the grooming table, it's time to move him to good old terra firma, and the more "firma" the less "terra"! Pick a free spot, indoors or out, where the footing is slip-proof. But before practicing standing or stacking your dog, take that nice new mirror and prop it lengthwise opposite the area on which you are going to work. Then, as you go along you can look up periodically from what you are doing to check your progress.

Toy dogs are generally examined and stacked on a table in the show ring, as are some other breeds; to determine which, go to dog shows and watch or ask your breeder about your particular breed—it makes sense to train them on the table. Simply move the mirror up higher so that it is even with the table. Dogs that stack on floor or table are a joy to work with.

Certain breeds—Collies, rough and smooth, Shetland Sheepdogs, and many of the Belgian working breeds are not stacked in the ring—that is, they are not held in position by head and tail as many other breeds are controlled. These breeds simply stand naturally on a loose leash in front of the handler, who spends little time, actually, with his hands on the dog. Nevertheless, it is an excellent idea for these breeds to be stacked in training so that they get used to people handling their legs, feet, and other parts of their bodies. With these breeds, practice in front of your mirror exactly as we are going to instruct owners of breeds which *are* stacked; it's an excellent way to teach yourself your dog's faults, because the more you handle a dog the more you know what's good and bad about him. But part of the time, practice in front of the mirror doing things exactly as if you were in the ring.

From this point on we are going to be using terms which may not be familiar to you to identify parts of the dog's body you will be touching, holding, and moving. The chart identifying parts of the dog should be of help.

"Stacking"

This term always brings to my mind a picture of about eleven dogs one on top of the other. Actually, "stacking" a dog simply means to set him up in a show position so that the judge can go over his body and at the same time see him in as natural and favorable a stance as possible. Years of teaching handling classes all over the United States and Canada have taught me that the easiest way for amateurs to learn how to stack their dogs is to tackle one section of the dog at a time.

THE FRONT

To anyone standing in front of your dog, the legs should be exactly the same distance apart on the ground as they are where they come out of the body. The feet should face straight ahead except in breeds where this is impossible due to body structure.

So let's start by facing the mirror dead on with your dog on a show slip-leash on your left side. *Do not lean on the dog at any time during stacking, and never under any circumstances touch his feet!* Lift up with your left hand on the leash so that the weight is not entirely on the dog's front. Now take hold of the dog's right elbow with your right hand and turn that leg either in or out, whichever is called for, so the dog's foot is pointing straight ahead. Take your hand away. Now all you have to do is match up the left leg. Change hands on the leash and, pulling up with your right hand on the dog's neck (don't strangle him now!—just take the weight off his front a little!), take hold of his left elbow with your left hand and position the left foot.

If your dog's toes tend to point out as you pick up either leg by the elbow, turn the whole leg *exaggeratedly in.* When you put the foot down on the floor, or ground, again it will probably balance into a pretty straightforward position. Work with it until it does, but don't fuss for a half an hour with each foot or leg. When you have things pretty parallel from the shoulders to the toes, let it alone for a second. Release the dog, then walk him around a bit and praise him before trying again. Concentrate on the straight-on approach in your mirror until you are satisfied.

Again, do not try to change the position of the feet by putting your hands on the dog's ankles or his feet. Stay up at elbow level and he'll fight you far less.

Never cross hands to set up a dog's front, and remember not to lean on him. With heavier breeds, you may run into a dog whose feet seem to be made out of pure cement. Perhaps you are a small person trying to set up a Dane; even a regular-sized guy or gal can get absolutely nowhere when a Newfoundland decides to stay put! Ah, but there are

The three dogs facing the cameras are "stacked," or positioned, to show the mistakes handlers make, often without realizing it.

The dog on the left is set up properly, his front legs perfectly parallel; the second dog's feet are too close together, so that he looks narrower in the front than he is; the dog on the right is set up so wide he looks like a bulldog!

ways to solve all things, so here is another handling "secret": if you cannot move that right front leg, for instance, without a derrick or a crane, drop your leash and take hold of your dog's head with your left hand and turn the head as far as it will comfortably go to the left. Now all the weight is off the right foreleg and you can do with it as you please. Once in place, change hands; swing the dog's head around as far as possible to the right with your right hand, and position the left foreleg with your left hand exactly where you want it. Let the dog's head return to the front position and praise him *quietly* so he does not erupt, in his joy at pleasing you, out of the position you have worked so hard to achieve.

Once you know how a dog should look in the front, as you walk him up and stop him in front of your mirror, take a quick look to make absolutely certain that you *must* rearrange his front legs. Y'know, it just could be that the dog is built so well in the front or just accidentally stopped so true, that a lot of fussing is unnecessary—always make sure you are going to improve a dog before you start moving his various parts hither and yon.

A final tip—small people working with high-stationed breeds (tall dogs) often prefer to stand in front of the dog facing him squarely. Then they kneel or crouch, hold the dog's head by the muzzle, and work below the head to set the legs straight. Many small dog handlers prefer this method. Try both and stick to the one that gets you the best results and makes you feel most comfortable. Remember, of course, to stand up and move to the dog's right shoulder when his front is in position.

THE REAR

Still with your dog on your left, position yourself in front of the mirror so that the dog's rear legs are visible in the mirror.

Never mind what the front of the animal is doing at this point, as long as both forelegs are on the ground and you have the front under control.

If you hold the dog's leash with your right hand, *pulling very gently up* on his neck and then exerting slight but constant pressure on his neck toward his rear end, you will find you are almost facing the mirror and can, again, tell what you are doing.

There are many stylized ways of setting up dogs' rears, all of which you can practice and experiment with to your heart's content when you have some idea of what you are doing. But in the beginning I want you to use the simple "rule of thumb"—your dog's rear legs should always appear perpendicular from the hock joints (or rear "elbows") to the ground, and be parallel to each other, turning neither in nor out at the hocks. *Parallel* and *perpendicular:* remember those words. As I said a moment ago, when you learn more about dog anatomy you can pull him out further in the rear or set his hind legs more under him than this, but in the beginning stick to parallel and perpendicular; you won't be sorry. His rear feet should be the same distance apart on the floor as his hip bones.

THE OUTSTANDING EXCEPTION

Before progressing one word further, we must take up the problem of stacking the German Shepherd. There really is no "problem" here, but this breed is set up differently than any other of his purebred brothers.

The German Shepherd standard calls for the dog's back to slope sharply and steeply downward from the withers (top of the shoulders) to the end of the croup (the point at which the dog's tail comes out of the body). To give the dog all the slope possible, he is set up straight

Rear positioning is just as important. Here, again, the dog on the left is positioned so that his legs are parallel and there is a perpendicular line from his hocks to the ground; the center dog, too close; the dog on the right, far too wide.

in front, as we described, but in the back the leg closest to the handler is set as far forward under the dog as his body structure will allow. The hind leg on the judge's side is pulled as far back as it can be and still maintain good contact between the dog's pad and the ground. How you take hold of his legs to achieve this position is described below, but "perpendicular" does not come into the picture, though the hind legs, separated as they are, should still be on as parallel a plane with each other as possible.

So in stacking your Shepherd puppy, be sure to practice equally the extension of either hind leg.

Keeping a weather eye on the mirror, you can achieve proper rear stance in one of two ways. First, if the dog isn't too tall and you are not too short, you can reach *over* the hind end and, taking hold firmly of the dog's legs at the top of the hock joint, with your left hand move those legs where you want them, one at a time. Again, don't fuss and nitpick; a fairly good picture that works is far better than a perfect picture that takes the stuffing out of both of you to achieve, especially while you are both learning.

If the dog is particularly tall, or chunky, you may find it more comfortable to reach under the dog's legs and grasp each leg, one at a time, in your left hand, at mid-stifle or hip. Again, once positioned correctly, praise soothingly for a moment, then release the dog and walk him around a bit before trying again. A reminder: fore or rear, never try to adjust the dog by his feet; dogs *hate* this and will fight you all the way.

In determining how he should look from the side, be sure you have first mastered fore and aft of the beastie. Then turn him sideways to the mirror. From the side, the front legs should be well under the dog but be slanted the very least bit forward. The back line or top line should be straight across unless the standard calls for something different. The hind end should be positioned so that it looks as if it gives the dog solid support.

Sometimes while stacking a dog the animal shows a tendency to lean against his handler for physical or psychological support. Or, the inexperienced handler who is having trouble controlling both ends of his exhibit will use his hip or leg to further brace the animal in position. Nothing is worse, believe me; and once this technique becomes a habit to the dog, it is very difficult to cure him of leaning. Stop this tendency to lean on the dog's part the moment it starts; make sure you don't unconsciously provide a brace for him, either. As you stack your dog, stand away from him so your body does not come in contact with his.

His body will turn whichever direction his head turns, so keep that head straight. If you can't control the head by holding the leash, hold the head itself until the dog is more familiar with standing for examination.

DROPPING

As you watch experienced people at dog shows, you will see many of them setting up their animals by picking up the dog either under his throat or just behind his forelegs and dropping him into position. It looks easy to you and quite impressive, so why not handle your dog this way? Because it's *not* easy and because you yourself need lots of experience and a *dog with an almost perfect front,* that's why!

I drop most of my dogs by lifting them just under the chin. But if you asked me why I always come out right, while I'd be very happy to explain to you about balance and what a difference the position of one finger makes, it would be difficult to tell you exactly how I do what I do—it's instinct by now.

Just to show you how tricky it can be, however, is a simple matter. Drag out that mirror and face your dog at it squarely. Now, taking hold of your dog by the skin way up under his chin on either side of his jaw bone, lift him off the floor and drop him; chances are his forelegs will be much too close together. Now move your hands down the sides of his throat to just above his chest. Drop him again—see how far apart his legs are? It takes a lot of practice to find out just where you must place your hands to wind up with a dog that drops true— legs exactly parallel when viewed from the front.

Until you have spent a long time posing your dog so that you can literally do it blindfolded in a very short period of time, set him up leg by leg; you'll waste less time and will achieve the desired result without having to correct yourself as well as the dog.

While holding a dog in a show pose you can either stand, crouch, kneel on one or both knees, or sit back on your heels, depending upon the size of your dog. There is no rule as to which dogs you kneel with and which dogs you stand with; again, use your noodle. Pick the position most comfortable to you and the least distracting to your dog and the judge.

THE TAIL

Tails should sometimes be held curved up over the back, sometimes straight out from the back of the dog, sometimes they should not be touched by the handler. Check your standard. But, from the very beginning, get your dog used to having his tail handled and brushed.

LAYING BACK

The way you handle a tail can sometimes help in the case of dogs that are "lazy" about assuming a show pose. These dogs tend to let you get them perfectly in position before "laying back," so that their front feet stick out at too much of a slant in front of them. It gives the appearance of a dog just about to sit down but not quite certain as to the exact moment. This position is also referred to as "posting" or "bracing." Take hold of the dog's tail firmly way up at the base where it comes out of his bottom, and pull steadily backward on it; when you suddenly let go, the dog will slide forward up onto his front feet where he belongs. You can, with practice, learn to time your pulling and your release of the tail to coincide the moment when the judge turns to look in your direction.

THE HEAD

Like his tail, your dog's head can be very useful to you in correcting his show position. If, according to your mirror, he is not "laying back" but is nevertheless still not stacked up on his toes where he belongs, go directly to his head and take it firmly between your two hands. Facing the dog squarely, hold his head between your hands and push it straight toward the floor until it will comfortably go no further.

Now pull the head *gently* toward you as you return it to a natural position. You will discover the dog is now up on his toes and his body is in the correct position. It takes a great deal of practice to do this without pulling the dog off his stance in the process. Don't be rough and don't expect an absolutely green dog or puppy to let you pull him around this way. You may wind up time and time again with the whole dog in your lap, but if you continue and are determined, this "trick" will stand you in good stead in the months to come.

How you hold a dog's head when he is stacked in show position is also important. It depends upon the breed and the type of head involved. I don't believe anyone has truly invented a control-proof or comfortable way to hold the head of a white or colored Bull Terrier, whose noggin is egg-shaped so that there is nothing to hold onto. With a dog whose head is so large or so strangely shaped that you cannot comfortably get your hands on the muzzle, use your collar well up behind the ears and let the head alone.

In case you are holding a setter's head or any head which tops a smooth, perhaps throaty stretch of neck, you can, with a little diligence, learn to hold it from *your* side of the dog, minimizing the throatiness and having control of the dog at the same time, without your hold interfering with the clean outline of muzzle and head which you wish the judge to see. Under every dog's lower jaw, that jaw bone forms a "V." Slip the middle finger of your right hand up into the apex of that "V." Now hold the dog's lip nearest you between your thumb and index finger. With your little finger and the one next to it you can gather in any excess skin detracting from the smooth throat line. The judge sees a clean throat and level muzzle which you can always control with your right hand alone, but this maneuver requires not only that you practice constantly, but that the dog get used to being handled in this way. On a green dog or wee puppy you must be very patient—but persistent! One step at a time, please!

While your mirror never becomes obsolete, now would be a good time to ask members of your family, kennel club cohorts, or knowledge-able neighbors down the street to criticize your work. In handling class, all novice handlers will take turns examining each others' dogs and criticizing each others' techniques.

Finally, make very sure you practice stacking with the dog on your right as well as on your left. In case the judge moves, you want always to be able to keep the dog between you and him. Get the dog used to standing still while you move around his muzzle—the shorter path— to his opposite side.

Moving

Now it is time to study your dog on the move if you are to learn what is the best rate of speed for gaiting him.

Just as it is impossible in a book this size to give you all the varying techniques for grooming each individual breed, it is equally impossible to go into the subtle differences in the gaits of all purebred dogs. Because of their body structure and the purpose for which they were originally intended, some dogs use their legs differently than do others. Many books have been written on the movement of dogs, one of the best of these being *Dog Steps,* written by a very dedicated, knowledgeable lady, Mrs. Rachel Page Elliott, and published by Howell Book House.

RATE OF SPEED

However, when learning to gait your dog at the speed that is best for him, there are certain standards you can use to help you get started on this project and keep you going in the right direction until you can learn, and get to understand, the refinements of movement.

I would like to start right off by debunking the theory that *fast* is always *good.* From time to time certain breeds catch the fancier's eye and become more popular than others; when this happens, very often movement comes to play such an exaggerated part of the picture that, far from enhancing the presentation of a breed, it turns into an affected style which is followed by handlers and breeders because it becomes the "in" thing. This is most clearly seen in Afghan Hounds, those lovely, elegant dogs which look so striking striding along with their luxurious coats parting in the wind like silk tasseling. The faster they go, the more striking the picture, but *the movement of the dog doesn't necessarily improve with that speed, a fact all too often forgotten.*

Show dogs are gaited in the ring at a trot, a two-beat gait in which the feet at diagonally opposite ends of the body hit the ground together. Assuming you are working alone at this moment, set up a chair to indicate the judge. In the beginning, get your dog to trot along beside you on leash; if he is a small breed you can sometimes walk along quickly with long, smooth steps as he trots; in the larger breeds you will have to run, but do so with long, gliding steps—never "chop" up and down. At the outset, concentrate on getting him even with you or just a bit behind you so that his body is in a straight line going away from the chair and in a straight line coming back. Never let him start off ahead of you, because you can rarely catch up and maintain control at the same time.

A show dog can move as far away from the handler as the full length of the leash sometimes, unlike the obedience or field dog, which is taught to stick close to your side. Remember, we are showing off the *dog* in breed classes, and the freer he moves on his own, with you all but out of the picture completely, the smoother and more spectacular he looks.

So from the very beginning of his gaiting sessions, keep him away from you. If he has a tendency to "cuddle," bump him with your

Nothing is much more impressive in the show ring than a beautiful dog gaiting along happily on a loose leash! If the handler stays a foot or so ahead of his dog, the dog's body is likely to stay much straighter.

hip, your knee, or your ankle, depending upon his size. Don't give in to the temptation to push him away with a light bash—it doesn't work! Keep talking encouragingly to him and *don't slow up on your turns*— a little behind you so he is straight—and away from you so he can be seen.

LOOSE LEASH

Until you have the dog trotting happily to and fro, keep that leash loose. Some dogs will hang their heads as they trot; some will hold their heads high. While some breeds are supposed to hold their heads lower than others, no dog really looks very snappy or stylish plodding along with his nose almost on the ground. In an effort to get a dog's head up, many novice handlers (and far too many experienced people!)

haul, jerk, and drag at the dog's neck until a true picture of his gait is absolutely impossible for anyone to determine. Right now we are not worried about his cranium; *leave it alone.* Keep the leash loose and talk to him. More often than not, as he learns what fun it is to run with you, he will start raising his head higher, in curiosity, each time you practice. If this doesn't happen, we'll give you suggestions to correct the problem later, but do not try to force a high head at this point or you could easily end up with a dog "sidewinding" as he does his ring patterns, and this is a very undesirable situation.

SIDEWINDING

Sidewinding means that the dog moves with his body at an angle to the line of travel, usually carrying his head in close to the handler and swinging his rear end out and away. Sidewinding (also called crabbing or yawing) is sometimes a matter of faulty body structure when a short length of back is combined with a rear end that is too much rear for the rest of the dog to handle. But in my experience over the years, I have found that most cases of sidewinding were caused by rough hands on a leash until the dog hated the whole process of gaiting so violently that, while he could not get his head free, he would move the rest of him as far away from the handler as possible!

Those of you working with older dogs may find that an earlier owner, or even you in your ignorance, has mishandled the dog so that he *does* have a tendency to sidewind. To discourage this, work the dog at a trot alongside a fence, a wall of the house or garage, a hedge— up *close* to this kind of running barrier, so that as the two of you move along there is no place for the dog to put his bottom except in a straight line beside you. Snapping or jerking your leash to cure this "disease" will only prolong it.

Once you have succeeded in getting your protégé to sail forth at a willing trot, perfectly at ease, and delighted with the whole procedure as you go round the ring and up and down with him on your *left* side, it is time to teach him to do the same thing on your *right* side, for some ring patterns require that you change sides in order not to block the judge's view of the dog with your body.

With some breeds, and usually with larger dogs, changing sides while gaiting isn't a good idea, because you interrupt a smooth flow of movement and swinging back into the same rhythm after you have changed sides is often clumsy and hard to achieve. But *all show dogs should know how to move on either side of their handlers,* so be sure to teach this to your dog right from the start.

Now we come to the point in training where you will need help. It's time for you to study your dog's movement from the front, side, and from the rear; obviously you cannot do all this and handle at the same time (unless you have discovered something I don't know about!). So whistle up some willing soul to move the dog at a trot in the directions you indicate.

As we explained earlier, it is impossible to go into all the variations of movement here. But in order to get yourself off to a good start, concentrate on the fact that the rear legs of your dog as well as the front legs should move as nearly parallel as possible. Completely parallel movement is impossible because the legs must compensate for such problems as depth of chest, length of body, muscle mass in the rear. The faster your dog goes, the further underneath him he gathers his legs; to achieve greater speed he needs his tools of propulsion close beneath him to give him greater push. Therefore, it stands to reason that the faster you move him, coming or going, the closer together will be his front legs and his back legs.

As your helper moves the dog away from you, have him try it three ways—first fast, then medium, then slow—always at a trot, of course. If when standing still your dog's hind legs are quite close together, you will probably decide on a slow or medium trot away from the judge so as not to add to the illusion of closeness. Use the same "yard-stick" in determining at what speed you should approach the judge in order to present the best picture possible. Sometimes it is necessary to train yourself, and the dog, to slow down or speed up either coming or going, because one end requires speed and the other does not. In making such changes in gait, practice until you can do it so smoothly that it isn't blatantly apparent to the judge that you are making such corrections.

Most dogs can afford a pleasant surge of speed when presented side-ways. Remember what we said earlier, however, and make sure the dog is moving and reaching *freely* and *comfortably* as he sails around the ring. You never want to give the impression that any animal is doing all he can, forcing himself to dig in, in order to keep up with the mere mortal on the end of his leash.

While you have your assistant handy, this might be a good time to discover whether a tight leash would be better than a loose one. Certain dogs have a tendency to trot with their feet close together, sometimes even crossing over each other, although they are wide through the chest or shoulders. Some dogs move pretty parallel in front but tend to throw their feet out to the side in a movement much like one you would make when flipping your wrists to shake water off your hands. And some dogs amble and sway in the center section because they are unusually long-backed. These faults can sometimes be minimized, even eliminated, by taking the dog's weight off his front as he moves and pulling back on him slightly to shorten and tighten or to seem to shorten and tighten the muscles between his fore and his rear.

American and Canadian Champion Wazat Shaka gaits across the ring on a loose leash beside his handler. Number one Rhodesian Ridgeback in Canada for 1976, with group placements from the classes in the United States, this stylish member of the hound group demonstrates the importance of co-ordination of movement between handler and dog. "Shaka" is owned by John and Pat Wilson of Ottawa. *Photo by Alice Bixler, courtesy Dogs in Canada.*

All these techniques may seem to be terribly complicated and mysterious as you start out, but believe me they are very simple to learn and to use. The only real difficulty sometimes lies in learning what remedy to apply to what problem when you are a novice—indeed, recognizing the problem is often the only bottleneck. In handling classes I have my students sit on the floor while dogs are gaited back and forth so that they get to view both good and bad movement from eye level. Still, even though I bring them what to me is a monstrously clear example of close rear movement in a dog, very often I have to have that dog moved time and time and time again before they cry, "Oh, I see it, now, I see it!" So don't belittle yourself for not "getting it" immediately when it comes to learning to identify good and bad movement in your dog. Rome wasn't built in a day, and no matter what you have heard to the contrary, handlers aren't developed in a single lesson or even overnight.

Go over it as many times as necessary until you are *sure* you understand. Don't hesitate to call on your kennel club buddies or to pay a professional to give you a lesson. If you *want* to learn movement, you *can!*

PACING

As a novice at moving a dog or judging movement, no one expects you to be able to cope with all types of movement in the beginning.

But you would be absolutely amazed at the number of experienced dog people in the United States and Canada who not only cannot "catch" pacing when a dog starts moving this way, but who haven't the foggiest idea how to stop pacing in a dog!

As you will remember, we identified the correct show-ring gait as *trotting*, a two-beat movement in which the feet at diagonally opposite ends of the body strike the ground together. *Pacing* is a four-beat movement in which the legs on each side move exactly as a pair, striking the ground almost together and causing a rocking or rolling motion. Pacing is frowned on in the show ring and can be caused by many things.

An adult dog that is squarely proportioned but tends to stand a bit lower in front than in the back will often start pacing to keep his legs from interfering with each other. In order to relieve strain on weary muscles, a dog will use the pace to rest himself sometimes. I think we see it most often in the show ring with a dog that is very short in length of back and a little more angulated in the rear than in front. Once in a while you will see dogs with too much arch, or roach, in the back; these dogs often pace due to the fact that the croup muscles are restricted. Once in a great while pacing results from lack of conditioning in an overweight or lazy dog who does not use his running gear properly. Any dog will move in the way that is easiest for him, whether he does so to prevent pain or to compensate for being poorly put together.

Whatever the reason, you should know when a dog is pacing and when he is trotting, and you should know how to get a dog out of a pace if he suddenly goes into that gait.

Two ways seem to make the most sense to amateurs or beginners working alone. First, close your eyes, making sure there are no trees or open manholes in your path. Now as you gait your dog, listen carefully for his footfalls and count out loud what you hear. "One-two-one-two"; if this is what you hear, the dog is trotting. If you hear four beats as his feet strike the ground, those beats run together so fast that there is little pause between them—"Onetwothreefour, Onetwothreefour" in staccato rhythm—it is pretty safe to assume he is pacing.

Now move him again, this time with your eyes open looking squarely down on the middle of his back. When a dog is trotting his body will keep time with his two-beat gait and will pull forward a little on one side on the count of "one" and a little forward on the other side on the count of "two." If he is pacing, however, and you are looking down on his back, you will see his body rolling or wobbling from side to side almost as if you had jostled a bowl of jelly. The ability to tell the difference between pacing and trotting sometimes comes hard for people, but this is one facet of dog education you should keep studying until you get the lesson straight. And once you do, we can practice the cure for pacing. There *is* a cure, though I didn't know what was happening when, as a very green professional, I was thrilled to be pulled out of the sporting group and asked to gait my Labrador again. As we went away from the judge, this dog on which I had put four or five group placements started doing very strange things with his feet. I thought he'd suddenly gone lame or something! When I got back to the judge he said, "Try it again." Hoping I was imagining things, I did just that—but now it was worse. By the time I got back to the judge this time I was frantic. I blurted out, "What's the matter with him?" The good man laughed and said, "He's pacing!" and that was the last look I got in *that* group!

As soon as I got out of the ring I went to someone I respected and got a long and proper lesson in pacing and what to do about it. Unfortunately, it requires a bit of muscle, but unless you are a pipsqueak and your dog is a Goliath, it's not at all difficult.

Remembering that no judge is going to look twice at a pacer in the show ring, if your dog is so inclined, you take measures to make sure he never gets a chance to err. As you start moving him, around or individually up and down, whether you customarily move him on a tight leash or a loose leash, fast or slow, you are going to start out on a *tight* leash and *fast!* As he starts to move, pull up suddenly on that leash and literally lift him into a fast trot. The moment the trot is achieved you can slow him down a bit, but I warn you, *do not lose speed on the corners or in making turns;* if you do the dog will slip back into a pace and, as we say in the words of the streets, "That will be all she wrote!" Don't change sides with a pacer once you have gotten him into a trot, as he may slip back into the undesired gait.

When the dog ahead of you is working, get ready early. Slide that leash or collar up under your dog's chin so that when you lift up you will be controlling the whole front end. Handling a dog that is inclined to slip into a pace from time to time is a nerve-wracking assignment, even when you've practiced so that you can do it in your sleep. You can never afford to relax for a single minute and you must keep your eyes on the dog most of the time, listening for the beat you want to hear.

The dog that does nothing but pace when he moves is in serious trouble and should not be shown. But the dog that, for one reason or another, sometimes paces, must be handled very carefully and demands a great deal of practice time.

WHEN TO START SHOWING

So now we've gotten the puppy or young dog used to people and places. He is happy and well-adjusted in society. Is it time to take the big plunge and go to an honest-to-goodness dog show? Is it a good idea to seriously campaign a puppy? Do puppies ever win points? Why show puppies at licensed shows? Would his record of losses as a baby hurt his chances as an adult? Do you leap into licensed competition or tiptoe into matches first?

There is only one fair answer to any one of these questions: "It depends." It depends on your capabilities and the condition of your nervous system; it depends on the breed of your dog, his maturity, mental and physical. It depends on your pocketbook, what events are available to you in your area, what the breeder or handler recommends. It often depends on the popularity of your breed and what is showing when you decide to start. I guess we could, in all conscience, safely urge you to go ahead whenever you or your experienced adviser(s) think your dog can hold his own without looking inferior against the competition. How's that for an answer? Did you notice I *did not say* whenever you or your adviser think your dog can *win,* etc., etc.? Sure that's what you want in the long run. But before we can run, long or short, it's wisest to walk a little in order to get the feel of the land.

Whether considering serious licensed or regular match competition, you must be very sure your dog is secure in his leash work. Certainly you can expect him to act up in an excess of good spirits, but if you suspect he might back off when approached by a stranger or put on the brakes and refuse to move on leash, then I suggest you return to classes and do some more confidence work.

A puppy starting his show career isn't expected to stand like a statue for hours at a time, but he must know that stand means don't resist, don't run away. While he may act giggly and curious, he must be perfectly agreeable to your fooling with his legs, looking at his mouth, or feeling around under his tail.

In deciding when to start puppies in competition, remember that in America or Canada cannot exhibit a dog under six months in a licensed show. So that takes care of that. Puppies younger than six months can get a lot out of sanctioned matches, and so can you as handler.

When one of my puppies goes to his first sanctioned match, I don't give a hoot if he kisses the judge or wiggles during examination or carries his leash or my arm in his mouth as he gallops about the ring. What I do care about is that tail—as long as it's wagging, the dog is ready to start at this level.

"What if the judge doesn't like a bouncy puppy?" I am often asked. Frankly, that's his tough luck. I go to sanctions with puppies *not* to win *that day* but because I want them to win *in the future.* As time goes by I can channel that exuberance, but oh, my friends, and ah, my foes, once it's gone you'll never, never put it back! When the moment comes to settle down my exuberant "angel" (and no two puppies are alike any more than any two children are alike), he'll be so convinced that the show ring is seventh heaven that he won't really mind having his wings "clipped" a bit.

Showing a promising but very immature puppy in licensed shows would be a waste of time and money; you would accomplish nothing more than to establish a record of losing for him, a record which won't do him any real good when and if he becomes mature enough to compete seriously. The "experience" you are seeking by showing an immature puppy at licensed shows is achieved in direct proportion to how he reacts to show conditions. So take care!

On the other hand, it is often advisable to show early and consistently if you wish to finish a particularly mature puppy, as some early bloomers have a nasty tendency to coarsen so that at a year or so they are almost impossible to finish.

Starting the average puppy off by throwing him into constant competition, being determined to campaign him straight through, is absolutely ridiculous, unless you have the one dog in a thousand that, because you know what you are doing, is capable of going Best in Show at under one year of age.

It's a rare puppy that can score points at six months. If you want to give him experience and let him perhaps establish a record which could lay the foundation for really important wins later, I suggest, as I will later in detail, that you campaign the puppy in Canada where Puppy Groups are available.

Otherwise, if at nine or ten months it appears (Glory be!) that you own a very good example of your breed which you believe in and of which his breeder approves, then go to it, have fun, don't push, and may the best dog win—provided it's *yours,* right? Right!

That older dog some of you might prefer can, of course, be started in shows earlier than can a puppy. But just because he's ten or eleven months at time of purchase doesn't necessarily mean he's not a "puppy" in terms of development or mental attitude. You may even find that because he has been left in the kennel longer—even in a good kennel—it could take a long time to bring him to the proper point to start competing.

But young or old, while you are getting him as ready as you can and making sure he has been given every advantage possible to help him to win, give yourself the advantage of reading the next chapter so that you'll know how to enter him, and where, and how much it will cost, and what rules and regulations can help or hinder you along your way.

3

Rules and Regulations
of Dog Shows

The general idea of dog shows is to improve purebred dogs. To a very large extent I'm convinced that in the long, *long* run, dog shows do exactly that, though it may not seem so when, on a given day, something less than the best dog goes home the winner. The trouble is that judges, being human beings just as you and I, all tend to interpret a breed standard a bit differently, and some place more emphasis on one point in that standard than on other points. As far as I'm concerned, the real value of dog shows and sanction matches is that they give all sorts of breeders, owners, trainers, and just plain dog lovers a chance to go and see other dogs of their breed and talk with people experienced in various phases of the dog world. There is boundless opportunity to cuss and discuss, sympathize, criticize, and exchange ideas and theories. Such exchange is invaluable both to the experienced dog person and to the neophyte.

KINDS OF DOG SHOWS IN THE U.S. AND CANADA

Any purebred dog eligible for registration with the American or Canadian Kennel Clubs may compete at licensed dog shows provided that animal cannot be disqualified under the stipulations of his breed standard or under the regulations of A.K.C. or C.K.C.

There are several different *kinds* of dog shows which the breeders, owners, and handlers of these dogs may enter.

In Canada there are:

Championship Shows
Limited Breeds Shows
Specialty Championship Shows
Field Trial Conformation Shows
Sanctioned Matches

The quite complicated rules and regulations regarding these shows are clearly defined in the rule book of the Canadian Kennel Club entitled *Dog Show Rules.* Copies of this booklet may be obtained by writing the Canadian Kennel Club at 2150 Bloor St., W., Toronto, Ontario M6S 4V7, and including seventy-five cents.

In the United States there are:

Member Championship Shows
Licensed Shows
Restricted Entry Shows limited to puppies eligible

for regular puppy classes and dogs which have placed first, second, or third in regular classes within a certain time period

Restricted Entry Shows limited to those dogs recorded as champions and those dogs credited with one or more championship points within a certain time period

A Member or Licensed Show with limited entries
A Specialty Show
An American-Bred Specialty Show
Sanctioned Matches

Again, the quite complicated rules and regulations regarding these shows are clearly defined in the rule book of the American Kennel Club entitled *Rules Applying to Registration and Dog Shows.* Free copies of this booklet may be obtained by writing the American Kennel Club at 51 Madison Ave., New York, New York 10010.

In both countries the most popular are: the *sanctioned matches,* which are mostly patronized by breeders, exhibitors, and handlers rather than spectators, and at which no points toward championship are awarded but which serve as a dress rehearsal and training ground complete with judges, best-of-breed awards, trophies, and ribbons; and, *licensed all breed dog shows,* at which championship points are awarded. These are the two types of shows with which we are primarily going to concern ourselves.

Benched Shows

Licensed shows in the United States and Canada may be benched or unbenched, although you'll meet up with very few benched shows north of the border. A benched show is one at which raised platforms (or benches) are supplied, divided into individual sections, each one numbered. You will be required to stay at the show with your dog on his bench (except when you are exercising, grooming, or showing him) from the arrival time to the departure hour, both listed in your judging program. Kennel Club representatives, empowered to report you and recommend that you be fined or otherwise disciplined for failing to bench your dog, will wander through the benching sections during the day to make sure everyone conforms to the rules. For the individual breeder or exhibitor, benched shows have the decided advantage of giving him somewhere to establish himself and his dog, and of being surrounded by other breeders and exhibitors of that breed. The day waxes long, and there is a golden opportunity to exchange gossip, feeding theories, and training tips. Even better, the general public wandering through the aisles gets a chance to see the breeds they particularly favor, to question breeders and owners to their hearts' content. The benched show is the breeder's showcase, as he has a captive audience to convince of the superiority of his particular kind of dog. Kennels sell puppies, sires for future litters are selected by the owner, of promising bitches, and all in all, many good things transpire at benched shows— *unless you happen to be showing more than one breed of dog!*

This is why professional handlers dislike benched shows. Certainly convenient for the one-dog exhibitor, "benched" means more work, inefficient supervision of dogs, many million more steps and extra help for the poor handler or multibreed exhibitor. These shows are also hard on the guy who has one or more dogs in both breed and obedience.

By way of giving you an example of the pros and cons of benched shows, let's take the Eastern Kennel Club show held annually in Boston in December. This is one of America's prestige shows. It is clean, centrally located, and draws an entry of thousands. The general public eagerly awaits this annual event and clogs the Prudential Center in their desire to locate breeds they would never ordinarily get a chance to see, let alone touch. The individual exhibitor also looks forward to this show because his dog is benched, shown, groomed, and exercised all on one floor. The trouble is that the show is held on *two* floors. Can you imagine what we handlers go through with, say, working, sporting and hound breeds on the second floor (where they must stay benched) and toys, terriers, and non-sporting breeds on the first floor? At the end of the day in Boston, those with different breeds know the back stairways of the Prudential Center better than the builder or the architect does!

There are only two exceptions to the rule that at a benched show *all* dogs must remain on their benches. The first is for bitches in season. Ladies in this alluring condition are not welcome at field trials or obedience competitions, of course, because of the distraction they would provide the male dogs. But since in breed competition animals are under judgment for "being" as opposed to "doing," it is very common for bitches in season to be exhibited. (In answer to the question, "But how do you handle a bitch in season at dog shows?" I invariably reply, "Very, very carefully.")

Anyway, when you arrive at a benched show with a female in heat, hie thee pronto to the show veterinarian's area—a small tent or table usually adjacent to the show superintendent's office. Explain what you want—permission to keep this female off the bench. The doctor will then examine the female, determine that she is indeed in season, and you will be given something that looks like a rather large baggage claim check. You will fill out on the card the required data about the dog, the vet signs it, and you hang that tag on the number holder of your bench section. Then, when the authorities come along to check up on you, all will be peace and tranquility. The bitch may then be kept in her crate either in the grooming section or at an out-of-the-way place convenient to your ring.

The second exception is for puppies—that is, male or female animals of less than one year. In the case of a two-day show, the puppy must be benched only on the day his breed is being shown, and no puppy is ever required to be benched until after the class in which he has been entered is judged.

A hundred years ago when I started out, we secured our dogs to their benches with benching chains which snapped into metal loops at the rear of the platforms. The other end was snapped on the dog's collar—usually rolled leather or flat buckle-type collars. While this method is still favored by some people, I am never happy leaving a dog unattended while tied. I'm happy to say that today the popular method is to place your crate right on the bench. The dog can change position safely and, while he can be seen, he has some protection against prying fingers.

If you must use a benching chain, use the type described in our Tools of the Trade chapter. Never use your leather or webbing leash— it takes but a moment for a dog to chew through one of these. And when fastening the dog on his bench, make certain he can neither get his feet over the front edge of the platform and possibly fall off and hurt himself, nor get his nosey muzzle around the partitions on either side of him. Who knows what the temperament of his next-door neighbors might be?

If you happen to be showing more than one dog of a breed, do not assume the people in charge will bench them together for you. When you submit your entry, be sure to attach a note asking specifically for "adjacent benching" for your dogs. If you arrive and discover they are not benched together, the world won't end—you'll just wind up walking many unnecessary miles. But a bit of forethought can be most helpful.

Finally, if you arrive at your benching section and discover your two or three dogs are benched next to each other, you are perfectly free to remove the partitions, converting your two or three stalls into one where your dogs can be together (if they get along!). By the same token, should you discover there is a partition on only one side of your stall, and you cannot find a person to alter this condition, be it known that these partitions slip out very easily and you can move one from another area if no one offers to help. No one is expected to leave his dog next to a strange, aggressive animal, rules be darned!

Unbenched Shows

Unbenched shows are in the majority, thank goodness, in both Canada and the United States. These are licensed events at which you may usually arrive any time prior to your class, and depart as soon thereafter as you please, though some programs specify an hour before judging as arrival time. (Of course, if you've gone Best of Breed you may want to stay to show in the Group in the U.S.; in Canada you *must* stay if eligible for Group.) You may "set up" and settle down in any area not considered off limits. Convenient for the exhibitor, true; but the spectator buying an admission ticket to see lots of dogs often comes away having missed the one breed he was interested in because he didn't know where to find it, judging was over, and he didn't want to wait until Group.

The United Kennel Club in Montreal experimented quite successfully in the winter of 1975 with an idea designed to accommodate the spectator, the all-breed handler, and the exhibitor of a single breed. The usual handlers section was set aside at their show, and into this area went all handlers and their great variety of breeds. All those exhibiting a single breed were asked to set up in spacious, clearly designated floor areas labeled by Group—all Sporting dogs here, all Terriers there, etc. The public could wander through the handlers' section and watch the highly specialized grooming of the professional, or he could seek out a specific breed and see many examples of it all gathered together in one spot, under large, easily read signs. Those bringing only one breed enjoyed spending the day with others having the same dogs, and all this without the dashing back and forth associated with benched affairs.

Most of us attending this show felt the idea was a simple solution, easily adapted by any show-giving club. But I doubt it would be acceptable in the United States just because it *is* so simple, so convenient for everyone involved!

Sanctioned Matches

The mechanics of attending Sanctioned Matches (i.e., "make-believe" dog shows held with the approval—or sanction—of the A.K.C. or C.K.C.) are infinitely easier. They are always unbenched, are very informal, and you may come and go as you please. The only problem with match shows is that you often wind up doing an awful lot of waiting. Since entries are usually taken the day of the match, it's impossible for the host club to plan ahead, as the show-giving club can. Consequently, you may have to be on hand to make your entries by 11 A.M. and may never get to show a dog until four in the afternoon. However, this is an excellent opportunity to give green dogs and puppies plenty of exposure to noise, congestion, and slippery floors, and a fine chance for you to get your own butterflies under control.

Matches and shows have one thing in common: they are both open only to purebred dogs capable of being registered with the A.K.C. or C.K.C.

PURPOSE OF MATCHES

I think it's important to discuss two particular things about matches.

Number one: matches are the place for puppies, wee puppies, just learning about walking on a leash, standing still while their teeth are examined, and not making puddles on judges' shoes. If more people would take more baby puppies to more matches, fewer judges would get upset in the rings at licensed shows because an amateur handler expected him to spend precious minutes on a dog that obviously had no idea at all what was expected of a show dog. Licensed shows operate on a very tight schedule, and there is no time to be spent on *training* a dog—there is little enough time to be spent *evaluating* it! And evaluating a dog that won't stand still and is either hostile to the thought of sharing his private parts with a stranger, or overly delighted that someone is paying attention to him, is nigh impossible. It isn't that judges at licensed shows consider themselves too good to take the time with such a dog, it's that they have an enormous obligation to all people who are scheduled to enter their rings with well-trained, correctly groomed animals the rest of the day. There is no point in wrestling with a bundle of wiggle and giggle, no matter how cute it is, because you cannot get a true picture of how it is built or moves. Such an untrained creature couldn't possibly be expected to defeat older, well-behaved dogs. On the other hand, judges at matches—I among them—have been known to get down on their knees with babies who were reluctant to move and we enjoy helping out at this kind of activity because we do remember puppies of our own who needed help.

MATCH JUDGES

Number two: sometimes you'll get a licensed judge who has a free day to help out with the home club, but more often than not, sanction judges are breeders, amateur and professional handlers, do-it-yourself-trainers, and just plain doggy people who have a fairly good background in the canine world, but who are chosen primarily because they meet people well, love animals, and will *encourage* the newcomer into the proper channels to secure his lasting interest in exhibiting dogs. Try to remember, then, that you are attending a match ot *learn;* if, incidentally, you come home with a blue ribbon, fine and dandy—but a Best of Breed at a match show doth *not* a champion make! One match judge has been known to encourage the owner of a prick-eared Collie to the extent of putting him Best in Match (a serious fault which would prevent any Collie from reaching his title); another one once denied a Golden Retriever Best of Breed because his topline didn't slope enough (Goldens are to have level toplines, moving or standing!).

In no way do I mean to malign Sanction Match judges—these are dedicated people, for the most part, who genuinely care enough about the future of shows and purebred dogs to stand all day in the pouring rain or the broiling sun explaining to Mrs. Smith, tactfully and kindly, that while her Shetland Sheepdog has great promise, "Shelties" are not shown with bows in their hair. I'm simply trying to point out that while winning at a match is "lover-lee," and could very easily be the first steppingstone on your road to Championship. *it ain't necessarily so!*

MATCH AND LICENSED SHOW ENTRY FEES

Since costs are rising constantly all over the world these days, it's impossible to advise you accurately of exact fees for matches or shows. But, generally speaking, I think it's safe to assume that you will pay from one to four dollars per dog for a Sanctioned Match; from seven to twelve dollars per dog for a Canadian Licensed Show including a one dollar per show "listing" fee, which is explained further along in this section headed *Two Common Misconceptions;* and anywhere from eight to twenty-two dollars each for U.S. shows.

These fees may be enclosed with your entry in the form of personal checks, certified checks, or postal money orders. Should you write a check for an entry in the U.S. or Canada and that check should "bounce" after the time the entry was accepted and before the date of the show, when you reach the show you will be called to the superintendent's office, where it will be necessary for you to pay for your entry in cash before you will be allowed to show your dog. Your NSF check will then be returned to you. (A very embarrassing situation to be scrupulously avoided!)

When entering U.S. shows from Canada, using a personal check, always write "pay American funds" on the bottom of your check.

MAILING LISTS, PREMIUM LISTS, AND PROGRAMS

Finding out about dog shows and matches can be a real problem to the greenhorn. If you are intending to exhibit the dog you are purchasing, consult the breeder from whom you are buying it. She can see that you are put on the mailing lists of local dog clubs and kennel organizations. If she is going to be attending licensed shows before you plan to, ask her to give your name and address to the show superintendent of each show she attends; toward this end, supply her with a dozen or so slips of paper on which your name, address, telephone number, and breed are clearly printed, as well as a statement of the fact that you intend to be exhibiting at all shows within a 500-mile radius of your home—then maybe, just *maybe,* you'll eventually get on the mailing list for licensed dog shows.

I suppose that one reason superintendents are so loath to put new names on their lists is that they want to make sure you don't turn out to be a one- or two-time dog shower—in a short time, in this case, you'll be throwing out truckloads of premium lists which might well be mailed to really interested parties. Also, the number of premium lists they are allowed to send out for each show is determined by the show-giving clubs, many of whom haven't changed the number of premium lists they print for the last ten years—and dog show attendance in that time has quadrupled. Getting on mailing lists for licensed shows is *not* easy; and no stone should be left unturned if you are genuinely interested.

Write to the American Kennel Club, 51 Madison Ave., New York, New York 10010, and ask for a list of kennel clubs in your area as well as a list of dog show superintendents. If your budget is limited, the one publication to which you must subscribe without fail is *Pure-Bred Dogs: American Kennel Gazette.* This is the American dog world's official organ; its monthly editions contain the results of all recent dog shows, field trials, and obedience competitions, as well as lists of all newly finished champions in each category, the dates of shows and field trials planned for most of the coming year, the names of the sponsoring clubs and their show secretaries.

The Canadian "bible" for serious-minded purebred dog people is *Dogs in Canada,* Suite 500, 3 Church Street, Toronto, Ontario

M65 4V7 a monthly publication whose pages offer official C.K.C. results, dates of shows to come, and changes in rules and regulations. Be sure to write to the Canadian Kennel Club, 2150 Bloor St., West, Toronto, Ontario M6S 4V7, and ask for a list of Canadian show superintendents; when you receive that list, write to them all and ask to be notified of coming shows.

Write to any person or agency connected with dog shows in your effort to be notified of coming shows, but don't feel that you alone are being boycotted for some strange reason—*everybody* has the same problem! Watch the newspapers and listen to local service programs on your radio and TV for dates of shows and matches in your area. Hie thee hence, entered or not, and at least introduce yourself and get put on the mailing list of *that* particular dog show or kennel club.

Prior to most matches, informal flyers are mailed by the match show committee giving you the necessary particulars. When it comes to Licensed Shows, however, in the U.S. and Canada, brochures called Premium Lists are sent out to reach exhibitors supposedly about four weeks prior to the closing date. Premium Lists are designed by the two kennel clubs to make sure the show-giving organization appraises the exhibitor of everything he needs to know about the forthcoming event—and then some!

A Premium List contains the names of the officers of the show-giving club with the address (and sometimes even the telephone number) of the show secretary, and includes the members of the show committee with the chairman's address. The names of the veterinarians assigned to the show, the names and addresses of all judges and a breakdown of their assignments for both breed and groups, a list of prizes being offered at all levels, and an explanation of any special classes or division of classes in addition to a list of regular classes, are all included in the Premium List. If any special standards for eligibility for various classes or groups are in effect, they will also be outlined, as will information about where the show is to be held, a map or directions for getting there, when it starts and when it closes, and hotels and motels in the area that accept dogs. With so many exhibitors, amateur as well as professional, traveling to dog shows in trailers or mobile homes, a description of facilities for these vehicles is usually given and advice as to whether or not food and drink will be available at the show. At least two entry forms are included, stating how much it will cost to enter your dog, where to send your entry, and when the entries close for that particular show. I warn you now that if the Premium List says that entries will close at 1 P.M. on Thursday, May 6, then that is *exactly* when entries will close. If the entries for a particular show are limited to the first thousand or fifteen hundred entries, this will be stated prominently, usually on the cover of the Premium List, and you had best mail early to avoid the rush. We'll describe how to fill out those entry forms later in this chapter.

If you should not get a premium list but you know from a friend or through a publication listing the closing dates of various shows that you still have time to enter, you may use any standard, official American or Canadian Kennel Club entry form, scratching out the name of the club and the date of the show printed on it and substituting the name of the club and the date of the show you are interested in. It's smart to keep a few blank entry forms on hand just in case. If you cannot find out the entry fee, send fifteen dollars for American shows and twelve dollars for Canadian, explaining you had no way to find out the proper amount and you wanted to make sure you sent enough. You'll get any refund you have coming when you arrive at Canadian shows; American show superintendents will refund your overpayment by mail.

When you get to that first show, go straight to the super's office and ask for some blank entry forms. He will give you some with blank spaces for filling in the name of shows you may have to enter in the future without benefit of the Premium List.

About a week before the show date, you will either have your check returned signifying you missed the closing date, or will receive an envelope for the show-giving club or dog-show superintendent containing the judging schedule or program of the show you have entered, an exhibitor's pass if necessary, and your dog's entry form with his number on it. In case of a benched show, that number will signify the number of your bench. For benched and unbenched shows alike, the number is also your armband number. In the U.S., if you are attending two shows in one weekend, you will have a different number and a different set of passes, entries, etc., for each show; in Canada, your exhibitor's pass, your number and all other pertinent data will remain the same for however many shows you attend over the weekend, provided they are all hosted by the same club, as they generally are. Your entry and your dog's will either be in the form of a photocopy of your entry form with ADMIT ONE stamped across it, or will be a separate thing, much like a theater ticket, stamped ADMIT ONE, etc., etc.

If you and your husband want to take two dogs to a show, make sure one is registered to Mrs. John Brown and the other to either John and Mary Brown or Mr. and Mrs. Brown—or one of you will have to pay a public admission fee at the door. The C.K.C. and the A.K.C. authorize the issue of one exhibitor's pass for every two dogs entered by one person, two exhibitor's passes for every three or four dogs entered by one person, etc.

The dog-show program arriving with your tickets will tell you what time the dogs are to be judged, in what ring, how many dogs, bitches,

and specials (more about them later) are entered in each breed, parking
information, more motel data, and any changes in judges. When it
comes to listing the entries in your breed, your program might read:

(30) Newfoundlands—10—10—9—1 ex.

This translates as follows, always in this order: of the thirty Newfoundlands entered there are ten class males, ten class females, nine champions
of record, and one dog on exhibition only.

Between the time the judges are announced in the Premium List
and the time the judging programs become final, it is entirely possible
for a judge to die, become very ill, or to wind up with more than the
175 dogs he is permitted to judge per day by the A.K.C. or C.K.C.

If and when this happens, the changes in judges will be stated in
your program and you have a right to withdraw your entries and your
entry fees will be refunded, provided you withdraw in writing and that
withdrawal reaches the dog-show superintendent or the show secretary
before the opening of the show. This rule applies only to breed judges
and and not to group or best-in-show judges, as you make your entry
originally *knowing* you will have to exhibit under the breed judge but
only *praying* you will get further!

Your program usually will also, as mentioned, provide you with directions for reaching the show site—either a list of highways with right
turns and left turns, or a map contributed by some well-meaning member
of the club who fancies himself a cartographer. If the road to hell is
paved with good intentions, the road to many a dog show is paved
with the same material. Suffice it to say that your best bet is to approach
all types of directions included in the program with extreme suspicion,
a will to win, and a well-studied travel map of the area.

THE REGULAR CLASSES

Now let's take a look at the regular classes offered at both U.S.
and Canadian shows in order to determine which dogs are eligible
for these classes and, in particular, to decide what class might be best
suited to you and your dog.

In the United States

The Puppy Dog or Bitch Class: for animals whelped in the U.S. or
Canada which are over six months and under twelve months on the
day of the show.

The Novice Dog or Bitch Class: for animals six months of age and
over, whelped in the U.S. or Canada, which have not, prior to the
closing date of entries for that particular show, won first prize in Novice

three times, or one first in a higher class (Bred by Exhibitor, American Bred, or Open). Dogs in this class may not have any championship points.

The Bred-by-Exhibitor Dog or Bitch Class: for animals whelped in the U.S. or, if individually registered with the A.K.C. stud books, for dogs whelped in Canada, that are six months of age and over, that are not champions and are owned wholly or in part by the person or by the spouse of the person who was the breeder or one of the breeders of record. Dogs in this class must be handled in the class by an owner or by a member of the immediate family of the owner (i.e., husband, wife, father, mother, son, daughter, brother, or sister). It should be clearly understood that if a dog wins this class, he may then be handled for winners or any subsequent competition at that show by anyone else—a professional, a friend, a fellow breeder; only in the Bred by Exhibitor Class itself must the dog be handled by the owner-breeder.

The American-Bred Dog or Bitch Class: for all animals, champions excluded, six months of age or over, whelped in the U.S. by reason of a mating which took place in the U.S.

The Open Dog or Bitch Class: for any animal six months of age or over. All imported animals, regardless of age, must be shown in the Open Class.

The Best of Breed or Specials Class; The Best of Variety Class: for dogs and bitches (shown together) that are champions of record, or for dogs which, according to their owner's records, have completed the requirements for a title but whose championships are still unconfirmed. Dogs are allowed to compete in this class without confirmation of their titles for only ninety days. If, at the end of that time, it turns out the owners' records were incorrect, the dog must return to the classes and remain there until he has secured the necessary number of points.

In Canada

You will notice that many of the classes are the same, but watch closely for different requirements for those classes.

The Junior Puppy Dog or Bitch Class: for animals at least six and under nine months on the first day of the show.

The Senior Puppy Dog or Bitch Class: for animals at least nine months and under twelve months on the first day of the show.

The Canadian-Bred Dog or Bitch Class: for animals born in Canada, champions of any country excluded.

The Bred-by-Exhibitor Dog or Bitch Class: for animals owned and handled in the ring by the breeder—unlike in the U.S., no family handler is acceptable. (Remember, after winning this class, a dog may be taken on in further competition by anybody, just as in the U.S.)

The Open Dog or Bitch Class: for all animals.

The Best of Breed or Specials Class; The Best of Variety Class: for dogs and bitches (shown together) which have attained championship status. Entry of a dog for Best of Breed or Variety is not prohibited, on the grounds that the title of champion has not been confirmed by the C.K.C. However, if it is established that an animal has been entered here before attaining championship status in accordance with the rules, then all awards earned at shows at which the dog was entered wrongly shall be canceled.

However, under recent legislation, no dog finished in Canada can be specialed in that country until and unless he has an individual C.K.C. registration number.

NON-REGULAR CLASSES, SPECIALTY SHOWS, BOOSTERS

Let's get one thing straight at the outset: a specialty show is not limited to Specials! Some people do get these two words confused, and it is not hard to do so when you are just starting out and all the doggy terms sound like so much Sanskrit shorthand.

A *Specials dog* is a champion of record in either country—we'll go into this in detail a little later. A *specialty show,* however, held in either country, is a licensed or sanctioned dog show limited to a single breed and usually sponsored by the so-called "mother club." You might be interested in the annual fall Specialty of the Golden Retriever Club of America, for instance, or perhaps the Northern New England Siberian Husky Club Specialty.

Sometimes a number of breeds will band together and hold a combined specialty; this might be for all dogs in the Terrier Group, or for all breeds of working dogs. In this case you might find yourself attending the Garden State All-Breed Sporting Dog Specialty at which all recognized breeds of Sporting dogs would compete for top honors.

While they may be held in conjunction with an all-breed show, combined specialties are often held independently. Single-breed specialties can be held independently or, as is most often the case, as a feature of a dog show offering regular classes in other breeds. By way of example, the Talbot Kennel Club might be the scene and date of the American Miniature Pinscher Club Specialty, in which case, as it would explain in both premium list and catalogue, the classes for Miniature Pinschers at the Talbot Kennel Club show would constitute that Specialty. In Canada, however, the Specialty held in conjunction with a regular licensed show is often considered a separate event. So you might attend the Dalmation Club of Canada Specialty at the Hochelaga Kennel Club three-day dog show. This would mean that in addition to having the three regular chances for points in the classes each day, you would have a fourth chance for points at the Specialty.

Incidentally, you should be aware that it is possible to finish your dog's show title by attending nothing but specialties, providing you meet all point requirements.

Booster shows, held to "boost" interest in a breed, work much the same way. The Papillon Club of Ontario could designate the regular classes at the United Kennel Club as its Booster or "Supported" show. This fact would be duly noted in premium list, program, and again in the catalogue; just before the listing of the various classes would be a statement something like: "The Bearded Collie Club of Canada will support the entries and consider the classes at this show as their Booster." "Support" means that the B.C.C.C. would offer trophies and prizes "through the kindness of its members and friends."

At specialties and boosters the points are figured per breed exactly as for regular licensed shows, which will be explained shortly.

Because they are trying to bring out all facets of their breed and give as many people as possible a chance to participate, clubs sponsoring specialties and boosters offer a variety of non-regular classes. These can range from Veteran Dog and Bitch to Brood Bitch, from Stud Dog to Field Trial Classes, from Braces (two dogs as nearly alike as possible shown together by one or two persons) to Team Competitions (four dogs as nearly alike as possible shown together by one to four persons). Dogs entered in such nonregular classes are not eligible for points unless they are individually entered in one of the regular classes. Later we'll discuss the reasons for not entering more than one regular class with a single dog; for now, suffice it to say you could safely enter any number of non-regular classes for which your dog is eligible plus one regular class and still be eligible for points if you should win your regular class.

When such non-regular classes are offered at specialty shows in the U.S., all single-entry non-regular classes are judged after Reserve Winners Bitch and before Best of Breed; this is because the winners of single-entry non-regular classes are eligible to compete for Best of Breed. Examples of this would be Field Trial Dog and Bitch Class or Veteran Dog and Bitch Class. In Canada, however, the Veterans Class is not competitive at all; it is merely a parade of dogs and bitches over seven years of age.

In both countries following Best of Breed judging, multiple-entry non-regular classes would be judged, such as Braces, Teams, Brood Bitch (the mother dog accompanied into the ring by two of her pups or "get"), or Stud Dog Class (the father dog accompanied into the ring by two of his "get"). The Parade of Champions usually finishes off the day—a heartwarming presentation in the ring of old and new champions of record.

Whenever non-regular classes are offered at boosters or specialties, they are duly noted in the premium list complete with any extra entry fees required, eligibility requirements, and other such data.

OTHER POSSIBILITIES
Local Classes

In order to encourage breeders and owners living close to the dog show to support the event, and to give people who perhaps cannot travel too far to show their dogs a moment in the sun, some clubs offer Local Classes.

Just what constitutes "local" is decided upon by the show-giving club and is explained in the premium list (e.g., "All dogs whose owners reside within ten miles of Tarrytown, N.Y., shall be eligible for Local Dogs and Bitches competition").

Local Classes are not divided by sex, and all entered males and females compete together following the Best of Breed class. Winners of Local Classes are then eligible for competition in Local Groups, tapering toward the ultimate: Best Local Dog in Show.

Exhibition Only

In both countries it is possible to enter a dog at a show purely for the purpose of having him on display. This classification is referred to as "For Exhibition Only." The registration requirements and age limits are the same as those for any dog entering a show.

In Canada you fill out a regular entry form putting "For Exhibition Only" in the box asking for Class. You will fill in all other particulars you would include on any entry. The fee will be determined by the show-giving club. Your dog will not be counted when figuring up championship points and cannot compete in any regular class or for any special prize. But at the option of the show-giving club, he can be entered and compete in any number of unofficial classes. Your premium list will outline the particulars you need to know for this classification of entry.

In the United States any dog that qualifies to be shown at any licensed show may be entered "For Exhibition Only" at the regular entry fee of that show provided the dog has been awarded a first prize in a regular class held prior to the closing of entries of the show in which the Exhibition Only entry is made. Some American show premium lists state that Exhibition Only is not available at that show. And in the U.S., a dog so entered shall not be shown in any class or competition at that show.

This class is often used by breeders who want famous, retired dogs to be seen by the public, or by those who wish to bring non-competing dogs along with them to the show without leaving them in the car or motel room.

Puppy Sweepstakes and Futurities

Puppy Sweepstakes is a non-regular class sometimes offered at all-breed licensed shows and sometimes at specialties. All entry fees paid for this class go into a special "pool," and the winners of the various puppy classes in the sweepstakes divide the money. The classes are divided into senior and junior puppies (determined by age) in the six regular categories. Four places are awarded in each class; sexes are rarely divided. After a winner is declared in each of the classes, the finalists come together and a single winner is selected. No championship points are awarded.

A Futurity is a complicated non-regular class sometimes offered at breed specialty shows. Wins in a futurity do not count toward championship.

Puppies competing in futurity classes are nominated for this competition before their litter is bred. A fee is paid per puppy nominated by the breeder of record before the dam is bred; another fee is paid after the puppies are born; and a third fee, before they are a specified age. The idea here is that the breeder is so proud of and has such confidence in his stock that he is saying, in effect, that he knows what his blood lines will produce before the puppies are born.

Since this is a non-regular class, futurities vary from show to show. Specialty clubs planning on offering futurities send exact information out to all members at regular intervals advising them of fees to be paid and dates for nominating litters, etc.

Combined Sexes

Every now and then, in an effort to give some rare breed an opportunity to draw an entry that will guarantee a respectable number of championship points (Sussex Spaniels, Kuvaszok, Manchester Terriers, for instance), a show-giving club will specify in the premium list that *the winners class will not be divided by sex.* In this instance, the bitch first-place winners in each regular class would enter the ring with the dog first-place winners in each regular class, and together they would all compete for a single *Winners* award. Championship points are then recorded for the dog or bitch awarded Winners, based on the schedule of points for the sex of the breed (or variety) for which the greater number in competition is required.

In other words, if six bitches and four dogs were present and the dog were declared Winners, he would figure his points on the basis of *ten males;* if the bitch went Winners, she would take that number of points which, on the chart, are to be awarded for defeating *ten bitches.*

JUNIOR SHOWMANSHIP
In the United States

The classes are as follows:

Novice: For boys and girls at least ten years of age and under seventeen on the day of the show, who, at the time entries close, have not won three first-place awards in a Novice Class at a licensed or member show.

Open: For boys and girls at least ten years of age and under seventeen on the first day of the show, and who have won three first-place awards in Novice. If a child wins his third Novice Class, he is eligible to enter and compete in Open that same day, provided there are one or more Juniors competing in Open.

Four placements are awarded in each class, and at the discretion of the show-giving club, the two first-place winners are allowed to compete for Best Junior Handler. The target in Junior Showmanship competition is to win the necessary *eight or more Open classes* in Junior Showmanship Competition in A.K.C. licensed or member shows held between January 1 and December 30 each year. These children must be at least ten years old and under seventeen at the time of each qualifying win, and their dogs must either be owned or co-owned by the junior and his immediate family, and must be eligible to compete in A.K.C. dog shows or obedience trials. In getting their eight wins, the lucky youngsters earn the right to compete at the prestigious Westminster Kennel Club Dog Show at Madison Square Garden, where America's Top Junior Handler of the Year is selected.

In Canada

While Canada's juniors are in no way as polished or sophisticated as their U.S. counterparts, due to the fact that junior competition is just getting proper recognition in Canada, these children are every bit as keen to win. Canadian rules state that they may use any dog they choose to compete in Junior Showmanship Classes.

The Classes are as follows:

Juniors: Boys and girls thirteen years and under

Seniors: Boys and girls fourteen to sixteen, inclusive.

These two classes may be divided by sex if the entry warrants it. In any event, the two or four winners compete for Best Junior Handler at the show. The children in Canada are aiming for Best Provincial Junior Handler or Best Junior Handler in Canada, based on five points for first place, four for second, three for third, two for fourth, and Best Handler, ten points. In order to be eligible for finals, the child must belong to the junior division of his local kennel club, and must report his wins and points collected at a minimum of three competitions within his province. At the end of the year, each club will nominate its top scoring junior for the Provincial Competition. In order to determine the single high-scoring junior in a club, the total number of points won by the junior handler is divided by the number of competitions in which the junior competed (competed, now—not necessarily placed!), and that figure will represent the total number of points awarded to that junior handler. The individual clubs are responsible for raising the money to send their top junior to the finals (in the U.S., the children have to get there on their own!).

The Provincial Competitions must be held on or before March 31 of the year following (i.e., points won by juniors in 1976 will count toward the Provincial Competition held in 1977). Provincial winners are eligible to compete for Top Junior Handler in Canada, and this competition must be held before May 31; the "Nationals" will be held at different locations across Canada.

It should be stressed that the Juniors in both countries are judged *not* by the quality of their dogs, but *solely* by the quality of their handling ability, their ring deportment, their appearance, and the grooming of their dog. These classes have gotten unbelievably large in both countries in the last few years, and consequently, even at the novice level, competition is very keen. Much waiting around and long, unproductive hours spent in crowded rings are often the case, but still there is no finer way to teach youngsters poise and good sportsmanship.

In Canada, these classes are most often judged by professional handlers who donate their time because they sincerely care about the handlers of tomorrow—"as the twig is bent so is the tree inclined."

Every now and then Junior judges are selected simply because they are "good with children" although they know zilch about show handling. Then the cutest little girl with the biggest dog wins, everybody gets a candy bar, and Junior Showmanship is set back a year or two. Fortunately these are infrequent occurrences.

For years, handlers just as dedicated judged U.S. Junior Showmanship classes, but because U.S. shows are so much larger for the most part and because U.S. professionals carry many more dogs than do Canadian professionals, we were soon running into the problems just beginning to face Junior Handling classes in Canada: a Junior class would be half completed and the handler would have to interrupt it to run off and handle a dog in competition. This is a most undesirable situation for both judge and Junior. Seeking to solve the problem intelligently, the Professional Handlers Association asked the A.K.C. to designate a one-hour lunch break at each show offering Junior Handling classes, and during that break interested professional handlers would judge the Junior classes. The A.K.C. flatly refused, fearing to tie up rings and drag shows out even longer than they run at present. Consequently, in the interests of the Junior, who deserves the undivided attention of some person of authority or knowledge as his talents are evaluated, the P.H.A. declined to continue judging Juniors and the A.K.C. gave this assignment to various licensed judges.

On the surface, this doesn't look like such a bad plan, until you realize that the judges, who often feel they get "stuck" with Junior Showmanship, are newcomers who get this extra assignment because they are only licensed to judge a few breeds, and who, because of their inexperience, can't afford to argue about it. If all judges had been handlers or even exhibitors before they got their licenses, things might be much better. But many judges were breeders who were never outstanding in the breed ring when they handled their own dogs, or people who themselves used the services of professional handlers. Never for a moment would I intimate that these people don't like children, but in most cases they are not terribly interested in what becomes of the youngsters once they have discharged their obligations to them, and let's face it, even the most gifted handlers are not always the best teachers!

The biggest problem in Canada when it comes to Junior Handling is that no matter how many competitions a child wins, if those competitions weren't held under "Scarborough Rules," the wins don't count! Hopefully someday the children in Canada will have the uniform regulations for national competition that the U.S. kids do, and the U.S. kids will again be judged by handlers.

A Doubtful Double Standard

In the mishmash of confusion surrounding Junior Handling in both countries, we come face to face with the fact that we seem to be teaching the children two methods of handling: one, how to win in the breed ring; and two, how to win in Junior Showmanship. This is due to the fact that too many Junior judges want to make sure the kids are always on their toes or they don't award them placements. This means that while handlers know perfectly well that when a dog in a large class is not under judgment you rest him, saving his wiggle and giggle for the moment when the judge again approaches, the kid whose dog is not set up in show pose 80 per cent of the time rarely has a chance for a ribbon in Junior competition. In addressing the judge during Junior Showmanship classes, the young handler knows perfectly well he must make a circle in front of the judge before starting, be it a clumsy maneuver or not; in the breed ring we only circle a dog before individually gaiting him, when it is needed to straighten out his approach to his pattern. These differences confuse the child with a double standard, which does nothing at all to develop a good handler.

I have sat with the mother of one of my pupils at ringside at a sweltering summer show and seen the judge disqualify a child because she took her dog out of the sun and over to the shade of the tent when he wasn't actively being judged, something any self-respecting handler would do automatically. I have heard judges fault children because "you never talk to a dog in the breed ring," which came as a distinct shock to me after finishing hundreds of dogs while babbling away encouragingly to them. And believe it or not, I once had to stand by and watch one of my more gifted protégés bite the dust because, as the judge explained to her, the dog was too perfect!

While most of these dedicated youngsters somehow survive the crimes of their elders and either become handlers, assistants, or poised, confident members in other walks of life, I fail to see the logic in teaching them false standards, in instilling in them artificial, stylized techniques that no professional would be caught dead using.

Mrs. Anne Rogers Clark did one of the greatest services to Junior Showmanship all over the world the year she did the finals at Madison Square Garden. As usual I was in the balcony, agonizing with many of my "chickens" who had happily qualified. Most of the young handlers were pictures of perfection—as were their highly trained dogs which could perform patterns and assume a show pose in their sleep due to weekend after weekend of competition. Then along came a young lady I had helped off and on with her Irish Setter. That setter, I knew, would have tried the patience of a saint, and he decided to pull out all stops for this most important occasion. He balked at gaiting, he soiled the ring, he snapped at his handler when she tried to adjust his foot, he refused to be examined. Writhing in agony in my balcony hideout, I went completely to pieces watching the performance; had I, an experienced adult, been handling the dog, I would have left him in the middle of the floor and fled to the Azores. But that little girl never got cross, never got rough, never gave up. Inch by inch, step by step, she worked and reworked, soothed, corrected, cajoled and compensated. A man sitting behind me scoffed: "Boy, she's some handler!" I whipped around and snapped: "She sure is some handler; she should win this class for the job she's doing!"

And because of the intelligent reasoning of a great lady, that child *did* win the award for Top American Junior Handler. A handler is somebody who can take a difficult dog and bring out the best in him—that's the name of the game. Someway, somehow, sometime we are going to have to get back to teaching this truth to the worthwhile hopefuls who compete in Junior Showmanship.

At the present time, in an effort to alleviate the complexities of this unique situation, the A.K.C. is pioneering a system of using qualified ex-junior handlers to judge Junior classes. This solution, while it has its good points, has some distinct drawbacks: the Junior Showmanship winner of 1975 may be in sympathy with the problems she faced during her Junior years, but still she lacks the experience of an older person in dogs.

While I seem to go on and on criticizing the existing system, I must admit that finding a solution is a lot like picking mushrooms—if you get the good ones, fine; if not, the results could be fatal. You cannot, in all fairness, experiment constantly with a system that grows more complicated each year due to increased numbers of children showing dogs.

Perhaps it would be possible for professional handlers who sincerely believe in the importance of the Junior program to give up, say, five shows each for the year. At the shows assigned them, then, they would not take any clients' dogs but would dedicate themselves to Junior Showmanship classes. All you need to make this one work is one thousand or so clients who feel the same way! Or, why doesn't the A.K.C. reconsider the proposal to take a break at shows to allow uninterrupted Junior classes under the supervision of professionals? What about limited entries at shows that draw enormous Junior entries? Certainly some children would be left out, but those who entered early enough would get much better attention and advice from judges; and with smaller entries there might be time for judges to use scoring sheets, so that even those who lost would know what they had done wrong. Such sheets might even be on file with the A.K.C. or C.K.C., so that judges setting their own standards could be controlled.

As the British put it, 'tis a "sticky wicket." Many American and Canadian children are getting sadly shortchanged. Actually, Canadian children interested in becoming handlers have one advantage over American kids—they can show *any* dog in Junior competition, and as the time of the class draws near, they are busily scurrying around "borrowing" dogs from breeders, owners, and handlers. I happen to feel that when children have to do a good job with a strange dog, they are accomplishing more than when they are showing the same faultlessly trained canine machine weekend after weekend. I would very much like to see the finals at Westminster require the last ten or twelve finalists to take dogs they have never seen before and for which they draw out of a hat.

Fortunately, I am not alone in my belief that we are letting down our professionals of tomorrow. Good people with plenty of "smarts" are working on this problem, and with a little bit of luck perhaps U.S. *and* Canadian juniors will be competing in programs that will bring out their best abilities and prepare them for a profitable, ethical future in dogs.

WHAT IS BEST FOR ME AND MINE?

Having studied all the regular classes and their requirements carefully, the novice is faced with the dilemma of which class is best for his particular dog. All too often a newcomer places a dog in a class simply because he's eligible for it—a puppy is entered in puppy class because he is, indeed, a puppy and puppy classes are for puppies. True, true— but there are puppies, and then there are *Puppies*.

The average nice, healthy, puppy-type puppy should of course be entered in puppy class if he is to be taken to licensed shows at all. (I happen to believe that in the United States, except at breed specialties, it's a waste of time and money to drag a daily-changing adolescent around when you could accomplish more by way of experience and exposure at matches or handling classes.) But then there comes along that certain puppy with a special something, a puppy that doesn't seem to know about the gangliness of adolescence. Or a very mature puppy growing up almost *too* fast. There is a chance that such a dog could make some points in licensed competition—but do we put him in Puppy class? Well, it depends. If he is really something special and you want the thrill of trying to finish him from the puppy classes, go ahead. Few indeed are the judges who will give a pup the nod for the points, but these brave creatures do exist, and if you can find enough judges who believe that the best dog on a given day should get the purple ribbon, regardless of age, go to it and more power to you! But if you have an almost *overly* mature puppy, puppy class is *not* the place for him—the judge is liable to look at him, ask his age and, after determining that he is eight or nine months old, turn him down by reasoning that if he is this big now, what's he going to be when he grows up?

Technically, of course, your puppy, if he is over six months, is eligible for *all* the regular classes! I didn't say he should be shown in any of them, but he *is* eligible.

Showing puppies in Canada is a different dish of tea. To begin with, puppy classes are divided, which means your six-month-old and one-week-old dollbump won't have to compete in his class with a "puppy" that is fifty-one weeks old. Also, there are special groups and Best Puppy in Show awards in Canada, now open to all puppies, Canadian and American alike, so if you don't make points it's still possible to come home with a puppy group win or a BPIS, which "ain't nutt'n to sneeze at, friend!" Entry fees are much cheaper in Canada, and when you consider the hours spent sitting around waiting to get into the ring at sanctioned matches for one or two dollars, it doesn't seem such a bad idea to enter in puppy classes in Canada, and for just a few bucks more get a crack either at points toward championship or puppy group wins, which look awfully good in one's kennel advertising!

I start most of my puppies in Canada, and when I get a client's dog which looks promising as a puppy, I insist he travel with me to Canadian shows whenever possible. By the time he has his Canadian championship or a few points or a couple of group placements under his chubby little tummy, he is a seasoned showman quite ready to compete in Open class in America. Canada offers a unique opportunity for puppies—a chance to get them ring experience, teach them what fun shows can be, an opportunity to get championship points and/or group wins—all for less than ten dollars! And remember—you can enter a puppy in Canada in any of the regular classes for which he is eligible, and he is *still* eligible to compete for Best Puppy.

The Bred-by-Exhibitor class was designed to give breeders a showcase for their wares. A breeder walking into the ring says to the world, "*This* is what I'm breeding and and I'm proud of it!" A win from the Bred-by-Exhibitor class is, as far as I am concerned, a real honor. I, myself, was only eligible for this class once in my life, and the fact that my Golden and I took a five-point win at Boston is one of my fondest memories!

Breeder judges (i.e., judges who were breeders of dogs at one time themselves) have a fondness for the Bred-by-Exhibitor class, but there are far too many judges who, in my opinion, always stick with the safe course and pick the Open dog or bitch for Winners time after time after time simply because "that's the way it is done" in their books.

I can think of no reason to enter a dog in Novice class except in a situation where I had a lot of dogs and needed a class for the odd one. But many people mistakenly believe that green dogs who aren't under one year *must* go in Novice. Not so—read your rules.

I finished twenty-four dogs out of the American-Bred class when I was starting out as a handler. It just so happened that in the breeds I was showing at that time, the Open classes were so crowded you couldn't find room enough to stand, let alone move. I reasoned that if I went into American-Bred and won it, even if I was the only entry, I would come back in against the Open winner in Winners, and with fewer dogs to wade through, the judge might see my dog more clearly. It worked then, and it's good psychology now, particularly at Specialty shows, where forty-five is not an unusual number in Open dogs and bitches classes.

Granted, the Open class at most shows, Specialties as well as All-Breed Shows, is where most of the Winners come from. It's the "big guns" class, full of good dogs with only a few points to go. It's the professional handler's home away from home, and handling techniques are as refined in this class as the competition is mature, experienced, and well-trained. If you enter Open, see that you are also mature, experienced, and well-trained. If, as a green handler, you are still finding yourself making mistakes in matches with the mumbled excuses, "Oh, I didn't know you could do that!" then stick with more matches and lesser classes at the smaller shows until you are ready to stand on your own two feet with confidence enough so that your dog doesn't lose because of *you*.

Again, seek out your breeder for advice as to classes. Call a local professional if there is one and make an appointment to get his opinion, being prepared to pay for same. Track down the successful breeder-handlers in your kennel club and ask their advice. Then try whatever class you think best. If you can be objective, a weekend of showing in the Open class will tell you fast enough whether you are in the right class or not.

The popularity of the breed has a lot to do with which class you will pick, as does the area of the country. Mastiffs, for instance, might draw heavy entries each weekend in West Virginia, but in South Dakota you might not see a Mastiff entered at all, show after show. You should be able to tell the popularity of your breed in your region by the number of people breeding and exhibiting in your club. If you are not sure, ask an experienced dog-show friend to let you thumb through her back catalogues, and this will give you a good picture of what to expect. Generally speaking, you will find that the bigger, more "famous" shows draw entries in even the rarest breeds. I could take an Akita out for six shows running and be lucky if I had a chance at a measly point in some of the smaller circuits. But sign up for Boston, Philadelphia, or Golden Gate, and look out, Josephine! Your breeder should be able to tell you which shows throughout the year draw the biggest entries in your breed. And if you are starting out, wobbly-kneed handler and know-nothing dog, for heaven's sake don't pick a show with a five-point entry for your maiden flight!

Most of all, don't get discouraged after a few shows because you don't feel secure in the class you have chosen and your dog is doing nothing to write home about, and *don't* let everyone else tell you that what you need is a professional handler! Funny, but the people singing this song—you'll notice if you look closely—are still handling *their* own dogs! Hmmmmmm—makes one right suspicious, don't it just? In summing up—getting you and your dog in just the right class may take a few nonproductive weekends. You can and should learn just as much from your failures, though, as from your triumphs—which *will* come in time, I promise you, if you use your noodle and stick to it.

ENTRY FORMS

On the following pages are sample entry forms for A.K.C. and C.K.C. licensed shows, as well as a santioned match entry form. You will notice how much simpler the match form is than the licensed entry. Match entries, as I said above, are usually made the morning of the match. But many clubs have started inviting phoned and written entries for a slightly reduced rate to give the club a better idea of what kind of entry to expect. Now let's take a look into the mysteries of making out entries for licensed shows.

Much of the same information is required on both the Canadian and U.S. forms, but you will notice that while there is a separate entry for each of two or three U.S. Shows on one weekend, a single entry form takes care of a three-show weekend in Canada; this is because in Canada all three shows are hosted by one club, while in the U.S., each show is under the auspices of a separate kennel club. Each club keeps complete records, hence two entry forms. We'll pretend that you are making out an entry, so we'll start right from the top. You'll need a pen and either your U.S. or Canadian registration certificate, or your U.S. or Canadian litter registration form. You may type out all of the entry form except for the signature. Many dog-show folks prefer typing their entries and make carbons in case any dispute should arise on an error in the entry form.

It might be wise to pause here a moment to straighten out two common misconceptions:

1. If I buy a dog which is not yet registered in my name with the A.K.C. or C.K.C., I cannot show him.

SAMPLE

SHAWANGUNK KENNEL CLUB, INC.

Sunday, February 1st, 19—

**PRE-WESTMINSTER
PROFESSIONAL HANDLER SLATE
50-FOOT RINGS!**

Entries Taken From 9:30 am   **Judging Begins at 11:30 am**

JUDGES	BREEDS	GROUP (Puppy & Adult)
ROBERT NORMAN	Sporting Dogs & O.E.S.	Working Group
JANE K. NORMAN	Terriers & Hounds (except Afghans)	Sporting Group
PHILLIP HARTLEY	Working (except O.E.S. & German Shepherds)	Hound Group
LOUIS GREENE	Non-Sporting & Afghan Hounds	Toy Group
KENNETH MOSS	Toys	Terrier & Non-Sporting Group
JONATHON HART	German Shepherds (at 1 pm)	

Best in Match Adult—Jane Norman   Best in Match Puppy—Louis Greene

Breed Classes: Puppy: 3—6 months; 6—9 months; 9—12 months
Adult: Novice & Open
FOR EXHIBITION ONLY—dogs with major points & Champions of Record.

Junior Showmanship classes: Age 8—10 years; 11—13 years; 14—16 years at 10:30 am

$0.00 entry fee per dog   Junior Showmanship $0.00   Spectators $0.00

Free Handling class, tips from Professionals at 10:30 am

TATOO CLINIC RUN BY SARAH DANIELS: $0.00 per dog

HOME-MADE REFRESHMENTS AVAILABLE   PHOTOGRAPHER
TACK SHOP FOR RING EQUIPMENT

No heavy grooming & mess **please!** No chairs or water dishes will be available.

The Greater N.Y. Bullmastiff Society will support their entry with trophies.

DIRECTIONS: N.Y. Thruway (North or South) Exit 19, take U.S. Rte 587 to Albany Ave, turn left to Manor Ave. Route 32 (North or South) to Manor Ave. Route 9W to Albany Ave, follow arrows to Manor Ave.

Information: Betty Nesmith (Show Chrmn) (914) 543-2109
Rose Manning (Pres) (914) 876-5432   Mrs Mead: (914) 765-4321

PRE-ENTRY FORM
Only $2.00 per dog if received by January 29th, 19—

DOGS PRE-ENTERED WILL BE PROCESSED
AT SEPARATE "QUICK LINE".

BREED_____   CLASS _____

Dog's name_____   SEX _____

Owner's name_____

Address_____   mail to: Betty Nesmith
_____   123 Shepard Lane
_____   Rye, N.Y. 12500

Make checks payable to: Shawangunk K.C. No refund unless show is cancelled.
Entries not received by 29th Jan or received without payment must re-enter at show.

SAMPLE

OFFICIAL CANADIAN KENNEL CLUB ENTRY FORM

ST. CATHARINES AND DISTRICT
KENNEL AND OBEDIENCE CLUB

SATURDAY, APRIL 2nd ☐   **SUNDAY, APRIL 3rd** ☐

BULL TERRIER SPECIALTY ☐

ENTRIES CLOSE 9 P.M., FRIDAY, MARCH 18th, 19—

Mail to: Mrs. J. L. Marsh
123 Highland Rd.
Pickering, Ont.
L1V 2P9

I enclose $_____ for entry fees. $_____ for listing fees. $_____ for recording fees.

TYPEWRITE OR PRINT PLAINLY

Breed		Sex:
Don't Use This Space	Enter in following Classes: (Give height, colour or weight if class is divided.)	
	Additional Classes (if any)	
Name of Owner		
Name of Dog		
Place of Birth	Canada ☐ Elsewhere ☐ Date of Birth	
C.K.C. Individual Reg. No.		C.K.C. Litter Reg. No. (if available)
	Breeder	
Sire		
Dam		

Owner's Address _____

Agent's Name _____

Address _____

I ACCEPT full responsibility for all statements made in making this entry.
I HEREBY CERTIFY that I understand the Dog Show Rules adopted by The Canadian Kennel Club and the regulations, conditions and provisions contained in the Premium List of this show; and I AGREE to be bound by same.

Owner's or Agent's Signature _____

I.D. Cards to Owner_____ Agent _____ PHONE_____

NOTE: Incomplete Entries will be returned.
AGENT'S NOTE: Names & Addresses of Owners must be filled in.

SAMPLE

OFFICIAL AMERICAN KENNEL CLUB ENTRY FORM

55th All-Breed Dog Show and Obedience Trial

CENTRAL NEW YORK KENNEL CLUB, INC.

SUNDAY—APRIL 25, 19—

ENTRY FEES: $9.00 for the first entry of each dog, $6.00 for each additional entry of the same dog. If entered for Junior Showmanship Only, the fee is $5.00; if entered as an additional class, the fee is $3.00.

DUE TO SPACE LIMITATIONS, ENTRIES ARE LIMITED TO 1400 DOGS. ENTRIES CLOSE: 12:00 Noon, Wednesday, April 7, 19 — (or when the limit is reached prior to April 7, 19 — at Superintendent's Office), after which time entries cannot be accepted, cancelled, or substituted. Entries received with the 1400th entry will be accepted.

MAIL ALL ENTRIES WITH FEES TO TOM SMITH, Superintendent, 234 Main St., P.O. Box 567, Madison Heights, Michigan 48071.

MAKE ALL CHECKS AND MONEY ORDERS PAYABLE TO MOSS—BOW DOG SHOW ORGANIZATION, INC.

I ENCLOSE $_____ for entry fees.

IMPORTANT—Read Carefully Instructions on Reverse Side Before Filling Out

Breed	Variety See Instruction #1, reverse side (if any)	Sex

	DOG Show Class See Instruction #2, reverse side (Give age, color or weight if class divided)	Obedience Trial Class

If dog is entered for Best of Breed (Variety) Competition—see instruction #3 reverse side —CHECK THIS BOX ☐	Additional Classes

If entry of dog is to be made in Jr. Showmanship as well as in one of the above competitions, check this box, and fill in date on reverse side. ☐	If for Jr. Showmanship only, then check THIS box, and fill in data on reverse side. ☐

Name of Actual Owner(s)   See Instruction #4, reverse side

Name of Licensed Handler (if any)

handler

Full Name of Dog

Insert one of the following: AKC Reg. # AKC Litter # I.L.P. # Foreign Reg. # & Country	Date of Birth	☐ U.S.A. ☐ Canada ☐ Foreign Do not print the above in catalog
	Breeder	

Sire

Dam

Owner's Name _____

Owner's Address _____

City _____ State _____ Zip Code _____

I CERTIFY that I am the actual owner of this dog, or that I am the duly authorized agent of the actual owner whose name I have entered above. In consideration of the acceptance of this entry, I (we) agree to abide by the rules and regulations of The American Kennel Club in effect at the time of this show or obedience trial, and by any additional rules and regulations appearing in the premium list for this show or obedience trial or both, and further agree to be bound by the "Agreement" printed on the reverse side of this entry form. I (we) certify and represent that the dog entered is not a hazard to persons or other dogs. This entry is submitted for acceptance on the foregoing representation and agreement.

SIGNATURE of owner or his agent
duly authorized to make this entry _____

2. If I buy a dog which is not yet registered in my name with the
A.K.C. or C.K.C., I can show him but he must be shown in the recorded
owner's name until my papers come through.

Regarding misconception No. 1: *in the U.S.* an unregistered dog that
is part of an A.K.C. registered litter, or an unregistered dog with an
acceptable foreign registration that was whelped outside the U.S. and
is owned by a resident of the U.S. or Canada may, *without special
A.K.C. approval,* be entered in licensed dog shows that are held not
later than thirty days after the date of the first licensed show in which
that dog was entered, *provided that* the A.K.C. litter registration number
or the individual foreign registration number and the name of the country of birth are shown on the entry form, *and provided that* the same
name is used for the dog each time. In the case of an imported or
Canadian-owned dog, that is to be the name listed on the foreign registration.

The American Kennel Club, I have always found, is usually most
helpful in matters pertaining to these rules. If you should use up your
thirty-day limit without being able to provide data to secure your individual A.K.C. registration *through no fault of your own,* call or write
the Show Records Department of the American Kennel Club. It may
be possible for you to get an extension enabling you to continue showing.
Sometimes several extensions have been authorized, but the A.K.C.
will want a written summary of the reasons you have not been able
to comply, and you will be able to continue showing only upon receipt
of a written extension authorization from the A.K.C.

In Canada the same thing holds true, except that such an unregistered
dog may be shown *indefinitely* as a "listed" dog, provided each entry
of that dog for each show is accompanied by a one-dollar listing fee.
In other words, your A.K.C. registered dog, for instance, could be
shown in any C.K.C. licensed show, provided you marked him "listed"
on the entry form and enclosed the one-dollar fee.

Regarding misconception No. 2: the rule is the same in Canada and
in the United States—a dog being shown in either country *must be
entered in the name of the person who actually owns the dog at the
time the entry is made.* (This is another excellent reason for insisting
upon a dated bill of sale signed by both buyer and seller when purchasing
any dog.) Therefore, if Susanna Smith purchases a dog from Bertha
Brown on a Tuesday and Susanna decides to show the dog on Wednesday, she would make out the entry for the dog listing Susanna Smith
as the owner of record. If Bertha Brown gave Susanna the registration
form on the dog signed over to Susanna at time of sale, then Susanna
would mail it out immediately and could write in the margin of her
entry next to owner of record: "Papers of transfer dated thus and such
are now being processed by the A.K.C." (or C.K.C., whichever applies).

If, for some perfectly legitimate reason, the papers were not forthcoming with the dog, Susanna has thirty days following that first show in which to see that those papers of transfer are mailed to the A.K.C. If she cannot straighten things out in thirty days, she may write the A.K.C. and, if her reasons are viable, she may be granted an extension. In the United States, in such a fix, you note on the entry form that the transfer application has been mailed or will be mailed shortly. Within seven days after the show involved, if the papers are not available for mailing, the owner should write the A.K.C. explaining the delay, and again, if the reason makes sense, the A.K.C. will grant any reasonable extension.

So with that bit of confusion clearly imprinted on our minds, we come to the first box on each country's entry form:

BREED: This is simply the breed of dog you intend to show.

VARIETY: Not all breeds have varieties. If you will check further on in this chapter under the explanation of the six groups into which all recognized breeds are divided, you will get a complete breakdown on which breeds have varieties. By way of example here, we'll use the Collie, which comes in a rough coat or a smooth coat. So if you were entering a Collie, on the U.S. form you would write *Collie* in the Breed box and *Rough* (or *Smooth*) in the Variety box. On the Canadian form, which has no Variety box, you would write *Collie (Rough)*.

SEX: In this box on either form you would write either *Male* or *Female;* or if you prefer, *Dog* or *Bitch.*

Now we come to DOG SHOW CLASS. In this box you write the name of the class in which you want to exhibit your dog—for instance, it might be *Open Bitch* or perhaps *Puppy Dog.*

If the dog you are planning to show is a champion of record, or you know he has completed his required number of points, then on either form you would write in the box labeled DOG SHOW CLASS, BEST OF BREED COMPETITION, SPECIALS DOG.

Which brings us to a point of much misunderstanding. Lots of people feel that when they finish a dog in the classes, they are not allowed to show him as a Special until they receive official confirmation of his title from A.K.C. or C.K.C. But it isn't so.

In the United States you may show a dog you believe has finished in Specials Class for ninety days without official notice of title, if you honestly think your carefully kept figures add up to the golden number of fifteen, including both majors. If, after ninety days, you haven't heard from "Big Brother," call New York. With a list of his points and wins lying right beside your telephone, ask why you haven't received notification of title. In fact, while I usually campaign like mad during those ninety days of grace, if I haven't heard good news in forty-five days, you can bet I'm on the long-distance line!

If the error is A.K.C.'s or C.K.C.'s fault, there is no need to get nasty; they are human beings too. Actually, they make surprisingly few mistakes when you consider the number of dogs they process every single day. In the United States, if the error is an honest one on your part, then you must drop that dog back into the classes pronto and get him finished right and proper. You don't lose any awards you collected while you were wrongly exhibiting your dog as a champion, but if, for instance, you won a group in that period, the points you might possibly have been entitled to for such a win would not count. *You must finish any dog by getting his championship points from the classes.*

In Canada much the same holds true, but there is no set time limit—you may continue to show in Specials class provided your dog has an individual C.K.C. number, indefinitely, although after two months I would call Toronto! If you were the one who miscalculated, then any wins during the period the dog was being wrongly shown will be canceled. You would have to return any awards and would then drop him back into the regular classes until finished properly.

On either side of the border, you are responsible for straightening out such tangles, and it is a wise handler who does not wait until the last minute; some of the saddest words in the world are, "Well, but I just assumed . . ."

Whether in the U.S. or Canada, when showing a finished dog in Specials Competition without official confirmation, simply leave off the prefix of Ch. until your certificate arrives.

CLASS DIVISION: For certain breeds, classes are divided by age, weight, or color. Some are always so divided; some, only when indicated in your premium list. Except for specialty shows at which such divisions may be carried out in other classes, the division usually applies only to Open classes for specific breeds, and those breeds with their unique divisions are listed on the back of all A.K.C. and most C.K.C. official entry forms. TO make certain the show you are considering isn't dividing classes for your breed, check your premium list carefully.

Let's suppose, for example, your dog is a Great Dane. Turn to the list of breeds in the Working Group in your premium list, because if the classes are going to be divided at that show, this is where such divisions would be indicated. In such an instance, your entry might read:

BREED: Great Dane   SEX: Male
DOG SHOW CLASS: Open Dog, Brindle

or

Open Dog, Fawn

or

Open Dog, Any Other
Allowed Color

It's always better to be safe than sorry, so include your dog's color on the entry form, even if it isn't called for.

On the U.S. form there is a line for ADDITIONAL CLASSES; there is no such line on the Canadian form. Nevertheless, the prospect of entering more than one class sometimes tempts a novice into the quicksands of disappointment and disenchantment.

While the entry form does not go into particulars, ADDITIONAL CLASSES means such non-regular classes as those provided by breed clubs at their specialty shows, or classes which do not qualify your dog to compete for championship points—such as Local Dog and Bitch, sometimes offered at regular all-breed shows.

There is no rule to prevent you from entering your dog in, say, American-Bred Dog *and* Open Dog; the Dog Show Superintendent or Show Secretary will happily accept your money for both, but what nobody bothers to tell you is that if you enter two of the *regular* classes, *you must win first place in both classes in order to be permitted to compete in winners class for points!*

The rules, buried deep in the morass of the rule book, clearly state than any dog defeated in the classes is ineligible for the Winners Class. But the novice show person doesn't normally dig far enough to find it; the "catch" to entering more than one regular class is not as clearly publicized as I think it should be, and year after year some innocent beginner falls on his face by reasoning that if he can win a ribbon in one class, perhaps he could win more in two classes.

Remember, then: the regular classes are Puppy, Novice, Bred-by-Exhibitor, Canadian or American-Bred, and Open. *Never, under any circumstances, should you enter more than one of these classes at a single dog show.*

The boxes for OBEDIENCE TRIAL CLASS and JUNIOR SHOWMANSHIP CLASS are self-explanatory on the U.S. form. Whether or not an additional fee is required for this class is indicated either at the top of the form or somewhere else in your premium list; some clubs charge nothing if a dog is entered in a regular class at that show; some charge a lower fee for Juniors; some charge the standard entry fee. But remember that in the U.S. any dog entered for Junior Showmanship must be owned by the handler or the handler's family. Also, at U.S. shows the dog in Junior Showmanship must be entered ahead of time, with the same closing date applying as to dogs entered for breed or obedience competition.

In Canada no fees are charged for Junior Showmanship, and the children enter at the show when instructed to do so over the loudspeaker.

NAME OF JUNIOR HANDLER is self explanatory. Check the reverse side of the entry form for further instructions regarding juniors.

Anyone in Canada can handle for money, and those who do are called agents. You will notice provisions for filling in information concerning your agent, and your agent could be anyone, even yourself (anyone in good standing with C.K.C., that is).

FULL NAME OF DOG means exactly that: the beastie's name exactly as it appears on his registration papers. You may always include the various titles your dog is entitled to use, but be advised that A.K.C. will print only show titles, obedience titles, and working cerificate letters won under American rules. Canada is more broad-minded, so Can. and Am. Ch. Fiddle-dee-dee, C.D.X., W.C., is a common sight in Canadian catalogues.

REGISTRATION NUMBERS are self-explanatory. I.L.P. numbers are those issued to persons who wish to exhibit nonrecognized breeds in Miscellaneous. In the U.S., foreign-born dogs may be shown for thirty days before they must be registered with A.K.C.; if the papers are held up in processing, extensions are available under proper circumstances as we've described. It is not necessary to register a dog with C.K.C. to exhibit in Canada, as noted previously, provided he is eligible for such registration and you pay a one-dollar listing fee per show. If yours is an A.K.C. registered dog, for instance, you would draw a line through or leave blank those areas calling for Canadian numbers and simply make a check in the box below CHECK IF LISTED. If no such box appears on your Canadian form, write "listed" in the box calling for registration number.

DATE OF BIRTH is easy enough. So is PLACE OF BIRTH on the U.S. form. On the Canadian entry, if your dog was not born in Canada, then he was born in that wonderful land of Elsewhere; goodness knows it must be an enchanted place, judging by the number of wonderful dogs that were born there.

BREEDER on either form means the breeder of record as written on your registration form—again, the exact name, please! If you are not sure, remember that the breeder is the owner or leasor of the mother of the litter which contained your dog at the time of the birth. SIRE is the father of your dog; DAM is the mother. OWNER'S NAME AND ADDRESS needs no clarification.

NAME OF ACTUAL OWNER means exactly that. This is where you print or type your name exactly as it appears on your registration form.

I realize that Joan Flores is a lot easier to write out than Mrs. Jason F. Eccholes Whiteside Flores, III, but if the latter form is the way you are listed as owner, then that's the way you have to write it on your entry form.

SIGNATURE OF OWNER OR AGENT must never be left blank or your entry will be returned. Either sign it yourself or, if you are telephoning your entry to a friend, have her sign her own name as your duly authorized agent. Actually, anybody can sign it, but don't leave it blank and never sign anybody else's name or suggest that a friend sign yours.

You will notice a place for a phone number on the Canadian form. Be sure to give one at which there will usually be someone around to answer and to accept collect calls from Show Superintendents and Show Secretaries, because if there is a question about your entry they very often are kind enough to give you a chance to correct your error. Also on both forms indicate to whom the show tickets and judging programs—I.D's—are to be sent.

In the United States, all such pre-show data is mailed to the owner of record, unless otherwise instructed in writing at the time you make your entry. There is no provision for a phone number on the U.S. form, but it doesn't hurt to include it on the bottom, just in case, and don't forget the area code. Actually, there is very little a U.S. Superintendent can do for you if your entry is faulty; it's against A.K.C. regulations and he could lose his license to stage shows for kennel clubs. But if your entry is sent early enough, he might call and give you a chance to send a new entry properly made out.

The one thing no U.S. Show Superintendent or Canadian Show Secretary can do for you is to accept your entry if it arrives late. That's a law over which they have no control; if the premium list says entries will close at 5 P.M. on July 1, all entries arriving after that time are returned.

Because the dog-show game isn't as unwieldy in Canada as in the States, and isn't, necessarily, as regimented, Canadian show officials can be much more informal about some rules and regulations. Show Secretaries run things for the most part in Canada, along with a few excellent dog show organizations, and these are friendly, knowlegeable, accommodating people. They can and do go miles out of their way to help you with paper work and often, in the case of mild infractions, will accept your entry providing you promise to arrive well before judging time to correct the form yourself.

To prevent frazzled nerves always mail all entries at least ten days ahead of closing date. When in doubt about postage, put on extra.

Mailing to Canada can present unusual problems, as this country seems to have postal strikes as often as South American countries have revolutions. Before mailing to Maple Leaf Country, check with your *main* post office to make sure mail is being accepted for Canada. If

SAMPLE

OFFICIAL AMERICAN KENNEL CLUB ENTRY FORM

49th All-Breed Dog Show and Obedience Trial

ONONDAGA KENNEL ASSOCIATION, INC.

SATURDAY — APRIL 26, 19—

ENTRY FEES: $9.00 for the first entry of each dog, $6.00 for each additional entry of the same dog. If entered for Junior Showmanship Only, the fee is $5.00; if entered as an additional class, the fee is $3.00.

DUE TO SPACE LIMITA... ...ARE LIMITED TO 1400 DOGS. ENTRIES CLOSE: 12:00 N... when the limit is reached prior to April 7, 19 — at ...entries cannot be accepted, cancelled, or substi-...will be accepted.

...ITH, Superintendent, 234 Main St., P.O. Box 567,

...PAYABLE TO MOSS—BOW DOG SHOW ORGANI-

ADMIT ONE
ONONDAGA K. ASSN.
Sat., Apr. 26, 19—
CEN. NEW YORK K.C.
Sun., Apr. 27, 19—

_____ for entry fees.

...ions on Reverse Side Before Filling Out

Bre...	Variety See Instruction #1, reverse side (if any)	Sex

DOG Show Class See Instruction #2, reverse side (Give age, color or weight if class divided)	Obedience Trial Class

If dog is entered for Best of Breed (Variety) Competition—see instruction #3 reverse side —CHECK THIS BOX ☐   Additional Classes

If entry of dog is to be made in Jr. Showmanship as well as in one of the above competitions, check this box, ☐ and fill in date on reverse side.   If for Jr. Showmanship only, then check THIS box, and fill in data on ☐ reverse side.

Name of Actual Owner(s)   See Instruction #4, reverse side

Name of Licensed Handler (if any)
                                                          handler

Full Name of Dog

Insert one of the following: AKC Reg. # AKC Litter # I.L.P. # Foreign Reg. # & Country	Date of Birth	☐ U.S.A. ☐ Canada ☐ Foreign Do not print the above in catalog
	Breeder	

Sire

Dam

Owner's Name _____

Owner's Address _____

City _____ State _____ Zip Code _____

I CERTIFY that I am the actual owner of this dog, or that I am the duly authorized agent of the actual owner whose name I have entered above. In consideration of the acceptance of this entry, I (we) agree to abide by the rules and regulations of The American Kennel Club in effect at the time of this show or obedience trial, and by any additional rules and regulations appearing in the premium list for this show or obedience trial or both, and further agree to be bound by the "Agreement" printed on the reverse side of this entry form. I (we) certify and represent that the dog entered is not a hazard to persons or other dogs. This entry is submitted for acceptance on the foregoing representation and agreement.

SIGNATURE of owner or his agent duly authorized to make this entry _____

SAMPLE

Breed: CHESAPEAKE BAY RETRIEVER	Sex: MALE

Enter in following Classes: (Give height, colour or weight if class is divided.)
JUNIOR PUPPY

Obedience Classes

Name of Owner	MARY REED & JEAN COLLINS
Name of Dog	HILLOCK'S PENNY ROYAL

Place of Birth	Canada ☐ Elsewhere ☒	Date of Birth 16 Day 3 Month 19— Year ■

C.K.C. Individual Reg. No.	Check if Listed ☒	C.K.C. Litter Reg. No. (if Available)

Breeder: ELLEN & THOMAS RANDALL   ■ By

Sire:	CH. HILLOCKS SWEET BASIL
Dam:	ROBBINS NEST MAJOR

Agent	Name MARY REED	Street THORNE ROAD
	City TAVISTOCK	Prov. ONT.

Owner This must be completed	Name JEAN COLLINS	
	Street 345 SHARON COURT	
	City NEEDHAM	Prov. MASS. Code U.S.A.

I accept full responsibility for all statements made in this entry. I hereby certify that I understand the Dog Show rules. Adopted by the C.K.C., and the regulations, conditions and provisions contained in the premium list of this show, and I agree to be bound by same.

Owner or Agents Signature
Mary Reed

Telephone
1-613-4567890

the mails are not moving, fear not: telephone the Show Secretary and she will either take your entry over the phone (you will pay your entry fee upon arrival at the show before exhibiting your dog), or will tell you of special pickup arrangements that have been made, in which case you will mail to a special U.S. address and your entry will be hand-delivered from there.

Most shows can be entered ahead of time at other shows. In the United States, you can hand the Show Superintendent your entries for later shows he is in charge of and not have to worry about postal foul-ups. In Canada, someone at just about every show is authorized to accept entries for any coming Canadian show. If it isn't announced over the loudspeaker, go to the Show Secretary and ask.

If you enter a show on either side of the border and then discover you cannot attend, you can cancel and expect a refund of entry fees only if you do so before the closing date for that show. You may call and cancel, but you will usually be asked to send written confirmation as well.

If you enter a show for which you couldn't mail and are to pay when you arrive, don't feel you can change your mind after closing and get out of paying. The club will bill you and C.K.C. can withhold your show privileges—and should—until and unless you pay up.

Sometimes two or three addresses are listed on the front of your U.S. premium list, all for the same Superintendent. Only one is indicated on your entry blank. Well, if you get caught in a last-minute bind and know you have a chance of mailing in time to an address other than the one on your entry, you may use the nearer office.

It makes good sense to duplicate a bunch of entries for each dog you are going to show. A.K.C. and C.K.C. provide free blank entry forms which you can pick up at dog shows. By having a batch on hand, all you have to do is sign the line at the bottom and fill in the show dates and name of the club at the top.

If you have no blank entries, you may use any official entry form for either country to enter any show, so save a few from premium lists of dog shows you are not planning to attend. Then carefully cross out the name of the show and write the correct club name and date above it.

Canada will accept entries on U.S. forms, provided all the necessary information is included; the U.S. cannot accept show entries on Canadian forms.

GROUPS

All recognized breeds of dogs in the U.S. and Canada today are divided into six groups or classifications. Each country lists the groups in the same order: Sporting, Hound, Working, Terrier, Toy, Non-sport-ing. But Canada almost always refers to them by number, while the U.S. uses the name (Group One is the Sporting Group, for instance).

Both countries include most of the same breeds in the six groups, but you will notice a few exceptions on the following Group charts.

THE "POINTS" OF IT ALL

While many of the rules and regulations are just about the same in both countries, the matter of points required to complete championship is quite another story.

In the United States, in order to be awarded the title of show cham-pion, a dog must accrue a total of fifteen points in competition at licensed dog shows. In the process of gathering these points, a dog must win two majors under two different judges, a major being a win of three, four, or five points won at one show. A total of three judges is necessary to complete championship in the U.S. To determine how many dogs constitute a major in your breed, consult your point scale (more about that in the next chapter) and notice that in the U.S. two dogs of the same sex are required for one point in any breed.

In Canada (at the time of this writing) only ten points are required for championship, and there is no system of majors. In the less popular breeds, you will see if you will consult the Canadian point scale, a single entry is worth one point. Before that final point is honored, *however,* a dog *must* defeat competition in either its own breed or in adult Group competition when that Group includes at least five dogs. As in the U.S., three judges are the minimum necessary for title.

Now let's proceed to just how you get points, and how to tally them for title. The progression of points within a breed is done exactly the same way in the U.S. and Canada. Except for the fact that in Canada puppies are divided into two classes, the regular official classes are the same in both countries, and these are the classes in which a dog *must* compete to be eligible for points. For purposes of clarification we're going to assume that at our mythical dog show all the regular classes drew an entry of at least three each. So here's the progression of points.

All class males are judged first (sorry about that, ladies!), and the classes are run in the following order:

UNITED STATES	CANADA
Puppy Dogs	Junior Puppy Dogs (6–9 months)
Novice Dogs	Senior Puppy Dogs (9–12 months)
Bred-by-Exhibitor Dogs	Bred-by-Exhibitor Dogs
American-Bred Dogs	Canadian-Bred Dogs
Open Dogs	Open Dogs

NAME OF GROUP	CONTAINING THESE BREEDS IN THE UNITED STATES		CONTAINING THESE BREEDS IN CANADA

SPORTING GROUP, referred to in Canada as GROUP ONE
 	
LIMITED IN BOTH COUNTRIES TO THOSE DOGS WHICH
 	
are basically the bird hunters of the world. Most of them are required to find and retrieve game on land and from water.
	Wirehaired Pointing Griffon
	Pointer
	German Shorthaired Pointer
	German Wirehaired Pointer
	Chesapeake Bay Retriever
	Curly Coated Retriever
	Flat Coated Retriever
	Golden Retriever
	Labrador Retriever
	English Setter
	Gordon Setter
	Irish Setter
	American Water Spaniels
		Britanny Spaniels
		Clumber Spaniels
		Cocker Spaniels, Black[1]
		Cocker Spaniels, ASCOB[1]
		Cocker Spaniels, Parti-colored[2]
		English Springer Spaniel
		Field Spaniel
		Irish Water Spaniel
		Sussex Spaniel
		Welsh Springer Spaniel
		Vizsla
		Weimaraner
			All breeds recognized by A.K.C. plus:
			
			German Longhaired
			  Pointer
			Pudelpointer
			Nova Scotia Duck
			  Tolling Retriever

[1] In the United States, each of our three Cockers goes into the Sporting Group; in Canada, the three varieties compete against each other to send just one into the Group.
[2] In the United States all English Cockers are judged together as only one breed; in Canada, English Cockers are divided into two varieties, Solid Color and Parti-Color, and only one goes into the Group.

NAME OF THE GROUP	CONTAINING THESE BREEDS IN THE UNITED STATES		CONTAINING THESE BREEDS IN CANADA
HOUND GROUP, referred to in Canada as GROUP TWO **LIMITED IN BOTH COUNTRIES TO THOSE DOGS WHICH** follow their quarry in one of two ways—the SCENT HOUNDS follow a trail with their noses using their power of scent to bring them to victory; the SIGHT HOUNDS which rely on exceptional eyesight and great speed to find their prey.	Afghan Basenji Basset Beagle not exceeding 13"[1] Beagle over 13" and under 15" Bloodhound Borzoi Black and Tan Coonhound Long Haired Dachshund[2] Smooth Dachshund[2]	Wirehaired Dachshund[2] American Fox Hound English Fox Hound Greyhound Harrier Irish Wolf Hound Norwegian Elkhound Otter Hound Rhodesian Ridgeback Saluki Whippet	All breeds recognized by A.K.C. plus: Drever Finnish Spitz

[1] In the United States, each sized Beagle is considered a different breed and both go into the Group; in Canada, the two sizes are judged against each other and only one goes into the Group.
[2] Although the U.S. recognizes the fact that there are miniature Dachshunds of all three varieties, both standards and miniatures are judged alike and only three Dachshunds go into the Hound Group; in Canada, each variety is separate, so six Dachshunds go into the Hound Group—the miniature and standard Longs; the miniature and standard Smooths and the Miniature and standard Wires.

NAME OF THE GROUP	CONTAINING THESE BREEDS IN THE UNITED STATES		CONTAINING THESE BREEDS IN CANADA
WORKING GROUP, referred to in Canada as GROUP THREE **LIMITED IN BOTH COUNTRIES TO THOSE DOGS WHICH** were developed to pull carts or sleds, to herd sheep or drive cattle. Others were trained for police and war work	Akita Alaskan Malamute Belgian Sheepdog[1] Belgian Tervuren Bernese Mountain Dog Bouvier des Flandres Boxer Bull Mastiff Collie—rough Collie—smooth Shetland Sheepdog Standard Schnauzer Samoyed Komondor Doberman Pinscher German Shepherd	Giant Schnauzer Great Dane Briard Kuvasz Mastiff Puli Newfoundland Great Pyrenees Old English Sheepdog Rottweiler Welsh Corgi, Cardigan Welsh Corgi, Pembroke St. Bernard Siberian Husky Bearded Collie Belgian Malinois	All breeds recognized by A.K.C. plus: Eskimos Old English Mastifs Bernese Mountain Dogs recognized in Canada a printing

[1] In Canada the Belgian Sheepdog is divided into three varieties as follows:

    Longhaired—Groenendael and Tervuren
    Shorthaired—Malinois
    Rough-Haired—Laeken

The three varieties are judged separately with the winners of each competing together to send just one into the Group.

NAME OF THE GROUP	CONTAINING THESE BREEDS IN THE UNITED STATES		CONTAINING THESE BREEDS IN CANADA
...RIER GROUP, referred to ...anada as GROUP FOUR	Airdale Terrier American Staffordshire Terrier[3] Australian Terrier Bedlington Border Terrier Bull Terrier (White)[1] Bull Terrier (Colored)[1] Cairn Terrier Dandie Dinmont Terrier Fox Terrier (Wire) Fox Terrier (Smooth) Irish Terrier	Kerry Blue Terrier Lakeland Terrier Standard Manchester[2] Terrier Miniature Schnauzer Norwich Terrier Scottish Terrier Sealyham Terrier Skye Terrier Soft-Coated Wheaten Terrier Staffordshire Bull Terrier Welsh Terrier West Highland White Terrier	All breeds recognized by A.K.C. except Soft Coated Wheatens

...ED IN BOTH COUNTRIES
...THOSE DOGS WHICH

...been known for years as
...varmint dogs". They are
...for their courage, hunt-
...bilities and willingness to
...o ground" after their
... Most Terrier breeds are
...crappers, and watching
...dging of any Terrier
...is a noisy and colorful
...ience.

[1] White and Colored Bull Terriers, while judged separately in the United States, are judged together in Canada.

[2] In Canada, Standard Manchesters are referred to simply as Manchester Terriers

[3] In Canada, the American Staffordshire Terrier is simply called the Staffordshire Terrier

...AME OF THE GROUP	CONTAINING THESE BREEDS IN THE UNITED STATES		CONTAINING THESE BREEDS IN CANADA
...GROUP referred to in ...da as GROUP FIVE	Affenpinscher Brussels Griffon Yorkshire Terrier English Toy Spaniel[1] Italian Greyhound Japanese Spaniel Maltese Toy Manchester Terrier Miniature Pinscher	Papillon Pekingese Pomeranian Toy Poodle Pug Shih Tzu[4] Silky Terrier[2] Chihuahua (Long-coated)[3] Chihuahua (Short-coated)[3]	All breeds recognized by A.K.C. plus: Cavalier King Charles Spaniel Mexican Hairless

...D IN BOTH COUNTRIES
...OSE DOGS WHICH ARE

...niatures of the canine
...They are coveted for
...andy small size. They
...al, devoted companions;
...xcellent watch dogs
...comes to raising an
...and perform in the
...nce ring with sparkle
...arm.

[1] English Toy Spaniels come in four varieties—King Charles, Prince Charles, Ruby and Blenheim. In the United States all are judged as one breed, as they are in Canada. In addition Canada recognizes the Cavalier King Charles Spaniel.

[2] In Canada, the Silky is referred to as the Silky Toy Terrier.

[3] In both the U.S. and Canada, Long-coated Chihuahua's are judged separately from Short-coated.

[4] In Canada the Shih Tzu is shown in the Non-Sporting Group.

...ME OF THE GROUP	CONTAINING THESE BREEDS IN THE UNITED STATES		CONTAINING THESE BREEDS IN CANADA
...PORTING GROUP ...d to in Canada as ...SIX	Bichon Frise Boston Terrier Bulldog Chow Chow Dalmation French Bulldog	Keeshond Lhasa Apso Miniature Poodle Standard Poodle Schipperke Tibetan Terrier	All breeds recognized by A.K.C. In Canada the Shih Tzu is a member of the Non-Sporting Group.

...IN BOTH COUNTRIES
...OSE DOGS WHICH

...ginally intended to
...eal role as a helpmeet
..."he breeds in this
...ve their greatest
...s companion dogs.
...ation, for instance, is
...the firehouse dog;
...le was originally a
...riever; Schipperkes
...d the Barges in

THE MISCELLANEOUS GROUP is another classification in both the United States and Canada. The Miscellaneous Group is for new breeds awaiting recognition by A.K.C. or C.K.C. In the U.S. dogs whose owners have been granted Indefinite Listing Privilege numbers (I.L.P.) compete in two groups, one for females, one for males, and four places are given in each class. When Canada offers Miscellaneous classes, the animals enter the ring and are paraded around; they are not judged, but people can see what they look like and perhaps support the development of one of these rare breeds of dogs.

One at a time these classes are called into the ring by the ring steward and are judged. It is possible to award four places in each class: a BLUE ribbon denoting first place, a RED ribbon for second, a YELLOW for third, and a WHITE for fourth. As soon as one class leaves the ring, the next one enters, and so on. When the judge has completed his examination of all dogs in the five American and five Canadian regular classes, the steward calls for WINNERS CLASS. At this point, the five first-place winners return to the ring. They are judged a second time. From this WINNERS CLASS the judge selects one animal only, and he is called winners dog (WD) or WINNERS MALE; it is to this dog and this dog only that any points toward championship available are awarded. The WINNERS ribbon is PURPLE, and this ribbon of course is what it's all about for any dog hoping to become a champion.

Immediately upon the selection of the WINNERS DOG, that fortunate animal and his beaming handler leave the ring for a while: the rest of the first-place dogs stay in the ring, to be joined by the second-place dog from the class from which WINNERS DOG has just been chosen. He now competes with the remaining first-place winners for RESERVE WINNERS DOG (RWD). The rules state that all classes with entries must be represented for competition toward the PURPLE AND WHITE RESERVE WINNERS DOG award.

To make sure you are straight on this, let's suppose that the first-place dog in the Novice Class was given the nod for winners. Then immediately the second-place winner in the Novice Class would go scuttling into the ring with the first-place winners of the other classes who are already in the ring, and from that batch of hopefuls would be selected RESERVE WINNERS DOG.

No points are ever awarded for RWD; consequently, some exhibitors don't get absolutely ecstatic about going reserve. This class, however, is the "safety valve class" and if, after the show, through some fluke, the male that took WD, and hence the points for the day, should be found to be ineligible, his points are then canceled. The heretofore down-in-the-dumps RESERVE dog, brooding at home because he was just an "also ran," receives a letter from the A.K.C. announcing he has won points because the WINNERS DOG proved to be ineligible for them, and Mr. Reserve may then bark for joy! To make sure of your point status, regularly check the show results section of the A.K.C. *Gazette* or the yellow pages of *Dogs in Canada*.

This finishes the competition of the class males in regular classes at a licensed dog show in the United States or Canada. They may all go home now, except for WINNERS DOG, which must stay around to compete on the next rung of the ladder. Remember, then, if you should place first *or* second in a regular class, stay hard by ringside because you will have to return for WINNERS, and should the dog that beat you in your class take WINNERS, and you were second in that class, *then you must get back in the ring for reserve.* Remember also that *no one is obligated to get you into the ring but little old you!* Stewards will usually call for classes, but sometimes they don't know enough to do so, are busy elsewhere, or call a wrong class. If you don't want to get gypped out of the chance for points, then it's up to you to stand by ringside ready to return either for WINNERS or RESERVE WINNERS. Also, when WINNERS is designated, do not wait to be called if you were second. March yourself right into the ring and occupy the position on the floor just vacated by the WINNERS MALE.

Now it's the ladies' turn, and they are judged exactly as the males were. The classes are the same, the order in the ring is the same, and just as in dogs, the female getting the nod for WINNERS BITCH (WB) is the only female taking home points and the coveted purple ribbon. Immediately after the judging of RESERVE WINNERS BITCH, all the girls can pack their bags and take off—except WINNERS BITCH, who must hang around with WINNERS DOG for the next foray into competition.

The next class into the ring following RESERVE WINNERS BITCH is referred to in Canada as either ALL GENERAL SPECIALS or SPECIALS CLASS; in the United States the steward may call for SPECIALS, but generally you will be hailed for BEST OF BREED COMPETITION. Into the ring for this class will come all male and female champions of record of the country in which the show is being held, plus WINNERS DOG and WINNERS BITCH.

Three awards will be made in the SPECIALS or BEST OF BREED class: (1) BEST OF BREED; (2) BEST OF OPPOSITE SEX to Best of Breed; and (3) BEST OF WINNERS.

BEST OF BREED: any male or female champion or WINNERS DOG or WINNERS BITCH has a chance to go BEST OF BREED (BOB, as it is commonly abbreviated).

BEST OF OPPOSITE SEX: if a male, should go BOB, then *any* female in the ring would be eligible for BEST OF OPPOSITE SEX (BOS).

BEST OF WINNERS: this award is open only to the WINNERS DOG and the WINNERS BITCH, and here is the *third way* to get points in the United States or Canada. Let's suppose, because of the number of class dogs entered at this show, WINNERS DOG is worth two points according to your point chart in the front of the catalogue. At this same show it turns out there were many more bitches entered, so that WINNERS BITCH was worth a whopping five points. If the WD goes BEST OF WINNERS (BOW), then the WD would also get that whopping five points! WB wouldn't lose hers, and WD would not add her five to his two, but would come home with five points also. If, on the other hand, WB took BOW, then each would be ultimately credited with their original points. It follows, of course, that if the roles of WD and WB were reversed and *he* had more points than *she,* then *she* would get the larger number of points if *she* went BOW.

No points are given to Champions of Record who are competing to see if they can amass enough BOB, Group, and BEST IN SHOW (BIS) wins to become one of the top dogs nationally or internationally. Some prominent breeders exhibit their best specials just as good public relations. The BEST OF BREED dog or bitch, whether class animal or champion, goes into the appropriate group for further competition.

We have seen the first three ways class animals can get points in the United States and Canada—WD, WB, and/or BOW. This is the end to the chance to get championship points at the breed level in the United States; not so in Canada.

Let's suppose Isadore's Eggplant, a very promising class bitch, beats four other bitches in the classes, which constituted one point in her breed, and then goes on to take BOB over two male champions and one female champion. Now the proud owner totals up the champions "Eggy" defeated for BOB and, regardless of sex, they "become" class bitches. He adds three "bitches" to the four "Eggy" defeated originally to come up with seven bitches, and adjusts his points accordingly.

At that same show, the judge, who obviously had a soft spot for class animals, gave BOS to the WINNERS DOG, a fine youngster called Blotto of Blop, who won three points when he took WD. His owner now includes any champions he defeated for BOS which were of his same sex (in this case, two), adds these to the number of dogs "Blotto" defeated in the classes, and adjusts *his* points accordingly.

So in the breed in the United States, a class dog or bitch can get championship points by going WINNERS DOG, WINNERS BITCH, or BEST OF WINNERS; no extra points are awarded for defeating champions of record.

In Canada, however, in addition to the same WD, WB, and BOW points available at the breed level, class animals defeating champions for either BOB or BOS could wind up with still more points.

There are still two more ways for a class animal to get points in the United States or in Canada at licensed dog shows.

If a class animal in either country should win his GROUP (Sporting, Hound, etc.) from the classes, then that beastie would get the most number of points won by any class dog from that particular Group at that show.

And, finally, if a class animal should win BEST IN SHOW from the classes in either country, then he would get the most number of points won by any dog of any breed at that show on that day.

In Canada, following the BEST OF BREED award, eligible puppies return to the ring to compete for BEST PUPPY IN BREED. If a puppy "went all the way," he of course is automatically BPIB as well as BOB. Otherwise, he returns to the ring to meet any puppies of either sex he has not already defeated in the classes to compete for the puppy award. After the judging of each of the six adult Groups, each of the six puppy groups are judged—SPORTING GROUP PUPPY competition following SPORTING GROUP, and so on. Now, this is where we get a bit complicated. If a puppy does not place in adult Group competition, then all eligible puppies enter the ring when puppy Groups are called. If, for instance, a puppy which went Best of Breed placed fourth in the adult Group, then only those puppies from the breeds which went first, second, and third in the adult Group return to compete with the puppy which went fourth in the adult Group—*because he has beaten all the rest with his placement.*

For instance, not long ago I went Best of Breed with a Bouvier des Flandres puppy. In the adult Group, a very fine Doberman adult was first, my Bouvier puppy was second, a German Shepherd adult was third, and a Samoyed adult fourth. When the puppy was called, it was comprised of only my Bouvier puppy and the Doberman puppy, which had gone Best Puppy in Breed that day—I had beaten all the other puppies by going second, see?

Finally, just as in grown-up competition, the six puppy Group winners compete, immediately following Best in Show, for the highly coveted award of Best Puppy in Show.

Finally, you cannot, of course, once you are entered, skip up into a Best of Breed or Specials Class from one of the regular classes just because you tallied your final point. For instance, if you entered the Open class for two shows on a weekend, and you got your finishing points on Saturday, you could not then leap into Specials on Sunday, but would stay in Open because the entries are closed for the second show and no entries may be changed or altered after a closing date. You are, of course, quite eligible to show on Sunday, if you wish to and we'll discuss your options in this instance later on.

So now that we've gone over the process of competing in breed competition and accruing points in both countries, let's see how it looks in a chart.

In the United States

(Shown in the seven stages from classes to Best in Show)

FIRST—MALE REGULAR CLASSES

Puppy Males	Open Males
Novice Males	Bred-by-Exhibitor Males
American-Bred Males	

SECOND—WINNERS CLASS MALES

Selecting Winners Dog and
Reserve Winners Dog

THIRD—FEMALE REGULAR CLASSES

Puppy Females
Novice Females
Bred-by-Exhibitor Females
American-Bred Females
Open Females

FOURTH—WINNERS CLASS FEMALES

Selecting Winners Female and
Reserve Winners Female

FIFTH—BEST OF BREED CLASS

Winners Dog and Winners Female
join all Champions of Record
in the ring to compete for
Best of Breed, Best of Winners,
and Best of Opposite Sex.

SIXTH—GROUP JUDGING

The six recognized Groups—
Sporting, Hound, Working, Terrier,
Non-sporting, Toy—judged one
after the other in whatever order
is announced at the show.
Four Placements.

SEVENTH—BEST IN SHOW

The six first-place winners of each
of the six Groups compete
for a single award of Best in Show.

In Canada

(Shown in the ten stages from classes to Best in Show)

FIRST—MALE REGULAR CLASSES

Junior Puppy Males
Senior Puppy Males
Bred-by-Exhibitor Males
Canadian-Bred Males
Open Males

SECOND—WINNERS CLASS MALES

Selecting Winners Dog and
Reserve Winners Dog

THIRD—FEMALE REGULAR CLASSES

Junior Puppy Females
Senior Puppy Females
Bred-by-Exhibitor Females
Canadian-Bred Females
Open Females

FOURTH—WINNERS CLASS FEMALES

Selecting Winners Bitch and
Reserve Winners Bitch

FIFTH—BEST OF BREED CLASS

Winners Dog and Winners Bitch
join all Champions of Record
in the ring to compete for
Best of Breed, Best of Opposite Sex,
and Best of Winners

SIXTH—BEST PUPPY

All puppy class winners, male
and female. If puppy entry goes
BOB, BP would be automatic.

SEVENTH—ADULT GROUP JUDGING

The six recognized Groups—
Sporting, Hound, Working, Terrier,
Non-sporting, Toy—usually judged
after the last breed in each Group,
but can also be done as it is
in the United States.
Four Placements.

EIGHTH—PUPPY GROUP JUDGING

Following each adult Group,
the best puppies of each breed
in the Group compete for
One Placement.

NINTH—BEST IN SHOW

A single winner selected
from the six first-place winners
in the Group competitions.

TENTH—BEST PUPPY IN SHOW

A single winner selected
from the six first-place winners
in the puppy Group competition

There will be more about the overall point system in Chapter 5, where you'll discover that there's a bigger difference than you might have thought between, say, a German Shepherd and a Norwich Terrier. You'll also learn what absentees (no-shows) can do to your scoring.

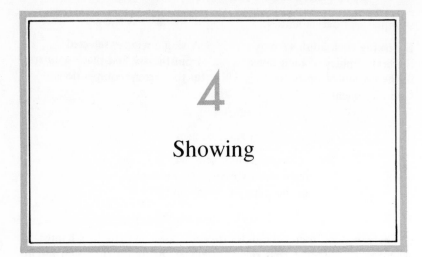

4

Showing

CONDITIONING

No dog can be expected to win, no matter how fine an animal he is structurally, if he is not in top condition. Keeping him that way demands that you know almost as much about his physical and mental condition as his veterinarian does; it is most important that you learn to identify warning signals that indicate all is not well.

Stools

Dogs that normally have firm, well-formed bowel movements, or stools, can suddenly come down with watery diarrhea at dog shows. Such a condition can be traced to nerves, heat, change of food, and particularly change of water. So carry your own food and water whenever possible. Your veterinarian can give you tablets to tuck in your tack box to be used in the event your dog is so stricken. Diarrhea can dehydrate a dog quickly, so don't deny him reasonable amounts of liquids. And if the situation doesn't start clearing up immediately, you can suspect other reasons and should consult a doctor. Most loose stools resulting from minor problems can be eliminated by feeding raw beef and boiled rice in small quantities frequently.

Allergies

Allergic reactions in a dog are characterized by swelling of the lips and around the eyes. The dog may try to paw at his face. Common causes are spider or insect bites, or food, or a drug to which the dog is allergic. An allergic reaction will occur relatively rapidly, usually within a half hour to an hour. If you suspect your dog is having an allergic reaction, contact your veterinarian to alert him, but most cases can be treated at home by giving the dog an antihistamine. Usually the symptoms will clear up within two or three hours. An allergic reaction can become more serious if the swelling of the throat does not go down after the first antihistamine tablet. Watch for difficulty in breathing and advise your veterinarian if the dog does not appear to be recovering.

Inoculations

Regular inoculation against distemper, hepatitis, leptospirosis and (so called) kennel cough is the only intelligent way to protect any dog, and dogs attending shows are particularly susceptible to these diseases. Such inoculations do not guarantee that the dog will not contract the disease, but it is the best way we know to lessen the possibility. In addition to yearly inoculations, "booster" shots are advisable whenever you feel that your dog is going to be unusually exposed. Regular rabies inoculations are equally important—don't overlook them!

Worms

There is nothing to be ashamed of in discovering that your dog has worms. But you should be very ashamed if you don't check your dog for internal parasites regularly, worm him under the direction of your veterinarian, and learn to identify the presence of these unwanted pests. Worms eat the food you buy for your dog, and thus rob him of needed nutrition. They can drain the tissues of life-giving moisture, cripple, paralyze, and even kill if allowed to thrive unchecked.

Round Worms (often called puppy worms) are in no way limited to puppies. Segments, resembling thin pieces of spaghetti, are sometimes found in soft stools as well as firm ones. Sometimes a dog will cough up a round worm.

Tape Worms (commonly believed to be carried by fleas) are easily detected because small segments, which look exactly like grains of rice, can be found in the stool as well as dried on the hair surrounding the rectum.

Hook and Whip Worms are the nastiest of all; they can do irreparable damage in a short period of time and are rarely seen in stools. However, gelatinous, particularly foul-smelling feces, white gums, rings around the dog's eyes which look as if he is losing hair, dry, flaky coat, foul breath—all these can mean the presence of hook or whip, which must be detected by a microscope.

Heartworm was formerly thought to be a serious threat only in hot climates, since the mosquito is the carrier. It is now acknowledged to be present everywhere in the United States. All dogs should be checked twice a year, at which time a sample of blood is taken by a veterinarian. Preventative medication is now a must for all canines during the months the mosquito is prevalent. Once contracted, heartworm will kill if the dog is not treated promptly. The treatment, unlike the other types of worming, is severe and extremely dangerous, so the best solution is to count on the available preventatives.

Itch'n 'n' Scratch'n

Many a glossy show coat has been ruined by a dog digging at himself to get rid of fleas and ticks. Both can be picked up at shows and, of course, from other dogs and animals. Flea and tick collars are excellent, provided your dog does not prove allergic to them and provided you follow directions carefully for their use. *Never medicate for anything or worm for any worm while a dog is wearing one of these chemically treated collars.*

Sprays and dips are also effective, but can be very drying to the coat. When either external parasite is found, make sure that while you are treating the dog, you are treating the bedding he sleeps in if he is in a kennel, or his rug or blankets if he is a house dog.

One of the peskiest problems facing show dogs is called "hot spots." Also erroneously referred to as "summer eczema," this condition can occur during any season of the year—summer, winter, spring, and fall. Sometimes you get a warning because a dog starts scratching and digging at himself for no apparent reason; sometimes there is no warning and you wake up in the morning to discover a spot as big as your hand where the hair has disappeared as if by magic. The bare area "weeps" continuously and the dog will not let it alone. If it is a true hot spot you can tell immediately by holding your hand just above the affected area but without touching it; the heat radiating from the lesion will startle you. Every vet has his own explanation and cure, but nobody knows what causes the condition. Cortisone is often effective, but almost everyone you meet at a show or kennel will tell you of a pet remedy!

Imperfections

We'll discuss exhibiting lame dogs later. When it comes to dogs that have been bitten or punctured or that are suffering from hot spots or skin conditions, provided the ailment doesn't completely ruin the appearance of the animal, there is no reason he cannot still be shown. So it is wise to instruct your veterinarian not to shave the affected area. A dog may not be shown with a bandage of any kind concealing a wound.

In the case of eczema, as unsightly as it may be, it is a condition very familiar to all dog people; it may cost you a placement but it's often worth the try. Dogs with stitches can be challenged, so it's a good idea to have in hand a certificate from a veterinarian stating the cause of the wound.

Many people, leaning over backwards to obey the rules and regulations, mistakenly assume that if a dog has had a skin tumor removed, or its appendix or tonsils removed, it cannot be shown any more because they feel he "has been changed in appearance by artificial means," which is the way the rules read. This is ridiculous! The rule was obviously intended to prevent deception. Nobody is deceiving anybody or presenting a different *type* of dog by exhibiting a tonsil-less canine.

Usually incorrectly called Kennel Cough, there is a condition that hits all dogs from time to time causing them to hack and choke as if they had something struck in their throats. Careless or uninformed handlers and owners drag these dogs to shows where they spread the ailment to any dog near them. Leave the coughing dog home and never locate yourself near a coughing dog at a show.

If you should need a veterinarian at a show, your dog show superintendent can advise you.

Basically, as described earlier, it is proper feeding, grooming, and exercise that will put your dog in top show condition.

GETTING TO THE SHOW

One of the most difficult aspects of dog competition of any kind is the trip involved. Today, with fuel conservation an issue for us all, "gett'n thar" is not always as simple as it sounds. There are, moreover, other considerations than just how much gasoline it will take and how many lunches you will have to skip to be able to *pay* for that gas!

Of the three destinations covered in this book—dog shows, obedience trials, and field trials—the first two, usually held in conjunction with each other, present by far the largest and most varied problems. So if the obedience folks will try, just this once, to speak sweetly to the show people, and the breed buffs will promise to smile nicely at the obedience trialers for just a little while, we'll tackle *their* problems initially and leave the challenge of locating and getting onto the grounds of a field trial until we get to that section.

In the United States in the past few years, shows and obedience competitions have become so popular that getting to one of these events sometimes seems to require the same inventiveness and fortitude that our pioneer forefathers needed to push back the frontiers of the Old West, while getting *into* the show grounds once you have finally located them demands all the cunning of a cat burglar, the bluffing ability of a card shark, the tact of a diplomat, an unquenchable sense of humor, the blessing of the Almighty, and the luck of the Irish!

The Ideal Solution

The ideal way to attend dog shows and obedience trials is to make reservations at a motel or hotel in the area of the event weeks in advance of the show date. Then you leave early the day before and arrive at your hostelry in the late afternoon. After settling into your room, you drive leisurely out to the site of the show so that, come morning, the route will be familiar. Then you drive back to your watering place, fill the gas tank along the way, have a nice dinner, and turn in for a good night's sleep, leaving a call for morning (and setting your own alarm clock just in case). In addition to being "ideal," this method can be horribly expensive, particularly if your entourage includes children. Then, too, not every businessman can close the office whenever he wishes.

Staying with Friends

To save money, if you can leave early on a Friday, you might arrange to stay with friends. But this procedure, if not handled with extreme tact and farsightedness, can boomerang. You see, friends are people who love you, have missed you, want to show you a good time. So the plot thickens.

Friends (even doggy ones sometimes!) do not always understand that a cocktail party to introduce you to the neighbors (none of whom you will ever see again, of course) followed by an intimate candlelit supper at Ye Olde Stone Inne (thirty miles out into the country, thirty miles back), after which you can "relax" by kicking off your shoes and reminiscing over highballs until 5 A.M., is not exactly the best preparation for tomorrow. Friends tend to forget that while additional dogs are just *fine* with them, the added noise level may *not* be just fine with the neighbors. And friends tend to exaggerate when they insist they have *plenty* of room for the dogs to run. "Plenty of room" has been known to boil down to a three-foot-wide strip of mud and thorn bushes, beyond which you mustn't let the dogs wander because Joe's putting green is on one side and Marion's herb garden is on the other, and the far end runs smack into—you guessed it—those nonaccommodating neighbors.

Then, because you *did* stay up so late Friday night, friends are those who tend to reason: "Lord, Martha didn't really mean to set the alarm at seven o'clock; she's *got* to have more than two hours' sleep! We'll just let her snooze until nine, and then we'll all hurry a little faster."

Arriving the Day of the Show

Since many of us can't afford the going rate of most motels yet want to keep those friendships we treasure, we are forced to travel to the show that same morning, sometimes starting in the wee hours, and lo and behold, there are more crises to circumnavigate.

I can remember way back when we used to get to a dog show at about 7:30 A.M. and have *plenty* of time to do what had to be done before our moments in the ring. *Plenty of time*—and in those days your dog had to stand in line to pass a veterinarian's examination before being admitted to the show building or grounds!

Today, should you plan to arrive at 7:30 in the morning, you no longer have to face a long line at the vet's table. Instead, what you have to face is the fact that 90 per cent of your fellow exhibitors *came the night before,* and between the point where you cough up your tickets and purchase a catalogue and the perimeter of the ring in which you are due to exhibit, lies an endless sea of travel trailers, tents, campers, converted buses, station wagons, all occupying just about every inch of space described in the premium list as "ample parking available."

It didn't take the American dog fancy long to tumble to the economic advantages of modern camping equipment and recreational vehicles. For the last several years, more and more folks have been turning to campers and trailers and cheerfully dispensing with the chore of unloading pounds of equipment and luggage at a motel at night and reloading in the morning. But the presence of these leisure vehicles on dog-show grounds not really designed to accommodate them presents problems we wouldn't have dreamed of ten years ago. Unfortunately, traditional methods die hard, and all too many clubs seem to have agreed to handle this problem in any one of several questionable ways:

1. *Ignore it and it will go away.* Only "it" doesn't, and the resulting traffic jams and displaced spectators see the show officials getting nastier and nastier until one wonders if the idea isn't to make it so unbearably unpleasant that "next year there won't be half these idiots to contend with." This doesn't work either, since new idiots are born every minute, many of whom will reach maturity deciding to follow in their parents' "idiotic" footsteps and become dog-show people!

2. *Appoint a committee to handle things:* On the surface a reasonable

idea. But who is the guy who fills these committees with parking-lot policemen who have never been to a dog show; sub-teen-aged draftees who would *much* rather be playing baseball and delight in taking their frustrations out on helpless, hysterical adults; and traffic directors from the local Girl Scouts who persist in stopping you just before the crest of a mountainous hill which is six inches deep in mud to inquire, "Where did you want to park?"

3. *Hire a Tent:* Then when things go wrong, the parking attendant simply points to it and explains carefully as if speaking to a four-year-old, "Unload here under the tent; park over there." These poor souls have never attended a dog show either. It is one of the two requirements they must meet when applying for their jobs. The second is that they are able to memorize, "Unload here under the tent; park over there." Unless you like to see grown people cry, do not, under any circumstances, try to explain, "But I do not *want* to unload."

4. *Mail out, well in advance of the show, directions for parking, camping, loading and unloading, etc.* Then, the night before the show, either appoint people to oversee these arrangements who have never read the fliers or don't appoint anybody at all, reasoning, "We sent out notices, so why do we have to have somebody on duty half the night?" So the guy who comes in and sets up at night and then has to move his rig in the morning because it turns out he's too close to the food concession, which was nonexistent when he pulled in, is purple with fury.

There is a fifth solution. Unfortunately, dog clubs, show superintendents, and the A.K.C. seem to have joined together to avoid it at all costs because—stop me if you've heard this before—it is at one and the same time sensible, practical, and exceedingly simple. This solution calls for gathering together a group of experienced people from the club, amateurs and professionals alike, who are constantly exhibiting at shows around the country. Direct them to the scene of the show, explain what areas can be used and what areas are off limits. Then let *them* set things up in a manner they know from experience will satisfy the needs of the greatest number of people. The Professional Handlers Associations will gladly delegate a member in the area to work with such a group, lending even more experience to the project. Granted, in spite of such intelligent attention to this national problem, there will *still* be bottlenecks and complaints; but they will be minor and the majority of spectators and exhibitors alike will return with a smile on their faces, year after year after year.

Well, let's progress to other topics. Suffice it to say that you should *never* plan to get to any show at the last minute. It is an unhappy fact of life that at today's A.K.C. licensed dog shows held in conjunction with obedience trials, you had better plan to arrive *with at least three hours to spare before your class is due*—that is, three hours from the time you arrive in the city in which the show is being held until your class is scheduled.

The Mechanics of the Drive

Having decided what time you wish to arrive at a dog show or obedience trial, get out the road map and study it carefully in conjunction with the map or directions you received with the judging program. Use the mileage chart to decide the approximate number of miles to your target, then figure your mileage at more time than you will probably need. In other words, if you feel it will take you a maximum of four hours, add at least one hour more to your Estimated Time of Arrival (ETA).

Never fail to have the car completely checked the day before: tires, oil, water in radiator and battery, spare tire (oh, and you *do* know how to use that tire jack, don't you, hmmmmm?), not to mention gas in the tank. Since I attend most of the same shows year after year, I have a habit, after the weekend is over, of attaching to the front of my catalogue the route I used, the time it took to get there, the motel I stayed at, etc. The next time I attend that show, it's half the work.

Speaking of motels, a number of such in Canada and the United States still accept dogs. Those that do not, I'm sorry to say, have whisked up the "dogs are welcome" mat due to the abuse of those facilities by dog owners who allow their dogs to go to the bathroom on the front lawn, where male animals raise their legs on bushes and flowers

The popular "van"-type vehicle is used by many professionals to move large numbers of dogs.

which cost hundreds of dollars to plant. These are people who refuse to leave their dogs in the car even though it is parked directly outside their motel door; instead, they turn the dogs loose in the room while they go off to wine and dine while the dogs chew up the bedspreads and soil the carpets or yap and bark from the moment they are left. In this department, the obedience folks get a few more gold stars than the show folks, but I have known many C.D.X.'s who were noisy, messy, unreliable, thoroughly unenjoyable beasts at home! If the shoe fits in this case, I would suggest switching to another style of footwear. In short, you should be ashamed! Did it ever occur to you that strangers judge you and your home by the way your dog behaves around other people's property?

I remember distinctly in my early days arriving to check into my New York hotel prior to the Westminster Dog Show. As I entered the lobby, I saw a well-dressed lady chatting animatedly to her friend while her Bloodhound urinated copiously all over a beautiful wall tapestry. I was young and innocent in those days; it never occurred to me that she was aware of what was going on. "Madam!" I called, hoping to stem the flood, "your dog—the tapestry—" She looked brightly at me, turned and looked fondly at the dog, then turned back to me. "You have no idea of how hard it is to get country dogs to do their business in the city," she explained, and went on chatting with her friend.

The Importance of Being Regular

She was right about one thing—it is hard to get country dogs to go to the bathroom in city situations. This is why exercise pens are provided at dog shows, the use of which we'll discuss in detail very shortly. But in the meantime, during your trip to the show, allow enough time to let Fido exercise somewhere along the road, preferably before he arrives in the neighborhood of the show and before he either uses the car or his crate as a "potty" or refuses to consider evacuating, both courses of behavior being due to the unnatural excitement surrounding him. The word "exercise" does not mean letting him frolic while he stretches his legs. It means giving him an opportunity to move his bowels and to urinate, and the importance of proper exercising cannot be overemphasized. Dogs who have to go to the bathroom and have not been given an opportunity to do so or who are too "uptight" to "perform" do not move as smoothly as they could in the breed ring or during the execution of obedience exercises. (Under similar circumstances, *would you?*)

While, to the best of my knowledge, no one has come up with a convenient method for getting reluctant dogs to urinate, it's a fairly simple process to get an inexperienced, distracted, or nervous dog to move his bowels, and this is how you go about it. First, you can use glycerine rectal suppositories such as are used for young children. *But* if you are not sure that your dog has to have a bowel movement and want to make certain he does relieve himself and is comfortable when he enters competitions, the suppository has a very obvious drawback: it is almost impossible to retrieve! Well, then, say you, leave it where it is. Not so, say I, for once upon a time I did just that and the dog was so uncomfortable that he drew one testicle up out of the scrotum and I had to do some *very* fast talking not to have the dog declared a monorchid and disqualified!

By far the best solution, with dogs that you feel might need "one more chance" before the hour of competition arrives, is the common book match. You simply tear off a single match for the average or small-sized dog and two for the giant breeds, wet the head of the match with your tongue so that it slips into the rectum easily, and insert it *gently,* headfirst, so that half of it is still very much in evidence. The dog will evacuate, if he really has to, in a few minutes—two or three at the most. If he obviously does not have to go, you can remove the match easily and you're "home free."

Getting to and into Canadian Shows

Traveling to dog shows in Canada is a mite easier. Bottlenecks to watch for in Canada are the secondary and lesser highways, many of which have old numbers posted beside them and entirely different numbers posted on the road map of the province. Maps themselves are very difficult to secure in Canada; your best bet is to allow enough time to stop at the tourist information centers. Superhighways in Canada are beautiful. Adjacent areas containing restaurant and picnicking facilities, camping hookups, garages, gas pumps, and toilets are located at regular intervals. Remember that while you are paying a bit more for Canadian gas, you are getting the imperial gallon, which is larger than the U.S. gallon.

Don't forget that if you are crossing from the U.S. into Canada and/or back in search of a dog show or obedience trial, you should be ready to present rabies certificates on each of your dogs. Canadian rules call for use of the one-year vaccine, which means your certificate must be dated within twelve months of your border crossing. On the other hand, the U.S. requirement at point of re-entry is that the dog must have had his rabies inoculation at least one month prior to crossing into the U.S. Most American veterinarians recommend using the vaccine that covers two and a half to three or four years. When presenting rabies certificates attesting to the four-year vaccine, it is wise to have your veterinarian's note of this on the bottom of the certificate.

While I've never been asked for it in all the years I have traveled back and forth across Canadian-American borders, in Canada you could be asked for some proof of U.S. citizenship as well as some proof of automobile insurance.

If you ship a dog by air to Canada, you may insure him for a maximum of $249 without filling out customs declarations. But a word of warning: having shipped a dog from, say, New York to Ottawa, when he is shipped back take along your copy of the shipping ticket proving you did not buy him in Ottawa but are getting your own dog back. Sometimes officials on either side of the border do not completely understand about show dogs, and it can become complicated.

Most border guards are courteous, pleasant, and helpful, providing you respond in kind. Since hippie-type clothing and appearance are inclined to be suspect to customs people, if you do not wish to be delayed while your entire car is searched, I suggest you present a respectable picture as you take your place in line—washed face, combed hair, etc.

From Montreal toward Quebec City, east and north, you can expect to run into areas where French is spoken and where all billboards and advertising are in French also.

Getting into the Canadian show once you have located the grounds is seldom a problem. In all fairness to U.S. shows, let's remember that Canadian shows are much smaller and therefore easier to handle. Canadians were camping out at dog shows long before the Americans considered it the "in" thing, so you can expect to meet up with lots of tents, tent trailers, and mobile homes. Ordinarily, it is possible to find cheaper motel accommodations in Canada, with a little looking around. Generally, food is higher.

Indoor Shows

While the problems we have been dealing with so far have been limited largely to outdoor summer shows, there isn't much difference when it comes to the indoor shows. People still arrive the night before. Getting inside hockey rinks and armories, high-school auditoriums and coliseums the morning of the show is more harassing than establishing a beachhead on the grounds of outdoor shows, for architects of these places seem to feel it's an unbreakable tradition to supply just *one exhibitors' entrance* and *one exhibitors' exit,* both being the same small single door or ramp, which ultimately becomes a more dangerous area than an active minefield.

Verily it may say in the premium list that exhibitors will be allowed to drive into the building to load and unload up until 11 A.M. the day of the show. Come five minutes before the deadline and cars are lined up for eight miles. But is the time limit extended? No, indeed! If you think that line of cars is frightening, I suggest trying to imagine the occupants of those vehicles dashing along burdened down with crates, dogs, picnic baskets, tack boxes, and children—only to get to the door of the building and discover nobody in the family knows where the exhibitors' passes are!

Trouble in Motion

If you are not able to get the car-sickness problem completely under control before a dog starts his show career, cheer up, you are not alone. *But* until and unless the problem is solved, bring along extra rolls of paper towels and make sure your supply of dog water is sufficient so that you don't use up all your own drinking water on the sick dog. Lots of water sloshing around in the tummy of a dog prone to car sickness is asking for trouble, but a paper towel soaked in fresh water and then used to wipe the mouth of your miserable passenger removes the smell, and he is less liable to upchuck again. Also, a few laps if he wants them, following an attack, will clear his throat.

Finally, try to remember how awful you felt as a child after you became ill in an automobile. Allow enough extra time after you get to the show for your dog to throw off the effects of car sickness.

It should be mentioned here that some people have great success with various patent medicines designed to cope with motion sickness in dogs. I, personally, dislike using this type of medication because I have found too many dogs are sleepy or sluggish for long periods after these pills have been used. If you decide to experiment, start your research weeks ahead of the planned dog show trip.

In the Final Analysis

Single-breed specialties held on the manicured lawns of ancestral estates, or obedience trials or tracking tests held independently of all-breed shows, are eminently more pleasant when it comes to arriving and establishing your right to be there. So look forward to them, enjoy them, treasure the happy memories they leave behind. For the rest, grit your teeth, take an extra nerve pill, and keep reminding yourself: you don't have to be crazy to put up with things like this, but it helps, ah yes, indeed, it helps! I don't want to discourage you at the outset, but I do want to be honest in preparing you, and this is, unfortunately, a dim phase of dog showing. But I haven't said it won't all be worth it when you and Tam O' Shanter trot out of the ring with your first ribbon!

AT THE SHOW

So now you have at last arrived. All "that" is behind you and you have even maintained some kind of composure. Surely you *deserve* some small reward for your initiative—something like Best of Breed, or perhaps you might even settle for Winners Dog! But remember, God helps those who help themselves! Sad but true, thy work is not quite done.

There are several things about dog shows and obedience trials which, if clearly understood, can make your show experience both pleasant and rewarding for you as well as your dog. These are, in order:

> The Handlers' Tent or Section
> The Dog Show Catalogue
> The Exercise Pens
> The Rings
> The Stewards
> The Armbands
> Disqualifications
> Show Photographers

We'll get to all of these. But first, where do you go now?

Indoor or Outdoor

We've discussed the procedures of locating your own little area at the benched show. But unbenched shows give you a wide variety of choices, and when you are brand-new to all this, the mere fact that you *have* a choice can be confusing.

Most obedience folks set up their chairs and stuff right beside the obedience ring. The show dog's owner can do pretty much the same thing except for the narrow aisles between the rings where you are not supposed to establish a base of operations, for very obvious reasons. If you are ever in a hurry to get to a show ring, I can assure you from personal experience that tripping and stumbling through a labyrinth of folding chairs while being asphyxiated by clouds of grooming sprays and powders is not a happy experience. In Canada, the aisles adjacent to the ring entrances are kept absolutely clear (by means of roped-off areas and stewards) of anyone except those waiting to exhibit. But apart from these aisle-ways, provided you arrive early enough, there are usually little nooks and crannies where the individual exhibitor can settle for the day and be close enough to the ring to observe it but far enough away to keep clear of traffic.

The main danger here is that other amateur exhibitors may become overly enthusiastic about your excellent choice of location and attempt to move in on you. Sometimes, at more crowded shows, it's a real challenge to maintain your small oasis of calm and quiet in the midst of a raging sea of confusion. Too many latecomers (who obviously have not read this book!) seem to feel that the rest of the dog show is waiting for their tardy arrival in order to make special concessions to their comfort.

People who arrive late in a flurry of hysteria, unless they've had real emergencies such as car breakdowns or highway accidents, get little sympathy from me, I'm afraid. When someone says, "You don't mind if I set up here, do you?" and plonks down in a manner which immediately isolates me from the entire dog show, I have no hesitancy in replying, "As a matter of fact I do mind, very much." I wouldn't do it to them and I don't expect them to do it to me—not and get away with it. There comes a time when one has to stand up for the things one believes in, such as the right to breathe. Which brings us to the matter of housekeeping.

Good Housekeeping

Certain breeds require a great deal of last-minute grooming, and in some cases this involves coat sprays (though new A.K.C. rules specifically discourage overuse of such grooming devices!), talcum powder, and cornstarch, which are bad enough indoors but which are murder outdoors on a windy day! While I am forever defending the amateur exhibitor, I cannot do so here, for it is not the professional who drives off leaving behind a wasteland of empty aerosol cans and balls of fur covered with white powder. And it is never the professional who plops his grooming table on top of my work area and then proceeds to cover everything I own, including me and the dogs, with a sticky film of hairspray. I do not take kindly to getting a black Lab all polished up for competition, then turning my back for an instant, and discovering I now have a particolored retriever. Such conduct is thoughtless, selfish, and rude. If you are in this category, gentle reader, I wish you every painful incident of social rejection you encounter—and many of them!

If meeting the challenge of existing independently at dog shows doesn't thrill you, you can go straight to the Handlers' Tent. This is just what it sounds like—a large tent, supplied through the generosity of the club, beneath which handlers can collect their crates and grooming equipment. At an outdoor show the tent is supposed to shade you from the sun (but it can become a furnace when there is no wind) or protect you from the rain (which it usually does, unless there is a high wind and it blows down, as has been known to happen). Handlers tend to congregate together under either a Handlers' Tent at an outdoor show or in the Handlers' Section at an indoor show, not because they are a bunch of snobs but because many of them work together, and all of them help each other out with grooming problems and ring conflicts. The point we want to make here is that you have a perfect right to set up right beside the professional handlers. So if you want a bit of shade or protection at an outdoor show, the Handlers' Tent is the place for you. If you want a spot at an indoor show where someone isn't liable to step *over* or, worse yet, *on* you as you groom your dog, then go to the Handlers' Section.

The amateur with only one or two dogs might prefer to leave everything in the car—dog, equipment etc.—park it, stroll back and "case the joint," then groom the dog at the car and bring him to the ring only when necessary. It will mean more walking but probably more peace and quiet. Leaving dogs in cars, however, brings us to the very serious subject of heat, the killer of dogs at summer shows year after year after year.

Heat and Cold

The public address systems at summer outdoor shows constantly warn of the dangers of allowing dogs to become overheated. Articles appear frequently in newspapers. The S.P.C.A. and humane societies of the world tack up posters, while radio and television shows repeat the dangers of leaving dogs in unventilated cars or kenneled in the sun. And still dogs die needlessly every summer because people just don't think.

These are the cold, hard facts: on a summer day when the outside temperature is 85°, the temperature inside a car parked in the shade with a window slightly open will reach 102° in just ten minutes! In thirty minutes it will climb to 120° even though the outside temperature is only 95°! The average dog's normal body temperature is between 101.5° and 102.2°. A dog can withstand a temperature of 107° to 108° for only a very short time before irreparable brain damage or even death occurs.

These statistics have been compiled by experts at the request of the Directors of the National S.P.C.A. and do not lie. I spend the greater part of my summers snooping about shopping-center parking lots making sure no helpless dog is being baked alive. With or without a policeman as a witness, I have smashed car windows and hauled out comatose animals just in the nick of time. Some of the owners involved were horror-struck at what their thoughtlessness had caused their pets to suffer. Others, beyond my comprehension, threatened to sue me for damaging their property. Unbelievable? Not when you cruise the parking lots at dog shows and are forced to slit the canvas of tents, pick locks, and smash windows to rescue valuable animals belonging to people who should know better. Worse yet, some of *them* try to sue also!

One episode still haunts me particularly. I was standing in the Group ring with a Toy and saw a woman carrying a very limp dog to the water spigot nearby. Bob Forsythe, the well-known handler who was also in the ring, also saw the pair. We took a step toward them but were blocked by the barriers of the livestock pavilion under which we were exhibiting.

"*That* dog is in trouble!" I said under my breath, I thought, but my voice carried and the woman raised her head and reassured me, "Oh, he's OK!"

"Like hell he is!" Bob replied. He yelled just one word at the top of his lungs: "Ice!" Because they had been carefully schooled for just such an emergency, the boys and girls working for the Forsythes appeared in less than a minute from two directions with portable coolers full of crushed ice. They lowered the dog into the cool puddle under the water tap and packed him solidly in ice. They massaged his chest, talked to him, slapped him gently about the muzzle, opened his mouth and fanned extra air into his lungs. The judging of the Group dragged miserably while we all hung over the half wall and encouraged the little dog's efforts to live. All the time they worked, the owner, *who later was identified as a licensed veterinarian,* stood aside watching as if the people administering to her dog had lost their minds. Even when the show veterinarian took over, she kept repeating, "I hardly think it's this serious!" The show vet thought it serious enough to carry the dog away for further treatment. That particular victim of heat prostration, who had been left in a car in the shade with only the window vents open, did recover, I am happy to report. Many more dogs at summer shows are not so lucky.

Those of us working from our vehicles at summer shows have awnings which stretch out from the sides of the van or bus. They give shade for grooming and trap any available breezes for the benefit of the dogs inside. We have coolers full of ice, and if the vehicles aren't air conditioned, we have electric fans plugged into portable generators. What I fail to understand is why it is so difficult for the amateur to handle the hot-weather needs of just *one* dog!

It is a well-known fact that black absorbs the heat like a sponge. But at show after show throughout the dangerous summer months, Newfoundland exhibitors drag their dogs to ringside hours ahead of their classes and sit there chatting with friends while their dogs literally broil. There are those who feel that plastic crates are ample protection against the rays of the sun; it is doubtful that the helpless dogs trapped inside these little ovens would concur. Affording animals protection from the heat doesn't take a lot of money or fancy gadgets. All it really takes is a modicum of common sense, the use of the good brain God gave us all.

The new "space" or "survival" blankets, which are coated with deflecting material on one side, are excellent for covering car windows. Backing your wagon under a leafy tree and then leaving all the windows and the back of your car wide open is fine; but be sure to keep a constant check *because the sun moves.* If the parking lot is unshaded, unload your crates in as shady an area as you can find and then have at hand plenty of large towels or blankets that you can wet and drape over the top of your crates as the day gets warmer. Andrea Martin, whose charming Best in Show Otterhound, "Boo," suffered greatly from hot weather, devised a slick system I have copied many times. She would remove the three- or four-inch-deep metal pan from the bottom of his wire crate. Next, she would line the bottom of the crate with bags of ice or large blocks of ice. Then she would replace the pan upside down over the ice and "Boo" would flump happily back into his very own air-conditioned crate. How about that for "smarts"!

Cars with air conditioning can be left running, provided you make sure your exhaust isn't threatening somebody else's dogs. But remember, motors have been known to kick off, and in a terrifyingly few minutes that icebox of a car can become an oven in which neither man nor beast could long survive.

While you are in the ring on a broiling hot day, when you are not having your dog moved or examined, it's quite all right for a helper to hand you a wet towel to drape over your dog. Wet a bath towel before you leave home and, while it's still dripping, tuck it down into the ice in your cooler. Small breeds can be placed *on* a wet towel while waiting in the heat. For hairy breeds whose coats would be ruined by covering them with a wet towel, try a hot-water bottle filled with ice chips and applied to the tummy, chest, or groin—or wipe those areas with your wet towel. And while waiting around in show rings on hot days, stand so that your dog is in the shade from your body.

I hope I have frightened you out of your wits about keeping a careful eye on your dog in hot weather; believe me, that was *exactly* my intention.

Moreover, never underestimate the danger at indoor shows, with their drafty aisles, or the risks you take when summer weather suddenly turns cold and wet! Every weekend dogs come back from shows coughing and sneezing and with high temperatures and who knows what else, simply because their owners left them near the door to the gymnasium or auditorium while they went off to locate benching or grooming areas.

Animals trapped in small enclosures and unable to move out of the draft or get out of the rain are candidates for all sorts of serious illnesses.

Make very sure your dogs are never left near doorways or loading ramps without being covered. If summer showers should surprise you at an outdoor show, plastic dropcloths used by commercial house painters are excellent protection and inexpensive enough to dispose of at day's end. Dry blankets are a must after the bad weather has passed, and no dog should ever be allowed to sleep wet in his crate.

Many people do not seem to understand the grave difference between taking a healthy retriever out for a day's shooting in sleet or rain or snow, and leaving the same dog for the night in a cage planted directly in the path of a cold wet wind. The difference could wind up costing you your dog!

Now let's go on to happier subjects. After settling your future champion in parking lot, at ringside, or under the Handlers' Tent, the next thing to do is to purchase a catalogue.

Catalogues

I know that a lot of people operating on slim budgets feel that $2.50 to $3.50 spent on a show catalogue is an unnecessary expense, but I disagree.

If you are serious about showing dogs and keeping records, your entire life will be brightened considerably by a neatly kept library of catalogues from shows you have attended. They contain a wealth of information, including a list of coming shows with closing dates and the addresses of the show superintendents and show secretaries, judges and their addresses, and all officers of the show-giving club.

All the information you had to put down when filling out your entry form is duplicated in the catalogue for every single exhibitor, plus a complete index of exhibitors' addresses. Here are also to be found the addresses of the official show photographers. Companies carrying hard-to-get dog supplies advertise in show catalogues, as do dog food companies.

By purchasing catalogues at each show you attend and marking the results of the judging of your particular breed, you can determine, over a long period of time, just which breeders and kennels are exhibiting and winning most consistently. I keep all my catalogues for two years and find I refer to them constantly.

But probably the most valuable service your catalogue provides, whether you are green as grass or moldy with experience, is a complete chart of championship points for the area of the country in which the show you are attending is located. These charts which must be present in all show catalogues, are devised and revised regularly by

C.K.C. and A.K.C. to prevent "cheap" championships and make the securing of titles as fair as possible to everyone.

You will notice by referring to the sample charts that, for instance, it requires many more German Shepherd bitches to be present in the ring than Vizsla bitches in order to get three points. This is because Vizslas are not yet as popular as Shepherds. Therefore, if the point requirements were the same for both breeds, it would take the poor Vizsla about ten years to complete its championship, while the Shepherd people could grind out titles like sausage weekend after weekend.

In certain breeds, research has turned up the fact that more males are regularly shown than females, so the powers that be make sure it takes more males in the ring than females to win five points. Also, certain breeds are more popular in one area than in others, perhaps due to population, accessibility, or simply because one area is more show-oriented than another. Whatever the reason, the Kennel Clubs divide up their countries into dog show zones and tailor the points required for championship to the activity in those zones. Canada has twelve zones: Alberta, British Columbia, Manitoba, New Brunswick, Newfoundland, Nova Scotia, Ontario North, Ontario South, Prince Edward Island, Quebec, Saskatchewan, and the Yukon Territory.

In the U.S. there are seven zones or divisions and their breakdown is a little more complicated because the United States represents a much more active and experienced dog-show community. These divisions are as follows:

Division 1: Maine, New Hampshire, Vermont, Massachusetts, Rhode Island, Connecticut, New York, Pennsylvania, New Jersey, Delaware, Maryland, District of Columbia, Virginia, Ohio, Michigan, Indiana, Illinois, and Wisconsin.

Division 2: West Virginia, Kentucky, Tennessee, North Carolina, South Carolina, Georgia, Florida, Alabama, Mississippi, Louisiana, Arkansas, Oklahoma, Texas, New Mexico, Arizona, Minnesota, Iowa, Missouri, Kansas, Nebraska, and Colorado.

Division 3: California

Division 4: North Dakota, South Dakota, Montana, Wyoming, Utah, Nevada, Idaho, Oregon, and Washington.

Division 5: Alaska

Division 6: Hawaii

Division 7: Puerto Rico

If you want to study further the differences in point requirements for Canadian shows, your copy of *Canadian Dog Show Rules and Regulations* will give you that chance. The A.K.C. does not print its point charts in the rule book, but an up-to-date copy can be obtained anytime, free of charge, by writing to their headquarters in New York.

We mentioned earlier that these charts are often revised; the reason

for this is that sudden surges in popularity in certain breeds can throw
the whole picture into imbalance; also, from time to time, once-popular
breeds fade away to almost nothing.

In America or Canada, as soon as a judge has finished an assignment
and turned in his judge's book to the show superintendent, a member
of the superintendent's staff rips off one of the duplicate pages from
that book and posts it either on a board beside the superintendent's
office or on a table close by. Some supers have an ingenious little clip-
board arrangement so that all the breeds can be clipped together by
Group, and obedience results by class. On the judges' sheets, classes
are divided and the entrants listed only by catalogue number.

A.K.C. and C.K.C. judges do not have access to the catalogue before
judging and while in the ring. It is felt, and rightly so, I think, that
by looking at a catalogue before or during competition, a judge is able
to identify dogs by their breeders or owners or by their famous names
and such information would prejudice his evaluations. All catalogues
are in the care of stewards.

As the judge goes through the classes, he marks which number placed
where as well as noting absentees or those dogs excused from the ring
or disqualified and the reasons therefore.

To keep your own score, all you have to do is spend a few minutes
copying the judge's results in your catalogue. *This is the only official
way to determine the results of the day's judging.*

Once you have completely marked a breed in your catalogue count
up the bitches or dogs present that day, turn to the point scale in the
front of the catalogue, and tally accordingly. *Dogs marked "Ab" (absent)
do not count.* However, when totaling points, be very careful about
dogs which the judge's book indicates were disqualified, dismissed, excused, or ordered from the ring. In Canada *these dogs count as having
been present;* in the U.S. *these dogs do not count as having been present
for points.*

One last thing: nobody in the A.K.C. or C.K.C. is going to appoint
himself as the personal guardian of your dog's points. That is up to
little old you. A.K.C. or C.K.C. will, or should, notify you when you
have completed points for championship by sending you a very handsome championship certificate. (In the case of a dog not registered
individually in Canada who finishes his championship, you will get a
nice letter from the C.K.C. stating you have "completed the requirements for a Canadian Show championship" and that you are entitled
to a certificate as soon as the dog is individually registered.) But your
show catalogue and your purple Winner's ribbons are the only positive
proof you have should a question arise. So until I have confirmation
on any dog's title, I mark my catalogues very carefully. Then, in the
upper right-hand corner of the cover I put the dog's award at that

U.S.A. POINT CHART

DIVISION NO. 1 (EFFECTIVE MAY 17, 19—) CONSISTING OF Maine, New Hampshire, Vermont, Massachusetts, Rhode Island, Connecticut, New York, Pennsylvania, New Jersey, Delaware, Maryland, District of Columbia, Virginia AND Ohio, Michigan, Indiana, Illinois, Wisconsin.

DOGS COMPETING TO OBTAIN RATINGS LISTED BELOW

SCALE OF POINTS	1 POINT		2 POINTS		3 POINTS		4 POINTS		5 POINTS	
	Dogs	Bitches	Dogs	Bitches	Dogs	Bitches	Dogs	Bitches	Dogs	Bitches
Pointers	2	2	3	3	4	4	5	5	7	8
Pointers (German Shorthaired)	2	2	7	7	13	13	18	18	27	26
Pointers (German Wirehaired)	2	2	3	3	4	5	5	6	8	8
Retrievers (Chesapeake Bay)	2	2	3	3	4	4	5	6	6	9
Retrievers (Golden)	3	2	9	8	15	15	22	20	34	29
Retrievers (Labrador)	2	2	7	6	12	11	15	15	20	21
Setters (English)	2	2	4	5	7	9	12	14	22	24
Setters (Gordon)	2	2	3	4	4	6	5	8	7	12
Setters (Irish)	4	4	13	14	23	24	39	40	67	71
Spaniels (Brittany)	2	2	6	6	10	11	13	16	18	24
Spaniels (Cocker) Solid Color, Black	2	2	3	5	5	8	6	12	9	19
Spaniels (Cocker), Any Solid Color other than Black, including Black and Tan	2	2	5	5	9	9	13	14	21	24
Spaniels (Cocker), Parti-Color	2	2	3	4	5	7	8	9	13	14
Spaniels (English Cocker)	2	2	4	5	6	8	8	11	12	17
Spaniels (English Springer)	2	2	6	6	11	11	18	17	32	28
Vizslas	2	2	3	3	5	5	7	6	10	9
Weimaraners	2	2	7	7	12	13	17	18	27	27
Afghan Hounds	6	5	18	18	30	32	42	45	65	69
Basenjis	2	2	5	5	8	9	12	13	18	21
Basset Hounds	2	2	5	5	9	9	13	12	20	18
Beagles (13 inches)	2	2	3	3	4	4	5	5	6	8
Beagles (15 inches)	2	2	3	3	4	4	5	5	7	7
Bloodhounds	2	2	3	3	4	4	5	5	7	8
Borzois	2	2	5	6	9	10	11	12	15	17
Dachshunds (Longhaired)	2	2	5	4	8	6	11	11	17	19
Dachshunds (Smooth)	2	2	4	6	7	10	10	16	16	26
Dachshunds (Wirehaired)	2	2	3	4	4	6	6	8	11	12
Greyhounds	2	2	3	3	4	4	5	5	6	8
Irish Wolfhounds	2	2	4	5	7	8	9	11	12	17
Norwegian Elkhounds	2	2	5	5	8	9	11	11	16	15
Rhodesian Ridgebacks	2	2	3	3	4	4	5	5	8	8
Salukis	2	2	3	4	5	6	7	8	10	11
Scottish Deerhounds	2	2	3	3	4	4	5	5	7	6
Whippets	2	2	5	5	8	9	10	13	15	19
Akitas	2	2	3	3	4	5	5	7	8	10
Alaskan Malamutes	2	2	7	6	13	11	20	17	32	29
Belgian Sheepdogs	2	2	3	3	4	5	5	7	7	11
Belgian Tervuren	2	2	3	3	4	4	5	6	7	9
Bouviers des Flandres	2	2	3	3	4	4	6	6	9	9
Boxers	3	3	10	11	17	19	25	27	38	42
Briards	2	2	3	3	4	4	5	5	7	7
Bullmastiffs	2	2	3	3	4	4	5	6	8	9
Collies (Rough)	2	2	10	11	19	21	30	33	49	56
Collies (Smooth)	2	2	3	3	4	5	5	7	7	10
Doberman Pinschers	6	8	18	21	30	34	40	46	59	69
German Shepherd Dogs	4	3	17	18	31	34	40	45	56	66
Giant Schnauzers	2	2	3	3	4	4	5	5	6	8
Great Danes	3	5	14	15	25	26	35	36	53	54
Great Pyrenees	2	2	3	4	5	6	6	7	9	10
Mastiffs	2	2	3	3	4	4	5	6	7	9
Newfoundlands	2	2	4	5	7	8	9	10	13	15
Old English Sheepdogs	2	2	6	7	11	13	14	17	20	25
Rottweilers	2	2	3	3	4	5	6	7	10	11
St. Bernards	2	2	7	8	12	14	26	28	51	54
Samoyeds	2	2	6	5	10	9	13	14	19	22
Shetland Sheepdogs	2	3	8	11	15	19	25	30	41	46
Siberian Huskies	5	5	15	15	25	25	36	33	51	49
Standard Schnauzers	2	2	3	3	4	4	5	6	8	10
Welsh Corgis (Cardigan)	2	2	3	3	4	4	5	5	8	7
Welsh Corgis (Pembroke)	2	2	4	4	6	7	8	9	12	13
Airedale Terriers	2	2	3	4	5	7	8	10	13	15

	1 POINT		2 POINTS		3 POINTS		4 POINTS		5 POINTS	
	Dogs	Bitches	Dogs	Bitches	Dogs	Bitches	Dogs	Bitches	Dogs	Bitches
American Staffordshire Terriers	2	2	3	3	4	4	5	5	7	6
Australian Terriers	2	2	3	3	4	5	5	6	6	8
Bedlington Terriers	2	2	3	3	4	5	5	6	6	9
Border Terriers	2	2	3	3	4	4	5	5	6	7
Bull Terriers (Colored)	2	2	3	3	4	4	5	5	6	7
Bull Terriers (White)	2	2	3	3	4	4	5	6	7	10
Cairn Terriers	2	2	4	4	6	7	8	10	11	15
Fox Terriers (Smooth)	2	2	3	3	4	4	6	6	9	9
Fox Terriers (Wire)	2	2	3	3	4	5	5	7	8	12
Irish Terriers	2	2	3	3	4	4	5	5	7	7
Kerry Blue Terriers	2	2	3	3	4	5	6	8	11	14
Miniature Schnauzers	2	2	7	7	13	12	17	17	24	25
Norwich Terriers	2	2	3	3	4	4	5	5	6	8
Scottish Terriers	2	2	4	5	6	9	8	13	11	19
Skye Terriers	2	2	3	3	4	4	5	5	6	7
Soft-Coated Wheaten Terriers	2	2	3	3	4	4	5	5	8	8
Welsh Terriers	2	2	3	3	4	4	5	5	7	8
West Highland White Terriers	2	2	4	6	6	10	10	16	18	28
Chihuahuas (Long Coat)	2	2	3	3	4	5	5	6	6	8
Chihuahuas (Smooth Coat)	2	2	3	4	4	6	6	8	9	12
Italian Greyhounds	2	2	3	3	4	5	5	6	6	9
Japanese Spaniels	2	2	3	3	4	4	5	5	6	7
Maltese	2	2	3	4	4	6	5	8	7	11
Miniature Pinschers	2	2	3	4	4	7	5	9	7	12
Papillons	2	2	3	3	4	5	5	6	7	8
Pekingese	2	2	5	4	8	7	10	9	13	14
Pomeranians	2	2	4	4	6	7	7	8	10	11
Poodles (Toy)	2	2	6	7	10	12	12	15	17	21
Pugs	2	2	4	4	7	7	13	13	24	25
Shih Tzu	2	2	6	6	10	11	14	13	20	17
Silky Terriers	2	2	3	3	4	4	5	5	6	7
Yorkshire Terriers	2	2	5	6	8	11	11	13	16	18
Bichons Frises	2	2	3	4	5	6	6	7	9	9
Boston Terriers	2	2	3	4	5	6	7	8	11	12
Bulldogs	2	2	6	6	10	10	17	17	29	30
Chow Chow	2	2	3	3	5	5	6	6	9	8
Dalmatians	2	2	6	6	11	11	13	15	18	21
Keeshonden	2	2	4	4	7	7	9	9	14	12
Lhasa Apsos	2	2	7	7	12	12	15	15	20	21
Poodles (Miniature)	2	2	6	7	11	13	15	17	21	23
Poodles (Standard)	2	2	5	6	9	11	13	14	19	20
Schipperkes	2	2	3	3	4	5	5	6	7	8
Tibetan Terriers	2	2	3	3	4	4	5	5	7	7
ALL OTHER BREEDS OR VARIETIES	2	2	3	3	4	4	5	5	6	6

show and the number of points he received. I staple the blue first-place ribbon, the purple Winners, and the blue-and-white Best of Winners ribbon to the page in my catalogue opposite my breed. The whole thing goes into my catalogue library until I have my letter or my certificate in my hot little fist.

The judging program, as we pointed out earlier, should arrive before **the** show date with your confirmed entry. If you should manage to leave it at home, don't panic! The same program will be repeated in the front of the catalogue.

CANADIAN POINT CHARTS

ONTARIO (SOUTH)
(South of 46° N. Latitude)

		Rating applies to each sex			
SCALE OF POINTS	1	2	3	4	5
GROUP 1					
RETRIEVERS (Golden)	2	4	6	9	12
RETRIEVERS (Labrador)	2	4	6	9	12
SETTERS (English)	1	3	5	7	10
SETTERS (Irish)	2	5	8	11	14
SPANIELS (American Cocker—Each Variety) ..	2	4	6	9	12
GROUP 2					
AFGHAN HOUNDS	3	7	12	17	22
BASENJIS	1	3	5	7	10
BASSET HOUNDS	1	3	5	7	10
BORZOIS	1	3	5	7	10
GROUP 3					
BOXERS	2	4	6	9	12
COLLIES (Rough)	2	5	8	11	14
DOBERMAN PINSCHERS	2	7	11	15	19
GERMAN SHEPHERD DOGS	2	6	9	13	16
GREAT DANES	2	5	8	11	14
SAMOYEDS	1	3	5	7	10
SHETLAND SHEEPDOGS	1	3	5	7	10
SIBERIAN HUSKIES	2	4	6	9	12
ST. BERNARDS	1	3	5	7	10
GROUP 5					
TOY POODLES	1	3	5	7	10
GROUP 6					
POODLES (Miniature)	2	4	6	9	12
POODLES (Standard)	1	3	5	7	10
ALL SIX GROUPS					
ALL OTHER BREEDS AND VARIETIES	1	3	4	6	8

QUEBEC

		Rating applies to each sex			
SCALE OF POINTS	1	2	3	4	5
GROUP 1					
POINTERS (German Shorthaired)	1	3	5	7	10
RETRIEVERS (Labrador)	1	3	5	7	10
SETTERS (Irish)	2	4	6	9	12
SPANIELS (American Cocker) (each variety) ..	2	4	6	9	12
GROUP 2					
AFGHAN HOUNDS	2	6	9	13	16
BASSET HOUNDS	2	4	6	9	12
GROUP 3					
COLLIES (Rough)	1	3	5	7	10
DOBERMAN PINSCHERS	2	6	9	13	16
GERMAN SHEPHERD DOGS	2	6	9	13	16
GREAT DANES	2	5	8	11	14
SAMOYEDS	1	3	5	7	10
SHETLAND SHEEPDOGS	1	3	5	7	10
SIBERIAN HUSKIES	2	4	6	9	12
ST. BERNARDS	2	4	6	9	12
GROUP 6					
DALMATIANS	1	3	5	7	10
ALL SIX GROUPS					
ALL OTHER BREEDS AND VARIETIES	1	3	4	6	8

Here is a sample of judging hours as they might appear in Canadian or American show catalogues or judging programs.

RING TWENTY ONE
JUDGE: Mr. Robert Braithwaite
(Also in Ring 17 at 2:15 P.M.)
9:00 A.M.
18—Italian Greyhounds 5–6–7
14—Papillons 5–6–3
10:15 A.M.
20—Pomeranians 10–7–3
4—Maltese 2–2–0
11:15 A.M.
19—Silky Terriers 4–10–5
12:00 Noon
Lunch
12:30 P.M.
33—Yorkshire Terriers
15–16–2
1:45 P.M.
10—Affenpinschers 5–4–1

118 Dogs

RING TWENTY ONE
JUDGE: Mr. Edward McGough
2:15 P.M.
9—Pekingese 2–4–3
12—Japanese Spaniels 8–2–2
15—Miniature Pinschers 5–6–4

36 Dogs

RING TWENTY TWO
JUDGE: Mr. Corson Jones
8:00 A.M.
27—Utility A Obedience entries
(Nos. 191–194, 231–252, 255).
12:15 P.M.
Lunch
1:15 P.M.
18—Utility B Obedience entries
(Nos. 9, 195–207, 253, 254, 256)

RING TWENTY THREE
JUDGE: Mr. Russell S. Breault
9:00 A.M. (The judge may take a one hour break at his discretion).
41—Open B Obedience entries
(Nos. 20, 191–230)

RING TWENTY FOUR
JUDGE: Mrs. Margaret McClintock
9:00 A.M. (The judge will take a one hour break at her discretion).
46—Open A Obedience entries
(Nos. 6, 7, 14, 15, 149–190)

RING TWENTY FIVE
JUDGE: Mrs. Ruth Kayser
9:00 A.M.
33—Novice B Obedience entries
(Part I)
(Nos. 5, 8, 10, 11, 12, 16, 18, 19, 23, 93–97, 104–122).

RING TWENTY FIVE
JUDGE: Mr. Paul Berkowitz
1:15 P.M.
32—Novice B Obedience entries
(Part II)
(Nos. 98–103, 123–148)

RING TWENTY SIX
JUDGE: Mrs. Beatrice P. Connelly
9:00 A.M.
36—Novice A Obedience entries (Part I)
(Nos. 17, 21, 22, 25–28, 31–59)

RING TWENTY SIX
JUDGE: Mr. Chester Monaghan, Jr.
1:30 P.M.
35—Novice A Obedience entries (Part II)
(Nos. 29, 30, 60–92)

Reading judging programs is as simple as eating apple pie, once you understand what you are looking at.

The single number printed just *before* the name of each breed denotes the total number of animals entered in that breed on that day: class males, class females, and all champions of record. The three sets of numbers immediately *after* the breed represent the breakdown of the total number of entries in this order: all class males, all class females, all champions of record or Specials. Sometimes there will be a fourth number followed by the abbreviation "Ex." This is the number of dogs entered for "exhibition only"; these animals will be at the show only to be seen by the public and will not compete for points or be exhibited in the ring in any manner. Very famous champions are often entered for exhibition only so that the public can get a chance to admire them.

A word of warning: these figures represent the number of animals *entered* at the dog-show superintendent's office; it does not necessarily follow that all who were entered will be *present* at the show. Absentees will not only affect points, as we'll see, but can also drastically alter the time you are due in your ring. Since there is no foolproof way to predetermine absentees, the only solution is to keep your mind pretty much riveted on how the classes in your breed are progressing. If you can stay at ringside, study whether or not your judge is a slowpoke. Is the ring steward a muddlehead who is slowing things up? If you cannot stay yourself, try to have someone else keep track for you.

You will notice that in Ring 21 the day starts off with 18 Italian Greyhounds followed by 14 Papillons. Both are scheduled for 9 o'clock, but if you were showing a Pap Specials you would not have to be on hand exactly at that hour, since the schedule tells you 29 dogs must be judged before your entry is due. Picture-taking may hold you up further. But beware of complacency. Judging schedules can be awful, artful liars. And watch out for those lunch breaks! Mr. Breault "may" take an hour to eat if he chooses—but he could choose to munch in thirty minutes or to skip the whole thing.

According to dog-show rules, no class can be started before the hour scheduled in the program; it will often run later, but it is not supposed to start earlier. Just make sure your watch and the judge's watch say the same thing. When one of my assistants goes to a ring to check on the progress of things, he automatically sets his watch by the steward's or the judge's watch, whichever individual is free and the more amenable. You might not want to go to this trouble with just one or two dogs in a single breed, but be aware that time marches on!

And when you look at your program and see that Boston Terriers will be judged at *approximately* 3 P.M. you have every right to start shaking. "Approximately" can mean anything from 2 till 5 o'clock, and often does.

In the U.S. the show programs usually state that Group judging will begin at a specified time and will be done "in the following order unless otherwise announced." The difference between this statement and a bald-faced lie is minimal!

Many a weeping exhibitor has returned to the show after a shopping spree or a fancy lunch to be advised that his Group was judged an hour before his return! He wails, "But I checked with the superintendent before I left and he told me . . ." Before you start yelling "foul!" you must understand that such muddle-ups are usually caused by one judge being unbearably slow, an unusually heavy entry at a specialty or booster show, the necessity of replacing a judge at the last minute— there are many such reasons, and the superintendent isn't always to blame. After all, he cannot put the hounds into the Group ring until Afghans are judged, so, since hounds aren't finished as expected, he has to slip in the Toy breeds who have been ready for some time. Every once in a while you'll run into a superintendent who is rude, inconsiderate, and sick and tired of bossy handlers, terrified amateurs, and prima donna judges. I locked horns with one once because he waved the Sporting Group into the ring even though Weimaraners weren't judged yet. We all hollered, "You can't do that!" But he did, indeed, do "that," snarling that he was fed up and we had entered in breed, not in Group, so it wasn't his concern if we missed out. This kind of situation is one I hope will never face you—but don't count on it. Be suspicious at all times.

If you want to go shopping, do so on Thursday; save that "special" restaurant until after the show is over; and if you are eligible for Group competition, hie thee to the show superintendent's desk to check the order not once, not twice, but as often as necessary to make sure you get your chance at the coveted Group first which qualifies you for that glory of glories, Best in Show!

In learning to handle Little Caesar dog-show officials, few and far between though they may be, you'll need extra cupfuls of tact, self-control, patience, and sense of humor stashed in the corner of your tack box. If you can develop a low-down, rotten, suspicious outlook while maintaining a pleasant facial expression, so much the better!

Differences Between U.S. and Canadian Groups

There are a few pitfalls concerning Canadian Group judging that bear close watching.

In the United States, Groups are almost always judged at the end of the day. This can happen in Canada also, but more often than not, Groups are called immediately upon concluding the judging of the last breed, alphabetically, in that Group.

This means that if Judge Hochenslopper were doing Non-Sporting breeds in Ring 1, he would start with Bichon Frise, then go to Boston Terrier, then to Bulldogs, and so forth, until he reached Tibetan Terriers, the last breed in the Group. As soon as Tibetans were finished he would commence judging the Non-Sporting Group without taking any break (except perhaps a short detour to the washroom while the steward got his breeds in the ring for him). Your Canadian judging program or catalogue will explain clearly which method of Group judging is to be used; make sure you check this out.

As we have explained earlier, Canadians are used to much smaller shows. They are only now learning to handle the sudden, enormous surge in entries, due in great part to the fact that more people are discovering what great fun it is to show dogs in Canada. But every now and then when a show will obviously be running very late, weary, hassled show secretaries will succumb to the temptation to run Groups concurrently (i.e., more than one at a time). This is never a popular move in either country, for many handlers have several dogs in all Groups; in Canada such a decision sends everybody into hysterics, so be prepared for great emotional upheaval and unexpected changes of mind and plan. Try to be an island of calm in a sea of storm!

Here is yet another difference between Group judging in the two countries: while in the U.S., you may stay for the Groups or not, as you choose, *you must stay and exhibit in any Group you are eligible for in Canada, or you could lose any points or awards you may have taken that day!*

For this reason, Canadian Groups are liable to take much longer to judge than American Groups because they are full. Spectators north of the border get an opportunity to see a much wider variety of breeds than is usually the case at U.S. shows. And when placing in a Canadian Group, you have the satisfaction of knowing you defeated a full representation of breeds in your particular Group classification.

Finally, remember, as we warned you earlier, that the Puppy Group competitions come directly after the judging of each Adult Group.

The Exercise Pen—Theirs and Ours

While we all hate to admit it, humans have to go to the bathroom too. Most of us dog-show regulars gravitate toward the coffee table as soon as we're set up at a show and soon find it necessary to locate the "human exercise areas." These can range anywhere from filthy wooden one- and two-"holer" accommodations in the middle of an unmowed wheat field, to tiled areas with automatic flushing devices and hot and cold running water. Some even come equipped with toilet paper and hand towels. They are located by asking around. I mention them in passing only because at some shows, whether the restrooms are indoors with lounges or circular tents with canvas curtains and specially dug holes, dog-show superintendents sometimes supply a lady or a gentleman attendant whose job it is to see that you have change, if necessary, or to provide you with hand basins of clean water. These nice people become very familiar faces to dog-show people. The ladies I've encountered have mended my hems, unspotted my dresses, zipped me up, and mopped my tears. In answer to whether or not you should leave a little change in their dish, my reply is a resounding *yes!* Incidentally, in the case of the individual porta-potties, long since dubbed "space capsules," you'll often have to supply your own toilet paper.

Exercise pens for dogs at shows are sometimes labeled "dogs" and "bitches," and sometimes not. In any event, they are square areas filled with sawdust over plastic indoors or sawdust over the ground outdoors, or just the ground. They are enclosed on all four sides with latchable gates (if the latches are in good repair). At the more famous shows there may also be gateless pens for those dogs being exercised individually on leash, as well as gated models where handlers, or others with more than one dog, will turn as many as ten dogs loose at the same time. There was a time when great resentment flared at U.S. shows when handlers usurped exercise pens with groups of beasties while the individual exhibitor just had to wait. This situation still occurs from time to time. But today, regardless of the rules, most professionals are forced to set up their own "ex" pens adjacent to their grooming areas.

Oh yes, we read the capitalized notice in the premium list and repeated in the judging program: "Individual exercise pens will not be permitted on the grounds under any condition!" But this rule is about as realistic as the handling of campers and trailers which we discussed earlier. Those of us who bring our own pens are forced to do so simply because, for one thing, two to four sets of exercise pens in the United States and one or two sets in Canada are woefully inadequate to handle the needs of animals entered in today's shows.

Before you start sounding off about those snotty professionals who consider themselves better than anyone else and who don't think the rules apply to them, close your eyes for a moment and try to imagine what those same exercise pens would look like if we professionals *did* use them instead of our own. Since we arrive ahead of other exhibitors, our dogs are exercised earlier; the rest of the show would never be able to get near the pens, let alone use them!

Then, too, as both amateur and professional breeders and handlers of certain smaller breeds will agree at the drop of a hat, some kinds of show dogs *cannot* be permitted to run around on grass, sawdust, cement, gravel, or even carpeting without breaking off the lustrous long "feathers" we have spent years growing and without which a Lhasa, for instance, or a Pekingese, or a Shih Tzu cannot hope to compete. The Afghan Hound in top show condition is a disaster once he has been turned loose in sawdust! The stuff is hard enough to get out of a Vizsla's flat coat, never mind that of a Chow Chow or a Setter.

When it comes to white dogs, public exercise pens are No Man's Land for *extra* sure! The small, pristine Maltese or the white toy Poodle has to be exercised on white shelf-type paper we beg, buy, borrow, or steal, because nothing looks worse in the show ring than a dirty dog, unless it is a dirty *white* dog. It takes over an hour to get a Maltese ready for the show ring so that he is sparkling; to have to reclean the animal and then groom it is simply impossible.

Show-giving clubs and show superintendents, instead of posting silly rules that no one can afford to obey, should face up to the fact that radical changes are necessary in the doggy bathroom department. The Professional Handlers Associations have offered year after year to work with these people to find a solution acceptable to everyone. To date, their efforts have been met largely with vague promises and sympathetic nods.

In the case of the amateur, I.think we must admit one more thing about public *or* private exercise pens—they are not healthy places. If waste is picked up and removed after each dog has used such a pen, the chance of the presence of germs is greatly reduced, but even if clubs start out picking up their exercise pens, as the hours progress and the weekend passes, these enclosures become ankle-deep in excrement.

One of the first things that attracted me to Canadian shows, indoors or out, were the many youngsters armed with pooper-scoopers who skittered around keeping the shows spotless. The famous Sportsman's Dog Show each March in Toronto—it is really seven all-breed licensed dog shows held in a single exposition building in nine hectic days— may be a bit messy when things are over each evening, but long before showtime the next morning, you could eat breakfast off the floors while electric spraying devices are fogging the building with deodorizing and sanitizing materials.

So what is the person with one or two dogs to do? Either get most of your pottying done during the trip to the show as we suggested earlier, and/or do any extra bathrooming out in the fields adjoining the show where you can safely walk your dog on or off leash. At indoor shows where you are not permitted to leave the building or show grounds for *any* reason, I'm afraid you are stuck with the area in and around the public pens.

If there are free dogs trotting around in the pen you wish to use,

Keeping a dog show clean is everybody's business. This dog can't read, of course, but his young handler can! Emergency situations are one thing; simply standing by as a dog soils the show grounds whenever and wherever he chooses is quite another. Such behavior has cost more than one club the use of proper facilities, and show sites are getting harder and harder to find. *Photo by Glenn Easton*

you can bet they belong to some professional and wouldn't be in there if they didn't get along. If your dog is temperamentally reliable, go ahead and enter, using your foot or leg to prevent loose dogs from escaping as you do. Kennel dogs are used to "obeying" feet, as most dog people know that slapping at them with hands is a dandy way to develop hand-shy dogs. Always close and latch an ex pen door when you enter and when you leave, *whether it is empty or full.* It's an automatic habit you should develop in your own kennels to avoid unpleasant situations.

Assuming you are lucky and nobody is in the pen, take your dog off leash and step outside. Without you to distract him he'll probably tend to business better. Or you can unsnap his leash and walk around inside with him, keeping him moving and therefore sniffing. But on leash or off leash, don't assume a distracted pose in the center of the pen and stare into space for ten minutes wondering why FiFi doesn't do her business. Remember, boy dogs have to be next to something so they can "tip up." Girl dogs do better in open spaces.

Earlier in this chapter we discussed "matching" dogs. Suffice it to say here that in starting a green dog at dog shows, I *never* take him into an ex pen and allow him to stand there, shifting from foot to foot, establishing negative patterns. I "match" him before entering, praise him for coming through, and leave promptly. He soon learns that an ex pen is something in which you do just two things and then leave.

The Rings

Having set up, coffee'd, exercised yourself and the dog, now is a good time to locate your ring, a fairly simple procedure one might think, right? *Wrong!*

I decided a long time ago that those who set up U.S. show rings have perfected a singularly unique way of counting which is obviously beyond me! If I were asked to lay out ten rings I would either do them in a single row from one to ten, or I would do them in two rows, one for odd numbers one through nine, the other for even numbers two through ten. But the Chief Show Ring Layer Outer, specialist that he is, counts 1-2-5-3-4-6-9-7-8, and if *you* can find ring 10 I'll give you a fur-lined chamber pot! I'm afraid there is no way I can give you a simple solution for finding your ring other than to be brave, start early, and maintain your cool. Each ring does have a number— at least it *usually* does—on a tall pole at one corner. This further keeps the exhibitor on his toes, as one is never quite sure if the marker that reads 8 refers to the area on its right or its left.

Obedience trialers have it easiest in this department in both countries, for obedience ring numbers always have an "A" tacked on; such as 19-A or 21-A, and obedience rings are usually located off by themselves.

In Canadian indoor shows, ring numbers are no problem, since rare indeed is the show having more than six rings. You can stand anywhere on the floor and easily find where you belong. At outdoor shows things are just about as simple. It should be emphasized, however, that very few Canadian summer shows are "outdoor" shows as we know them. With only a few exceptions, Canadian summer shows have some sort of pavilion or building in which many of the classes are held, and Canadian handlers are just learning the advantages of working out of their cars at summer shows, rather than loading and unloading.

There are several reasons for locating your ring early on.

First and foremost, if you are *really* early, you can go in and walk around it looking for holes, mud puddles, treacherous bumps, etc. Note particularly if the ground slants, because for reasons we'll discuss later you never voluntarily want to face a dog downhill. Although stewards do not take kindly to having empty rings used as practice areas, if you get to your ring before anyone has taken charge of it, I can see no reason for denying a nervous pup—or a self-conscious you—a few laps around your ring "trying it on for size," providing your dog doesn't foul the area in the process. If he does, see to it that it is cleaned up immediately! *Obedience rings are never used as practice areas at any time under any circumstances.* But there is no law to prevent a crack-of-dawner from walking alone around an obedience ring looking for hazards to navigation.

If it's an indoor show, determine the design in which the ring mats are laid; most thoughtful judges try to invent gaiting patterns that allow you to stick to the mats. Later on, while watching other classes, study the patterns he asks the dogs to execute; chances are he'll keep to that same pattern with each breed all day long. Locate the entrance to the ring; is there more than one? If your dog is the least suspicious about crowds and dark shadows, perhaps you would be wiser to ignore the entrance under the tent and use the one on the opposite side of the ring. If there is no alternate entrance, nothing prevents you from hopping over the side of the ring and entering from an uncongested point.

Indoor rings, while not boasting muddy potholes or poison ivy, nevertheless can be very dangerous. Since most indoor shows take place in gymnasiums or armories or on hockey rinks during off season, you can expect the footing to be slippery. Most clubs put down rubber or tarpaper matting, but it is placed so near the edges of the rings that even if you are built like a lead pencil, it is almost impossible to get both you and the dog on the matting at the same time.

While moving a dog on a slippery floor calls for a great deal of care, setting up a dog or stacking him on a highly polished floor is literally impossible. You get the front just right and, as you progress to the rear, the front of the animal slides out from under. Because you *feel* insecure and the dog knows he is, he tends to try to grip the floor in a futile attempt to stay put; consequently, his body is rigid in all the wrong places!

Those with experience in keeping themselves and their dogs perpendicular during competition on slippery floors swear by any number of solutions. Coca-Cola wiped on the dog's pads before entering the ring is a wonderful emergency solution. Or you might prefer to purchase a product called Sticky Finger at a stationery store. It comes in a tin box resembling an ink pad for a rubber stamp; secretaries wipe their fingers across it when counting pages. Concessionaires at dog shows carry an aerosol spray called Tacky Foot, which is sprayed on for added traction. All these things can be used on the handlers' shoes as well as on the dogs' feet! Gaiting your dog during practice sessions on a variety of indoor surfaces pays off in the long run. Even so, be sure to tuck some helpful product into that trusty tack box and don't be afraid to use it!

Stewards

Once you have located your ring, it is necessary to then locate your ring steward and determine whether or not he or she is of the type you can depend upon when the going gets rough. Stewards are the people who work in the ring with the judge. One is usually at the table handing him ribbons, advising him of absentees, and making certain all trophies are properly distributed. The other is supposed to be at the gate to the ring giving out armbands, keeping children and stray dogs and irate losers out of the ring, and getting classes to come lined up somewhat ahead of time. All of which sounds dandy; unfortunately, stewards come in four delicious flavors.

First, *the Prestige Steward*. He has been appointed to lend "class" to the show because of his prominence in the community. Then we have *the Social Steward,* who believes that in order to claim to have "arrived" socially, one must preside in some capacity at dog shows. *The Courtesy Steward* is a poor misfit who has been tried on every other committee in the world and been found wanting; not knowing what to do with him, the show chairman makes him a steward.

All three of these types of stewards have one awesome thing in common—they know absolutely *nothing* about the rules and regulations of dog shows; they are the greatest bottlenecks in the world of dog shows because, even if they condescend to make a stab at the rule book, they are way over their heads and they know it. What is more, the judge soon knows it, and the most gracious judge in the world can turn surly, dictatorial, and downright mean when he discovers that in addition to evaluating dogs all day in the broiling sun or pouring rain, he is also responsible for getting his own examining table, sorting his own ribbons and trophies, chasing down late or absent exhibitors, finding some lunch or some coffee on his own, and teaching some disinterested imbecile how to mark a catalogue without himself looking at it.

These kinds of stewards are easily identified if you go about it in a common-sense manner. Approaching the ring in which, say, Scottish Deerhounds are being judged, you clear your throat and, speaking in a gentle but positive tone, say, "Steward?" If the face which then turns in your direction is wild-eyed and twisted into a sickly grin denoting abject terror, you can begin to suspect all is not well. Obviously the only reason he has responded to your call is that he is praying you have been sent to get him out of there. To clinch your diagnosis, you try once more, enunciating clearly: "Steward, what class is this?" If after proper consideration of the dogs in his ring he replies, "Scottish Deerhounds," just say, "Thank you, Steward," and you know that from this point on you will be fending for yourself!

Fortunately, in addition to having put on this earth such good things as spring twilights, water lilies, grandparents, and the flash of fireflies at dusk, the dear Lord, in His munificent wisdom, also created the *Working Steward.*

Working Stewards—those belonging to organizations whose members hire themselves out to show-giving clubs for such remuneration as expenses for the weekend and free passes to the shows—are usually middle-aged, retired show folks who don't want to give up the fun of dog shows. They've usually forgotten more than us whipper-snappers will ever know and are absolute gems. Then, there are bright young club members who take pride in knowing the rules and a joy in doing their jobs well. In Canada, the dog-show organizations, of which there are very few, supply their own capable stewards. Dog Show Associates, located in Ottawa, is the best in Canada in my opinion. In the U.S., Foley is the most experienced. Both organizations supply and understand the value of good stewarding.

In case you haven't guessed, I have absolutely no sense of humor where bad stewarding is concerned. Whether I have brought one dog or ten to a dog show, I feel my support warrants at the very least capable persons in positions of authority. Just like any other exhibitor, I highly resent being hassled in and out of rings in the late afternoon without being given my fair share of a judge's time just because some stupid steward has caused that judge to be an hour or two behind schedule. It's not a difficult matter for clubs planning shows to send for a list of stewards' duties as outlined in A.K.C. or C.K.C. rules, and then, after picking their stewards, hold a couple of practice sessions to make sure these people realize how important they are to a successful show and to teach them how to do their jobs properly.

Armbands

Once you locate your ring at U.S. shows, you must ask the steward for your number. She will hand you an armband bearing the same number as that on your dog's ticket, the same number that appears opposite your name in the catalogue.

On-the-ball stewards have their catalogues propped open to about three breeds ahead of yours. After you have consulted your own catalogue and deduced that you have about half of a large entry to go before your breed is due, or two or three breeds with only one or two entries each, you can be reasonably sure the steward has your armband ready for you. So, if you were showing a Miniature Pinscher, for instance, you would get the steward's attention and ask politely for "Minpin Open Dog Seven, please." She would hand this to you and then make a mark in her catalogue indicating that you had "picked up." Later on, if for some reason you were late to the ring, the steward would not be as likely to think you were absent.

Securing your armband to your arm in a manner which leaves you free to move without losing it, takes a bit of experience. You will wear it on your left arm because you will gait your dog by circling to the left, and the judge who is in the middle of the ring can then see your number clearly at all times. There are three kinds of armbands, each one designed in a unique way to drive the uninitiated exhibitor bananas—unless some sneaky authority like me tells him the truth about *rubber bands!*

The first style of armband is simply a rectangular piece of heavy paper. All dog-show people, in addition to collecting stomach ulcers, blisters on the soles of their feet, swollen ankles, and enlarged muscles in one arm, *always* have a large supply of rubber bands. When dressing for a dog show, even the most style-conscious men reach for a wad of the things to affix to their left wrists before reaching for their wrist-watch. And the possibility of the runs in ladies' nylons is of little import compared to the size and stretchability of her rubber bands! In the case of armband No. 1, make a slight horizontal tear near the upper right- and lower left-hand corners. Now fasten the number to your arm using two thicknesses of rubber bands *diagonally* across the number.

The second style is designed the same way but comes supplied with its own rubber band fastened to a hole in one end and two notches already cut on the other end. *This does not work!* Throw away the wispy rubber band and, using your own nice fat ones, fasten armband No. 2 exactly as you did No. 1.

Finally we come to the double armband—somebody was trying here, and you can't really knock a guy for trying. *But this does not work either!* In case of armband No. 3, two armbands, each with the same number, are stapled together, the theory being that you are to poke your arm through the hole and the band will stay put. *Another bald-faced lie!* Go ahead and stick your hand through, slide it up your arm—and fasten your rubber bands under one corner and over the other. A final word of warning about armband numbers: be sure you don't get sixes and nines turned upside down. If the lettering does not make it clear which way is up, check your catalogue and dog-show ticket. If you are "six," draw a line under the number, so that if you get in a frazzle at the last minute you won't make a mistake. And as you enter the ring and the steward checks you in, repeat your number out loud, making sure her number agrees with what you said You don't want to win—or lose—for somebody else!

In Canada the three types of arm bands are also present. They are all located at a central table presided over by people trained to find your number quickly and give it to you. Since you don't get your number from the steward at the ring, it is wise to check in with her shortly before your breed is due to be shown, so that she knows you and your dog are present; this prevents her marking you absent if you should be a few moments late getting to the ring. In this country the two or three shows on the weekend will be hosted by a single club and the same number will be used each day.

If, for some reason, you lose your number or it gets so crumpled or torn that it cannot be used a second time, fear not—you can get a fresh number every day if you so desire.

One final tip about armbands in either country: if you are showing more than one dog, take a moment before the show gets underway and your butterflies wake up, and write the name of each dog on the back of your armband. This saves much confusion when the going gets hectic.

Special Problems

No matter how carefully we do our homework, evaluate our potential show dog, keep records, and read entry forms, things do go amiss from time to time. Ignoring the possibility of the existence of foul-ups does not, unfortunately, make them go away. We have to be prepared for them and be able to deal with them correctly and intelligently.

THE NUMBERS GAME

Every once in a while you will get to the show and discover, in looking over your catalogue, that the number assigned to you next to your dog's name in that august book is not the same as the number on his show entry form. It's a good idea to trot right over to the superintendent's office. A member of his staff will go with you to the ring, tell the steward which number you will be wearing on your arm-band, and will correct the judge's book so that one number and one number only will be yours and yours alone when judging time rolls around.

WRONG CLASS

The same thing could occur in the case of classes. You might have entered your dog as Open and the catalogue might have you in Puppy.

Go right back to the superintendent again, and he'll get you straightened out, making sure, again, that the records in your ring are so corrected.

Or you might find your Bred-by-Exhibitor Bitch entered as a Bred-by-Exhibitor Dog—and away we go to the poor superintendent again, the magic fixer-upper who will straighten it all out.

I suggested earlier in this chapter that it might be a good idea to make a carbon of each record you mail out, in case something goes wrong. As you can see, these are instances where your duplicate entry form, stuck in your purse, might be a very handy thing to be able to pull out. The show superintendent has your entry in his "baggage" too, and he can find it quickly and check things out. If the error in sex or class is his error, then he'll correct it all the way from the steward to the judge and back again. If the error was yours, the U.S. superintendent can do nothing about it and you've just driven to the show for nothing. In Canada, however, if your error is a minor one, very often it can be corrected so that you will be able to exhibit.

Disqualifications and Other Dilemmas

Sooner or later in the life of every exhibitor comes that gray day when you enter your ring full of confidence and enthusiasm, and the next thing you know you are standing *outside* the ring. If you were *excused* because in the judge's opinion your dog seemed lame; *ordered to leave* (heaven forbid!) because you were perhaps foolish enough to argue with the judge for some reason; *dismissed* because your dog acted in an aggressive manner to the judge; or *had all ribbons or awards withheld* from you because the judge felt your dog was an inferior example of the breed—all is not lost. Certainly such awful moments cause acute embarrassment and the memory of them is painful. But in the case of such actions being taken by a judge, nothing prevents you from exhibiting the next day or whenever you wish to from then on. These instances represent the opinion of a given judge on a given day and in no way reflect on or restrict your future show plans—unless, of course, (could it be?) the judge was right. You have no recourse on that day; the judge has a right to his opinion just as you have a right to yours. You can write letters of protest and certain other courses of action are open to you if you feel you were unfairly condemned, all of which are carefully outlined in the A.K.C. rule book.

When you enter any show ring, even if you are the only one in the ring, the judge does not have to give you any award whatsoever. It is his right to give a second ribbon or a fourth ribbon or to withhold any ribbon at all. In larger classes he may give second, third, and fourth, or only one ribbon if he is so inclined. Keep this fact uppermost in your eager little heart, and sometimes those fourth-place pieces of white don't look half bad when you consider the grim alternative.

Now, then, if you should get the old heave-ho because the judge *disqualified* your dog, you may not then exhibit that dog at licensed shows in the country in which the disqualification was made until that disqualification is lifted. Again, there are avenues open to you, and A.K.C. or C.K.C. will review the disqualification, making no promises of course, providing you fulfill the requirements for protesting such a ruling. You must ask for such a review in writing within a certain number of days of the show, you must pay a fee which will be returned to you only if the disqualification is lifted—and other such "musts" are listed clearly and in great detail in your rule book. The American Kennel Club representative or Canadian Kennel delegate present at that show can answer any questions you might have and will be happy to do so provided you conduct yourself, throughout this traumatic experience, in good taste and with good manners. Always carry that li'l old rule book with you; you just never know when it might become the very best—almost the only—friend you have in the world at a given moment!

Disqualification is automatic in the United States if a dog is blind, deaf, castrated, spayed, changed in appearance by artificial means (except as specified in the standard for its breed, such as removing dewclaws or docking the tail); or if a male does not have two normal testicles normally located in the scrotum. Lame dogs must be excused and cannot be given any awards in the U.S. In Canada a dog excused for lameness at three championship shows during a two-month period assumes the status of a disqualified dog. Remember now, in such instances there is no point in making an effigy of the judge and sticking pins in it each night when the moon comes out! *He has no choice*—he is governed by the same rules you are.

A disqualification in either country could also occur if the dog has a characteristic which is listed in the individual standard of a breed as *disqualifying*. Many breeds have no disqualifications in their standards. Others have quite a few. In the United States, for instance, entirely white or black Boxers *must be disqualified,* as must a Golden Retriever with an overshot or undershot bite; in Canada, by way of example, a French Bulldog which doesn't have "bat" ears, or a Schipperke of any other color than solid black, *must be disqualified.* These disqualifications are obvious and easy to spot. But now and then certain breeds turn up with height or weight disqualifications. When a judge suspects a dog may be over or under the weight limits, or taller or shorter than the permitted size standard, he is obligated to have it officially weighed or measured by a committee of officials of that show-giving club plus the C.K.C. or A.K.C. official. If the process determines the animal is within the weight or height limits, the dog can continue competing. If the weighing or measuring proves the dog does not lie within legal limits, he is disqualified then and there; he cannot compete further at that show or any other show unless, through channels I explained earlier, he is reinstated.

If you suspect your dog's weight or height may be challenged when you get to a show, there are steps you may take to protect yourself, all of which are outlined in the rule books. Suffice it to say that you should know the disqualifications if there are any in your breed, and you should be sure at all times that his height or weight are not disqualifying.

In weighing large breeds of dogs you'll have to use the larger scales some veterinarians have, or go down to your local grain store and ask to borrow theirs. For dogs that can be held, climb on the scales at home, weigh yourself; then have someone hand you the dog. When you subtract your weight from the combined weight of you and the dog, you'll have his weight.

When measuring a dog's height, be sure to set him up on a level, nonslip surface. Position him in a natural stance, front legs dropped under him and rear legs positioned so that the hocks are perpendicular to the ground. For best results use three people: one who does nothing but soothe the dog and hold him firmly in place; a second to hold a yardstick (low numbers down) straight up in the air even with the dog's shoulder blade, and a third to lay any straight edge (a piece of heavy cardboard, a ruler, or even another yardstick) lightly on the dog's withers (the top of his two shoulder bones). The point where the straight edge crosses the yardstick is the height of your dog.

Again, read your rules and regulations about disqualifications regularly, so they are always fresh in your mind should an "ungood" moment darken a day in the life of you and your show dog.

Nose Printing

In order to be registered in Canada, a dog must be either tattooed or nose-printed. If you choose the latter, you can have it done for you while waiting around at Canadian shows. There is no charge for the service and it is painless.

You may do your own nose-printing at home if you wish by attaching three unsmudged prints to the official form, which you may obtain by asking for it at any Canadian show. I know it is possible to do because I did it myself, once—*once and only once!*

I consider it to my credit and everlasting glory that, after only five and a half hours, I came up with three suitable prints of Canadian and American Champion Native Shore Jock of Wooltop. Prior to this experience, "Jock" was one hundred pounds of Chesapeake Bay Retriever with the disposition of a perfect angel. By the time we had "compromised" and done things my way, we both hated each other mightily! There was more ink on the walls, on me, and on the dog than I would have thought possible, and the floor was hidden beneath layers of smudged index cards. The entire do-it-yourself project probably cost me about ten dollars in equipment and put the kind of strain on my nervous system I never wish to duplicate.

Shortly after this horrid experience I discovered that a C.K.C. representative is usually present at most Canadian shows, complete with numbered blanks for the prints and experienced help. The entire process takes all of five minutes per beastie. All other requirements for C.K.C. registration can be explained to you when you take a dog for nose-printing.

Show Photographers

Just as horrid, embarrassing things happen in show rings to everybody, now and then, no matter how carefully and correctly you go about things, wonderful moments occur too. The time you spend in that magical place called the Winners Circle more than makes up for the days Lady Luck wasn't smiling in your direction.

It may be the occasion of the first point you ever put on your dog; it may be the day he finishes his title, takes a major, goes best of breed from the classes, walks off with "the whole thing" at a National Specialty, or places in the Group. When events like this happen, most of us want a memento of the victory, something we can look at year after year and experience the thrill of victory over and over again. The obvious solution is a picture.

In the United States, each licensed dog show has a professional show photographer assigned to it. These men and women are experts in their field, very experienced in getting nervous dogs to "say cheese." They can be counted on to tell you to pull your skirt down, straight your tie, move the dog's outside foreleg under him—all the little things that are so important in making your picture as perfect as possible.

If you win and want a picture taken, your first step is to say to the judge, "May we get a picture?" or, "Do you have time to have a picture taken?" Judges won't stop in the middle of a breed, for obvious reasons. If, for instance, you went Winners Bitch, you wouldn't bother the judge before he finished Best of Breed. As soon as the breed is finished, however, ask his permission. If he says yes, go to the ring steward and ask her to call the photographer. You may wait inside the ring with your ribbon and trophies, if any. When the photographer comes up, indicate whether you want black-and-white or color and tell him what award you have won—"Best of Breed" for instance or "Best of Winners." Most photographers carry little signs which indicate all of the possible wins. Hand the ribbons to the photographer and he will give them to the judge as he positions him in a level spot in the center of the ring, puts down the correct sign for you and your dog, and lines you up next to the judge. He may take several shots to make sure he gets a good one. He has squeaky toys and a vocabulary of interesting noises to make your dog pick up his ears. Follow his directions—don't argue with him!—and you'll soon have the deed done with a minimum of inconvenience and almost no delay of the show. Following the picture-taking, thank the judge for his courtesy. If he asks for a copy of the picture, of *course* you will be polite—and grateful— enough to assure him it would be your pleasure to send him a copy. Be sure the photographer gets your armband number, as this is the way he identifies you so that he can send your picture to you—in a week or so.

When the picture arrives you do not have to accept it if it is not a good one. But most American show photographers know when a photo is not up to snuff, and they often send a little note saying something like, "I'm not pleased with how this came out; let's shoot it again at a later show." In all probability, you would not get that judge in the second picture, but you will get a good job for the money you pay. If you do accept the picture, there will be a price scale for reordering in the envelope; indicate your preference and enclose your check or money order. If you want a picture sent to the judge, include a little thank-you note and the photographer will be happy to attach it to the picture and send it on to Mrs. So-and-So. (Include the judge's full name and address from the front of your show catalogue.)

The only reasons a judge would have for refusing a picture would be if he was way behind in his assignment or was perhaps due immediately in another ring. In these cases, he will suggest that you "catch me later." Let the show photographer know that you want a picture with this particular judge before the day is over. He'll keep an eye cocked on the judge, watching for spare moments when he can slip you in, but he can't devote his entire day to arranging *your* photograph; it's your responsibility to stay on top of the situation too. Generally, there will be several of you waiting to get pictures with a certain judge, and there usually comes a time when he is free, ditto the photographer, and using a spare ring you all line up and get the shutterbugging done one at a time.

A scrapbook of color prints of your show dog winning in the ring is an excellent thing to show people who might be interested in using your dog at stud later on, or when you get ready to have puppies. For the same reasons, it's an excellent idea to place a good picture of your dog, as he finishes his title, in one or two of those dog magazines subscribed to by doggy people.

Dog-show photographers make their living taking pictures at dog shows. Technically, they are the only ones on the ground allowed to photograph the dogs for money. Sometimes, however, the husband or wife of the family is a camera bug and wants to take pictures too. I don't think anyone objects to this as long as you keep out of the professional's way and don't expect judges to pose for "family portraits."

In Canada, the process of getting show pictures taken is about the same as in the U.S., but the whole dog-show "thing" is just coming into its own in Canada and some show photographers there are liable to be very inexperienced. Some of them insist on money before they send the prints. Make sure before agreeing to this that you have a right to return the pictures and get a refund if they are bad.

Don't expect the majority of Canadian show photographers to have any idea of how a dog looks best in a photo. If you have to work with an inexperienced person, make sure *you* take over politely and firmly and tell him exactly how you want things done. If you are as green as he is, your best bet is to have the dog face just a bit into the camera—flat side-on shots can be most unflattering. And you may need a friend to talk to the dog to make him look alert.

The handful of experienced show photographers in Canada are excellent. They want to learn and are always open to suggestion. You are better off, for the most part, if you have the duplicates sent directly to you and then you send them on where you want them to go. Give these people another two or three years and they'll be as on-the-ball as their U.S. counterparts.

As green and clumsy as some of the Canadian photographers may be, there is no reason for you to act superior and behave in an impatient, rude manner. Everybody has to learn his trade, and I have found that if you let these people know you are not trying to *embarrass* them but to *help* them through your experience, you usually get grand pictures—and you've made friends who could be most valuable to you and your dog in the years to come!

IN THE END

Surviving dog shows is a great deal like having a baby; when it's all over one tends to remember, more clearly than anything else, the *good* things that happened along the way.

Somehow we put up with and live through the stupid stewards, inadequate facilities, and careless show officials because of things like the judge who "dumped" you your first time in the ring and then spent ten minutes of his valuable time encouraging you to continue because you had a good dog. After a while the long drives and lousy weather seem to pale beside the memory of the time your Chow Chow puppy bitch beat the No. 1 Chow Chow of all time and took the whole thing—yessir, Best of Winners, Best of Breed, the works! That in itself was wonderful enough. But guess who took the time to help groom your puppy for you before the Group showing—yep, the owners of the No. 1 Chow Chow of all time!

Who cares if they sold out of catalogues in ten minutes in the morning? The important thing to remember is the professional handler who flagged you down when you were late and very lost, turned you around and led you triumphantly through the gates to the show just in time for your class.

Of course we could do without high-priced motels, half-cooked hamburgers, and armbands that fall apart in the rain; on the other hand, we couldn't do without the thrill of "almost" winning the National Specialty and the people who came running up to say, "You were robbed!"

We do it because we love it, that's why. In the merry month of May we scowl, complain, write letters of protest, and wave our fists in the air at club meetings; we swear we'll never go to such-and-such a show again. But when winter rolls around and I'm sitting next to a roaring fire with a lap full of cats and the heads of dogs, the remainder of which won't fit in anybody's lap, I am apt to start giggling quietly as I turn to you and say, "Hey, remember that time in New Jersey when the cop said we couldn't take our dogs into the building?" You chuckle and reply, "That wasn't half as wild as the time we locked ourselves in the hotel room with the dogs and couldn't get out!" And I say, "Will you ever forget that idiotic Canadian show secretary who couldn't speak English . . ."

On and on it goes until the fire burns to embers, just as do all flaming injustices once they have a month or so to burn into the dear, funny, happy memories which are the real reasons we go to dog shows.

What in the world would our lives be without them, hmmmmm?

5

The Art and Ethics
of Showing

Most of the instruction you have received up to this point was concerned with your dog—conditioning him to maintain a happy attitude, suggestions for moving and grooming him. Now it's time to tackle the other end of the leash—you! *Your* grooming, *your* movement, *your* attitude—these factors greatly influence the results you seek in the show ring.

YOUR ATTITUDE

It's up to you as handler to present your dog in such a manner that when you enter the ring with other competitors in your class there is an aura about you that separates you from the "herd." First impressions mean almost everything in the show ring. Whether or not you have the best dog in the class is something the judge will have to decide. Your job is to achieve a better job of presentation than the rest of the class by entering that ring looking as if you are proud to be there and as if you believe in your dog—as if maybe you know something about that dog nobody else knows!

Your attitude will determine, in large part, your dog's attitude. There is a very old, very true saying that all your feelings "travel right down the leash" to the dog, and they do. Let me give you an example of what I mean.

I was waiting to show at one of the summer outdoor competitions. My dog had squeezed as much of himself as possible into my lap and was happily cleaning my left ear while I absent-mindedly stroked his head. Along came a lady with a group of children and a very nice dog. He was trotting along, wagging his tail, happy as a clam; he was going somewhere with his family, and that was obviously his idea of paradise. Well, in the next fifteen minutes I never saw a dog so "abused" in my life. Obviously very nervous about showing, the lady screamed at the kids, yanked the leash of the dog until the tail wagged less and less. She yelled at him to lie down. He did so, and when some oaf stepped on his paw she slapped him for moving. By the time this poor animal got into the ring he was absolutely miserable. When the judge tried to examine him he pulled away sulkily. He didn't place, needless to say. And as that shrew of a woman rounded up her whining children and dragged her long-suffering dog off into the sunset she was heard to mutter, "I didn't think I'd win, he just *hates* dog shows!" *Dear Heaven, who wouldn't?*

If I were asked to cite any one thing about the majority of newcomers—and a few of the old-timers, too!—I see in show rings every weekend, it would be that not very many people seem to be having *fun* with their dogs! Now, don't misunderstand me. Showing dogs, as we have explained, is a costly and sometimes wearing proposition. Certainly you aren't expected to bounce into the ring and start frolicking with your dog. Of *course* you want to win, of *course* you must be businesslike and tend to your knitting. But more than being a handler, you are a salesman when you enter that ring. You have a product to sell; the judge is the potential buyer. Why, Dale Carnegie would faint dead away if he could see some of these "salesmen" in dog-show rings as they approach the "buyer" with, "Well, I know he's not perfect and I don't blame you for not being terribly interested—in fact, I know this is a waste of time for both of us. Please let me apologize for bothering you!" If that's the way you feel about the whole thing, you'll never get anywhere in competition of any kind.

"That may all be very true," I can hear someone wailing, "but my dog isn't a show dog. Irish Water Spaniels (or any other breed) and dog shows just don't go together." Let's take a moment to debunk this bit of balderdash. Just what are we asking of a dog when we take him to a dog show? Oh, it may be rough on the people, but all the dog has to "put up with" is being admired by strangers, brushed and fussed over, fed delicious tidbits, petted, praised, and adored. Tell me, please: what in the world is so awful about this? There are exceptions to the rule, of course, but in nine cases out of ten, if your dog is miserable at dog shows, it's because you are miserable at dog shows due to the fact that you have succumbed to a very old, very serious disease. It's called stage fright. It can lay you low without warning, I'm the first to admit, but like a broken heart, it is rarely fatal.

The quickest cure is to simply admit the truth. If someone says to you, "Are you as scared as you look?" take a deep breath and reply, "I'm terrified!" Second, take my word for it that you are not the only nervous wreck at the show. Third, your best bet for a quick cure is not two shots of brandy or a couple of tranquilizers. Actors and actresses on the legitimate stage all agree that if you're not a little nervous, you won't give your best performance. Turn to the one friend you can count on to help out—your dog. Scratch his ears, pat him, tweak his tail, encourage him to put his paws up on your tummy. Play with him as if you were the only two creatures on earth. Believe me, this is the neatest trick in the world and it works.

As you enter the ring in a relaxed manner, obviously having fun with your dog, obviously glad to be there, a strange sonar emits from you to the judge with the message, "Ah, ha! That must be a good dog. She certainly seems to believe in it!" Keep one eye peeled for instructions but concentrate all your energies on getting the dog to relax. In watching his delight you'll soon forget your hang-ups, and the next thing you know you'll be handling like—you should pardon the expression—a professional!

YOUR GROOMING

Nothing adds to a man's or woman's self-confidence more than knowing you are dressed correctly and attractively. This is particularly true in the show ring. In addition to being you dog's handler, you are also his backdrop, the background against which he will either stand out or disappear into the surrounding foliage. The following true story will show you how important color can be in relation to your show dog.

Many years ago there was a charming lady who showed a Border Terrier. She was an Irish lassie and had the most mouth-watering collection of tweeds I have ever seen. She took great care to dress casually and always looked as if she had just stepped out of a bandbox. Unfortunately, her idea was to match her little dog as nearly as possible, and against her brown-and-beige tweed her brownish-beigeish dog virtually disappeared! He never got looked at and probably never would have been had not a good friend put a bug in the lady's bonnet. The next thing we knew, she was putting points on her little dog like crazy— by wearing bright, complimentary colors which framed her dog for all the world to see.

Royal blue, kelly green, red, gold, orange—all dogs look great next to such shades. But in no way does this mean you must spend hundreds of dollars on getting costumed to show your dog. For women in the summer, cool, inexpensive cotton shifts, khaki skirts and blouses, and hardy denim culottes are easily within the reach of most pocketbooks, and today's patterns make them a cinch to whip up at home. In the winter, such inexpensive materials as corduroy, washable knits, or again denim with color co-ordinated sweaters and blouses, give self-confidence and a great freedom of movement. Pantsuits are rapidly taking over the show ring and are always in good taste, where slacks and shirts are *definitely not*. However, here's a secret men have known for years: once you kneel on a dusty gym floor or in six inches of dewy grass, your knees are going to give you away. Try for the more neutral colors, which don't tattle so much.

And don't weep, ladies, if that dress you are pining to purchase because it would look lovely next week at the dog show is sans pockets. Just rush it over to your friendly neighborhood dressmaker and ask her to slit the right-side seam about five or six inches below your hip line. She can then fashion a pocket in a jiffy out of scrap material. As a matter of fact, as undomesticated as I am, I can do the same thing right at home.

Bright sportcoats which can be whipped into the washing machine make dressing well easier than ever before for today's male handlers. As I said to the ladies, if you are going to have to kneel with your breed, get neutral-colored slacks. Whether or not to take off your jacket at stifling summer shows has always been debatable. The rule of thumb seems to be that if your judge removes his jacket at a hot show, off come the handlers' jackets too.

I hear many of you complaining, "But I thought judges were supposed to be judging dogs!" Of course they are, and of course they do. But it's almost impossible to separate you from your dog in trying to get a true picture of the latter. You brush Fido and bathe him and buff him and fluff him—you may be almost too exhausted grooming him to consider anything but blue jeans and a sweat shirt. But make an effort. If you don't believe me, look around you at a few dog shows and see how the people who are winning points, breeds, and Groups are dressed. They must be doing something right!

Speaking of movement, if you are going to be able to stretch out your legs and run fluidly so that your dog looks fluid too, flat-heeled, rubber-soled shoes should be your main investment. Sneakers (tennis or running shoes) are ideal and no great financial outlay is necessary. Whether you are a man or a woman, showing indoors or out, comfortable, safe footgear is absolutely vital. *How* you move with your dog influences the way he looks as he moves. If you take choppy, short little steps, your whole body goes up and down; because he's silhouetted against you, your dog looks as though he's moving choppily too. In gaiting a toy, walk flat-footed and take long steps; in gaiting larger breeds, run, using the same long steps. Place your weight on the bottom of your feet, not on your toes. In practice, close your eyes and listen to your dog moving beside you. Try to hit the ground *once* for every *two* times he does. Your rhythm should be "you-dog-dog-you-dog-dog-you."

The Afghan standard may call for long flowing hair, but it is not any help on the handler, believe me. I love long hair, but nothing is more annoying to me when I am judging a match or to a licensed judge at a show than to have to part the fur of the handler to find the dog. So tie it up or back, girls: it will also help you to keep a closer eye on the judge!

There is a very prominent school of thought which believes that the sexier a girl looks in the ring the better chance her dog has to win. I must admit there are certain judges who go for such nonsense; trouble is, novices who grasp at any straw for an edge in the ring tend to forget there is a vast difference between *poor taste* and *sharp grooming.*

If you have a good figure and nice legs there is no reason why you shouldn't dress to show off such blessings. But if every time you bend over your dog, the world can behold the center seam on the crotch of your panties, take it from a woman who has stood at ringside and listened to the handsomest and most sought-after of the male handlers: you are showing your least attractive asset! Oh, the men will *look,* all right, but they do so because they can't believe any woman would be so blatantly crude in public. End of lecture.

If you do *not* have a *Harper's Bazaar* figure and your legs, like mine, are not your best feature, then dress to complement what you "is," not to imitate something you "ain't got." Short skirts on heavy people make their legs look even thicker, tight clothes only make these people look fatter; and snug waist lines turn stout people into two bags of potatoes tied in the middle.

SOME CONTINGENCIES

Assistance

Every once in a while you may need assistance while you are in the ring—you might run out of liver or have forgotten your comb. Or on a hot day you might want a cold towel to drape on the dog while he is waiting to be gaited or examined.

It is perfectly correct for someone to hand you what you need from ringside, but no one may *enter* the ring to bring you anything except in case of a genuine emergency. And no matter how badly your dog is behaving or how much someone (owner, co-owner, or mate) may disapprove of your efforts, no one may come into the ring to bail you out or threaten mayhem or offer suggestions for better handling from ringside.

I distinctly remember a Terrier Group in Toronto one awful day when a poor little amateur lady was fighting a losing battle with a white Bull Terrier who had decided he was hungry enough to eat all the other terriers. The more she tried to reason with him (it is rarely possible to "reason" with a Bull Terrier!), the more fractious he became. And as he got louder and wilder, so did every other dog in the ring. Finally, just as the judge was about to throw the poor soul out on her ear, in came her very French, very annoyed husband, sixty miles an hour, screaming at the judge, "Zees is reedeeCUEluss. You are all mad! Fini!" And taking both his wife and his dog literally by the backs of their necks he dragged them out of the ring and out of the auditorium while the rest of us stood there with our mouths open. Then everybody burst into laughter.

This kind of action is just not done in correct dog-show society, but I must confess many of us were in sympathy with that husband. Many's the time I have longed to say, "Oh, to hell with it!" and run for the boondocks!

Double Handling

There is another kind of assistance from outside the ring which is absolutely illegal. But you will see it used again and again in certain breeds, and no action taken to stop it. "Double handling" has become the "in" way to make German Shepherds, Doberman Pinschers, Great Danes, and some other breeds look sharper and more alert; because "everybody does it," everybody else is supposed to look the other way.

I realize that by taking a stand on this very controversial subject I will antagonize a lot of handlers and owners, but I do not believe in double handling. Just because it has become tolerated as a kind of handling technique doesn't make it right in my mind!

Double handling is practiced when the handler takes a dog into the ring after making certain the dog is watching while his owner or someone he is very fond of walks away into the crowd. For the rest of the time that dog is in the ring under judgment, the "helper" moves around the perimeter of the ring waving his hands over his head, whistling, coughing, scratching his head with his catalogue, so that wherever he goes the dog can follow his movements while being encouraged to do so by the handler. The helper positions himself wherever his services will make the dog look his best to the judge.

I suppose my chief objection to this folderol stems from the fact that as a professional handler it is my opinion that when someone is considered an expert in a breed, and gets paid a lot of money for handling that breed, he should be good enough at his job to win without assistance from anyone else. And if the dog is so emotionally unstable as not to be showable without such inducements, then I don't think he should be finished or bred. I have either pointed or finished dogs in breeds notorious for double handling and never had to resort once to this ploy.

Since I have made no secret of my feelings on this subject, I have been accused by double-handling owners, breeders and handlers, of "not understanding" the temperament of these dogs. My reply to this charge has always been and always will be that if you are referring to acutely hyper animals whose eyes are wild with anxiety, dogs who slink on their bellies at the slightest suggestion of trauma, hysterical dogs who are a joy to absolutely no one and could never be considered "companions" to man by even the wildest stretch of the imagination— then, yes, I confess, I do not understand such temperament. Nor do I want anything to do with it. And I feel anyone who sanctions such behavior by exhibiting dogs who can only be controlled in the ring by two people is not interested in the future of purebred dogs!

Recently, a dog had the points he had won at a Canadian show canceled when it was discovered that the owner was walking around in the crowd with a transistor radio, a receiver for which was attached to the dog's collar! I have stood by at ringside in the United States and seen a prominent woman professional handler physically shake the owner of her dog in public, loudly berating him for having cost her the points by "not doing what you were told"! These instances make me ashamed to be part of a system that permits such practices. I would welcome any move to eradicate double handling forever!

"Starting" a Dog

There is only one instance in which handlers may be changed on a dog already in the ring—barring emergency situations, of course. This is when a professional handler finds he is tied up showing one dog at the exact moment another one is due in another ring. When this occurs, as it does quite often, another handler or a helper or even the owner will "start" the dog, getting at the end of the line and hoping against hope that the professional will be able to come in and take the dog before the class has gone on very long.

Many people who handle their own dogs resent handlers who come in to a class late, not realizing that we must do so if we are to behave ethically on behalf of the person who has hired us. And once we start a dog in the ring, we may not leave that ring for another until the class is judged. However, once an entire class has been individually gaited and examined, a handler may be denied the right to take over a dog, even though he must act to prove he tried to fulfill his commitment. There are still judges who do not agree with this ruling and those who have misinterpreted it. So the perfect solution has not been found, but certainly efforts are being made in that direction.

In Canada there is no such rule and one often sees a handler start a dog, then have an assistant come in and finish the dog while he runs to another ring. I disapprove of this practice and, were I the judge, I'm afraid I would interpret such action as an indication that the handler thought *me* less important than the other judge!

Public Punishment

Except in the case of dogs trying to bite the judge, or dogfights, which we will discuss in detail later, physical punishment in public at a dog show is something one should avoid. I don't care how much your dog needs a good swat, nothing looks worse in public. Since those who see you take a crack at the animal have no notion of your motivation, they naturally assume that you are abusing the creature. All too frequently an amateur who does not know what he is doing and cannot control his dog in other ways will haul off and take a crack at it. In public or in private, striking a dog never does any good when you turn to such a solution simply because you don't know what else to do. Children who are allowed to handle animals too spirited or too large for them often resort to such solutions.

Most unpleasant situations involving public punishment arise because people aren't paying attention. One dog wanders too close to another animal who is not in the mood for company; or someone else's nasty dog is permitted to get too close to yours. Other unpleasant incidents occur when an overeager amateur puts a dog in competition before it is trained or under control. In these cases I feel the owner should be slapped, but unfortunately it's usually the poor dog who suffers.

There are moments, however, when an experienced dog who knows better gets in the ring and decides he's going to make a fool of you. This cannot be permitted because dogs are smart cookies, and once you let them imagine they can avoid all discipline just because they are in the ring, *they* will soon be showing *you* weekend after weekend.

Shaking the dog violently and swearing at him in threatening undertones are two solutions which leave a lot to be desired. Whenever public discipline is called for, is truly justified, figure out for yourself some quick, subtle correction which can be seen and felt only by the dog. Then make sure you keep smiling as you apply it.

I have found that a severe pinch on the dog's side nearest me does wonders for a beastie who has decided he doesn't want to stand on four feet; of course, you always run the risk that he will squeak loudly and draw everyone's attention to you. But don't get flustered. Keep smiling, reach down and pat the little devil; chances are that now when you set him up he'll stay put. Be sure to praise him the moment he gives you an opportunity to do so *sincerely*.

I love all dogs and would die rather than abuse them; on the other hand, I am not going to let intimidation pass, simply because a dog is the culprit. I was raised by a mother who was a primary supervisor at twenty-one. I can remember going through a stage when I figured she wouldn't dare spank me in public. Spank me she didn't. But she got her point across quickly and painfully, and very few people standing around us knew what had happened. I, however, learned only too well what I had suspected for years: my dear mother was indeed smarter— and faster—than her naughty daughter Martha! I never loved her less, and those around us loved me more. It's the same thing with dogs.

Dogfights are horrid, savage affairs which leave anyone connected with them weak in the knees when they're over. Since few fights end without at least one dog getting badly ripped or punctured, I do not think I will be accused of nagging if I say again: *when in public anywhere with your dog, pay attention!*

If your dog should be involved in a dogfight, do not drop the leash and start yelling and screaming. And under no circumstances stick your hands between the two angry animals. They are both too excited to realize it's *your* hand, and you will get badly chewed at the very least. And never mind running for buckets of water; by the time these arrive the dogs could be torn to bits. Grasp the animal, male or female, in that private area most sensitive of all, and apply enough pressure to cause it to forget the other animal. Then immediately withdraw to a far, far corner by yourself where you and the dog can calm down. As we've said, veterinarians can be called upon if needed.

While Waiting

Just as it is important for you to know how to move and stack your dog in the ring, still there are moments when the best thing you can do for him is to do absolutely nothing at all.

Big classes of twelve dogs or more are hard on dog and handler. It should be obvious that posing for long periods takes the fire out of any animal; constant fussing or nagging by the handler will make you stand out all right—yours is the dog that just quit cold! Yet most novices who find themselves part of a large class demand that the poor dog be on his toes every single second they are in the ring. The dog gets tired, the handler gets cross, and the whole thing becomes a battle of wills—and won'ts!

After the initial go-round, the judge usually starts looking at the dogs individually. This is your cue to break the tension by letting the dog jump up on you. Scratch his ears, let him sit or lie down. Feed

Dogfights at ringside are only slightly more common at dog shows than at obedience trials. A Bloodhound, a Welsh Corgi, and an Irish Wolfhound become hopelessly tangled as their oblivious owners check catalogues, watch the judging, or just think it's cute. If one of these dogs gets belligerent, the other two will follow suit instinctively, and suddenly we have a nasty situation. To assume that because *your* dog is friendly, every other dog is friendly too, is asking for trouble. Taking chances like this is never worth the heartache that can result. *Photo by Glenn Easton*

him a tidbit. Play little games with him; it loosens both of you and is usually fatal to butterflies. Then, when it's your time to be gaited and examined, you wind up standing out in the crowd because you have the only fresh, bubbly dog left in the ring. How your dog looks to the gallery is of monumental unimportance! *They* don't give the points!

Don't hand me the line, "But I thought it was against the rules for a dog to sit in the show ring!" What rules? In the show ring about the only "rule" you must try to remember is never to get between the dog and the judge. If there is one "rule" about showing a dog in enormous classes, it is this: that you are honor bound to conserve him over the long haul so that when your precious moment comes to "do your thing," the dog is up on his toes, looking sassy and sharp, not lost *in* but standing out *from* the crowd.

In the process of studying how to present you and your dog to the waiting world, let's not overlook the most important person in that world: the men or women who have the power to ration points and all sorts of other goodies—the judges!

Once you get into showing regularly, you will be sharing most of your weekends with the people who wear the purple ribbons. Their uniquely different position in the dog world sometimes makes their actions seem particularly difficult to understand. Wise indeed is the amateur dog-show enthusiast who does his best to learn early all he can learn about judges.

THE CARE AND FEEDING OF JUDGES

I was educated mostly at parochial schools after I left senior high. Perhaps it was because I was the only Protestant on campus, but I can remember that during my first few months I tended to address the nuns and priests in tone never above a whisper.

When I started in dog shows as an amateur, I felt the same way about judges. I guess I figured they slid into the show ring on a sunbeam straight from Heaven, and at the end of their assignments were spirited away in the same manner. For months, as a neophyte, my mouth was constantly agape in wonder and my eyes discreetly downcast as I blundered around and around the rings. If my jaw muscles hadn't begun to ache and if a constant view of nothing but grass, dog feet, and dog manure hadn't begun to bore me to death, I might still be in this unrealistic position.

But one sunny day I put all the courage I possessed into one big effort and as I said "Thank you" to a judge, I stood up straight and looked him in the eye. It was dear old Dr. Mitten and he looked like a real live human being. There were no little wings sticking out of his shoulders! It was a very warm day on the eastern shore of Maryland and he looked hot and tired and extremely wilted, just as I did. He smiled. I smiled. And he replied, "You're welcome, young lady. Thank *you* for bringing me such a nice dog!"

At that moment I decided that if he were judging on the moon I would be the first one in his ring. I thereby entered into Phase Two of any beginner's development, during which you believe all judges are wise, wonderfully kind, helpful, and polite. This phase lasted for me just about as long as it does for any other greenhorn. My rude awakening came one afternoon when I had just executed a perfect "T" pattern and returned proudly to the judge to be hit with his sarcastic bellow which carried, I am sure, at least ten miles: "Madam, if I want you to execute a 'T' I will ask you to execute a 'T'. In the meantime, I'd appreciate it very much if you would listen to my instructions—

you *do* speak the language, I suppose?" Oh, if only the ground could have mercifully swallowed me at that moment! I prayed that his next assignment was in Hades. Phase Three gave me the experience to realize that just as there are good and bad doctors, teachers, and plumbers, so there are good and bad judges.

During my years as a handler I've been most fortunate to have been able to exhibit dogs under some great all-rounders (all-breed judges) such as Alva Rosenberg (who never forgot a dog), Percy Roberts (who would actually slap your hands if you overhandled), and Marie Meyers (who always wore enormous picture hats, whose dresses all had "V" necklines in the back, and whose uninhibited ways and speech terrified as many exhibitors as it delighted).

These judges and many others taught me much about self-control, ring manners, good sportsmanship; about lack of control, no manners, and bad sportsmanship. They made me glad enough—and mad enough—to cry. Their sense of humor—and their lack of it—have sent me into gales of laughter. Their conceit—and their humility—have brought me up short more than once, and their kindness—and cruelty— have taught me what we all sometimes tend to forget: nobody, not even a dog-show judge, is perfect!

Sometimes judges have to honor assignments when they are tired, sick, or maybe a teensy bit hung over, just as you and I once in a while wind up in the ring a little slow on the uptake. Sometimes they are beautifully taken care of by the clubs they accept assignments from; sometimes they barely get a "thank you" as they dash for a taxi to make their flight at a distant airport.

No matter who they put up in the ring, somebody is going to object, sure as shoot'n! They are expected to be patient, pleasant, businesslike, fast; their heads are crammed full of a list of rules and regulations that would make a quarterback's play book look like a copy of *Wind in the Willows,* and there's always some real or imagined "authority" a few feet away to pounce if, heaven forbid, they should be normal enough to make an error. They are expected to memorize enough breed standards to choke a horse. If they suddenly go blank and call for a book of standards, as is their right, you can hear everyone whispering, "Fine time to learn about a breed—in the ring!" If the poor judge decides to "wing it," he's shot down because "you'd think he'd at least know his standard."

Your Responsibilities to the Judge

In putting your best foot forward with any judge, try to remember that he has to finish his assignments on time if he is not to hold up the rest of the show. So be prompt at ringside and don't delay him by engaging him in long conversations about the record of your dog or by forcing him to explain his instructions over and over again. Watch those ahead of you and when your turn comes, move out quickly and confidently. If you don't understand what he wants, don't try to invent something that will annoy him and delay things even more. Admit you're confused and be done with it: "Sir, I'm afraid I don't understand."

Among the responsibilities *you* have to any judge is to bring him a dog prepared in all ways for competition. No judge is under any obligation whatsoever to put his hands on a dog that is obviously filthy, temperamentally unreliable, or completely untrained. In fact, as we've pointed out, even if you're the only one in the class, he doesn't have to give you any ribbon at all if he doesn't feel your exhibit warrants recognition.

It is equally important that you do not antagonize or interfere with a judge while he is examining your dog. Stay out of his way and see to it your hands aren't where his hands are. While we all have to hide something—or try to—sooner or later, the quickest way to make a judge suspicious is by attempting to cover any part of a dog with

Just because the judge takes hold of one end of the dog is no reason to turn the animal's control blithely over to him while you rearrange other parts. *(left)*

Control over the dog's body at all times is essential, no matter what part of it is being examined by the judge. Make sure you exercise that control and at the same time stay out of the judge's way. *(right)*

flamboyant or clumsy actions. If you feel he is overly rough you may ask to be excused, but you never have the right to argue with his methods or his decisions.

Position your dog where it can be seen; no judge is obligated to sort out your dog from the middle of a crowd in order to evaluate it. When a judge asks you to change a position—"Face me, please" or, "Bring that dog up here"—do what you're told promptly. Don't look around comically with "Who, me?" written all over your face and have to be called a second time. Believe me, he who hesitates in the show ring is often lost!

Some judges tell you to relax once they have gone over your dog, and mean it. Some are sneaky and keep looking back over a shoulder to see what the dog looks like when the handler is not on the job. Good handlers, amateur or professional, are *always* on the job! It's fine to swap recipes with Gloria Glopnagle who is next to you in line, but while swapping, keep one portion of your noggin tuned in to the judge's wavelength and keep the outline of that honorable offical in the corner of your eye at all times. If he *is* a "checker-backer," swap recipes some other time and keep your dog looking sharp at those moments when you know you're being peered at. Now, that doesn't mean keeping the dog stacked for *hours on end!* You can let him stand free and bait him when the judge is peek-a-booing; just make sure the dog's angle to the judge is his best angle.

I don't happen to think it's good form to chat with the judge when he's going over your dog, because I think you put him—and yourself— in an awkward position with the other exhibitors, all of whom are just as suspicious as you would be in their boots. I don't care if the woman judge bounced you on her knee when you were teething; swapping "Remember when's" is out of place in the ring or immediately before judging commences. Bill Jenkins and Margaretta Rob may be dear enough friends for me to address them by their childhood nicknames *between shows.* But in the show ring I do not think it fitting or proper to refer to them as "Binkie" and "Skeeter." "Thank you, sir" and "Yes, ma'am" are all that is necessary.

Incidentally, while "thank you" comes easily for first-place ribbons and winners awards, it is not quite so easily issued when your lot is second, third, or fourth. *But say it anyway!* You just never know when you may wind up showing under this person again. Let all his memories of you be good ones. If you cannot learn to lose gracefully, *whether or not the loss was justified,* I suggest you get out of dogs and try guppies—better yet, piranhas! You should be aware that extreme rudeness of any kind could *cost you your right to exhibit dogs for short periods or forever,* both in the United States and Canada!

The Judge's Responsibilities to You

While you may lose privileges, a judge can lose his license for various reasons. Both of you are bound, through simple common sense, to behave with restraint while in each other's company. But a judge has certain other obligations to you as well.

I think it is every judge's duty to be on time for his assignment. While I think he deserves a competent steward to work with, I do not think that lack of such dependable help should be taken out by him on exhibitors, no matter how bad things get.

Courtesy may wear thin after six or seven hours on one's feet, but I believe he owes each exhibitor good manners whenever permitted to use them. I feel he should make all his directions crystal clear, and while I love them dearly as people, those two or three judges who are famous for directing their rings with the vague gestures of drunken symphony conductors can be very annoying to experienced handlers and the source of abject terror to newcomers.

Never under any circumstances should a judge be seen drinking on the show grounds or acting intoxicated in his ring. Never should he physically handle any dog in a manner that suggests roughness. While he is under no obligation to lead an obviously inexperienced exhibitor around by the hand, neither does he have any right to publicly embarrass such a person, as trying as some of them do get.

While there are moments in life when one wonders whether two cents wouldn't be overpayment for the services of one judge, many people *do* wonder how judges get paid. They are paid in as many different ways as there are different judges.

Some charge so much per dog. Some get a flat fee per show plus expenses; some include their expenses in their fee. Since travel can be costly, dog clubs will often split expenses by hiring the same judge for a weekend. He will do Terriers, Toys, and Sporting Dogs at the Saturday show, for instance, and Non-sporting, Working, and Hounds on Sunday. No judge may do the same breeds both days at back-to-back shows.

Judges licensed for all breeds are referred to as All-Rounders. By the time a man or woman gets to that exalted plane in his judging career, he is very liable to have passed his thirtieth birthday. Recently some of our most revered All-Rounders have retired or passed away, and replacing these people is extremely difficult.

Some judges are more popular than others either because of personality or because of knowledge, or both. Clubs scramble to try to get these people because their names on judging programs draw bigger entries. But even the average judge is sometimes booked three years ahead, and the most popular ones, the busiest ones, are often almost impossible to sign up.

Every now and then the American Kennel Club or Canadian Kennel Club will give its permission for a person to judge who is not licensed to do so. This occurs at specialties where prominent breeders or ex-handlers or other persons famous in a given breed are honored by being asked to judge by a breed club. Sometimes, also, well-known, highly respected dog people from other countries are granted permission to judge specific shows.

The American Kennel Club has strict rules about how often a judge may officiate in a geographical area. So before you start moaning and wailing because your club hasn't engaged the judges you like most, be fair enough to take all the reasons into consideration—and there are many of them!

One of the first things you learn in exhibiting dogs is not to enter under judges who have seen your dog once or twice and have made quite clear the fact that they did not share your good opinion of your entry. On the other side of the coin, everyone looks forward to returning to a certain judge once he has voiced his approval of your dog. But I think you are asking for trouble which you richly deserve when you "follow" judges too closely. Sooner or later, out of fear someone may challenge why they are always putting up a certain dog, you get dumped with a bang. It's called "going to the well once too often." Like everyone else, I have my favorite judges and know which of my dogs are their favorites. Because I respect these people, I am very careful not to put them in a position where they might think, for a moment, that I *expect* them to put me up whenever I appear. Remember, nobody wants to be taken for granted.

Most people who show dogs are as mature, businesslike and honorable as are most of the people who judge dogs. Just as there are bad exhibitors, without whose presence the dog-show game would be much better off, so is there a small coterie of judges whose behavior and attitude nobody needs.

In the heat of competition it is sometimes difficult to be broad-minded enough to give anyone the benefit of the doubt, but if we would all make just a little more effort to understand each other's needs and feelings, the dog-show game—all of civilization, in fact—would be a smashing place to spend the rest of one's life.

RING PATTERNS

Whether or not you take my advice about running *after* certain judges, like it or not, indoors and out, you can expect to run *for* them whenever you enter the ring. And "what makes Sammy run" *well* is a complete understanding of the various traffic patterns he may possibly encounter in any judge's ring. So let's take a look at those.

Round About

When you originally enter the show ring, whether you are alone in your class or accompanied by other exhibitors, the first moving you will do will be around the ring to your left, or counterclockwise. You will, of course, gait your dog on your left so that, as the judge presides from the center of the circle, your dog will always be between the judge and you. This is, in all probability, the only time you will move together, at the same time, with all the other exhibitors in your class.

If you are alone in the ring or are first in line, watch the judge for his signal to move around him in a circle. He may come down the line of exhibitors or just to you, and either stand beside you contemplating your dog, or walk down the line giving every entry an initial "once over." At this point you may either have your dog stacked or let him bait free, whichever is best for you both.

Sometimes the judge will direct, "Take 'em around." If this is the only command you are given, check back for a moment to make sure those behind you are prepared to move. If someone seems asleep at the switch, you might say, "Everybody ready?" Then take off at a stylish gait and do not stop again until you are directed to do so by the judge. *Remember, unless a judge clearly says to you,* "Take them around once and stop when you get back to this spot," or, "Circle the ring three times and line up under the tent"—*keep going!* As leader, your fellow exhibitors will not thank you for periodically slowing down so that everybody piles up on everybody; and if you're alone, your side gait will seem rough and unsound if you stutter back and forth between forward and neutral.

And do not enter a ring at a dead run and start circling while the judge is busy elsewhere. Take your time and do exactly what you are told to do.

After this initial go-around, the judge will probably examine all dogs individually, or he may wait and do this later. In any event, when he moves his dogs again it will be one at a time, and he can ask you to gait in any one of the following "patterns."

Up and Back

The simplest pattern you will be asked to execute is Straight Up and Back. This means that you will take your dog straight away from the judge, wherever he is standing, to the furthest point you can go in the ring and straight back. You will move your dog at a trot.

When the judge motions you out of line to gait individually, you will either be on his right or his left. In either case, walk forward and position your dog in front of the judge with your back to him. Pause just a moment to collect your thoughts and your dog, then start off smartly. This small pause in front of the judge just before "take off" is called "addressing the judge"; what it actually means is that you are taking a moment to be very sure that you have placed your dog so that the two of you are moving *straight* out from the judge and he gets a true picture of the rear movement of your dog; you will come *straight* back so he can clearly see the dog's front action. At no time *ever* do you leave the line where your dog was examined and take off with your dog before first going to the judge. No matter where you are, walk to the judge first, then execute the pattern, unless he should walk down the line of waiting dogs and pause behind each, asking that they be individually moved.

There is a school of thought that advocates making what is called "a courtesy turn" in front of the judge before moving your dog individually. This means you would approach the judge and make a complete circle in front of him before starting off in a straight line. At the risk of toppling the towers of tradition, I find the courtesy turn outmoded, clumsy, and dizzying in the extreme. It is wasted effort, consumes time foolishly, and does nothing I've ever been able to determine to help you, the dog, or the judge.

Instead, as I explained, I recommend marching up and pausing a moment in front of the judge, then moving your exhibit as directed to do.

Because that unwritten rule about never getting between your dog and the judge is so overemphasized in most handling courses, lots of amateurs insist upon either changing hands and bringing the dog back on the right side when executing the straightaway pattern; or they make a "U" turn with the dog on the inside. Either is perfectly acceptable, of course. However, I find that with any dog, I boggle the rhythm of his gaiting by switching him from hand to hand or perhaps bumping against him making an inside turn. The few seconds you are between the dog and the judge, if you don't change hands on a straightaway pattern, are ridiculous to worry about, in my opinion. When I get to the end of this pattern, I turn to my right and come back, making sure that I turn early so that when the dog turns he is a little behind me and his body is straight.

I would like to repeat a warning here: unless you are the first dog in line or alone in the ring, there is no necessity to ask what pattern the judge wants. Pay attention and do exactly as the person ahead of you did.

There seems to be a great deal of confusion about what to do upon returning after gaiting individually. One does not simply make a sharp turn and flee back to the safety of the line; neither is it recommended that you concentrate so on the dog that you run the judge down. Both solutions are "no-no's." As you are returning toward the judge, begin slowing down so that when you are about a yard away you can stop and let the dog stand free at the end of his leash as you bait him from directly in front. Be careful that you do not block the judge's view. As you come to a stop, a few quick steps will swing you into position for free baiting with the dog at a bit of an angle to the judge and you out of the picture on the far side of the dog. As you keep one eye peeled to be sure the dog is keeping alert, turn the other eye on the judge. He may walk forward to touch the dog again as he is standing free; keep out of his way. Do not remove the dog from this spot until you are told to do so. He will dismiss you either with a wave of his hand or he will say, "Thank you." Reply, "Thank you, sir (ma'am)," and return to your place in line.

If you are alone in the ring after gaiting individually, the judge will indicate, "Number one, please," or "Take her to number one." Go to the placement marker he has indicated and stay there until he presents the ribbon. Help him to read your armband by holding your arm up a bit toward him; to make sure your win is recorded correctly you might even say, "Thirty-four, sir."

The Triangle

The next easiest pattern is fortunately becoming more and more popular with judges. It is the triangle and it allows the judge to see a dog going away, from the side, and coming back. Even the most inexperienced handler can execute this pattern with ease, for there is no cause to worry about changing hands. The entire pattern is done with the dog on your left. Start out from the judge after pausing briefly in front of him to collect, then make a triangle starting away from the judge to the right on a slight angle. Go as far as you can on that leg; turn left and go as far as you can across; turn left and come back to the judge on a slight angle from the left. Nothing could be simpler—unless, of course, the dear soul wants you to execute the triangle *backwards*. This makes for clumsy handling, necessitates at least two changes of hands, and because most exhibitors "choke" when they see this pattern coming, the dog is a bit uptight too. Don't ask me *why* some judges call for it; the reason is unimportant. The point is that you must practice at home and in class until the changes involved in "backward patterns" hold no terror for you or for your dog.

Backward patterns—any pattern in which you are instructed to start off on the left and turn to the right—may be executed in one of two ways. When you see one coming, in the case of a triangle, you can switch your dog to your right side and still not have to make any changes; this is a dandy solution of the dog is familiar with working on your right and is as comfortable there as on your left. Yard practice insures this. Or you may start out with him on your left, change hands at the first corner as you turn right, keeping him on the judge's side, then change hands again on the final right turn.

Few people have trouble changing hands in handling class or in yard sessions *while moving the dog in a straight line;* but everybody gets snarled up when they practice *changing hands on a turn.* Don't make it complicated! As you approach a right turn with your dog on your left, without stopping or breaking stride, reach across your tummy and take the lead with your right hand—the last few steps before the turn are taken with the dog still on your left but with your right hand on the leash. At the moment of turn, take a giant step forward, beyond your dog. Now pivot one complete revolution to your left and the dog will fall in by your right side. Don't try to turn the dog or step over him or pass him behind you—*ignore the dog completely!* Just be sure, as you hit the point where you must turn, that you and he are still parallel to each other, with him slightly behind you due to the giant step you took. Now turn toward him one full turn and, lo and behold, you have "got it, by George, you've got it!"

At the next turn you'll want him back on your left. Tackle it exactly the same way.

"L" to the Left

This is another easy pattern: straight away from the judge, turn left, go along far enough to give the judge a good picture of your dog's side movement, change hands and bring the dog "home" over the same path you used going out.

"L" to the Right

Here we have another "backward" pattern. Handle it as you did the "backward" triangle; either keep the dog on your right the entire time, if you start out with him on your left, or change hands at the first, second, and third turns. Again I advise you to practice, practice, practice on "backward" patterns to lay to rest those pesky butterflies.

The "T" Pattern

A judge wanting you to use this pattern will usually not describe it. He'll probably just say, "Make a 'T', please."

Do exactly that—gait off an enormous capital "T" on the ground with your dog. Since most dogs work best on the left, start off with the dog in this position and make the left bar of your "T" first—in effect, execute an "L" to the left. When you have gone as far as you can on the left side of the top of your "T," change hands, keeping the dog on the judge's side and go all the way across, this time passing the stem of the "T" and continuing an equal distance beyond it to the right. Now change hands again and come back to the stem. Turn left and gait straight back with your dog on your right or your left, whichever is easier. It's perfectly correct to start into your "T" at the top of the stem by turning right, but it does mean you'll have to change hands more often.

Over and over again we have discussed the unwritten rule about keeping the dog on the judge's side. Please do not misunderstand— you don't *have* to change hands and keep the dog in sight at all times unless you want to. Frankly, I play it a lot by ear. If I have a giant breed, changing him will interrupt his gait, so I leave him on my far side; he is big enough so he'll be seen anyway. With Shepherds few handlers risk disturbing the desired smooth, effortless stride with a change of hands. With toys it is a different matter. Since most of them are so small a judge could lose them in tall grass or behind size 9½ shoes, such as I wear, you almost *have* to keep them between you and the judge; however, they turn so easily it is no "big deal." If you are taking an unfamiliar dog in for someone else, the show ring is no place to find out if he "changes sides." *Don't try it.* You are much better off sailing smoothly along, even if he is "shrouded" for a moment or two, than winding up in a snarl of arms and legs and leash which ruins the picture for everyone. I think it is an excellent idea for a dog to be as familiar with working on your right as on your left, and it is essential you know how to get him from one side to the other with grace and dispatch whether in a turn or on the straightaway. Then, whether or not to use these maneuvers depends on the moment. Is the dog hot and thinking of quitting? Don't switch—pray, and keep going! Is he high as a kite and gaiting *you?* Then switch, by all means, and steal an extra moment to settle him down a bit in the process.

A final word about turns: the smoothest gaiting job in the world can be totally ruined when dog and handler bump into each other on a left turn when a change of hands is not involved. This happens when the dog "sneaks out from under you" and takes the lead as well as the upper hand as he progresses along the pattern. Take it from an expert bungler—you *cannot* get a dog back under control, once he has the bit in his teeth, without manhandling him in public. You *must* keep your eye on that dog *constantly* so that you can correct him *before* he takes charge. If you do reach a left turn with your dog on your left and realize the two of you are going to collide, you can sometimes

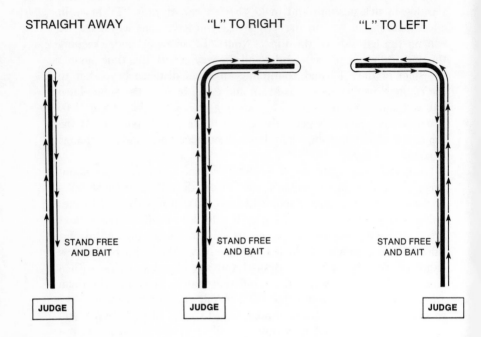

STRAIGHT AWAY

STAND FREE
AND BAIT

JUDGE

"L" TO RIGHT

STAND FREE
AND BAIT

JUDGE

"L" TO LEFT

STAND FREE
AND BAIT

JUDGE

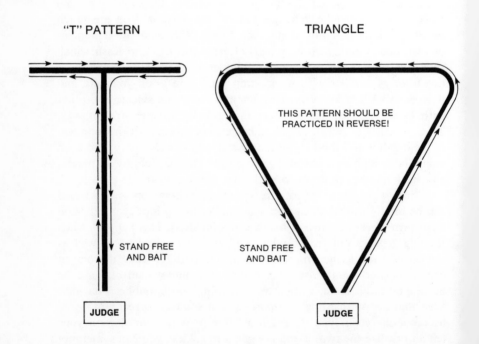

"T" PATTERN

STAND FREE
AND BAIT

JUDGE

TRIANGLE

THIS PATTERN SHOULD BE
PRACTICED IN REVERSE!

STAND FREE
AND BAIT

JUDGE

FADING for control on L. Turn
when dog is on handler's left

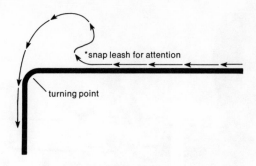

*snap leash for attention

turning point

SAFETY TURN for control on L. Turn
when dog is on handler's left

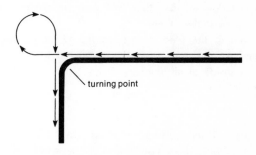

turning point

Pattern of MOVEMENT AROUND ENTIRE RING
alone or in company of other exhibitors

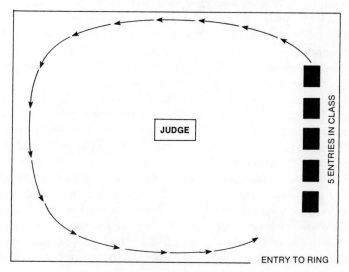

JUDGE

5 ENTRIES IN CLASS

ENTRY TO RING

Sometimes a judge will ask that two dogs be gaited together so he can study one against the other.

Coming or going, the idea is to keep the two dogs together so the judge can compare the animals. Unless instructed to do otherwise, keep the dogs on the inside at all times.

regain control by either "fading" or making a "safety turn."

"Fading" does not mean you abandon the whole project and slip unnoticed into the crowd! The moment you sense that the dog is going into the left turn ahead of you—which often happens when a dog gets "ring-wise"—give a snap on your leash and fade off your track to your right. As he follows, a bit confused you hope, slip around the corner to your left and he'll be right where he belongs. If he should shoot way out past you just as it's time to "turn for home," instead of turning left, make a small complete circle to your *right,* making absolutely certain that you come out of it ahead of the dog.

The best solution of all is not to get into such "fixes." This is most effectively insured by using that momentary pause before the judge, when first entering a pattern, to slip half a step ahead while the dog is still waiting for the command to start. If you begin a few feet ahead of him, you can generally stay there.

You will never lose control with your dog on your left going into a *right* turn if you take a few quick steps before the actual turn in order to place yourself ahead of the dog as he reaches the corner.

There are, of course, all sorts of weird and wonderful things that can befall you in the show ring. Most of the time you have no idea of what you did to perpetrate the particular crisis; but if you will draw up a toadstool and sit at my feet, I will tell you "What to do" to get out of such difficulties and at the same time maintain your dignity.

"WHAT TO DOOF'S"

Over the years, during speeches, handling classes, and clinics, when questions from the floor are solicited, person after person prefaces question after question with, "What should you do if . . ."

More often than not, the words "do" and "if" run together. This is how "What to Doof's" got started, and these days wherever I spend a lot of time teaching or lecturing, rarely an occasion goes by but someone rushes up with, "Hey, I've got a new Doof for you."

The following "Doofs" concern problems that can usually be solved in a few words, but they represent situations that are constantly cropping up at indoor and outdoor shows, benched and unbenched, in the United States and in Canada.

By carefully reading about "Doofs" today, you could avoid panic or out-and-out failure tomorrow.

A Judge Says You Can't Bait Your Dog in the Ring?

This is a problem indeed! Actually, while I do not feel that a judge has the right to forbid your use of any method you choose to bring out your dog's best points, arguing with him is no way to guarantee your eventual triumph.

There is a dear lady and an excellent judge officiating in the ring in the U.S. and Canada at the present time who has become unreasonable to the point of annoyance about baiting in her ring. Originally, I was in sympathy with her as she was against baiting while moving a dog, because it caused the dog to leap and bounce all over the place and she couldn't get a true picture of the animal's movement. She took the time to explain her reasons and she was absolutely right. But over the years, I guess, she has gotten so fed up with explaining over and over and over again that now all you have to do is have a piece of liver on your person and you are practically banished to Siberia. I feel that she is overstepping her authority; however, I am not going to say so to her in *her* ring! Therefore, I bait very carefully when her back is turned or she is concentrating on another exhibit. Everyone else I know handles this problem the same way.

A judge is in a ring to give his opinion of my dog. As long as I am not breaking any rules or conducting myself in a manner that makes it impossible for my dog to be correctly stacked or moved freely, then it is my business what transpires!

Which brings us to another "Doof" that illustrates an opposite problem.

A Judge Asks You to Do Something You Know Will Not Work with Your Dog?

Recently, a young friend told me a tale of woe. His dog was not moving well and the judge suggested he try baiting him to get him trotting along in a more energetic manner. My friend knew that if he showed his bait to the dog while moving him, the dog would "go ape," but he did it anyway, with the predicted results, because he was afraid of irritating the judge by not accepting his directions.

This judge was just trying to help, as are most judges when they make such suggestions. In this particular instance, I think I would have thanked him and told him I would try to get more animation. Then I would have moved the dog again and perhaps talked animatedly to him or clapped my hands; these actions, too, could be considered a form of baiting.

Years ago a famous handler and I were asked to move our dogs together down the ring and back. "I want loose leashes," the judge directed. I therefore dropped my leash; the other handler did not— and still won the class. His dog had a notoriously bad front, which fell to pieces unless the dog were strung up on a tight leash. The handler knew that if he dropped the leash he was all through—so he gambled and won!

You have to play these situations by ear; sometimes you can make it *look* as if you are following orders when actually you are not. I'm afraid there is no pat solution to this particular "Doof"—experience helps, as does a lot of nerve. The only thing I can advise you *not* to do is argue with the judge or try to make a lengthy explanation as to why his idea won't work.

Your Leash or Collar Breaks in the Ring?

Call the dog quietly to you, or have anyone who can catch it do so. Then take it to the side of the ring and either knot your broken leash together or borrow equipment from anyone who offers it. Then take your place in line where you were before. It is possible to carry extra leashes or collars at all times, of course, but if you carry extra everything from combs to bait to leashes to collar, you won't be able to move! The best bet here is to check all tack or equipment carefully before entering the ring, and to have your dog sufficiently under control by the time you get into a show ring so that he is not going to act in a manner calculated to break chains and snap leashes.

A Judge Asks You to Set up (Stack) Your Dog Facing Downhill?

In stacking a dog so that his body is square and relaxed, his legs in natural positions, his topline (his back) showing the proper angle called for in the breed standard, it is necessary to place the dog on level ground. Stacking a dog *up*hill can sometimes enhance a show pose, particularly if the dog is supposed to have a slanting topline. But to the best of my knowledge and belief, there isn't a dog alive anywhere today that looks good set up facing *down*hill.

In order to remain in position as he was trained to do, a dog standing headfirst down the side of a hill or slope must brace himself in order not to move forward. The handler is forced to assist him, further bracing the dog so that his shoulders are pulled backward into his chest while his hind section is pushing against the fore section. *This is not good!*

This particular problem occurs at outdoor shows, where show rings are often set up on uneven ground because there is no other place to locate them. This is why we urged you, earlier, to get to the show enough ahead of time to at least look at the lay of the land in your ring.

Most judges, through years of experience, have learned to "case the joint" upon arrival and plan just where they will gait their dogs so than when it comes time for a dog to be stacked for examination, it will get the advantage of as level an area as possible.

But sometimes judges become careless; sometimes, too, there just *isn't* any level ground. Then what?

If you are alone in the ring and the judge instructs you to "Set him up," you are quite free to pick a level spot anywhere near the judge, if such is available. If the whole thing is on a slant and the judge positions himself thoughtlessly below you, smile sweetly and say, "I'm sure you won't mind if I stack him uphill," and then do so promptly, as close as possible to the judge. If he (or she) is absolutely adamant and insists you do things the awkward way, then you have to oblige. For the moment at least, this is *his* ring. But never be embarrassed by trying and failing; it's your job as handler to get the best possible breaks you can for the dog you're handling, and as long as you remain polite and businesslike, no criticism is implied or taken.

If you are one of a group asked, for instance, to move out from under the tent and stack the dogs, and you see the leader heading for a downhill area, suggest in a quiet voice, "Why don't we move around more and try and get level ground for everybody?" This usually works. If not, again, you are quite free to ask the judge for permission to have everyone move to a level spot. If he concurs, thank him graciously; if he ignores the request, you can sometimes set the dog a bit crossways in line so that he isn't facing 100 percent downhill, but whatever you try, you're in a bad situation and you'll have to make the best of it.

The only sure solution is to try at all times not to get in a downhill position to begin with. Look ahead whenever possible.

The Person Behind You Lets His Dog Run Yours Down?

This is a quite common problem. It is called "running up on a dog" and, in addition to being distracting to your dog, could cause serious trouble if either animal decided to take advantage of the close proximity to indulge in some canine fisticuffs.

Before giving you two solutions to this problem, I would warn you to make very sure the person seemingly intent upon running you down is doing it deliberately. I know it may seem otherwise, but you are not, gentle reader, the only nervous amateur at the show!

The few times this has happened to me, I was able to handle it in one of the two ways described below and nobody got hurt. The one time in my life when I was so angry I turned to the person who was literally stepping on the heels of my sneakers and gave her a piece of my mind, it turned out to be the wrong time! She looked at me with great round eyes from which the tears began to stream and whimpered, "I didn't mean to, but I've never been in the ring before and I'm s-s-s-cared t-t-to d-d-d-death!"

I felt about as high as a runt pygmy! I mopped her up, gave a quick handling lesson, and concentrated on my victim so hard, in an effort to make amends, that she wound up with the points I was paid to get!

Also, make certain in your mind that it's not so much a question of the guy behind you running you down, as it is a case of you being entirely too slow. If your dog is an "iffy" mover, position yourself whenever possible at or near the end of the line.

Whenever I say to my handling classes that I have never known a professional to run up on me in a ring, I get lots of "Oh, yeah's?" from the audience. Person after person will insist he's been run down by someone he knew was a pro—until I ask if they were very sure it wasn't their fault for moving entirely too slowly. Then come the "Well, no, buts." Dogs forced to run up on anyone do not move well and suffer in the effort. Very few handlers would jeopardize a dog's chances in this manner.

However, it is true that some people, amateurs as well as professionals, who see a good dog ahead of them and feel it might give their dog trouble. So they do everything possible to unnerve both dog and handler of same. If you are absolutely convinced without a shadow of a doubt that this is the case, you have two options.

Cut toward the center of the ring, giving your pursuer a chance to get more moving room by staying where he is and continuing at his rapid pace. This is the reverse of the solution for handling the dog ahead of you that moves too slowly. Now, if the handler of the dog behind you sticks with you as you cut in, you can be jolly well sure you are, indeed, being run up on. In this case *stop dead in your tracks.* Yep, I mean it. Watch carefully out of the corner of your eye and, taking careful aim with the back of your lap, halt suddenly, making very sure you don't telegraph your intentions ahead. The effectiveness of this particular ploy requires that your opponent be taken *completely* by surprise. The very second that contact is made, spin around dripping with regret: "Oh, I'm terribly sorry!" Then, with no further ado, take off again minding your own business. The "enemy" will either decide you are out of your gourd, or he will be convinced you are not to be taken lightly. Whatever his opinion, I can guarantee you he'll steer clear from that point on.

Step out of his way and motion him around you. There is an unwritten rule that one does not pass another in the show ring except under unusual conditions or unless waved on by the judge. Part of being a handler, amateur or professional, is learning how to position and space yourself and your exhibit to avoid such problems as crowding. But extenuating circumstances do arise. If you can't solve the problem by the two methods just given, simply step back and motion your competition past you.

Use any of these solutions in any order you prefer; they are all time-tested by the author and are all very effective. But once again, in the words of a great philosopher, first and foremost; "Be sure you're right, then go ahead!"

Your Dog Snaps at the Judge?

Before I tell you what *I* do and what I recommend *you* do and why, I might as well confess right at the start that I have little or no sympathy for the dog or for his handler in this instance. Oh, I know, there are all sorts of "reasons" for such behavior and most of them are aimed at pointing out that it was the *judge's* fault—he shouldn't have worn a hat, he shouldn't have worn a raincoat, my dog doesn't like people to wear sunglasses, etc., etc. Dogs bite, in my book, out of fear, because they are just plain nasty, because they are in pain, and because they are undisciplined. But whatever the reason, as far as I'm concerned, such behavior cannot be permitted in the show ring.

The minute a dog snaps, I correct him. If he is a nasty dog and has a history of such actions, I'm probably not going to solve his problems with one swat, but he's not going to get away with such rudeness as long as I'm attached to the leash. As I said, swat—don't stop to think but slap him hard and smartly across the muzzle, then set him up again and just pray the judge doesn't throw you out (which I think he most certainly should!) or that, if he is gracious enough to return again (which he is under no obligation to do), there is no repeat performance. If the judge does come back to your "exhibit," loosen your hands—holding him too tightly will make your dog even more apprehensive. If the examination is concluded successfully, praise the dog.

Many years ago I watched a little girl of about fourteen or fifteen with an obviously evil Fox Terrier. When the judge approached with every consideration, the dog literally flew at him and, bless her heart, the young lady slapped him a "good 'un." The judge simply pointed to the exit; that was that and she left in tears. Whereupon her mother came up and began to lace her up and down, inside out, for being cruel to the poor little doggie! I couldn't believe my ears! I sailed over to the pair and, putting my arm around the child, informed the mother what I thought of her advice and her child psychology. "It is obvious to me, madam, why this dog has a behavior problem!" I finished as I stalked off.

I know people will criticize you if you strike a dog in public. In a way they are right—you should have struck the little so-and-so at home where training is supposed to be done. But to permit such a performance in public, thereby giving the dog the idea that once he gets into a show ring he can do as he pleases, could easily finish a show career before it begins.

You have absolutely no business bringing into a licensed show ring a dog that is temperamentally unreliable, particularly if you are not 100 per cent sure you can present him without jeopardizing anyone who approaches. But there are high-strung dogs who get mouthy when they are tired, though they may go six to eight months without an incident. Showing the just plain mean dog—and there are a few around, I'm sorry to say—is not my idea of "improving the breed."

Every once in a while a judge will startle an otherwise gentle dog and without thinking the dog will snap. This is something else again. Most judges who do this feel terrible about it and will join with you in making amends. Soothe the dog a moment or two, walk him around, then set him up again, *but do not hold him in position*—it will only cause him to become more and more uptight. Sometimes, if this doesn't work, a quick shake with your collar will let the dog know that you do not approve, and this very action may give him confidence. When such an accident does occur, the moment you get out of the ring and away from the crowd, get friends to go over the dog *immediately,* praising constantly so that he never leaves the "arena" with a bad taste in his mouth.

Finally we come to those judges who believe it is their duty either
to stack the dogs themselves or to loom over them in a way that would
frighten Jack the Ripper. These judges are in a minority, thank goodness.
Experienced exhibitors know who they are and show only their bravest
stock under them—never, never puppies! But if you unwittingly draw
such a nudnik, watch him as he falls all over the other dogs. Stack
your dog early. The moment he arrives, step *completely back out of
the way* and let 'er rip. Without both of you pushing and pulling at
him, the dog may be able to control himself—it's the best choice you've
got, anyway. If it doesn't work, the judge, in my opinion, is "asking
for it" and deserves what he gets. Nevertheless, the dog who snaps in
this situation *still* must be corrected. Do so with voice and collar, both
showing your disapproval.

If, heaven forbid, your dog draws blood without provocation, you
are both in big trouble and should be, generally speaking. A report
of the incident will be taken by the A.K.C. or C.K.C. representative
and or the Show Superintendent; the dog will be immediately barred
from shows unless and until you effect reinstatement through proper
channels. You may get an opportunity to present your side, but I
wouldn't count too much on the sympathy of those around you.

Your best protection against something like this is lots of home training and intelligent discipline in puppyhood, lots of traveling to matches
and classes. A truly unreliable dog will show his colors from the cradle
and, just like leopards, won't do an awful lot of spot changing.

But always, *always, always* take time to apologize in person to the
judge. I don't care whose fault it was or what the outcome, take a
moment before you leave the ring to say something like, "Sir (Madam),
I'd like to thank you for your considerate handling of my dog I'm
very sorry we caused any unpleasantness." Period, end of apology.
The one exception to this is the judge who deliberately insists upon
forcing his overbearing intentions on a dog and then gets into trouble.
This is the time you steal quietly away, like the Arabs with their tents.
If the man (or woman) should stop you on the way out of the ring
and explain that he wanted to place you but that it was your dog's
attitude that cost you the win, just reply, "Thank you," and keep going.
Don't go into a long discussion or argue. Go away. Remember, you
don't ever have to show under this person again, so thank heaven for
small favors and forget it.

Your Dog Gets Ahead of You in the Ring?

Every now and then, careful as you are, when you start gaiting individually for the judge your dog takes off in several gears higher than
you intended. *Then* what to do?

Well, if it's a matter of galloping a few steps instead of trotting and you can settle him down immediately, do so and keep going. But if there's clearly a lack of control and co-ordination between you and your dog, simply stop dead, walk quietly back to the starting point with a sweet, "I'm very sorry," and take off again.

A lot of this kind of thing can be eliminated if you don't go into orbit the moment your moment of truth looms clear. When it's your time to "do your thing" with Fido, walk with the dog to directly in front of judge. Pause a moment or two until you are certain friend dog is paying attention to you, and until you are sure that when the two of you start to move, *you,* and not your dog, will be managing things.

Always move away from the judge in a straight line and return on the final leg of any pattern in a straight line.

You Become Ill in the Ring?

Most of us at one time or another have received a call of nature to which it was impossible to turn a deaf ear; sometimes, one becomes so keyed up that the old stomach threatens to embarrass you momentarily.

Whatever the cause, there comes a time when there you are in the dog-show ring and, as lovely and balmy the day, as dear and sweet the judge, and as nice and flat the terrain, that that particular spot is suddenly the last place you would like to be.

Don't fiddle around until the worst occurs! If you are in line, say in a rather loud voice, "I'm sorry, I will have to be excused!" and flee. As you get to the steward say, "I'm sick!" and hand her the dog; or, say, "I'm sick" to the steward and hand dog and armband to a friend.

If you are in serious trouble, get out of there; rings are usually surrounded by lots of helpful souls who will do the best they can with Fido until you are either able to return and continue or can send for the dog.

Almost every ring has at least one chair in it for the judge's convenience, but in an emergency you have every right to confiscate it. Sit down immediately, for instance, lower your head and say, "I think I'm going to faint," which, while hardly an original line, does get your point across.

No matter what the immediate problem, leave the dog behind you if you have to seek privacy; he will be well taken care of, believe me. Dog-show folks can be most provoking at times, but they seem to rise to superior heights when one of their own is in trouble.

Your Dog Starts Blowing Coat Just Before a Show?

Why, you steal a line from David Copperfield and "Wash him, madam." Oh, I know all the arguments: "But it will all come out; he'll be naked!" It's gonna come out anyhoo and he's gonna be naked anyhoo, so why not get the whole thing over with, once and for all? Wash with a good shampoo especially made for dry hair. Lather heavily and rinse; repeat. Wipe excess water off with your hand and let him shake. Now pour out a little Alberto V-O 5 hair cream on one palm, rub hands together and, starting at top of head, rub him all over while still wet-dry. Now comb or brush him dry. Use an electric blower-dryer if you have one. Give him daily rubdowns with a terry-cloth or corduroy mitt and keep combing. We increase vitamins while the shedding process is going on, as I'm convinced the whole system undergoes change while the coat is getting straightened around. Some dogs shed until they are absolutely hairless; this kind of dog is best scratched from shows for a while. But if your dog is the average animal who blows coat and grows coat in orderly due process, and if he is in good condition otherwise, I can see no reason to waste entry fees. Coat isn't everything, you know.

Your Dog Starts to Go to the Bathroom in the Ring?

Answer: you do absolutely nothing—he can manage just fine without your help! I fail to understand why some people go into orbit because an uncomfortable beastie has to "spend a penny." And it is *not* true that if you soil the ring you are as good as disqualified. Utter nonsense! Oh, I'll admit there was a day when such goings-on shook me up a bit. But then came the memorable night at Madison Square Garden when my Chesapeake Bay Retriever, in the middle of sailing down the long carpet in the Group, suddenly stopped and evacuated. After your dog has so performed in the Group, at Westminster, with *thousands* watching—and you and he being televised coast to coast—well, nothing makes you self-conscious any more, believe me!

I have developed a kindly, vacant stare which I use while the dog is relieving himself. I have worked on my expression very carefully and by now I hope it conveys to all watching: *"What* dog? Oh, you mean *this* dog, the one whose leash I'm holding? Why, I never saw him before in my life. I was just standing here in the middle of this ring with my hand out, and a perfect stranger came up and said, 'Would you hold my dog a minute?' and he hasn't been back since!"

The one thing *not* to do is start dragging the poor dog across the ring toward the exit—one pile is *much* easier to collect than eighteen individual blobs! The best thing to do is stand still and pray hard for a firm stool so that the gossips at ringside won't decide you have worms in your kennel. And if it happens when you are not center stage, call the steward and ask her to send for the guy who used to be called a clean-up man and is now referred to as a sanitary technician. In the meantime, if she doesn't have presence of mind enough to put a chair over your intestinal contribution to purebred dogs, walk over to the nearest empty one, carry it back, and place it strategically yourself. When you are next to the judge so he can hear you, apologize for soiling his ring, and forget it.

The Dog Ahead of You Moves So Slowly Your Dog Cannot Gait Properly?

This is a very simple one to solve. There is no excuse for running up on anybody in the ring, no matter how fast your dog moves. Fast or slow, when the judge starts you all moving, allow the dog ahead of you to get three or four lengths away before you start. Usually this will keep you out of trouble. However, if your dog is distantly related to Secretariat, all you have to do is make a *square* as you run instead of a circle, and each time you turn a sharp ninety-degree corner, you gain feet of running room ahead of you.

The Judge Is Rude or Commits Some Error Against Current Rules and Regulations?

You report him, of course. I happen to think this is your duty, not your privilege. I also happen to be of the opinion that it's a crying shame that judges don't report more exhibitors for misconduct or bad sportsmanship!

I just happen to be violently in love with anything having to do with purebred dogs, and I resent exhibitors who shame me and the entire fancy with poor sportsmanship and bad manners, just as I resent judges who discourage amateur and professional handlers alike with rudeness or inattention to the dogs brought to them for their evaluation.

Let's back up here a moment and make sure we are both—you and I—defining the word "rude" in the same manner. Rude does not mean your dog was beaten, you know—start reporting every judge who puts you down and you'll soon have quite a reputation of your own. But if the person with the purple ribbon is inebriated, if he flatly refuses to acknowledge the presence of the dog and of you for no reason whatsoever, if he takes back awards he has made *after* he has marked his book and changes his rulings, then you should report him.

Go *quietly* to the superintendent's tent and ask to see the A.K.C. or C.K.C. representative. If the show superintendent asks if he can be of help, thank him kindly and refuse to discuss your grievance with anyone else except the representative. No point is served by wailing to everyone within earshot that you have been insulted. The official will take down your complaint and listen politely. Keep emotions out of it. He can solve nothing on the spot. But he will take your complaint back to "the office" with him, where it will remain confidential but where it will be investigated completely, I can assure you. In fact, you usually get a letter informing you of the action taken.

In order to make it very clear how careful you must be that your complaint is a warranted one, let me tell you a short story.

Many years ago, when I had just received my A.K.C. handling license, I was showing a lovely male Chessie on which I needed just one more point. In those days it was a constant battle to get enough dogs of this breed together for any points at all, let alone majors, and as a member of the show-giving club, I had been delighted when our judge turned out to be a very great and experienced gentleman who had forgotten more about this breed than most of us will ever know. In fact, the Chesapeake people were so impressed with the man's reputation that it turned out to be a five-point major. Well, I proudly tromped into Open Dogs with my marvelous animal who had never been beaten in the classes; I was confident of my one puny little point. The judge was obviously impressed until he examined the dog's mouth. He backed off, excused himself, and sent for a book of standards. He read in it a moment, shut it with a snap, and said quietly as he returned to me, "Martha, I'm terribly sorry but I will have to disqualify this dog. He is badly undershot, and in this breed that fault is a disqualification." I was thunderstruck. I somehow made it out of the ring with all the grace of a wounded hippo and ran for the book of standards myself. Sure enough, undershot was disqualifying—and I, a professional handler, had been showing the dog *without checking my standard!* It was indeed a bitter pill to swallow and taught me more than one valuable lesson, for the owners of the dog, far from being furious at me, as they certainly should have been, immediately and without my knowledge reported the judge to the A.K.C. I later learned that they had impugned his ethnic origin, criticized his attitude, maligned his judgment, and demanded he be reprimanded. Believe me, I was heartsick. I did the only thing I felt was fair. I sat down and wrote a letter to the owners in which I explained that, instead of trying to ruin the man's reputation, they should be glad we at last had found a judge who *knew* the breed standard and *adhered* to it. I said that the fault for this embarrassment was entirely mine. I then wrote the A.K.C. vindicating the judge in every way, assuming complete responsibility for the error, and stating that his attitude was courteous from beginning to end. I added that if all judges knew their breed as well as this man did, we'd all be better off. And finally, I wrote to the judge apologizing for putting him in this position. The owners never did get the dog reinstated, for he was, even to the most inexperienced eye, undershot. But their bad manners and unfair attitude in reporting a judge where there was absolutely no reason for doing so did their breed and their own dogs great harm, in my opinion.

The Person Next to You Is Distracting Your Dog with His Baiting?

Oh my, this is a sticky wicket—because you have to be sure the distraction is being done deliberately. Some novices get so involved with their dogs that they drop liver all over with complete oblivion as to what they are doing to the next dog in line. If this is the case, touch the person gently on the arm and ask him, politely, to please keep his bait in his own area. This should do it. If, however, there is an experienced person involved who baits his own dog and then, when the judge is not looking, throws a piece of liver directly at your dog, you must, of course, take action to protect your entry fee if nothing else. The solution is simple here, too—nasty, true—but if you are convinced it is being done deliberately, than I don't think you have to take this kind of nonsense for one single moment. Pick up the offending bait, wait until the judge cannot possibly miss your action, then walk the few steps to the offender so you approach him in a manner obvious to everyone. Be sure to speak loudly but *very* politely as you hand him his bait and say, "I beg your pardon, but I believe you dropped this." Then go back to your place in line and continue showing your dog.

Your Bitch Comes in Season Just Before a Show?

Some bitches show 100 per cent better when they are in season; some become quite flighty. If your female is one of the former, then by all means go to the show. You'll just have to play it by ear until you know your particular young lady.

Suffice it to say there is no reason to scratch her. The only time you will actually come in contact with the males is if you go WB and have to compete for BOW and/or BOB, but there again, the class bitch is usually last in line. Even if she's not, those who show with any regularity know the economic problems of showing girl-type beasties, and no one whose opinion you value is going to think you crude or ill-bred, *provided* you keep your alluring dumpling in proper seclusion until her turn comes to be judged. It is considered *very* bad manners to stand in the gateway into the ring with a bitch in season and calmly watch the dogs entering erupt into jealous fights and wind up frothing and frazzled. "Oh," you say, "nobody would to *that!*" Wouldn't they just!

A really funny one happened to me at the Sportsman's Show in Canada one winter. I brought my dog early to the ringside as he needed to settle down, and there, big as life, was this innocuous idiot female with a bitch in flagrant season. She chatted away to friends and cronies as dog after dog attempted to do that which comes naturally. All the amateur dog handlers were in a swivet, which was nothing compared to the state of their male dogs. I was the only professional in miles, so I took it upon myself to tap her on the shoulder and say quietly, "Miss, is your bitch in season?" "Oh, yes," she replied as proudly as she would have answered me if I had asked, "Lady, did your dog win the Nationals this year?" She turned back to her socializing, and I tapped again. "Miss, your bitch is really distracting everyone's male. Don't you think it might be better if you took her over . . ." I got no further. She turned on me in a rage. "Look, lady, I paid my money and I've got a right to be here just like you." Bang!

Now, dear friends and gentle readers, I am normally a peace-loving soul. But inconsideration and gross stupidity rile me a mite. I loosened my dog's leash just enough and he assumed the position. Feeling the sudden movement at her side, she looked down, and then, horrified, started to turn on me again. I smiled and said, "His stud fee is two hundred and fifty dollars."

We all doubled over as she fled with her chaste child.

When the judge, in examining your bitch, finishes with the front end, I usually say, "Sir, she's in season." I think the reasons for this courtesy are obvious. Always make sure any handler of a male near you knows your bitch's indelicate condition. If you make the Group, warn those around you immediately. And when not being examined or gaited, keep as out-of-the-way as possible. We explained earlier about bitches in season at benched shows.

The Steward Calls Your Class into the Ring in Catalogue Order or the Group into the Ring in Alphabetical Order?

Every now and then, particularly at Canadian shows where the practice is becoming quite commonplace, Irish Setters, Open Dogs, for instance, will be called into the ring in catalogue order. This means, of course, that the first Irish setter listed in the catalogue as an open dog will enter the ring first, followed by the second listed dog, etc. Sometimes this is done to make the steward's job easier as she is responsible for checking off each exhibit by number as it appears. Sometimes the judge requests this system because it does away with giving unfair advantage to the amateur or professional who has a dog that is difficult to control when back in the pack. Frankly, I think it is a good idea and I never object to this procedure. You see, I have no sympathy for the "handler" who admits that he has to go first because he can't control his dog otherwise. In the first place, if he is so inexperienced or inept that he doesn't know how to make room for a fast dog in a slow class, he has no business calling himself a handler; in the second place, if this were true in my case, I certainly wouldn't be stupid enough to say so out loud!

There are many handlers in both countries who are convinced they cannot win if they are not first in line. Toward this end they position themselves in the ring entrance well ahead, preventing anyone else from getting ahead of them. This is ridiculous, and making everyone stay in catalogue order prevents a sharpy or a prima donna from dominating a class which should offer equal opportunity to everyone.

I do, however, object strenuously when some genius decided it would be nice to line up the dogs eligible for Group judging in alphabetical order. Whoever dreamed this one up is for the birds! Let's use the Hound Group by way of example.

For years the Afghan led off in the Hound Group; even if he came in late he was put up front automatically without anyone batting an eyelash, not because the handler was famous and deserved preferential treatment, but because he was probably the fastest dog in the group. He was followed by the larger hounds which were happily welcomed to the front of the line by the Basset or Dachshund folks. We all adjusted ourselves comfortably with the biggies "here" and the littles "there" and the problems were minimal. Now along comes somebody—usually a steward who is frantic she won't be able to get everyone's number as they arrive—and behold!, the giant Wolfhound is looming above the smaller Whippet; the Foxhound breathing down the neck of the Dachshund, and the poor Basset being chased by the faster Beagle who is trying to outrun the Coonhound. As I said, ridiculous! Handlers are frustrated, dogs are nervous, and the judge couldn't get a true picture of group movement in a million years.

Having gotten everybody's number as they entered, the steward now does what she should have done to begin with and goes down the line a second time. Then the judge comes along and says, "Ok, all big dogs up at the front!" EEEek!

When the steward calls my group to the ring alphabetically, I get into the ring as ordered. The minute I'm in, however, I go to the part of the line that makes sense. If this disturbs her, I explain that I will be glad to move at the judge's indication. Be polite but firm— don't be pushed, if you can avoid it, into a ridiculous situation which could be deterimental to your chances.

Nothing Works?

There you were, all my loyal little chickens, clustered around the Rhodesian Ridgeback ring at Atlantic City, and I had "Ché" looking splendid and could smell the delicious aroma of success. We were put at the head of the line and kept there, and Madame Judge kept coming back to us. Ah, yes, wondrous, calm, efficient, know-it-all Martha Covington Thorne was in her glory—until, with feet of clay clearly exposed for all to see, the idol toppled from her pedestal. "Ché" decided not to move.

I tried everything I had ever heard of and invented a few tricks of my own—*and nothing worked.* We had "it" in the palms of our hot little hands and the dear dog simply died. It was very hot, the class was very big; he baited magnificently but he simply decided someone else, *anyone* else, could do the moving, *he* was just not interested. Never could I have dreamed up a better example of the point I am trying to make. There are, indeed, times when all one's knowledge, inventiveness, cleverness, and inventory of prayers are of no avail. You *fail.* Period. It's not that you do a bad job—it's just that at this particular moment, even the Heavenly Father couldn't succeed; it's not in the cards.

So what do you do? You take the dog back, give him water, exercise him, and tuck him in for a nice long nap. There's no point in swearing at the dog, punishing him for letting you down (which he most certainly did!), or jerking him around so everyone can see what a genuine ass you are. It's over, done with, the day is shot. The thing to concentrate on is the fact that the dog must forget it, too, before it comes time for him to enter the ring *the next time.* "The next time"—that's what you should be worrying about. You can't do a thing about what just happened except cry quietly in your brew when you are alone. But perhaps you can do something to make sure it doesn't happen again. Concentrate *ahead* of yourself, not *behind.*

It is healthy for all of us to realize that everyone fails. It's the way I keep telling you: nobody's smarter or luckier or more gifted in the ring than *you* are—but *not all the time,* lamb chops!

DIFFICULT DECISIONS

To Show in Classes After Championship Points Have Been Won

Now we have to face a chronic "hot spot" in the world of dog shows, and I don't suppose in that world there is any more inflammatory subject than this one: "Is it ethical (right, proper, fair) to continue showing in the classes once you have finished a dog?"

We are going to tackle this monster at some length because it is absolutely imperative to present all sides fairly and completely. Personally, I have very definite feelings on this matter born of long years of experience, and after we have examined it from every possible angle, I will give you my humble opinion. But when all is said and done, you will have to make up your own mind and take your stand.

To Pull or Not to Pull

Now, then, arguments in favor of continuing to show in the classes after you are reasonably sure you have completed the required points for championship include:

1. Why not? I'm eligible!
2. I want to get "insurance" points.
3. I've paid my entry and I'm going to show.
4. It's good experience for the dog.
5. To heck with anybody else. It's my dog and I'll do as I darned well please.

In discussing the "in favor" standpoint, one has to agree with No. 1, No. 3 and the latter half of No. 5: the dog *is* eligible; the owner *has* paid his entry; indeed, the dog *does* belong to him. Where we run into trouble is the first half of No. 5 ("To heck with everybody else"). This attitude can be just as wrong as the counter-attitude (i.e., that in order to be a "good sport" it's your job to help everyone else finish their dogs). The idea of "insurance points" is valid only when the dog finishes "on the nose" (i.e., with exactly fifteen points in the U.S., or ten in Canada). Then I think most people would agree it's a good idea to try to get another point or two in case you counted wrong or, after some prior show at which you took points, some dog was found to be ineligible, thereby perhaps reducing your point total. I seriously doubt, however, that your dog truly needs ring "experience" if he has finished his championship.

Now let's look at arguments against continuing to show in the classes once you're finished:

1. It's not fair to everyone else.
2. You're not giving the other guy a chance.
3. You're taking the points away from somebody else who needs them.

Unfortunately, none of these arguments make a great deal of sense, in my opinion. As for No. 1, life itself is unfair; that's the fact, man, and the sooner you accept it, the quicker you'll start enjoying the process of living. Nos. 2 and 3 are based on a completely unfounded supposition that just because a dog won points on Saturday and finished, he is therefore going to do the same thing on Sunday, automatically. Oh, Lordie me, wouldn't it be wonderful if this were true?

In taking a fair look at both sides, I like to recall the definition a famous philosopher once gave of good manners. "Good manners," he said, "are what you do when no one else is looking." I'll paraphrase that for good sportsmanship: "Good sportsmanship is what you do when you don't *have* to do anything." And I think good sporsmanship as well as good manners must always be taken into account in any competitive situation.

You cannot make a flat, black-and-white ruling here, because we must consider the type of dog involved. While I have never knowingly brought a "bad" dog into the show ring (i.e., a rotten, substandard example of a breed), I have put titles on dogs I felt were not as good as other champions I have finished. If I take a dog that I feel is justified in having his title, period, I make it very clear to his owner that we would get this dog's championship and then retire it immediately, because while it had much to offer as a stud dog or brood bitch, it was simply not a show dog. If such a dog finished on Saturday and one were sure enough of points to feel "safe," then the dog should most definitely be "pulled" (not shown) on Sunday. Knowing the dog was in no way, shape, or form, group winning material, it would be, in my eyes, unethical, bad manners, unsportsmanlike, and just plain wrong to show the animal further. In the case of the breeder-handler, you would be admitting that you really didn't know a good dog when you saw it and were probably suffering from kennel blindness; neither impression would help when it came to selling puppies or establishing a good reputaton for your kennel. In the case of the professional it would be a clear-cut case of accepting money under false pretenses.

Then along comes the dog everybody has been waiting for. He enters the classes, but instead of merely racking up points, he explodes onto the dog-show scene with BOBs over Specials, majors right and left, Group placements galore, all indicating the very real possibility of a Best in Show from the classes! He finishes on a Saturday—now tell me, were you the owner, breeder, or handler of that dog, would *you* pull him?

I tend to think not! And in my opinion, pulling this kind of a dog would be just as unethical, unsportsmanlike, and stupid as pushing a dog in the classes when you know there is no place for him to go. You would also be showing the worst possible kind of bad manners toward a fine dog who deserves his moments in the sun. When you have an ordinary champion, you have an obligation not to demean him by placing him in positions with which he cannot cope; when you have an extraordinary champion, you have an enormous obligation not to hold him back or deny him any laurel he is worthy of winning.

Decisions of this kind require a great deal of that very rare ingredient known as guts. But please notice that in these two theoretical cases, the decisions I have favored have nothing to do with whether an amateur or a professional is involved or with what is best for the other exhibitors. They have to do *only* with *what was best for the dog.* And this particular outlook is one I think all of us tend to turn our backs on when we are sometimes tempted to practice "inlook" instead of "outlook."

Of course the heady wine of winning has a lot to do with your decision. But that winning doesn't just represent silver trophies. It represents the dog's eligibility for national, perhaps international, recognition, and that recognition means a better reputation for his kennel name, his owner, his breeder, his handler. It means an opportunity, in the case of a bitch, to have her puppies recognized for what they, in turn, might contribute to the breed; in the case of a dog it means stud services not just to bitches but to the *finest* bitches in his breed, and his imprint on that breed could be invaluable. The day he is "pulled" to give somebody else a chance might be just the day he could go all the way— or the day on which another member of his breed does exactly that thousands of miles away, and then our "quiz kid" is playing catch-up ball, unnecessarily.

In an effort to embarrass someone who has decided to show his finished dog, some handlers and amateur exhibitors will congratulate that person loudly at ringside when they are sure the judge is within earshot. "Hey, Martha, heard you finished that dog yesterday. Way to go!" More often than not this backfires, since you are in effect telling the judge what to do, and that *never* goes over well!

Quietly asking someone if he hasn't already finished his dog is quite OK in my book, if you have the intestinal fortitude to do so. Problem is, How are you going to know if he's telling the truth when he explains he's not sure about the two points he got April 2nd at such and such a show and wants insurance? You have no way of checking up on what he says, so why bother?

Why doesn't everyone just show their own dogs and leave the backbiting to tigers in the zoo? Just make sure you are playing by the rules and not belittling either yourself or your fellow exhibitors. Amateurs and professionals alike make entries on behalf of *their* dogs, not on behalf of *yours.* The old political saying, "If you can't stand the heat get out of the kitchen," may sound cruel, but winning isn't always pleasant, and losing doesn't always have to be sad.

Majors

Majors, in popular breeds where they occur frequently, as well as in less popular breeds where they turn up only once every six months, are never to be taken lightly. So now we come to a dilemma: you enter a pair of shows which turn out to have majors on both days. All the stars are in proper orbit, and you win the major on Saturday. We'll assume that this is either your second major and leaves you with just one point to go, or it finishes you.

Now what do you do? If you stay in the Sunday class you may take the points, but you don't need the major and every one else is very desirous of collecting same. Your dog has little chance for anything beyond Best of Winners, due to the judges involved or any number of other factors. So you decide you'll pull and give everyone else a whack. But if you do pull, the major will be broken.

Here are your options. The professional with just one point to go *has* to enter. He has contracted with the owner to finish the dog, and if he can finish it with three majors instead of two, so much the better.

The amateur with just one point to go should feel, I think, exactly the same way, but he is governed only by his own feelings and can do as he pleases. I don't think he should be censured for staying in there, particularly, if it is a popular breed in which the opportunity to win majors occurs frequently.

If the dog was finished at the Saturday show, then it seems reasonable for you to go to the other class people and explain the predicament. Would they like you to pull and break the major, or would they prefer you to perhaps send the dog in with someone less experienced? The professional handler should settle the problem with the owner before the show, so that the decision is made by the owner and the handler is only doing what he is told.

The main thing to remember is to give people a chance to do the right thing. Don't start jumping up and down over a broken major until you are very sure of your facts. Perhaps the major is being broken unintentionally by someone who, if you explained the situation, would be only too happy to help.

Several years ago I went to chat with a group of people I knew by the Pointer ring but it was immediately obvious a bad brannigan was brewing. It seems that Mr. Smith, who took the major in Pointers the day before, was sitting "right over there" and wasn't going to show today because he didn't need the major. He was breaking the major and "there oughta be a law . . ." etc, etc. "there *is* a law," I explained. "If the dog is with him 'right over there,' then he can be forced to show it because the dog is present on the show grounds—that's what it says in the book!" Very proud of myself, I found the A.K.C. rep and brought him back to the group, who explained the situation with much emotion and indignation.

Thank goodness the rep was the calm, deliberate type! He agreed that he could force the man to show if the dog were on the grounds and would be happy to step in if necessary. "But," he counseled, "has anyone asked the man his intentions? Don't you think it might be a good idea to approach him in a friendly way first?" Much grumbling and grumping followed. Since I had nothing better to do, I strolled over and, after talking with him a bit, asked him what he planned to do. He smiled pleasantly and said, "Why, I thought I'd let my nephew here show the dog; Jeff's only thirteen but he's been practicing and I thought this might be a good time for him to try his wings."

I reported to the group, all of whom were quite shamefaced, I'm happy to record. Jeff did quite a nice job, but someone else got the major.

By way of another example of giving the other guy a chance to be as thoughtful and considerate as you are (ahem!), I remember a three-show circuit in which I had a Wolfhound who needed to go Winners Dog all three days to finish. We made it the first and second days and during the classes I spoke several times to a very attractive, very small, and *very* inexperienced young French girl who was attempting to show an enormous dog and getting nowhere. The dog wasn't trained, the girl had no idea what was expected from her or her dog, and it was just "bad news." I made a few sympathetic overtures, but she left the ring both days in tears.

Her experiences were so traumatic that she decided to withdraw the dog the third day, which would make it impossible for me to finish my dog and would reduce the points for everyone else. My owner came to me weeping tears of her own. Remembering the lesson I had learned from the incident I have just described to you, I suggested she go to the girl, explain the situation, and ask if she would reconsider. I suggested that since the dog was obviously a handful, I would be happy to supply an experienced person to handle for her at no charge if she would show the dog the last day.

The girl was flabbergasted at the thought that she might be inconveniencing anyone. She agreed to show, I found her a very capable handler, and when the smoke had cleared from the Wolfhound ring that day, I had my precious championship and the green dog went Reserve Winners Dog, the first award of any kind he had ever won at a dog show.

Everyone was delighted and again the tears fell—but happy ones this time.

Sometimes it seems that no matter how hard you try to practice good sportsmanship, things still go wrong. I once sent one of my Chesapeakes in with a very green young assistant in order to give my fellow competitors a chance at a major I didn't need. She was carefully informed that we did not need the points that day—and still she won. In fact, she took the breed from the classes!

There's still another facet of majors: is it "ethical" to enter hoping for a major (which you need to finish) and, if the show doesn't draw a major, stay home? Of *course* it is! Certainly it may cut down the points of the others who entered. But since no one has found a foolproof way to predict majors, this is what everyone does "wot needs 'em." You enter with hope and a prayer, and if the show draws only one or two entries in your breed, then you stay home, trying not to think what you could have done with that entry money, but at least you've saved on gas, motel, etc., and may hope that the next show has more to offer you.

I enjoy helping fellow exhibitors at dog shows whenever I can. And I never cease to be warmed by their thoughtfulness of me. But I will say here as I say in my classes: your first obligation is to your own dog. Just make very sure that when you win it's something you can be very proud of. The rest of the world won't always like you, or always hate you, or even understand you much of the time. But the guy in the mirror each morning when you brush your teeth—what does *he* think of you? Every decision you make in handling these problems will not be fair to everyone. Sometimes you'll make decisions that will turn out to be not so hot for *you!* But if you take all the rules and all the facts into consideration and then make as *honest* a decision as you can, in the long run things will even out for everyone, winner and loser alike.

THE SPIRIT OF SHOWING

Campaigning a Champion

Too many people don't seem to understand the purpose of showing a dog after he has finished his title and is a champion of record.

Once it is decided that a dog is Specials material and worthy of going on (we discussed earlier the sort of dog to be retired after finishing), he is on the road almost constantly. We know we have a champion. We have a hunch he is better than a lot of other champions, so we set out to prove we're right, and every time he takes a breed or wins

The first time he stuck his very busy nose into a show ring it was Best of Breed from the puppy class over champions of record, followed by a fourth in adult and a first in puppy Terrier Groups!

Winning seemed duck soup to this Colored Bull Terrier; getting him to stop wiggling long enough to get his picture taken was the hard part! Note that his armband number is "lucky" 13! He is Ch. Baymarket's Great General, owned by the Voodoo Kennels of Mr. and Mrs. F. Austin, Ste. Anne de Sabrevois, Quebec, Canada. *Photo by Bob Streeter*

a group, people say, "Oh, he's a Such-and-Such Kennel dog, isn't he? Such-and-Such must breed good dogs." The more the dog wins, the more people are impressed, the more bitches are brought to Such-and-Such Kennel to be bred, the more Such-and-Such stud dogs are used, the more good puppies appear with Such-and-Such blood lines—and this is why dogs are specialed. This plus that wonderful thrill of owning (or handling, or both) a top winning animal which you can look at with pride and say, "This one is what I believe in, world! Beat him—if you can!"

American and Canadian Champion Long John Silver is a powerful moving, strikingly marked Landseer Newfoundland. He holds the title of Canada's Top Show Dog by winning the prestigious Show of Shows competition during which he defeated over fifty Best in Show dogs by one of the highest scores ever recorded in this event!

A true Canadian product (Canadian bred, owned, and handled) "L.J." belongs to Lynn Raymond of Ottowa, Ontario. This magnificent example of a working breed is shown with one of his biggest boosters, Judge Anthony Hodges, who gave the dog some of his earliest wins.

In addition to having won multiple Specialty shows, as this book went to press Long John had over twenty all-breed Best in Shows to his credit!

When to Stop Showing

Knowing when to start a dog on a show career is tricky; knowing whether or not to special it is not always easy. But the hardest decision in the world to make regarding that show dog of yours, is knowing when it's time to *stop* showing.

The glossy color photos in the dog magazines, the roar of the crowd at ringside, the beautiful silver, and the deference extended by authorities you respect—these comprise a heady wine! Pulling from competition, at just the right moment a "hot" dog with a long record of wins is a sticky wicket. No one can promise you won't always wonder, "What would he have done if I'd kept him in there another six months?" There will be Helpful Harrys who will swear you took him out too soon, and others who will say you should have pulled him months ago.

Everybody has his own definition, I am sure, of what is meant by cruelty to animals. To me, the height of cruelty is to keep pushing a dog after he has secured his place for all times in the record books, after he has made his name (and yours). There is, in truth, a season for all things, and when a dog is at the top of the heap, when he has beaten the best and could probably keep beating them a little longer, that is the time to hang up the show leash. That word "probably" is crucial. There's always a *chance* a great dog will bite the dust every time he enters the ring; it's always *possible* he will lose. But when a defeat looms as "probable," that's the time to walk away from it all with an "is" at your side, not a "has been." Quit while the dog is where he deserves to be—on top—and while people remember the things he stands for *now,* not what he used to be.

Truly great dogs wander through a person's life all too infrequently. They deserve a crack at fame and fortune, and it is your responsibility to give them that chance if you have to sleep in the car and eat peanut butter and kibble in order to afford the entry fees. They never ever deserve disrespect. So don't wait until you are leaving the ring one day and have a whisper break your heart: "Yeah, he's great—but you should have seen him in the old days!"

The toy breeds are generally "toy-like" only in size. They are hardy, active, opinionated "little people." In this picture, American and Canadian Ch. Cadaga's Saluté accepts another group placement from judge Michelle Billings. "Toot" won many groups with his sound movement and sparkling personality. He is owned by Tom and Susie King, Saratoga Springs, New York. When not collecting prizes at dog shows, this animated charmer with his butterfly ears spends his time "running" a household of Doberman Pinschers and Rhodesian Ridgebacks —and there is no question who is boss! *Photo by William P. Gilbert*

Another Look at Standards

At the beginning of this book when we were concentrating on picking just the right show puppy for you, we urged you to read your breed standard. We explained what a standard was and urged you to study it carefully until you understood it completely. Now let's take another look at that breed standard and try to put it in as clear a perspective as possible.

Time after time a novice comes out of the ring after a disheartening loss and complains to family and friends, "I don't understand why he loses, he fits the standard perfectly." If this is true—and it often is!—does the fault lie with the judge? The handler? The dog? The breeder? The standard?

Just as often as this occurs, a dog wins while breeders stand around the ring shaking their heads and muttering dolefully, "He's just beautiful but he's *not* a Ridgeback!" (or Bulldog or Dalmatian or whatever). If this is true—and it often is!—where does the fault lie in *this* instance?

In none of the three phases of the dog world we are dealing with is there more room for personal opinion and interpretation than in the judging of show dogs. In the field, there is enough room for personal opinion to allow one judge to feel it is a serious offense for a dog to wriggle around on the line, while another doesn't give a darn as long as the dog doesn't go before it is sent. And one obedience judge may take more points away for a slow sit than another judge will. But in obedience and in the field there are very strict rules which prevent any judge from flunking or throwing out any dog that completes the designated test. In the show ring, the only rule or guideline the judge has to go by in evaluating each of many different dogs is the breed standard. And because judges are individuals, very few of them see alike in all matters.

Unless we are considering a disqualifying point in a standard, in which case a judge's preference has nothing to do with his ultimate decision, there is, and I think there *should* be, room for differences in the opinions of people who are considered experts in their field. Otherwise, we would wind up with such a rubber-stamp animal that individual characteristics would count for naught. A judge whose heart flip-flops when a happy, stylish, sound dog flies around the ring can be forgiven for placing him over his less exuberant brother who is just a shade better in shoulder angulation.

However, when a judge reads in the breed standard that the body is to be "not too short," that the stop is "not too pronounced," that the ears should be "fairly long" and the muzzle "quite wide," you must admit, in all fairness, that he is *forced* to be interpretive! These ridiculously vague terms are to blame for much confusion on the judges' part and much dissatisfaction, therefore, with their rulings.

Just as bad as equivocal descriptions, are terms that are familiar only to limited groups of people. The Schipperke standard, in describing correct coat, uses the words "cape," "jabot," and "culotte"—all dressmakers' terms.

Or how about those standards that call for things impossible to determine in a breed ring? The Basenji is supposed to have "far-seeing" eyes, and the bark of the Old English Sheep Dog is supposed to have a "pot-casse ring." I really can't remember having ever shown a Basenji who was asked what distant point he was staring at. And I have yet to exhibit an Old English who was required to bark upon command in the ring.

Other standards commit the ultimate crime: they leave out *any mention* of certain points. While every Pug breeder worth his wrinkles knows that pugs should move soundly with a rolling motion, the gait of this toy dog is not mentioned at all in its breed standard.

This last crime—that of omission—seems to incense some judges. At one time I campaigned a fine dog to many group wins. The only fault anybody was able to single out was that the dog was slightly undershot, a problem we all wished was not present. Unfortunately, many of the dogs of this breed have imperfect mouths, and the mouth is not mentioned in the breed standard. During the years I handled this dog I was sometimes "dumped" for this fault and was perfectly prepared when it happened, though I have always resented judges who turn dogs down with everything else going for them except a single factor. However, I shall never forget one judge who took the time to explain his feelings and the conversation went, as best I can recall, like this:

"He's a nice dog but he's undershot."

"I know. What else didn't you like about him, sir?"

"Nothing. He's absolutely perfect otherwise."

"I know. It's a shame really—especially when the standard doesn't even mention mouth."

"Oh, it doesn't? Well, it certainly should!"

End of Discussion.

Just as I think it's unfair to blame judges for ambiguous standards, I feel it is even worse when a judge decides to impose his own criteria.

So who is to blame for breed standards that contain confusing terminology, nondescriptive phrases, and completely overlook certain important points? Why, every member of every breed club anywhere in the world! Breed standards are written by breed clubs, and breed clubs are composed of people most directly affected by and affecting the improvement of a specific breed of dog.

In the opening paragraph of this chapter I suggested that you study

The tallest dog in the world and the largest member of the Hound Group, the Irish Wolfhound is a "pussycat" where kids are concerned and a loyal, undemanding member of the family. This particular "Woofer" is Ch. Finnegan of Elmbrae, shown taking one of his many breed wins under judge Howard Tyler. A multiple group winner, "Finn" was always one of my favorites. His owner is Dr. Gilles Bernard of Montreal, Canada, a truly devoted breeder and an active member of breed clubs in the U.S. and Canada. *Photo by William P. Gilbert*

your breed standard until you understand it completely. Well, then, tell me, *do* you understand it? Oh, I'm not talking now about terms like *layback, harefoot,* and *cobby.* I'm talking about the adjectives and adverbs which are supposed to form a clear enough word picture for you to be able to close your eyes and envision what a good example of your breed should look like.

If you have doubts and questions, certainly other people do also, and if enough of you feel strongly about this, you can go to your national organization and demand that your standard be clarified. Then a committee is appointed and the task is under way. And, friend, this is some task!

Verily, it is said that the reason the Good Lord was able to create the world in seven days was that he did not belong to a breed club!

In the rewriting of any standard, forget seven weeks, or months; seven *years* is more like it. Not long ago I "sat" upon the standards committee of a national breed club. The chairman was in South Dakota, two members were in California, I was in Vermont at the time, and the other members were in far-flung locations such as Florida and Michigan. This is all very democratic, to be sure, allowing representatives from all sections of the country to participate in the task of making this particular breed standard as easily understood as possible. But at the end of a year and a half I just gave up and resigned. We hadn't progressed three feet, and I doubt if the brave souls who are still working on this project will *ever* agree on a standard they can present to the membership for a vote. And when they do present it, do you know what will happen? It will *not* be approved and will be returned to committee for more "clarification"! The problem would be bad enough if all the committee members could sit down at a great oak table in a nice warm room and be locked inside until they came up with a "perfect" standard. But while Mrs. Jones in Idaho agrees that the correct depth of chest for an East Indonesian Scatterhound is level with the elbows of the dog, Mr. Smith in West Virginia thinks you should have a leeway here of a half inch. Mr. Rogers in New York City feels that's too much leeway, and Miss West of Illinois wants the chest to be measured in distance from the floor. When Chairman Snicklefritz in Kansas gets Mrs. Jones, Mr. Smith, and Mr. Rogers to agree with the first suggestion, Miss West has married, is honeymooning in East Africa, and won't be available to vote for six weeks. It's an impossible task.

What, then, is the solution? To my way of thinking, the only solution is for the A.K.C. and C.K.C. to set up immediately a universal format to which all breed clubs must quickly make their standards conform. Since this could never be accomplished in under a hundred years, we'll have to limp along as we are, making the best of a bad situation.

This leaves us wondering if the standard of any breed is worth considering at all. Certainly we need some sort of guideline for the dedicated breeder, some sort of yardstick for judges. But how much emphasis should we put upon the standard as breeders, exhibitors, judges, and owners? I think there is a great lesson to be learned from the following fable, which was first printed in the *St. Bernard Bulletin,* then reprinted in the *Mount Diablo DTC News:*

A FAIRY TALE, by Robert Hope

Once upon a time, four St. Bernard exhibitors were coming home from a big show. They were driving over a mountain pass in the middle of a violent snowstorm when suddenly their car went into a skid, hit a guard rail, and went careening down a slope about a mile into a ravine. The trailer which they had been pulling, containing their four dogs, landed relatively undamaged next to their car. No one had seen the accident in the blinding storm. As luck would have it, the Saint breeders were trapped inside their car. The door to the trailer, however, had popped open.

The first dog was a very "typey" Saint, as this was what his breeder cared about the most. He made it about a quarter of a mile up the slope before he was gasping for air, and his nasal passages began to freeze because of his foreshortened muzzle. After another 200 yards he was blind and hopelessly lost because the driving snow was piling up in his haws.

The second Saint out of the trailer was bred for the "important things" like prettiness, size, color and perfect markings. He was a beautiful sight to behold, but unfortunately, he too collapsed after only a few hundred yards from the ravages of hip dysplasia.

The third dog to try to summon help had been bred for "soundness." His breeder wouldn't have dreamed of using a dog that wasn't X-rayed free of hip dysplasia. He made it halfway up the slope before he collapsed from exhaustion. He could not cope with the high drifts. His breeder hadn't realized that there was more to "soundness" than hip dysplasia and had neglected to include the head, back, shoulders, forelimbs, feet, chest, lungs, heart and hindquarters in his "breeding for soundness."

The fourth breeder was conscious by now and knew that at last all those years of breeding would pay off. He had bred for type, being careful not to shorten the muzzle so far as to obstruct the breathing or ruin the bite. He was proud of his dog's "tight eyes." His dog had "storybook markings," a "richly" colored coat, and was a very "powerful, proportionately tall, strong and muscular figure." He had an OFA number, of course, but was also big-boned, a "very strong and powerful neck" that was properly muscled; his shoulders were "well laid back." He had a "good rib spring"; he had "strong pasterns" and "strong, tight feet." He had perfect rear angulation and his hocks couldn't have been any stronger. When moving, he was absolutely flawless. . . . With great pride and tears in his eyes, the breeder saw his big, beautiful Saint Bernard drive off into the blinding storm just like the hospice dogs of old.

The last Saint made it up the slope to the road almost effortlessly. A passing state trooper saw the dog and stopped to investigate. As he got out of the car, the dog attacked and ate him. . . .

Standards remind us that there is more than one facet to any dog; when all is said and done, we have to consider the overall, the complete dog. And when it comes to determining the definition of a great dog, is the standard all-important? Or, as we suggested earlier, because a dog is winning, should we perhaps tailor our standard to that particular dog?

Of course a standard is important in evaluating a good show dog; but it is not the only means of evaluation. There are certain things about great racehorses, great ballet dancers, great sports cars that you simply cannot put in words because no words have been written to describe the feeling that particular "champion" inspires in people.

There's a dog who, for the last three or four years, has led his breed in the country in which he is being shown. He is flashy in the extreme, very personable. His record of Best in Shows is unrivaled in many breeds. He fairly shimmers when he enters a ring, but his front movement leaves a lot to be desired and his rear movement is close. To picture him doing the work for which his breed was intended is difficult,

When this picture was taken we called her "Rebecca-bottom." Clearly showing her disdain for the informality of such a nickname, she finished her title in short order so that we simply had to call her Champion Tumac's Rebecca. Her proud owner-breeder is Mrs. Joan MacVicar of North Gower, Ontario, Canada.

"Becky" is shown making her ring debut under judge Mrs. Georgina Lane, who gave her Best of Breed from the Junior Puppy class, and her first points.

A typical Bulldog, she is exceedingly affectionate and also strong-minded.

if not impossible. He does *not* truly conform to standard, but this dog
has made thousands of friends for his breed, and he has done possibly
more than any other dog in that country to convince the public that
show dogs are happy, well-adjusted, healthy animals worthy of admiration and respect. But if you asked one of the thousands of people who
adore him to describe what makes him so great, they, as I, would
stutter and stammer and never be able to explain it at all.

Developing an Eye

So how do we go about getting to the point where each one of us
can truly say, "I know a good dog when I see one."

Read your standard, study it carefully. Then, with that information
tucked securely in your cranium, watch all the dogs you can watch
and study some more. Watch Labradors in the field clearing stone
walls with birds in their mouths. Watch Newfoundlands swimming
along towing boats. Watch Terriers digging holes, and Toys sleeping
in the sun. Watch sled-dog races, Whippet and Greyhound races, coursing events, and obedience trials. Study canine anatomy. It doesn't matter
whether you can list the bones of the foot by memory. But it does
matter that you understand how the foot is attached to the ankle and
what happens if it is not attached correctly and what happens if it is.
Concentrate on the furry breeds until you can tell what their legs are
doing under all that fancy coat as quickly as you can tell a Doberman's
faults as he gaits around a ring. Why is a Chesapeake able to hit the
water like a Mack truck? Why can a Deerhound stop on a dime and
pivot almost in midair? Study still pictures, motion pictures, and old
paintings. Become familiar with all types of temperament, from fawning
to defensive shyness. Try to fit the dog you see today to the history
that produced him.

While you are studying, don't forget "type": probe it until you understand that there are different kinds of dogs in which different things
are important. I started out in sporting dogs and, as I trained them
in obedience and ran them in the field, I learned the importance of
soundness to these working animals. When I began handling toy breeds,
I was fortunate in starting out with a toy that moved soundly and
truly. When we were beaten, I would get quite hot under the collar
because the dog that won, like most of the other dogs in this particular
breed, did not move well. Finally I sat down with an internationally
respected breeder, handler, and now judge of toy breeds, and he explained to me about type. "Certainly soundness is important; but remember, toy dogs were not bred to carry messages in wartime, to pull
carts, or to hunt birds all day. They don't have to do a great deal of
heavy labor. They spend much of their lives on laps just being loved

The silky-coated, sweet-dispositioned English Setter is a breed that retains its popularity in the Sporting Group year after year. This particularly charming young lady is American and Canadian Ch. Guys and Dolls Taste of Honey owned by David Ruml, M.D., of South Strafford, Vermont. During her show career, "Tastee" gave her many fans plenty of opportunity to celebrate with multiple specialty wins and groups. She is shown here going Best in Show at Sherbrooke, Quebec, Canada, under judge Gordon Parham.

because they are beautiful. That is really their role in life; in this case, I personally find that type is more important than movement." And while I sat there like a balloon from which the air was slowly leaking, I came to admit that he was, of course, quite right.

When you can admit there is *always* more to be learned, then maybe, just maybe, you'll develop what is known as "an eye for a dog." Most often people are born with this gift, but it certainly can be developed to a great extent. The trouble comes when, after you feel you have it, you try to describe what it is to somebody else!

What Makes a Great Show Dog?

Maybe it's particularly difficult to describe greatness, because it means something a little different to all of us. If I see a Chow Chow that turns me on and say, out loud, "Isn't he great?" and the guy next to me says, "I hate Chows!" I know I'm not talking to a dog person. There are certain breeds I favor more than others; I'm sure we all feel this way. But the "great" dog transcends this preference because there's that magic something about him, no matter what the breed.

Without the standard to guide us we couldn't develop the great dog; without the mystery of greatness, the standards wouldn't mean a thing.

Once I knew a Mary Poppins-type lady who had the loveliest, naughtiest Golden Retriever that ever flunked obedience class. I once asked the owner why she had named her "Sherry" and she replied, "Because she is the color of sherry and she warms the heart."

Maybe that, after all, is the answer. The Best of Breed Ridgeback with the ridge that isn't exactly perfect, the Group 1 Papillon whose butterfly ears could use more fringe, the Best in Show Bouvier des Flandres whose coat is a little too soft—one could argue for hours how important it was that they did not conform 100 per cent to the standard. But no one could ever deny that they "warm the heart."

All breeds of dogs are divided into six Groups. One of the hardest jobs any judge faces is to compare the merits of many different breeds—some large, some small, some long-coated, some short-coated—within a single Group. Four placements only are awarded in each Group.

6

Professional Handlers

Weekend after weekend you are going to be sharing show rings across the country with that form of life known as the Professional Handler.

In this country, professional show handlers until recently had to be licensed by the American Kennel Club. Working with other organizations, such as the Owner-Handlers Association and the Professional Handlers Association, the A.K.C. has done a good job of keeping standards of handling up and ethics among handlers and exhibitors at an equally high level.

In Canada, there has never been licensing of handlers by the Canadian Kennel Club or any other body, and anyone who feels competent, whether he is or not, can charge to take dogs into the ring. When I first went to Canada, I was shocked at the lack of professionalism. Then, little by little, I began to hear rumors about handlers associations, and soon, the Professional Handlers Association of Canada, once defunct from lack of interest, was regrouped. At the same time, the long-dormant Canadian Professional Dog Handlers Association came to life, and suddenly the quality of handling started to improve, and with this we began to see a much better quality of dogs in the rings in Canada.

GETTING STARTED

Many young people with some small background in dog shows aspire to become professional handlers. "Handler" to them means a white show lead and a purple ribbon with a mink-clad client running along before you covering your path with gold coins. The ones who "make it" as handlers are those who learn from the ground up over a period of years. If you are interested in being a handler and believe you have the personality for it, work around dogs: that's the best advice you can get from anybody. Work for veterinarians, cleaning out cages until you can look at a stool and know instantly whether it's a healthy one or not, and why, and until you can identify worms in your sleep. Work for a grooming shop, bathing, trimming, scissoring, de-matting. When you can handle the average owner of the dogs you'll be grooming and go home smiling, you'll be halfway there, believe me! Start early to apply to handlers to help at their kennels or at shows on weekends, but don't get discouraged if we don't send a private car to pick you up the moment we get your letter. Most of us have people who work with us year after year, and taking in new, unknown people, is often hard on everybody. Letters of recommendation help. But as well-recommended as you come, there's no way to tell how you'll do "under fire" until you are put in a tough situation at a dog show. And by the time I discover that if, in a nervous moment, I raise my voice to you, you will dissolve in tears and run for the lady's room, I could have lost a client. So it isn't that professionals are unsympathetic to newcomers; its just that our livelihood depends upon dependable people, and if we have such creatures around us we're not panting to take a flier on an unknown.

If you hope to be a pro, get every bit of dog experience you can. Read everything you can get your hands on; learn how dogs are bred, whelped, trained, groomed, fed, vetted, disciplined, put down, bought, sold, shipped, exercised—learn everything you can about *every kind of dog*. Before you're through, you'll admit many times, I promise you, that you are floored by what there is to learn and by how little you know. And when you accept the fact that in any field of dogs you can *never* afford to *stop* learning, you are on your way at last!

WHETHER OR NOT TO USE A HANDLER

With more and more excellently trained amateurs handling top dogs and winning, it is not always as easy to identify the professional handler as it was in the old days. There was a time when the professional was identified as "the one who's always smiling and isn't nervous," or as "the one who always wins." Today, the breeder-exhibitor is showing more and enjoying every minute of it. So just what makes a professional different from an amateur—what else, that is, beyond the obvious answer: he makes his living, or a part of his living, showing dogs?

Remember the old rhyme, "Twixt the optimist and the pessimist the difference is droll/The optimist sees the donut, the pessimist sees the hole."? Some dog wag once paraphrased: "Twixt the amateur and the professional the difference is funny/The amateur sees the dog, the professional sees the money." The actual picture is hardly that cut and dried. There are professionals who refuse to take bad dogs out regardless of the money involved, and there are amateurs who want to campaign a dog because it is the "in" thing to do, to heck with whether it's a good dog or not, and money is no object.

One of the greatest changes in recent years is in the relationship between the amateur and the professional. When I first started out, I was blasted because I gave handling tips to people who asked me. I was warned by other pros to stop such practices or I'd "teach" my way into the poorhouse. I never found this to be true, and today professional handlers are teaching clinics and holding handling classes everywhere. Some do it to augment their income; some do it to drum up interest in their field of endeavor; some donate their services as their "contribution" to the field they have chosen. There is plenty of room for both amateur and professional and an enormous need for both. In fact, in my view, each faction is interdependent upon the other in order to survive in the highly competitive field of purebred dogs.

Unless the professional handler has staff and backing enough to breed extensively himself and still be free to travel almost constantly, he needs the breeder-owner to create new "stars" for him to finish and campaign.

Some amateurs can't always make all the necessary shows, due to business or family pressures. Some like to handle now and then but hate traveling long distances or the nervous strain of the larger shows. Some amateurs are not able to handle due to health reasons. Some get a kick out of watching, not doing, and others find they can actually send dogs to certain shows with a handler for far less than it would cost if they went themselves. These people are dependent upon the professional handler. Each one scratches the other's back, or should.

There are other, more complicated considerations. Specialist handlers are identified as such by judges long used to seeing them with winning dogs. In toy poodles, for instance, you'd not be likely to win often, especially at first, against the poodle specialist handler. This happens to be one of the less pleasant facts of life. Here it is strictly up to you; with a good dog, eventually, of course, you *will* break through, but whether you want to take one year to finish your dog yourself, or two months to finish him if you hire a professional known in this breed, is a decision *you* have to make.

Whether we like to acknowledge it or not, judges, like the rest of us, may feel insecure and be liable to go with the person they *know* has a reputation for good dogs in a particular breed. So it might be "smart" to start the dog out with a well-known person in that breed so that judges get used to seeing him in the limelight. Then, once he's started, you could take over yourself.

There are also certain breeds in which the competition is so stylized and the classes so large that majors are almost impossible to attain by the novice amateur. In German Shepherds, for instance, it takes over 70 class bitches, present and shown, for a five-point major! It makes good sense in this instance to hire a handler to get your majors at least.

There are lots of folks who show their own dogs regularly and win but who absolutely believe you *cannot* win in Group competition without a handler. (Oh dear, how many BIS's I could have won if this were true!) But true or not, they *believe* this, and therefore are better off with a handler at that level.

There *are* judges who are professionally oriented; to deny it would be ridiculous. There are also more and more judges coming along who delight in giving the Bred-by-Exhibitor entries the nod whenever they can; and more and more of the new judges truly do judge the dogs and only the dogs, be it in breed or Group. Knowing this, the wise amateur doesn't waste his money exhibiting under those few people who are blatantly political. If, however, he knows one of these judges will flip over his dog if handled by a particular person, he has the option of plugging away himself or hiring that particular pro.

Of course, there are certain dogs that simply demand a professional touch. These are the dogs that are very different in type from most of those being shown in a breed; or dogs that are exceedingly fractious in public; or dogs that are so "at home" with their owners that they are bored to death in the ring and show it.

There are so many considerations to be taken into account when deciding whether or not to use a handler that it becomes a very personal, very involved decision. But I have never felt that you should have to apologize for using a professional or for *not* using a professional.

Certainly there are big differences between the amateur and the professional, but they are just that, differences, not barriers, as some people imagine.

When Joe Dokes decides to make a show dog out of his pride and joy and constantly loses, he can blame it on anything he wishes— crooked judges, lousy weather, influence peddling, dishonest competitors, dirty professionals. But in the long run he is perfectly free to turn his back on the whole thing and quit. No one is depending upon his attendance at dog shows to put bread and butter on the dinner table. If he's too stubborn to quit, he is equally free to keep on exhibiting and losing for the rest of his life. After all, its *his* dog, *his* money, *his* business what he does with *his* time!

But when you start fiddling with somebody *else's* pride and joy and charging money for it—somebody *else's* money—then the picture changes drastically. The professional puts his reputation on the line every time he walks into a ring, so he'd better be darned sure he knows what he is doing or there is going to be trouble in the teepee!

So, it behooves the professional to be seen in the ring with dogs that not only *can* win but that *do* win with some regularity, or it might just occur to the owner that perhaps somebody else could do a better job. Also, there are more capable people waiting in the wings these days than ever before. If the professional loses his dogs, he loses his ability to make a living.

Viewed from this realistic angle, winning takes on a much more serious implication for the pro than for the amateur. *Everybody* wants to win, that's for sure! But if the amateur loses, he can always hope for better luck next time; when the pro loses he is in danger of there not *being* a next time, and therefore he takes every possible care to insure that his dog is as ready to win as human ability, knowledge, and experience can make him. He is groomed to perfection, he is conditioned within an inch of his life, he is coddled and jollied into being a happy, eye-catching, heart-stopping sight to behold. The handler picks his clothing carefully to complete the picture he hopes will put him in the winners circle, and his dog's tack is as clean and correct as possible for that particular dog. He knows which judges favor what kind of dogs and how they like a dog to be presented; he tailors one to the other carefully, so as not to waste judges' time bringing them dogs they won't look at twice and so as not to waste entry money and handler's fees in a situation where his dog has absolutely no real chance of doing anything. He recognizes there is a difference, sometimes, between the dog that fits the breed standard as absolutely as possible and the dog that has Best in Show potential although he may not be so perfect standard-wise. These are the reasons why professionals do win much of the time in whatever breed they are handling.

Now, then, instead of sulking and pouting in fourth place weekend after weekend, damning these people because they win too much, it might be an excellent idea to take a deep breath and face the truth squarely: *none of the things listed above are beyond the means or the abilities of the average amateur handler, not a single one!*

If you are fortunate enough to have a really good dog, then I think you have a serious obligation to that dog and to his breed to do your absolute best on his behalf once you have decided to engage in competition with him at any level.

It most certainly does *not* always follow that a professional can do what no amateur can! It is *not* a fact of life that dogs lose simply because they are not professionally handled. Good dogs lose because they are badly presented. If you apply yourself, study, practice, learn, compete to win with an open mind at all times, and if you have a really good dog, you can win with the best of them; it happens every day. But it is unbelievably hard work and demands a concentration on the ultimate goal worthy of a chess master. If you do not care to exert this much effort, then hire someone who will make it his job to give that dog the chance he deserves. But whatever you do, please don't blame the professional because you don't know what you're doing, or are too lazy, or too busy elsewhere to learn what you must know to do top winning at dog shows.

CHOOSING A HANDLER

Once you have made up your mind to go with a pro, the big problem is how to choose the best man or woman for your dog. The dog's personality must certainly be taken into account. Timid, sensitive dogs can be given confidence, which often develops into that star charisma, when placed in just the right hands. The high-strung, opinionated quiz kid needs another kind of personality on the other end of *his* leash. But how to decide?

Leaving your dog at home, go to some dog shows. *Watch* the professionals at work. How are they received by those around them? Winning is important, so find out if they win with their dogs. But make sure of what kind of dogs they are winning with. Are the animals well-conditioned and anxious to please? Watch as they feed their animals, as they groom them. Do they give the dogs ample time out of their crates? What about the assistants: do you like them too? Wait until the handler you might be interested in is taking a break and introduce yourself. Tell him why you are there and what you have on your mind. Above all, *never be ashamed for not knowing and never apologize for asking questions.* Talk to your friends and ask them for their recommendations, but run these recommendations down yourself, firsthand. Never forget that what Mrs. Jones might like in a handler could easily drive you and your family right up the wall. Personalities are very much involved, and if you and a certain handler strike sparks the first time you meet, then no matter how highly recommended he comes, neither one of you will be happy with the relationship.

Again we find that absolutes are leaky buckets in which to put much faith. It does not necessarily follow that the top handler in the country at a given moment will automatically be the best for you and your dog. He has other commitments to long-standing clients, and as his newest client, you will be low man on the totem pole in case of ring conflicts with other dogs. On the other hand, it isn't always a good idea to pick the smallest handler you can find on the theory that he'll have more time for your dog and fewer conflicts; this may be true, but what experience has he in your breed, what reputation for winning with it? There is always the possibility of picking a specialist—someone who handles *only* your breed. But this too presents problems, for he can take only a very few dogs at a time under ordinary circumstances and you may find your dog will take longer to get finished even though he may do more winning than he would otherwise.

For instance, let's imagine you are interested in finishing your Blood-hound. It becomes important for you to know if he is handling any other Bloodhounds before you hire a specific handler. Except at specialty shows, where considerations and conditions often prevail with the co-operation of several different clients, no one handler can ethically take more than one class dog, one class bitch, and one special in any one breed; even then there are going to be problems. For instance, if the class bitch goes winners and the class dog goes winners, then who is going to handle what for Best of Breed? Or if the judge gives your handler Winners Dog, will he be unbiased enough to look at your bitch, with the same handler, for Winners Bitch? Or, if yours is the class dog and he loses, won't the judge be tempted to put up the class bitch for Winners because he has "dumped" the handler in dogs? And if this is so, what will the judge do about the Specials dog if it happens to be yours and if your handler has already won in the classes? While he was not a dog-show buff, the King of Siam put it very well, I think: " 'Tis a puzzlement!" It requires a lot of give and take between the handler and the owner, a lot of trust, a lot of understanding. If you don't have a foundation of mutual respect and downright affection from the very beginning, a normally rocky road is going to be rockier than you could possibly imagine!

If necessary, as you do your handler shopping, make a list of things that come to mind. "Who will handle in your place if you are tied up with some other dog and can't get to the ring with my dog?" "What do you do with the dogs at night?" "Will you continue specific medica-tion my dog is used to (heartworm preventative, for instance)?" "Who is responsible for inoculations and wormings—me or you?" "Am I to make entries?" "How far ahead of the class do you want me to bring the dog to you?" "Who pays vet bills?"

Then narrow your choice of handlers down to two or three and visit their facilities, if at all possible. *Make an appointment* and be on time. Expect to be shown the grooming and bathing area, exercise yards, and runs. Allow enough time to sit down and ask him your questions. And remember, *he'll* have a lot of questions, too—make sure you under-stand them and answer them *honestly*. Let him know just how much you have to spend and get his financial policies down in detail.

Most of the misunderstandings that erupt between clients and han-dlers are based on a simple lack of understanding, so never be afraid to ask about whatever is unclear to you. This is your *right* and it is the handler's duty to do everything he can to make sure you are clear about what is involved if he agrees to handle your dog. Some handlers, like myself, give clients an involved fact sheet, which discusses everything that might be unclear to a green dog person. In addition, my clients sign an "Alternate Handler Contract" in which the reasons for unavoidable ring conflicts are explained, and on which the client indicates his preference for a substitute handler in case I cannot make the ring: himself, another handler, a member of my staff, or "I don't care—I trust you, do the best you can." He is given another form explaining how we handle entries if we are to make them, how much deposit we require, and after all this he signs a slip to the effect that he has read all this information and is in full accord with it. These forms, with the client's signature affixed, go right along with me in his file in my briefcase—and *still* we have misunderstandings from time to time!

Beware of the handler who takes more than one class dog in the breed in which you are giving him a class dog. But if he takes your Open dog, somebody else's Puppy, and some other person's Novice dog in, say, Labradors, what happens if all three win their classes? Only one of the three of you is going to get the professional for Winners; the other two are going to get alternate handlers. Make sure you understand this and make sure your potential handler understands that you understand this kind of pitfall.

Beware of the handler who takes four or five champions out to campaign in the same group—a Shepherd, a Newf, a Bouvier, and a Corgi, for instance. What happens if more than one of *them* wins the breed? Who will handle your dog in the working group?

I am not suggesting that anyone would take a dog with the deliberate intention of deceiving or misleading you. I am only insisting that you take it upon *yourself* to get these things clearly out in the open between you before you start.

YOUR RELATIONSHIP WITH A HANDLER

Once you have decided to go with a handler, *give that person your absolute trust and absolute obedience.* He has very specific obligations to you as owner, which we will go into in a few moments. But what many clients don't understand is that *you* have very definite obligations to *him* also, and not to recognize these and accept them is stupid, nearsighted, and can cost you an awful lot of money.

There are very formal pros with whom you deal largely through assistants or bookkeepers; there are very informal pros you can sit down and share a beer with after the show. There are pros who have a lot of artisitic temperament and get quite emotional under pressure;

there are others who are at their quiet, icy best when facing three conflicts with three top dogs. To learn which kind of a person your employee is, you'll have to know him for more than a weekend or two. But while getting to know him, and even after, *you always owe him the benefit of any doubt.* Question whatever you don't understand, by all means, but never forget he's a human being and, like you, has both strengths and weaknesses.

He works for you—you pay the bills—and you have every right to critize his handling of your dog if you feel deeply about it. But if you are displeased, for *goodness sake* wait until the two of you can sit down alone and hash it out. Nothing sounds worse than an owner talking to another owner derogatorily about her handler, for all the world to hear. If you have decided to hire a person, then it is understood you trust him. *Don't check up on him behind his back* via another owner. The only one who will suffer from such behavior is *you,* believe me.

Now, I do know of a few handlers who enter dogs and do not show them and then tell the owners a tale of woe about their being beaten. But these crooks are in a very tiny minority and, believe me, they cut their own throats! Sooner or later the owner finds out and then all is very "unwell"—it's a nasty business "when first we practice to deceive." Dog shows are like small towns—everybody knows everybody else and you can't cheat for very long, as clever as you may be, before the wrong person happens to be on hand at the right moment. Cheating clients is something that happens only rarely because it is so very difficult to achieve and because it is the quickest way to Disasterville in any business. So expect your handler to level with you, and take his word when he gives it. But if you *are* disturbed, go directly to him when the gossip is fresh, and give him a chance to protect himself—and incidentally, you—if the gossip is untrue, which you'll find it *usually* is!

Once you've placed your faith and trust as well as your dog in the hands of a particular handler, *do as you are told.* That may sound a bit strange, but it makes no sense whatsoever to pick a professional in any walk of life and then proceed to tell him how *you* want the job done. Nobody *I* know would hire a plumber (especially at today's prices!) and proceed to tell him how to fix the leak in the kitchen sink; nor would you get away with telling a surgeon just before the operation where he could or could not cut!

THE OBLIGATION OF THE HANDLER
TO THE OWNER

On the other side of the coin we come to the obligations a pro has to you, his client. First of all, he has an obligation to make very sure you understand what you are getting into and that your financial situation is up to the expensive business of showing dogs.

And he has an obligation to do everything possible to see that you get your money's worth. It's his job to present your dog to his best possible advantage, to feed him well, groom him correctly, exercise him adequately, and keep him happy mentally as well as physically healthy. If you request complete marked catalogues, he must supply them. Otherwise, he will send you the appropriate pages from the catalogues, clearly marked. These pages (or catalogues) plus all ribbons and rosettes and nonbreakable trophies should be mailed to you promptly after each series of shows, along with a statement of your account brought up to date each weekend so you are not suddenly faced with an enormous bill. If you want him to telephone you on the road in case of special wins, then he should telephone—collect, of course—but be prepared for some late night calls; it's not always possible to stick your hand out of the show ring and latch onto Ma Bell's machine, you know!

Most of all, it's his business to keep you informed of *everything* that is going on with your dog. "Tell them the truth and tell them *now*" has always been our policy at Quickstep, whether it's good or bad news. If something comes up and he can't reach you, he'll have to and should go ahead on his own as your representative, and if he doesn't make emergency decisions when necessary, he is letting you down.

He owes you his allegiance all the way. He doesn't talk about or against you or your dogs or your kennels publicly and he does his best to help publicize your breeding program and to help you sell your young stock.

If he agrees to finish your class bitch in a given breed, then I don't think he has any right to accept another class bitch in that breed to show at the same time or at the same shows. Since different judges like different things, its perfectly all right of course, to have other bitches in his string which are shown on different weekends than your animal.

Because people are human beings and judge you and your values by the people who represent you in public, I feel your handler has an obligation to dress well at all times, to treat his fellow competitors with courtesy (even when it hurts), and to maintain his working area at shows in a clean, considerate manner. An occasional dog sitting in a soiled crate is something that happens now and then to the fussiest of us. Consistently filthy cages and setups are beneath a conscientious professional, and such conditions reflect on you, the owner.

I'm a drinking woman, myself—*after the show is over.* Handlers who drink at ringside and whose areas are littered with beer bottles do great, great damage to the profession and to the dog game as a whole;

fortunately, these people are very, very few and they get the level of patronage they deserve.

I feel that a handler has just as much an obligation to tell a client when *not* to show as when he *should* show.

HANDLING COSTS

When it comes to how much it costs to hire a professional handler, the picture gets complicated. It is almost impossible to give you a fair picture of what to expect, as every handler makes his own arrangements with individual clients, arrangements that can vary in any number of ways. All reputable handlers will supply you with their "price cards" upon request. Some of these simply list costs—boarding, grooming, handling, etc. Some present a more detailed sheet. Happily, there are those marvelous individuals who can pay for handling and all the other services and never feel a thing. Unfortunately, these people do *not* own all the great dogs of the world, and when a really promising prospect comes to a handler owned by people who are sincere but not exactly well-heeled, it is often possible to make "arrangements" that keep everyone happy.

Some handlers charge a flat fee for finishing a dog; they take the animal when it is to be started on its show career and return it when requirements for title have been met. Some handlers, if certain the owners will take care of the dog properly between shows, prefer to have the animal brought to the show, after which it goes home again with its owners. Some handlers charge bonuses for championship points in addition to their regular fees; there are others who charge a bonus upon completion of title; there are some who charge more for specialty shows and major wins; several charge more than their standard fee if they accept a strange dog at the last minute at ringside. Almost all of us charge bonuses for group placings and Best in Show wins.

So you can see how difficult it would be for me to tell you exactly what it will cost you to show your dog. I think we could quite fairly assume however, that you could expect to pay between twenty-five and fifty dollars per show as a basic handling rate. Settling happily on costs and prices is as vital to the handler as to the owner, so you can be quite matter of fact about asking for a professional's system and prices *before* you launch into this partnership. Make very sure you understand your handler's *complete* financial policies and get them in writing if possible. Then uphold your end of the deal by paying your bills when they are presented.

Another point that bears clarification: if your handler is tied up in another ring with somebody else's dog and cannot get to yours, he will usually ask a fellow professional to stand in for him. In this instance, *you are still liable to pay the handling fee to your handler.* Standing-in is a professional courtesy handlers extend to each other.

There is no denying that it is expensive to hire a handler. But strange as it may sound, most clients of professionals will quickly assure you that they couldn't possibly travel with their own dog for as little as it costs them to send him with a handler. For instance, I charge thirty dollars per day expenses on top of handling fees when I am on the road. (I do not charge board for dogs while traveling.) But all the people whose dogs I am taking along for two shows on a weekend will split that sixty-dollar charge for expenses. Now, if my arithmetic is correct, carrying six dogs mean each owner would have to chip in ten dollars in expenses for two days. *Could you do the weekend for this?*

The professional and the amateur—I can't imagine what it would be like in the dog game without both. I think each inspires the other to better things, challenges the other to goals he might not otherwise dream of obtaining, heckles the other into trying harder, looking longer, understanding more.

PART THREE

HANDLING
FOR OBEDIENCE

1

Something For Everyone

The task of compiling an obedience manual is a great deal like trying to bail out a boat without first fixing the leak—there always seems to be something left over!

Nevertheless, being of stout heart, we have gone ahead and tried to put together our theories on obedience training in a manner that we hope will make this section as useful to the shy, middle-aged lady who has never owned a dog before and has suddenly inherited a brace of adolescent Boxers, as it will be to the outdoor-loving scuba diver who has owned dogs all his life and now wants to train a Papillon. We have compiled ways to make noisy dogs be still; to make "deaf" dogs come when called; to make bellicose dogs cease devouring the neighbors' pets; to make a hyperactive dog slow down enough to give his master at least a soupçon of peace and quiet. Bearing in mind the countless varieties of canine and human personalities, we have tried to offer methods that will be of most help to the greatest number of dogs and people.

There are lots of obedience books on the market, lots of theories, lots of methods. All of them have something good to offer if you look at them objectively. But to my knowledge, this is the only manual written to be used in three ways:

1. As a guide for the trainer working alone with one dog;

2. As a supplement of suggestions for making your own experience in any trainer's class a richer, more rewarding one, and, incidentally,

making you a more receptive student and, therefore, a more successful teacher of your own dog between classes;[1]

3. As instructions for a group of amateurs deciding to join together to train in the absence of qualified, experienced instructors.

There is no set order for the exercises, so that you can go ahead at your own pace, teaching what seems most important to you first, and so on. The entire format is based on a theoretical 10- to 12-week course in novice obedience. It is highly recommended that those who have never trained a dog before spend the full twelve weeks learning and perfecting the novice exercises offered in the following pages. Dogs thoroughly schooled in fundamentals at the novice level are the ones that quickly become and always remain dependable, happy workers. Slipshod attention to the basic principles outlined herein will lead only to sloppy work and disinterested dogs.

Of the three fields of endeavor covered in this book, none is more readily available to the average family than obedience. Entry fees are rising, but they nowhere nearly approach those to be paid at retriever trials. While many fine show champions are also obedience dogs, an expensive breed specimen is not necessary in obedience competition. The equipment can almost always be homemade and is not difficult to maintain. Professional handlers in obedience are in a minority because obedience exercises are built progressively, from Novice through Open to Utility, so that almost anyone can teach a dog the things he has to know. Obedience classes are available in almost all communities today in the U.S. and Canada, and those who do not wish to compete for obedience titles are just as welcome as those who aspire to high-scoring national awards.

Obedience training any animal is the best way in the world to get his attention and his love; it's a wonderful hobby, either at the teaching or the competitive level, and one in which the whole family can take an active part. Special rules now permit even handicapped people to do their own handling in obedience competitions in the United States and Canada.

While altered males or females are ineligible for breed competition, spayed bitches and altered males are welcome to compete in obedience trials. They may not do so if blind or deaf, but the definition of blind is "having useful vision in neither eye"; and of deaf, "without useful hearing"; so, there is some latitude not present in breed rules, although

---

[1] If you plan to attend an already established class, then of course you will do things the way your instructor wants them done; in no way would we presume to suggest that our method is the only method! But whether you teach "down" by pulling the front legs out, or by pressing on the dog's back, there are still universal attitudes and precepts we can all share in common and which make any teaching and any learning more easily assimilated.

bitches in season may not be shown. Dogs that cannot be shown in breed because of stipulations outlined in the standard can be and often are entered in obedience, although only purebred, registerable animals may compete in trials in the U.S. or Canada. Particolored Poodles, for instance, are not eligible to compete for breed championships, as the standard for all three sizes of Poodle stipulates that the animals must be of one solid color. These charming, multicolored dogs are seen quite often in obedience competitions. Unfortunately, there are those who feel that such exceptions prove obedience dogs are not good enough for any other kind of competition. Certainly many of the animals in obedience aren't show dogs; but many, many of them *are* champions, and in more than just one country! Proud owners would twist the question around and ask: "What makes you think your show champion is smart enough for obedience?"

We'll go into rules and regulations later on. Right now we just want to point out that it is often cheaper, simpler, and more convenient to find a dog that can compete in obedience than it is to locate a show animal and do a lot of winning. Obedience training can be enjoyed simply for the purpose of developing a more mannerly pet, and in so doing the owner assumes a community responsibility which could well be adopted by show-dog owners.

Obedience is easily understandable to everyone. The public who attends dog shows often gets bored or confused watching conformation classes, but they cluster in great crowds around the obedience rings where the greenest neophyte can understand what is going on. Obedience has won many, many friends for purebred dogs. In fact, many people who eventually rise to the top in breeding, handling, training, and judging dogs get their start in obedience.

And let's not forget that some people are great and undying fans of the mixed-breed dog. While he can't compete at obedience trials, he can be trained, and almost to a man his owners will insist the mixed breed is smarter than his purebred cousin. There is no basis in fact for such a statement, of course, but such loyalties are strong, and one of the charms of obedience is that you can train any kind of a dog you want to, papers or not, and reap the rewards of a special companionship.

2

Picking an Obedience Puppy

When you are picking a puppy to be used mainly for obedience training, as much as I love my own "house mice" (who are mixed in the extreme), I must urge you to choose a purebred, registerable animal for two very important reasons.

First: temperament is paramount with animals that are to be trained to do specific tasks. It is much easier to predict the disposition of a Newfoundland or a Maltese than it is to guess at the probable mature disposition of a mixed-breed dog, as we don't usually know the breeds that contributed to it. There are exceptions to every rule, of course. There are Poodles that are abysmally stupid, Basset Hounds that are overly aggressive. But generally speaking we know that the average Chesapeake is very protective of his family; the average Papillon does a lot of yapping; the average Scottish Deerhound is highly adaptable. And because most purebreds follow pretty obvious behavior patterns; it's an obvious advantage to be able to approach training when the human being has a little more knowledge of his dog than the dog has of his human being!

Second: I'd like a nickel for every person who started in obedience warbling, "Well, I don't care about papers, because I just want to train my dog to make him easier to live with!" Sooner or later the innocent newcomer gets caught up in the training program and begins to regret very much that his sharp, smart, attractive mixed breed cannot compete at A.K.C. or C.K.C. trials. If his interest continues, of course, he'll go out and purchase a purebred with which he can compete in licensed and sanctioned trials. Oh yes, many a mixed-breed doggie has sparked a lifelong interest in purebred dogs, but always the owner regrets, in his heart, that his first dog, the mixed breed, couldn't go further in his training than merely weekly classes and demonstrations at hospitals and schools.

In the chapter on Picking a Show Puppy we covered how to find reputable kennels, secure healthy animals, and examine litters for soundness. The obedience puppy buyer can be assured that the same rules apply from initial inoculations to individual registrations. But the buyer looking for a dog to *train* has to look harder than other buyers for a dog with that particular spark God seems to put in some of them, an extra teaspoon of moxie, if you will. It's a good idea to find out if the sire and dam of the puppy you are considering have any obedience degrees or were working animals, such as hunting or herding dogs. In talking to the breeder it is a simple matter to determine his interest in temperament and disposition, keystones to biddable, smart animals of any breed. Also, I think you must consider that some breeds seem to be born for training; other breeds, while perfectly capable of learning, nevertheless do so grudgingly without any special flair.

I will have to disappoint you if you are waiting for me to recommend certain breeds above others as candidates for top obedience scores or easy conversion into companion dogs. I'm too smart and too fond of life to fall into *that* trap! Also, I am too experienced not to acknowledge that the exceptions to the rule, as to trainability in dogs, are legion.

You should decide whether a companion dog that you can train to be a pleasure to have around is your main interest, or whether you are also interested in competing for obedience degrees. Your age and athletic ability will have great bearing on whether you select a big, rugged, outdoor breed, a more easily controlled middle-sized breed, or perhaps one of the sparkling toys.

As we advised in picking a show puppy, it might be wise to consider, under certain circumstances, purchasing a slightly older pup so that you won't have to contend with early house training and can get on with formal obedience work much sooner.

TESTING

When looking at a litter, there are lots of ways to test puppies as well as older dogs for alertness and intelligence. Of the many evaluating systems, I personally favor the Seeing Eye program, which puts great emphasis on retrieving. Take along a tennis, ping-pong, or golf ball. Roll it past the whole litter and see which puppy is most interested in chasing it. As I mentioned with the prospective show pup, never mind if he picks it up or brings it back—*interest* in a moving object, curiosity to see where it is going and what it is, are excellent indications of a quick, "thirsty" mind.

After rolling the ball a few times, ask to have the puppies that chased it most avidly removed from the litter. Then all alone, one at a time, roll the ball again for each of these. Pups that function well in their peer group sometimes are insecure by themselves; put those back with the others.

While the "finalists" are jumping and frolicking around together, have a friend retire a good distance and then either drop a book or clap his hands without warning. The "normal" puppy will "start," of course, and look to see the source of the sound. Insecure puppies will cry or scuttle to hide. Remove these from sight and mind.

I think you can safely consider any of those left as promising obedience dogs. If you have in the back of your mind that you might perhaps be interested in conformation showing with this pup as well, now is the time to check for movement and body structure, as advised in the section devoted to selecting a show puppy.

TRAINING THE INCUMBENT PET

Sometimes people become interested in obedience training after they have had a family pet for several years and decide to use "Fido" to learn on. In the case of a dog acquired when very young and still spunky and outgoing, this is a fine idea. But for dogs that have settled into a family's routine and have given no trouble for three or four years, staid dogs that have gained mature dignity and have been satisfactory in every way for a long time, I doubt if this is a good idea. I think it is unfair to uproot these animals from their secure niche just because *you* get a brainstorm. Dogs over four years of age can certainly be trained and learn very readily in most cases, but I think you want to seriously ask yourself if this is being kind to an animal who has long since settled into the activity pattern of "his" family.

BRINGING THE PUPPY HOME

If you decide to allow the beloved family retainer to continue without formal training and settle instead on getting a new puppy, you will come up against the very common problem of introducing the stranger into a household the older dog has considered his personal property for some time. In most cases it is possible to handle this situation satisfactorily for everybody concerned, but it takes a little common sense and sometimes a great deal of patience.

Head-to-head confrontations between four-footed creatures are always best settled *before* they take place. Bearing this in mind, introduce the dogs *outside* the home, preferably on some sort of neutral ground about which the resident dog feels no particular possessiveness. Never, for instance, pop a new dog in a car with the dog that has been riding in it for years. This is his car and he would quite naturally protect it from strangers. Instead, let the pup and the mature dog size each other up *off leash* in the park or on a neighbor's lawn. (On leash, your tensions are quickly transmitted to the dogs.) Keep your voice calm and matter-of-fact. Don't stand still and wait for trouble. Walk away from them and call merrily to them to follow. Make sure you pat the family dog every time you pat the puppy; in fact, at this point it's a good idea to make more fuss over the old friend than over the new buddy. When it comes time to go home, if you have a crate, put the new pup in the crate and the older dog up front with you—a sign that he is still very special. Once home let the puppy out first; after a few minutes, release the older dog and keep busy at anything you can think of while they run around together. Then enter the house, letting the older dog lead the puppy in. Never bring a new dog into a house while the family dog is guarding the threshold. Keep the puppy in the crate for periods of time each day while you spend a lot of time with the resident dog. At the beginning, never mix the two at feeding time. Never throw something when both dogs are available to retrieve it. Eventually, the two could become quite good friends if you take a bit of care and spend an ounce of intelligence at the start.

If the family dog is a male and you are bringing home a female your problems should be few indeed, for dogs have a perfectly lovely arrangement whereby it's quite OK for a female to pick on a male, but it is rare indeed that the male will retaliate.

Two boys can usually be socialized in time except in rare instances. Particularly if the new puppy is *very* young, things should simmer down quite soon. But two females that take a dislike to each other are quite devoted to the proposition that "one of us has got to go and it ain't gonna be me!" Still, this situation can be handled, too, if you use your noodle. The main thing to remember is that *you* must stay calm; if a fight occurs, the solution is not to isolate one in the dining room and one in the bathroom for the rest of their lives! Let tempers cool awhile, then try again. Don't do stupid things like giving them big bones to chew on together. Don't you remember when you were a kid that *Johnny's* orange balloon was always much more desirable than *your* orange balloon?

Be very fair at all times. It's no more right to let the older dog hiss and spit at the puppy without correction than it is to let the puppy constantly hassle his elder without interference. Sibling rivalry is pretty much the same in kids and dogs; the solutions are pretty much the same too. Just keep proving to them both (particularly, in the beginning, to the older dog) that there is love enough in this house for everybody.

Success doesn't always result, but it will much of the time.

As for those of you who have selected an older dog to start with, try to bear in mind at all times that dogs of any age are "puppies" when they start their training. Which brings us to the subject of childhood—a vital part of any dog' development, no matter at what age it arrives. True indeed is that little poem so familiar to obedience buffs everywhere:

> The older you grow the more you'll find
> That the happiest dogs are those who mind,
> Who know that someone cares for their good
> Enough to make them do as they should.

But not too soon, not too soon!

Housebreaking and leash training can be handled by the obedience enthusiast exactly as was suggested earlier in our section on show dogs. But because the obedience-ite will be dealing with training to *do* as opposed to training to *be,* he usually needs constant reminding (as, I have found, does his brother in the field with a retriever) that pushing puppies too far and too fast can do permanent damage.

3

Preliminaries

THE MIDDLE ROAD

Puppyhood is all too often treated indifferently because it presents certain hardships to the human. But to the animal, it is a vitally important part of his mental and physical development. The childhood of a human baby forms many of his future life patterns, and it is no different with dogs: one model has two feet, the other four, but both species need a time to be children.

I realize that a very respected, widely followed school of thought holds that puppies removed from the nest and carefully sculpted along the lines the owner has in mind between the fifth and seventh weeks of life are the most well-adjusted animals in the world. Well, the author of that theory wrote *his* book and I'm writing *my* book, and I don't go along with that idea at all. To begin with, I'm old-fashioned enough to raise an eyebrow the moment I hear, "Statistics prove that. . . ." Why, I don't even trust computers!

I don't have any computers and/or statistics to prove what I say. I have only years of experience during which I have seen far too many perfectly trained puppies under the ages of six months with a heartbreakingly beseeching look at the back of their eyes. Their whole attitude was one of trying endlessly to please, constantly fearful they might fall short of the mark. To me, *that* is cruelty to animals!

Nor do I hold with the school of thought that says anything a child, two- or four-footed, wants to do while he is growing up is OK because he's "expressing himself." This kind of upbringing leads down the road to doggy delinquency just as it does to human delinquency.

The middle road is the one I recommend, because it teaches the puppy just enough to let him enjoy being a child while not dominating his family, and gives the novice obedience trainer the opportunity to enjoy this precious period with his dog, a time that is gone all too soon and never will come again.

The puppy's childhood is a period when *dog* teaches *man*. You don't need a leash and collar in your hand to observe. When is the pup's most receptive period of the day? When is he his sharpest? His quietest? What times does he establish as his bathroom breaks? Does he remember a "No-No!" (such as attempting to nibble the sofa or attack the cat) from one day to the next? What kind of correction does he best respond to: a harsh word? a swift swat? Or perhaps the punishment of being ignored works best with him. Puppyhood is the time for the owner to remember that just as all children need the reassurance of discipline, they also need the confidence of approval. From the very beginning, correct instantly when evil strikes, and reward good behavior just as instantly with the warmth and reassurance of physical contact. Hugging and squeezing and kissing have been proven to be vital to the psychological development of children; I believe this is so, also, with young animals.

Perhaps this might be the place to digress a moment and discuss one of the few criticisms I have of most obedience people: they are so busy training they don't take time to enjoy their dogs, to have fun with them. When they first get a puppy they rush to get him heeling and housetrained so they can boast how quickly they accomplished these feats; then they rush on to get him ready for his first match; then rush some more to push for high scores. From such an attitude comes the sometimes fair, sometimes unfair criticism that training dogs in obedience is no more than an ego trip for the human involved. Unfortunately, it's all too easy to force your will upon a friendly, willing animal, and of course that's exactly what we do, ultimately; force our will on them. But there is a right way and a wrong way to do so, a right and a wrong reason, attitude, time. It's not a matter of what you *do,* my friends, as much as *how* you do it!

An example of what I mean is this: a friend of mine was wrestling with his new puppy on the floor. They were rolling over and over and having as much fun as I was having watching them. Up until this moment the puppy had been doing pretty well on his housebreaking and hadn't erred in days. Now, the violent exercise and unusual excitement triggered an enormous puddle. My friend immediately scolded the pup severely and threw him outside. I immediately laid into my friend for stirring up an enjoyable game with the dog, then at the pinnacle of delight, punishing him when the predictable results occurred. Horrified at what he had done, he raced out and attempted to undo the damage. Not too *late* because he *did* care; but certainly too *bad!*

Top obedience dogs are wonderful to watch; they achieve fantastic scores not just because they do what they are directed to do, but because they go about their work with such obvious joy that they are impossible to ignore. And this kind of worker is the result of a happy, fun-filled childhood, coupled with well-thought-out schooling. So handle housebreaking and leash training just as we described in the chapter on show dogs, choosing whatever way seems most convenient to you and fits in best with your lifestyle. But in the process, take time to invest in the privilege of the sheer enjoyment of sharing fun and love—you and your dog—and both of you will be better adjusted for it.

Informal Training

During that wonderful period when you are enjoying your puppy while he is enjoying growing up, there are numerous opportunities to "train" him without his being aware he is going to school. While he is following you around the kitchen as you put dinner on the table, a delicious tidbit might be in order. The moment his attention focuses on your hand holding the munchie, raise that hand. His head will follow the movement. As his head goes up it is a simple matter to push him down on his rear end, gently, saying, "Sit!" The moment he does, give him his cookie and ruffle him up with delight. Then forget it and go on about your business. Do the same thing at *his* mealtime. Feed him in his crate, but the moment he sees his dish in your hand, raise it and press down for the sit command. Then pop him in his crate with much happy talk.

When he joins you in the den for TV after dinner and comes up beside your chair, after scratching his ears for a few minutes, carefully and gently position your hand on his back just behind his shoulder bones and press quickly, saying, "Down!" Once he has collapsed, keep stroking his head *quietly;* do *not* hold him down, and if he gets up in a few seconds, so what? As often as possible start his "down" exercise in this manner, and when it comes time to get serious about the command it will hold no real fears for him.

In fact, from the moment you bring your puppy home, whatever beginner work you do should, I feel, be integrated into your family routine. Entirely too many so-called obedience dogs that regularly score 199's in the ring are absolutely impossible to live with in the home because, for some reason, their owners equate the *ring* with *training* and the *home* with *recess.*

I don't think there is anything more foolish than the notion that if a dog is going to be trained for obedience competition he should be started one way, and if he is going to be trained simply as a member of the family he should be started another way.

All untrained dogs of any age commit the same crimes. Great Danes can see no reason why they shouldn't climb into horrified Aunt Agatha's lap. Wet Cocker Spaniels tend to flood the whole house when they shake. Basset Hounds all love to take their owners for walks. Some of these dogs may shine in the ring, some in the home; in the meantime, they have all got to learn the same shocking truth: it may be a dog's life, as some wag wrote, but it is a *man's* world. Your dog as well as my dog must live in it under the rules that govern *human* society. It may be quite OK to bark up a storm when meeting a fellow canine in the world of the dog, but in our society it is most definitely *not* OK!

One fact must be faced squarely by *all* dog owners: *Not everybody likes dogs!* Oh, I know, this is a horrible thought; it is also a fact of life. Your chances of altering the situation don't amount to a hill of beans, but you can make things much easier on you, your dog, and the anti-dog-ites of this world by proving that not all dogs are worth disliking. There is nothing wrong with daydreaming of 200 scores, provided you realize it is as important for your dog to be respected outside the ring as it is for him to "shine" in competition.

While you have responsibilities for seeing to it that your dog is well-fed, well-groomed, and healthy, you also have a responsibility to give your dog a set of rules he can count on 100 per cent. A few simple commands will make him a good citizen welcome anywhere; purebred, mixed breed, family dog, or obedience titlist, this is the very least you owe to this animal who is to be so integral a part of your life. Whether you ever enter a ring or not, the whole idea of obedience training is to increase the joy *you* get from owning a dog because *he* has a set of rules to live by and knows his boundaries. I cannot understand people who have to hire a dog sitter when they want to attend a movie. A dog sitter for a C.D.X., U.D. dog, yet, already! And I have indeed known several such "families." I have known obedience dogs who wouldn't dream of opening their mouths in class or in the ring but bark for hours in the home without ever being commanded to hush. I have seen dogs that sit next to other dogs on the stays with complete disregard for their neighbors go absolutely wild when a strange dog passes by, while their "trainers" either laugh it off or ignore it completely.

These poor animals are what I call *trick* dogs, as opposed to those I refer to as *trained* dogs. I urge you to start at the very beginning with two words for every puppy: "No!" and "Come!" Both could be lifesaving; both are always temper-saving. And they teach the most important thing for any animal to know from the earliest point of his relationship with his humans: that "my master never lies."

If you will make a point of taking that obedience puppy everywhere you go from the moment his inoculations are up to date, you can do more for him than you could by enrolling him in class too early. The main thing to teach him is that his leash and collar represent happy things. Make quite a production of putting on his training collar and leash whenever he is to go somewhere with you. It won't be long before he wriggles delightedly at the mere sight of this equipment. These early days are the perfect time to start lining up your local obedience stronghold so that when the puppy is ready for kindergarten or first grade, you'll know where to take him.

OBEDIENCE CLASSES

Novice, intermediate, and advanced training classes are held in almost every community in the United States and Canada these days. They are sponsored by all-breed kennel clubs, humane societies, the 4-H, breed clubs, various departments of public parks, and training clubs specializing in obedience.

The American Kennel Club *Gazette* and *Dogs in Canada* list obedience clubs throughout both countries. Check with veterinarians' offices, your local department of parks and recreation, and chambers of commerce. Sometimes individual persons experienced in training hold private classes. The kennel from which you purchased your dog should be able to help. While the puppy himself is still too young for class, it's a good idea for you to go alone and observe to get an idea of what is offered and who is conducting the training. Here we must pause and issue yet another warning.

The Trainers

Unfortunately, there is no control over obedience handlers and trainers in either the U.S. or Canada. There is a National Association of Dog Obedience Instructors in the United States, but this group has no real authority to act against unqualified persons teaching classes. As I have known two excellent, long-established trainers who were turned down when applying for membership, I'm afraid I have little faith in the groups existing at the present time, although I believe there is a real need for some kind of monitoring.

There is no point in denying the fact that a lot of inexperienced, incompetent people are holding obedience classes. There is a real and ever-present danger of innocent newcomers walking into such a class and having their dog systematically ruined while they look on with complete faith and trust simply because they don't know enough to resist.

At classes sponsored by one licensed kennel club I know of, sitting at heel is taught by having the handler stamp heavily on the floor each time he wants his dog to sit. At another kennel club's class, dogs that bark in class are "cured" by having cigarette smoke blown directly into their noses and eyes. One kennel club simply refunds the money of any dog who is aggressive to other dogs after the third night, explaining to the owners that such dogs are vicious and should be destroyed.

Finding a good class under the supervision of qualified personnel is not always a simple matter of a few letters or phone calls. As I said earlier, while your puppy is still a preschooler, find an accessible training class and observe; there are telltale things to look for.

Just because an instructor slaps a dog, do not head for the door. Attend these sessions with an open mind and try to think what you would do in a given situation. Did the correction work? Are the dogs generally happy? Do the trainees seem relaxed? How many of these people are getting obedience degrees? Are mixed breeds as welcome as purebred dogs? Are puppies expected to stay on the floor the entire class period, or are their owners encouraged to work only a few moments at a time? When the instructor approaches a dog to work it for its owner, does the dog look forward to this period or does he back away as the teacher approaches? One or two such reluctant trainees might signify a neurotic streak in the dogs, but if all dogs in the class act this way, things are not being done correctly. If the trainer feels that first you must knock the dog to his knees physically and psychologically and then win him back so that he becomes "your" dog; if he does not exhort his class to "praise your dogs" as often as he directs them to discipline the dogs; if his methods with the shy, sensitive dog are exactly the same as with the brash, bouncy dog—run, do not walk, to the nearest exit.

Certainly before you finish training your dog for competition he will need the experience of working around other animals. But for now, in the beginning, *no* class is far better than a *bad* class! If you have any doubts at all on the qualifications of the people who are teaching obedience in an area convenient to you, get started on your own; when the dog is older and you have gained experience through having learned you can teach your dog exercises by yourself, then you can try the class in safety, for you will know enough to say "No!" to anyone who, you feel, is approaching your dog in an attempt to cow him rather than control him.

On the other hand, don't delude yourself into thinking that nobody in the whole world understands your dog except little old you! This cloying, stifling attitude is just as deadly as the overly aggressive trainer can be. Training alone can be rewarding and fulfilling for you and your dog just as long as it doesn't develop into the Mama's Little Darling syndrome. Tying a dog to your apron strings is as cruel as it is disgusting.

I am reminded of a lady who brought a Mastiff to one of my training classes. She came early to explain that this dog was so shy it had bitten several people; not badly, but very deliberately. I appreciated her honesty, although the dog looked anything but a problem to me. However, years of experience have taught me that it is often a good idea to listen carefully before making a fool of one's self. So I watched the two circle the floor for a while. In spite of my repeated directions to loosen the leash, my Mastiff lady held tighter and tighter. Finally I walked over and took the dog from her. The woman was perfectly willing, but I literally had to pry her fingers off the leash.

The dog did beautifully for me, though we both watched each other very carefully. It took several tries before I could get my hands on the dog, and when I finally touched her shoulders she was braced so hard she felt as though she were made of cement! Slowly she began to loosen up, and when I took her back to her "mother" she lifted one paw very slowly; I shook it politely. Whereupon she put both her paws on my shoulders and gave me a big slurpy kiss. "She doesn't seem terribly shy to me!" I said, joining in with the laughter of the rest of the class as I dried my face. "Well, she *is!*" the lady snapped, so nastily that I could not believe what I heard, and I looked at her; in her eyes was pure, unadulterated hate, if I ever saw it. You see, that lady didn't *want* her dog to love anybody else but her, and by holding the dog as close to her physically and mentally as she possibly could, she was turning a perfectly dear dog into a fear biter. Happy ending: she saw the error of her ways and had a far richer relationship with her dog from that moment on. I just mention this incident to ask you to make sure *this* shoe doesn't fit *your* foot.

While we're on the subject of neurosis, you might as well face the fact that sooner or later you will meet up with the "nut" who will vilify you for training your dog because you are "breaking his spirit." Like people who hate dogs and people who think putting dogs in "cages" is cruel, you are not going to change the minds of people with far-out views such as these. But if the thought had occurred to *you* once or twice when the going got a little rough, instead of turning your back on the thought, take it out and look at it straight on. Ask yourself: "What is to become of the countless dogs abandoned on the highways, or turned in at already overcrowded humane societies just because they were so uncontrollable that they ceased to be wanted?"

Starting Your Own Group

While the increase in popularity of obedience training throughout the world makes it hard to believe, there are, nevertheless, areas where classes are not available. The instructions in these pages can be shared by a group of determined beginners as class exercises. Like weight-watchers, there are groups of people who need training and, failing to find experienced help available, band together and help each other. Many of our established training clubs in both the United States and Canada started this way.

Reaching other people who, like yourself, might be interested in forming a do-it-yourself group for obedience isn't as difficult as it might sound. Place an ad in your local paper, and post a notice in the laundromat and at the veterinarian's office. Usually such offers are snapped up quickly and you're off and running. Just be sure, as most training clubs are, that all dogs have been properly inoculated for distemper, hepatitis, and leptospirosis.

THE PROFESSIONAL OBEDIENCE TRAINER AND HANDLER

I think we must pause here and deal with the fact that not everybody wants to train his own dog; not everybody is able to do so. Physical infirmities sometimes make it impossible for a dog-loving person to enjoy a pet unless someone else trains it for him; and there are people in this world who are nervous wrecks and all thumbs when it comes to teaching any animal to do anything. While you and I may be convinced you have to participate with your own dog in training and obedience trialing in order to really enjoy your dog, there are others in this world who get their thrills out of simply sitting back and watching somebody else win with their dog; theirs is a pride of ownership.

Picking a good obedience professional for your dog is a little simpler than picking a show handler, because the results you obtain in competition depend more on the dog's working ability than on the opinions of the judges. In the heel-free, for instance, the dog either heels free, under control, or he does not. Whether the judge *likes* a particular handler or dislikes a particular breed of dog is immaterial. If the handler and the dog do the work, he must be passed. It isn't a matter of opinion, it's a matter of performance.

However, I have seen more damage done by people who set themselves up as professional trainers in obedience than I have seen in any other line of training. The professional is relatively new to obedience; the field of opportunity here is wide open and much damage can be and is done by unqualified people, some of whom honestly have no idea of the harm they are doing, and many of whom don't care as long as they make money.

I remember when I was starting out in Boston with the New England Dog Training Club. I finished my first C.D. with three first places,

won the Lu Wood Memorial Trophy, and thought I had found my
true niche in the world. Obviously, I was good, good enough to teach
others. Today, the thought of my brashness makes me squirm all over!
But then I was too green to realize my limitations and I promptly let
it be known around the city that I would teach novice obedience classes.
And I would have, too, with what dire results I hesitate to even contem-
plate, had I not received a phone call from a well-established obedience
trainer in the area. He began by praising my record and then very
gently suggested I was not ready for teaching classes. Before I could
get huffy, he asked me a simple question: "Tell me, Martha, what
would you do if you were conducting a class and two Boxers suddenly
began fighting?" After a few moments of silence on both our parts, I
gently returned the receiver to its cradle—I hadn't the *vaguest* idea
what I would have done! Years later this exact situation did indeed
take place in my class—two Boxers decided to eat each other. Both
owners panicked, dropped the leads, and ran off. Alone, I stopped it
in short order by rubbing the two dogs' muzzles together until they
couldn't wait to get out of sight of each other. As I sat back catching
my breath and quieting my vibrating knees, I thought of that long-
ago phone call and gave thanks that someone cared enough about dogs
to question me, and that I'd had brains enough to listen.

Only last week I took in a dog who may never be "normal" again.
He was sent to a professional obedience trainer who sent him home,
after six weeks and six hundred dollars, cringing, so that you had to
crawl on your hands and knees to heel the poor dog. A formerly clean
house pet, he now widdles if you look at him cross-eyed. Several months
ago another lady brought me a delightful beast who was a cross, we
believe, between an Airedale and a St. Bernard. Bigger than the average
Saint, he resembles an enormous shaggy dust mop and has the disposition of a pussycat. But he did need some basic obedience. I was not
holding classes at that time and recommended that she attend the summer classes sponsored by the parks department in a nearby metropolis.
She made inquiries, but fortunately she called me before reporting for
class because she was concerned about the requirements. After inter-
viewing the lady and her big shaggy dog, the "trainer" insisted she
purchase a spike collar, a length of chain, and that she attend with
not one but two men beside her for the first six weeks of the eight-
week course. You can imagine I stopped that in a hurry!

Admittedly, these awful tales occur in *all* fields of dog handling,
but I honestly and sincerely feel that finding a competent obedience
trainer to train your dog and handle him to his degrees is much more
difficult than finding his counterpart in the field or the show ring. It
is one thing to take your dog to a class and watch for the danger
signs, which we outlined earlier, that denote a poor trainer; it is quite

another to hand your dog over to someone who walks off into the blue with him, out of your sight and control, for six to eight weeks.

So get good references on your professional trainer, whoever he or she may be. You can find one in the same manner we suggested you find a trustworthy show handler earlier in this book. And once you have located a qualified individual, rest assured you will have fewer political ramifications to contend with in showing in obedience, and far fewer conflicts than in breed. Therefore, you can expect quicker results in obtaining obedience degrees once the basic training is accomplished and the dog starts competing.

Put your complete faith in the person you have chosen, but check regularly to make sure your dog is in good weight and coat, and that his attitude is that of a contented, well-adjusted animal.

The costs involved in hiring a professional obedience trainer and handler are considerably less than having a dog professionally handled in the breed ring or at retriever trials. Above all, watch for the person who may seek your business by boasting that, once your dog has graduated from his school, it will be so well-trained you won't have to work with the dog, that all you'll have to do is just sit back and enjoy, enjoy. Believe it or not, there have been innocent, unknowledgeable people who have actually fallen for this line of hogwash!

The reputable obedience trainer wants you to know how to handle your dog when you take it home, because he knows that dog is his best—or worst—advertisement. If the dog goofs because *you* don't know what to do, it's still the trainer who will get the bad press. Expect regular progress reports by phone or mail. If you can't get to see the dog often because of distance, ask for photographs now and then. And allow enough time before taking the dog home to make sure you know which buttons to push, so to speak.

Sometime before I die I would like to see the show handler and the obedience trainer working together, but I'm not holding my breath until it happens. I mention this sorry state of affairs in order to spare you the embarrassment of asking your obedience handler to work in conjunction with a show handler so that your dog can be shown in breed and obedience at the same time. *Forget it!*

The obedience trainer wants the dog fresh for obedience, so he doesn't want him off being groomed for hours by a show handler; the breed handler wants the dog fresh for conformation classes, so he doesn't want the edge taken off the dog in obedience classes. Each is quite willing to co-operate as long as his field comes first, and each has legitimate reasons for feeling that way. Since breed classes can run far behind, it's impossible to ask one of the two to stand at attention in case the dog is needed by the other. And there are only a handful of professionals who take dogs for both types of competitions at the same time.

So pick your show handler, if you are going to use one, for that kind of competition, and your obedience handler, if you are going to use one, for that kind of competition. If you want to do both, as we stated earlier, you are generally better off concentrating on the show ring first, though of course complex personalities and circumstances make exceptions to every rule.

KINDS OF OBEDIENCE DOGS

Just as the professional show handler will advise you what kind of show dog you have, so the professional obedience trainer can be expected to tell you whether you have: (1) a dog that should get his degrees and then come home; (2) a dog that should be trained, period, and not exhibited; or (3) that super sparkling kind of dog capable of competing for high scores on a national or international level.

If you are training your dog yourself, it is wise to determine as early as possible what kind of dog you have. Is he a worker who is happy but not overly accurate, an animal who is easily distracted, though he takes punishment well and tries because it's you who are asking him to? Get his degrees and call it quits. Does he bore easily and need to be constantly jazzed up and fired with enthusiasm through your antics? Perhaps you should think twice about using him in competition. Ah, but what if he is the kind of dog that fairly vibrates when you bring out his training leash, a dog that obviously gets as much kick out of learning as you do out of teaching? What if he heels along without so much as once taking his eyes off your face? What if it seems that when you tire and slow down he is always still ready for more? If that is the case, then I will tell you the same thing your professional trainer will tell you: *"Go, man, go!"*

SHOWING IN BOTH BREED AND OBEDIENCE

Showing a dog in obedience and breed classes at the same time is entirely possible if you are doing your own training and handling. However, I think you should be advised that this is never an easy row to hoe. More often than not, obedience classes are scheduled at exactly the same time you are due in the show ring. The rules state that obedience judges can, if they wish, agree to judge competitors out of order, and if you go to the obedience ring early and explain that you have a time conflict with the breed schedule, many judges will do their best to help you out of a tight situation.

But it is never easy to spend the day keeping the dog "up" emotionally for the breed ring without wearing him "down" emotionally for obedience. It involves a lot of running back and forth between breed and obedience rings, which are usually located at opposite ends of the show grounds, and one's mind is rarely free to concentrate entirely on whatever field you are competing in at the moment. It takes a very special kind of person and, more importantly, a very special canine temperament to handle this combination of interests happily. If you can do it, my hat is off to you and your dog. But if you can't, don't feel badly— lots of the rest of us didn't feel the hassle was worth the rewards, either!

DO'S AND DON'TS IN TRAINING

Now, let's get on with the actual business of training. Here is a list of tips which will help you and your dog over many a rough spot. Since, as we explained earlier, this section on obedience is written for group or solo training, we've divided our Do's and Don't's accordingly.

Accentuate the Positive

If You Are Training Your Dog in a Class: *Do* get to class on time. An hour may seem long in the beginning, but you'll soon discover that sixty minutes is barely time enough in which to review last week's work and learn your new assignment. You've paid for your course; don't waste your money.

Do let your trainer know if you can't hear, or if you don't understand a command. Why hesitate to admit you are confused? Your trainer is your salaried employee; you are the employer, so haven't you the right to expect every consideration?

Do attend every single class! If "Esmerelda" is in season, *you* come to class and watch from the sidelines. You would be amazed at what one can learn by watching the mistakes of others! And there is no reason you can't train at home for the three weeks or so that your female must be isolated; this way you won't fall behind your class. Be sure to inform your trainer of the reason for your dog's absence— some trainers will bring a substitute dog for you to work until your own is welcome in mixed company once again. Most classes have a rule that three unexplained absences mean you cannot graduate, and this is as it should be. It's hardly fair to expect any trainer to hold up the entire group while he brings you and your dog up to date. Besides, no matter how eager a pupil your dog is, nobody can really do a good job of training by going about it in a hit-or-miss fashion.

Do feel free to have a friend or members of the family attend classes with you. But remember that obedience classes are not social gatherings; they are schoolrooms. The person in charge usually teaches all evening long, handling anywhere from one to four classes, and it isn't right to expect the trainer to compete with chattering spectators for the right to be heard. Bringing very young children to training classes where you'll spend most of the evening escorting them off the floor, mopping tears, and locating the washroom or a drinking fountain, is intolerable. If you can't find a baby sitter, then train at home. It's hardly necessary to point out that unentered dogs are not welcome at classes unless special permission has been given beforehand.

If You Are Training Your Dog by Yourself: *Do* select a training area that will allow you and your dog to work without undue distractions. Visitors and busy locations are excellent *after* you and your dog have got the hang of things. In the beginning, work somewhere alone, just the two of you.

Whether Training Solo or in a Group: *Do* remember that the only reward your dog is looking for is *your* approval. He needs to be constantly assured of that approval when he is right, just as he needs your disapproval when he is wrong. In an intelligent handling of these two extremes rests a dog's security. So be just as quick to tell him when he has goofed and you are not pleased with him as you are to tell him he is the smartest, sweetest, cutest, cleverest, most valuable animal on earth when he is on the ball!

Do remember to exercise your dog before training. Solo trainers who take a dog out of a kennel or out of the house to work in the back yard or the garage should let the dog go to the bathroom before and after the training session. Ideally, you will set aside one section of the property for bathroom duty and another area for lessons. Since the unnatural excitement of traveling in a car to a training class can easily cause the most circumspect dog to forget himself, be prepared to take the class dog outside the building or training area whenever he looks as if he might want to relieve himself. Male dogs love to "christen" strange buildings, so be a good citizen and watch your boy to prevent leg-lifting on chairs and the corners of buildings.

If excitement makes it impossible for your dog to evacuate before class, you might wish to resort to "matching" as discussed in our breed chapter under The Importance of Being Regular.

Do wear sensible clothes in which you can move with a maximum of freedom and a minimum of worry about getting things snagged or dirty. Low-heeled shoes are a must for ladies, just as full, swishy skirts are out. Sneakers, blue jeans, wash-and-wear clothing—these are the backbone of any trainer's wardrobe.

Do give your dog a few minutes of training each day. Just fifteen minutes a session is plenty—fifteen minutes in the morning and again in the evening should send you and your dog soaring into the "cum laude" ranks. *Do* use your common sense about training in the heat of summer, and try to remember, as we've said earlier, that a day off once in a while is just as welcome to your dog as it is to you.

Do remember that a *positive impression* in your training practices is the most important, single facet of your dog's education. For instance, if you can *praise* him for executing a *short* sit-stay perfectly, you are miles ahead of the game. If you have to *punish* him repeatedly for breaking on a *long* sit-stay, you have accomplished absolutely nothing, and in the bargain you have convinced him that training is anything but fun. Dogs are animals, animals are creatures of habit; they learn by doing. Scientific research has proved that dogs that learn the quickest are dogs that are constantly successful at their work. See to it that your training is always *positive and happy* and your dog will build on these *positive, happy* impressions, will gain confidence in you and in himself, and will progress rapidly in all his work.

No matter how inadequate your dog's performance may seem to *you*, it is essential that *he* feel he has done something *right*, something that merits *your praise*, which he wants more than anything else. If your dog has difficulty learning a new lesson, go back and repeat an earlier lesson that he already knows. You'll then have a legitimate reason to praise him, and he'll be ready to tackle that new lesson again.

Do give commands in a loud, clear voice which tells your dog you are full of confidence. You don't need to scream, but *don't whisper!* No dog can be expected to obey when he needs a hearing aid to get the message.

Do limit yourself to one decisive command per exercise—unless the dog refuses and you must start from scratch. If you start at the outset to teach him that you are only going to tell him something once, then he'll never start waiting until the second or third command before obeying you.

Eliminate the Negative

If You are Training Your Dog in a Class: *Don't* let your dog sniff other dogs. Never mind the fact that your dog and that little Poodle over there play together at home. You are not at home now, you are in a classroom; the dog is there to work. So many beginners have unhappy experiences thrust on them because they *assume* that because *their* dog never fights, the strange dog he is nose to nose with in class won't fight either. Rarely has a novice dog who is attending class for the first time in his life seen so many dogs so close before. It's an exciting thing for your dog, for any dog, and the halo he wears during the day can very easily slip a bit under the circumstances. So if you keep your dog on a short leash, minding his own P's and Q's, you will avoid unpleasant encounters with other nervous beginners.

Don't concern yourself with the dog and the handler next to you; their progress is *in no way* comparative with yours! No two dogs are alike, ditto no two people. Your dog may have an *awful* time with the down command when everyone else gets it "like that." Cheer up; next week you'll probably do the stand-stay best and first, while everyone else struggles. So pay attention to your own problems and let the rest of the world go by.

Don't bring any tidbits—dog cookies or candies—to class! You are here as an intelligent human being to demand obedience out of respect. It should be absolutely beneath you and completely unnecessary, except in rare cases, to "bribe" your dog to do your bidding, and it is certainly no compliment to your dog for you to feel he's that stupid.

Don't try to get your dog to do the complicated routines you see the advanced dogs doing. The ladder of success is best climbed one rung at a time. The advanced dogs who jump and retrieve and drop at a distance worked *first* at the fundamentals; that's why they are doing so well now.

Don't shirk your responsibilities if your dog has what we call "an on purpose" in class. (The old-fashioned term was "an accident," but we don't see it that way!) Every class in the world has special equipment for just such emergencies, so ask one of those in charge. Any member of any training committee will be glad to help out by holding your dog for you and showing you what to use and how. But they will not be glad to pick up after your dog *for* you! They wouldn't expect such service from you, so don't expect it from them. They have all been in the same boat you are in, they sympathize—but they didn't volunteer to be your dog's nursemaid! If your loving pet decided to "express himself" while you are heeling in class, *stand still!* Don't run for the door until it's all over, or it will be, literally, *all over!* And never assume it "couldn't be *my* dog!"—because it could so *too!*

If You Are Training Your Dog by Yourself: *Don't* let anyone else (friend, child, or neighbor) work your dog until you have completed the exercises in this book, and until you *know* the dog knows the commands and is in no way confused on any of them. Even then, make sure the person working your dog knows the correct commands to use. Switching dogs with other trainers is excellent for the dogs as well as the people, but it should never be attempted until the dog is really obedient.

If training by yourself means you and your husband (or wife), make very sure each of you issues the commands in exactly the same way. If father is working Fido, then mother disappears completely, and vice versa.

Whether Training Solo or in a Group: *Don't* nag and don't overtrain—overtraining being just another form of nagging. Nothing is more miserable to behold than a bored, disinterested dog who loathes his work. Generally speaking, such a dog has been nagged and trained over and over until he couldn't care less.

Don't assume that just because you and your dog took to obedience like ducks to water, *all* dogs and *all* people will do as well. There are dogs who should *never* be trained, just as there are people who should never try to train a dog. By all means spread the good word about obedience, but bear in mind that it takes all kinds, etc.

Don't train your dog in such a way that all he gets out of his work is a negative impression. Concentrate on never putting him in a position where he *might* disobey if you can keep him in a position where he will *probably* do a perfect job. Punishment, as you will read later, is a must; it is not, however, the "be-all-end-all." Punishment is a trainer's "ace in the hole" when he has tried everything else with no success and when he is *absolutely positive* the dog knows what is expected of it and is simply not doing it. It's the old confidence theory again.

Don't feed your dog directly before training him. It will make him sluggish, and a full tummy plus a room full of other canines often causes "upchucking." We always advise that, if you are training alone, the dog be fed about half an hour after his lesson, providing, of course, your training hour falls somewhere around the time or times you usually feed. If you are attending a class, wait until you get home before feeding. In both cases, it is easy to see that feeding after training can serve a double purpose: it nourishes and it rewards. Also, it calms the dog and he sleeps quietly. If you are worrying, as so many do, that the dog will simply *die* if he isn't fed on time, stop behaving like a ninny about it.

Don't try to smoke and train at the same time. The only exception to this rule is the person who has three hands.

Don't attempt to train without proper equipment. Unless given permission by the trainer of a class or unless your dog's veterinarian or some training authority feels your dog needs special, nonstandard equipment, each dog should wear a chain-link training collar attached to a standard six-foot training leash. (Exceptions to this are, for instance, tiny dogs whose necks won't support a heavy collar and leash.)

Don't expect your dog to turn into Rin Tin Tin overnight! There is no shortcut, no "gimmick," no magic obedience juice involved in turning your budding superboy into a genius. It does help, immeasurably, to keep that leash well oiled with elbow grease!

Don't, please don't, become an authority overnight. It's amazing what half a dozen lessons can do to one's ego. But a know-it-all attitude will endear you to no one, and no matter how easy it looks to you, no matter how quickly you can spot what Mrs. Jones is doing wrong— even though Mrs. Jones hasn't been able to see it after weeks of work— *never forget that knowing how it should be done doesn't make a trainer!* The trainer is the guy who knows what to do when the obvious correction doesn't work. And that sixth sense, my friends, is developed over many years of working with all breeds, all temperaments of dogs *and* people. Just because you could make your German Shepherd do an exercise with the aid of a pet theory, the fact in no way guarantees that *all* dogs will succumb to such strategy. The danger here lies not in any embarrassment you may suffer; the danger lies in the possibility that you could easily *ruin* a perfectly nice dog through your "little bit of knowledge."

SOME COMMON WORRIES AND QUESTIONS

Self-consciousness is the disease that keeps many novices from asking questions at the beginning of their training. They are afraid they will sound "silly" or that they are asking a "stupid question." This is too bad, for the quicker a trainer can get to know the people studying under him, the quicker he can help them and their dogs. For some strange reason, most folks are almost ashamed to admit they love their dogs and worry about them. They feel that because they are in the company of a professional, or working with an amateur who has trained *many* dogs, their feelings will be laughed at. *No attitude was ever wronger.*

Professional or experienced people who work with dogs in any capacity are just as sloppy about their dogs as you are about yours. They are in a profession that offers great personal satisfaction in return for a lot of hard, back-breaking work and no great monetary rewards, so it stands to reason they love what they are doing. Because these people *are* experienced, however, they have heard all the standard questions and protests umpty-ump times. Because they have met and worked with a great cross-section of novices learning to train their dogs, they know what you are going to ask almost before you ask it. There are certain things *all* beginners worry about and question.

In order to save you embarrassment and to save time in class or give you peace of mind as you heel around your back yard by yourself, we've listed below a number of the things that "bother" beginners. Granted, they sound silly, amusing when you read them on the printed page. But they are all "dog-eared" refrains spoken by uneducated trainees whose only crimes were *loving* their dogs. And if you think anybody is going to laugh at you for that, *you're crazy!*

1. *"I can't understand the way my dog is behaving tonight! He does everything perfectly at home!"* wails the lady trainer during the second or third class session.

Nobody doubts for one second that her dog does, indeed, obey perfectly at home. And the reason nobody doubts it is because *everybody's dog* works well in his own territory with no strange dogs, sights, noises, and smells to distract him. The fact that the dog in class is more excited and more difficult to handle than the dog at home is no mystery at all when you stop and think a moment. Of course he's rattled—aren't *you?* This is the reason class work is invaluable. It teaches dogs to mind in the face of many distractions, and it teaches the handler how to make the dog pay attention when he'd rather flirt with the Poodle two dogs down the line.

2. *"My dog never growled or snapped before in his life! Do you think this training is going to make him vicious?"* asks the man who has just forced his dog to lie down on command when the dog obviously didn't go for the idea.

Make the dog vicious? *Hardly!* To begin with, the word "vicious" is sadly misused. After all, the only way a dog has of showing his feelings is to either wag at one end or snap at the other. When you and I get mad, we can use a bad word, throw a tantrum or a couple of pieces of china. But the only way a dog can show he is angry is by growling or snarling or biting. *Don't tolerate such behavior for a single, solitary moment!* After all, you are making no cruel or unreasonable demands of your dog, so if he throws a temper tantrum, tough! He'll live through it and so will you; if nothing worse ever happens to you, you'll both die happy! In the meantime, the first bite your beloved aims at you is best squelched by prompt assurance that such antics gain dogs nothing but front-row seats in Unhappyville!

A *vicious* dog is a "depraved, wicked" animal, according to Mr. Webster; the dog that snaps when his sacred opinion is challenged is simply a *brat.* And all *good* parents know how to handle this tendency.

3. *"Oh dear,"* the housewife with the Sheltie moans, *"I guess my dog will never mind me!"*

She is absolutely correct—he probably won't if this is her attitude. As far as we are concerned, *never* is a long, long time, and *can't* and *won't* are words we don't even discuss. Anybody who sings this lady's refrain is *really* saying, "I haven't the guts to make the dog do what I want him to do." And, frankly, we feel this is a shameful thing for anyone to admit to himself, to his dog, or to the world.

We've graduated dogs with three legs, a middle-aged lady whose hands were partially crippled with arthritis, a very ancient dowager who stumped through class with the aid of a cane, deaf dogs, one-eyed dogs—and *you* think *you* have problems?

4. *"If I have to make my dog do all these things, won't he end up hating me?"* a junior handler wants to know.

The answer here is simple—very few people grow up hating the parents who taught them to say "please" and "thank you" and the fundamentals of good manners. Right? Right!

5. Last but not least, we have the man or woman who complains, *"My dog is sensitive and high-strung. I'm wondering if all this confusion will be too much for him."*

It probably will, indeed: he'll quit worrying about his own problems and decide it's quite a nice world, after all. As we said earlier, there *are* dogs that should never be trained, but they are in a minority; in the vast majority of cases the sensitive, high-strung dog is owned by a sensitive, high-strung man or woman who has never permitted the animal the dignity of his own personality. Obedience is the best therapy in the world for the dog that is not outgoing. If your beloved is in this category, *don't sympathize!* Just reassure the dog by behaving, yourself, as if this were the most normal thing in the world, as if you weren't the least bit concerned about a blinking thing.

The above points of concern are closely coupled with a virus known as *First-night Fever.*

You look forward for weeks to the first class, and when the night arrives the balloon bursts! All of a sudden you are surrounded by strange people and too many strange dogs. Your own dearest Fido has turned into a monster who acts as if he owns the joint. You seem to have three arms, two left feet, your hearing is obviously failing—and where in the world should you stow your purse or hat? You have been told to put out your cigarette, but you don't dare let go of the d____d dog long enough to locate an ashtray. Somebody says that your "leash" is a "lead," that your "collar" is a "chain," and that you are a "handler" and not an "owner." The fixed, stiff smiles masking the real feelings of the other members of your class make you only slightly less nervous than the disgustingly confident expressions on the faces of the know-it-all members of the Training Committee. As that first sixty minutes drag by, you grow more certain, moment by agonizing moment, that "I must have been stark, raving *mad* to have signed up for this fool thing!"

Calm down, relax. That man over there is *not* staring at you; that woman in the corner does *not* think your dog is funny-looking; nobody thinks you are stupid or clumsy. *You* may be convinced that you stand out like a sore thumb, but you really don't. You are among friends. Every single member of the Training Committee was in your shoes not too long ago, and they know your agony from firsthand, personal experience.

If you listen to the instructions, spend your class time training, concentrate on your own dog, and are faithful with your homework, you'll find that a trainer *can* train *you* to train your dog.

P.R.D.: These letters stand for the password to dog training; they represent the magic touch—*P*atience, *R*epetition, *D*etermination. Mix these three well, and you are bound to get the hang of it, P.D.Q.— *Pretty darned quick!*

PUNISHMENT AND PRAISE

Most owners coming to a training class for the very first time arrive with a king-sized chip on their shoulders, a chip labeled: "Nobody had better try to push *my* dog around, boy!" If you said to these people: "But it's ok for your dog to push around the members of the Training Committee, is it?" they would be floored. It simply doesn't occur to many dog owners that you don't have to be at your dog's mercy twenty-four hours a day. They would never tolerate being dictated to by a child, but it is accepted as standard operating procedure that if, for instance, a dog wants to bark all night, and you can't shut him up by yelling at him a few times, then you are simply out one good night's sleep!

A dog, no matter how wonderful or beautiful or pedigreed or beloved, is first and foremost a *dog.* He may seem human to you but he is *not.* He is a canine, an animal, period. Because he *is* a dog, he learns things best when they are presented in a simple black-is-black and white-is-white manner, so the quickest, kindest way to teach him anything is to *praise* him when he is right, and *punish* him when he is wrong—it's that simple. Promise your dog at the start of his training that pleasant things happen when he is right, unpleasant things happen when he is wrong, and make sure you never *break* that promise!

For some reason, "punishment" is a word that conjures up visions of innocent little puppies being tortured by black snake whips and thumbscrews. Actually, it is simply a word that stands as a base for one of the oldest theories in civilization: *devotion* comes with *respect; respect* comes with *discipline;* and *discipline* is the foundation of any adult society.

"I love my dog! Why do I have to punish him at all?" is a cry often heard from beginners. Well, maybe you won't ever have to punish him. It has happened—rarely—but it *has* happened. But if your dog deliberately disobeys you, you will punish him *because* you love him.

Then, too, there are ways and ways to punish. You can "punish" a dog by merely looking at him or by using a severe tone of voice or by actually bopping him on his behind. You can even follow the mother dog's procedure and shake your dog by the scruff of his neck.

But whatever is called for, the emphasis should always be on the *timeliness* of the punishment, not on the *severity* involved. And equally important is balancing the quality and severity of the punishment with the quality and severity of the crime.

Small dogs are corrected in a manner that takes their size into consideration—usually, that is. But some small dogs are veritable lions and must be chastised more firmly than is necessary with their bigger brothers.

Large dogs take more convincing to emphasize the errors of their ways—usually, that is. But some large breeds are overly sensitive and must be handled as if they were tiny things. But no dog, big or little, hard-headed or sensitive, will resent you or the punishment you dish out *if* you balance that punishment with praise and affection in *equal proportions.* Keep it simple and clearcut: never punish unless the dog is wrong, never praise unless and until the dog is right.

Whether it's child or dog, spanking is what usually comes to mind as an obvious method of punishment. But with dogs, there are some rules and techniques.

1. Never call a dog to you under any circumstances and then spank it. Go to the offending animal yourself. If you can't get your hands on the dog, have someone else get him and hold him until you reach him. Never chase him around.

2. Take a firm grip on the collar with one hand and position the dog crossways in front of you. Hold the dog close to you and in such a way that there is absolutely no possibility of his getting away while you are administering the spanking. He *must* learn that you spank only when serious crimes are involved, and that while you will hurt him, you are not trying to drive him away from you.

3. Swat him repeatedly and meaningfully on his backside with your free hand. Accompany your swats with a thunderous tone of voice as you repeat some standard word that can be reserved for future use and will always ever after let the dog know you are displeased with him. "No!" is a good word, and one all dogs should be familiar with from puppyhood. "Phooey!" is a word borrowed from European trainers; it sounds deliciously disgusting and is a favorite oral weapon. Remember now—it's not how hard you swat, it's the sound and the fury that accompany the spanking that really impress the dog.

4. Make your spanking brief and meaningful. As soon as it is over, if his crime was a serious infringement of a training rule, put the dog on leash, lead him through the exercise until he does it right once, praise him lavishly, and turn him loose. It's time for you both to "take five."

Don't thump and whack a dog every time he is wrong; soon your blows will lose all meaning except that he will learn to duck and cringe. Always try using your brains before resorting to your muscle. Utilize your leash and collar for the majority of your corrections; your body movements and your sense of balance and timing are just as important. You can usually do more by changing your tone of voice than by almost any other method. Above all, never resort to striking a dog just because you lose your temper or because you don't know what else to do. Whatever your method, *make it mean something*—do it right once, and get it over with. Don't nag! Don't threaten!

Slapping or swatting a dog in the face is a correction that is rarely used, but there are specific circumstances when such a correction is called for—when a dog is snapping, for instance, snarling or biting or refusing to stop barking. The trouble is, most folks only encourage more of this same kind of behavior from a dog when using this correction, because they don't administer the slap correctly. They flick their pinkies in the dog's teeth, or flutter up and down on his nose like a butterfly, or make repeatedly empty threats that drive the dog into a nervous tizzy. He retaliates by barking louder, snapping faster—or he tries to catch that hand and swallow it whole. Such bad training results in a hand-shy, snappy dog who ducks every time you scratch your ear or light a cigarette.

Whenever you *must* resort to this kind of correction, *make it mean something!* Do it *well* or don't do it at all. Slap or swat solidly just *once!* Then it is *over* and soon forgotten by all concerned.

Throughout this manual you will find various exercises in which you are directed to slap a dog sharply across the muzzle; in each case the reason for this unusual correction is carefully explained. Unless you are *specifically* directed to correct in this manner, save your swats for the dog's *bottom,* not his *top.*

Now we must combine punishment and praise to make them work. Correction balanced with praise is the ideal training outlook. There has to be a difference between right and wrong. If you are fair about correcting the dog as promptly as you praise him, he will never be confused.

Correction and praise are *absolutely dependent upon each other for effectiveness.* To use either one alone renders it absolutely useless. To use both at the same time is utter confusion.

Correct your dog the *instant* he is wrong, when the error is fresh in his mind, not twenty minutes after he has disobeyed a clear-cut command you know he understood. Most novices are loath to crack down at the first infringement; they wait to see if maybe the dog will behave and they won't have to correct. But the moment they start giving the dog a second chance, they let the dog in for more correction than is fair to him, because his handler goofed, not the dog. The dog didn't know better; the handler did!

Praise your dog the *instant* he is right, at the actual moment he executes the command correctly, and praise in proportion to the correction you made earlier. If the dog erred just a bit, a few quick pats are sufficient when he does things right. But if it has given you a number of unpleasant moments before you could get your point across, take time out to really love him up with sincerity because he finally did things *your* way. Make it wonderful for him to please you, not just a bloody bore.

One of the worst crimes in this category comes in teaching a dog to sit when the handler halts. Over and over you will see novice trainers whop a dog for not sitting promptly, then lean over patting the dog with, "Good doggie!" The "doggie" wasn't "good" at all. He was so in error that he had to be whopped. Wait until the whop isn't necessary, *then* goo over him.

Always bear in mind what we stress over and over throughout this book: no two dogs are alike. All dogs need regular practice sessions, but some do best when worked for *very* short periods; others require longer, more demanding sessions. Some need a firm hand and a gruff voice; some require an unusual amount of praise and a high voice. Study your dog's needs constantly. He may require the use of a continuation of these techniques, depending on what you are trying to teach. Stay alert for signs of overtraining—boredom, slow-heeling, hanging head.

Left-handed persons and any hunters training sporting breeds may wish to work their dogs on the *right* side instead of on the left. This is perfectly permissible. Simple reverse all right or left commands given in the training exercises, but once you start a dog on a certain side, stay with it. Don't switch sides in mid-course, or you will become the rueful owner of a crazy, mixed-up canine. (Bear in mind that in the ring, both in Canada and the United States, obedience dogs *must* work on the handler's left.)

Don't pick the side you are going to train your dog on the assumption that all gun dogs work on the right (because they don't), or because it's "fashionable" to work your dog on the left (which is ridiculous). Most trainers work dogs on the left because most trainers are right-handed, and with the dog on the left their right hand is free to train with or shoot with. Make up your mind based on what is comfortable for you.

A GLOSSARY OF OBEDIENCE TERMS

Here are a number of basic words and expressions used in obedience training. Knowing their meanings may help you to avoid feeling, "It's all Greek to me!"

Training Collar—a chain-link collar that tightens when the dog is wrong and lies loosely when the dog is right. The *training collar* is to be worn *only* when a dog is in training, unless it is locked to prevent an unsupervised dog from hanging himself. (The fitting and locking of a *training collar* were explained in the section on Collars and Leads in Tools of the Trade.

Training Leash or Lead—a six-foot (approximately) length of leather or cotton webbing, with a loop handle at one end and a sturdy snap or catch fixed to the other. Long leashes of chain link, plastic, or plastic-coated wire are not *training leads,* because it is impossible to "feel" through these kinds of materials how the dog is responding to your commands. Also, they are unbearably hard on the hands. Many novices feel that chain is the only thing that will hold a big dog, but you "hold" or control the largest dog by the way in which you use your leash, not by the size or thickness of the lead itself.

Heel—this word can be confusing. Heeling means that the dog is walking freely at your side. The command "Heel!" means the dog comes to your side, or that he starts moving as you move after having been stationary. When you *return to heel,* after having left him for some distance, you face the dog and walk past him and around behind to return to his side so you are again standing as you were before leaving him. In the obedience ring, *at heel* means the dog is on your left. As we explained earlier, in our classes your dog may be at heel on either your right or left.

Forging—your dog is out too far ahead of you.

Finish—the process by which your dog returns to heel position after having come to you when so directed on the recall.

Lagging—your dog is dragging his heels and is too far behind his handler.

Recall—to call your dog to come from where you have left him to where you are standing.

Wide—your dog is working too far afield and should be closer to your side.

Crowding—your dog is interfering with the progress of his handler by pressing too tightly against his handler's leg. Or it could mean he is interfering with you on his left turns or cutting across in front of you when you halt.

Degree—when talking about a degree in conjunction with obedience, the word has nothing to do with body temperature or the weather. There are four Obedience Degrees which can be won by any registered dog when he completes certain requirements established by the American or Canadian Kennel Clubs. These degrees are won at licensed obedience trials which are held sometimes alone and sometimes in conjunction with licensed dog shows. The degrees are usually referred to by initial, so to prevent confusion for the greenhorn, here they are:

C.D. (one judge)—Companion Dog degree: novice level; most work on leash, but some work off leash, including heeling, coming when called, staying while sitting and lying down; and the dog must stand without moving while the judge touches his head and back.

C.D.X. (one judge)—Companion Dog Excellent degree: high-school level; all work off leash, including more demanding heeling, dropping on command while coming when called, longer stays, retrieving on the flat and over a high jump and a broad jump.

U.D. (one judge)—Utility Dog degree: college level; all work off leash, including giving directions with hand signals, long stays while standing, finding objects by hand direction, directed jumping, and scent discrimination.

T.D. (two judges)—Tracking Dog degree: dog required to follow man-laid track a specified distance; working on a long tracking line, or leash, to find a previously dropped object.

Since these degrees were originally set up to build upon one another as the dog progressed from novice to advanced work, it is required that the dog start with the C.D. degree and achieve his subsequent degrees in the order given above. The Tracking Dog degree is the only exception to this rule. A dog may try for his T.D. at any time, contingent upon a few prerequisites clearly outlined in the rule books.

To secure copies of the rules for obedience competitions, write the Canadian Kennel Club, 2150 Bloor Street West, Toronto, Ontario M6S 4V7, enclosing seventy-five cents and asking that you be sent the *Regulations and Standards for Obedience Trials.* Or write the American

Kennel Club, 51 Madison Avenue, New York, N.Y. 10010, for the pamphlet *Obedience Regulations.* If you are in need of a single copy there is no charge; ordered in quantity (by a club, for instance) the booklets are fifteen cents each. Whether or not you ever enter an obedience ring with your dog, these two books are informative and educational and are well worth having in your doggy library.

To complete our glossary of terms, here is a list of non-regular classes (those classes in which no credit is given toward obedience titles) sometimes offered by clubs at obedience trials, at specialties, and at sanctioned trials:

Pre-Novice—a pre-C.D. class seen at many sanctioned trials. (As in dog shows, sanctioned obedience trials are those in which no titles are awarded. It is an excellent place to practice, a real dress rehearsal opportunity.) In this class all C.D. exercises are included, but all are done on leash.

Graduate Novice—This class is offered, usually at sanctions, for dogs with C.D. titles who are working on their C.D.X.'s. C.D. and C.D.X. exercises are combined, the only on-leash work being the heel exercise (however, the figure eight is done off lead).

Brace Class—two dogs of the same breed, not necessarily of the same sex, performing novice exercises. They may work coupled or uncoupled and are handled by one person only.

Veterans Class—open to dogs with an obedience title who are eight or more years old prior the the closing of entries. All novice exercises.

Versatility Class—This is a fun class for dogs with U.D. degrees. It's a grab-bag affair where the handler draws a card telling him which six exercises two each from Novice, Open, and Utility) his dog will have to perform. The handler never knows which exercises he will draw until he gets to the show, so his dog must be prepared for everything from heeling to directed jumping, seek back to scent discrimination articles.

Team Class—a class in which four dogs (an alternate may be entered at no entry fee) perform novice exercises together, each dog with its own handler.

The above non-regular classes have specific rules which may be found in the A.K.C. rule book. The Canadian Kennel Club does not officially recognize non-regular classes in their book of regulations for obedience.

These, then, are the most important terms and definitions you will have to know. Other terms unique to obedience will be explained as we go along.

4

Basic Novice Training

BASIC COMMANDS

No matter how many degrees you hope to get with your dog, a firm foundation in novice work is an absolute *must*. Many of you will not compete in the ring but will use your dogs in the bird fields, in duck blinds, as companions in the home, as protectors of property, as working farm animals. But no matter what training the dog receives later, there are few areas in which the dog would not do better with a basis of standard, novice obedience training. Some breeds should get their work earlier than others; some sporting breeds should get their commands in different order than others. But all dogs of all breeds are never harmed by obedience training *if* it is taught correctly. And no matter what you want to do with your dog when he comes "of age," the following commands will be invaluable to you both for years to come:

Heeling—fast, slow, normal, right about turn, left about turn, circle to the right, circle to the left, figure eight.

Sit and Sit-Stay

Down and Down-Stay

Recall—come-fore with walking finish, standard recall, standard finish.

Heel-Jump-Heel—over solid high jumps as well as bar jumps.

TRAINING BY TWOS

Theories, theories, theories—*everybody's* got a theory! Why should we be an exception? Our pet theory, then, is that starting with you

(1) and your dog (2), the whole world of obedience training is based on a system of *twos*.

Since one picture is worth a thousand words, we felt it would be much easier if we cut a person in half to demonstrate our theory; trouble was the lack of volunteers. Then we decided to draw a trainer and divide the picture with dotted lines; trouble was that the author, obviously, is no artist. However, it was felt that our readers were people of imagination, so we went ahead with our "picture." (It's a girl trainer because our author can't draw boy trainers.)

The Two Sides of Your Body

THE ENTIRE RIGHT SIDE OF YOUR BODY will be used when you are *working against* your dog, or when *leaving him behind* or when *punishing him*. It might be summed up by simply stating that the right side is the wrong side.

The right hand is used only for punishment and correction. Keep your surplus training lead tucked neatly in your right hand so that it doesn't flop distractingly in the dog's face. If you want your dog to sit straight at heel (on your left) never pat or praise him with your right hand, as he will come across in front of you to sit where he is nearer the source of what he wants. Do the majority of your leash correction with your right hand, saving the left for when a severe jerk is in order you need both hands for strength and balance.

The right foot is the foot you lead out on—step off on, if you will—when you are leaving your dog behind you.

The right side of your body and your *right leg* must be off limits to your dog. If your dog should cross behind you and come up on your right side, correct him by slapping back sharply with your right hand or, with larger breeds, by swinging out threateningly with your right foot and leg. Encourage him back where he belongs and leave with him the impression that *right is wrong!*

THE ENTIRE LEFT SIDE OF YOUR BODY will be used when you are *working with* your dog, or when *taking him with you,* or for *reassurance and praise*—therefore, keep it in mind that the left side is the right side.

The left hand is used for encouragement, praise, reassurance. Your left hand should stay off the leash, except when it is needed for strength or balance as an aid to your right hand in severe corrections. Make your dog *want* to stay near your left hand: never let him worry that it will slap him or yank at him or snatch for him. Scratch his ears with your left hand when he is sitting properly. If you can reach your dog without bending, pat his shoulders occasionally as he heels along. Point with your left hand to show the dog where he belongs. Pat your

THIS IS A TRAINER

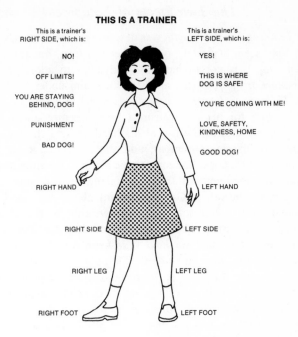

This is a trainer's RIGHT SIDE, which is:	This is a trainer's LEFT SIDE, which is:
NO!	YES!
OFF LIMITS!	THIS IS WHERE DOG IS SAFE!
YOU ARE STAYING BEHIND, DOG!	YOU'RE COMING WITH ME!
PUNISHMENT	LOVE, SAFETY, KINDNESS, HOME
BAD DOG!	GOOD DOG!
RIGHT HAND	LEFT HAND
RIGHT SIDE	LEFT SIDE
RIGHT LEG	LEFT LEG
RIGHT FOOT	LEFT FOOT

left leg to encourage the dog to stay in position. Never punish or correct with your left hand.

The left foot is the foot you lead out on—step off on, if you will—when you are taking your dog along with you.

The left side of your body and your *left leg* must represent safety, security, home to your dog. He must never be afraid to press close against your left leg or to come to your left side for sanctuary.

The Two Voices Used

A low, firm voice is used if the dog is to be left behind while the handler moves away from him, and when the dog has failed to obey the first command. This tone of voice is used to indicate *disapproval,* or to give extra emphasis.

A high, bright voice is used on any command which puts the dog in motion with or without his handler, and to show praise for a command executed correctly. This tone of voice indicates approval and encouragement.

From now on, all commands outlined herein will be followed by "L" for low voice or "H" for high voice. Since your most effective training aid is your voice, follow these directions carefully for the most effective training.

The Two Pieces of Equipment

1. *A Training Leash or Lead:* was described in the Glossary of Terms. Six feet may seem at first to be five feet too long, but the purpose of so much "rope" is not to hang anybody, but to allow you to get a good distance from your dog and still have him under control.

2. *A Training Collar:* also described in the Glossary of Terms. To measure a dog for his collar, run a tape measure under his throat and up over his ears to the top of his head, pulling the tape snug but not tight. To that measurement, add three inches for big dogs and two inches for little dogs. Take your tape along to the store and measure the collar flat on a counter from the farthest rim of one ring to the farthest rim of the other. Get lightweight chains for small dogs and somewhat heavier —but not overly so—weights for the larger breeds.

To get the maximum effectiveness out of these two pieces of equipment, it is essential that you *hold your leash correctly.* Grasp the end with the handle in your right hand. Don't wind it around your wrist or stick your arm through the loop handle. Just wad up the surplus any way you feel comfortable holding it. Correctly used, there should be a "U" in your leash from your right hand to the dog's collar, leaving the dog a reasonable area for error. Too much slack and the dog will trip over his leash, if you don't do so first. Too little slack and the dog will be fighting you every inch of the way. The length always depends on the height of the handler as well as the size of the dog. But, ideally, you can tell when you are about right if, when making the dog sit by pulling up on your leash, your right hand never goes higher than your right shoulder. The Statue of Liberty is a noble lady, but her arm is cement; yours is not, and you'll wear yourself out and throw yourself off balance if you have to "carry a torch" every time you pull up. Your left hand hangs relaxed and loose at your side.

It is very important to make sure your collar is on correctly. Go back to the show section and double-check the directions for putting a choke or chain collar on a dog in the correct manner. If working in a class, keep asking to be reassured each night until you are positive you understand. If working alone or with other novices, inspect each other's collars constantly to avoid errors.

We also described earlier how to lock a training collar so that it will not choke. To be completely safe, never put a dog in a kennel or crate or turn him loose to run free wearing an unlocked training collar.

The Two Golden Rules

1. *Teach only one thing at a time.* Perfection in any occupation comes in stages, never all at once. For instance, when teaching the recall,

concentrate on getting the animal to come to you happily and quickly; crooked sits and anticipated commands and automatic finishes can all be solved *after* the dog has learned the prime reason for the command—to come when called. It's rather nerve-wracking to watch people ruin an enthusiastic worker by nagging about little details which couldn't matter less in the long run.

2. *Get your dog's attention and keep it.* Once you manage this, all else is duck soup. How you accomplish this is up to you. Anything that works is correct. Watch your dog so that you can tell the moment his mind is wandering. Move briskly so that the dog is too busy keeping up to daydream; talk to him as you move along—the alphabet with rising and falling inflections can be as effective as *Evangeline* recited in singsong fashion. If the dog looks at you as if you'd lost your cotton-pick'n mind—well, he is looking at you, isn't he? Or, you might try changing direction without warning. Sneaky? Sure—but that's *his* problem. If he doesn't like being suddenly yanked off balance or getting a knee in his ear, all he has to do is pay attention. The minute your dog becomes convinced he'd better pay heed to you just in case you come up with something new, you've "got it made."

The Two Kinds of Commands

1. *The command of attention:* Before each command you give your dog, use his name to establish the fact that you are speaking to a specific dog. Never say: "Down, Fido." This is backwards. The correct method is: "Fido! (Hey, dog, I'm speaking to you) Down!" The dog's name or command of attention is given in a quick, high tone.

2. *The command of execution:* This has absolutely nothing to do with a firing squad. In the above paragraph, the "Down!" was the command of execution—it was the command you gave your dog after you got his attention, to tell him what you wanted him to do. All together it works like this:

"Fido!" (Hey, friend, pay heed, I'm about to tell you something.) "Down!" (That's what I want you to do.)

But no matter what theory you use in training any animal to do *anything,* never let it be in doubt that *you* are boss! No matter how many hours you spend training an animal, no matter how much help you get, no matter how many rules you memorize—nothing you do will give you a trained dog—or horse or monkey—unless you have

A POSITIVE ATTITUDE

Certainly, as you start your training, you will have misgivings. But this is something you should not share with your dog. You must approach every single moment of your training with the belief that your dog will obey. You must never *ask* a dog to sit or stay or come; you must tell him he's going to sit or stay or come.

When your dog disobeys you, never sag, inwardly or outwardly. If you sag inside, the dog knows he's got you confused. If you sag outwardly, you've relaxed your control for a minute or two—and that's long enough to give the dog even more naughty ideas.

Keep going. Mentally and physically you must behave as if you had an end in sight, and as if you never had a moment's doubt that you would reach that end with the dog.

In a class situation, the moment you don't understand, say so. If you don't like training as much as you thought you would, quit. But if you decide to train an animal, never waver once you start. Behave as if you've done this all your life. Your fumblings with your leash and your slow responses and faulty co-ordination in the beginning can be corrected by others. But only you can convince your dog he will mind you; only you will give him the notion that he doesn't have to mind if he doesn't feel like it.

You are a human being; your dog is an animal. It may be tough sledding from time to time, but how disgusting to imagine, even for a moment, that this four-legged, furry bit of beloved wiggle and wag could ever dominate you! Sure, he's got your heart all sewed up, and that's as it should be. But if he's got you licked mentally, you are both in serious trouble.

If you are working in an established class, watch the trainer as he or she takes your unruly child and he behaves like a lamb. The trainer isn't smarter than you are; the dog doesn't like the trainer better than you. But the moment the trainer's hand touches the leash, he is in command; it never occurs to him it could be any other way; it shouldn't occur to *you* either. Therefore, make sure you never lie to your dog!

Stop to think a moment. Isn't that exactly what you do when you say to a dog, for example, "Heel!" and then let him pull you around for goodness knows how long before finally saying: "Look, Buster, I wasn't kidding—I said, 'Heel!' and I meant it!"? Good trainers don't lie to their dogs. When they tell a dog to do something, they level with him; the dog who is calm and happy in his work knows his handler always tells him the truth. He can *rely* on his handler; he can *believe* him, every single time.

Trainers who lie are lazy people. It's more work to tell the truth with your training methods—more work in the beginning, that is. But in the end, the truthful handler spends less time and effort than anyone else—because his dog can count on him and he can count on his dog.

ON-LEASH EXERCISES

Just as student pilots sometimes "freeze on the stick," student trainers often "freeze" on the training leash. Because you are confused and unsure, your tendency will be to grab that lead and hang on for dear life until the dog starts slowly turning purple!

Don't pull steadily against your dog—you just can't win. Even the smallest breeds can tow a man a city block without tiring. So don't fight the system. *Jerk,* don't *pull.* A *jerk* is a sudden tightening of an otherwise loose leash, then the leash is loosened again. *Loose, tight, loose,* that's a *jerk.* The opposite of this is the constant pulllllllll.

Remember, keep that left hand off the lead when it is not needed. But if the situation calls for a healthy correction, put both hands on the lead and really *jerk* (or *snap)* that lead once, so that it means something.

Fear not! A dog's neck is well-constructed. If you use your leash and collar *correctly,* it is impossible to injure your dog. People who complain that their dog's neck is raw from a training collar or that the dog spits up or chokes when he is training, are blaming the collar when it is really their fault. They are pulllllllling, sawing away endlessly on the poor animal. Jerk! Don't pulllllll! Jerk! Don't pulllllll!

The following obedience commands are given in conjunction with a trainer's commands. If you are working alone, you will only use those directions labeled "Handler's Command":

Heeling

INSTRUCTOR'S COMMAND: HANDLER'S COMMAND:
"Forward!"   "Fido, Heel!" (H)

The *At Heel* position is "home base" for most exercises—they all begin with the dog sitting *At Heel.* You will tell the dog to "Heel!" when you want him to come along with you, or if he is too far afield and you want him closer to your leg.

How to make a dog move forward at this command: Forget you are at training class and pretend you are at a bowling alley. The gesture you use to put a bowling ball in motion is the same one you will use to start the dog moving. Swing out on your *left foot,* shoving your *left hand* forward at the same time, pointing to your *left leg;* give the vocal command at the same time. Snap your leash briskly with your

When first starting out with a dog, it is often necessary to exaggerate the motion of the hand and the left leg when giving the command, "Whiskers, heel!" This is particularly true with those breeds built close to the ground, like this Cairn Terrier. Since their eyes are not on stalks, it is helpful, until they have become used to watching you for signals, to bend a little nearer to them so that they are very aware of your movements. *Photo by Glenn Easton*

right hand as you start off, then *keep moving.* Once you start, *don't stop, don't slow up, don't wait for the dog,* no matter what he wants to do.

Don't reach back to tug at the dog with your left hand or to pat him when he's behind you; teach him at the start that if wants approval he'll have to come up beside your left leg to get it.

Apply the old Rule of Opposites.

If the dog is *wide,* you go *wider,* snapping your leash sharply and making him come close to you by encouraging him with your left hand, patting your leg encouragingly.

If the dog is *crowding,* walk into him—*you* crowd *him* right back! Shove him with your knee or with your hip. *Never shove him with your left hand.*

If the dog is *lagging,* speed up. Encourage him with voice and hand while insisting with your leash. Generally speaking, the faster a trainer goes, the faster the dog will go trying to keep up.

If the dog is *forging,* slow down. Back away from him at an angle to your right, throwing him off balance. A number of quick right-about turns will help here. But remember to snap the leash hard, don't pull against the dog.

How to Make a Dog Sit

INSTRUCTOR'S COMMAND:	HANDLER'S COMMAND:
"Halt!"	"Fido, Sit!" (L)

Dogs are like seesaws; that is, when one end goes up and is *kept up,* the other end goes down and *stays down.* Also, dogs are like deck chairs—if you follow the directions given by the maker, they fold easily.

So to make your dog sit promptly and neatly pull up and back on your collar briskly with your right hand *at the same moment* you push him down sharply on the outside (far side) of the dog's derriere with your left hand.

Don't pinch or dig with your nails; don't use the dog's tail as a handle or his surplus skin as a grip. Synchronize a sort of slap-push with the left hand with the up-and-back snap of the right hand.

Never turn your body toward the dog. Keep facing straight ahead, bend your knees, apply the slap-push to the *outside edge* of the dog's bottom so that in forcing him to sit you pull him in tight against your left leg. Give one command only.

And *never wait to see* if the dog is going to sit—he's a beginner too, you know, and he's not *that* smart! If ever you have to "wait and see," *he's not sitting fast enough!* Staring fixedly at his rear won't help; neither will leaning over and screaming in his ear. Stand up, bend knees, jerk up with right hand, slap down with left hand. If the dog sits properly, your left hand will miss him; but the times he is slow, you'll be ready for him.

Circle to the Right

INSTRUCTOR'S COMMAND:	HANDLER'S COMMAND:
"Circle to the right!"	"Fido, Heel!" (H)

When you hear this command as you are heeling along, you will make a complete, individual circle, swinging away from your dog to start your circle. Make only one complete circle, then continue on in the direction you were going before. The idea is to make a tight enough circle to require your dog to adjust his pace to yours without dragging back or forging. Short, brisk little jerks on your lead will best control the dog here.

Right about Turn

INSTRUCTOR'S COMMAND:	HANDLER'S COMMAND:
"Right about turn!"	"Fido, Heel!" (H)

You will turn away from your dog and go in the opposite direction from the one in which you were heeling when you were given this command. As you give your command and turn sharply to your right, give your leash a quick jerk or snap; then loose leash again and keep moving in the opposite direction. A lot of encouragement with the left hand against your left leg is helpful here. As you make your turn-about, *don't hesitate, don't halt.* Keep going. Don't swing the dog around like a sack of potatoes or wheel him into orbit like a yo-yo. Try crouching down a bit as you turn and exaggerate your left-hand encouragement to show the dog where he belongs. Praise him lavishly as soon as the turn is made and you are both on the straightaway again.

Circle to the Left

INSTRUCTOR'S COMMAND: HANDLER'S COMMAND:
"Circle to the left!:   "Fido, Heel!" (H)

This exercise is executed exactly as is the *circle to the right* except, of course, that you turn into your dog to start your circle, not away from him. Again, make only one complete circle, then continue on in the direction you were going before. The idea is to make a tight enough circle to require your dog to get out of your way and out from under your feet as you walk into him. So as you swing into the left circle, bring up your *right* knee sharply and bump him once solidly, encouraging him immediately thereafter to stay close to your left leg, but "out from under" by patting your left leg with your left hand. Keep your eye peeled and the moment he starts to crowd, use your knee again. Tiny breeds are too far below your knee, so use your right instep to push them out of your way. When using your leash here, snap backward sharply on it as you turn into the circle.

Left about Turn

INSTRUCTOR'S COMMAND: HANDLER'S COMMAND:
"Left about turn!"   "Fido, Heel!" (H)

Just as you changed direction in the *right* about turn, so you will change direction in the *left* about, but this time in so doing you will turn to the left, or into your dog. As in the circle to the left, this command is designed to teach the dog to keep out of your way, so as you make your turn remember that right knee or right foot, and don't forget to snap backward on the leash as you turn. Don't try "begging the question" by walking obliquely around your dog. Try to keep in mind *who* is training *whom.*

Three Speeds Heeling

INSTRUCTOR'S COMMANDS:	HANDLER'S COMMANDS:
"Fast!" or "Double!"	"Fido, Heel!" (H)
"Normal Pace!"	"Fido, Heel!" (L/H) [1]
"Slowly!" or "Slow!"	"Fido, Heel!" (H) [1]

This is another way of teaching your dog to adapt his pace to your pace and is a great aid in getting the dog to pay attention to his handler. While you shouldn't be unreasonable about changing pace so suddenly that the dog has no chance to correct his rate of speed and therefore is *unable* to adapt to your speed, still you should change briskly enough so that the dog is forced to keep his mind on his business. *Your normal pace* is the rate at which you heel through most training exercises—a brisk, military walk, never an amble. Fast or double is a dead run for you and usually a gallop for your dog if he intends to keep up. But while this gait is a pell-mell-ish sort of thing, it is *still a controlled exercise,* so be sure you aren't racing each other. *Slowly* is a studied, artificial pace, almost a slow step. But be sure you aren't going so slowly that the dog is expecting you to halt every minute and keeps trying to sit. In the beginning, to get prompt response to your changes of pace, exaggerate those changes. You can become normal in your rate changes as soon as the dog starts adapting on his own without a jerk or encouragement from you.

Figure Eight

INSTRUCTOR'S COMMANDS:	HANDLER'S COMMANDS:
"Forward!"	"Fido, Heel!" (H)
"Halt!"	"Fido, Sit!" (L)

[1] Please notice that in giving the command for these types of heeling, the command for the *Fast* or *Double* is *always given in a high voice,* because you want to speed up your dog whenever you start running.

With the *normal pace* both *high voice and low voice* were recommended for these reasons: if you have been running at the double and want to slow the dog down for the normal pace, you certainly wouldn't give him an enthusiastic command which would excite him even more. Instead, give your "Heel!" in this instance with a low, warning tone which says, "Watch it, son, we're going to calm down now." On the other hand, if you have been progressing at *slow* speed and want to resume the *normal* rate of speed, naturally you would use a *high tone of voice* to "jazz up" the dog.

With the *slow pace,* always use a *lowered inflection* because you are trying to slow the dog down, to hold him back a bit. It would be quite unfair, obviously, to excite him *forward* and then snap him *backward* because he believed you!

By the time you get to the Figure Eight, it should be duck soup. You have learned the *circle to the right* and the *circle to the left;* now all you have to do is put them together. You start this exercise at the mythical center of a large "8" drawn on the ground. One circle is on your right; one is on your left. The instructor will tell you in which direction to start. When the trainer gives the command "Forward," give your dog his heel command and start off to your right or left— whichever way you were instructed. When you have completed the first loop or circle, *keep going* right on into the next loop or circle. You will halt frequently at different places whenever you are told to by your trainer. But you should *not* stop automatically at the center of the "8"—simply cross it and keep going until told to halt. This exercise has two values. One is obvious: the dog is taught to keep up and to keep out from under his handler's feet. The second is that it also teaches *you and the dog* quick and *straight sits.* Since you will get the "Halt!" command at various spots around the Figure Eight, you will sometimes have to stop on a curve; keeping a sit straight in this instance takes concentration. As you travel your Figure Eight, *never change your rate of speed.* Start with a speed at which the dog can keep up when he's on the outside of the circle, and it will be a good speed when he is on the inside of the circle. If you feel him start to lag, speed up. When using friends or chairs or objects to serve as "posts" for your Figure Eight, don't cut your left post too sharply or you'll cut off your dog and make it impossible for him to keep with you; and *don't* exaggerate your swing on your right circle or he will have more than reasonable difficulty trying to stay with you here too.

The ideal Figure Eight is executed in two identical circles of equal circumference, negotiated at a steady, even rate of speed. In using your leash for this exercise, try giving your jerks *as you cross the center of the "8"* just to remind Mr. Fido that you have not left the country.

Sit-Stay

INSTRUCTOR'S COMMANDS:	HANDLER'S COMMANDS:
"Leave your dog!"	"Stay!" (L)
"Return to your dog!"	
"End of exercise	
or	
"Exercise Finished!"	

This is the first time you have left your dog behind you. Remember that *lowered inflection,* and also note that the handler does *not* use the dog's name preceding this command. This is because "Fido" is the command of attention, and until now each time the dog heard it he sat up ready to move out. You want him to stay put now, so why get him all set to move?

To leave your dog: With the dog sitting at heel, place your left hand, palm up, around the leash just *below* where the snap connects to the collar; throw the rest of the leash out on the floor in front of the dog. Stepping out on your *right foot,* swing around facing the dog, bringing your right palm to a sudden halt just in front of the dog's nose. As you swing out, and at the same moment that you bring that right palm into position, give your command "Stay!" (L). Now, start quietly backing away to the end of your leash, letting the leash slide through the fingers of your left hand so that there is always a steady, taut pressure on the leash. You are, in effect, pulling the dog toward you, though you want and expect him to resist that pull. Keep your right hand out level with the dog's nose as you back up. *Keep quiet unless* the dog does get up and start toward you. Then quickly step

While performing the "Figure Eight" exercise on your way to a Companion Dog degree, the dog is required to work around human "posts"; ring stewards are used. In training, however, the dog must learn to work near and around all sorts of obstacles. Two lawn chairs or a pair of wastebaskets will do; or, when working with fellow trainers, other dogs in various stages of training can be used. The working dog will find them distracting at first; and the "posts" will have to get used to a dog moving around them as they stay put. *Photo by Glenn Easton*

forward—and the trick is *quickly*—bringing that right hand smartly in contact with his erring nose. Repeat "Stay!" in an even sterner, more warning tone. When you reach the end of your leash, stand up straight, holding the leash loosely. Hesitate only a moment before returning to heel. Never jerk or rattle the leash, or you will make your dog break his sit. Don't warble; that, too, will make him nervous and unsure. Shut up and stand still. If the dog breaks, correct with your right hand, smacking him smartly on his muzzle; or, if you didn't catch him soon enough, go back and start from scratch. The psychology of the Sit-Stay is simple: teach the dog from the beginning that the place where you left him is safe and on that spot only nice things will happen. But if he trespasses into the no man's land between the spot where he was left and the spot where you are standing facing him, life will become unpleasant.

Return to your dog: Start back to the dog, keeping him on your left and circle around behind him and up into heel position. To discourage the dog's natural inclination to swing around as you pass him and follow you, keep your *loose leash* high in your left hand and on the left of the dog as you approach him. Since he is busy worrying about "cannons on the left of him, cannons on the right of him," chances are good he'll be so unsure *which* way to turn that he *won't* turn. At any rate, by the time you are at heel, it will be too late; it won't matter what he wanted to do, as he never got a chance to do it.

End of Exercise, or Exercise Finished: This means that the exercise has been completed and it's time for you to show your approval and appreciation. Step away from the dog *first,* then tell him "OK! Let's play! Good doggie!" Let the dog bounce and slurp and show off for a few moments. Then settle down and repeat the exercise. Always step away from your dog before releasing him so that he doesn't get the mistaken impression that the moment you get near him or are standing beside him he can move.

Come Fore

INSTRUCTOR'S COMMAND: HANDLER'S COMMAND:
"Come Fore!"   "Fido, Come!" (H)

The first step in teaching a dog to come when called, this exercise utilizes the old theory that dogs chase things that move away from them. This is why dogs chase cars, balls, cats, other dogs, and also why they chase people—and the "people" in this case is going to be you.

As you are heeling along, suddenly shift into reverse, dropping all of your wadded-up leash except the end of it. *Don't turn your body at all. Just start backing up, backing away from the dog, and don't wait to see what he's going to do. Keep backing.* When you get to the end of your leash and Fido is still six feet away, couple a solid snap or jerk with the "Fido, Come!" (H) command. Keep backing until you dog is chasing after you. When you are sure that he wants to reach you *more* than you want him to chase you, start gathering up your slack leash but keep it loose, so that as he finally catches up, all you have to do is pull up on that leash, tell your dog to sit, and there you have it—dog sitting happy and wagging in front of handler; handler standing panting and exhausted facing dog.

Incidentally, while your instructor, if any, gives you the "Come Fore" command to start you off, *when* you halt is entirely up to the individual. A large dog sometimes requires more backing to bring him into line than a small dog, so the trainer just waits until all is quiet again. The most important thing to remember here is *not* to simply back up two steps and stop as the dog, lost and off balance, bangs into you. If the dog is to learn to come, he must *come toward his handler.* Keep going until he is trying to reach you. Also, while most exercises include the warning, "Don't warble, give one command only," the "Come Fore" allows you to warble all you wish. "Fido, Come!" (H) should be followed by, "That's a good girl, come along, honey," or "Come, come, attaboy!" in order to make reaching you an irresistible thing to your dog. When he is sitting in front, take *both hands* and, scratching him behind the ears, coo more endearments at him. To come must be a glorious thing— which brings us to why so many dogs don't come when called!

Stop and think a moment, now. When you call your dog at home, *why* do you do so? Sure, you want him. But *why* do you want him? Be honest about it. Isn't it a fact that you call your dog to scold him, to give him a pill, to put him in his kennel or on a leash—all things that mean the dog's freedom is ended and something unpleasant is in store? Dogs, as some educated scholar once pointed out, ain't stoopid! Why *should* the dog come if it's always going to mean "un-fun"?

Call your dog to you frequently *simply because you want to smooch him or pat him or give him a tidbit.* Then turn him loose again. When you want to scold or medicate or confine, go *to* the dog. He'll soon be coming like a flash.

Now back to the "Come Fore." You will have a dog sitting squarely in front of you, just as he was instructed to do. Which is loverlee, except that now there is no way to get around the dog in order to continue your training unless you walk on, through, or over said animal. So how to get him out of the handler's path is the next problem, which brings us to the

Walking Finish

INSTRUCTOR'S COMMAND: HANDLER'S COMMAND:
"Finish!"   "Fido, Heel!" (H)

With the bulk of your leash in your right hand, put your left hand down the leash to the snap. Now, with your right foot, take a giant sliding dance step to your right, giving the command "Fido, Heel" (H). As you start walking briskly forward, snap that leash with your left hand. Remove your left hand from the lead as soon as the dog falls into step beside you. When you are both side by side again, give the Sit command. As you practice this command following the Come Fore, try taking fewer and fewer steps after getting the dog in at heel, so he gradually lays the foundation for the regular finish during which you stand still and he does all the moving.

During the execution of the Come Fore and Walking Finish, concentrate on the fact that never once do you ever turn your body. If you start out walking north, you do the Come Fore by walking south; to complete the Walking Finish, you walk north once again.

The Recall

INSTRUCTOR'S COMMAND: HANDLER'S COMMAND:
"Call your dog"   "Fido, Come!" (H)

The recall is the final step in teaching your dog to come when called. The psychology of this exercise and the vocal commands and leash work involved are the same as in the Come Fore. The only difference is that this time the *dog* does *all* the moving while you just stand and wait.

It has been truly said many times that the hardest part of any recall is the last six feet. Happily, this is the length of your training leash, so if you train your dog to come quickly from the end of his leash when he hears your "Fido, Come!" command, and to sit straight and promptly when he reaches your toes, you are home safe. After that, whether the distance of your recall is six feet or sixty, he can usually be relied upon to do it stylishly and happily.

To teach the recall correctly, leave your dog on a sit-stay exactly as if you were going to do a long sit. But when you reach the end of the leash and face your dog, separate your feet a bit and put both hands on your leash squarely in the mid-tummy area. Give your command and, as you do so, *stand up straight!* There is a natural and universal yen to bend over as in coaxing the dog, but to do so will only cause him to sit too far away from you, especially with small breeds to whom the looming you resembles nothing so much as a weeping willow! Accompany the "Fido, Come!" command with a firm snap on the leash, *whether or not the dog needs it.* As we said before in the exercise dealing with having a dog sit at heel, if you have to wait and see if a dog is going to obey any command, he is not responding promptly enough; and if you have to give a second command, then you are teaching him that he has permission to goof once. Obviously this is no basis for training *anything!* So give your vocal command in an encouraging but firm voice, snap the lead as you speak the words, then encourage him all the way in with your voice. Gather up your surplus leash as he advances toward you, but *keep it loose at all times.*

The leash work in the recall is very important. Do your jerking smoothly from tummy level, your hands close to your body. Keep patting your tummy as you gather the surplus leash so that the activity of your hands keeps your dog's eyes riveted on them. When the dog is about two steps away from your toes, with your fingers going like mad and both hands still together, start raising your hands. Keep raising them and when you say "Fido, Sit!" (L) as the dog is in position for sitting, watch his bottom go down. Why not? His head is so high in the air that sitting is quite natural at this point.

Remembering our foremost training rule—*teach one thing at a time*—two dogs graduate from "Come-Fore" on a training leash to "Come" on a longer check line. Because we do not want to confuse them with the difference between staying put and coming when called, the instructor holds the dogs gently until the trainers give their commands. Notice that we use a considerably heavier line with the Irish Wolfhound than we do with the tiny mixed-breed dog. *Photo by Glenn Easton*

Remember to praise *with both hands* when the exercise has gone successfully. In conclusion, a word or two about why the hands are together and the feet apart. The accuracy of the finished recall depends on teaching the dog accurately in the beginning. And to teach the dog accuracy, do it simply, in terms he can most quickly understand. By separating the feet a bit we give him a "landing strip," a "garage," an area to come to bordered by your feet, the presence of which, one on either side of your dog, will tend to keep him straight. Now, if his body is to wind up straight, it is necessary that his head be aimed straight at his handler; a dog's head is always pointed where his eyes tell him to look. So keep his eyes busy and on *one single spot* and the rest comes naturally.

Last but far, far from least: always *praise* your dog when he comes to you and sits in front of you looking up at you. He does so because he *expects* that praise; never deny or disappoint him and he will never deny or disappoint you. Now that the dog is sitting in front, you will next teach the end of the exercise, i.e., getting the dog around at heel so he is out of your way and ready to work again. But don't slip into the sloppy habit of praising only when the dog has returned to heel. Praise for *coming,* and praise for *finishing.* Then both parts of this two-part exercise will be done well. Also, you will avoid the pitfall of "teaching" a dog when you call him to come directly to heel, because that is the only place he is rewarded.

The Finish

INSTRUCTOR'S COMMAND: HANDLER'S COMMAND:
"Finish!"   "Fido, Heel!" (H)

The Finish is done in two ways, depending upon your personal preference, the size of your dog compared to the size of you, or the personality of your dog.

The Standard Finish requires that after coming on the recall and sitting in front of the handler, the dog, upon receiving the command "Fido, Heel!" will get up and walk to *his right* in a circular pattern that winds up with him sitting at heel at his handler's left side.

The Baltimore Finish requires that after coming in the recall and sitting in front of the handler, the dog, upon receiving the command "Fido, Heel!" will get up and walk to *his left,* coming *behind* the handler and up into heel where he will sit without further command.

Both methods are taught in two steps to make it easier for the handler; it is necessary only to decide *before starting to learn the exercise* how you are going to do it; then all that remains is to stick with your decision. Once you have started to teach this exercise in one manner, it is obviously unfair and quite foolhardy to switch the dog back and forth.

We come now to the difference between the finishes, or why one is used in preference to the other. The only difference, really, is in actual traffic patterns. Some sporting-dog men say they like their dogs to return behind them so that they are out of the way of the guns; other sporting-dog men say no, that when a dog is behind a shooter he is out of the shooter's range of vision and that they want to know where the dog is all the time.

As far as we are concerned, the methods described are both excellent. The Standard Finish can be executed in a more flashy style sometimes, particularly when an enthusiastic small dog learns to "flip" straight up in the air on the "Fido, Heel!" command, coming down for a perfectly square, three-point landing at heel. But the Baltimore Finish, we find, usually guarantees more consistently accurate sits, as the dog comes into heel position facing forward and doesn't have to turn out of a circle on as much of an angle. Also, the Baltimore Finish seems easier for people with big, long breeds of dogs which weren't built to turn corners neatly, and also for little handlers (small of stature, that is) who are not strong enough to force a dog back and then turn him correctly for a straight sit. We don't care at all which finish you use. We recommend that handlers with big dogs, handlers with handicaps such as a bum knee or a lame arm, junior trainers, and elderly people use the Baltimore Finish. But remember, we *only recommend.* The real choice is up to you, so make up your mind, because *here we go!*

The Standard Finish

INSTRUCTOR'S COMMAND: HANDLER'S COMMAND:
"Finish!" "Fido, Heel!" (H)

In order to learn this exercise carefully and correctly you will first "walk through it" with your dog. The position for beginning the Standard Finish finds your dog sitting squarely in front of you and close to your toes.

In step one, when you give your "Fido, Heel!" (H) command, *do not move your left leg or foot.* This is the "post" or "target" your dog must learn to come to when told, so keep it stationary. As you guide him around to heel position, you are going to make what amounts to an old-fashioned curtsy. Cross your right leg back behind your left leg to give you the balance you need to direct the dog *away from and behind* that left leg. In step two, bring your right foot back into position to give you the balance you need to direct the dog *up from behind and into position beside your left leg.* Pull dog's head up and give Sit command.

While the whole thing may sound as if a trainer has to emulate a pretzel, actually the finish is very simple to get across to your dog if you remember that *dogs need room to turn in*. You can't pull the dog straight along your left leg and then force him to turn around with no turning area. You'll get crooked sits and a pugnosed dog. So remember to make the dog's circle into heel position one which (STEP 1) pushes him away from your left leg far enough to allow him to turn into it and which (STEP 2) takes him behind your left leg far enough to allow him to come up into heel in a straight approach rather than on an angle.

Don't strangle the dog by dragging him into heel position. Start him with short jerks and keep encouraging him along so he wants to get to home base and doesn't spend his time fighting the leash for breath.

It should be unnecessary to point out that the moment the dog is properly at heel, he should be praised highly with your *left hand*.

The Baltimore Finish

INSTRUCTOR'S COMMAND:	HANDLER'S COMMAND:
"Finish!"	"Fido, Heel!" (H)

Again, first "walk through it" with your dog. The position for beginning the Baltimore Finish finds your dog sitting squarely in front of you facing you, just as if he had completed the recall.

Without turning your body, pass your leash around behind you until it is looped with *very little slack* around your right hip, across the back of your knees and up to your tummy again, this time the surplus being held in your left hand. Your right hand should be way down the leash near the snap.

STEP 1—When you hear the instructor's command "Finish!" step back with your right foot, then snap backward behind you with your right hand on the leash. As you do so, your command is "Fido, Heel!" (H). This motion on your part should be strong enough to carry the dog a bit past your right side, still facing behind and away from you.

STEP 2—Now quickly transfer any surplus leash from your left to your right hand, which is free the moment it has given the leash the initial jerk. Your left hand should now start patting your left leg as your right hand snaps the leash with short, sharp jerks, and you give vocal encouragement to heel. As soon as the dog is sitting beside you, praise highly with the left hand.

As soon as this is going well, stop moving your feet. Keep giving the start-off jerk with your right hand only as long as necessary to start the dog moving. Be sure to use your left hand to praise and encourage; don't drag the dog or strangle him.

THE HALFWAY POINT

No matter in what order you have learned the exercises given so far, or whether you are working alone or in a group, now is a good time to pause a moment and review to make sure both you and your dog are absolutely clear about each exercise you have learned.

If you are working alone, ask a friend to check you out at this stage of the game. The more unfamiliar your friend is with obedience training, the better. Ask him to answer to his own satisfaction the following questions:

Does the dog work happily?

Does the trainer move as if he knew what he was doing?

Is the trainer repeating many commands for a single exercise without realizing it?

Is the dog obeying on the first command or waiting until the second or third?

Because your critic is ignorant of the whys and wherefores, he can be absolutely objective in his "grading" of your performance. It may make you a bit hot under the collar, but you'd be amazed at the things you do without ever realizing you are doing them until somebody "peeks!"

If you are working with an organized group, now is the moment for you to take advantage of the offers usually made repeatedly by members of such groups regarding outside-of-class help for those who want it. Extra, private instruction in any club is almost always available if you ask for it in advance. Don't hesitate to speak up if you don't understand—who knows, maybe nobody else does either. This is the point at which you should stop being afraid of being wrong—who's perfect all the time?

Whether solo or in a training class, this is the time in your training known as "the point of no return." You must face the fact *right now* that you and your dog are no longer beginners. Your dog knows the commands given so far; you know how to enforce them. So from now on, you *must* insist the dog do his part or he will never be a trained dog, just a dominated one.

For example, it's high time your dog should be sitting *automatically* when you halt. If he doesn't obey your "Fido, Sit!" (L) command, swat his behind smartly, snap up on your leash. Stop *making* him sit and start *giving him a reason to do it himself.*

Here's a Checklist of questions to ask yourself:

Is your dog's collar always on right?

Is the leash loose enough?

Is your voice always audible and positive?

Is your normal rate of speed brisk enough to keep the dog's attention?

Does your command of attention always precede your command of execution?

Are you guilty of being careless with your training habits because you are more relaxed than you were at the beginning?

No truer saying was ever coined than, "A little knowledge is a dangerous thing." It seems the more obedience trainers learn, the less they feel it necessary to make themselves clear to their dogs. They seem to feel after a few lessons that because they know what is expected of the dog, the dog knows too. Consequently, when the dog is across a room from them or down the block a few yards, they suddenly yell "Fido!" in a commanding manner—leaving their poor dog to puzzle out whether they mean "Come!" or "Sit!" or "Down!" If one is foolish enough to question one of these neophytes, chances are he would turn on you with: "He knows what I mean!"

Be honest now—isn't this a bit ridiculous? If you are guilty of this very common training booboo, admit it and break it up, fast!

Beware of Boredom. In obedience, particularly at the novice level, one of the greatest enemies of the trainer and his dog is boredom. After all, the variety in novice commands isn't exactly mind-boggling.

At this point in your training you should be reminded that if boredom is not to slow down your prodigy, it is up to you, the trainer, to keep things interesting and challenging. Don't always give your dog his exercises in the same order, at the same time, or in the same location. Try doing your finishes separately before you do your recalls, for instance. Most dogs love to jump, and we'll get to that in our next training exercises. While it is another chance to maintain control under slightly different circumstances, it serves largely to put a little fun into going to school. Now on to new exercises.

MORE ON LEASH EXERCISES

Down on Command

INSTRUCTOR'S COMMAND:	HANDLER'S COMMAND:
"Put your dogs down at heel!"	"Fido, Down!" (L)

The Down Command is taught first *at heel* because it seems easier for new handlers to control their dogs at heel and because the down command given from in front of the dog often presents a perfectly natural problem in temperament. This is what we call "a punishment command." In other words, your hand is going to be raised against your darling, probably for the first time. Since many dogs sincerely resent this and make no bones about showing their resentment, we start a little lower down the ladder and work up.

The biggest bottleneck in the Down is the fact that novices insist upon trying to achieve results by pushing on the dog's neck or head, which forces only the front part of the dog into submission. So if you want your entire dog on the floor and not just his nose and chin whiskers, do your pushing on the part of the dog's back immediately *behind his shoulder blades.* Another word of advice: dogs are uniquely built machines, well-braced in the hinges. If you push straight down on any dog, chances are he'll grin at you and remain solidly in place. Make your push an off-balance thing, pushing to one side or the other and a bit toward the front of the dog.

When you hear the instructor's command "Put your dogs down at heel!" your dog should be sitting at heel. Simply lean over and place your left hand on the animal's back as directed above. As you give your command "Fido, Down!" (L), push sharply to either the right or left. If you encounter resistance, and most of you will the first time, *don't release your pressure until the dog is horizontal.* If you push hard enough and quickly enough, the dog will be prone before he knows what happened.

Anything goes in getting the dog down the first time. But we do not feel it necessary to pull the dog's legs out from under him or tap the floor beseechingly in order to achieve this command. All you are asking is that he lie down. This requires no great personal sacrifice on his part, so don't make a project out of it. You may use both hands to push if you are small or if the dog is large. You may use your leash as a pully, sliding it under your instep for leverage; as you pull up on your leash you are pulling the dog down at the same time. But whatever method you favor, get the dog down and get him down fast.

Now we come to the part where the dog decides he's had enough. He doesn't want to be pushed around—up *or* down—and he snarls or snaps or tries to bite. Don't you dare back off! If a young child stamped his foot and screamed, "I won't!" most parents would plop said child across the lap and change it to, "I will!" Don't act a bit differently because this tantrum is being staged by a four-footed child instead of a two-footed one. If he tries to bite, make sure it's his one and only try; teach him that hand he is aiming for can bite back! Slap him sharply and solidly once; thunder "No! Phooey!" at him in your most horrible tone of voice, then immediately start all over again to put him down.

Once success is reached and the dog is lying on the floor, lovingly praise him by scratching him on the *top* of his head and stroking his

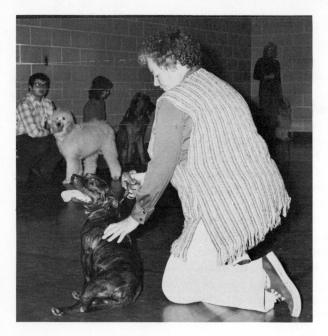

No matter what size dog you are training, if you push on him just behind his shoulders *in the direction he is leaning,* the down is rarely a difficult command. Pushing straight down on any dog's body usually produces little more than cement-like resistance. As you can see in the case of this Staffordshire Bull Terrier, he is "listing" toward the trainer, who is about to push down in that direction.

back. As you pat soothingly and quietly, you might croon, "Staaaaayyyyy! Staaaaayyyyy!" Whatever you do to reward his obedience, be careful that your excitement at his coming through for you doesn't pop him right back up into a sit again.

Once the dog is down, *never try to hold him there.* Dogs don't like to be held down; even small puppies become terrified if you try to hold them flat. Get your hands off the moment the dog is lying down—and never mind *how* he is lying. If he is down, what does it matter that his feet are straight up in the air, or that he is lying on his right side? Don't nag—position in life is *not* everything. He's down, and that's good enough for now.

Down Command from in Front

INSTRUCTOR'S COMMAND:	HANDLER'S COMMAND:
"Leave your dogs and take two steps forward, face your dogs; put your dogs down!"	"Fido, Stay!" (L) "Fido, Down!" (L)

The Down Command from in Front of the Dog is the next step. By the time you get this far in your "downing," most of the battle will be over. This command is given the dog when you are about two

However, even the smallest dogs can be very determined, and sometimes an inexperienced handler is not co-ordinated enough to manage with the push alone. So, if necessary, snap down on a very shortened leash as you push down on the dog. If that is not sufficient . . .

Try slipping your leash under the arch of your foot and pulling *up* on your leash as you push down on the dog. This maneuver gives you added front leverage. At any cost, do not cease the battle until the war is won!

steps in front of him facing him. At the instructor's command to "Put your dogs down!" this distance allows you room enough to take one step toward your dog as you raise your right hand in a Hitler salute. Only, instead of screaming "Heil!" you say firmly and with lowered inflection, "Fido, Down!" As you speak, lower your hand to the dog's withers—that area we described in the paragraph on getting the dog down at heel—and keep pushing until the dog is prone. Never give two hand commands any more than you would give two voice commands. Push down briskly and firmly, again at an angle. Remember, you are now in front of your dog and, because of the way he is constructed, you will do your pushing to one side or the other but slightly toward the dog's rear section.

Once the dog is down, praise as you did in the Down at Heel exercise, then return to heel. Watch as you return that the dog doesn't start to sit up. Push him down again smartly at the slightest indication, and repeat your lowered "Fido, Down!" To avoid this natural inclination to rise on his part, as you return to heel stand about six inches away from him. Keep your eyes straight ahead and listen for the slightest movement indicating he is changing his position. He's perfectly free to flop from one hip to the other or to roll over; don't pounce unless he sits up. Then pounce good and proper!

The moment success is achieved, pat him with the same hand that was raised against him and act as if nothing unusual had happened. Don't apologize and don't sympathize! If this small difference of opinion is the worst thing that ever happens to either of you, you're *both* lucky!

Down-Stay

INSTRUCTOR'S COMMAND:	HANDLER'S COMMAND:
"Leave your dogs!" (in the down position)	"Stay!" (L)

Remember, as was explained in the Sit-Stay, we use no names, *no command of attention when leaving a dog behind.* We don't want to alert him in case he might alert himself right into following us as we leave.

The Stay in the Down Position, or the Long Down, is executed exactly as if you were handling your dog on a Sit-Stay. The only difference is that your hand command for the Down-Stay is given from a point just *above* the dog's head to further encourage his remaining down; and when you pull your leash taut, keep it *parallel* to the ground, even though you may have to crouch a bit to achieve this.

Handle any infractions exactly as you would correct a break on the Sit-Stay. Limit yourself to one command, and stand ready to use that right hand to block the dog if he decides to move.

Distractions for the Stays

Since the obedience dog must remain at the stay, either lying down, sitting, or standing up for varying periods during which all manner of distractions can occur, it is a good idea, once the dog knows what stay means, to deliberately test him by introducing distractions he is liable to run up against sooner or later.

1. If you are training at home alone, leave him in the hallway and drop a pan in the kitchen; have somebody knock on the door or ring the doorbell. Rock music on the hi-fi or a quiz show on TV are good training aids. Ask friends or neighborhood kids or members of the family to walk by the dog whistling or singing; do this yourself, swinging you arms.

2. In a class, clapping is excellent, as applause is often heard at dog shows. Get half the class to walk around the other half while on stays. Have all dogs form a circle and, after placing a few weenies on the floor in the center of the circle, give the stay command and see what happens.

3. If you honestly think you have done your leash pulling correctly and haven't cheated, test yourself by having a stranger come along and pull on the leash.

But don't try these distractions until you are certain in your own mind that your stays, either sitting or lying down, have been made perfectly clear to the dog. Also, don't overdo the time of your stays until your dog is breaking his sits and downs regularly. If you are training for three-minute sits, then it's fine to clock the dog at four minutes; it's wrong to hold him to eight or ten. Research has proved that dogs learn by *succeeding*. Failure teaches them to dread their work and to sneak out of it whenever possible. You are much further ahead with a one-minute Sit-Stay executed perfectly so that the dog leaves his training remembering the praise he got for doing right, than you will be if you repeatedly nag, correct, and scold because he breaks a ten-minute stay over and over again.

Jumping

When the handler gets ready to teach his dog to jump, he is permitted to use any word he chooses to signify that the dog must leave the ground and clear a barrier. Good words to use are: "Hup!" "Up!" "Over!" "Jump!" Just make sure you always use the same word and that you give it at the point at which the dog is to take the jump. Don't just aim him at the barrier and let nature take its course. We start our jumping, as do most classes, using the solid rather than the bar jump. This is so that the dog learns *first* that he has to go *over* a hurdle *before* he discovers there is a way to go *under* it!

The only danger in jumping exercises is that the moment most folks see their dogs jumping, they are so delighted and proud that they start building up the hurdles until the poor dogs need rotor blades on their heads to scale the obstacle! The American and Canadian Kennel Clubs limit all jumping in licensed and sanctioned events so that the dog never jumps more than one and one-half times his height at the withers, or three feet, whichever is less. More than this can cause a dog serious injury. ("But you see police dogs jumping more and they aren't hurt by it!" somebody is wailing right now.) The truth of the matter is that these animals *don't* jump six and twelve feet, they *climb* that height; they claw and scramble their way up. And the minute you give a dog something to jump that is beyond him, he'll do just that, claw and scramble and climb. Then there is the devil's own time teaching the dog to clear the hurdle without touching. So limit your jumps to low heights until the dog is sailing over them happily with inches to spare. Then start raising your jump a few inches at a time, but use your noodle, please!

The Jump Command

INSTRUCTOR'S COMMAND: HANDLER'S COMMAND:
"Jump your dogs!"   "Fido, Heel!": (H)
                                         "Fido, Jump!" (H)
                                         "Fido, Heel!" (L)

This is taught with the dog a good distance from the solid high jump to allow plenty of room for take off. *Be sure to approach straight.* The jump is ridiculously low at the beginning, so that you may step over easily as your dog jumps. Start the approach to the jump with a happy, brisk "Fido, Heel!" command. At the point where you feel he should start lifting himself, tell your dog, "Fido, Jump!" And *keep moving* as you pull (or jerk) out and up on your leash! No matter what the dog wants to do, *never slow down or back up.* If he refuses, you are in a perfect position to insist and encourage from the other side, so see that no matter what *he* does, you *clear* the barrier! If all goes well, the moment he lands on the far side of the jump he'll be going faster than usual and will have a tendency to forge. So the moment his feet hit ground after he has jumped, snap your leash toward you smartly and this time in a *lowered* tone of voice tell him, "Fido, Heel!" When he is in position again, make a big fuss over him and heel around to the end of the line to await your next turn.

In getting your dog to clear a jump of any kind, hold your leash in the way that is most comfortable for you. Some prefer to hold it in the right hand, sliding the left hand down on the leash to insure straight approach. Others put all the leash in their left hands for jump-ing. The two-handed control of the leash is especially valuable when it comes time for you to go around the jump as your dog goes over. But however you hold your leash for jumping, remember it should never be used to force a dog into a jump, and it should never be so loose that the dog might trip on it, or that it might catch on the jump and check the dog severely when he is not expecting it and has done nothing wrong.

Your speed in approaching the jump is equally important. You should arrive at a brisk walk. But don't run at the jump so that the dog must throw his body over or so that he slams into the jump if he refuses; many good jumpers learn to hate this exercise because they were hurt at a hurdle by the stupidity of their handlers. If you feel your Fido balking, keep going until you are on the opposite side of the jump from the dog. Then you can wheedle and encourage with short jerks on your leash. But let him jump on his own; don't wheel him, choking to death, through the air. The sooner you teach him, really teach him, what the word "Jump!" means, the sooner you will be ready for the bar jump. Start this low, too, so he goes over before he learns to duck under. And if he does scoot beneath the bar, snap him back and lower the jump so he can't do it again. Never let a dog complete his turn at jumping by going around or under the jump. Positive, remember? Never negative!

If you or your training group don't have and can't afford standard jumps, a sheet over a broomstick between two chairs is great. Or two chairs on their sides, or a garbage pail on its side between two chairs. "Jump!" means "Jump!" and should have nothing to do with what is being hurdled.

The Sit from the Down at Heel

INSTRUCTOR'S COMMAND:	HANDLER'S COMMAND:
"Have your dogs sit!"	"Fido, Sit!" (H)

Instead of the usual lowered inflection used with the Sit command, a high tone of voice is used here to encourage the dog to raise his head while he is lying down, thus making it easier for him to move into a sit at the handler's command.

Having your dog sit from the down at heel position is possibly the easiest command you will teach your dog.

When you hear the instructor's command, tell the dog, "Fido, Sit!" in a high squeaky voice. At the same time, jerk up on your leash with your right hand and slap your left side with your left hand. Praise as soon as the dog is sitting.

Don't bend over—you are trying to make the dog sit up to get praise, so why would you put yourself so close to him he needn't move a muscle to get patted?

Don't haul him up like a dead fish either. A few times doing this and he'll hug the floor for dear life. Wouldn't you?

If nothing inspires him to do this exercise (an unusual situation, but it *could* happen!), bend over just long enough to start scratching your ankle. The moment the dog turns his head to see what you are scratching, start moving your twiddling fingers slowly up your leg. He'll probably follow them with his eyes and will end up sitting, thanks to his curiosity!

The Stand-Stay

INSTRUCTOR'S COMMANDS:	HANDLER'S COMMANDS:
"Prepare to stand dogs!"	"Stay!" (L)
"Stand Dogs!"	"Fido, Heel!" (H)
"Return to Heel!"	

The Stand-Stay is an especially valuable command if you are planning to show your dog in conformation. In the breed ring a dog never sits but always stands, unless moving, since in this position the judge is easily able to evaluate the animal's physical structure. If you are hoping to compete for obedience degrees in the show ring, the Stand-Stay is an important part of the Novice and Utility requirements. If you have no such plans for your dog, this command is still valuable as yet another way to keep your dog under control, and can be very useful when he has to visit a veterinarian.

The danger of this command lies in the fact that for many weeks you have been teaching your dog to sit when you stop moving. Now you are going to teach him to stand when you stop moving, and the transition is likely to be confusing unless you are very careful that your command is given *while you are out in front of the dog* and not while you are standing at heel or anywhere near heel position. Later, of course, the dog will know the difference; but he will learn the difference effortlessly and with little confusion if you remember *to get away* from him at the beginning when teaching the stand.

Note that the handler, as is true in the Sit-Stay and the Down-Stay, does not use the dog's name before the command. The reason here is the same as the reason given before: we don't want to make the dog too alert. Also, any word you choose to use here is fine—"Whoa!" "Stop!" "Stand!" are just as good as "Stay!" We use the latter because we feel the dog already knows what stay means (in the down and in the sit), so it might make his stand a bit easier to assimilate.

The stand is taught in three steps:

STEP 1. While heeling around the room the instructor will give the command, *"Prepare to stand your dogs!"* When you hear these words, transfer all your leash to your left hand but don't stop, slow down, or hesitate; *keep going!* Then you will hear the instructor say (STEP 2) *"Stand your dogs!"* At this command, imagine to yourself that you are teaching the Sit-Stay or the Down-Stay. Move forward suddenly, swinging your body out in front of the dog so that you are facing him. Keep the leash taut and discourage the dog's continued movement with that extended right palm. Keep the leash low and the dog will be less liable to sit than if you pull his head up. Keep your right hand low too.

You will be just as unsuccessful in this exercise if you move too quickly, causing the dog to be startled into sitting, as you will be if you move too slowly, allowing the dog to wander after you until he sits out of confusion. Treat the whole thing exactly as you would a Sit-Stay or Down-Stay.

STEP 3. When you have slid the length of your lead through your hand and are at the end of it, loosen it carefully. Stand still a moment. Then circle around the dog as on a Sit-Stay or Down-Stay. But as you walk into heel position, tell the dog to heel and move right on out with him. Don't halt for about fifteen paces. This will give the dog no chance to wonder if he should sit when he feels you beside his shoulder. *Never have your dog sit immediately after a Stand-Stay.* Even when this command becomes familiar to the dog, always make it a point to walk a few steps with the dog at heel after finishing a stand before asking the dog to sit.

As soon as your dog is standing on command, start hesitating longer each time you reach the end of your leash. When this is going well, start hesitating for longer periods when returning to heel position. And when the dog is standing firmly for you at heel for perhaps the count of four, start running your hand down his back saying, "Stay, stay" in a soothing voice. If this can be achieved without collapse of canine, add a springy push on his hind quarters, repeating the command "Stay" soothingly.

Finally, your trainer should be able to examine the dog as you stand at the end of your leash ("examine" means to touch head, shoulders, and back of the animal) without the dog showing resentment or moving away.

There are a number of things that can be tried if all does not go well:

1. If the dog sits after the command to stand, don't jerk on the leash or get upset. Simply walk back to the dog, lift him gently but

Step 1. Heeling a dog into a standing position is not difficult if the trainer remembers the "Stay" command must be given from *in front of* the dog, not at heel where the dog is used to sitting.

We start with the dog heeling alongside the trainer, the leash held loosely, with sufficient slack, in the trainer's right hand.

Photos by Glenn Easton

Step 2. When the dog is heeling along freely, we transfer the leash to the left hand. While making this switch, the trainer does not slow down or in any way change his forward momentum. The leash is shortened only slightly so the dog does not trip over it. If you are working in a group, the instructor's command, "Prepare to stand your dog," would be the signal to transfer your leash to your left hand.

Step 3. Now give the vocal command "Stay!" but make very sure that the moment you open your mouth, you are ready to take a giant step so that as you speak you are *in front of the dog*. The gesture you make with your free hand is the same you would use when teaching sit or down-stay. Note that the trainer in the picture holds her leash loosely; if she pulls up, the dog will probably sit as he has been trained to do earlier in response to this pressure. You can see that as the dog comes to a halt, the trainer is facing him, blocking him with hand and body. *(left)*

Step 4. The trainer holds the stay position until the dog is completely stopped. In the beginning, pause only long enough to make sure your point is made with the dog. Now return to heel exactly as you would following the down or sit-stay, but as you reach the dog's shoulders, give the command, "Fido, Heel!" and move out smartly, giving him no opportunity to sit as he usually does when he finds himself at your side. As the dog becomes more secure, you can begin stopping briefly at heel upon your return until you can stand beside him without confusing him. *(right)*

firmly into a standing position by pulling down toward the floor on the collar with one hand while stroking gently upward under the tummy with the other hand.

2. If the dog lifts but doesn't stay up on his own, tickle his tummy soothingly and remove your hand gradually.

3. If the dog still doesn't "get it," slip a leash under him and support him with that, or have a helper walk behind the dog supporting his rear half. (With male animals, the leash being used in this manner must be handled with due respect to the animal's equipment.)

Generally speaking, your main trouble will inevitably stem from your failure to get out in front of the dog before giving the stand command.

Helpful Corrective Exercises

FOR SLOPPY, INATTENTIVE HEELING

1. Change pace and direction frequently, and without warning.

2. Start off at a dead run and don't fuss too much about square sits—your aim right now is speedy starts.

3. Weave in and out around real or imaginary obstacles.

4. Make sudden left and right turns without warning.

FOR QUICKER DOWNS

1. Stop waiting to see if the dog is going to obey your first command. Give it and bring that hand down to the dog's withers immediately.

2. Put the dog down while heeling along by suddenly plonking him down, smacko! Balance the necessary extra firmness with extra praise.

FOR MORE SPIRITED RECALLS

1. After giving the come command with the jerk on your leash, run backwards clapping your hands and whee-ing. Let the dog jump up on you when he catches you.

2. Off leash: Call the dog, then immediately disappear around a corner or into another room or out of a door. Keep calling and turn it into a game of hide-and-seek!

3. On leash: Before calling the dog, sit on a chair. For some reason dogs love to hurl themselves upon low-slung objects.

FOR QUICKER SITS

1. Do a series of heel-sit-heel-sit-heel-sit commands with only enough steps in between to get the dog moving and on his feet.

2. Stop giving vocal commands when you halt. Just slap the dog's bottom sharply the instant you stop. Praise lavishly the moment he does it on his own. Whether the dog requires it or not, get that left hand down by the portion which needs "guidance." If the dog sits quickly you'll miss him, but the times he goofs you'll be Johnny on the Spot. *Always have that hand ready!*

TO EMPHASIZE THE AT-HEEL POSITION

1. With the dog at heel, give him a stay command and take a giant step to the right. Then tell him to "Heel!" by patting your leg and snapping the leash with your right hand. Praise lavishly at home plate.

2. Try the same technique with the dog one step behind you; then one step in front of you; then one step to your left.

FOR BETTER SIT-STAYS AND DOWN-STAYS

1. Stand beside the dog with a loose leash, the extreme end in your hand. Let the surplus lie on the floor sloppy-like, as if you weren't paying attention. Tell the dog to stay and have a helper roll a ball past his nose. When he lunges forward, dig your heels in and stand pat. As the dog hits the end of the leash and flips himself, repeat the "Stay!" command. Encourage the dog back to his original position and try again. Let the dog correct himself; your role is to praise highly when he's right.

2. Try a chair dragged back and forth when the dog is steady to the ball. A lawn mower, a vacuum cleaner, other animals—all are excellent when appropriate. But be sure your dog is calm and steady before making him so nervous he runs for a hiding place.

OFF-LEASH WORK

The Importance of Hands

Before going into the intricacies of off-leash obedience, let's take a moment to consider some words by Mr. Stanley Dangerfield, noted dog judge and former Secretary of the Labrador Club of England, who maintains that "the link between man's ambition and his achievements is hands."

"Man has in his hands," Mr. Dangerfield continues, "the most powerful weapon when dealing with dogs. These hands can tame, subdue, punish, heal, exact obedience, charm, comfort and cherish. Make no mistake about it—the dog knows this. When *dog* deals with man, he looks at his hands!"

"No dog should ever be taught to fear those hands. Foremost among bad habits which are more thoughtless than cruel, is *grabbing* at dogs. I know it is tempting to grab at a dog that has just changed his mind about coming to you, but it startles the life out of him and soon builds up a determination to stay out of arm's length at all costs. The casual cuff or slap which the dog does not quite deserve also builds up the wrong sort of awareness of hands. Although this may seem a novel idea, it is easy enough to prove the truth of it.

"Distract a dog's attention from your hands by talking to him, thereby causing him to look up into your face to see where the noise comes from and try putting your hands in your pocket while you are doing so. You will find the dog's eyes register the move. Try taking a swipe at the next dog you meet, hiding a ball he wants, throwing this ball without any warning at all, or hurling a stone at him. In each case the dog's reaction is automatic and immediate. He reads the language of our hands correctly every time, and either runs, ducks, wags his tail or approaches. All of which should make us a lot more careful with our hands than we are!"

The reason for including Mr. Dangerfield's words in this book is that we want to do everything possible to make sure that in dealing with your dog, yours are always *helping* hands.

Unfortunately, two things seem to happen the moment a novice trainer takes the leash off his dog for the first time:

1. Realizing with terror that he has nothing by which to hold on to his dog, the novice handler snatches nervously at the dog whenever the animal looks as though he might be thinking of disobeying. Instead of making the dog aware that the handler is wise to his tricks, the nervous hands simply drive the dog further away. They also tell the dog that the human is panicking and is losing confidence in himself.

2. After a few turns around the lawn or the training floor off leash, a great surge of conceit rushes over the handler. "My dog's off leash! By gosh, I'm a great trainer!" And for some weird reason he has to be forced to put his dog back on leash when the dog needs it, probably because he feels his leash means he's a "learner" again and not a "teacher." Off-leash work seems to be a status symbol to green trainers. They actually tend to sneer at others who must put their dog back on leash after having been off leash for a while.

No one should ever have to tell a good trainer when to put his dog back on leash. A good trainer *knows* the moment his commands sound frantic rather than positive. A good trainer knows the instant he has lost perfect control of his dog. And the good trainer, because he is an intelligent human being, knows that his best training aid is that six-foot lead he started his training with, the same six-foot lead he will count on from his C.D. through his T.D. A dog who doesn't perform perfectly off leash probably wasn't performing perfectly on leash.

Heeling

1. Start by working with the leash dragging on the floor behind the dog. Arrange the leash before you start so that it lies between you and the dog.

2. Also, remember to begin by reaching down and giving that leash a brisk snap with your left hand as you give your command to heel.

3. Then get your hands off the leash and start moving. The secret here is to move quickly and *keep going!* Remember the rule of opposites: if the dog seems to be moving faster and faster and is obviously going to slide out from under you, slow up and lower your voice. If the dog tries to stay wide, veer to your right and lower your voice as you repeat your command to heel.

4. Don't chance a dog that is running out of control. If your dog discovers he is free and takes off before you can step on his leash, simply crouch down and call him. Open your arms and welcome him with praise and affection—he *came,* didn't he? Then go right back on leash with a series of turns allowing you to snap your leash to remind him you *are* in control and that he goofed. Then drop your leash and try the same pattern in the same tone of voice and at the same rate of speed. When this is going well, unsnap the leash without making a project of the process. Heel on out briskly, talking a blue streak, clapping your hands, keeping the dog's attention on you every minute of the way. And the instant you feel "Whoops, thar she blows!" give the sit command and halt.

Sits

1. Slow down a bit gradually before giving the sit command to your dog. Warn him that something different is coming with a few low "Ah, ah's."

2. When you give the "Fido, Sit!" (L) command don't snatch wildly at the dog's collar. By the same token, don't wait hopefully expecting that each step the dog takes after the command will see him sitting until the dog has walked right out from under you. Then you must punish, and it's really *your* fault, you know.

3. As you give the sit command, slap down sharply with your left hand. If you have taught this command correctly, the dog will expect this motion and will duck it—right into a sit! So use the hand to praise him with. But as we have pointed out a number of times in this book, the time he doesn't sit you will connect automatically when you should connect, so that the dog will *never* succeed in disobeying, not even *once!*

4. The moment the dog obeys, praise him at heel, of course.

Stays (Stand, Sit, and Down)

1. You will start teaching off-leash stays by dropping your training lead while doing a stay on leash. Never bend over when dropping your leash. The dog sees you bend toward him and he thinks you want him, so he comes to you. Or he thinks you have found some interesting object on the floor and he wants to see it, too. So *stand up straight, open your hands, and let the leash fall to the floor.*

2. When your stays are going perfectly with the leash dropped, unsnap the leash before beginning a long sit or down. Fold it neatly and place it on the floor behind the dog. Move on out exactly as if you had a leash on him and it will probably go beautifully. If not, go right back on leash and pull the leash taut until he resists. Then try going off leash again.

Note: The Sit-Stay, the Down-Stay, the Stand for examination are all performed *off* leash in novice obedience training in the U.S. In Canada, the Stand-Stay is always done *on* leash. So it's a good idea to practice both ways.

Since you don't want to confuse the long stays with the recall, be sure to use a slightly different position for the stays than you do for the recall. We recommend that when doing long stays you stand facing your dog, feet *together,* hands clasped *behind your back.*

Recalls

1. Start by doing a series of on-leash Come Fore exercises, snapping the leash smartly as you give the "Come!" command.

2. When this is going well, do the same exercise with dropped leash.

3. Next, do regular on-leash recalls with snapped leash at the "Come!" command.

4. Then, dropped leash regular recalls—be sure and chatter up a storm of encouragement as the dog comes toward you, and make it really worth his while to get to you. Never mind straight sits. We're training the recall now—*one thing at a time, remember?*

5. The regular off-leash recall starts with you unsnapping the leash, folding it neatly and placing it behind the dog on the floor. Step right out as if you were doing the exercise *on* leash, and go the same distance from the dog that you would go if you had a leash in your hand. Stand still a moment and then call the dog to sit in front. Praise with both hands.

6. Your correct recall position: feet slightly apart, hands folded in *front* of you across your tummy, just below your waist.

Jumping

1. Try a few on-leash jumps, snapping the leash with your command.

2. Now, as you approach the jump—just as you *begin* the approach and are heeling along—lean down and unsnap the lead, letting.it fall where it will.

3. Your hand commands at the jump should be made as if you were using the leash, but be careful you don't spook the dog into going around the far side of the jump by too exaggerated hand commands.

4. Make sure that your approach puts the dog, not you, in the center of the jump.

5. The problem here is the landing off leash. Most dogs take off with great glee the moment they land on the far side of the jump. Be ready for it. Before the dog lands on the far side of the jump, *snarl,* and we do mean *snarl,* "Fido, Heel!" (L) as you take a step to your right away from the dog. The sudden movement of your body should pull the dog to you; the unexpected severity of your voice will alarm him also. "Why snarl at him if he hasn't done anything wrong?" somebody is protesting right now. The idea is not to let the dog misbehave. A wasted snarl or two from you won't kill the animal or break his spirit, and it will certainly save him from a firm correction.

6. The moment the dog has landed and is again heeling along with you, praise by patting him lovingly as you heel along. After all, he's done a clever thing—so have *you,* but we rarely have time to scratch trainers behind the ears!

Finishes

1. Most dogs have trouble with the finish for some reason, and the danger of taking them off leash too soon is that they will learn to hate the exercise and you have to snatch and grab at them to make them move when off leash.

2. So stay on leash until you know that dog is going to finish when you tell him to every single time. If the dog finishes usually or on the second command, or if you have to bend your body at a secret angle, he is not ready to go off leash.

3. But when you feel you are both ready to try it "cold turkey," take the leash off the dog and put it out of the way. We don't teach this with a dropped or dragging leash, as it seems to bother the dog in his circle.

4. Lean over and snap the collar each time you give your finish command until the dog is doing it almost before you snap.

5. In the beginning, go through your body movement for either type of finish. When all is going well, stand still, but try tracing the dog's

path to heel position in the air with your finger. As he gets more positive about this command, gradually cut down on your finger work until you only have to start him into his traffic pattern with your finger or hand.

Downs

1. Downs at heel off leash present no problem, as your leash wasn't really used in this exercise from the beginning. Just increase your push downward in quickness and force, and lower still further the tone of your voice.

2. Downs in front are little more of a problem, except that the dog is liable to scoot away when he sees that hand coming and realizes he is not fastened to anything any more. Drop your leash and step on it until this is going well, always remembering to praise when the dog is down with the same hand that put him there.

3. If you are honest about your hand in the down, you'll have no trouble. If the dog can count on your hand to always come to rest upon his withers where it will push, he'll never shy from it. If you flop and wave it threateningly in his kisser, he'll scoot.

Sits from the Down-at-heel Position

1. This is quite simple, as was this exercise *on* leash. If you teach your down-at-heel correctly on leash and your sit-at-heel correctly on leash, your off-leash performance will be a cinch.

2. Do a quick series of "Down! Sit! Down! Sit!" commands at heel. If they are going well, unsnap the leash as the dog is being praised for a sit, and then instantly give another down, moving your hand briskly down toward the dog's shoulders, exactly as you would do it on leash. Then pat your leg briskly and quickly and squeek your sit command—it should all fall into place smoothly. If it does not, back on leash.

WORDS TO THE WISE

Especially at the outset, being off leash requires great concentration on the part of the trainer.

You must concentrate on *not grabbing,* as well as on *anticipating* your dog's inclination to err, so that you can prevent it by a counteraction of your own.

With the leash off, you must depend on your second greatest training aid, *your voice.* A warning tone *before* trouble has happened is money in the bank. Since you have been shorn of your artificial aid, use your natural aids: the movements of your body, the various speeds at which you can move, the *positive* tone and the *positive* approach.

And once again, never forget that the *good* trainer knows when to put his dog back on leash. Don't cheat, don't con yourself into thinking all is well when you know perfectly well that it isn't!

When it comes to dropping a dog from a distance or giving jumping commands by hand signal, it is most important to keep in your mind the picture you present to your dog. To make sure your signals cannot be misinterpreted, keep your spare hand tucked tightly against your body.

5

Rules and Regulations
of Obedience Trials

Since I started in obedience many years ago, the rules have changed in many respects.

When I was actively teaching people who went on to their C.D.'s, their T.D.'s, C.D.X.'s, and U.D.'s, it seems to me there was more emphasis on the companion element than on high scores. In those days, Utility dogs had to pick their scent articles out of a pile including metal, wood, and leather; today in the United States they work only with leather and metal; in Canada they still work with three sets. In Canada the Stand-for-Examination in Novice is still done on leash; in the United States it is done off leash. The Seek Back exercise in Utility is still done the old way in Canada, using a plain, neutral-colored glove the dog must retrieve by sight or scent; in the United States this exercise has been replaced by the Directed Retrieve using three white gloves, only one of which is retrieved by the dog when given the direction by the handler.

One of the *worst* commentaries on obedience in both countries is that obedience dogs are still being required to do their stays in broiling heat or heavy rain without benefit of shelter, while their brothers and sisters in breed get whatever shelter is available in case of heat or inclement weather.

One of the best innovations is the recent inclusion of handicapped people as eligible to handle in obedience competitions in the United States and Canada.

In the United States the handicapped person fills in the entry form exactly as does his unhandicapped counterpart. Provided his dog can perform all parts of all exercises as described in the regulations, and provided he, himself, can move about the ring without physical assistance or guidance from another person except in the group exercises, he can attend and compete in any obedience trial for which he feels his dog is qualified or eligible.

In Canada the handicapped person sends a letter to the Canadian Kennel Club listing his background and qualifications and outlining the extent of his handicap. The Kennel Club, through its Obedience Council, approves or disapproves the request on a *one-time basis.* When the handler arrives at the obedience ring he presents his letter of approval to the steward, who presents it to the judge. If, after the initial experience, it is obvious the handler can be held responsible for himself and his dog's behavior, then he is free to continue showing to his heart's content.

EQUIPMENT

Equipment for competing in the obedience ring in the United States and Canada is very similar. Canada does not specify what kind of collar is to be worn in the ring, or stipulate its fit, but it does mention that the leash should be approximately six feet long and made of fabric or leather. American rules call for well-fitting plain buckle or slip collars, the latter made of leather, fabric, or chain, and having a ring in each end. The leash may be of fabric or leather and need only be long enough to provide for adequate slack in the heeling-on-leash exercises.

DEGREES

Earlier in this section we listed the titles available in obedience. However, each class offered in the process of securing these titles or degrees is divided into "A" and "B" classifications. We have detailed these differences below with the understanding that, unless otherwise stated, the same regulations apply in the United States and Canada. A perfect score in either country, in all degrees, is 200.

The Companion Dog Degree (or C.D.) may be awarded to any dog at least six months of age, purebred of any breed and either sex, that has been certified by three different judges [1] to have received a score of better than 50 per cent of each of the exercises and a total score of at least 170 points out of 200. In the United States there must be at least six entries in the regular novice classes for the score to count toward title; in Canada there is no such limit.

[1] Canada calls for qualifying scores under *two* different judges except in the Provinces of British Columbia, Ontario south of 46° N. latitude, and Quebec, which require three judges.

To get a C.D., the novice dog must compete in either Novice A or Novice B classes at licensed obedience trials, and no one dog can enter both. The "A" class is for dogs owned by their handlers or members of the immediate family. The handler in "A" must handle only one dog, and handlers who have taken other dogs to other degrees are not eligible, nor are licensed handlers or professional trainers. In Novice B, the owner may handle his own dog if he chooses. This class is also open to professionals and more than one dog may be entered by one handler, provided he has a handler for each of his entries for group exercises. People who have secured degrees on other dogs must show in Novice B. There is no difference in the tests, and the judging is the same. Dogs that have won C.D.'s in other countries must be entered in Canada in Novice B.

The Companion Dog Excellent Degree (or C.D.X.) may be awarded to any dog at least six months of age, purebred of any breed and either sex, that has won the title of C.D. in its home country but has not won the title of C.D.X. All other requirements listed above for C.D. apply to C.D.X. The "A" and "B" differentiations apply equally for Novice (C.D.) or Open (C.D.X) except that in Open B, dogs holding C.D.X. *and* Utility degrees may compete at any time and do so hoping for "Highest Combined Score" given for Open B and Utility dogs. Dogs that have won C.D.X.'s in other countries must compete in Canada in Open B.

The Utility Degree (or U.D.) is for purebred dogs of any breed and either sex that have already won the title of C.D.X. in their own countries. Anyone may handle, amateur or professional, and anyone may enter more than one dog provided there are individual handlers for group exercises. Dogs may continue to show in this class after securing their U.D. titles in order to compete for Highest Combined Score (Open B and Utility). In the United States a club may choose to divide its Utility Class into "A" and "B," leaving "A" for those without a U.D. and "B" for those who already have a Utility Degree.

The Tracking Degree (or T.D.) is available in the United States or Canada to any registered dog, six months or older, of any breed or either sex, that has been certified by two judges to have passed a licensed or member tracking test in which three dogs actually participated. Tracking tests are never given at dog shows or obedience trials but are held on separate dates at separate locations. The length of the track is not less than 440 nor more than 500 yards, the scent to be not less than one half hour nor more than two hours old. The dog is required to locate a specified object at the end of a track; he does not have to pick it up.

In Canada, if a dog has a C.D., a C.D.X., and a U.D. degree, he can then use the initials O.T.Ch. before his name—Obedience Trial

SAMPLE

OFFICIAL AMERICAN KENNEL CLUB ENTRY FORM

(NOTE: For Field Trials, use space below marked additional classes.)

I ENCLOSE $_____ for entry fees.

IMPORTANT—Read Carefully Instructions on Reverse Side Before Filling out

Breed	Variety See Instruction #1, reverse side (if any)	Sex
	DOG Show Class See Instruction #2, reverse side (Give age, color or weight if class divided)	**Obedience Trial Class**
	If dog is entered for Best of Breed (Variety) Competition—see Instruction #3 reverse side —CHECK THIS BOX ☐	**Additional Classes**

If entry of dog is to be made in Jr. Showmanship as well as in one of the above competitions, check this box, and fill in data on reverse side. ☐

If for Jr. Showmanship only then check THIS box, and fill in data on reverse side. ☐

Name of Actual Owner(s) See Instruction #4, reverse side

Name of Licensed Handler (if any) handler

Full Name of Dog

Insert one of the following: A.K.C. Reg. # A.K.C. Litter # I.L.P. # Foreign Reg. # & Country	Date of Birth	Place of Birth ☐ U.S.A. ☐ Canada ☐ Foreign Do not print the above in catalog
	Breeder	

Sire

Dam

Owner's Name _____
(Please print)

Owner's Address _____

City_____ State_____ Zip Code_____

I CERTIFY that I am the actual owner of this dog, or that I am the duly authorized agent of the actual owner whose name I have entered above. In consideration of the acceptance of this entry, I (we) agree to abide by the rules and regulations of The American Kennel Club in effect at the time of this show or obedience trial, and by any additional rules and regulations appearing in the premium list for this show or obedience trial or both, and further agree to be bound by the "Agreement" printed on the reverse side of this entry form. I (we) certify and represent that the dog entered is not a hazard to persons or other dogs. This entry is submitted for acceptance on the foregoing representation and agreement.

SIGNATURE of owner or his agent duly authorized to make this entry _____

Champion. The A.K.C. has also recently established a Championship obedience title.

Finally, it should be pointed out that a purebred U.S. dog not registered with the Canadian Kennel Club can continue to show in obedience indefinitely, provided the handler or owner pays a one-dollar listing fee for each trial in which the dog is entered. Should such a "listed" dog complete requirements for any obedience degree, he will receive a letter from C.K.C. stating he has met all requirements and will be sent his certificate as soon as he is registered in Canada.

In the United States, purebred nonregistered dogs may show in obedience for the same thirty days their show cousins are allowed to show (Chapter 16, Section 1 of the dog show rules) unless A.K.C. tenders written extension, which it will do only if the registration is being held up by forces beyond the control of the owner. Nonregistered dogs completing obedience titles receive a letter from A.K.C. so stating. Certificates are sent when registration requirements are met.

Another rule applies equally to show dogs and obedience trial dogs: they cannot compete if lame, taped, or bandaged. Under certain circumstances, the entry fees for bitches that come in season after you've made the entry can be refunded. Check your rule book.

ENTRY FORMS

While we have included a sample entry form for your perusal, entering dogs in obedience trials involves filling out the same particulars you were asked to give with breed dogs and which are explained in Part I Chapter 3. Check your premium list to make sure the classes you want to enter are offered and whether or not nonregular classes such as teams and braces are included. Remember to sign your entry and mail well ahead of closing date. Since dogs and bitches are shown together in the same classes in obedience, you indicate, for instance, that you are entering Obedience, Novice A, but need not indicate Dog or Bitch after the entry. Be sure to indicate the sex of the animal in the box marked "Sex," however. Canadian entry forms sometimes don't include a specific line for indicating obedience classes; in this case simply use the line marked "Additional Classes."

6

At the Obedience Trial

Sometimes obedience trials are held alone, separate from anything else; sometimes they are held in conjunction with breed specialties or all-breed licensed shows. But alone or in conjunction, all obedience trials may be defined as "a system of public demonstrations designed to prove to as many spectators as possible the innate superiority of the intelligence of the dog over that of man." Whoever the obedience wag was who devised this tongue-in-cheek definition, he had a sense of humor, and a sense of humor is as necessary to the person attending an obedience trial as it is to the one showing his dog in breed.

Earlier, in our show section, we discussed the program, which usually is mailed to you before the date of the show, and in which you are given all necessary information as to the time you are judged, ring number, etc.

RULES REGARDING TRAINING

The procedure for enjoying a day at an obedience trial with an entered dog is the same as that for a dog show, with one possible exception: you may do all the grooming you want on your show dog on the show grounds, but you may not, repeat *not,* train your obedience dogs on the grounds at the show. This is a written rule in the U.S. and an understood one in Canada. I myself can see absolutely no reason why a person shouldn't give his dog a few warm-up exercises, but that is the law. So if you feel you need such rehearsals, I suggest you retire to the parking lot, which is not generally thought of as the show grounds.

Just as you are not supposed to train on the grounds prior to competing at obedience trials, you are not allowed to train while in the ring.

If you do so, substantial deductions can be expected. However, this does not consider the ring-wise dog who, for instance, gets to a point where he runs around the jump on the way back from retrieving only when he's in the ring, where he knows he will not be corrected. In this case, I strongly recommend that the moment he sticks his dear little snoot around the edge of that jump, you run out and force him over. Substantial deductions need not frighten you, as you are "out" anyway the moment he pulls such shenanigans. If you ask the judge's permission, the effectiveness of instant correction is gone forever. Most judges, I believe, are secretly sympathetic with trainers sharp enough to realize the value of positive training at home or abroad, though they cannot of course sanction it. However, while they may deliver a lecture and read you the rules, they cannot banish you to Siberia or take away your exhibiting privileges, your driver's license, or charge cards, so what's to lose?

This does not mean I or anyone else would sanction your chasing around a ring for ten minutes to catch a dog and force him to do an exercise right. But if you see your standing dog starting to sit in Novice or in the Utility signal exercise, and you know a firm reprimand can make him change his mind, then give it. You have flunked anyway, and at least you can return home having made a valuable training point in the ring, though you did not place. But never correct your dog in a group exercise lest you disturb another dog.

WHILE WAITING

We recommend, as we did to owners of show dogs, that you arrive very early, bring your own water, exercise the dog (get him to go to the bathroom), etc. Read the section "At the Show" to refresh your memory.

Remember that obedience trials, like dog shows, are very rarely canceled on account of weather, so go prepared with boots and raincoat.

Obedience rings are very often quite separate from the show rings at all-breed shows, and this is as it should be. Because the novice can enter only one class at a time, conflicts are not going to harass you, so settle yourself in your chair at ringside with your catalogue and watch the other dogs in your class. Make sure your own dog is in a shaded area if the show is outside, or in an inactive area at an indoor show. I know that many people sit at the obedience ring with their dogs under their chairs, but I personally feel the dog works much better if he is allowed to "miss" his handler for a while directly before he is called upon to do his thing. So while it may mean a little more lugging, I recommend, for your dog's sake, that you bring along his crate lined with a nice comfy pad.

When space is limited, obedience rings sometimes have to be shared with show dogs, but in this case the rings are always cleaned between breed classes and obedience classes.

SCORES

In licensed obedience competitions in the U.S. and Canada, judges may not give out score sheets to individuals. Just as judges' sheets are posted in breed competitions, carbons of the judges' sheets for each class are posted at the superintendent's desk so that obedience exhibitors may know the scores they received on individual exercises.

If you fail one of your individual exercises, don't forget that you are required for the group exercises, the long sits and downs. This holds whether you "goofed" one of your earlier exercises or not. Since the stays are sometimes done halfway through a large class, or at the end of smaller classes, it is wise to check with the steward to make sure you are within hailing distance when it comes time for you to participate in these group exercises.

STEWARDS

You will find obedience stewards generally more knowledgeable and helpful than stewards in show rings. Usually you are called into the ring for obedience competitions in numerical order as listed in the catalogue. However, sometimes special concessions are made for people showing in conformation classes as well, since it is not always possible to be in two places at once. Upon arriving at the show, go to the steward and give her your number so she knows you are present and can call on you if need be.

There seems to be now a distressing tendency on the part of some obedience exhibitors to abuse the courtesy extended to those who are also exhibiting in breed and who are customarily allowed to compete "out of order." If scheduled for early in the morning, certain obedience folks simply decide they have no intention of inconveniencing themselves at such an ungodly hour, and report to the ring when they feel like it, misusing the original intention of this privilege. This means that those obedience exhibitors who show up promptly when their classes are scheduled are forced to wait around for group exercises until the latecomers see fit to appear. It also means that obedience competitions drag on interminably and that obedience judges are still on their feet working long after the breed judges are tucked snug in their beds.

It is inconceivable to me that one group of people can so inconvenience those around them and get away with it. Obviously we need more rigid policing of obedience entries and some sort of time limit after which a dog whose owner has not appeared will be marked absent.

AT RINGSIDE

Very young children are frowned on at the ringside in breed; they are murdered upon sight at obedience trials, unless they are as well-trained as their parents' dogs! If your children are demanding, overactive, and inclined to tire easily, leave them at home, I beseech you. You would feel awful if they wrecked your own dog's scores, but imagine your guilt if their antics caused somebody else's dog to goof!

Because, as I said, novices are limited to one class (if you are competing in "A"), obedience allows lots of time for getting to know your fellow trainers. Firm friendships that last a lifetime are born at the ringside during obedience, for there is more time to be social, more opportunity to be informal and friendly, than is usually the case among conformation exhibitors.

To my mind, there is only one thing that quickens the heart more than the sight of a happy, enthusiastic, high-scoring obedience trial winner, and that is the day-to-day obedience of a family dog whose manners make him welcome—and beloved—everywhere he goes. My hat is off to the handlers and their dogs who score the top marks in obedience trials. But I salute from my heart the hundreds of plain ordinary people with their mixed breeds and purebreds who never compete in trials but who love their dogs and respect their neighbors enough to make sure that every dog is a gentleman and every bitch is a lady. That, my friends, takes real dedication; on the other hand, its rewards are manifold.

7

Obedience Training for Special Problems

A good course in novice obedience training covers many problems that occur in day-to-day living with any dog. There are other behavior riddles, however, which can't always be solved in a training class or alone by yourself with no experienced person to guide you. No matter how carefully you train, new challenges pop up constantly.

THE CONSTANT BARKER

Before deciding how to stop a dog from barking, it must be clearly understood that dogs bark for many, many reasons, not all of which should be considered punishable offenses. It doesn't take long for even the greenest neophyte to learn the difference between the bratty, no-one-is-paying-attention-to-me-and-I'm-mad bark (which is generally a monotonous yap, yap, yap or a long, drawn-out keening with little or no particular feeling behind it) and the bark that clearly says, "Something is the matter, come in a hurry and look!" (a medium-pitched, quick-paced barking with great excitement behind it), or "This is serious, and I mean it!" (low-pitched and growly, extremely intense), or the sharp, high-pitched yipe which transmits, "I am in trouble and I need help fast!" Such calls should be investigated with dispatch.

Now that we know each other better, I must confess a "funny" to you. When I was living in Germany right after the war, a great deal of pilfering and stealing was taking place. Consequently, my husband and I kept our two Irish Setters in the house at night. They slept in the kitchen to guard the castle; we slept upstairs. The only time they ever disturbed us at night, I leaned over the banister and yelled, "Hush!"

They were instantly silent and I congratulated myself—until morning, when I discovered we had been cleaned out, wall to wall! They even stole the dogs! So I would recommend that you listen to your dog's message before you leap into action.

Still, except when dogs are startled, or strangers arrive unannounced at your home, or in time of fear or undue excitement, there is absolutely no excuse for allowing any dog to sit in his yard, his kennel, or his home barking his head off day and night for no reason other than that he likes to make himself heard. Constant shrill screaming at a barking dog drives him to even more frantic vocalizing, as does trying to clamp his mouth shut with your fumbling fingers.

Pick a word, from this moment on, which is going to mean, to put it as succinctly as possible: "Shut your mouth!" "Hush!" is a good word when spoken with meaning and force; so are lots of others such as "Quiet!" or "Cease!" The trouble is, by the time a dog is really barking away he is in another world and your word, no matter how it is delivered, will slip right on by him unless it is accompanied by some sort of physical attention-getter which will break the hysterical concentration he is enjoying while barking. So accompany the command, particularly in the beginning, with a firm wallop across that part of the dog's anatomy most readily available. The moment the dog looks up, and I guarantee you he will if the vocal and physical are simultaneous and decisive, repeat your command again; then have the dog do something other than what he was doing when the barking started. "Go lie down!" or "Sit!" or "Heel!"—anything to break further the train of thought that brought on the initial barking. If necessary, take him by the collar and lead him away from that particular area; don't lock him in another room—simply move him around a bit.

I remember delivering a first-night lecture to an obedience class years ago through the yapping of a dog sitting beside his mistress. I was telling the story, as I always do to novice classes, of the man who wanted to sell a mule. He advertised that the animal was trained to saddle or to buggy with lovingkindness, and that due to this training the animal was trustworthy in the extreme. Eventually a buyer showed up and the man sold his mule. However, when the new owner took the animal home, no matter how loving or how kind he was, the mule refused to do anything but stand and stare into the distance. The buyer called the seller to complain and the man offered to come over and see what the problem was. When he got there, he picked up a two-by-four, walked up to the mule, and hit it squarely between the eyes— whereupon the mule performed perfectly. "But," complained the buyer, "you told me this mule was trained with nothing but lovingkindness." "Oh, he was, he was," the seller explained, "but first you gotta get his attention!"

As I was working my way through this story, the dog never stopped barking for an instant. Finally I gave up and turned to his owner. "Madam, you will have to silence your dog. He is disturbing everybody."

"I know," she agreed. "I told him to be quiet, but he doesn't seem to be listening."

I walked up to the dog, took his leash and told him firmly to "Hush!" He continued his monologue without batting an eye. Whereupon I hauled off and landed a healthy swat across his bottom as I told him to hush for a second time. By this time he was so wound up in himself that this didn't work either. So I took his head firmly in my hand and, giving the command a third time, slapped him sharply across the muzzle. The resulting silence was delicious.

"Humph!" the lady complained. "I must admit it worked, but didn't I hear you say something about lovingkindness?"

"Your dog was making so much noise I'm afraid you missed the punch line to my story," I explained. "Lovingkindness is all well and good, Madam, but—" And before I could complete the sentence, about six voices from the audience called out, "First you gotta get his attention!"

Dogs that live alone in a kennel often feel sorry enough for themselves to tell the world about it at 2 A.M. Again you must synchronize your vocal command with a physical one. But because there is more distance involved in this instance, you will save yourself a lot of time and develop more rapport with your neighbors if you can convince the animal out *there* by dint of a noise in *here* that he'd better shut up because reinforcements are forthcoming. One good way is to throw up a window so that it makes a noise to accompany your original "Hush!" As you open it, be sure and rattle it deliberately. Then scoot out to the kennel and deliver a good thrashing with either a rolled-up newspaper or an old hunting boot (boots make horrible noises as they connect with the dog, but do little physical damage; this is true whether on the foot or held in the hand). Do it well and get it over with the first time. If you are faithful about developing the Pavlovian relationship between the noise, the command, and the spanking, you should soon have late-night serenades under control. Then opening the window should be all that is necessary.

While riding in a car, if you don't have your dog in a crate (and even if you do), nothing is more nerve-wracking and potentially dangerous than a dog that lunges at the windows barking hysterically at everything that moves. Obviously, you can't train a dog not to bark and safely negotiate complicated traffic patterns at the same time. If the dog is to be loose (which, in case you didn't get the message, I do not approve of!), before starting out the next time, take about four or five empty one-pound coffee tins and put a healthy handful of good-sized stones in each, then tape them firmly shut. Pile your ammunition on the front seat beside you, load the dog in the back, and take off. Drive slowly. The first time he opens his mouth, yell "Hush!" at the top of your lungs and start firing your coffee cans over your shoulder into the back seat until he stops barking. ("What if I hit him?" one lady asked. "It will probably hurt him," I replied.) Now pull over, collect your cans, and start again. Once he settles down, praise him quietly but always be ready to let fly a barrage of rattling coffee containers the moment he forgets. If he is in a crate, carry a supply of chain collars. Give the "Quiet!" command and throw the chains, singly or in bunches, over your shoulders at the crate.

I must pause here a moment to sing the praise of the electric anti-bark collars, which are most effective when used correctly and intelligently on dogs that have resisted all other attempts to teach them to be seen and not heard. I have personally used these devices and have recommended them in specific situations, always with excellent results. The thing that must be constantly remembered is that they are no good in a kennel situation, as all barking will trigger the electric mechanism; in other words, the dog wearing the collar gets "zapped" each time any bark is registered. Using these devices in an area where your dog is liable to get punished because nearby dogs are barking is inhumane. Used on the otherwise undaunted night serenader who lives alone, it is very much in order. In a remarkably short time the electric collar can be discarded for a narrow, leather, dummy collar which the dog is buckled into each time he is left alone in his kennel.

THE DOG WHO WON'T COME WHEN CALLED

Sometimes even the most beautifully trained dog seems to go deaf when the handler calls him to come from a distance. Off leash in the obedience ring he is as reliable as the seasons. On leash you can't fool him. But decide to take him for a lovely walk in the country, and forget it—his auditory mechanisms are temporarily out of order.

The moment you call a dog that is perfectly familiar with the word "Come" and all its ramifications, and he turns his tail and keeps going, start after him. Do *not* chase him, run, or start screaming and yelling as you set forth. Take a leash in your hand and walk briskly to the spot at which the dog thumbed his nose at you. Drop something at this point—a piece of tissue weighted with a stone, a glove, a head scarf. Then keep walking until you can quietly come up beside the dog and snap your leash to his collar. Now take a deep breath and, backing away without any undue warning of your intention, give that beastie a come-fore snap of the leash accompanied by the "Fido, Come!" command which he will not soon forget. Shorten up your leash and as you make your way back to the spot you have marked, jerk it often, repeating "Come!" each time you do so, this time in a stern, reproachful manner. When you get to the proper place in the field, have him sit, go to the end of your leash, and call him, jerking very strongly. When he gets to you, praise him, then heel him back to the car and forget it. This technique works in most cases, though once may not be enough.

Remember always that running after a dog, shrieking dark threats as to his future in this world, is a pattern that absolutely delights the animal. He senses the excitement in you and suddenly the whole thing is a big game which *he* will ultimately win, I assure you.

Another variation to the corralling of the runaway involves the dog that gives you the impression you have won the battle. Lowering his head, he thunders toward you at top speed; then, at the last minute, he veers off. You, of course, make a wild grab, missing everything except perhaps a handful of hair, and *voilà—he* has invented a new game and *you* are "it!"

The first thing not to do is what I did when I was young and foolish. I took dead aim and slipped my middle finger into the ring of the choke collar on the neck of my very large, very fast Irish Setter. Those moments between the time friends got my finger out of the ring, and the instant when the doctor in the emergency ward reduced my dislocated finger, were some of the most horribly painful I have ever spent. I must admit it cured the dog, but there has to be an easier way, and of course there is!

The solution is to turn, again, to the rule of opposites. As the dog wheels by on your right, *do not grab*. Repeat "Fido, Come!" and back away. If you will pay attention to the rhythm of the dog's sweeps, you can quickly get the knack of turning away just before he does and, lo and behold, soon *he* is chasing *you*.

A check line is very much in order if you suspect this is what might happen when you turn the dog loose. Make it a long one, but be very sure to untangle it and lay it flat before beginning, so that neither you nor your dog wind up in a dangerous snarl of rope. Thirty feet is a good length. Once you fasten the line to the dog's collar, keep only the very end of the check line in your hand. The proper use of such a training device is to allow you to allow your dog to discipline himself. Each time he runs wildly by you, deaf to your commands, watch carefully so that just as he hits the end of the line going in his direction, you jerk it in your direction—then loosen it again and repeat your command. As the old saying goes, Give him enough rope and he'll hang himself. Check lines made of various weights of rope and cord are available at pet shops and at dog-show concessions; they are also very easy and inexpensive to make yourself.

There are still other solutions to the bolting problem. If the dog takes off in a situation where he can get into trouble, such as toward a highway or an approaching car, scream suddenly and start running hell-bent for election in the other direction. The scream is a sound which, since he is not used to it, will catch the dog's attention long enough for him to see you are running away; it is possible he will try and catch up with you. A friend of mine had a house guest who inadvertently let her three Borzois loose on a busy road. A professional actress, she immediately dropped to her knees and rocked backward and forward, sobbing, moaning, and groaning; in a split second the dogs were at her side trying to see what was the matter with her, and she was able to hold them until help came.

If your dog and you are alone in the country and he takes off over the horizon and out of sight, your best bet, believe it or not, is to drop your jacket in the field, get in your car and drive away. Stay away—sometimes until dawn if you have courage enough and are in an area where you know no harm will come to the dog. Usually when you return there he is, on the jacket, scared to death and overjoyed to see you. Very often this will end such disappearances once and for all. But this solution takes a strong heart and acres of private land.

Again, I can heartily recommend the electric collars which work from a control box held by the handler at a great distance, sometimes as far as a quarter of a mile. For the chronic runaway, after fitting the collar to the dog, turn him loose in a situation where you are certain he will take off. When he is a good distance from you, give the come command. Unless he *instantly* wheels in his tracks, press the button. The dog is then the recipient of some very unpleasant electric shocks which frighten him more than hurt him, but suddenly he realizes that if he disobeys you, bad things happen. Take your finger off the button and call again. Usually, he'll come flying to be praised and petted, while he explains to you about the bees which attacked him "out there." You explain sweetly, as you scratch his ears and reassure him, that the bees can never get him if he comes when he is called. Hard-core cases sometimes demand more than one treatment. Some dogs require reminders every few months. In between, dummy collars are all that are necessary. The psychology is marvelous, the effects quite often miraculous. But again, this device loses all value as a training aid and becomes only an instrument of torture when not used with prior planning and a great deal of intelligence and consideration.

THE DOG WHO IS AGGRESSIVE

When you discover one day, to your utmost consternation (I hope), that the dear little darling you love so much has taken to eating up or otherwise mauling all the cats and other dogs in the neighborhood, you have a real problem.

It is a sad fact of life that in the vast majority of these cases, the owner knowingly or subconsciously encouraged the feelings that triggered this kind of delinquency in the first place. Let me give you a few examples.

Not too long ago I invited an acquaintance whom I thought was lonely to come for the weekend with her rather large dog. She explained that I should know the dog was a cat killer. I thanked her for being honest and replied that my two cats were very fond of all dogs and we would have to be very careful. When she arrived, she took her dog out of the car on leash. My friendly Himalayan cat trotted up as the lady pulled her dog in the opposite direction, soothing it. "Discipline her now!" I shouted, when it looked as though the dog would have its way before I could rescue my cat. "What for?" she screamed back at me. "She hasn't killed it yet!"

Some years ago, I was handling one of the terrier breeds that has quite a reputation for not readily tolerating other animals. At a terrier get-together following a show where we were fortunate enough to go Best of Breed, a licensed judge, who was a breeder of these dogs, congratulated me on my win and began asking me about my dog's temperament. I described his lovely disposition, how easy he was to travel with, and what fun it was to have him in my home from time to time because he loved all my house animals. The man's face got grimmer and grimmer as I went on. "He likes cats?" he asked. "Evidently. He gets along fine with mine!" "Sorry to hear that. Yep, never was a _____ terrier worth his salt that didn't kill cats. Used to be lots of cats on my street; isn't a one left. Old Hank, he took care of 'em all—what ye think of that?" he wanted to know. "I think," I concluded the discussion, "that I am going to be violently ill!"

I guess I had better go on record right here and now as saying that, except in the wild state where such things are dictated by the need to survive, I see nothing glorious or laudable in the killing of one animal by another; in my opinion, human beings who tolerate such behavior, either by sanctioning it from afar or excusing it as a personality quirk of particular breeds, are morally unreliable, temperamentally unstable, and in need of immediate psychiatric help.

The drives that allow approval of such antics are not terribly different from those that lurk behind the owner who allows his "pet" to lunch on human fare. A lady with a small, hardy breed of dog came to me at a show and asked if I would handle for her the next day. "Cyrus has his C.D. but I can't seem to get him to animate in the ring. Would you try?" I said I could and suggested I call at her trailer that evening to get to know Cyrus a little better. "What does he do in the breed ring?" I asked. "Oh, he won't walk and he's afraid of the judges." "Does he cringe?" "Oh, no, Cyrus wouldn't cringe. He's not a coward! He tries to bite them." "Oh."

When I came to call that evening I was welcomed by the lady, who held Cyrus under her arm. I was immediately impressed by his beady little eyes. They told me his impressions of me were not favorable. I sat down quietly in a chair while his mistress sat across from me on a padded bench. She put Cyrus down beside her. The minute she released him he made his move. I have never seen anything so fast in my life. He ripped my sleeve, opened a sizable gash in my forearm, and returned to his "Mommy's" side almost before I knew what had happened. "See how smart he is, how quick?" she asked me as she took out her knitting.

I sat there open-mouthed as she made no attempt to correct the dog or to comment on the blood now staining my slacks. Somehow I found my voice. "Would you mind holding Cyrus again, please?" "Well, no, of course not, but why?" she wanted to know. "Because," I explained, "I am now going to leave, and if that dog moves as much as an eyebrow in my direction, I am going to drop-kick him the length of your trailer!" I will long remember Cyrus and his beady little eyes and the open mouth of his speechless idiot of an owner!

You think this is unbelievable? Then how about the breeder of one of the larger breeds which is generally one of the more placid whose beast pulled free from her during one of my handling classes and attacked a little Poodle on the far side of the room for absolutely no reason whatsoever. While the hound owner looked on yelling, "Don't hurt him, don't hurt him!" the Poodle owner and I beat the brute off, no small feat, as he obviously meant to kill the smaller animal. I was in the midst of administering a serious thrashing to the enormous hound dog when I felt his owner beating on me screaming, "How dare you touch my dog, I'll take you to court!"

I literally threw the animal in her face, dispatched the Poodle to the local veterinarian and its owner to the emergency ward of the hospital to have her mangled hand attended to. Then, nursing my own nicks and scratches, I sat down with the owner of the bully. I swear to you this is the conversation that actually followed:

"Mrs. _____, do you realize your dog almost killed that dog?"

"Well, he must have had a good reason!"

"What on earth do you mean, a good reason?"

"We humans can't always know what goes on in a dog's mind."

"True. But we certainly can show our disapproval of antisocial behavior."

"Antisocial by whose standards, yours or the dog's?"

"I don't believe you are at all sorry this happened. Haven't you any feelings about this incident?"

"I think we should talk to that lady with the Poodle; we never had any trouble till she came to class. I think you should refund her money and ask her not to come any more."

And this woman was a presumably intelligent person and an important figure in her breed club!!

These stories, funny as they may be to read, are not amusing at all. Sadly, they are all true, and if I had the space, I have fifteen or twenty more I could throw in. The people I have just told you about are all responsible for turning otherwise perfectly nice dogs into biters and killers because they believe their dogs are different from any other dogs and therefore have different rights and privileges in our society.

I feel we must pause at this point and admit that, like it or not, there is a certain "sick" section of society which equates its superiority with the aggressiveness of its dogs. These people are from no particular religion, race, or color—they are simply the misfits of the world who cannot or will not exert themselves enough to make themselves noticed as individuals. Instead, looking for a crutch to lean on, they procure a poor, dumb animal, usually a dog, and encourage him to be the tiger they have not guts enough to be themselves.

Many years ago I was training with a man who had a young Doberman. As we were attending the same obedience class some miles from our home area, we took to traveling together to and from classes. When he was called away, his wife volunteered to keep the dog working, and she and I made the trip each week to class. During one such trip the dog refused to stop barking. The lady turned around and said, "Hush!" pointing her finger at the dog. He promptly attacked his mistress and she lost most of the offending finger. I pulled the car over to the side of the road, thrashed the dog within an inch of his life, and drove her to a hospital. The next morning at 8 A.M. the husband was at my door with two policemen. He was going to put me in jail *for beating his dog!* This is the kind of mentality we are dealing with when I refer to "sick" dog owners who turn dogs into liabilities.

Certainly there are dogs born into this world that are temperamentally unstable. But man can and does seem to develop some perfect horrors on his own, using for raw material innocent animals who are never permitted to realize that there are rules we all, two- or four-footed, have to live by. Dog owners who permit their animals to bite or maul other animals should not be permitted to own pets of any kind. But many amateurs acquire dogs with a tendency to start trouble and no knowledge of how to stop the dog from stirring things up. There are other people who want to stop such activity but are afraid to do anything for fear it might be wrong. Still others believe that certain breeds are not trustworthy and therefore tolerate snapping, biting, and fighting because it goes with a breed. Many people believe if you are bitten by a Chow, "What can you expect, it's a Chow!" Some acquire Boxers, Doberman Pinchers, or Shepherds, tie them up for long periods, then when they run amok upon release, blame it on careless breeding.

No emotionally stable dog, unless he is defending himself from abuse or is being hurt, has to bite. If he does, the first time should be the last time. That initial experience should be so unpleasant, so awful for him, that he has no desire to try it again. Permitting young puppies to snap because it looks so cute is asking for trouble; at maturity, 120 pounds of snapping dog is no longer a laughing matter. Toy breeds are often excused their transgressions because they are tiny and therefore "frightened." At maturity, even a Chihuahua's jaw muscles can do a lot of damage! Introducing dogs to other dogs or to strange people on a tight leash "to control him in case something goes wrong" is inviting disaster. The tight leash tells the dog all is not well, and his apprehension often overcomes his "won't" power.

I certainly don't mean to imply that as long as you go through life with your dog off leash, he is going to love everything. All I'm saying is that it is never "normal" or excusable or acceptable for dogs of any size or breed to attack other animals or people, and that when it happens you should not hesitate to make your disapproval immediately and violently apparent. When introducing two animals, keep your voice calm, rather high-pitched, and pleasant. If on leash, loosen that leash while they smell each other. Then take them apart for a few minutes and try again. Once the tails start going you are usually over the hump, though not always.

Dogs and bitches usually get on splendidly; the usual thing is for the female to show her disapproval of the male's curiosity by snapping. He will then retreat apologetically. Seeing that she has the upper hand, she will encourage him to try and make friends again, and chances are all is well. Two males may be fast friends until a bitch shows up. Then extra care should be taken by the owners involved, as jealousy in dogs causes just as much trouble as it does in humans. Two females, should they decide to fight, are three times as dangerous as the males of the species.

The only sure way to prevent trouble on your block between your dog and the others on the street is to see that your dog is never at large with the others unless you are in attendance. Your control over your own dog is often the only weapon you have to prevent disaster, and you will thank your lucky stars over and over again for your obedience training when emergency situations arise.

If a fight should occur, remember never to reach between the warring dogs. Sometimes, if there are leashes on the dogs, two of you can pull in opposite directions and, when both are tight against their leashes, drive your foot hard at the point where their jaws are connected. Probably the best method in the case of male dogs is to grasp the scrotum firmly and sink your nails into the testicles. This is drastic, but methods less painful than this one will not even impress the fighting dogs, let alone deter them. Whatever solution you choose must be one that hurts the dog more than the other dog is hurting him. He will then turn on that new source of pain and, if you are quick and expecting such a reaction, you can suspend him in the air awhile until he can be controlled and calms down a bit.

The experience of taking part in an organized obedience class where the dogs come in contact with other males and females of all sizes and types and temperaments cannot be underestimated. Once, many years ago, when I was teaching obedience classes on the eastern shore of Maryland, a club asked me to divide my classes so that small dogs worked with small dogs and large dogs with large dogs. I refused, explaining that in my opinion this would be a great disservice to all the dogs, as the outside world consisted of dogs of all sizes and our trainees had to learn to live in that world without fear, suspicion, or antagonism. They did it my way, and were everlastingly grateful that I didn't give in to their wishes.

THE HYPERKINETIC DOG

Help for the hyperkinetic child has progressed dramatically in the last few years. Certain drugs, a curtailing of artificial food colorings and additives, and various handling techniques have been most successful in dealing with these unfortunate youngsters who cannot seem to stop moving, stop doing, stop performing.

Up until very recently, however, the high-strung dog was thought to be just that—a throwback to a breeding nick somewhere along the line, a product of too much inbreeding. And certainly there are nervous dogs that are the result of such things. But more and more we are beginning to see evidences of the hyperkinetic dog, and finally veterinarians and research agencies are beginning to tackle this problem.

High-strung dogs are those who all their lives urinate at the slightest bit of excitement. They jump at the smallest noise. They immediately distrust unfamiliar situations and people and spend much of their time pacing in kennel runs or moving from spot to spot in the house. Careless breeding practices are as responsible for these sad animals as are certain environmental influences. We see much of this in some hunting dogs who never have contact with the human world except when they are working, and then they go, go, go! Certain breeds can be expected to be calmer than others due to their backgrounds. Intelligent handling, regular exposure to the world at large, inclusion in a sound family-type atmosphere, patient introduction to the reassuring boundaries, rules, and regulations of obedience training—all can do wonders with a dog like this, though he will never be completely cured.

The hyperkinetic dog, however, is difficult to reach; he resents human physical contact because he feels he has more important things to do; his attention is so inward-directed to his own needs that he has no time to pay heed to a handler's commands. He resents everything that seems to interfere with his inner clock. He rushes by other dogs and ignores sights and smells that would attract other canines—in search of what? He does not know.

While, as I say, this kind of dog can look for help in the near future, finding relief for him at the time this book goes to press would be unlikely, except in certain areas of the country where research is being directed toward this unique condition. If you suspect you have this kind of dog, I heartily suggest you seek help at one of the larger veterinary colleges or hospitals, such as Guelph, in Canada; Angel Memorial in Boston, Massachusetts; Cornell School of Veterinary Medicine, in Ithaca, New York; the Veterinary School at Michigan State University at Lansing. There are many, many more.

In a high percentage of cases of hyperkinetic dogs, in spite of present and probable future progress, painlessly disposing of these unhappy, unfortunate animals is the only humane decision.

In bringing up this particular subject we come face to face with a fact we should never lose sight of: obedience training, as wonderful as it is, does not and cannot cure all the ills in the world of dogs.

It can bring you and your dog close and keep you that way; it can give courage to the shy dog and teach self-control to the overly aggressive dog. Obedience training contains the ingredients to do many wonderful things for dogs everywhere, but it is no good whatsoever if administered by a human who feels that obedience training is strictly for dogs. Teaching is the best way in the world to learn. Make sure you learn as much as your dog and—who knows?—someday they might invent obedience titles for people. If you work hard, you might find yourself, with your dog's patience and assistance, a winner! But still, obedience training cannot solve *all* problems.

FEAR BITERS

This is true, also, in most cases of fear biting. Fear biters, whether their insecurity is related to poor breeding practices, which is often the case, or is man-made, can rarely be changed. There are exceptions to everything, of course, but these are miserable animals one can rarely trust. Their sickness causes them to be defensive about everything, and they lash out, for no reason, usually when your back is turned or when you least expect it. I'd love to be able to give you a training cure for such a problem, but if the dog is a true "fear biter," there simply is no such thing. Again, the kindest thing to do is ask your veterinarian to put the dog to sleep.

JUMPING ON FURNITURE

I myself have no objection to dogs sharing my living-room couch; but I want them to get off when I tell them to and lie elsewhere.

If you want your dog to stay completely off sofas and chairs, then never let him on to begin with. A warning "ah-ah!" in a threatening tone of voice makes a good warning. The word "Off!" is a good command to use from the start. Sweep the pup off the furniture as you give the command. A blanket, basket, or crate of his own makes such training easier.

If you are faced with the bad habits already instilled by someone else in an older dog, your job will be harder, but it doesn't mean you have to give up. Since you can't be with him every minute, put him in his crate when you have to leave him alone in the house. If you don't care to do that, tip lighter chairs over on their faces and place a light ladder over the length of a couch, which will make it uncomfortable enough to discourage a visitor. Shut bedroom doors, and that should be that. Many people use mousetraps with success, setting them and then deliberately leaving the dog to learn for himself that furniture bites back.

Again, a mat or blanket of his own often helps get the lesson across more painlessly. But it takes consistent supervision.

CHEWING

The great majority of puppies chew; it is part and parcel of being a puppy. But older dogs who persist in destroying chair legs, ripping up linoleum, munching shoes and books, present a serious problem that can sometimes only be curtailed but not completely cured.

Chewing can be caused by a diet deficiency or internal parasites. Certain horses are acknowledged "cribbers," which means they bite constantly on any wooden edge available to them and suck in air. You can't cure them; I think there are some dogs like that.

Putting pepper or mustard or soap on the thing the dog has shown a preference for chewing sometimes works, but the damage has already been done. Dogs left alone a lot chew because they are bored. Toys of their own for these animals sometimes work, sometimes not. Again, the best cure, here, is not to give the animal a chance to start chewing. Crate or kennel him when he is left behind; and don't laugh at his chewing as a puppy and expect him to know this is suddenly a "no-no" just because he's grown up.

DIRTY DOGS

Over the years I have had many dogs brought to me because they could not be housebroken. I must tell you honestly that I can count on the fingers of one hand the dogs who were truly dirty; the rest were nervous wrecks, so afraid of bed-wetting that they did little else.

When I first started handling Bouviers des Flandres I was warned that this was a "dirty" breed that evacuated in their crates and slept in the filth quite happily. I can state unequivocally that I have *never* known a dirty Boov. People also tried to tell me that Italian Greyhounds were filthy little beasts. The ones that travel with me aren't; nor, in my humble opinion, are most dogs that are properly exercised and housebroken with intelligence.

There are, of course, dirty dogs, but these are in a definite minority. The rest who make puddles, sprinkle chairs, and leave surprises on the kitchen floor, do so because they are screamed at and swatted and thrown out the door and because somebody rubs their nose in their excrement until they are so confused they don't know which way to turn. I once fired a kennel girl because she left a dog in a dirty crate for three hours. When I asked her her reason, she said she was "teaching him a lesson." I don't know whatever became of this charmer, but she surely left *me* in a hurry!

Puppies need to be exercised frequently—*very* frequently! They are more liable to have to urinate after drinking and heavy roughhousing than immediately after eating. Bitches are inclined to have to urinate more while they are in season or coming in, and a very common vaginal infection also can cause such reactions. Dogs will quite naturally christen a strange place if they get the chance. It is a heritage from the days when wolves and wild dogs marked their territory and honored the areas so marked by others of their kind. And bitches in season can cause males to urinate copiously and continually.

If you should "inherit" a dog because nobody can housebreak him, chances are excellent that you can turn the tide by scrupulous attention to his moods and *absolute* refusal to acknowledge his mistakes, which will be many to begin with. Match the dog (as described in the section on showing) at regular hours, same times each day. And when you do so, always take the animal to the same area. As when housebreaking a puppy, all fluids cease from early evening until morning, so pick up his water bowls and drop the toilet-seat lid. Keep him on leash at all times either beside your bed or on it. In the beginning, set your alarm for four times a night. Take him out even if you have to wake him. Praise when you are rewarded by success, but don't overdo that part of things either. If he should err, let him see you cleaning it up, and hum as you do so, in a high key, not in a threatening lower key. Feed less than you will later on after he is trustworthy, and early in the day so he's cleaned out for night. If the dog isn't wormy, doesn't have dysentery or colitis, and is otherwise well oriented mentally, you can lick it.

Truly and verily, most dog problems are man-made. Sometimes it puzzles me, the things man does to man's best friend. Occasionally I wish dogs could talk; most of the time I think it is exceedingly fortunate that they cannot!

PARTING PARODY

When you're ready to spit because Fido won't sit and you're dreaming of puppy-dog stew:

When you huff and puff, "Enough is enough!"—is it the dog? or *you?*

You tell him to stay but he comes anyway till you're ready to coat him with glue!

You are fit to be tied 'cause his heeling is wide—is it the dog? or *you?*

Have you made things quite clear to the dear little dear? Have you given him every chance?

While he was a-walking, weren't you talking to Jane about Saturday's dance?

You told him to stay with your thoughts miles away; when he didn't **you** thought it a joke.

With a thundercloud frown you ordered him "Down!"—then walked off to catch a quick smoke.

Well, why should he bother to try and rate? He can see *you* don't bother to concentrate!

If you want *him* to work for a ribbon of blue, *you* have to be willing to work hard too!

So you're set to get mad because Fido is bad? Well hold it a minute or two!

Cancel that blow-up! Take time to grow up!

IT ISN'T THE DOG—IT'S YOU!

PART FOUR

HANDLING
FOR THE FIELD

1

The Retriever Mystique

No matter what dog endeavor you select, doing your best is a challenge, and the sweet reward of success is always a thrill. But no thrills, in my mind, quite approach those which come as the result of your first placement in a field trial, the awarding of your first working certificate, your first field trial championship, your first duck retrieved by your very own retriever. This is because no matter what you set out to do with your retriever, each step is a test of the intelligence and flexibility of you both; also, we are dealing here not only with obedience but with the natural instincts of a particular kind of animal created to do a specific job.

Show, obedience, field—each requires a partnership of sorts between dog and handler. The partnership that must exist between the retriever handler and his retriever is so unique, to my way of thinking, as to have no counterpart in any other relationship, for it demands fierce concentration on the one hand and nonaction based on absolute faith on the other. It requires of the trainer that he teach without subjugating and control without conquering; it requires of the dog that he obey without question, trusting completely in the ability of his handler to get him what he wants most—a successful retrieve. At the same time, the animal must be able to fall back on his own instincts when he realizes the handler has taken him as far as man can go; and he and his handler must each have the intelligence to recognize this moment.

No two tests at a field trial and no two opportunities in a duck blind can ever be counted upon to be exactly the same due to sudden variances of wind, light, cover, and the fall of the bird. Therefore, each time you stand beside a retriever in competition or in the shooting field you must be prepared to handle an unknown situation, extemporaneously. To achieve this on your own would be quite a feat. To do it through and with a dog you have trained yourself and who has as much faith in you as you have in him, and to do it better than another twosome to go before or come after you, is pretty heady wine!

THE LANGUAGE OF THE FIELD

Before going one single step further into the discussion of retrievers, we will have to face the fact that if you are going to run field dogs, then you must learn to speak two languages—English and Retriever-ese!

There was a very brief glossary of terms in our obedience section; in the show portion of this book there was no glossary at all. The words peculiar to retriever activity, however, are so numerous and so interlocked that it would be impossible to explain field work without giving the reader some idea of the meaning of the terms we will be using. So right now we'll take time to translate the lingo. Some of these words are important only to those trialing their dogs; most, however, are used and reused by retriever folks, no matter what level of retrieving they are pursuing.

The Line—This is a nonexistent spot from which all tests are run, in training or at trials. It is the point at which the dog leaves you and goes forth to do his thing; the area where you stand with your hands clenched in your pockets, leaning in the direction of where the bird went down, praying like mad; the place to which your dog will deliver his birds. At a trial you are given a number and when your turn comes you are called: "Number eight on line!" If something goes wrong with the birds or the guns, you will be told to "Take your dog off line." In other words, go back in the direction from whence you came, relax, and wait until you are called again.

A Line—The direction a handler indicates to his dog by use of his voice and his hand or his finger. This process is called "giving a dog a line" and is used when sending a dog for a bird he did not see fall. In "lining a dog" the handler draws an imaginary line between himself and the bird, and the object is for the dog to continue in that direction with as little correction or assistance as possible after the initial command to go fetch.

Cast—You "cast" a dog out as when fishing. It means your original command to go and retrieve when you mentally "throw" him in the direction you wish him to go. If he continues true for a good distance, the dog is said to have taken "a good cast."

Back!—This is the command most people use to send their dogs to retrieve. It means, "Go beyond where I am and find the bird." Some handlers send their dogs with a snap of their fingers; some use the dogs' names; some say "Fetch!" But of all the commands to retrieve, "Back!" or "Get Back!" are the most commonly used in the United States and in Canada. When a dog has been stopped at a distance from a handler so that the handler may give him directions to go deeper into the field or further out in water, the command, again, is "Back!"

Mark—Here is another term that has a zillion meanings. If you want a dog to notice an oncoming bird he hasn't seen yet, you draw his attention to it by whispering or saying in a soft, excited tone, "Mark! Mark!" If a dog fails to find a bird he has seen fall, he is said to have "missed his mark!" A dog's "marking ability" refers to his ability to see birds fall at a great distance and to remember more than one fall at a time. All field trials are run on marked falls or blind retrieves either alone or in combination. "Marked falls" are birds shot for a dog so that he can see them go down, and may consist of a single (one bird) and double (two), or triple (three), or even, sometimes, four birds.

Blinds—A "blind retrieve" is a dead bird planted in a field or in or across water before you get to the line with your dog. *You* know where it is located, he does not. You must then direct the dog to the "blind" by whistle, voice, and hand signals.

There are many kinds of "blind retrieves." A "cold water blind" has nothing to do with the temperature of the water but refers instead to a blind planted across or well out in water. The dog is brought to the test "cold" (without practice or prior knowledge), with no diversions to warm him up and get him in the mood. He is simply told to retrieve. Land and water "blinds" are often used together. They are sometimes given in conjunction with one or more shot birds. "Channel blinds" are quite common in trials today and require that a dog be handled to a bird hidden at the far end of a channel (a rivulet or stream), being kept in the water at all times, going and coming. "Blinds" are also given with the distraction of a shot being fired in the opposite direction before the dog is sent for the "blind"; or the dog may be required to be steady while a shackled bird is dropped in front of him, then turned from that flapping duck and sent *first* for his blind retrieve.

The word "blind" is often used casually to refer to the bird the dog must find on a blind retrieve. A trainer (or a helper) is said to be "planting a blind" if he goes out to hide a bird before running a dog.

A "blind" can also be a portable piece of training equipment simulating a duck blind; it is often used in training gun dogs who must learn to go out of a hole or hatchway in the front of the blind to get the birds and return around there with their retrieves. It is generally constructed of lightweight plywood and can be brushed with pine boughs to camouflage it for hunting. It is sometimes used in field trials.

A "waiting blind" is shaped like a training blind but it is made of a long piece of canvas or burlap and tied to steel stakes which are driven into the ground. The "waiting blind" is where you and your dog are told to wait by the line marshal when you are the next to compete. It is high enough so that the dog is not able to see over it and allows you to wait near enough to the line to save time between dogs without jeopardizing somebody else's chances by allowing your dog to watch the test before he runs it (although many of us feel that so doing is more of a hindrance to a dog than a help).

Shooting Stool—This is a small round or square platform used in swampy areas to give a dog someplace to lie or sit above water which is frequently almost over his head, and to allow him to see incoming birds without thrashing around and distracting game. You will also see a "shooting stool" used in some field trials.

Open Dogs—Those competing for Field Trial Champion and/or Field Trial Champions Running in Amateur All-Age or Open or Limited All-Age Stakes.

Derby Dogs—Young retrievers under two years of age. The term is usually applied to trial dogs running in either sanctioned or licensed Derby Stakes open to all dogs over six months and under two years.

Bumpers—The training substitute for birds. Made of plastic or heavy canvas, they can be purchased at most boating stores and marinas, for they really are boat bumpers, the kind you hang over the sides of yachts so the crafts don't rub against the dock. They are also referred to as "dummies" and come in different sizes and weights if purchased through stores that handle retriever training equipment and advertise in dog and sporting magazines.

Cover—A term used to describe the type of area through which a dog may be asked to work (i.e., the topography of a piece of land). Dense cover could be brambles and thickets; light cover could be a just-mowed wheat field; clover is thick cover.

Honoring—Usually after a dog runs a test, but sometimes before he runs, he may be asked to sit quietly at heel under perfect control without any physical restraint while another dog works. The purpose of this is to simulate actual gunning conditions wherein one dog who failed might be aided by a fresh dog standing by. At retriever trials, two dogs never work at once, but frequently there are two dogs on line at the same time—one "honoring," one working. When it is called for on land or water, it is always a supreme test of control and discipline. Dogs ordered to stay on line to honor are under judgment until released by the judge.

Fall—The area in which a bird or a bumper falls to the ground.

Check—That with which you pay entry fees. It is also the process by which a dog investigates something in the field that drew his attention. You might say "He checked back"—he doubled back thinking he had found something; or "He checked the old fall"—he went to the spot where an earlier bird had landed.

No Bird—A "no bird" is called at a field trial or during training when the bird or bumper does not land where it was supposed to.

At a trial, if the judge feels that where a particular bird landed for a particular dog was too easy or too hard for that dog, compared to the birds of the other competing dogs, he will call "No bird!" In stakes involving younger dogs and sometimes in championship stakes, the judges will both start repeating loudly, "No! No!" to help enforce the fact that the dog is not to go. When a "No Bird!" is called, you also may repeat "No! No!" to your dog to get him off line. Particularly in the case of a young, eager dog, never turn your back and walk off assuming he will follow your "Heel!" command. Simply keep slapping your leg on the dog's side, repeating, "No! Heel, boy, heel!" until you are several feet behind the line. Then you may put your leash and collar on him, and find out when the judge wants you to return for your rerun.

Rerun—Most judges explain to you that you can go right back and run the test again immediately, or you may wait and come back after two or three other dogs have run and the placement of the "No Bird" is out of your dog's mind. Take my word for it, in ninety-nine cases out of a hundred you should take all the recess the authorities are in the mood to extend to you. The only exception would be in the case of a very lackadaisical dog who needed perking up, and then only if the fall wasn't too far out of the intended area. If at all in doubt, *don't!*

Steady—Retrievers competing in field trials must be "steady to shot." This means that the dog must sit on line, beside his handler, without more than the initial "Stay!" command which is permitted just before the judge asks you to "signal me when you are ready." No other vocal or physical restraints are permitted between the time the first bird of the test is thrown and the moment when the judge calls your dog's number, at which point you may send your dog.

Breaking—If a dog is not steady he is said to "break," or to "break shot." If, under certain circumstances, when a dog commits himself to retrieve before all birds are down, and the handler can stop the dog in midflight so that the dog stays put until his number is called, the dog is given a "controlled break" for which he will be severely penalized. In most instances of "controlled break" after the dog's number is called, the dog must be brought back to the line by the vocal commands of his handler before being sent for his birds. "A breaking bird" is a bird thrown at close proximity to a dog under judgment. "Breaking birds" are used to test the staunchness of retrievers under fire by testing their resistance to the highest form of temptation. "A Breaker" is a dog that, because of overenthusiasm or inadequate training—sometimes a combination of both!—consistently "breaks."

Thrown Out—A very unlovely term, but accurate in the extreme, meaning that you and your dog committed such an awful blunder, or blunders, that you are summarily removed from competition. Breaking dogs are "thrown out"; so are dogs that chew up their birds instead of retrieving them, go deaf when called, fail to find their marks, or refuse to go out to retrieve when commanded to do so. Judges allot one page in their books, each test, for each dog. The worst sound in the whole wide world is to be standing on line sweating out a dog that is not doing a particularly dandy job and hear behind you the "rrrrriiiiippppp!" of your page as it is torn from the judge's book, to be followed by the crackling sound as it is wadded into a ball. At this point, no one needs to tell you that you have just been "thrown out."

Field—Another innocent little word which causes troubles sometimes. A "field" trial, for instance, is a test of dogs' abilities on land *and* water. The "field" at a trial consists of the people following the progress of that trial—judges, spectators, committee members, and participants.

Field Trial Committee—These are the members of the trial-giving club directly responsible for running the trial. The *Gun Captain* is responsible for lining up men and women to shoot and for replacing them frequently; he is also the one who finds out how many guns a test will require, whether the birds are to be killed or shackled and thrown, and for telling his guns where the judge wants the birds dropped. The *Field Trial Marshal* has all the headaches of all his sub-chairmen and committee members—his word is law. The *Line Marshals,* of which there are ideally two, keep the dogs and handlers coming to line quickly so that no time is lost, take care of returned birds, and indicate when new ones are needed. There are many other members of many other committees, but these people are, along with the *two judges* necessary for each series of each stake, the ones with the most authority and usually with the most knowledge.

Guns—Field trials or training would be impossible without the dedicated services of those men, and a few women, who stand long hours in pouring rain, freezing snow, chilling sleet, and numbing winds to make it possible for all dogs to have an equal opportunity to win or a chance to train under conditions simulating those at field trials. They are called "guns." They have to be more than just good shots. Retriever trial shooting is a very specialized thing, for it requires not only that a gun "hit" a bird when the judge gives the signal, but that the "gun" drop that bird in the same area for each of the dogs running in a particular stake. They are the unsung heroes of field trials and field training. While they are quite rightfully wined and dined and put up during the trials by the grateful club hosting the event, they take no money for their services. In return, whenever the wind starts doing crazy things and the pheasants won't fly or the pigeons won't drop— guess who gets blamed for being slow, stupid, and blind? Yep, the "guns!" The only group of people to whom we retriever addicts owe more and give less are the bird boys.

Bird Boys—"Bird boys" get paid for throwing at licensed trials; usually volunteers do the work at sanctions and working certificate tests where championship points are not at stake. The art of throwing live, unshackled birds in a manner that lets the guns bring them down where the judge instructed, requires talent and a consistently reliable throwing arm. The ability to put twenty-seven shackled ducks in the water exactly one-foot three inches from a given lily pad, not once but twenty-seven times, is something inexperienced critics should try before blaming their dogs' errors on the poor "bird boys." In addition to throwing birds, "bird boys" lug boats, tie and untie game, haul ammunition, set out and pick up decoys, and plant blinds. Usually teen-agers trying to earn money for school, or farm kids picking up a few extra bucks in their spare time, or the sons and sometimes daughters of trainers, kids who just like to help, they are the backbone of any trial and all training. It is a wise handler who brings along a pair of dry socks or an extra-warm sweat shirt for his "bird boy."

Refusals—This term generally refers to a dog's failure to take direction or to stop on whistle for his handler during the execution of a blind retrieve. Three refusals on a test are serious enough; any more could mean that sound of ripping paper behind you. The word is also used when a dog fails to retrieve upon command, or "refuses" water.

Deeks—The familiar term for decoys, artificial ducks or geese made of papier-mâché, wood, or cork, used in hunting to lure birds and in trials to test a dog's concentration and intelligence. Many "deeks" are used in hunting; rarely are more than six at a time set out in one spot at a trial.

By-Dog—A dog not competing in a given stake but asked to *stand by* and either honor with a working dog under judgment or work with an honoring dog under judgment. The idea is to make all tests and all test situations on line as uniform as possible for everyone.

Test Dog—A dog not competing in a given stake whose purpose is to run the new test the judges are proposing in case they're not sure it will be feasible, and/or for handlers competing in that stake to watch before bringing their dogs to line so they can get an idea of the problems involved in a test. Test dogs are not always used, but they are most welcome when they are. By offering to run a test dog, a handler just dropped can often get useful experience for his dog. If you volunteer, just make sure your dog is up to the work involved.

Handle—Here is another word used with such casualness that it can be very confusing. When a trainer is asked of a young dog, "Is he handling yet?" the translation is: Does he do blind retrieves? A good "handler" is one who works a dog well in competition. "The dog didn't 'handle' well" means he argued with his trainer during the course of a blind retrieve. "He 'handles' his birds well" means that the dog picks his birds up cleanly and delivers them with no mouthing.

Diversions—Pretty girls are "diversions" (i.e., they take a man's mind off his work). "Diversions" at field trials and in training are used for exactly the same reason—to see if the dog can be sidetracked from the job at hand by various methods. A "diversion bird" is thrown close to a dog to find out if he will rivet his attention on it and miss other marked falls which follow. A "diversion shot" is sometimes fired before a blind to see if it will distract the dog from his handler's commands. Sometimes helpers in light clothing are sent into the field and told to do nothing at all but stand there while a trainer tries to send a dog past or beyond this "diversion." "Diversions" of all kinds are used, not to see what it will take to trick a dog into making a fool of himself and his handler, but to test a dog's span of attention, his intelligence, and the amount of control his handler has over that dog under pressure.

Bird—This word can mean pheasant, duck, pigeon, or whatever other feathered creature is being used. It can also refer to a training bumper. "Pick up that bird!" can sometimes mean "Whatever you threw, get it up off the ground!" Birds at trials or in training are sometimes shackled (i.e., used live but temporarily tied wing and foot so they remain where they have fallen until the dog finds them) or shot (i.e., killed on the wing by skilled men and women who work in twos to insure equal distance on all falls for all competing dogs).

Switching—A dog that goes to the area of a fall, hunts, fails to find, and then leaves that area to hunt for another bird; or, that drops a bird he is retrieving and goes for another shall be considered to have "switched." This is one of the gravest of crimes and must be discouraged at every opportunity. We'll discuss this in detail later on. Any dog that "switches" while under judgment is instantly disqualified.

Then there is a group of terms used at field trials that are easier to understand if we use them together:

Licensed or Sanctioned Field Trials offer the entrant certain *Stakes,* such as Qualifying, Derby, or Open, just as the Dog Show offers Novice or Bred-by-Exhibitor Classes, etc., and the Obedience Trial lets you choose between Novice, Open, or Utility.

Once your Stake begins, the first *series,* or inning, will consist of one *test* designed by both judges to evaluate your dog's abilities as a retriever. Every dog entered in the stake in which your dog is entered will run that same test. When all have done so, this would mean the end of the first *series.* After the judges have decided which dogs should be allowed to continue, the numbers of those dogs will be announced by the Marshal as *call backs.* The dogs *called back* will then prepare to run the second series in your stake, which consists of a second test devised by the judges. And so on, until, by process of elimination, only the best dogs are left to receive awards.

If, on the other hand, the judges feel your dog's work did not merit much consideration, chances are you will not be called back, but will be *dropped* from competition.

Picked up—If, during a test, your dog begins thumbing his nose at your commands, goes deaf to your whistles, or is otherwise thought to be out of control, the judges will tell you to *"pick your dog up, please."* There are moments, believe me, when you would like to do just that—and then throw him as far as humanly possible! When told to *"pick your dog up,"* however, you are to get the dog back to his crate as promptly as possible so as not to hold up the rest of the trial or foul the working area for the dogs that follow you. You are then free to sit back and watch the rest of the trial. And vow to do better another day.

2

Field Trials

THE WORLD OF RETRIEVERS CHAMPIONSHIPS

Finding the right dog, raising him from puppyhood, special training exercises—all these we'll get to in time. But before we get under way with the particulars, let's talk generally about a retriever championship. No title of the three we are discussing in this book demands a more exacting regimen than does the securing of an Amateur or Field Trial Championship for a retriever in the United States or Canada.

If you set your sights on this lofty goal you will need more self-confidence than Hannibal had when he decided to take his elephants over the Alps. More than just intelligence, you'll need a particular kind of gray matter that permits you to think on your feet and gives you a special intuition not always easily explained. A Field Trial Championship requires more work at stranger hours than many people are willing—or able—to give. Some of the equipment necessary can be hand-made; much of it cannot. It can be costly in the extreme, not always easily accessible and, in the case of birds, must be constantly replaced. Entry fees are sky-high due to the rising costs of running field trials these days, and the prognosis of the cost of trials in the future is not bright. The asking price for a dog with the potential to compete with the unbelievably fine retrievers we are breeding today, and win, is often more than three times that of a promising show or obedience prospect. The distances you must travel to train, not to mention in order to reach field trial grounds, are not only far but often over bad roads in out-of-the-way places. If you don't like the sight of blood, are against killing things, avoid physical sports like prizefights and wrestling matches, and are not comfortable around guns, you are in a heap of trouble if you have decided you want the letters F.T.Ch. in front of your retriever's name.

If you goof at a dog show, at best you'll bring home a ribbon, at the worst your dog gets the experience of being examined by a stranger; if you fail in one exercise of an obedience trial you can still continue all tests, and nonqualifying scores have been known to be high enough to place; again, at least you benefit from competing. If, however, your dog should break on the first bird of a licensed field trial, that's all, my friend—no valuable experience, just hours of driving, another entry fee down the drain, and failure. Back to the drawing board!

The rhythm of competing at trials once your dog is ready is absolutely necessary. It's foolish to pick a trial one month, and another two months later. He needs to run, and on birds, every single weekend, and you need to handle him under pressure every single weekend, once you make up your mind you want that retriever trial championship.

During the week he needs to work at basics and blinds, lining and marking, almost every day, winter, summer, spring or fall, wind, sleet, snow, rain, or hail, particularly in the beginning. This requires not just little old you, but also bird boys most of the time.

Obviously you have to be very well-off financially and pretty much your own boss to be able to take every weekend off and train most weekday afternoons and evenings. If married, you have to have the understanding and co-operation of the entire family.

In obedience or in breed competitions, professionals and amateurs compete constantly. Once you make up your mind to get a field trial championship, you might as well face the fact that everyone you'll be competing against in open and amateur stakes is good enough to be classed as a "professional." Some of these men and women earn their living training other people's field trial champions; some run their own, either trained by themselves or others. But by the time you get to the stakes you have to win to get either your Amateur Field Trial Championship or your Field Trial Championship, the amateurs out there with you are just as clever and experienced and wise and sharp as most professionals. You will have to be just as good in order to beat them.

The people running in retriever trials every weekend most of every year are a world and a law unto themselves. Fanatically devoted to their interests, they are usually so well-to-do that if they decide to go down to Georgia for January to get a head start on training for the spring trials, they simply pack up their four or five dogs, a couple of bird boys, a load of pheasants, ducks, and pigeons, and take off. Professionals join together to help each other shoot, train, cook, and drive. Amateur and professional alike, they are all busy people with constant deadlines of the next trial by which they have to have a certain number of dogs ready not just to run but to win. Glamorous as it may seem to the spectator to watch them in their white handling coats at trials, there is no harder working group of people alive on the face of the earth. For the most part, they are helpful and encouraging to newcomers who are serious and whose dogs merit their admiration. But they have no time to waste on also-rans or fair-weather handlers. These people talk their own language, live by their own code, and by their very existence control and direct the flow of retriever activities. They are triggered by an absolutely fanatical determination to protect their sport and preserve the way of life it stands for at all costs and against all encroachments of social demands, political bickerings, law, time, and the tides. Constantly under the pressure of competition, they anger fast, forgive fast, move fast. They spend 75 per cent of their lives in the field training or competing, and 25 per cent of it eating well and drinking hard. If you can't train all day Friday from dawn to dusk, compete all day Saturday from sunup to sundown, participate in a hearty meal and talk dogs half the night over endless Dead Soldiers and still be in the field in command of yourself and your dogs at daylight on Sunday, you'll just never make the grade, never in a million years!

I make all this clear to you before you start, because if you have a good dog and have settled on nothing less than a F.T.Ch., you should know the whole picture. You *can* do it—other amateurs have. I don't in any way mean to discourage you. I do, however, feel you must have an opportunity to look objectively at the whole, true picture before making what amounts to an enormous commitment.

Today there are a number of nonwealthy amateur trainers running their own dogs and finishing them. They sacrifice a lot because it means a lot to them to get this very special recognition. They live on hotdogs and peanut butter and sleep in their cars or trucks to save money for entry fees, gas, and birds. Many of them get their first championships in Canada, where the competition is no less tough and the dogs and tests are every bit as fine as those in the United States. But in Canada you are not allowed to shoot to kill at retriever trials. All land work is on birds already dead before the trial begins; on water tests, ducks are shackled or wrapped. Therefore, because you are liable to get more uniformity in falls and the hazard of dogs breaking on squawking cock pheasants released in their faces is not as great, you have two advantages from the start, and these two particular advantages do a great deal toward stilling vibrating knees and murdering abdominal butterflies.

Before deciding whether a retriever field trial championship is your dish of tea, take a moment now to look into the rules and regulations surrounding retriever trials, and what is involved in picking the proper stake in which to run your dog.

RULES AND REGULATIONS

A field trial is a competitive event designed to test the heart, nerve, intelligence, nose, memory, and tractability of a retriever under conditions which simulate, as nearly as possible, natural hunting conditions. Two judges pass on the performance of every dog.

All dogs entered in a specific stake or class, as we noted in the Glossary, are given exactly the same test each time around until the winners are decided by a process of elimination.

There are many, many ifs, ands, buts, and whereases in field trial rules and regulations. To make sure you know the whole story, write to the American Kennel Club, 51 Madison Ave., New York, N.Y. 10010, for *Field Trial Rules and Standard Procedures for Retrievers,* and a copy of *The Standing Recommendations of the National Retrievers Advisory Committee.*

In Canada, write to the Canadian Kennel Club 2150 Bloor Street West, Toronto, Ontario M65 4V7, and ask for *Field Trial Rules and Regulations for Retriever Trials.* The Canadian equivalent to our *Standing Recommendations of the Retriever Advisory Committee* is included in their booklet on retriever field trial rules and regulations and is called *The Supplement to the Standard Procedure for Non-Slip Retriever Trials.* It costs seventy-five cents.

Current changes in rules and regulations are to be found in *Dogs in Canada* and in the American Kennel Club *Gazette.* Both of these publications also list licensed trials, dates, and results. And you simply cannot get along without the *Retriever Field Trial News* (1836 East St., Francis Avenue, Milwaukee, Wisconsin 53207), which is a "bible" no matter what you intend to do with your retriever.

To get the dates of sanctions or fun trials, locate the kennel club in your area and they will direct you to their field-orientated members. Or the mother club (the Golden Retriever Club of America, for instance) can usually refer you to activity in your neck of the woods. The secretaries of these organizations are listed in the American Kennel Club *Gazette* or *Dogs in Canada.* Check with the rod and gun clubs, the local gun stores, game wardens, and forest rangers. Once you make contact with one other retriever "nut," you're on your way!

In retriever competition, unlike many sporting-dog events, no money prizes are ever awarded. Trophies and ribbons for the first four places in each stake are usually given, and it is encouraged that J.A.M.'s (Judges' Awards of Merit) be awarded to dogs that have passed every required test in a stake and have proven themselves to be well-trained, qualified retrievers.

Official Stakes

While retriever clubs may hold such nonregular stakes as puppy, gun dog, or veteran, the only regular official stakes to be offered at a retriever trial are as follows:

Derby (Junior in Canada) is for dogs which have not reached their second birthday on the first day of a trial at which they are entered, and are at least six months of age on the first day of that trial. No championship points are awarded by reason of Derby or Junior wins, but there is a national rating system in both Canada and the United States listing the top Derby dogs each year by reason of their placements in licensed Derbies.

Open All-Age is for all dogs over six months of age.

Limited All-Age is open only to those dogs over six months of age which have previously been placed or awarded a Judge's Award of Merit in a licensed Open All-Age Stake; or, that have been placed first or second in a licensed Qualifying Stake; or, placed or awarded a J.A.M. in an Amateur All-Age Stake carrying championship points.

Qualifying: The Qualifying Stake is for dogs over six months of age which have never won any placement or J.A.M. in an Open or Limited All-Age Stake; or, any placement except a J.A.M. in an Amateur All-Age Stake; or won two firsts in a licensed Qualifying Stake.

Amateur All-Age: The Amateur All-Age Stake shall be for any dogs over six months of age if handled (not trained now, just handled) in that stake by persons who are amateurs. (The definition of an "amateur" is to be determined by the Field Trial Committee of the trial-giving club, but it is generally considered to mean any person who has not derived any part of his livelihood from the training, handling, or showing of field or hunting dogs in the calendar year preceding the trial in question.)

Special All-Age: (Canadian only) is for dogs that have placed or been awarded a J.A.M. in an Open All-Age or Special All-Age; or, placed or awarded a J.A.M. in an Amateur All-Age; or, placed first or second in Qualifying during the year preceding that of the stake in which the dog is to run.

Kinds of Trials

Four main kinds of field trials are open to American retrievers: *A Member Trial* is one at which championship points are awarded and given by a club or association which is a member of the American Kennel Club. *A Licensed Trial* is one at which championship points may be awarded and that is given by a club or association which is not a member of the American Kennel Club but which has been licensed by that body to give that specific trial. *A Sanctioned Trial* is one at which dogs may compete for prizes and ribbons, but no championship points are awarded. These may be sponsored by a member or nonmember club by obtaining the sanction of the American Kennel Club. *Working Certificate Trials* will be described later.

In Canada there are only *Licensed Trials* (licensed by the Canadian Kennel Club), at which championship points are awarded; and *Sanctioned Trials,* which are defined as the American Sanctions are. The regular official stakes in Canada are Junior, Qualifying, Open All-Age, Limited All-Age, Special All-Age, and Amateur All-Age, but the Junior, Open, Qualifying, and Amateur Stakes, with requirements similar to their U.S. counterparts, are the most regularly offered. The qualifications for these stakes parallel the U.S. qualifications.

The Point System

Placements in Limited, Open, or Amateur All-Age Stakes in licensed retriever trials in the United States or Canada represent points toward championship as follows:

First Place	5 points
Second Place	3 points
Third Place	1 point
Fourth Place	½ point
J.A.M.	No championship points are given for Judges' Awards of Merit

Field Trial Championships

There are two types of field championships available to retrievers in the United States and Canada: Amateur Field Trial Championship and Field Trial Championship.

In Canada, to acquire an Amateur Field Trial Championship a retriever handled by an amateur must win The Canadian National Amateur Championship Stake or must win a total of fifteen points as a result of running in Open All-Age, Limited All-Age, Special All-Age, or Amateur All-Age Stakes. In those stakes in which he places there must be at least eight starters, each of which is eligible for entry in a Limited All-Age Stake. During the accrual of his fifteen points, the dog must win at least one first place in at least one of the stakes listed above which is open to all breeds of retrievers. In other words, while specialty trials would count toward points for a retriever championship, that dog must win at least one of the major stakes competing against all other kinds of retrievers, not just his own breed.

To acquire a Field Trial Championship a retriever handled by an amateur or a professional must win The Canadian National Retriever Championship Stake or must complete requirements outlined above for an Amateur Field Trial Champion title, except that the total number of points (including the five-point win) required is ten gained as the result of wins in Open, Special, or Limited All-Age Stakes.

In the United States, things are a bit more complicated.

To acquire an Amateur Field Trial Championship a retriever handled by an amateur must win:

1. The American National Retriever Championship Stake, or
2. The American Amateur National Retriever Championship; or
3. A total of ten points in Open All-Age or Limited All-Age Stakes in which there must be at least twelve starters eligible for entry in Limited All-Age Stakes, or
4. A total of fifteen points in Open All-Age, Limited All-Age, or Amateur All-Age Stakes in which there must be at least twelve starters eligible for entry in Limited All-Age Stakes.

As is true in Canada, within their total points the American dogs must also win a first place, five points, in one of the major stakes open to all breeds of retrievers.

To acquire a Field Trial Championship, a retriever handled by an amateur or a professional must either win the American National Retriever Championship Stake or take a total of ten points exactly as outlined in the Amateur qualifications (including the one five-point win), as a result of competing in Open or Limited All-Age Stakes.

The "National" stakes in the United States and Canada are the ultimate in field trial competition. The retriever year is marked from National to National for Field Trial Champions and from Amateur National to Amateur National for Amateur Field Trial Champions. Only one National Championship Stake and one Amateur National Championship Stake are offered annually. Only the top-winning dogs in both countries are eligible, and qualifications are set by the Boards of Directors of the A.K.C. and C.K.C. You can imagine the caliber of the work at these stakes! Each event must go at least ten series (or tests), during which the dogs are tested equally on land and water. One, and only one, winner is selected. He (or she) then becomes that year's National Retriever or National Amateur Retriever Champion.

While A.K.C. and C.K.C. issue certificates for Fld. and Amt. Fld. Championships, no certificate is available for Dual Champions. But if your dog has completed requirements for and has been granted a championship in the show ring and in the field, you may refer to him as a Dual Champion.

Licensed Trials

Licensed Trials are held throughout the United States and Canada during almost every month of the year. Sponsored by field trial clubs and associations, they must be entered ahead of the trial date before a specified date of closing, in writing with fees enclosed. The requirements for registration of purebred retrievers—and only purebred retrievers eligible for registration with C.K.C. or A.K.C. may run in sanctioned or licensed trials—are the same as those for licensed and sanctioned dog shows. Licensed trials usually last three days, from Friday through Sunday, offer two stakes in which championship points are awarded, and one other regular stake such as Derby (or Junior) or Qualifying. Canada manages to offer both of these lesser stakes at one licensed trial far oftener than does the United States. You are guaranteed absolutely nothing at a licensed trial except that you may run your dog until the judges say "out!" Fees are much higher at licensed stakes than at sanctions—$35 to $50 in the U.S., $20 to $25 in Canada— but there are no spectator or parking fees. Usually food is available from a caterer's truck. The only trial I have ever known to be canceled was called off by the Forestry Department because of fire danger. The birds used are usually pheasants and ducks, some shot, some shackled, except, as we have explained, in Canada where there are no shoot-to-kill tests.

Bitches in season are more unwelcome at trials than a Bull Terrier at a cat show. If your female comes in heat between the time you submitted your entry and the morning of the trial, submit to the Field Trial Committee either in person or by mail a veterinarian's certificate stating her condition, and most of the time your money will be refunded.

The rule book clearly states there is to be *no training* done on the trial grounds at a licensed or sanctioned event. However, since trials are held in the country it is quite simple and perfectly legal to slip into a field "down the road a piece" and throw a few birds. In fact, most adjacent fields are quite crowded! Sound carries, however, so shooting and whistling anywhere near enough to the trial so that there is a possibility of the wind carrying the noise to competing dogs should be carefully controlled.

Working Certificate Tests

While Working Certificate Tests are sometimes offered separately by retriever breed clubs, they are usually held in conjunction with a national or regional specialty show of that club—such as the Irish Water

Spaniel Club of America Specialty Show. They are judged by two people.

The entry fees for these events are very low and all prerequisites are carefully outlined on a sheet you will receive with a premium list for the show. Requirements for working certificates for Irish Water Spaniels are included for you to look over. It becomes immediately apparent that the idea of these tests is to determine a retriever's *natural* ability, his intelligence, and his desire to do the work for which he was intended. Fancy whistle work, steadiness on line beyond that involved in reasonable control, honoring—these things count for nothing, for they come about only as a result of man's refinements of the dog's unrefined instincts. Therefore, the qualifications are within the reach of many dogs and many handler-owners who would not otherwise be able or might not otherwise be interested in putting a dog in the field.

As is true of Derbies and Sanctions, working certificate tests are a marvelous place for breeders to keep in front of the sporting-dog world the fact that their dogs are capable of "singing for their supper."

Here's an example of specifications for a working certificate trial and award:

IRISH WATER SPANIEL
WORKING CERTIFICATE

SCOPE: The purpose of the IWSCA in establishing and making available a *Working Certificate* to all owners of Irish Water Spaniels is to encourage the use of and to maintain the natural hunting and retrieving abilities in these dogs which is genetically vital to the breed.

In establishing the criteria for the *Working Certificate Stake,* the IWSCA realizes that most Irish Water Spaniels will not be as thoroughly trained as those competing in field trials, and therefore, for the WORKING CERTIFICATE STAKE have devised simple land and water tests, using ducks, game birds, or pigeons. The tests are designed to show a retriever's hunting and retrieving ability, courage and perseverance in the field for sport and for the conservation of fallen game.

REQUIREMENTS: Working Certificate Stakes may be held at any retriever field trial or any event held in the name of the IWSCA for any number of Irish Water Spaniels. Permission must be granted by the IWSCA, and the stake is to be conducted and judged under the requirements of these articles.

All retriever clubs, other than the IWSCA, desiring to hold a *Working Certificate Stake* shall submit a written request to the Secretary of the IWSCA thirty (30) days prior to the first day of the trial, listing the trial location, date, judges, and the estimated number of dogs to be tested.

All IWSCA-sponsored retriever field trials for Irish Water Spaniels only shall have a *Working Certificate Stake* and will be indicated in the premium list whenever possible.

A fee may be charged for giving *Working Certificate Stakes.* The cost shall be known to the owners of dogs before the Stake is held.

Working Certificate Stakes shall be conducted and judged under the *Standard Procedure* and the *Supplement* to the *Standard Procedure* for *Derby Stakes* as described in the A.K.C. Field Trials Rules, for non-slip retriever trials. The following exceptions shall apply in the *Working Certificate Stakes:*

1) Artificial decoys are not to be used.
2) Dogs may be brought to line on leash and held but shall not be sent until their number has been called.
3) Hand delivery of birds not necessary, but is, to area of line.

There shall be two judges for the *Working Certificate Stake* whose combined retriever field trial experience equals or exceeds three (3) A.K.C.-licensed field trials.

TESTS: Test for the *Working Certificate* shall be:

1) The retrieving of two (2) birds on land (double) in moderate cover with birds approximately 40 to 50 yards from line and at least 90° apart.
2) The retrieving of two (2) ducks in swimming water as back-to-back singles, in light cover with ducks approximately 25 to 35 yards from line.

CERTIFICATE: A *Working Certificate* shall be awarded to the owner of those dogs who, in the opinion of the judges, satisfactorily complete the tests of the stake. The Certificate and copy shall be *completed and signed by both judges.* The owner shall receive the original, and the copy is to be sent back to the IWSCA Secretary, along with any unused Certificates left.

Working Certificate blanks will be issued by the IWSCA Secretary to the person responsible for the *Working Certificate Stake.*

Working certificate folks are a close-knit, friendly group of people in all retriever breeds. Limited by time, other interests, and money, they have settled for proving to the world that their dogs are perfectly capable of doing a day's work in the field and are therefore a more all-around dog than their cousins who do just obedience or just show work. They don't feel it is necessary to trial a dog all his life to prove his working ability, and of course they are right. These folks seem to share an enjoyable secret with their dogs and with each other: field training can be just plain, downright fun. They are proud as punch of their certificates and rightfully so. Their theme song is as follows (with apologies to Mansfield):

I must go down to the fields again
To the lonely fields with my dog
To rush through the mud, browse through the brush
And plow through brambles and bog
And all I ask is a friendly duck
Or a pigeon fat as a plover
And a working certificate on my wall
When the long trek's over!

ENTRY FORMS

For entries to field trials, write the Field Trial Secretaries listed in *Dogs in Canada* or *Pure Bred Dogs, American Kennel Gazette.* To locate working certificate tests, contact the Secretaries of the mother clubs as listed in either of these publications.

Entry forms for trials or working certificate stakes are filled out as are obedience and dog show entries—very carefully. But while evaluations for working certificates are usually offered in conjunction with a national or regional specialty which will send you a judging schedule with full particulars after your entry has been accepted, licensed field trial particulars such as locations of the trial, the specific days on which certain stakes are being run, and "suggested" starting times, come along with your entry blanks in your premium list. After that, you get no more communications from the trial-giving club unless some emergency necessitates the altering of original information.

When you arrive at the trial you will be given a trial catalogue listing each dog and his particulars by stake. At this writing there is no charge for your field trial catalogue, but with prices rising there could be in the next few years.

Sanctioned Field Trials

Sanctioned Trials are also available through the United States and Canada during most months of the year, and are sponsored by field trial clubs and associations. You may enter the day of the trial. The birds used are shot and shackled pheasants or pigeons or ducks, and you will get more birds shackled or killed on a previous test than shot. No championship points are awarded, but Open, Qualifying, and Junior (or Derby) Stakes are offered. The tests are liable to be a little less demanding than those in licensed trials, for Sanctions primarily offer rehearsal opportunities. Food is not often available; there are no spectator or parking fees. Usually each dog, regardless of performance, is guaranteed two series, one on land and one on water, so that you get your money's worth in experience. These are informal events and once you are washed out, an offer to the trial committee to help throw birds, tie birds, marshal, shoot or direct traffic, often finds you in a job where you can learn much. As always, there are two judges for each stake.

Picnic and Fun Trials

Sponsored by the same groups which sponsor Licensed and Sanctioned Trials, these are where, ideally, all newcomers should start. These are very much family events, and there is the time (simply not available at Licensed and Sanctioned events) to have questions answered and to sit down and listen to more experienced people who are more than willing to put you and your dog on the right track. Fun Trials offer a variety of nonregular stakes such as puppy, gun dog, etc. The entry fees paid as you arrive rarely exceed five dollars, and you couldn't duplicate the experience for three times that amount. This is where contacts are made which will keep you in touch with retriever activities in your area, and this is where your Poodle or Newfoundland should be welcomed for a spot of experience in public.

Competitive Work Trials

As I flitted back and forth across Canada and the United States teaching clinics in the field and helping retriever clubs get started, it became more and more apparent to me that there was really nothing available to the run-of-the-mill retriever lover who hunted over his own dog each year but now and then got a perfectly natural urge to show off. So a few of us got together and invented some nonregular stakes which would give the hunter someplace to go with his retriever and perhaps come home with a ribbon instead of a duck, someplace for the working certificate dog to go after he got his certificate if the owner wasn't able to get him into serious trialing. And we found we started quite a few junior handlers who fit into these more relaxed stakes until they were old enough to slug it out with the adults. By setting up these "special" stakes, which any club could offer at any nonsanctioned trial—we called them "competitive work trials"—we found we encouraged whole families to participate in the sport. I include these stakes with their requirements now, to be used by any group of people who want to have fun in competing with their dogs in the field. These stakes have been used with great success in Massachusetts, Maryland, Vermont, Virginia, and various parts of Canada.

PUPPY STAKE

1. Open to all dogs three to five months of age.

2. Dog need not be steady and may be held any way handler wishes.

3. Dead pigeons with training pistols used for land and water tests. Three series in this stake.

4. Judgments will be made on basis of style, enthusiasm, and natural ability. Delivery of birds to area of handler is sufficient. You may encourage puppies in any way at all times, provided you do not go more than ten feet from running line.

BEGINNERS' STAKE

1. Open to all dogs over five months and under one year of age who have never competed in any stake at a sanctioned or work-type trial above beginners' level. Dogs may win this stake twice before being declared ineligible.

2. All dogs in this stake are guaranteed a minimum of two series. There will be a maximum of four tests offered in this stake.

3. All land game will be dead. Live ducks will be used on water, with a maximum of two retrieves (two singles or one double) using ducks.

4. Dogs in this stake may be held in any way their handler wishes. They need not be steady, and older dogs which *are* steady in this stake will not get extra points or consideration for their steadiness. All vocal encouragement necessary, in handler's opinion, is permitted, and handlers may move up to but no more than ten feet from the running line to physically assist their dogs without being disqualified. While dogs should be encouraged to deliver to the handler, dogs in this stake will not be penalized for putting game down on ground in front of handler, or for adjusting hold on game, except that, in case of a tie, the dog doing the neater job will, of course, get the edge.

5. *All* dogs in this stake are brought to line on lead.

6. Dogs in this stake may be expected to work single retrieves on land and in water, and no fall will be longer than seventy yards. *This does not mean that all falls will be this distance.* On the water, dogs will be expected to work through a maximum of three decoys. Dogs may be expected to complete a simple double on land or in water in which *both birds are to be in plain view and widespread.* Any double offered will consist of two birds on water or two land falls; doubles will not consist of one land and one water bird, and no doubles will require a change of bird (i.e., one pigeon and one duck).

7. Dogs in this stake need not wait for a number to be called, but handlers are to send their dogs as soon as they wish after the last bird in each test has hit the ground.

8. Disqualifications in this stake are as follows:

a. Handler going more than ten feet from the line to the bird to physically encourage his dog to retrieve.

b. Failure of dog to return a retrieved bird close enough to the handler so that the handler may get the bird by taking one giant step.

c. Failure of dog to go out to retrieve after second command to do so by handler. One recast is permitted but will be penalized.

d. Injurious mouthing of game, live or dead, by the dog and/or rough handling of the game by the handler.

e. Bringing two birds back at the same time, or bringing no bird back at all.

Note: Since this is probably the most crucial stake, training-wise, handlers are encouraged at all times to ask assistance from judges, guns, and bird boys to make sure dogs complete a retrieve whenever possible. Once a dog is obviously not going to complete a test, whether in training or competition, handlers are advised to leave the line and go out and make sure such errors as trying to bring both birds of a double back at once are *never successful for the dog.*

9. The emphasis in this stake from a judging standpoint should be entirely on the natural ability of the dog. Handlers' refinements or errors should not count in scoring the performance of the dog.

INTERMEDIATE STAKE

1. Open to all dogs over nine months of age who are steady under physical restraint on line. Dogs are ineligible for this stake if they have won first, second, or third place in a Gun Dog Stake, or if they have placed above Beginners' level at a competitive work trial of any other club, or if they have placed, c.m.'s included, at a licensed or sanctioned trial anywhere. Dogs may win this stake twice before being declared ineligible.

2. All dogs in this stake are guaranteed a minimum of two series. There will be a maximum of four tests offered.

3. In addition to regular use of shackled ducks, dogs in this stake must be prepared to handle both live and dead pigeons.

4. Dogs in this stake may be held on line by handler either by the collar, leash, or a "sending line." They may sit or stand at heel. Talking to a dog to restrain him is permitted but should be kept to a minimum, and obviously, in the case of two dogs doing equal work, the dog working with the least amount of restraint and direction by the handler would get the edge. Game must be delivered to hand, although dogs will not be penalized for putting game down to get a fresh hold, or to

shake leaving the water, provided the pickup is made quickly and neatly. The term "to hand" means that *the bird reaches the handler's hand before it is put down on the ground, or dropped, at the handler's side or feet.* Sitting to deliver will not be given extra note. Handlers wishing to run their dogs in this stake, under judgment, without holding their dogs, will get no extra credit for steadiness. Such dogs will be disqualified if the dog goes before the number is called and the handler cannot stop him within six feet of the line. Quietness of handling is to be encouraged at this level. Handlers may feel free to move about in an area no greater than six feet from the established line without being disqualified for leaving the line.

5. Dogs may be brought to line on lead. Those who feel their dogs are under control enough to come from the waiting blind to the line *off* lead may do so, but *if their dog leaves heel position and runs into the bird field out of control,* they will be marked down by the judges.

6. Dogs in this stake may be expected to complete gunning-type tests, including long singles on land and in the water, the distance of the fall in this stake to exceed ninety yards. *This does not mean that all falls will be ninety yards.* Dogs will be expected, on water, to work through a maximum of six decoys, and could be asked to complete a double where one bird was on land and one in water, necessitating a change of bag (i.e., one pigeon and one duck, either bird on land or water, in a double). Dogs should be prepared to work out of a boat anchored off shore, or through the opening of a training blind, or to do simple single walk-ups on leash. They should also be prepared to do singles with replacements in plain view. Honoring could be given after the first two series of this stake have been completed. If included, honoring dog will honor *on a loose leash* from a point at least six feet behind the working dog; a tightening of the leash of the honoring dog constitutes a commitment to break.

7. Dogs in this stake must remain at heel until the judge has called the dog's number. A judge will call the number only once after the last bird is down on each test, after which the handler may pick up birds in any order he wishes without further direction from the judge. The normal order of pickup is to be encouraged on doubles (i.e., the first bird the dog retrieves is the last bird downed). Should the dog miss the last fall, he will not be penalized for picking up birds in reverse order, provided he finds both birds without assistance. Should the handler commit his dog to one bird, but the dog chooses the other, this is not to be considered a switch (see disqualifications for definition of switching).

8. Disqualifications in this stake are as follows:

a. Dogs which put down game before putting it in hand will be disqualified if the handler is unable to make the dog pick up the bird after reasonable commands to do so. *This disqualification holds only on single retrieves* . . . many young dogs or green dogs, which usually deliver to hand, are so anxious to get the second bird of a double that they tend to throw the first bird at the handler on the way to the second; we feel their memory and desire for a second bird should be encouraged rather than their delivery in this situation. Therefore, on doubles, dogs not delivering first bird neatly to hand will be marked down but not disqualified.

b. Handler going more than three feet from line to assist dog.

c. Failure to go out and retrieve after first command. Recasts are permitted in order to help dog complete the retrieve, but dogs which have to be recast are disqualified.

d. See "d" under disqualifications in Beginners' Stake.

e. Switching is an automatic disqualification. This means that after definitely committing himself to the area of one fall and hunting that area unsuccessfully, the dog quits that area without finding the bird, and goes to area of other fall. Handlers are always encouraged, when they sense a dog is ready to switch, to go out and prevent this training crime from ever happening.

Note: The emphasis in this stake, from a judging standpoint, should be entirely on intermediate work—work more polished than that of the beginners, yet not expecting work up to the advanced level. Since, ideally, we are building toward learning the fundamentals of field trial handling as well as the refinements of top gun dog performance, more attention here should be given to the development of rapport between dog and handler.

Since these stakes have been carefully constructed to bring dogs along in their training step by step, great care should be given by judges that the intermediate stake neither hold back a precocious dog nor force an average working dog beyond his scope.

DERBY STAKE

1. The Derby Stake will be run in conjunction with the Intermediate Stake. The same rules and requirements will apply for Derby Dogs as for Intermediate Dogs *with the following exceptions:*

a. Dogs eligible to run in the Derby must be *over* six months of age and *under* two years of age on the first day of the trial.

b. *Derby dogs must be steady on line* without physical or constant vocal restraint.

GUN DOG STAKE

1. Open to any dog over eleven months of age which has not placed

in a Licensed Open, won a Licensed Qualifying, or won first place in two Sanctioned Open stakes in the United States or Canada. Handlers must be prepared to conduct themselves and to handle their dogs exactly as if they were running in a Licensed or Sanctioned Field Trial.

2. All dogs in this stake are guaranteed a minimum of *three* series. A maximum of five series will be offered.

3. On land, live and dead pigeons will be used at discretion of judges. Shackled ducks will be used on water. Mixed bags should be expected.

4. Dog must be steady without vocal or physical restraint beyond the initial handler's command to stay given prior to informing the judge he is "ready." In the case of a controlled break or a creeping dog, after the last bird of a test is down, the handler will call his dog back to heel and his number will not be called by the judge until the dog is back at heel. The individual judges are asked to carefully specify to all handlers, before beginning this stake, just where the point is at which the dog is to be considered having crept "off line." A controlled break may be defined as a dog making a definite commitment to retrieve without being sent, whereupon the handler is able to stop him with whistle and voice, after which the dog remains where stopped without further inducement by the handler. A controlled break entitles a dog to continue competing in this stake provided he does the retrieving work satisfactorily, but he cannot be placed first. Dogs running in this stake are allowed a fresh hold on bird, but must deliver to hand, and any fresh holds are to be noted by the judges. The area of the line in which the handler may move about freely without disqualification will be clearly established by the judges prior to the stake, either with logs on the ground or some such indication. Handler must remain in the area of the line and will be disqualified for shouting or calling dog's name while in the field. If a dog misses a mark and can be handled promptly to the bird, the handler should do so, though he will be penalized for handling on a marking test. If he wishes to emphasize the marking work of his dog, he may ask that the bird be thrown for his dog if the dog is obviously lost, whereupon the bird shall be thrown *in exactly the same place it fell the first time,* with bird boys or guns calling dog's attention to the fall.

5. Dogs in this stake may be brought into the waiting blind on leash, but are under judgment between that point and the line, coming and going, and must in this area be off leash with leash left behind in waiting blind, or completely out of sight in handler's pocket from the time he leaves the waiting blind. Dogs must be run without collars. Dogs that run out of control into the bird field, having to be recalled to heel by their handlers, either before or after running a test, will be removed from the field promptly and will be put last in running order. If the dog breaks into the bird field a second time, he will be disqualified,

but may run not under judgment as long as his work remains satisfactory, being thereafter brought to and from line on leash.

6. Dogs in this stake may be expected to complete marking tests at any distance specified by the judges, ranging from long singles to doubles to triples, over-and-unders, walk-ups and work through any number of decoys, land or water. Dogs should be prepared to handle as many as four birds on a test. Handlers should be prepared to have dogs honor on land or water. Honoring will not be required, if at all, until the third series, and multiple honoring or walk-ups while honoring could be expected in later series. Handler may direct dog to falls in any order he chooses if not otherwise instructed by the judge.

7. Once they have signified they are "ready," handlers must be prepared to have their dogs remain at heel under judgment until their number is called to retrieve, and they are to stay on line after honoring until excused by the judges.

8. Disqualifications:

a. Disqualifications in this category follow, in essence, those outlined in recommendations of the Retriever Advisory Board, and this list can and should be procured by every handler from the American Kennel Club, 51 Madison Avenue, New York, N.Y. 10010.

Note: This stake is for dogs which are capable of doing licensed marking tests. The tests should be constructed to give ample opportunity to prove a dog's ability to mark, and handlers in this stake should be expected to be treated as experienced sportsmen, and to conduct themselves as such.

3

Your Field Puppy

All retrievers should be started the same way, whatever their ultimate role or goal will be. So we're going to begin at the beginning and make it possible for *you* to get a good puppy, raise it, train it, and get it into sanctioned competition or Working Certificate tests. From that point on it's up to you.

WHICH BREED?

For years people have tried to trap me (and every other professional retriever trainer) with the innocent little question: "What kind of retriever is your favorite?" I have always replied very truthfully (but also, I feel, quite cannily!): "My favorite retriever is a happy-working, hard-going dog." It still is and always will be.

Picking one breed over the others is a sure way to alienate the breeders of the five kinds you didn't pick! And, frankly, I don't happen to think a Labrador is better than a Chesapeake, or that an Irish Water Spaniel isn't as good as a Golden. I believe quite honestly that each of these breeds was developed for a certain job, for a specific kind of hunting. There are good dogs to be found in all six retriever breeds. But I do believe certain people are happier training a particular kind of canine personality, and vice versa.

So, after twenty years of experience training many different breeds to do the work of a retriever, I would be remiss in my job here is I didn't share with novices what I have learned about retriever breeds through experience with them in the ring, in obedience competitions, in the home, in the kennel, in the whelping box, in duck blinds, at controlled pheasant shoots, and on line at retriever trials. I hope breeders will knock the chips off their shoulders and put the shotguns back in the hall closets, for I mean no disparagement of any breed; in each there can be "happy-working, hard-going dogs."

One final swipe at some old wives' tales: You will not find me recommending the Chesapeake as a water dog because he has webbed feet, any more than you will find me recommending the Irish Water Spaniel because of his protective heavy coat.

All dogs have webbed feet! Everything from Chihuahuas to Irish Wolfhounds have a connecting piece of skin between the toes. Bigger breeds have more webbing, smaller dogs have less, but it is always there and, of course, if any animal is swimming, the webbing helps his paws pull him through the water.

Dogs work with their hearts! Sometimes a dense coat is a help, sometimes a hindrance. But ask any retriever trainer and he'll tell you that what makes a dog hit cold water hard or race through briers is not his protective coat but the degree of "want to" or the amount of good old-fashioned guts The Guy Upstairs put into that particular dog.

Many people bring me a retriever that is not a Lab and that works indifferently. I'll explain in detail why he won't make it as a field trial dog, and I get the reply, time after time, "Well, he's a Curly (or any one of the other retriever breeds). He's not supposed to work like a Lab!"

A Lab works in no particular "way" that sets him apart, honestly, except that dog for dog, the average Lab shows more style in water and on land than the average dog of the other breeds. If you feel you can discount this, then why are field trials the world over dominated by Labradors? It is not because these dogs are Labs; it is because they are fast and exciting to watch and aggressive in their approach to their job. If you haven't got these qualities in a dog, you haven't got a field trial retriever. Oh, certainly, there have been Champions and Nationals winners which were criticized by others competing with them because they lacked style. Even so, these few exceptional dogs had more of that in them than the average gun dog. Curly or Irish Water Spaniel, Chessy or Golden, Flat or Lab—if they don't hit the water hard and hustle getting their land work done, forget trials and start hunting.

The Labrador Retriever

Since, as we've noted, these dogs dominate field trials by number and performance, there has to be at least one reason; actually, there are many. Labs are very easy to keep, for their flat coats (which come in chocolate, yellow, and black) are easily groomed and they can be quickly whisked from field to ring. They are also very easily trained and are anxious to please. The majority are hardy, temperamentally and physically, which doesn't mean there are no soft, unexciting Labradors.

Because it is a very adaptable breed for show, pet, obedience, or field, good Labradors of dependable breeding are quite easily located by the prospective buyer. They have good noses, good brains, and good dispositions, on the whole, and fit in beautifully in a suburban community, a country estate, or even in a condominium. A very social animal, they usually get along well with males and females of other breeds. Very few I have known were ever bullheaded or true fighters. If you were given ten Labs and ten of each of the other three breeds, more of the Labs, I must say, would naturally prove to be "happy-working, hard-going dogs" than would any of the others.

In conformation there seem to be two different types of Labrador Retrievers. One is higher on the leg and longer in the body and usually proves to be a result, largely, of U.S. or Canadian breeding; British and Scottish blood lines produce a much shorter coupled dog with heavier bone, a bigger head, and shorter legs. Today there are several outstanding field-show kennels producing a dog that strikes a happy medium between the two and is the most attractive for my money.

There are useless Labs with no desire to retrieve and shy Labs who hate everybody. But they are rare, and it is hard to imagine going wrong with the choice of a Labrador Retriever for your shooting or trial dog. One word of caution: of the three colors, the black seems by far the more stylish and the one with the more positive personality. Granted, there are fewer yellows and chocolates being born, but even so, finding a good chocolate or yellow (by "good" we mean aggressive, stylish, anxious, fast, outgoing) is not as simple as locating a "good" black.

The Golden Retriever

In color the Golden ranges from an almost flat white (seen more from English breeding) to a pseudo-Irish Setter red, found mostly in U.S. blood lines. I am happy to report that the days of labeling this wonderful breed as a "lady's hunting dog" are gone forever. The most flossy of the retriever breeds, the Golden was disregarded for many years by serious trainers who mistook beauty for weakness or softness. Granted, there is a very real, very captivating gentleness in many Goldens which, while it doesn't hurt their work, doesn't make them terribly exciting to watch. And dog for dog, compared to the Labrador, you'll find it more difficult to locate a hard-going Golden, though "happy" is the middle name of most of them. The most exceptional noses I have ever had experience with belonged to Golden Retrievers.

Today it is much easier to find one that will take a swift kick or a lick of the whip and not quit than it was in the days where I was starting out. Field trial Goldens are being seen in much greater numbers now than ever before because *finally* there are breeders who want this animal accepted for the fine, positive hunter or competitor he has the ability to be. For many years breeders treasured and nurtured the idea that the Golden was gentle and loving and quiet and dear; this description just didn't cut the mustard with hunters and trialers. Also, because of their longer, lustrous coats, it was felt that their feathering would be a nuisance in marsh or thicket. Again, breeders fostered this notion by refusing to put their dogs into the field until they had finished their show championships for fear it would ruin their glossy guard hairs. Actually, nothing could be further from the truth. The Golden takes a little longer to dry off and certainly does attract burrs in heavy going, but his coat is silky and doesn't long retain weeds and brambles. He takes more grooming than the Lab, but not much more, really. And contrary to popular opinion, I don't think he sheds a bit more than the Lab.

Lab and Golden share a personality that loves people, is great with children, and learns quickly. I find the average Golden takes a little longer to mature, mentally, than the average Lab. He makes a heartstopping show dog, a stylish obedience worker, a dependable trial dog, and a good hunter. He can and does work well in the water, and his water entry can be everything you ever dreamed of, but you'd have to give the Lab the edge in swimming speed. The run-of-the-mill Golden doesn't take quite as much pushing around as the Labrador, but then, he rarely needs much. The outstanding field Goldens in the world are every bit as rough as tough Labs, however, so don't hand me that "sissy" bit. I have bred both Goldens and Labs for field and for the ring, and while my Goldens were hard, positive, aggressive, and dominant at work or at play, I must admit they were not the ordinary dogs I found in other very-well-thought-of kennels.

The Chesapeake Bay Retriever

No dog has ever had so much damage done to his reputation and his development by his "home town" than the Chesapeake. Years ago when field trials first became really popular, they were dominated by the Chessy. By the time I came along, while I was located in the heart of the Chesapeake Bay country, it was almost impossible to find a good working one, a good-looking one, or either kind with registration papers! Careless confidence in these rugged dogs by the people who bred them for the rigors of working in the treacherous Chesapeake Bay in Maryland had led this owner to breed his "water dog" to that neighbor's "Peake" and to hell with registration—all they wanted was a dog to bring in ducks a few weeks out of every year. The rest of the time the animal was tied out behind some waterman's shack on three feet of chain and fed when somebody remembered he was there. Believe me, he *had* to be rugged! Chicken farming was big business in eastern Maryland, and many of these dogs were trained to discourage pillagers who thought all they had to do was reach through the window of the chicken house when they wanted fried drumstick. These dogs were meant to be mean, and, take it from me, they were! Since papers rapidly became "old hat" to all except a few fine kennels that held the line and hung on for dear life, there were many "Chesalabs" or "Labrapeaks" running around and being referred to as Bay Dogs.

In the process of helping to establish the Talbot Kennel Club in Easton, Maryland, I was determined, as the date of our first licensed show drew near, to have a good turnout of Chesapeakes. With the help of several others who were just as determined, we waged a tireless hunt for eligible dogs. We combed old warehouses, the shacks of the slums bordering the local dump and fish-packing plant, and traveled, I'm sure, hundreds of miles on Maryland's worst back roads, coming to a screeching halt every time we saw something, tied or otherwise, that vaguely resembled a Chesapeake Bay Retriever. The next step was to go up to the door and knock, with crossed fingers, to ask— was it a real Chessy and was it registered? If it was, we begged to be permitted to spend our own money to enter it and we would provide a handler to train, groom, and get it to the show and home at no charge. (We also wound up inoculating and worming most of them, if and when we could get our hands on them!)

To make a long story short, we wound up with twenty-five Chessies entered under the internationally famous all-rounder Alva Rosenberg. When he realized he had this many he turned to me and said, "My God, Martha, I didn't know there were twenty-five purebred Chessies left in the United States!" That's how bad it was twenty years ago!

Happily, things have changed for the better. Fine Chessies are being seen regularly in the show ring, the obedience ring, the duck blind, and on the line at field trials. But they are still very much in a minority. It is almost impossible to find a truly top show Chessy in Canada, but the Canadians have good working retrievers in this breed. The best trial blood lines seem to be located, for the most part these days, in California; they'll stay there, because those who cared enough to develop this fine breed to its true potential are loath to let their good dogs get away. It is from the California blood lines that Chessies used as Seeing Eye dogs are chosen.

The Chesapeake Bay Retriever is not for everybody. If you get an unusually good one, he is bright, adaptable, strong, tireless, and devoted. If you get an average puppy from an average litter, he is liable to be softer than the Golden ever thought of being and quite sulky when things aren't going his way. The common Chessy takes correction when and if he is sure he cannot get his way; he'll suffer punishment ungladly and will either quit cold or turn on his trainer. For this reason, I don't recommend him as a beginner's dog. The typical Chessy's devotion to his family and to any children in that family can be quite touching— until the day Susie gets socked in the eye by the kid next door, who sometimes winds up needing stitches from Susie's "adoring" Chesapeake Bay dog. Chessies in a suburban setup where they are not kenneled can, and often do, spell trouble. They are not, as a rule, good with other male dogs. As a comparatively successful breeder of Chessies for a long time (I was once the Breeder of the Year with my dogs going Best of Breed [dam], Best of Opposite Sex [sire], and Best of Winners [puppy] at Madison Square Garden!), I can tell you quite frankly, I have never encouraged a prospective buyer who wanted to purchase a Chesapeake because he had liked a picture he saw in a dog magazine.

Chessies do much better in the homes or kennels of experienced dog people. They need training early and will require either a light touch or a very heavy hand; it seems there is no in-between. Still, nothing is hardier hour after hour, in fair weather or foul, than a good Chesapeake, thanks to their rough, wavy coats which dry with a shake or two. (Chessies range in color from beige—dead grass—to mahogany red; black is illegal.) They are marvelous watchdogs; it is not so hard to find Chessies that will make excellent gun dogs; and good show specimens can be discovered with a little more effort. But locating field trial-caliber Bay dogs is a quest somewhat akin to searching out the Holy Grail.

There is a very popular theory that Chessies cannot be kept as house dogs because their coats have a special oil gland which makes them smell like a combination of wet seaweed and dead fish. Wet Chessies smell like wet dogs; dry Chessies don't smell any more than any other breed; in fact, the smelliest dogs I ever housed were Goldens though that odor was not an unpleasant one. One other small point: *all* Chessies do not automatically know how to swim any more than do all dogs of any other breed. And it is equally a bunch of claptrap that this breed swims better than other retriever breeds because he is higher in the rear end than at the withers. The way the standard is written leads the inexperienced breeder to believe the animal should be as sway-backed as Don Quixote's horse! This breed swims powerfully but so do lots of other breeds whose backs are shorter and straighter.

The Irish Water Spaniel

This is the only Spaniel breed that runs and competes in field trials with retrievers. He is a big dog which should carry a chocolate brown, curled coat all over, except for his face and his long tail; the latter is why this dog is sometimes referred to as the Rat-Tailed Spaniel.

For years and years, while the Irish Water Spaniel has been excelling from coast to coast as a no-nonsense gun dog, particularly good in swamps, marshes, and cold water, other professional trainers and I have been looking for a good field trial Irish. So far nobody has come up with one that lasted more than one or two seasons.

For one thing, his heavy coat, loaded with water or the burrs which cling to it fiercely, slows him down. He usually has an eager water entry, but his return on land or water is understandably not fast without special coaching. For another, he is a real clown and loves to leave you with egg on your face. Also, while he looks rough and tough, too many examples of this breed have a yellow streak right smack down the middle of their backs. A change of handler, a change of location, a change of training territory will throw them every time. I have sent home close to twenty Irishers I was very enthusiastic about as young dogs; but when the pressure of high school arrived, I had no dog left to work with.

I have trained with many Irish Water Spaniels and am so partial to the breed that I kept one of my own for many years. I worked with a lady who breeds what I consider to be some of the very best temperaments in Irishers; we never got but one really good dog—and he, too, had his insecurities, although I know he was raised with every consideration imaginable. Thinking perhaps that other blood lines might be the answer, I went looking and was given a lovely puppy I was quite high on. He, too, failed miserably when it came time to quit being a puppy.

I believe that the right dog in the right hands might make it in field trials, but so far the hands and the dogs are missing. The best one in the country at present loves everybody and everybody loves him. He is a show dog who is fussed and fawned over and petted twenty-four hours a day; what he would be under the pressures and demands of field training, who knows?

The Irish Water Spaniel being field-trained is difficult to keep clean and requires a lot of daily grooming to make him presentable for every-day family living. He is a one-trainer, one-family dog, there is no doubt about it. The truly gregarious ones, unfortunately, find it very difficult to keep their minds on their work. In training they present a real challenge, but nothing an amateur couldn't learn to cope with, provided that amateur is determined and a little more bullheaded than his Irisher.

The Curly-Coated Retriever

I once handled in the ring the No. 1 Curly-Coated Retriever in the United States. Since I have always had a "thing" about the more unfamiliar breeds, I became quite excited when I was told by the owner what a marvelous retriever she was. I tried her out and almost died— I have never watched anything more boring in my life! She did her work with all the enthusiasm of a wet tea bag. Because she was pushed hard in obedience at the same time she was hunting and being shown, I gave her the benefit of the doubt and blamed her lack of enthusiasm on her early training and conditioning. The others I have worked with, however, have done no more than she did to stir my heart with their performances on land or water. Gun dogs, yes; field trial dogs, good luck! If, as a breed, they do possess this special colorful drive, how come you rarely see them in trials?

The Curly is a fascinating animal to work with. He is affectionate but never fawning, and tolerates strangers politely though not going out of his way to win their approval. Because comparatively few breeders are dedicated to doing anything constructive with this breed in the ring or at trials, there tends to be a great variety in type. The Curly's coat, which may be black or liver-colored, is absolutely fascinating and requires little work; it thrives on water and weather. If the stray wisps are kept snipped off and the ears are trimmed flat, this can be a most attractive dog at all times. Ideally, he is built along the lines of his other retriever brothers, a tiny bit leggier, perhaps, and covered all over (except his face) with crisp, tight "Shirley Temple" curls. Amazingly enough, some of the best blood lines producing today come from Australia and New Zealand, two countries which have doted on the Curly's ability as a gun dog since the late 1800s.

The Flat-Coated Retriever

This grand breed is often accused of being a long-coated Labrador, and to my eye he looks very much as if he could be. Temperamentally similar to both the Lab and the Golden, Flat-Coated Retrievers seem to have the tractability of the Lab and the more luxuriously coated beauty of the Golden. They may be black or liver in color.

The Flats I have trained or shown were fun dogs to work with because they were dying to please in the most engaging, happy manner. Fast as the dickens, the few who have made it to the line in competition at trials were show-stoppers, but for some reason most of these never made it past the Derby stage. In my own experience representative Flats were dispositionally a little harder than representative Goldens, a little softer than representative Labs. They are lively without being high-strung, and I am forever looking for a good field trial-caliber Flat-Coated Retriever, but then, so are lots of other people—good luck to us all! Again, as with Irish Water Spaniels and Curlies, I think the problem lies in the fact that not too many breeders are field trial oriented.

The Flat is a canny dog, quick, nimble, and flashy. He doesn't sulk at correction but he's no rough, tough customer when it comes to discipline. He learns after he has been corrected, and he remembers. The outstanding ones have plenty of flash for trials and are such smooth, quiet workers that they have the job done almost without your realizing it. If you can find a good one, it should be a wise choice for a beginner trainer-handler; unfortunately, Flat-Coated Retrievers, good, bad, or indifferent, are not found on every street corner.

Now then, I've gone out on the forbidden limb, but before you start sawing it off behind me, listen well; at no time do I remember saying this breed was better than that breed. I told you at the outset of this portion of the book that I felt I would be cheating if I did not give the benefit of my experience with the six sporting breeds that compete in retriever trials. I have trialed, trained in the field, and shown many specimens of each of these fine breeds; I have bred three of them most successfully for many years. But I have never felt that because I bred, say, Goldens, therefore all Goldens are perfect. There are advantages and disadvantages, plusses and minuses, in any human and in any animal. I have honestly outlined what I have learned firsthand over the years. So please "translate" my findings as honestly and with as open a mind as I have always tried to have in approaching any problem or any breed of dog.

Other Possibilities

"Does it have to be a Retriever breed?" Heavens to Betsy, no! I was field trainer for the Poodle Club of America for three fascinating years. Now here is an eminently trainable, hardy breed which learns like lightning. My own shooting dog for many years was a big white Standard. "Chally" and his field buddies drew great response from died-in-the-wool field trial folks who made it possible for us to run these dogs, not under judgment, at sanctioned trials. I have trained two Moyen Poodles for dove and pigeon and they were most successful. The Moyen is halfway between the Miniature and the Standard in size. The Minnies and the Toys are just as trainable, but their size is a great disadvantage.

Unfortunately, Standard Poodles have two things against them as working dogs—their coat, and the majority of the people who own them. The first problem can be handled if you care enough about developing the breed in the field; it must be groomed and clipped constantly, but the coat is such that dried mud shakes off easily. Unfortunately, reckoning with owners who want Poodles recognized as shooting dogs only if they can stay in clean water and who do not want their dogs to have to put dirty old birds in their mouths, makes the project almost hopeless. There are a few sensible Poodle people, bless them, but they are so outnumbered that, while they win a battle from time to time, it's going to be a long, long haul to win the war!

Springers are an excellent choice, particularly if your water retrieving is largely limited to ponds, although I've trained and used the Springer Spaniel in the Chesapeake Bay with great success. Here is an easy keeper, bright, smaller than the larger sporting breeds, very affectionate, and marvelous with children.

I have seen a Boxer work all day on pheasant, although their short nasal passages are supposed to ruin their scenting ability. One of the finest duck dogs I ever sent home was a cross between a willing Great Dane lady and an ingenious Labrador suitor. His owners called him— brace yourselves—"Ducky." When he hit our training pond the water was displaced for at least three feet all around. But gangly glump that he was, "Ducky" put hundreds of water fowl on his master's table before he was through. German Wire-Haired Pointers, German Short Hairs, and Weimaraners are all fine retrievers.

Looking back over the "retrievers" I've trained, one of my happiest experiences was with a brace of Boykin Spaniels. Developed and cherished in the south—Tennessee, I believe—specifically for use on wild turkeys, they were prized and hoarded; rarely were Yankees entrusted with a Boykin. Smaller than our American Cockers, longer in body and shorter-legged, with a head more on the type of the English Cocker, these are tremendously game little creatures and tireless workers. Despite their size, they handle ducks and even geese as if they didn't know these were big birds. They swim like eels, learn easily, and have a pleasant, adoring-without-fawning disposition.

But take a moment to remember that, as adept at retrieving as almost any breed can become if he has a natural desire, only Labs, Goldens, Chessies, Flats, Curlies, and Irish Water Spaniels can compete under judgment at retriever trials. Also, when you're starting out, I think it is generally a good idea to pick a breed already established as being proficient in returning to hand that which you are hunting. Nevertheless, nonretriever breeds and mixed breeds can and do excel in waterfowl work or in pursuit of upland game.

I think it is interesting to note that in these days when, in spite of the efforts of ecologists, our bird cover is rapidly disappearing, more and more hunters are turning to the retriever breeds to point and flush as well as retrieve. They are close workers, which is an enormous advantage in heavy going. They are quiet, not as high-strung as some of the larger pointer and setter breeds. They train up faster and are more easily kept and kenneled. But again, they cannot compete in bird-dog competitions.

For any of you who might be confused by the terminology here, bird dogs are the setters and pointers, whose primary job is to locate the bird and stay with it until the hunter arrives, or the spaniels, who flush after finding game. These dogs cover the ground ahead of the hunter at some distance as they search for game. Because the retriever stays at heel until directed to pick up whatever has been shot, he is used to being in closer proximity to his handler, and when doubling as a bird dog still stays quite close at heel.

Retrievers, as I said earlier, make excellent bird dogs, but first, I believe, they should have at least one season as a retriever under their belts.

CHOOSING A PUPPY

Locating reputable breeders of retrievers and finding retriever litters may be tackled in the same way as earlier in this book we looked for show or obedience puppies. But selecting just the right dog to be worked as a retriever and used for hunting or trials is even more demanding than finding the best available obedience puppy.

You'll save a lot of time if you aim for litters from sires and dams that either work as retrievers themselves or at least come from hunting or field stock. Your best means of quickly locating such litters is to subscribe to *Retriever Field Trial News,* 1836 East St. Francis Ave., Milwaukee, Wisconsin 53207.

This is a unique publication which covers all phases of the retriever picture, from training equipment to trial results to national ratings of individual dogs to pedigrees on outstanding dogs, articles of information and general interest, and a series-by-series report on all the licensed trials held in the United States. Whatever the subscription cost, it is worth twice that if you are seriously interested in retrievers or trials. There is no publication like it in Canada, where your best bet is *Dogs in Canada,* which we mentioned earlier, and which prints the dates of forthcoming trials and results of past ones. Retriever puppies are advertised, but I'm afraid you don't get the background you need to make a safe selection of a working retriever.

Buying a working retriever puppy, sight unseen, is an iffy business, but there are some instances when it is impossible to do otherwise; you are wise, in this case, to purchase from reputable field kennels which advertise in field publications. Don't overlook adventure magazines, hunters' annuals, and hunting and fishing directories.

Don't be afraid to trust your hunches, but back them up with all possible research. Remember, there are exceptions to every rule. One of the finest field trial champions I ever watched was picked up, spayed, at a dog pound. Years ago I trained a great young Lab who was purchased at our local country fair from a bushel basket full of puppies priced at twenty-five cents each. Without a doubt, the best trial Chessy I ever trained and handled was the last one to go from her litter. Nobody wanted her because she was leggy and quite ugly with a soft disposition, so that she ran whimpering if you dropped a dish in the kennel. She sat at the back of the pen when strangers came in, and, in short, was everything we warned you earlier to stay away from. I took her into the field at about nine months because nobody wanted her and I felt sorry for her—and, lo and behold, I had me a dog! She blossomed, to put it mildly. We named her "Howdy." I steadied her without a check line in just one session, and she always hit the water like a Mack truck. She could mark like an arrow and she won a forty-dog derby stake on her first birthday, the only Chessy running in a field of Labs and Goldens. We finished her on the bench with ease. So you just *never* know!

Selecting the retriever puppy by looking for all the qualities we outlined in looking for an obedience dog or a show prospect, *plus* natural instinct, can be rough. It would be just lovely if, because the pup's sire and dam were field trial champions, all their puppies would therefore, automatically, be trial dogs. Of course such lineage guarantees nothing—it's just the best we can do. But you will find some breeders who, because the blood lines of their pups are highly field oriented, feel that this, alone, is enough, and you are expected to pay their price and feel honored. *Don't do it!* You should expect the breeder to answer your questions about the puppies.

Remember when you are retriever shopping to look, if at all possible, for a breeder whose puppies are raised with an eye to developing naturally, from the moment of birth, their curiosity and sense of adventure. Good field dogs are born with a natural desire to retrieve; great retrievers are developed from these good field dogs by giving the animal every opportunity to develop his nose, his memory, his brain. The difference between teaching a dog something, and giving him the opportunity to teach himself, is the name of the game when it comes to retrievers. It is a process that continues from birth to death.

Puppies fondled a lot while still in the whelping box are easier to train and to handle, no matter what their role in life is to be. Early vocal and physical contact is not only absolutely necessary for the retriever pup, it is vital to the owner of the litter if he expects to be able eventually to determine which of his litter is the most promising, either for himself or for a potential buyer. And plenty of opportunity to explore fields, water, stone walls, anything and everything gives a proper start. Retriever puppies should be raised like retrievers, not

It is essential that puppies to be used as retrievers get a chance to investigate the world in which they will spend their working lives. This means "puppy walks" on land or in water. The smart owner carefully studies his pup's natural reactions to new experiences and lets the youngster figure out his own solutions whenever possible.

like lap dogs. Look for this kind of a background when you are shopping: lots of love, lots of handling, lots of opportunity to grow in experience and to explore the natural world they will soon be expected to handle with one paw tied behind their backs.

There are breeders who will throw up their hands at such theories. "What about the puppies being subjected to disease by all this handling in the nest? What about them getting sick from drinking stagnant water or chewing on a rotten fish? What about cut feet, etc., etc.?" Well, what *about* all this? Personally, when it comes to retrievers, I'd rather have a well-adjusted extrovert of a puppy with a cut pad or a few fleas than all the clean, uptight, sterile puppies in the world. Of course, it is to be understood that all puppies must be wormed and inoculated regularly.

So look for puppies that have been raised close to the earth and treated as little animals. And if you find a litter of this kind within striking distance, a litter from seven to ten weeks old preferably, hop in the car accompanied *not* by a screaming load of kids but by a shackled live pigeon, a stuffed sock, and your wife or husband, in that order, and go see for yourself.

Using the elimination process described in the chapter on picking an obedience dog, try the puppies as a group on the sock, then singly. Ditto with the shackled pigeon. You are looking for aggressive behavior and great curiosity. Don't worry about the puppies bringing the sock back to you or actually picking the pigeon up in their mouths. If there's one little character who sits on the bird and defies her brothers and sisters to take it from her, snatch her up and stuff her in your pocket. Don't be afraid of the smallest one in the litter. Sometimes the so-called "runt" of the litter is the most aggressive. And remember that little girl dogs at about six weeks tend, sometimes, to spurt in their development mentally and physically for a while. Little boy dogs catch up quick, but don't be fooled if the male pup you like is a little behind his sister. If he's a "good 'un" he'll be right up there with her very soon.

This ten-week-old Lab puppy has just been introduced to his first dead pigeon, and he has no intention of relinquishing his discovery!

Chewing and mouthing of birds must be discouraged from the outset, but the handling of a very young pup in this kind of situation calls for intelligence, firmness, and understanding.

BRINGING THE PUPPY HOME

If you've made up your mind that you are going to have a working retriever and are a parent, then I'm afraid you've some "homework" to do. As I said earlier, retrievers are not pets. Nothing ruins a dog faster than having it retrieving sticks and balls for all the kids on the block. Your own children are going to have to face the fact that, while they can love and squeeze the puppy and kiss and hug him during his periods of socialization in the house, his work and his training have got to be up to one person only—mother or dad, as the case may be.

Having run up against this problem many times, I find you are more successful if you say "not yet" instead of "no." If you can enlist the co-operation of the children by promising them they can be a very great part of the pup's future when he is old enough, co-operation is not difficult to get, particularly in the case of older kiddies who will sit still and listen to you explain. With younger children, I'm afraid you just have to lay the law down and be done with it. If you can't train your kids, how can you expect to train an animal?

The new pup should have, from the very beginning, a run of his own, a house of his own, and a crate of his own. He is fed in his run two or three times a day, depending on his individual needs. Take him wherever you go, but he travels in his crate. At least once a day he gets into the house to learn about the untrustworthiness of throw rugs, kitchen smells, television and radio noises, and slippery floors. At least twice a day he should get out of his run for a short walk and romp in his family's back yard with kids to cuddle and fondle him. One work session a day is ample as long as it never gets skipped; Dad can do it before work or after he gets home. If Mom is the retriever nut, she can plan her work periods with the pup when the wee ones are napping or the older kids are in school. Distractions during early puppy training are not a good idea.

What can you do to "train" an eight- to ten-week-old puppy? Millions of things. Nothing formal or serious, of course, but let me give you this little story to show you what I mean.

My mother and father were married before father finished his training to become an M.D. and orthopedic surgeon. Mother, naturally interested in learning *anything* with her background as a primary supervisor, took all of her husband's psychology courses right along with him. Till the day she died, she loved to tell the story of the woman in class who one day asked the professor: "I have a two-year-old son at home; when should I start training him?"

"Madam," the good doctor replied, "we will excuse you while you rush home. You are two years too late now!"

NURSERY SCHOOL

In the case of very young puppies, two or three, never more than four, retrieves per day with the stuffed sock are all that is necessary. It is vitally important to remember that baby everythings—lion cubs, kittens, humans—have a very limited attention span. Once you lose their attention you cannot teach them and succeed in doing nothing but nagging. To produce a good marriage or a good retriever, *don't nag!* Always quit before the puppy wants to. We have reiterated this rule in other portions of this book, as it holds true for show and obedience dogs as well as field dogs. But retriever babies have another childhood problem—their young eyes can't see beyond a very limited distance. So when you sling that sock out there for Midas Ace of Spades, remember to keep it close enough so he can see it fall. If he doesn't but keeps trying, tiptoe out there and draw him to it with the motion of your body before he quits. Never let a real youngster feel foolish, confused, lost, or wrong. *Never let him fail!*

At least two or three times a week, get the puppy out for a swim if it is warm and summery—and only if it's warm and summery. If you are the one introducing him to water for the first time, walk out into it with him in your arms. When the water is knee-deep, lower him, gently, using your locked hands as a basket; his feet will be paddling before he hits the water! Later, he'll follow you in, but if you start him *away* from the shore he'll never have the opportunity to refuse to enter the water and no negative impressions will upset his confidence. As he's swimming in toward shore, after he has learned to do so happily a few times, throw his sock directly into his path between him and the shore. He'll probably snatch at it as he goes by and one more lesson is learned. Incidentally, if he's too little for a bumper, slip a piece of styrofoam into that sock so it doesn't sink.

Remember that retriever training is not a process by which we determine just how much punishment a dog can take. Retrievers who love to retrieve barely feel icy water. But first they must learn to love their work. To throw a small puppy or dog that has had little water experience into a lake or creek in early spring or early winter is not only cruel, it's stupid. Before you've got the animal turned on to retrieving as the most wonderful game in the world, you turn him off with an experience that is not only uncomfortable but frightening. If he wants to splash around in ice water, fine, don't discourage him; just don't take this as a sign that he would enjoy swimming across Lake Michigan in a sleet storm! Use your head, please! Stop me if you've heard this before, but build on positive, not negative, impressions.

A BRACE OF TROUBLESOME TERMS

I should like to digress a moment to discuss the two most misunderstood terms in retriever-dom: *hard mouth* and *gun shy.* So much misinformation has been circulated about these aspects that an amazing number of amateurs firmly believe puppies are always born with either one of these deficiencies bred into them. Actually, with certain exceptions, both problems are usually caused by bad training practices, overtraining, misguided correction, and too early introduction to guns and birds. In other words, most cases of hard mouth and gun shyness are not the dog's fault but the trainer's. Let's make sure *you* don't create these problems with your dog!

Gun Shyness

In seven out of ten cases, this problem, if it arises, can be cured, because it isn't a matter of shyness at all but rather a matter of overawareness that something is being waved over a pup's head and, if that isn't scary enough, the whatever-it-is makes a large noise. Nothing happens—just noise! Several years ago I sold a lovely little Labrador bitch to a young couple who were full of questions. "Is she gun shy?" was high on their list. "Brandy," as they decided to call her, was only eight weeks at the time, and I told them to take her home and play the same "games" I'm going to teach you to play with your retriever, and not to worry about guns until the time came and she was old enough. What did they do? They took her home and walked to the top of a hill. The woman held the puppy while the man fired a twelve-gauge over her head. Brandy was gone for twenty-four hours! Realizing they had goofed, they didn't tell me. I might never have known and a grand shooting bitch might have been lost to the world. But I agreed to do a field clinic for a club to which they belonged. I wrote them and told them to be sure and bring the puppy. Since I am a rather overbearing female, they were afraid to stay home (and terrified, I'm sure, at their impending betrayal!).

Anyway, everything went beautifully because we started on bumpers and yelled bang to simulate the noise of a gun. The Lab puppy was fast, happy, and couldn't seem to do enough to please. Then came the awful moment when I threw a dead pigeon for the young dogs and fired a training pistol at a distance. It wasn't even Brandy's turn, but she broke her leather leash and headed for their convertible. She dove right through the top, shredding the canvas, plowed into the back of the car, ripped up the floor mat, and wedged herself under the front seats. Everyone stood stock-still with their mouths open. When I could talk I said, "Well, you went right home and did it, didn't you?" The girl fled to the car in tears and the husband just stood there so shame-faced I actually felt sorry for the jerk. "Is she ruined for good?" he asked me, his face a mask of despair. "No thanks to you!" I snapped, but I weakened because he was so obviously ashamed of his stupidity and I could tell he genuinely loved the dog by the way he had handled her earlier. "No, no, I don't think so. Now go and get in your car and get her the hell away from these guns. There's a Howard Johnson's up the road. Go order a couple of hundred cups of coffee, and when I'm through I'll come up and we'll see if we can fix it, OK?"

They did as they were told and over the next few months, by dint of careful handling and associating all noises with something falling, we did cure the poor little bitch. But just stop and think for a moment how a human baby might have reacted if you had fired a shotgun over her bassinet! You'll rarely have trouble with gun shyness if you teach the dog that the noise of a gun signals something good is coming. Never shoot a gun of any kind around an inexperienced dog unless something is going to fall from the sky immediately after the bang. Locking him in a car at a skeet range for an afternoon is imbecilic! Doesn't mean a thing. Neither does the old system of shooting while a dog is eating. Now, if you shoot while carrying the food *out to the dog* in his kennel—see the difference?

Hardly a week goes by but what I get a call for help because somebody has a "gun shy" dog. When I ask, "What makes you think he's gun shy?" I get answers like: "He lies down on the floor if I raise my hand over my head." Or, "Every time I get my gun out of the case he cries and backs away." Or, "If he sees me raise my gun up to my shoulder he cowers." Which might be serious if the dog were a year or two old. But in most instances, it's ten weeks, or two months, or three months old! I have never been able to understand how anybody expects a wee infant to look at something as big as a shotgun being waved around in the air and sit there saying to himself, "Hmmmmmmm, let me see now. I'm a retriever, so that must be a gun. Yep, it's a shotgun. Mother told me about those. They shoot birds and I retrieve them. Interesting, verrrrrrry interesting!"

Truly gun-shy dogs that I have known weren't crackerjack retrievers. Oh, they'd retrieve but they were easily distracted, and once corrected, they didn't want to "play" any more. Any loud noise upset them, and a gun shot from any distance caused blind panic; after which they didn't trust anyone for days.

Healthy, normal, curious retrievers raised around healthy, normal households where dishes get dropped and people sometimes scream at each other and kids fight and the television argues with the radio for top billing, will take shotguns and their noises in stride if they are taught the love of retrieving *before* being introduced to guns. We'll show you how this works as we go along in our training manual. Just don't get ahead of yourself.

Hard Mouth

These words are whispered as if one were discussing a social disease. Everybody knows that a hard-mouthed dog chews on his birds, and everybody agrees that isn't good; very few people stop to ponder what causes it, because very few people care; they just want it stopped and they don't want a dog of theirs to even hear the word.

A dog can damage a bird in many ways. He can destroy it by putting it down, holding it firmly with his paws, and then tearing at it with his teeth. He can roll it over and over in his mouth until it resembles a feathered sack full of cornmeal mush. He can clamp down on it and hold it firmly in his mouth, doing little damage until someone tries to pry it loose. He can chew on it, hard, as he's carrying it, so you sometimes get two pieces of bird instead of one when he finally comes on with it. Or he can pick it up gently as can be and then drop it repeatedly until there's nothing left to share over a bottle of white wine except perhaps the feet.

Generally speaking, you can tell when you are going to have trouble with mouthing birds by the way dogs handle their bumpers. If they are started right and are taught from the beginning that holding things is good and mauling them is bad, the introduction of birds rarely presents a problem in survival for the bird. If wee puppies are given things too heavy to carry, they will learn to drop and pick up, drop and pick up, because they *can't* manage any other way. If "high school" dogs are allowed to play catch-me-if-you-can games with bumpers, they will play the same games with their birds. If a dog that is "ready" to run in derbies is still delivering "to hand" because, and only because, his handler has lightning reflexes and is a good guesser, real trouble is dead ahead. These are training hazards we'll avoid as we go along. Hard mouth is caused by other influences as well.

People who snatch things from retrievers' mouths as they dash by at sixty miles an hour are laying a lovely foundation for hard mouth. If you let your son or daughter play tug-of-war with your young retriever when he brings them something they threw for him, you are asking for it, friend. If you think it's cute to loosely tie a pigeon and watch your puppy tear into it, thus drawing everyone's attention to his enthusiasm, you are going to regret it!

There are certain dogs that are so high-strung that they go through a period in which they will "freeze" on birds. It's a form of hysteria. They refuse to give up a bird through no fault of their own—their jaws lock and excitement causes their muscles to tense so that they are physically incapable of obeying the command to "give" or "out." This is a unique problem which is handled in the same manner as other forms of hysteria, and we'll go into it later.

For right now let me just say that rarely is hard mouth incurable. The sooner it is stopped the easier; the longer it goes on, the more difficult it is to break. Frankly, I would much rather have the task of breaking a dog who was hard on birds than of correcting what I call the "flannel-mouthed" retriever who carries his birds as if his jaws might break if he opened them up and took hold with enthusiasm.

Dogs that handle ducks and pigeons with dispatch often leave their inexperienced handlers slack-jawed with amazement the first time they get a shot pheasant. Pheasants are "soapy" birds; a mallard can be carried by one feather, but a pheasant's feathers come out at a touch, and the dog really has to take hold of the body of the bird to carry it with any degree of success. A dog isn't born automatically knowing these things!

Experience, training, a complete distrust of old wives' tales—and "poof!"—the problem fades into obscurity. Concentrate on the dog, one step at a time, one day at a time, remembering you have to crawl before you walk and walk before you run. You'd be surprised at how things fall into their proper places if you don't get ahead of yourself. So let's get busy.

AT THE VERY BEGINNING
Proper Exercising

Dogs running under judgment at field trials will be penalized for soiling the field in which they, and other dogs, are running. Dogs that relieve themselves on the way to the bird are considered as having really committed a great and awesome crime, and I'm inclined to agree. After picking up a bird, the release of tension is so great that some dogs get that urge to let go. That's not good either, but it is a far lesser crime than stopping to "spend a penny" on the way out.

Dogs that are permitted to go to the bathroom in the field in training will do it under pressure. Break up the inclination as soon as you can and you and the dog will both be better off. While tension and excitement can cause animals to forget their manners, when dogs soil the working area it is generally because their handlers haven't exercised them enough.

The rhythm to retriever training, whether for trials or shooting, is: first, we exercise the dog (give him a chance to clean himself out); then we run him; then we exercise again. Exercising—taking two or three dogs out off leash between tests to let them relieve themselves— can never be overdone. Start the habit in puppyhood. When you take the dog out of his pen, let him run around and get the tinkles, booms, and sniffs out of his system; then train him; then another exercise period. Keep this rhythm going from puppyhood to the day you retire him to the hearth rug, and one of the biggest problems in retriever training will never rear its ugly head.

There are retrievers who are so high-strung that you can exercise them at trials until you are blue in the face but with no results—all they want to do is run. I suggest you resort to matching, as we described in the show-dog section. It works wonders and will save you points when you most need them.

Incidentally, it's well to remember that older dogs just as well as puppies of either sex are encouraged, by the feel of water on their privates, to want to urinate.

Body English

You will notice that up until now no specific training equipment for the puppy has been described. This was not an oversight. While I certainly believe that retriever puppies, like their show and obedience kinfolk, should get used to a leash and collar early in life, I am really not an advocate of continuing use of this kind of control for the baby retriever. You see, much of the show or obedience dog's life is spent on leash; but a retriever's life is largely *off* leash; in fact, when he is ready to run in stakes giving championship points, he works without a collar as well. (Hunting dogs, which might have to be out of your sight from time to time, should work either with a buckle collar, locked chain, or no collar at all for their safety.)

But most important of all is that the retriever handler must learn from the beginning to use body english and his natural hand and leg movements to control his dog. The earlier he learns the better. The more secure he is in his knowledge that he can control his dog without leash and collar, the more secure the dog becomes and a better team develops.

Never take chances, of course, and always use a leash and collar (properly introduced, fitted, and put on as described earlier) in situations where a puppy might spook at unnatural noises (down at the shopping center) or bolt into trouble (crossing streets). But for the rest of the time, start from the beginning teaching the pup that as your body moves, so does—or should—he.

In *heeling,* for instance, walk briskly along with the pup, patting your left side with his stuffed sock in your left hand. He'll follow fast enough! Stop frequently, tucking the sock out of the way as you pat the pup and cuddle him close to your left leg with your left hand. (Or use your right side if you prefer, and right hand—but whichever side you are going to be working him from, start now and stick to it.)

As for *lining,* he's much too young to worry about blinds, of course, but if you teach him right now that the hand nearest him will always send him where he is supposed to go, his later training will be 100 per cent more easily accomplished. Every time you send him for something, give your command in a positive, happy voice and sling that hand out as if you were bowling a ball. In the beginning he won't even be aware of it, but always use it because it will become a habit *you* need to establish and a motion you want him to be very aware of throughout his life. To keep him returning to you speedily, keep running away from him until he gets to you; just as he does, swing your business side toward him and kneel down, patting your leg. He'll soon learn to always return to that spot.

Teaching the pup to sit without using a leash and collar is easily done by using body english. As you are standing in front of the puppy, chucking him under the chin, stiffen your index finger as if the end of it were covered with something delicious, and poke it in his direction. The minute he sticks his nose out to investigate, raise your finger steadily upward. His head will follow the motion of your finger, and as the pup's noggin is elevated, it naturally follows that the rear end is lower; it is a simple matter to say "Sit!" And if he doesn't slide into that position automatically, a two-fingered little push on his hind quarters as you give the command will usually do it.

While this book is not going into Open training, as I explained earlier, there is no reason not to teach the pup that one short blast of the whistle also means sit. In fact, the earlier he learns to sit to a whistle command, the better. His whistle training can become a real game as you are getting dinner, washing the car, or watching television. Learn now to say "Sit!" with a whistle in your mouth, so you can follow the verbal command with a blast. As you go about your ordinary chores. let him accompany you and suddenly give a quick, unexpected "Tweet!" You'll be surprised how soon he'll catch on and how much work you'll save yourself later on.

Delivery to Hand

Your hand motions when taking from the puppy are most important—never reach down over his head or out away from you. Keep your hand close to your business leg and low with the palm up. And

always say whatever you decide to say for release—"Give!" "Out!"—
even though the puppy is too young to understand.

At this stage of training, nothing is more important than the problem
of delivery. Force training comes soon enough, and it is, at best, a
necessarily unpleasant period. You can lessen that period now, even
avoid it entirely in certain instances, by never letting the pup get in
the habit of dropping at a distance. Always remember to keep your
hand close to your leg at the moment of delivery. This rule holds all
through your training. Handlers who stick their hands way out in front
to take birds usually get the bird only as close as the end of their
fingers and no further. Keep it close!

Apart from that rule, there are several methods from which to choose:

Choice No. 1—run away from the puppy, yelling and whistling to
him constantly until he catches up with you. As he nears, don't quit
running, but keep your feet pumping up and down while covering little
distance—that way he thinks he's catching you and he'll be especially
pleased with himself.

Or, Choice No. 2—you can crouch down with your knees spread
and pat your tummy so the pup comes literally walking up to your
chest. But watch his approach carefully—if he slows down, take off
as in No. 1.

When working on water, you are in great jeopardy, as the shoreline
is where most pups start dropping if they never did before. Wade out
a few steps and, the minute the pup's feet hit the bottom, start running.
Teach him that shorelines are for starting to run, not stopping to shake.

Never allow that puppy to deliver to anybody else; never allow anybody but you to take anything from him; and never, never, *never* try
to break a puppy that is prone to dropping, on land or water, by shoving
a bird or a bumper down his gullet and swatting him repeatedly under
the chin while you scream, "Hold it!" There is time for this command;
the time is not now. The puppy is just learning to love his work, and
now all of a sudden he comes in with something, drops it, and gets
the hell beaten out of him. He isn't old enough to understand why
you're mad or what's going on. You can start all sorts of problems
this way—if he's a gutsy baby and doesn't quit cold on you, he'll start
running away just before he reaches your side; or he'll start hanging
on so tight he'll soon be ruining bumpers and killing birds; or you'll
make him spit out birds at greater and greater distances—I could go
on and on. The point to remember is, with a baby puppy or a green
dog, don't force-train in the high chair.

Holding the Puppy

A foolproof method for holding a squiggly puppy while you throw for it in a manner that enables him to see what is falling, hasn't been invented yet. I doubt it ever will be; until it is, when you first start a wee retriever, don't attempt it. Simply start walking a little faster, yell something to perk his ears up and catch his attention, something like "Heyheyhey!" Then heave the sock forth. When he gets a little bigger and you want to start restraining him, crunch down or kneel beside him. Tuck him between your front legs with his back against the middle of your tummy. Then run one hand under the elbow and up across his chest to the other side. Throw with your free hand (after yelling) and immediately transfer that free hand to the pup's chest. In his excitement he'll probably stand up. Fine—one hand is set to support him so he can see; the other keeps him from leaving too soon. The very second that sock hits the ground, release both hands and give your command.

I'm sure you can see what an important part your body will play in the training of your retriever. However, there are certain items of teaching equipment which will replace the well-worn stuffed sock all too soon, so now is the time to start ordering or making them.

Equipment

A Training Collar, Chain Link—described in our show-dog section. Get a heavy enough one so it doesn't saw into the dog during correction or break at the wrong moment.

A Training Leash—the standard six feet of leather or webbing with a very strong catch.

A "Traffic" Leash—used for taking more mature dogs back and forth to line or in and out of cars in congested areas. No more than two feet long with a heavy bolt. When not in use, snap it to the belt hook at the back of your slacks, or to the pocket on the side opposite the dog. It doubles beautifully as a training whip.

A Training Whip—commercially produced "persuaders" which sting but do not cut.

Check Lines—for controlling dogs at a distance. These can be home-made or purchased commercially. You should have two—one about thirty feet long of medium-heavy clothesline with a strong catch, another about ninety feet long of very lightweight nylon so that it slips easily through heavy cover, minimizing the chance of snagging.

Training Bumpers—Regular boat fenders, in medium and large sizes, are available at marinas and boat supply houses. Those manufactured especially for dogs come in canvas, pebbled or smooth, and in knobby red and white plastic. There are smaller (narrower) ones for puppies, medium-sized and larger ones. The canvas ones are very good for a person with one dog, but they do rot more quickly, and while the plastic ones cost more, they are virtually indestructible. Some of the plastic bumpers can be filled with water to make them heavier—when training dogs for geese, for instance.

All bumpers come with a gromet in one end to which a rope can be tied. Triple-knot one end of the rope to the bumper; make a small loop in the other end for hanging bumpers up to dry when not in use, but make it a very small loop. Double ropes on bumpers or ropes with large loops can catch on things and pull it from the dog's mouth, encouraging him to drop. (Trying to get good height when throwing bumpers is almost impossible unless you can swing them up by a rope "handle.")

If pooling bumpers with other trainers, make your own clearly identifiable by using colored throw ropes or marking them with colored tape or a special type of knot. Purchase no more than four puppy-sized ones, about a dozen regular-sized, and maybe two heavier ones. This should take you through a number of stages and the puppy ones can be used with the older dog if you run low. One word of warning: if you start on canvas, be prepared for your dog to refuse the plastic the first time you use it. Also, the white plastic is very easy to see, and while this is a help in working with a dog that is a mediocre marker, it can develop into a crutch your dog doesn't need. I cover all my plastic bumpers, red or white, with strips of old burlap bags. I slather the bumpers first with Elmer's glue, wrap them, then bind the ends of the burlap with old fashioned electrician's tape. They throw well, are not obvious in the field, and new dogs don't balk at the plastic surface.

I know it seems that twelve to sixteen bumpers is a foolish investment for someone with just one dog. But think a moment. Time is always precious—to the pro it means money, to the amateur every time he has to walk out to a bird boy with a handful of bumpers, he has sacrificed five to ten minutes of training. If you set up a double with two bird boys and ten bumpers, that means they can stay out there for five tests without coming in.

Training Whistles (two, in case one jams)—No, you don't *have* to use a whistle. You don't *have* to wear shoes while working on gravel; you don't *have* to pull on thermal underwear to go hunting in a blizzard—but when you don't you usually wish you had! Screaming at a dog from far distances does nothing for your voice, hunting buddies, field trial judges, or wild birds. So do it our way and get a lanyard and two whistles, plastic ones. (In cold weather the metal ones stick to your lips and you can't remove them without removing said lip; also, you can't "talk" as fluidly through a metal whistle.)

A Blank Pistol and Blanks—You don't need to spend a fortune, but the very cheap ones are not reliable. Those which handle 22-caliber blanks are best.

A Shotgun—12-gauge preferably, because "popper loads" (blank loads) are manufactured only for this size. When buying ammo, if you can't get the poppers, use light loads, 8's or 8½'s for training.

Air Pistol—preferably CO^2 BB pistol. You do *not* want the varmint-killing kind—they are lethal. The kind you want has a screw in the base plate for adjusting the force of the projectile, takes standard BB's and only the smaller CO^2 cartridges, such as used in cocktail shakers. You probably won't use your air pistol until well into your training, but you might as well have it on hand just in case.

The Sending Line—From the moment you begin to work at steadying your dog, your sending line will be one of your most valuable pieces of training equipment. You cannot, to my knowledge, purchase one but must make it yourself, and while you're at it, turn out two or three, as they are easily misplaced and somebody is always wanting to borrow one.

One of the biggest problems in training arises in handling the semi-steady dog. He's not foolproof yet, and you don't want to chance his breaking and missing his mark or marks. If you hold him by his collar, your position is unnatural and he's too aware of you. If you use a leash, you must reach over and unsnap it after the fall before sending the dog, and this too is distracting. The sending line fills the bill beautifully. It is worn on the wrist of the hand with which you will send the dog.

Using a medium-thin flat length of nylon chord about thirty-six inches long, first burn both ends so they don't fray. Now tie a loop knot in one end through which you can pass the other end. Put your wrist in the loop and pull it snug. Run the free end of the line through the free ring on the dog's collar and hold the end in the hand nearest the dog. When it is time to release the dog, make a forward bowling motion of that arm, as we described earlier, and simply open your hand as you do so. The line slips clear of the dog's collar quietly and without distracting him.

Decoys—Like the air pistol, decoys come later on in school. But

1. The loop of the "sending line" is passed over the wrist of the arm with which you intend to send the dog, and pulled snug. Then the free end is threaded through the "live" ring in the dog's chain collar.

2. During the retrieve, the handler checks the not-quite-steady dog, if necessary, by holding the free end of the "sending line" tightly in his hand.

3. When it comes time to release the dog to retrieve, instead of having to reach down and unsnap a leash, which can be time-consuming and distracting, the handler merely opens his hand and sends his dog. The line slips through the collar ring without taking the dog's attention from his mark. *(facing page)*

lining them up early is wise. You don't need good ones—use old jobbies, perhaps some you or your buddies have discarded because they are minus heads. Seal the cracks and holes with caulking compound and paint some of them brightly with leftover dabs of red, yellow, white, or blue enamel. Why? Because dogs that learn to work through brightly colored decoys as well as through the more normally colored ones will balk at nothing when you get to that trial or working certificate. Attach regular heavy-duty lines and weights to them and wrap them individually for easy carrying. Half a dozen should be ample.

Burlap Bags—People used to throw burlap bags away and they were *free* for the taking from feed stores and farms. Today feed in burlap bags costs more, and farmers get a rebate on bags they turn back when empty. So you'll have to pay your friendly neighborhood farmer twenty-five to seventy-five cents for a bag, but they are essential for putting bumpers in, carrying decoys and birds, and drying a wet dog on a cold day.

Feathered Bumpers—a darned good idea for intermediate bird work, or for people who have limited access to birds. Either cover commercial plastic or canvas bumpers with wings and tail feathers of pigeons, ducks, or pheasants, or take a piece of styrofoam and wrap it in burlap, taping feathers to that. Four of these should be plenty.

Except for the burlap bags and feathered bumpers, everything else listed above is available by mail (except the guns, of course) from supply houses listed in *The Retriever Field Trial News* or in the back of sporting magazines.

Things You Can Live Without

The Retriev-R-Trainer—This piece of equipment is optional, and I've trained hundreds of dogs without it. I have also used it. I am sold on it for planting blinds at great distances without disturbing cover, thereby minimizing the possibility of a dog tracking the blind planter to the bird. It is an automatic device which, held in one hand, will fire a plastic bumper as it emits a very loud bang. I feel it is *much* too much equipment, in terms of noise and distance, for young dogs, and I find that green trainers who use it tend to steady inexperienced dogs too soon and to use it to save doing a lot of physical labor. This is fine and dandy, but the gadget gets to be a crutch and a gimmick too fast and much learning is lost by both the dog and the handler. Also, I have been around guns all my life; they hold no terrors for me, but the Retriev-R-Trainer is a dangerous piece of equipment and, used casually, can cripple or maim. I don't happen to think its value is worth its risks. It was originally designed for trainers who were short on help, but, it prevents the handler and the dog from working as a unit, and the dog tends to freeze on the handler instead of looking in front if it is introduced, as it often is, too soon.

Scent—It is possible to purchase bottles of pheasant, duck, or goose scent with which to permeate your bumpers. I don't believe in this idea. When I train a dog I want him to go and get whatever he sees fall. It is my theory that a dog running through a clover field checks when he has a nose full of clover one moment and some other scent interrupts that odor the next instant. I don't want a dog dependent upon running across a specific smell. So I don't use scented bumpers, but lots of trainers do.

An Electric Collar—This is a marvelous device, as we discussed earlier, but individual owners or trainers rarely need to purchase one. They are very expensive, and if in the later stages of training you should require such a training aid, they can be borrowed or rented.

EXCUSES

I'd like to pause here a moment and debunk a few notions new retriever folks sometimes fall prey to. Many people who purchase retrievers have a genuine interest in training; some of them get to work, locate what they need, and spend wonderful years enjoying their dogs more than they ever thought possible. Others—especially working certificate candidates,—never get to line with a dog because they have a list of excuses. Others get as far as sanctions or working certificate trials when they fail and trot out the same excuses. This is too bad. Stating flatly that "I can't do it!" without trying can rob you of some of the most rewarding moments of your life, steal from you memories you could cherish forever. Let's look closely at some common examples—and remember that nothing in life worth having is the product of wishful thinking!

If you desire a C.D.X. with your obedience dog, you have to build or borrow jumps. If you have your sights set on a bench championship, you had best be prepared to do some traveling. By the same token, there are problems facing those who decide to have a well-trained field trial winner, or a dog with a working certificate. These problems can be solved by facing them squarely and handling them with the same common sense and determination with which you confront all life's problems.

"We Haven't Any Place to Train"

Nonsense! This country is full of places to train. Get into your automobile and start driving. Sooner or later you will see a juicy field or a delicious pond. Drive up to the owner's house and introduce yourself like a lady or a gentleman. Explain what your problem is and ask permission to use the property. Every once in a while an owner will say "No." But more often than not, he'll be fascinated; in addition to lending his land, he'll provide a gallery of interested onlookers, which will help you get over the butterflies which materialize at the sight of field trial galleries.

When you are property shopping, bring your dog along. Dogs are great ice breakers. And be sure, at the beginning, to explain that, unlike bird dog or hound training, you are not going to hunt the natural game on the property or shoot anything. Just ask to yell, throw bumpers, and work your dog. By the time you have to switch to birds and guns, the landlord will more fully understand the purpose of a retriever and you'll usually make the transition with little or no effort. Many state game preserves have no objection to retriever training during certain months; contact your local game warden and ask his help when looking for land.

A word of caution: once you get permission, *don't ruin it!* Pick up your litter; close all pasture gates securely behind you; always let your host know when you are on the property even if he insists it isn't necessary; and ask permission to bring a friend or two before descending upon the area with half a field trial in tow. Remember the words *"Thank You"* are rarely overused. A bottle of fire water, a box of candy, a few birds during the season are gifts which do wonders.

"We Never Get a Chance to Work with Birds."

Why not? Birds are as available as property to work on. And anyway, how *dare* you take a lovely dog who is working well on bumpers and then pull the rug out from under him so that he falls on his face in public when he sees his first real bird—through no fault of his own? How inconsiderate can you get! Birds are bound to be available *somewhere;* you just have to get out and do some detective work. Attend farmers' markets, talk to your butcher and find out where he gets his ducks—all *roast* ducks were once *live* ducks. Telephone the local hatcheries—no matter what they are hatching, they very often know where you can locate ducks, pigeons, or pheasants. Call, write, or visit the nearest professional trainer you can find; even if he's a day's drive away, one trip would probably get you all the feathers you need for one dog's schooling. And don't be a breed snob—if there is a pointer or setter club working in your area, ask for help with your bird dilemma. Watch for notices of trials—there are always birds at trials; attend, go to the bird truck, and beg. If you only need one or two, they are much more liable to be agreeable than if you were trying to buy a hundred or so. Sometimes local pigeon clubs are excellent sources of supply—racing enthusiasts who breed their own birds often destroy those which are not good breeding quality, and that's where you come in.

"We Live in the City and We Can't Keep Birds"

Of course you can keep birds if you want to—even if you don't want to, you simply *have* to for a while at least if you want that working certificate or ducks on the table come fall. All it takes is a dog crate or a homemade wire box. Pigeons and ducks cohabit beautifully, subsisting happily on your wilted lettuce, a little corn, bread crusts, and water. If you keep their newspapers clean, they don't smell *that* bad!

"I Haven't Anyone to Help Me"

This usually continues: I have to work alone and the dog gets all confused when he sees guns and bird boys in the field." That's your fault, not his—nobody has to work alone. Put a notice in the local want ads reading something like this: "Retriever owner seeking another retriever owner to train with." Put up a card on the bulletin board of the local high school offering part-time work after school. Teen-agers are great people. It won't bankrupt you to pay them, and they enjoy watching the dog develop. Swap baby sitting for bird throwing with a next-door neighbor. And you'd be surprised what a seven- or eight-year-old can do to help if you keep sessions short and are long on praise. If you are really isolated, call your local Scout troop leader or Campfire Girl counselor. Explain your problem and see what they can do to help. I know one gal who got all the training help she needed from a rod-and-gun club in return for taking the dog out during hunting season and "picking up" for the boys—*me!*

"My Dog Is a City Dog"

"He retrieves but he doesn't seem to know how to use his nose!" Neither would you if you spent your life on carpeting and linoleum. So you'll have to teach him, and *nothing* could be much simpler. Take him for long walks in the country with a pocketful of small dog biscuits. Every once in a while call him to you and throw a handful of cookies into the tall grass. As he roots them out he is learning to use his nose and never realizes it. After a bit, hold him back until the yummies are down, then let him find them. Keep making your cookie-falls in more and more difficult cover until you feel you can graduate to bumpers—use the same technique and never let him quit. Get out there and help him if you have to, but *never let him leave an area empty-handed.* Learn to study the wind yourself, so you know just where the dog should be when he first gets the scent. Now, that wasn't so awful, was it?

"I Have No Conception of Distance"

"How am I supposed to know if I'm working at forty or fifty yards?" Don't feel bad, friend. When people ask me to pace off any yardage, I just look as feminine and helpless as possible. Twenty years of training retrievers and three husbands haven't helped a bit. Well, there's a way. If your working certificate qualifications call for a fifty-five-yard fall, get a yardstick and measure sixty yards of surveyor's twine just to make sure the dog gets more distance than called for. Then take two pegs into the field you intend to use and stake out sixty yards. Leave the far stake with a paper cup over it. Put a branch down where the first stake was and work from that point. Remove stake No. 1 and the twine to prevent someone tripping.

The rules also say that the falls should be about ninety degrees apart. That's simple, too, Just close your eyes and picture your front door: the corners are ninety degrees—right angles, in other words.

"I Think It's Cruel to Use Birds"

"Why can't we just use bumpers?" The answer to this is very simple—because there is no open season on bumpers! Using birds with dogs is not my favorite part of training either, but there are parts of any hobby or pastime that are not as much fun as other parts. Retrievers are bird dogs, and if you can't bring yourself to look at this side of training in an adult manner, then forget the whole thing. I've seen thoughtless people do more damage to birds than dogs do. If you tie your feathered friends with soft binding, untie them promptly after using, handle them with consideration and demand your dog do the same, there is no reason for the bird part of retriever training to be objectionable to any person who loves all God's creatures.

"My Dog Doesn't Like Deep Water"

Then teach him to swim! Warm weather is ideal for going in with your dog (wearing sweat shirt and jeans and sneakers please, cause toenails scratch). Forget retrieving and teach him a love of water. Be calm and very matter-of-fact about it all. A gentle older dog who loves water is a great help. And trips to the water absolutely every day are necessary until he plunges in with enthusiasm. Never throw a dog in, never punish a dog for showing fear, or laugh at him. Fear is overcome best through love and positive thinking. (So are most of the world's problems!)

"Who's Got Money These Days for All That Equipment?"

Nobody, my friend—well, almost nobody. If you're as poor as I usually seem to be, don't despair. Most of the items I listed a few pages back you can make yourself or borrow. A training leash and collar do not represent a big investment. Forget the traffic leash and whip—use your doubled leash when chastisement is called for. Bumpers can be made by binding styrofoam (ask your florist for leftover pieces) to odds and ends of wood in anybody's home workshop (try your high school shop teacher) with butcher twine, then wrapping with any heavy material. Secure with waterproof tape and attach a piece of old clothesline to one end. One whistle (a little over a dollar) you must invest in—sorry about that! I told you about using old decoys and finding burlap bags. Go to your local feed store and pick up pigeon feathers at the base of the silo. Guns you can borrow. (I understand some people make them at home, but I don't recommend this.) If you have your own shotgun, you can load your own shells or buy reloads at a fraction of the cost of new shells. Lots of reloaders invent their own blank shotgun shells using cornmeal.

There, now, we'll see you in the field, right? I hear that out behind the A&P on Sunset Street there's a great creek . . .

SIGNS OF GREATNESS

As we have gone along we have referred several times to pups that might have field trial potential, even the stuff to make championships. Before we start off on early training exercises, let's point out what to look for in deciding whether or not a dog might wind up in the Nationals. During the first weeks of training is the time to start looking for that touch of greatness.

Does he snap training collars regularly in sheer exuberance, just in the process of heeling into a field? Does he get so wild at the sight of anything in your hand that he's almost uncontrollable? By the time you get him into the field to work, or down on the water's edge, are his teeth chattering and is he shaking all over even though it's ninety degrees in the shade? Does he hit the water hard and swim furiously, churning white water behind him? Does he squeak and whimper with desire while you're waiting to work? On land is he just as fast coming back as going out? Is he always looking for another retrieve—and another—and another? Does he remember his lessons from day to day with only occasional lapses? Does he tackle unpleasant cover (thorns, briers) without hesitation? Is he exceedingly restless in his crate before he works, and almost impossible to stuff back in when his turn is over? Does he seem to be a good judge of distance? Does he take a boot in the pants or a crack with the whip without sulking or quitting, and does he learn from correction?

All these *can be* signs. But don't expect them all to happen at once. They could pop up gradually as the dog matures and his training progresses. Without intelligence and trainability, the fastest, most stylish dog in the world is hopeless in a duck blind or at a field trial. So don't assume, because you've got a wild Indian, he's automatically going to become a champion. Don't assume, either, that because your dog doesn't show *all* of these signs he's not good enough to take a chance on. Many a trial has been won by the dog that just went about his work steadily, series after series. Perhaps he wasn't the most stylish, but you can't penalize a dog very much if he remembers all his marked falls and lines all his blinds.

These are only some indications to look for as you go along. Keep your eyes open and your fingers crossed.

IF YOU NEED A PROFESSIONAL HANDLER

If it turns out that you do, indeed, happen to be the owner of a dog who could make his field championship and perhaps go even beyond this, and you can't afford to campaign him or just aren't interested, *do* you have the right to keep the dog as a pet? This is a real dilemma. But if it should happen to you, take heart from the fact that you aren't the first, nor will you be the last, to be faced with such a decision.

It may not come to you immediately, but it won't be long before you realize that if this is a dog with true field trial championship personality, *he'll* never be what *you* want any more than *you'll* ever be what *he* wants. A frustrated, undertrained field dog of any breed becomes a big fat pain in the neck all too soon. And it's not his fault, He was given certain desires and instincts which he is quite powerless to control. He can never be a pet, as I explained earlier, in the true sense of the word. He needs to run and run and retrieve and retrieve and swim and hunt and smell birds. He'll never be happy lying as a baby's play mat in front of the family hearth until he can control the itch to be in the field. You'll come to hate him as the frustrated, pent-up delinquent he will soon, inevitably, become. The thing to do, when all is said and done, is what's best for the dog. *You,* after all, can make choices and decisions and start anew; *he,* on the other hand, is dependent on others to see that he gets what he needs.

There is no licensing or control over professional retriever trainers in the United States and Canada by A.K.C., C.K.C., or any other body. In the United States there is the rapidly enlarging Professional Retriever Trainers' Association. This is no more a policing agency than P.H.A. or P.H.A.C. But it does its best to see that its members maintain high professional standards and receive the formal recognition they so richly deserve, for certainly in their world they are the true experts.

Finding a professional to train and/or handle your dog at trials is not difficult; there are many good ones to choose from. They may be located in the publications I have listed earlier in this section, especially *The Retriever Field Trial News.* You may also find their advertisements in the backs of sporting magazines. But word-of-mouth advertising is the best way to judge; talk to people who have used one. Attending sanctioned and licensed trials is another good way not only to find a pro to suit your needs, but also to watch him at work and talk with him. The prices for professional services vary widely depending upon whether it is gun dog or field training in which you are interested.

Very few men and women who run dogs regularly in the licensed field trial circuit have time, for obvious reasons, to take on gun dogs or working certificate candidates.

In fact, if you are starting out an untested dog, your best bet would be *not* to select one of the top trial handlers. Except in rare instances, these people are already committed to owners who support them year after year with champion after champion. There is little opportunity to start a new pup or to give him much personal time and attention. So I would suggest you start out with one of the less busy, less exalted members of the profession.

Moreover, there are many excellent trainers who are not on the licensed trial road every weekend; just as experienced and well thought of, they prefer the training and developing of dogs rather than the constant competition. So shop around. As in choosing a professional for the show ring or obedience, the selection of the field trainer just right for you and your dog is a very personal, important decision.

Whomever you pick, make sure that person knows everything *you* know about your dog's idiosyncrasies, habits, likes and dislikes, weak and strong points. The professional retriever trainer will ask you all sorts of questions when he first accepts your dog, but what the owner answers in response to our queries usually differs entirely from what we had in mind when we asked the question!

THE PRO'S QUESTION	THE OWNER'S ANSWER	FREE TRANSLATION
Does the pup like the water?	Loves it!	*Sits in his water dish by the hour.*
Does he retrieve naturally?	He'll pick up anything you throw.	*Sure—then try and catch him!*
Have you tried him on feathers?	Oh, he loves pigeons.	*In fact, he swallows them whole!*
How is he around other dogs?	No problems.	*. . . because he can lick any dog twice his size and does so regularly.*
Is he a good, hard dog—does he take punishment well?	All you have to do is raise your voice and he responds.	*. . . by lying down and urinating straight up!*
Is he gun shy at all?	I never noticed it.	*. . . because the moment I take out my gun he disappears for half the day.*

If you expect these men and women to level with you, please do the same with them.

While it's ideal to be able to use a pro who is located near enough so that you can check on the dog's progress in person, sending a dog far away is sometimes necessary. If you want to be able to handle the dog yourself when he is returned, make sure the pro understands this. If you can't spend a weekend with him training at the close of your dog's stay, perhaps he can recommend a fellow professional in your area who can guide you along until you get the hang of things. Or ask him to send you detailed written instructions. A trainer who isn't interested in how you fare upon your dog's return is to be avoided.

Lots of trainers send monthly typed reports; some call; some ask you to call. Get in touch with your pro regularly, but don't nag. Results with young dogs don't come overnight. Don't drop into trials or training sessions uninvited and unexpected. A pro is a businessman with a rigid schedule. If he knows you are coming he can juggle his time, but he is under no obligation to drop his other dogs and spend a whole day with you and yours without warning. And if you do go to a trial to watch your dog, the same rule holds as for obedience and show: *Stay away from the handler and the dog until the handler says the coast is clear!*

4

Early Training

BASIC PRINCIPLES

Upon going into the field with a promising new puppy, the first thing most people do is reach for a book. Now, most books dealing with retriever training start right off with how-to-do-it advice—which is excellent psychology, as it gets the neophyte trainer ambulatory immediately and gives him a positive approach. The trouble is, most amateurs have no business starting off with a new pup until they know exactly what *not* to do! This is not a negative approach—because I'm positive the beginner will go off in all directions at once. Enthusiasm overpropels most amateurs, I've observed, to the point where a promising pup either becomes a plodding, obedient, unexciting machine or quits completely.

Every person who sells a trial prospect retriever puppy or a green older dog should be compelled to send with the buyer the following list of pitfalls, making the new owner promise to read them over, aloud, three times each day before starting training:

1. *Any animal starting retriever training is a puppy, be he three months or three years of age.*

You cannot assume that because a dog is two or three when you start him he automatically knows all those "silly little details" like marking and staying and holding. Lots of people start with older dogs and have a grand time, provided the dog is a natural worker to begin with. My first retriever was a three-year-old pet-reject. I had good coaching and started him off as if he were eight weeks old. We went ahead faster than if he had really been a puppy, but he did well because

he learned everything in order, step by step, just as if he'd been a
real baby instead of a big baby.

2. *Twenty minutes a day, every day, will get you and the dog ahead
faster with less confusion than three and a half hours straight once a
week.*

The professional trains dogs all day long. This is what he does for
a living. When the amateur goes to the office, the professional trainer
goes into the field. He doesn't have to try to sneak in a few minutes
with his dog when he gets home from work, providing Johnny doesn't
need a chauffeur to get to the basketball game.

The amateur knows this and is determined to catch up with the
professional by spending half the time trying to cram twice as much
into his poor dog's head. Pity the poor canine! All week long he's
been sitting in his kennel; now, in one Saturday or Sunday afternoon,
he is to learn to be steady, deliver to hand, do doubles, and honor.
He returns to his kennel, in most cases, delighted to see the place,
his eyes crossed in hopeless confusion. Father goes in for a highball,
puffed up with pride—"Boy, honey, did we accomplish a lot today!"
And Fido sits in his run for the rest of the week; come the weekend,
it will start all over again.

Now, I'm writing a book on dog handling, not a marriage manual,
but it seems to me that each partner in a marriage has a right to a
few moments a day to do something he or she really wants to do. So
why shouldn't Dad or Mother announce, "Attention, troops! From
now on, at five o'clock each day, I am going to give Blackie twenty
minutes of training. I do not want to be disturbed. You may watch
through the window if you like, and later on, you can help me with
Blackie. But right now he needs to go to school alone with me. When
I'm through training, I'll be glad to help you do anything you like.
OK?" If any adult human being can't steal twenty minutes out of each
twenty-four hours for himself and what *he* wants to do, then I think
he's in trouble.

Often, it's more than a matter of taking the twenty minutes regularly—it's more a case of it being very unglamorous to train alone,
behind the house, with no admiring eyes to drink in the spectacle of
what a great trainer you are. There is a wee bit of the "ham" in all
of us, I'm afraid, and it's much more exciting to put on that orange
whistle and your new white handling jacket, don that suede hat with
all the dog club buttons on it, and prance around a field with others
who love showing off too. And there's nothing really wrong with it—
except that the dog is being sadly shortchanged, and so, in the long
run, you are being shortchanged too. Field champions are *finished* at
field trials; they are *made* in the back yard, or behind the barn, or in

the driveway, or wherever it is you spend that twenty minutes a day laying down a good foundation of fundamentals learned in order, one thing at a time.

And then, all too often you think, after a hard day at the office, that you are simply too pooped to fool with the darned dog. But you look out in his kennel and he's all hunkered down with anticipation of your nightly session. You weaken, and before you know it, that exhausted, tense feeling you brought home has vanished. Dog training is one of the greatest unwinders I know—and beats martinis all hollow!

3. *Until the dog is ready to start serious qualifying training, do not combine marking and handling.*

A dog learns to mark because he has nothing else to fall back on. But dogs are smart. If you teach him hand signals and handle him when he loses his marks as a young dog, he'll *never* learn to mark dependably. Why should he? After all, he's got you to fall back on. Of course, there comes a period in his training when he must learn to stop on whistle with a nose full of a bird he knows is there and take direction to a hidden bird—*but not now!* Even with gun dogs whose field responses can be far less exact than those of their trial brothers, foolish indeed is the guy who says to a pup after a few moments of futile hunting, "Never mind, fella, it's over here!"

Granted, it's much easier to stand where one is and direct the dog to the mark he missed than it is to go pelting out into that field a hundred yards or so and take charge of the situation in person. But "easy" isn't where the action is in the retriever world. And "lazy" is a word that never yet produced a good mark even on an asphalt parking lot. Take my word for it: marking and handling don't mix in the early stages.

4. *Decide what you want to accomplish before you start training, not after you're in the field.*

One of the gravest mistakes new retriever enthusiasts make is not having some training pattern or format in mind when they move out of the yard and into the field. While I am always ready to join the gang for an afternoon of training, I'm afraid I'll have to confess that I rather dread what lies ahead when I go out the first time with a new trainer. I know from experience that his idea of "training" is throwing as many bumpers as possible, one test setup for marking, another for steadying, another for something else, no lesson quite learned before we're on to something else. There is no progression of the training level, no point to what is supposedly being taught.

Training a child with two legs or a dog with four feet is not so different. Kids learn the alphabet before they are expected to read *The*

Decline and Fall of the Roman Empire. Dogs should learn their profession the same way: first things first, one thing at a time, each thing learned turning into a steppingstone for the next lesson.

So when you move into the field with bird boys to help you, don't get drunk with power. Just because your dog is sitting at heel in a corn field instead of on the neighbor's tennis court doesn't mean he knows a thing today that he didn't know yesterday. If you've been working on steadying in the back yard, stick to steadying in the field until he's steady. If you've been having double trouble on the side lawn, stick with doubles in the meadow until you no longer doubt him. And when you go out with a bunch of friends to train, sit down first and decide what you're going out to accomplish. Then everyone can help everyone make as much sensible, intelligent progress as possible.

5. *Take time out, before you get into complicated training routines, to sit down with your bird boy and make sure you both understand what each of you is responsible for.*

We discussed bird boys briefly in our Glossary, but let me say again that behind every successful retriever trainer is a bird boy who knows his business.

Trainers joke that if we couldn't blame mistakes on the bird boys, what would we do? But it's one thing to joke about venting frustration on the bird boy because he, or she, was the nearest victim to yell at, and quite another to heap vindictives upon the head of the poor bird boy who has goofed because you didn't take time to let him know what you wanted him to do. Not only are you liable to go through quite a few bird boys, who simply don't have to take such guff to make up for your own stupidity, but you are liable to ruin quite a few dogs as well in the process of learning the value of prior planning.

To keep bird boys happy and prevent you from blowing your stack, your first step is to sit down "over a cuppa," as the English say, and explain in words of one syllable what you are trying to accomplish with the dogs, and what your assistant is expected to contribute. Make it vitally clear that when you signal him he is to yell (or shoot) first, *then* throw. Take a few minutes to teach him *how* to throw a bumper to get height, which is the most important thing, particularly when starting green dogs. Emphasize that the moment he has thrown, he is to stand absolutely still with his eyes riveted on you and the dog; he may move his eyes and breathe, but that is *all* he may do until the dog is well on the way back with the bird. Teach him that as soon as the dog nails the bird, he's to signal you *unobtrusively,* for sometimes, in high cover, it's difficult to tell from your vantage point.

Teach him early that bird boys who bend over to tie their shoes or get another bumper while a dog is working, who empty the chambers of shotguns or light cigarettes, comb their hair or hum to pass the time, die an early and exceedingly unpleasant death. Start with simple things for both dog and bird boy, so they get used to each other and to your ways. Set up a bunch of prearranged signals you can give to tell him how to help in unusual circumstances rather than hollering directions at him over the head of an already confused dog.

For instance, if you raise both hands over your head, he is to yell "Bang!" to draw a drifting dog's attention back to the mark he is losing; if you put your hands on your hips, then the dog is truly lost and you are turning it completely over to him, lock, stock, and barrel. He is to immediately get the dog's attention and at the same time run toward the area of the fall. The idea is to have his movements and noises attract the dog to follow the bird boy while you stand still and shut up. By moving away from the dog on the far side of the fall, he can draw the dog to the bumper or the bird. The minute the dog finds his mark, the boy is to freeze and stay put silently while you take over again. Overhelping in this manner can cause dogs to become too dependent on bird boys, so you never want to issue a flat order to always help—have him wait for your signal. When a bird boy learns that a dog's success or failure can often be entirely up to him, real interest is born; some of the finest trainers in the world started out as bird boys. Bird Boying is a great place for a green handler to learn, as you see the whole picture from the dog's point of view.

Introducing a dog to a bird boy takes a little effort. The dog's natural instinct is to bring the bumper back to the person who threw it, and now, all of a sudden, there are two people in the field and he's to return to the "other" one. So until you're sure the dog isn't confused, keep your falls short on a lawn—no cover in the beginning. Start with the bird boy beside you on your right. Each time he throws, he should move out away from you at a slight angle. The minute the dog, as he is returning, seems to notice the bird boy, you start running in the opposite direction. If, in spite of your careful programing, the dog goes to the bird boy, discourage it immediately the first time. See that the boy knows that he is not to push the dog away with his hands or swat at him with a spare bumper. A thunderous roar of rage will break this bad habit in a young puppy, but lest he then be afraid of bird boys, after the test have your assistant immediately play with the pup and pat him. Then run the same test again. With an older dog I favor having the bird boy put the sole of his sneaker into that chubby little backside—but, again, you have to know your dog. "Be quietly un- friendly" is a good way to put it to your helper. If this upsets the dog so he starts running back in without his bumper, it's time for the

Particularly in early or puppy training, it is important that the bird boy be clearly visible to the working animals, and that his throws be high so they are outlined against the sky before they fall. By standing on this rock in the water, this bird boy is not easily accessible to novice retrievers, who might want to return the bumper to him instead of to the handler.

trainer to get out there and help the dog find his mark. Then praise and run the same test again until the bird boy ceases to seem so all-fired interesting.

Never let bird boys put piles of birds or bumpers at their feet. Keep extras of both in those burlap bags we mentioned; once a dog gets away with stealing from the bird boy, you have one more headache you can well do without.

If you can find a long-suffering buddy or a teen-ager or two to throw for you, by all means do everything possible to keep their interest. Take them to a few trials; if they are good, try to get them a paying job throwing at trials; let them hear you publicly give them credit for the long hours they stand out there helping you. Because the moment a bird boy or girl feels he is part of the training, you'll get the kind of results you read about in the headlines the day after the trial.

No matter how good your bird boy is, all of us goof, and every now and then a bumper will land on his head or someplace else it is

GETTING A DOG USED TO A BIRD BOY

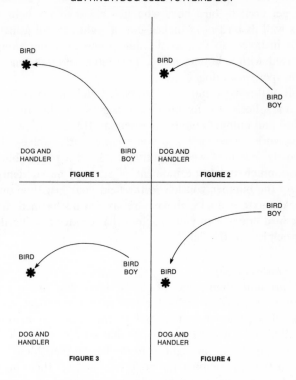

not supposed to be. Establish before you start that when this happens he is to pick the bird up immediately and stand still again. You will call it a "No Bird," get your puppy off the line, and throw a few on your own for him to get his mind off the error. Then try the test again.

While we're on the subject of bird boys, remember that their position in the field is important. If using guns, station the bird boy as close as possible to them. Bird boys should never be directly in the path of a dog as he comes toward his bird; nor should they be standing close beside the bird, or the dog is liable to start marking the bird boy instead of the bird.

Wise is the trainer who has his bird boy throw sometimes to his right, sometimes to his left, so the dog gets used to working on both sides of the "guns." Even wiser is he who sets up tests, from time to time, that require the dog to go beyond or past the bird boy to get his bird. Dogs must get used to bird boys who stand out like sore thumbs because they are dressed in white (an excellent way to start young puppies), as well as bird boys dressed in hunting clothes, which make them harder to spot (excellent for advanced work). Very advanced dogs must get used to bird boys who just stand in the field and do nothing, as well as bird boys tucked out of sight around a little point of land, for instance, so that as the dog comes charging along he is suddenly faced with a human being. This latter situation has thrown many an inexperienced dog.

When out of throwing material, bird boys should never come pelting in on the dog's heels waving his empty bag as the dog returns with his bird. Bird and bumper counts are essential. If you take twelve bumpers out to work, make sure you come home with twelve—they are not only costly, but next week, fighting a dog to a trucky blind, you won't like it much if, at the moment of success, he suddenly spins and picks up the bumper you left in the field your last time out. And if you shackle sixteen ducks, make sure sixteen unshackled ducks go back in the bird crate—can you imagine what chance a mallard would have lying helpless in the field?

6. *Honor individuality.*

All dogs are individuals; it is, of course, important that a given test be completed one way in order for you to get a perfect score, but every dog, while completing that test in the approved manner, will have little differences in his performance that set him apart. Some dogs always drift a tiny bit to the right or to the left on their blinds. Instead of hacking at them, remember the preference and set them up accordingly. One dog may shake immediately coming out of the water, while the next will deliver his bird and then shake; as long as he doesn't put the bird down between the shore and your palm, who cares? One way is no better than the other—but the handler who knows the individual preferences runs a smoother trial. On multiple marks some dogs need to be settled down and "collected" between birds; some should be released for the second bird the moment they deliver the first. Some need to be jollied along as you go to line to psych them up; some need to be growled at or intimidated from car to line and back to the car. Know your dog and make yourself intimately aware of his individual characteristics and habits.

7. *Know when to stop training.*

Let me reiterate the bit about always quitting before the puppy wants to. There is one more thing to add: always *quit on a positive note.* If things aren't going well, try at all costs to leave the field when the pupil *has succeeded at something.* If you get to a bit more complicated work with your puppy and he's simply not getting the message, drop back to an earlier lesson—just sling a simple single out a short distance, for instance, teasing him into dashing out and dashing back with it. Then praise and put the pup away until next time.

CORRECTION AND PUNISHMENT

During early training it is reasonable to assume that there will be moments when you and the pup, or dog, do not see eye to eye. So let's discuss crime and punishment before we meet them face to face.

Correcting any dog of any age for any crime depends on what kind of personality you are dealing with. Once upon a time I knew a field trial champion to whom the words, "Don't you *ever* do that again!" spoken in a sepulchral tone while pointing the index finger at him, were all that was necessary. This treatment completely cowed him. But after such "awful" punishment, he would pull himself together and do the job correctly. The most feminine retriever bitch I ever owned, on the other hand, was a holy terror. Because she was so adorable she got away with murder. "Isn't she darling?" cooed the gallery at trials as she tippytoed by them with a pheasant as big as she was in her mouth. She cost me about a year of training progress because I couldn't believe something that little and dear required physical chastisement of the most meaningful kind before the message got through! When I began lacing her britches with a field whip and even resorted to an electric collar, "Darling" actually started acting like a field trial winner—which she indeed became!

Physical chastisement with small retriever puppies is rarely necessary if you keep them going on a positive bent by never putting them in a position where they can do things that get dogs in trouble. If Junior is *caught in the act* of chewing up Grannie's cashmere earmuffs (and only if caught in the act), shaking the devil out of him by holding him just above the ground by the back of the neck, as his mother did when he got too fresh, should suffice. The most important part of such correction is not the damage done to the dog, but the sound and fury of the experience, which will dent his ego, nothing more. Roar a lot but carry a very small "stick"!

Young pup or older dog, no matter what you are correcting for, *never* begin the correction when you haven't got a firm hold on the animal; do not release him until your point has been made and you have made up with each other, unless you elect to leave him alone in his crate to think on his misdeeds for a period. Threatening "You just watch it, Bracken, or I'm gonna let you have it!" over and over again is senseless. Once you commit yourself, carry through.

In all forms of punishment and correction, the *timeliness* is what counts. If you can't punish precisely when you are absolutely sure the dog knows what he is getting thumped for, don't thump.

From the whelping box to the grave, your tone of voice is your most powerful weapon. Use it. When older dogs working far afield start thumbing their noses at handlers, most trainers have their own little verbal message which means, loosely translated, that patience is absolutely exhausted and results had better be forthcoming, *or else!* One well-known trainer would yell, "Allìlllllllright, now!" and his dogs would freeze. This was the moment of truth and his dogs knew by his tone and the inflection of his voice that they'd "had it." Over the years I seem to have developed a special rhythm and tone to my words. "I wouldn't do that if I were you!" during a land test, or during a water blind, "I can walk on the water!"—and I usually get co-operation. All my dogs know these phrases mean "Mother's on the warpath," and suddenly they are refreshingly eager to please.

Because there are available today such aids as air pistols, electric collars, slingshots, and cattle prods, people often feel that these implements are a means in themselves, which, of course, they are not.

When the chips are down and all else has failed, nothing, to my mind, beats a good old-fashioned licking (provided you can get to the dog quickly!), followed by a successful rerun of the same test. There are many times, however, when dogs are working away from their handlers, and here is where the ability to correct immediately, from a long distance and at the moment of disobedience, is worth its weight in gold. Air pistols, electric collars, and slingshots can go beyond the range of your itching fingers. Therein lies their greatest value.

The biggest problem with any artificial training device is not the device itself but the person using it. The guy starting out reads about this wonderful method of training advertised as "foolproof"—he doesn't stop to think the only fool it's not proof against is himself. There is no such thing as instant training. All these devices are excellent only when used in direct relation to the fundamentals of yard training. They are not the solutions to anything; they are a means to the solution of problems. They are, as I said earlier, aids, nothing more, nothing less. Before using any of these aids, the trainer is wise to ask himself:

1. Have I really taught my dog what I want him to do? Am I absolutely certain the dog is disobeying me out of sheer willfulness, rather than out of confusion? Remember now—not "I think so"—*absolutely sure?*

2. What kind of a dog am I training? Is he bullheaded and wayward because he's smart, or because he's stupid? Does he cringe when I raise my voice because he is soft, or because he gets sympathy?

3. Am I contemplating using a slingshot (or an air pistol or an electric collar) because it's easier for me, or because I think this is the only

thing that will make the kind of impression I want to make?

If you don't care enough about yourself and your dog to question your motives and methods every step of the way, then raise guppies and sell your retriever. But if you want to learn *with* your dog, accepting the fact that he may have some things to teach *you* along the line, then you are ready to accept the fact that cruelty comes from people, not from devices.

When I first started training other people's dogs, I wore a short training whip around my neck. My dear mother was convinced that when the owners were around I should put it away, but I have never done this. Lots of trainers believe that the best time to punish a dog is when its owner isn't around, but I happen to believe that if a person trusts me enough to leave his dog with me, then he must trust me enough to believe that I know when to "get in on" a dog and when not to. Since, over the years, my retrievers have all had to be coaxed away from me and into their owners' cars when it came time for them to go home, I must have been doing something right. And to expect any rational human being to believe I or anyone else trained dogs with a cup of sugar in one hand and a dog biscuit in the other would insult the intelligence of the village idiot!

As I said, my field whip nestled around my neck most of my professional life, just in case it was needed. The dog who was being "evil" never saw where it came from until it landed, and was therefore never afraid of my hands, a danger we went into in detail earlier in this book.

But to this day my favorite means of correcting mature, experienced dogs who are deliberately disobeying me is to take them on either side of the neck, swing them around to face me, and then whomp them first with my right leg, then with my left, then right, then left, repeating the command which had been broken each time I connect. Because I am very susceptible to poison ivy, I must train in "mucking boots"—high, loose-fitting rubber boots made popular by pictures of Christopher Robin in the rain. As I slam my leg against the dog, the air rushing out of my boot makes an awful whooshing sound, and I make a deep impression without leaving a mark on the dog.

All sorts of things are done to retrievers in the process of correction. It takes a lot of time for people starting out to recognize the fact that certain dogs have an emotional makeup that demands they be physically hurt in order to gain their respect. This was a hard, unpleasant lesson for me to learn as a novice too—but I know it is a true fact of life. Over the years my attitudes regarding crime and punishment have changed greatly because I have seen the good things that can be accomplished by punishment and the awful waste perpetrated in the name of compassion.

The point I am trying to get across is that it is vital to keep this matter of correction in proper perspective. It may well be you will train your dog without ever needing to resort to anything more than a boot in the rear. But while dogs that train this easily do exist, they are in a minority. All I ask is that you turn thumbs down on preconceived notions.

You don't have to try anything you don't want to try, but if you are going to be a good trainer, then I think you owe it to your dog to approach his schooling with an open mind. Just don't get cruelty and deliberate meanness mixed up with punishment in the field. There's a world of difference.

In the clinics I teach, it becomes quickly apparent that my idea of "cruel" and the definition of the word by my amateur pupils are miles apart. To them, kicking a dog or whipping him or physically roughing him up in any way—all these things constitute cruelty. Anybody who would shoot a dog with buckshot is a monster. To use an electric collar is an action of one who is obviously depraved. I sit there biting my tongue until they get all done with their opinionating, and then comes *my* turn!

"Mrs. Jones," I commence, turning to a handsome white-haired matron, "today I told you to give your puppy three bumpers, maximum, on each test. Behind my back you went to the far end of the field and threw bumper and bumper after bumper until that four-month-old baby quit from sheer exhaustion. Then, having overworked him mentally and physically and having removed all of his enthusiasm, you became really disgusted and grabbed him up by the back of the neck, threw him into his crate, and slammed the door in his face. That, in my humble opinion, was cruelty of the highest order!"

Everyone immediately turns accusing stares on Mrs. Jones. I go on to Shirley. "You were having trouble steadying your Lab. I told you we would wind up the day with steadying exercises and to put your dog up until then. But instead, you tied him to the bumper of your car in plain sight of the working dogs and let him hurl himself against his collar again and again while you stood there smoking a cigarette. I think that was cruel and just plain stupid. What was the point of it?"

She opens her mouth to argue as I turn on Jim. "You complained that your dog was spitting birds and I told you to forget it until after we had finished doubles and I'd show you how to cure this with yard training. But every time that dog brought you a bird today and dropped it, you grabbed him and slapped him around and shoved the bird halfway down his throat. And when he missed his marks you couldn't understand why. That was cruel, in my book."

With apologies to Mr. Webster, I have my own idea of what "cruel" means. To me it is a word describing *unnecessary harassment which teaches nothing*. It is the timeliness of the punishment and the attitude with which the correction is made that makes it either valuable or *mean*. If somebody invents a device that will let me correct an animal at the exact moment of his disobedience, then I don't consider it cruel to use that device.

A good example is teaching dogs to stop on a whistle at a distance. Years ago when I was just starting out, you taught the dog to sit in yard training every time you blew a specific command. You taught him line work and, when you were sure he understood what one short blast of a whistle meant, you set up a blind and prayed and sent the dog. When you hit your whistle and the dog ignored it, you took off like a banshee whooping and screaming behind him. Very few humans can outrun a retriever who senses there is a bird dead ahead. So when you got to the place where he should have stopped, you dropped a weighted handkerchief and went on to catch the dog. By this time he was proudly coming back to you with the bird, so you whaled the daylights out of him, after yanking the bird from his mouth and replacing it. Then you led him back to the handkerchief, made him sit, and sent him back.

Now, in my humble opinion, this kind of correction in the beginning stages of handling training leaves a lot to be desired. There comes a time when this exact correction is necessary to prove to the dog who knows better that we *know* he knows better. But in the beginning, talk about cruel! How confusing can a human make things for the dog who has spent months learning to use his nose properly and to rely on it? Suddenly he has done something wrong by finding a bird and bringing it back! This is where the electric collar is the answer to a maiden's prayer, for it can correct at the moment of disobedience. If used correctly, it keeps the dog from making negative moves and creates a confidence in him born of positive moves. Dogs learn best, scientific research has proved, by *succeeding*. And the electric collar, used in his instance as an aid, keeps the dog succeeding with a minimum of physical abuse, in a minimum of time, with a maximum of quiet control. Is this, then, to be considered cruel?

Some of the roughest professional trainers I know seem to inspire in their dogs a love—devotion, if you prefer—which would make the dogs follow them to Hell and back, not through fear, but because they *wanted* to. And some of the gentlest trainers I have ever met produce well-trained dogs, year after year, which cower at the least excuse.

Part of it is, as I said, the personality of the dog; part is the personality of the person administering the punishment. But I will repeat again that, to me, timeliness is the reason you can rough up a dog when he is wrong and, in so doing, build a bond between the two of you which is hard to break.

So as we go along, if you are called upon to really work a dog over, do it in the name of all that is humane; do it honestly, quickly, and decisively. Get the bad over with and get on to the good.

One of the greatest dangers in correcting dogs is *where* you do your correcting. I'd hate to think of the dogs that were almost ruined not because they were corrected, but because, after the correction, the trainer forced them to work again in the area of the unpleasantness.

Let's say, for instance, that your dog went through water for a duck which landed near the opposite shore. Instead of swimming straight back with it, he got up on the opposite bank and, in order to keep him from running around and returning by land, the bird boy had to really fight him off. Never send him back to *that* shore in *that* pond again for at least two weeks! If you have only that body of water to work with, run him from the *other* side of the pond. The same holds for fields—after an unpleasant session in a certain field, stay out of there for a while. You've made your point; don't beat it to death.

I know one dog writer who cautions his reader never to discipline a dog when angry. This instruction has amused and confused me for years. To begin with, how do you work yourself up to the emotional pitch necessary to really work a dog over if you are all sweetness and light? In the second place, how do you keep from getting angry at a dog who is thumbing his nose at you? I have been looking for a way to answer these questions for a long time; I still don't know how.

What I *do* know is that I am incapable of being *un*mad if I feel a dog is deliberately defying me. Actually, I'm not just mad—or angry, if you prefer. I'm furious! Far from wishing to keep my feelings a secret from the dog, I am exceedingly anxious that he know exactly the depths of my displeasure.

However, there is a limit beyond which a wise trainer never goes. I love all my dogs, I'm afraid, the good ones and the bad ones, the fast ones and the slow ones, the stupid ones, the smart ones, the rough ones, the nasty ones. But there has rarely been a dog I have loved that I didn't truly hate at least once in his life. It takes years of experience before you can understand what I mean by that, but anyone who has trained a variety of dogs will know. And once or twice in my life I was so filled with rage that I was completely out of control!

The first time this happened to me I was training a dog whose breeder had raised him for the entire first year of his life on leash! He was a hard-going, high-strung Golden, but after about two retrieves, the dog would just take off and run and run and run. Twelve months of constant restraint was just too much for him; he couldn't contain himself. It wasn't until I had turned him loose on a friend's farm for three whole months, to get the running out of his system, that we were able to get to first base with him. But I remember clearly the last day I worked him before I gave up and sent him off to the farm.

I was down on the eastern shore of Maryland working land singles with a young assistant named Othar. This fine, sensitive, understanding fellow was without a doubt the best bird boy anybody ever worked with. We had been schooling this dog so carefully that we were both finally convinced we had the problem licked. Then after three straight days of perfect work, the dog broke loose again. I watched him dash past me several times and I began to tremble. I was so filled with helplessness in the face of this problem, so discouraged that such marvelous talent was going to waste, so imbued with disgust for the woman who had done this to a perfectly nice dog, that I could feel the vomit rising in my throat. I don't know what would have happened if it hadn't been for Othar. I felt him touch my arm. "You're all upset now," he said. "You don't want to touch that dog! Now, you just go back to the car, you hear me? I'll take him home. Then I'll come back and we'll work the other dogs. You hear me now?"

Yes, I heard him, bless him, and I did as I was told. If anybody had tried to tell me I could ever have been this furious over a dog, I would have laughed. It was a sobering, frightening revelation. I loved that dog, but I'm sure I would have almost killed him if I had got my hands on him. I like to think I would have come to my senses without Othar to snap me back; but frankly I don't know. The lesson here is: Never correct a dog when you don't have complete control of yourself. Have someone else put the dog away for you until you have calmed down.

Nobody enjoys physically chastising any living thing unless that person is unbalanced. But when it has to be done, do it in an intelligent, constructive way. Then remove the bad memories from your mind and from the dog's and go forward together. End of lecture.

USING THE WHISTLE

The proper use of your whistle is vital to your training. The guy who lets a green dog run all over the place with no hint of a whistle is no worse than the overzealous neophyte who is "whistle happy" and drives everyone within earshot, not to mention the dog, up a tree with his constant toot-el-ing! The idea in the shooting field or in competition is to get the job done as smoothly and unobtrusively as possible, and piercing the air with unnecessary noises isn't called for.

The "come in" whistle is a call best described as sounding as if you were imitating the hoofbeats of a galloping horse, one long trill and two short all run together: "Ttttttttwwwwwwwweeeeeeettttttt-tweet-tweet!" It is most important that you develop a clear-cut call your dog will recognize whenever and wherever he hears it. It's quite true that, while any trained dog will obey any kind of a "come" whistle, each handler unconsciously develops his own individual trill, and it can be an intriguing game to turn your back and try to identify the handler by his whistle work!

On Land

On land it's a good idea with a young puppy to synchronize your whistle with the moment he ducks his head over a bird. But if he doesn't pick up what is lying there, shut up until he does. You can very easily become so quick on the whistle that a pup, or green older dog, being a bit confused, would start leaving his bird and coming to you because, after all, he *was* called. Ideally, the time to whistle is when you see the bumper or the bird in the dog's mouth; that is why, as we explained earlier, it's a good idea to have your bird boy trained to signal you *every* time the dog picks up; that way you never miss. If the dog starts racing back to you, no more whistling is necessary after the initial two or three blasts as he picks up and turns around— obviously he knows where you are and he's coming as fast as he can get there, so why keep tweeting at him? *But keep your eyes trained on him constantly. Anything* could distract him, and you can't give added reminders with your whistle if your back is turned. Study the way the bumper is lying in the dog's mouth. If he has a firm, central grip, there's not much danger of it slipping away or of his feeling that a new grip is necessary. But if he has the bumper by one end or is holding it unsteadily, watch his head like a hawk. The moment it lowers the least little bit, hit that whistle to remind him we do *not* put birds down anyplace but in the handler's hand! Low, encouraging little trills as he approaches the line are sometimes in order to remind him you are still in command, and they are quite acceptable in competition when the yelling and calling and clapping, often so necessary in training, are not allowed.

Whenever you get a bird boy's signal that your dog has picked up in cover where he is invisible to you, keep whistling until you can see him and are sure he has located you. Keep reminding Blackie with that whistle that you are waiting right over "here" until you are both visible to each other again.

Sometimes a dog will pick up a bird, particularly pheasants, in such a way that a wing covers his eyes and he is truly blind. Concentrate hard if this happens; don't whistle constantly after your initial signal upon pickup, but regularly give him little trills as he gets closer and closer. You'll find that a dog in this situation usually slows quite warily as he gets near the handler; keep up a steady encouraging trill at this point and pat your leg; that sound can help too. Remember, before sending that dog out again, to give him a moment to get his bearings!

A great deal of self-consciousness is involved in using the whistle in the beginning. I remember how embarrassed I used to feel when my buddies said I sounded like a leaky tea kettle! The only place I could practice in complete privacy was the bathroom, so I used to sit there and shrill away like mad. The practice paid off. When you stick that whistle in your mouth, hit it hard—there's no such thing as too loud when you are calling a dog in the field.

It is important that your whistle always represent command never punishment. In time you will learn to make it say quite clearly to a dog who has been goofing off: "You better get your bottom in here, laddy, or you and I are going out behind the barn!" Or, "That's a good dog, fella, I didn't think you could do it!" Or, "It's OK, pup, I'm right here, easy now!" But don't ever use your whistle to call your dog in and then punish him. In no time he'll turn a deaf ear to that whistle because it represents something bad.

Once you start your obedience training you can use your whistle to speed up his return by leaving him at a sit-stay and calling him from a distant point with your whistle, letting him jump up on you when he arrives. There is nothing more exciting than a dog who races to a bird with the speed of light and returns to his handler the same way! And if you'll stop to think for a minute, you'll realize that the dog that returns the fastest has the less remembering to do when it comes to multiple falls and has less time for "no-no's" in the field, such as relieving himself or dropping birds.

On the Water

Proper use of your whistle on the water can keep you out of a lot of trouble. When the dog is picking up a bird in the middle of a pond, hit your whistle the moment his mouth is around the bird and keep whistling until he's turned toward you. Then lay off until you see his feet hit the bottom—this is the area of a water retrieve where most things go wrong, so remind him that the same rules apply in shallow water as they do three feet from the line on land. Whistle low and positively so that he doesn't get any silly notions.

When you first start giving the dog falls near a far shore, it is vital you start your whistling when he's about two strokes away from the bird, so that by the time he has nailed it he is quite aware that you are behind him and that behind is the direction he should go! Same

thing if he comes out of the water and must pick up on land. Usually
the dog will go to the bird and shake, then pick it up. Get your two
cents' worth in early, while he's shaking; you want that "come home,
all is forgiven" sound to be ringing in his ears when he picks up the
bird. (We warned earlier against whistling too soon, but by the time
a dog gets to this more advanced work it's unlikely he'll come back
rather than pick up.)

When a dog is coming out of the water through high reeds or cattails,
even if you can see him, keep whistling until he's free of them until
and unless he's a seasoned worker.

From the moment you start to train, your whistle becomes part of
you. You never take it off in the field. Learn to hold it firmly in your
teeth, leaving your hands free. In time you'll become quite adept at
talking while holding your whistle in your mouth—also yelling, swearing, laughing, and crying.

As we noted, always wear two on your lanyard. You can tell if
one is not right because suddenly, instead of a tweet, you'll get a little
peep, as if a baby bird had just broken out of his egg; the ball is
stuck; fix it later; switch to the other whistle and keep going. In very
cold weather the little cork balls in your whistles can easily freeze.
While standing around, keep at least one cupped in your gloved hand.
If your dog's reactions at a distance lead you to believe he is not hearing
you, stiffen your palms and put one hand on either side of the whistle
tight up against your lips to form a megaphone effect. But don't make
the mistake of cupping your hands so closely around the whistle that
you cut down on its carrying power. Many people clamp down on
their whistles so hard that they get sore teeth—so they cover the shank
with a protector made of wide rubber bands.

Whatever you do to or with your whistle is up to you, but use it
wisely. A good soap-and-water cleaning with a tooth-brush is in order
from time to time.

CHECKING THE WIND

Early in any budding trainer's career, he should start thinking about
using the wind to his dog's advantage. Two terms will soon become
commonplace: *Upwind* and *Downwind.* If a dog is *Upwind* from a bird,
it means he cannot scent the bird because he is above the fall and
the wind is blowing the scent *away* from him. When a dog is *Downwind*
he will wind his bird because he is below the bird and the wind is
blowing the scent *to* him. Some people feel that the direction the wind
is blowing only affects blind retrieves, when it pays to be able to line
a dog either upwind or downwind. But marking is just as involved
with wind direction, if not more so.

In puppy training, getting a puppy out a long distance can become considerably easier if you drop his bird so that as he approaches it he winds it. Later on, in more advanced training, it is vital to train on marks set up so that he doesn't wind his bird until he has gone beyond it. It is especially important to study the wind before setting up doubles, as all sorts of problems arise when a dog on the way to his first fall winds his second fall, which was foolishly planned with no thought to the dog's nose. You will find that in the face of gale-force winds such as you sometimes get in late-fall trials, complete with rain, snow, or sleet, few dogs will head directly into the wind; the degree to which you can expect an individual dog to fade could cost you a trial if you haven't studied your dog.

You can check the wind by watching the grass, the trees, or by holding up a piece of tissue or lightweight cloth. Or you can wet your finger and hold it up; the side that becomes cold first indicates the direction from which the wind is blowing.

Once you discover that direction, don't take it for granted it won't change. Check frequently as you train or trial to make sure that Old Mother Nature doesn't try and pull a fast one on you. Using arrows to indicate the direction of the wind, we have included two diagrams illustrating what is meant by *Upwind* and *Downwind*.

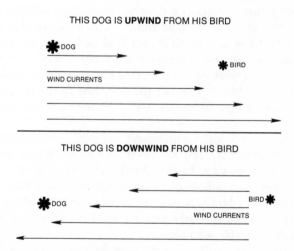

THE SINGLE
Getting Started

Probably the most underrated test in the world is the single retrieve, yet it is the foundation for more complicated work, and it is through the medium of the single that the new dog develops his marking ability. Notice I did not say "learns to mark." It is my theory that some dogs are born without that ability, and I don't believe it can be developed if absent; I do feel, however, that with a correct start, you can improve the latent marking ability of any willing animal.

We spoke earlier about certain training precepts being so simple that novices don't pay them much attention. The single falls easily into this category because the greenhorn blithely defines the single as "one bird." The single retrieve involves only one fall, true enough; but it is where that bird lands and how far afield it falls, past what diversions the dog must go to reach it and across what types of natural barriers that make the single not so simple at all!

Until the puppy is about four months of age you have been holding him yourself and throwing. It doesn't take a genius to realize that unless you steady him far too soon, you are severely handicapped in your throwing, because the range is pretty much always the same and you are working with only one free hand. Stick to that system too long and the dog is soon convinced that nothing falls beyond your throwing radius. This is a bad rut to get into.

So as soon as your youngster is dashing out and back with his bumper in various kinds of cover, on land and in water if the weather is right, call on the bird boy and go to a nice field of low cover. Why low? We are teaching just one thing at a time, right? Right! So first we have to get the dog working with the bird boy, as we explained earlier, and next we have to get you and the dog used to the fact that you are going to hold him differently now that both of your hands are free.

From now on you will stand behind the pup, legs spraddled, and your hands gripping the dog on either side of his throat below his cheeks and under his ears. In each hand grab a handful of loose skin so that you have a firm hold on the pup but he is quite free to move his head. Signal the bird boy with a nod of your head. He is then to yell "Bang!" or some similarly exciting word in order to attract the dog's attention. Double warning:

1. You are *not* to push the dog's head or yell at him in order to make him look in the right direction, or do anything to distract him from the world in front of him. If you do, you will not be helping at all but just hopelessly confusing the animal.

2. The bird boy is *not* under any circumstances to *throw* that bumper

until the pup is looking at him. He may have to move in closer—start at about twenty to thirty yards—and even have to do a war-whoopy Indian dance to get the dog to look at him. The *second* that furry head turns in his direction he is to let loose—high in the sky—then stand perfectly still.

The usual reaction from the young pup is for him to surge forward into your hands, pushing with his hind legs. Give with the dog but don't release him yet—he'll probably be standing and leaning into your hands as the bumper hits. At that very moment simply open your fingers and say, "Back!" Don't push at him or make him sit first or anything ridiculous—one thing at a time, remember! Today we're getting him started on singles with a bird boy, and that's *all* we are going to put into his pointed little head.

The instant he leaves you, pop your whistle in your mouth; the instant he ducks his head over the bumper and comes up with it, start whistling, clapping and calling, all at the same time, sounding as if you had just discovered gold. If he starts to slow down, you start running away until he catches up to you, as we explained earlier.

The Danger of Old Falls

One of the biggest dangers when a novice starts to work his dog on land is that he is unintentionally careless and sometimes asks a young or inexperienced dog to cross an old fall to reach another bird. Nothing could possibly be more confusing to the youngster who has just learned to use his nose to find that while his nose says "stop!" there is nothing to retrieve. It is very discouraging and can set back even the most promising pup.

An old fall is, quite simply, the piece of ground on which an earlier bumper fell. Scented or unscented bumper, pigeon, duck, or pheasant, the grass (or clover or corn stubble or whatnot) on which that bird lay, however briefly, still bears the scent of said bird. While it is impor-tant, as we will see in a moment, that dogs eventually learn to handle old falls without losing confidence, kindergarten is a poor place to start. Avoiding old falls while increasing the distance of your singles is very simple.

Lengthening Singles

When you first go into the field with your bird boy, station him at a certain spot and insist that he stay put. Emphasize that every bird he throws is to drop in about the same spot. If he has to come in for more bumpers or blanks or a jammed gun, make sure he marks the spot from which he was throwing by leaving his hat there, or one bumper, or the bag.

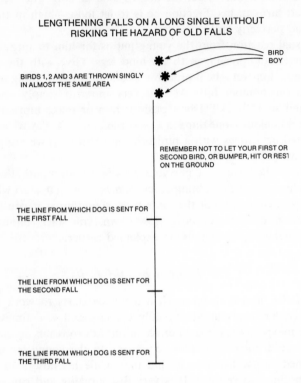

LENGTHENING FALLS ON A LONG SINGLE WITHOUT
RISKING THE HAZARD OF OLD FALLS

BIRD
BOY

BIRDS 1, 2 AND 3 ARE THROWN SINGLY
IN ALMOST THE SAME AREA

REMEMBER NOT TO LET YOUR FIRST OR
SECOND BIRD, OR BUMPER, HIT OR REST
ON THE GROUND

THE LINE FROM WHICH DOG IS SENT FOR
THE FIRST FALL

THE LINE FROM WHICH DOG IS SENT FOR
THE SECOND FALL

THE LINE FROM WHICH DOG IS SENT FOR
THE THIRD FALL

When you bring the pup into the field to work, start quite close to the bird boy, twenty to thirty yards with a very young pup as we suggested earlier. If the dog nails that first retrieve as he is returning to you, back up another ten yards to a second "station" (or line). When he has delivered, stuff that bumper down your shirt front, in your pocket, clamp it between your knees, tie it to your belt—but don't put it down! Now turn the pup around and send him for the second retrieve; since he has already been to that spot once, he'll take off with confidence and enthusiasm, not realizing that you have added several yards to his retrieve.

Keep backing up in this fashion until you feel he is driving out a good distance for his age and experience. If he "wobbles" on the last few yards (acts a bit unsure), give him one more fall after moving up nearer the bumper a "station" or two so that he quits on a positive note.

Getting Unusual Distance

As we've said before and will doubtless repeat again and again, confidence is what that puppy has to have, and now is the time to give it to him.

Every once in a while it doesn't hurt to push him beyond himself, distance-wise, on long singles, as long as he doesn't know what's going on. And this is the way you do it.

Get things straight with your bird boy before you begin, establishing what signals are to be used. Let him know what you are trying to accomplish so he can better do his part.

Keep the dog sitting with you watching the bird boy disappear further and further into the field. Whisper "Mark!" at him and other exciting little things so that he is full of curiosity as to where the boy is going and wondering when he'll get to find out.

When the boy reaches the agreed-upon point in the field, he is to start "Bang! Bang!"-ing! and yelling and at the same time swinging the bumper around and around in the air above his head. He is not to stop yelling or stop swinging until he gets your signal.

The moment the noise starts, tell the pup "Back!"; stand still and shut up. His curiosity about the movement and the noise in the field should carry him out there as fast as his legs can take him. When he's just about ten yards from the bird boy, signal him to shut up and let the bumper go. The pup reaches it, of course, just as it hits the ground, delighted with his great coup and blithely unaware that at four months he has gone about ninety yards all on his own!

This exercise doubles by achieving distance experience and relieving the tedium of doing the same thing the same way time after time. Use it sparingly so that it keeps its allure.

Variations in Cover

Land singles can be infinitely varied once you get the dog into the swing of things. Day to day changes from high cover to low cover to no cover are vital from puppyhood on. A variety of cover on one single is excellent also—from clover into meadow grass, from low corn stubble into high, or vice versa.

Interruptions of Cover

One of the tests that seems to throw dogs who haven't been correctly trained is the long single across a natural barrier. In other words, the dog's path between you and the bird is interrupted by a stone fence, a narrow creek, a country lane, or a hedgerow. A unique problem arises here because to the dog's eyes this is an optical illusion. Unless he has experience on this kind of "fooler," he sees the bird go down, for instance, behind the old stone wall, and that's where he hunts and hunts and hunts.

This dragon is easy to slay. Station the bird boy *well* out in the field beyond that stone wall. Instruct him to throw always in the same spot. Now bring the dog up to the stone wall and over to the other side. With the wall at your back, send him for his first fall. End of step one. Staying in the same spot, signal for a second retrieve. The moment he leaves you, climb back across the wall and stand in the field where he can clearly see you—no more than twelve feet from the wall—so you can encourage him to climb over if need be. End of step two. If this goes well, send him for the bird from where you are now standing and stay put the first time. If he doesn't hesitate going or coming, you can feel free to keep backing up until you get the entire distance you are after.

When introducing puppies or young dogs to this kind of test, always start them on the far side of the barrier so they never learn that it is possible to stop and hunt where they don't belong. And make sure the very young dog is tall enough before choosing a stone wall—best settle for dry ditches or country lanes.

A Dog's-Eye View

It is amazing the number of people who don't stop to realize that the dog, being considerably shorter than his handler, rarely gets the same picture of a test that his handler does.

The handler is looking *down* on the field or the water; on a water retrieve, the dog is on eye level with the fall, and on land his sight line is rarely more than thirty-six inches above the ground.

When working a dog in high or uneven cover it is always a good idea, and perfectly permissible at a trial or during a working certificate test, to kneel down beside your dog until your eyes are on the level of his. You'd be amazed at what you sometimes see—and equally amazed at what you sometimes can't see at all!

So when placing your dog on line, make very sure that what *you* consider that silly little insignificant bush in front of him isn't, to him, a formidable barrier around or through which he can see absolutely nothing. If, in competition, your dog winds up behind such a barrier, it is perfectly permissible to break it off, pull it up, and throw it away unless the judge has specifically requested that bit of cover be used by all dogs as a diversion.

Using Singles to Teach Lining

While marking is your prime objective when starting any dog, the single retrieve can help you get started on lining. After running the same single at increased distances, return to station No. 1, having made prior arrangements with the bird boy to place an unseen but very white and obvious bumper on the ground while you are collecting your last long single. As you walk the puppy back toward this line of the shortest fall, keep talking to him excitedly: "What's up there do you s'pose, fella? What's out there, watch it now. . . ." When you get to the spot you are going to work from, hold him as you would for a straight single and signal the bird boy, who then yells, "Bang! Bang! Bang!" Send the pup immediately with much gusto. He's used to going at the sound, he's already been to this area many times, and if you start close enough, just about the time he realizes nothing fell following the bang, he'll see the bumper on the ground. As soon as he scoops it up, have the bird boy place another light-colored one in the same spot. Now collect rapidly, and before the pup can think about it, turn him around and send him back. Gradually, as he gets older, it's marvelous training always to line him back for one bird over the path of his last long single of the day.

If for any reason he hesitates in the early stages, make sure you have instructed your bird boy not to wait for a signal but to "Bang!" immediately. As I said earlier, keep it *very short* to start with and you should have no real difficulty.

The Baby Blind

Now is also an excellent time to introduce the Baby Blind, which is another good way to teach a novice dog that he doesn't have to *see* something fall in order to go get it.

While the dog is on the way out to a long single, move quietly in the opposite direction from the one he is taking and place a nice, shiny, white bumper in the grass about six feet from the line. If you have to prop it on its end with a rock, fine, but take *no* chances that it isn't as visible as a tuna in a goldfish bowl! If you sneak back to the line (you obviously have to be quick about this!) and discover that from there the bumper isn't as visible as you thought it would be, forget it entirely; send the pup on another single while you fix it!

See to it that as you collect the long single from the dog, you are facing the "blind." If he sees it immediately, send him immediately. If he doesn't, hold him long enough for you to draw his attention to it and not a moment longer. *Voilà,* the dog's first blind retrieve! You can lengthen this *very gradually* as you go along. It never hurt any retriever to feel there always might be something else dead ahead!

Exercise for Varying Distances on a Single

As you become more experienced in your training techniques, you should find yourself inventing little exercises or drills which make sense to you and seem to pick the dog up on marking, lining, taking directions, whatever. It's a strange thing, but many of these routines just happen as you're going along, with no real prior planning. This is how I came by my Quickie Marking Drill. It consists of one exercise: four single retrieves of different lengths, and the opportunity to teach a dog about crossing old falls without confusing him. For a puppy or green dog, work on a flat lawn or a parking lot if you have to; later on when the dog is mature, experienced, steady, etc., you can do the same thing in heavy cover, and you can use it early on or later in the water as well.

Imagine, to begin with, that your training area is covered by a giant "X." Put your bird boy out about sixty-five to seventy yards at the point where the four legs of the "X" meet. You and the dog work from a point directly opposite him halfway between the bottom two legs of the "X." His first throw is a single mark slung out high following the line of the upper leg of the "X" to his right. When that bird is delivered and out of the way, he throws a second single, low and past the dog's nose, along the path of the bottom right leg of the "X." The third single goes high and toward the upper leg of the "X" to his left as long as he can make it. The last single goes low and short along the line of the lower left leg of the "X."

You can see from our diagram that in order to go for No. 3 bird, the dog must cross the fall of No. 2. But it will not slow him down or bother him *if* you let him go just before No. 3 hits the ground. Stay with this drill on lawn or low cover until you can hold him until all birds hit the ground and he is not bothered by No. 2. If he should hesitate to sniff, make sure you have instructed the bird boy, well in advance, to give an attention-getting yell. Use only big, white, easily seen bumpers.

The Water Single

If it's the right time of year for it, puppies and inexperienced dogs can learn a lot in the water.

It is much easier to teach the runaway retriever to return to the handler if you can start him in the water. If you heave your bumper out into the briny, the beastie's got to come to shore somewhere, and

VARYING FALLS WITH A SINGLE RETRIEVE TO TEACH DOGS
TO IGNORE OLD FALLS IN THE SAME FIELD WITH WHITE
BUMPER AND NO COVER TO SPEAK OF

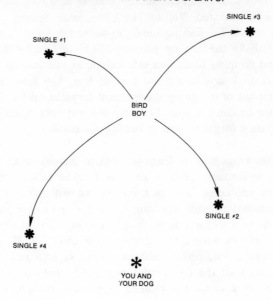

since you can run faster than he can swim, you can "head him off at the pass," so to speak. If it's too hot for land work and/or if you have a dog who has been slowing down a bit on you, short singles will perk him up and give him a day off without losing the rhythm of training.

Always start a dog on the water only a few feet from the edge. Don't throw too far to begin with. Your bird boy can eventually be stationed on the shoreline, in a boat out in the water, or on a point of land sticking out into the water. Make sure at the outset that he understands all bumpers are to land well out into the water and not nestled up against the shoreline—that sticky wicket comes later.

You'll run into all sorts of problems on water singles that you will never get on land. The time to solve them is now, in the early stages. (We're assuming that you have taught your dog to swim, as we suggested earlier.) Here are some of the things you will have to look out for:

Running Water: By this we mean water shallow enough so that the dog runs through it instead of swimming. This kind of water is found, for instance, in swamps, and young dogs often tend to forget their jobs and put their birds down for a quick refreshing frolic in the shallows. Worse yet, they sometimes choose this kind of area for mauling ducks. This cannot be tolerated. Yelling like a demented banshee, wade right in (another reason for waiting until the water temperature is less than frigid!) and shake the dog up properly, holding him by the scruff of the neck and flopping him from side to side as you roar at him. Then pick up that duck and toss it out beyond him. Tell him "Back!" and start running out of the gloop the moment he picks up the duck. Keep running until he catches you. Then try the test once again—and only once again; then forget it; you've made your point.

Dead Falls: Dogs have to learn to work in marshy areas where they must navigate through, around, over, and under fallen trees and old stumps. Any obstacles such as these are known as dead falls. It is just as dangerous to wait too long to give a dog experience in such conditions as it is to force it on him too soon when, for instance, he is too physically immature to negotiate these obstacles. Whenever you decide to work in swamps or marshes, make sure there is a boat out in the proximity of the fall so the dog can be helped to succeed, if necessary. Since it is not practical to expect bird boys to walk on the water and dash hither and thither helping a dog who has lost his mark, as may be done on land, make sure the boat contains a goodly supply of large stones which can be splashed in the direction of the fall to give an unsure dog renewed confidence.

Swimming Water: Long swims into nothing but lots of deep, still water can be discouraging in the extreme and should be handled carefully in the beginning. Get your bird boy and his boat beyond the fall and make sure you lay early plans for when and if to chuck stones out toward the fall. Too much help, as we said earlier, can be just as foolhardy as too little. Don't forget what we warned you about earlier: *you* can see a duck or a bumper far out in the water because you are looking down on it; the *dog* as he swims along is at eye level with the retrieve and doesn't get a clear shot at it until he's almost upon it!

Combining Land and Water

Another type of long single combines land *and* water and gives you even more experience in training with natural barriers across the path to the bird. Finding areas in which nature has been kind enough to tailor the topography to your training desires is not always easy. You are after a pair of narrow bodies of water each surrounded by land. Remembering the training through hedgerows and over walls, start your training for *land to water* on the shore of the farthest body of water. Move backwards through four singles until the dog is going the whole route; the moment he wavers—at station No. 3, for instance— stay there and repeat another single from this spot before moving back. *The bird falls in the same spot each time!* Follow the same technique for water to land to water.

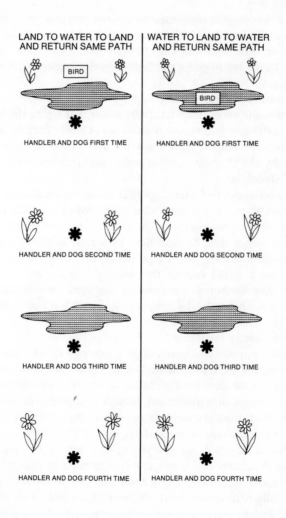

LAND TO WATER TO LAND AND RETURN SAME PATH

WATER TO LAND TO WATER AND RETURN SAME PATH

HANDLER AND DOG FIRST TIME

HANDLER AND DOG FIRST TIME

HANDLER AND DOG SECOND TIME

HANDLER AND DOG SECOND TIME

HANDLER AND DOG THIRD TIME

HANDLER AND DOG THIRD TIME

HANDLER AND DOG FOURTH TIME

HANDLER AND DOG FOURTH TIME

In either case, make sure to hit that whistle at the crucial time. On land, you don't want the dog to even consider the fact there might be a path around so he could conceivably return by land; in the water, as we warned earlier, if you can turn the dog back toward you the instant he connects with the bird, he's out of trouble and you're home free. Remember the one-thing-at-a-time precept, and if your dog is liable to scoop up his water bird and try for a nearby hunk of shore, place your bird further away from land than you would with a more experienced dog.

Again a warning against expecting baby puppies to complete this test. If you can find two little rivulets with about two gallops of land between, fine; otherwise wait until junior is doing water and land singles the length he'd have to go for our land-to-water exercises before starting in on this drill.

A dog must learn early to pick up a duck or a bumper across water near the opposite shore, then return by water, not trying the land route. Working certificate judges and hunters don't really care by what route the dog goes or comes; field trials require, however, that a dog go and come by the shortest possible route, and that does not include by way of Philadelphia.

People sometimes feel that dogs that make for land when it is close by, or prefer to run the shore rather than swim back with their birds, don't like water; this isn't true in the majority of cases. Dogs can make much better time by land than by water, and fast dogs will opt for terra firma whenever they are presented with a choice, unless trained not to do so. I would suggest that even if you are not going to trial your dog, you discourage his running the bank or returning by land whenever it is obviously the long way home. It's a bad habit to start, because dogs can get into all sorts of trouble on land that they don't run into swimming back.

With baby puppies and green dogs don't *ever* throw in a place that would encourage them to seek land. If you don't put them in a position where they realize they have a choice, they may *never* realize it. They aren't old enough or experienced enough to handle the correction at this stage. By throwing carelessly on water singles, much damage can be done to a dog's confidence and his love of the water.

But when a dog is doing everything else hard, fast, and right, and going long distances, and you know him enough to recognize the fact that he doesn't intimidate easily (at least nine months of age unless he's unusually precocious), start throwing closer and closer to the opposite shore. Before starting, however, have your bird boy well oriented. Have him cut a leafy, soft branch off a tree, a big limb, and have him stand with it over his shoulder, not moving it at all as he stands near the shoreline and throws near the shore. The fall should be located near to him so that he can correct if necessary. The bird boy is instructed not to move unless the dog makes a definite commitment to head for the shore on which he is standing. If this happens he is to roar "No!" and slap the branch on the ground at the edge of the water. One such deterrent should do the trick. But if it does not, the bird boy should be instructed to keep slapping at the water or land with his branch, keeping himself directly in the dog's path, until he has turned him into the water again, even if he has to hit said dog with the branch.

Meanwhile, you on the opposite shore will be whistling and calling like mad until the dog is in the water and swimming toward you. The secret of this test is to conquer it the first time out. Instruct your bird boy that under *no* circumstances is he to give up and let the dog up on the land. If he can't stop him with the branch, he is to drop everything, tackle the dog bodily if necessary, heave the bumper back out into the water, and then freeze.

To practice *across water up onto land,* start in a situation where there is no way for the dog to run around land on his return; a riverbank is best. This is a foolproof way to get the message across to a puppy without resorting to force. He can run up and down merrily, but sooner or later he'll have to come back by water because there *is* no way to make it by land.

This is the first step in teaching straight returns once dogs have crossed water to a land fall. It's the same old story—never put the dog in a position where he can run around. Sooner or later, of course, when the dog is experienced and old enough, he'll have to learn that, while there is a path back to the left, the right, or in either direction, he'll be much happier if he ignores these options and does things your way. You have no idea of the training setbacks you can secure for yourself by not planning your defense in advance, and in detail, against his running around. Once a dog learns that he can outrun you or a helper or two, it becomes a wild and exciting game and one that you can seldom win. And every time the dog gets away with making it home on foot, he becomes more convinced that he can outguess you as well as outmaneuver you. If you let this crime go unpunished and uncorrected long enough, you'll either have to jump the dog so hard you might ruin his desire to set foot on the opposite shore; at best, you'll go through any field trials you enter never knowing what he's going to pull in this kind of a situation. The trainer who explains to his bird boy, "Watch him on the right, he'll never try breaking through those briers on the left!" has just made one more contribution to the Famous Last Words Department.

You'll need a fairly small pond that you can throw across so that, if need be, you can swim it yourself. You'll also need two bird boys, each with a leafy branch, each hidden on the opposite bank, one to the right, one to the left. You might even walk the dog around the pond before starting to train, to prove to him there is indeed a path around it.

Now, then, before we go any further, make sure you take time to explain to the bird boys that once any dog gets by you, it's hopeless to pursue him. The idea is for them to erupt out of nowhere before the dog reaches them. They are to move straight across his path, swatting and swinging the branch and yelling dreadful threats at the dog. If the dog stops dead, the bird boy stops dead—but don't let him be lulled into thinking he can relax. The dog could elect to turn back and start across water as he's supposed to, but it isn't likely. It's more probable he will try and run around the boy on the other side—or turn and try running around in the opposite direction. If he heads for the other bird boy, the one the dog just challenged should fall flat and stay motionless until and unless the dog "tries him" again. If the dog can't elude his guards by running between them and the shore, count on it—he'll try going up and around. *Stay between the dog and his obviously chosen route, backing away if necessary to keep ahead of him.* As I said earlier, once he's even with a bird boy, he's won, so you've *got* to turn him before he gets to you.

It sometimes takes a while to get a dog to try and run around. If the first two falls don't lure him, throw at such an angle that in picking up his bumper he is almost halfway around and the land is more tempting. Once you get him cornered on land, it sometimes takes a bit of doing to convince him those boys mean business. As they "guard the pass," you keep calling and whistling. If it seems to be getting you nowhere, make a splash in the water on your side so that the dog sees it; it may encourage him to hit the water. While he has his back to the bird boys and is coming in, have them hide again. Praise the dog and put him up for a while—yes, I said praise him. What for? Why, for bringing you the bumper, of course—it's too late now to expect him to know that you are mad on *this* side of the pond because he goofed on *that* side.

Work a few other dogs or sit down and relax. Remember, we have corrected in this spot, and if we are to reuse it we'll have to be cagey about it to avoid cowing the dog or getting a quite understandable refusal. When you take him out again, throw a few in the water and make them fun retrieves, no staying involved. Then put one on the edge of the opposite bank. If that goes well, make a big fuss. Tease him with the bumper and let it fly a bit up on the opposite shore. If he looks warily about him, keep talking, whistling, and splashing. The bird boys are to stay put until challenged. If he should freeze on the other side with the bumper in his mouth, take another bumper and swing it wildly around your head. Let it fly high and behind you. If that doesn't work, try a stone hard in the water directly in front of him on the far side of the pond. If that doesn't work, kick your shoes off and swim straight over to him and, taking him quietly by the collar, swim back with him. Then a few in the water for fun and try the one on the bank again. It doesn't have to go very far up the bank to prove your point—and once that point's been made, he's through for the day. For reasons we explained earlier, don't go back to that pond for a week or two, and when you do, use the other side as the line.

If you are working alone and it is impossible for you to get this much help, use a check line but *use it carefully*. Pick a small pond with no cover on the far shore to snag the line. Before taking the dog out of his crate, make sure (1) that the line will reach across the pond to the fall (you can test this by tying the check line to the bumper and trying a practice throw), and (2) that the line is strung out, clean, in a straight line behind you and the dog; never mind neat little sailors' circles of rope. If it snags on itself you'll snub the dog on his way out, and that could be serious. Fasten your check line either to a buckle collar, or lock your chain collar as we described earlier so that in pulling on the dog you are not choking him. Now get him out and set him down so that the line trails down his back from the collar. Don't hold on to the line when he takes off, but only after he's started to swim. Throw a few close ones with no stays involved to get him fired up and trusting the line. Now let your long one go. When he takes off, pick up the line with either hand, and holding it shoulder high at least, let it run through a circle made with your thumb and forefinger. This keeps most of the rope out of the water for one thing; for another, there's less chance of it getting snarled around the dog's legs, and as he climbs the opposite bank it gives him less interference.

Don't use your line until the dog has shaken, if he is prone to, and actually has the bumper in his mouth. Then give a little yank accompanied by a firm, "Ace, come!" followed immediately by your whistle command. Use both voice and whistle as long as you are getting static from the dog.

If he tries to run around the pond to your left, yank hard and run down the shore to your right. A check line infuriates some dogs; it intimidates others. Use it positively but calmly and keep talking and whistling, using encouragements when you think they are necessary, and punitive tones when you think these are called for. It usually takes a combination of both. You and he may play shore games for a long time, but it's well worth the effort—just make very sure you come out the winner!

Water Singles at an Angle

This is another variation of the no-shore-running water single we just described. This time we want to make sure the dog will continue into the water from land on an angle, if that's the way his handler casts him off. This test, like others before it, is not for babies or greenhorns.

Start at the water's edge as usual. Each time you throw, instead of backing up in a straight line, do so at a slight angle. Keep the bumper quite close to shore in the beginning so its proximity lures him straight in at the point he entered the first time. Don't go too far back when you start this—make haste slowly, remembering that one yard's worth of clean angle is far better than ten yards of hacking away and calling the dog back repeatedly. Remember, also, that you are teaching *only* an angle into the water—one thing at a time. Later on you may need people on the bank for long angles; if you are working alone you can build a barrier with your training boat or dead brush. But in the beginning, keep that angle simple and short, and always start on the shoreline. Exaggeration of your hand command as you angle a green dog into the water often helps.

Moving Water

Retrieving from a lake or still river is one thing, but dogs also have to learn to handle currents, how to cut across them at an angle, and how to judge where the floating bumper will be when they get to it. It is much easier for a dog to "chase" a bumper floating away from him, it seems; trouble usually comes when the dog has to swim against the current for his retrieve. Kindergarten-grade white water can be found sometimes at the bends in little streams. Always remain on guard that the inexperienced dog of any age doesn't get discouraged or quit. Walk along the shore encouraging him, and as usual start your falls quite short. Do your own throwing when introducing any dog to moving water, and always have stones and spare bumpers on hand so that he never comes back empty-handed.

The Water Single Through Decoys

Decoys are best introduced on water singles when there are no other distractions. If you are blessed with your own pond, I heartily suggest you stake down four decoys and leave them there forever. The puppy gets used to seeing them and soon takes them for granted. Make sure that if he should swim over to check them out, they are so firmly anchored that it is impossible for him to bring one in.

If you have to use public water, you will save time and make decoy retrieving much more difficult for your dog if you take a few moments and rig what I call a decoy raft. When I started with my first retriever,

I didn't own such a grand thing as a boat, so I learned to tie my decoys to the shore or a bridge in order to retrieve them when the session was over. I designed the decoy raft so that the dog learned he couldn't swim through the decoys and therefore went around them from the very beginning. I know there are those who will argue that a dog might lose his mark doing this, but I would frankly have a wobbly mark rather than a dog so tangled in decoy lines he quit and came back to shore. "Dogs learn not to get tangled!" I have been told, but how do you "learn" not to brush up against something you can't see? The decoys are visible; the lines are not. Incidentally, decoys are not used in retriever working certificate tests.

You can make my decoy float either by using two pieces of wood that will float and which you fasten together in the form of a cross about 36 inches square, or you can use a 36-inch-square solid piece of wood. To the center of either model, on the under side, fasten two screw eyes. One is to anchor the float to the bottom; the other is to tie it to the shore. For an anchor you can use a piece of cement block, a stone, a length of old chain. Give yourself enough anchor rope and enough tying rope to allow you to use a fairly deep pond or river. If you have to use a stone, put the stone in a burlap bag and tie the bag to your anchor line—losing the anchor on your decoys can cause problems your dog doesn't need. To each of the four corners of your cross or piece of wood, staple, nail, or strap a decoy. By using the float idea you can use pretty banged-up deeks without fear they will sink on you.

Use a very fine line for your shore rope and a heavy, thick rope for an anchor line, as this is less liable to hurt a dog if he should get tangled. If you fasten small leash snaps to one end of each of your ropes, they can be coiled separately and carried more easily. The decoy float itself will fit easily into the back of a wagon, the trunk of a car, or on the roof of any automobile.

Fasten the far end of your shore rope to something solid. Now, holding the float in one hand and the anchor and line looped loosely, heave them out into the water as far as you can. You might even have to wade in a bit to get them placed. Working from a bridge is ideal.

Bring the dog, two bumpers, and a pocketful of rocks to the shoreline. We are teaching only that decoys are *"verboten!"* No holding or staying—just yell and heave your bumper out past the decoys and a good distance away from them at the outset, but in clear view of the dog.

If the dog should suddenly spy the deeks, don't start yelling and screaming at him. He may do a little "just checking" detour and swim right on for his bumper, in which case your hollering would have been wasted. If he starts for the deeks, you aren't going to stop him by

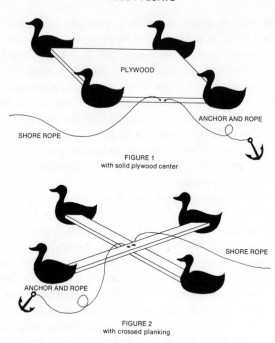

FIGURE 1
with solid plywood center

FIGURE 2
with crossed planking

screaming, I can assure you. So grab one of those big rocks in your pocket and wait to see what happens. Give him a chance to check and go on about his business. If he checks and then turns around and is obviously lost, yell to get his attention and then chuck a stone at the bumper. Much praise when he comes in.

If he decides to nibble the float, this is the time to start showing your disapproval, but don't have hysterics. "No, George, no! Bad dog! Leave it! No!" repeated over and over is fine. And the moment he gets your message, help him with a rock.

It is one thing for a dog to pick up a single deek in his mouth and come in with it, but quite another to wrastle in the whole float. I've never had a dog succeed in moving the float, but if he *won't* let go, there's nothing for it but for you to hustle out there and whomp him good. I prefer to push the dog's nose right into the nearest decoy and tell him "No!" repeatedly as I shake him by the back of his neck. All in all, I make it so completely unpleasant in the neighborhood of the decoys that he is not going to look on those fake ducks as something representing fun and games the next time he sees them. Now turn him around and make a splash at your bumper and praise him when he comes in.

Usually, when done correctly, the first correction is the last one necessary. You should keep throwing to the right of the float, the left, short of it, beyond it, near it, and far from it, until it might be sedge grass for all the attention he pays to it. Skip a few days and try again in a different area. You can't go wrong by placing the float on the lawn for a few land singles by it. When all is going well, throw a bumper right at the center of the float. He'll get it if it's a nice, big, fat, white bumper or a dead duck, even if it lands on the wooden part.

Baby puppies shouldn't be introduced to decoys too soon. Make sure, first, that they are really hitting the water and retrieving long water singles.

A perfectly nice dog who never thought of looking at a deek can be all messed up by the idiot who encourages him to pick up the decoys after hunting because "it saves time." It does nothing more than cost more time or even money for a professional to straighten out the poor animal.

Water Singles From and Near a Boat

Boats are used in most field trials and working certificate tests, of necessity. Early in the game, get the dog used to seeing them on the water loaded with the bird boy and his bumpers or game. Always instruct your boated assistant to throw well away from his craft, but set up a few tests where the dog must swim past the boat. If he pulls to the boat and actually puts his paws up on it, have the bird boy swat him soundly either on the top of his head or the end of his nose— then loft a rock to the actual fall to remind the delinquent of where he was going. Run the test again, immediately.

While dogs are never asked to work out of boats in a working certificate test, and rarely in a sanctioned or licensed trial, simply because it takes so much time to run such a test, nevertheless retrievers should be familiar with riding in boats and entering the water from a boat to pick up a bird and return it to a boat. Hunting dogs work under these conditions constantly, of course. This kind of training can be fun for everyone—dogs seem to love it, and even puppies benefit if handled with care.

Start out where nothing can go wrong—on land! With wee puppies, pick them up and put them in the boat with you as you sit there and play with them. If they jump out, fine; they'll want to come back in soon enough. If they are too small to struggle over the gunwales, practice getting them back in exactly as you will do it on the water, and nothing could be simpler. When the pup puts his front feet up on the side of the boat, reach behind his head and place your forefinger lengthwise about midway down his neck. He'll do the rest—he'll push his head back against your finger to give himself leverage to get in. Then you can help him so that he doesn't injure his private anatomy as he finally tips into the boat. (This is where girl-type retrievers have a very definite advantage.)

Big or small baby, retrieve with them on the lawn in and out of the boat until it is a fun game for everyone. Now move your operation to the water. When you first shove off, just row around awhile and let the dog get the feel of it. To prevent his jumping out ahead of schedule, I loop my training leash around my waist and fasten the dog to me. This way he isn't threatening to upset us and I can soothe him if and when needed. Anchor well away from land so that the shore won't be a temptation. Now stay seated and unsnap the leash. Tease the dog a bit with his bumper and then, yelling "Bang," toss it only about the distance he can leap from the boat. *Don't throw him overboard!* Keep encouraging him to jump with an excited voice, patting the side of the boat. It just might be that you will have to boost him in the first time, but do it gently. The minute he grabs his bumper, sit down in the bottom of the boat and lean over the side, clapping your hands and patting the side of the boat. When he puts his paws up, stick that finger behind his head and get him back in. Let him shake and tell him what an extraordinary creature he is. Then throw from the other side. Keep it up, throwing short, until he's coming and going with enthusiasm.

With a pup too small to manage getting in and out, throw your puppy bumper, holding him so that he can see the fall, then very gently, with much exciting chatter, settle him into the water with your hands beneath him. Pluck him out the same way. It's wonderful experience and, as I said, fun for dog and trainer.

Heavy Shore Cover on Water Singles

There are two problems to be reckoned with on this test. First, the dog goes busting through the heavy cover, sedge grass or cattails, for example, reaches the open water and stops dead. "M'Gawd, where'd it go?" It's another example, obviously, of optical illusion or change of cover. So, in the beginning, see that your bumper lands just beyond the cover so that he sees it the minute he breaks into the clear. Small pups can benefit from this kind of test if you start them on the far side of the cover and walk back through it with them before throwing again.

The second problem is that in returning from the water, as we said earlier, most untrained dogs want to put their burdens down. Well, the heavy cover pushing against the dog's bird or bumper doesn't do a thing to discourage this inclination. So see to it you keep him coming back fast through the reeds and give him no time to think about bumping into and against things. If he does get the bumper knocked out of his mouth, tell him in a matter-of-fact way to fetch it up; stop moving away from him and give him a chance. If he does pick it up again, keep going and offer a prayer of thanks. If he does not pick it up after dropping it, run back, heave it out again, and keep trying. Tests like this can be frustrating, and when we get to them in training it usually means the dog has come along far enough for his first taste of yard work in obedience and his first experience with force training. So it's out of the field and back to the garage or the lawn or the driveway or wherever.

5

The Intermediate Stage

HOW DO YOU KNOW THE TIME HAS COME?

As we said earlier, it's a good idea to keep the puppy working at ordinary leash and collar obedience from the first, providing you do not overdo it and that in the beginning you never mix this kind of training with his retrieving. It's one thing to do heel, sit, and sit-stay on leash in the yard two or three times a week, and quite another to be dragged into the training field by an enthusiastic puppy who is getting all excited over nothing and then lug him kicking and screaming back to the car as he does his darnedest to choke himself to death. With baby puppies, carry them out and carry them back. But how do you know when the time has come to start demanding a little more of the dog as far as control is concerned? It's just as dangerous to keep him in rompers too long as it is to turn him loose too early. Retrievers who bolt into the field ahead of their handlers and out of control alienate every other hunter and can get themselves thrown out of trials before they ever get a chance to run.

It is not easy for *me* to tell *you* if your dog is ready for the next stage because, as we have long since agreed, dogs are individuals and I don't know your individual dog. I do know that this is the hardest differentiation for the beginner to make with his dog, so let's see if we can come up with some reasonably safe rules of thumb which may help you decide by answering a few questions *honestly!*

Is the dog's work suffering because of *your* inability to control him to a point where he can concentrate on his marks? Has he begun to drop his birds (bumpers) so far from you that you can't really call it retrieving? Be honest now—is he actually running the show most of the time, out of control because you're afraid to do anything for fear it might be wrong?

If you answered yes to these three questions, then we'd better get to work. While there are exceptions to every rule, a puppy at five to six months can usually begin to combine his obedience training with his retrieving if the handler uses good judgment. Short sessions and no retrieving is the winning combination.

OBEDIENCE WORK

Flip back to the obedience part of the book and study directions for getting dogs to heel beside you on a loose leash, sit beside you when you halt, and sit-stay on and off leash. For two or three weeks concentrate on these commands, cutting your retrieving to one or two sessions a week. Remember to use a short blast of your whistle for sit as often as you use the word. In the beginning, work at home, behind the garage, in the rumpus room, anywhere *alone* without distractions. But as soon as the pup is walking happily on heel and sitting when you stop, you can start taking him to the local shopping center to practice. If there is an obedience class in your area, ask for permission to attend on *your* terms. If necessary, pay for the course, but do just heel, sit, and sit-stays, and only for short periods, no matter what anybody else is accomplishing—remember, you are out for distractions, not perfection. Be very sure the puppy looks forward to his obedience sessions as eagerly as he does his retrieving sessions; he *will* if he has learned by now, as he should have long since, that all good things come from you and that pleasing you pleases him.

Once this is going well, take him into the field where you trained the day before. Make him heel out and around the places he worked yesterday and then back to the car. While it is not necessary for a field dog to stick to your side as exactly as is required of an obedience dog, nevertheless see to it that he stays out from under your feet and that he works on a loose leash—holding him back on a tight leash only makes any dog twice as frantic. And by using a standard six-foot obedience leash, if the dog does try to take off, six feet is as far as he'll get. Let him check himself, and when he finally comes back to your side, to your command and encouragement, be sure to praise him. It is interesting to note that dogs trained on a six-foot leash rarely misbehave when the time comes to steady further than that six feet they have become so used to.

Once Fido is heeling around the field under control on leash, the next step is to put your bird boy out in the field to stand quietly.

Now practice heeling to the line, praising the puppy as he sits and looks, then heeling off the line and back to the car—*on a loose leash.* If he's got anything going for him at all, even with nothing falling, you'll find it's much harder to get him *back* to the car than it was to get him *out* to the line.

Once you get the dog heeling to and from the line with control—bouncing along a little ahead of you is fine provided the leash is loose and you *know* the dog is aware of where you are and has part of his mind tuned to the fact that you might ask him to do something different at any given moment—the time has come to combine the obedience with the retrieving for the first time.

Put your bird boy in the field with a bumper, ready to throw, but caution him to stand absolutely still. Take the dog from the car and start toward the line. After about six steps, tell him to sit—never mind if he's a foot out ahead of you as long as he obeys the command promptly. Now bend over and pet him soothingly down the outside of his flank, repeating the words, "Stay, good dog, stay." After a few seconds, it's "Fido, Heel!" and off you go for another eight or ten steps. Then stop again—repeating this routine until you reach the line. Three stops out should do the trick. Don't forget to keep that leash loose! When you get to the line, have him sit, and praise and soothe him again. Now slip off the leash and collar (don't take your hands off him so he can break and ruin your good work) and hold him on either side of the throat as usual and begin training. When it's time to quit, have the bird boy freeze again as you slip on the dog's leash and collar and take him back to the car. Once he's in his crate, lean in and ruffle him up a bit with approval. You should both be very pleased with yourselves.

STEADYING

Again, whether to begin steadying depends on the individual dog. If he's five months old and doing well by being held by the throat on line, I'd leave it at that until he's six months. I really don't like to introduce this restraint until the dog has learned to mark and to "count to two" (been introduced to doubles). If, however, you feel he is being held back by the small degree of control you have over him, if he is a big or a rough pup, if he is willful and stubborn and you're not sure but what he's learning less while you are getting only pulled muscles, the time has indeed come to steady the dog. Six months (or a bit earlier if it is called for) is no time to suddenly crack down so hard on even the most precocious pup that you lose in enthusiasm what you gain in control. But there is a happy medium, and if you can just get it across to the dog that if he sits still long enough for the bird to get down you'll let him get it, you are over the hump, so to speak.

Steadying is the first real test of a dog's character and potential. No matter how carefully you go about it, this will be a traumatic time for both of you. But as mother always said, "You won't learn any younger, dear," so let's get cracking.

From the very beginning one of the most important things for any retriever to learn is that nothing bad will happen if he stays put at heel. A dog who is trained this way has a much better chance of turning into an exceptional marker. His mind is free and clear and he isn't *afraid* to watch the birds fall. Dogs that are kicked, jerked, slapped, or screamed at while at heel are naturally apprehensive about this position. The greatest dog in the world can't be expected to watch out for your corrections and at the same time remember where his birds are landing.

The point of teaching dogs to be steady is not to see how long we can make them stay put when they want to get going, but because once they learn to sit still and stay put, they are granted the opportunity to go after what they want more quickly, and given the chance to find it more efficiently.

Steadying, Step 1

So here we are in the backyard, the garage, or the side lawn—no cover, please!—complete with bird boy and bumpers. Your dog is at your side wearing a chain slip collar attached to a six-foot training leash. You are to stand upright beside the dog—don't crouch over him or hover apprehensively—with the middle of the leash touching the ground, making the dog think it's just lying there. Hold the loop end of the leash squarely in front of your tummy with both hands. Before bringing the dog to line, instruct the bird boy to yell bang in a moderate tone until you tell him to get louder; also establish just how far all bumpers are to fall—never more than thirty feet away— always in plain sight and the first to his right, the second to his left, the third to his right, the fourth to his left, and so on. And instruct him that the minute he sees you nod your head, he is to shout and throw.

You heel the dog to line, lean down, and give the "Stay!" command in a firm voice, at the same time giving a good snap to the leash. Now stand up straight, holding the leash as directed, and nod. Chances are excellent that the dog will take off hell-bent for election the moment the bird boy goes into his act. Hang on to your leash, bend your knees a bit, and as he hits the end of the leash, repeat "Stay!" Now, using a combination of jerks on your leash and pats on your leg, woo him back to heel position. As soon as he sits there, bend down and praise him *soothingly;* he's plenty excited enough without jazzing him up even more with your excited approval. Stand up straight, drop the leash, and send the dog for the retrieve.

It is very possible he may refuse you now—after all, for the first time in his life he has started for something and been corrected for it! Don't bat an eyelash, simply repeat your command, flinging out your hand toward the bird (as you always do), and taking that bowling step forward at the same time. It should be obvious by now why we are keeping the bumpers close and in plain sight of the dog.

When he returns, praise him and play with him a bit. Then have him sit at heel and take up your leash again for the next attempt. If he gets to the place in this first lesson where he doesn't go before being sent, count to three in this manner (inaudibly to yourself, please!) before sending him: "One-gobble-gobble-two-gobble-gobble-three-gob-ble-gobble-back!" Send with more enthusiasm and oomph than you would do normally, because this is not a normal situation; it is a time when the dog needs added incentive from you to offset his vague insecurities.

One quick word about the "sitting" at heel—a dog doesn't have to sit either while shooting or at a field trial, licensed or sanctioned. In field talk, a dog is steady when he doesn't make a commitment to go for a bird until he is sent. Lots of dogs stand on line; some move about quite a bit, adjusting themselves to the different areas they must focus on in the case of multiple falls. So don't whang on the dog if he stands when the bird goes down. Don't give a second command—it can become a bad habit. Give one command, "Stay!" Then stand still and shut up until and unless the dog makes a try for the bird before you have completed your gobble-gobbling. It is just as damaging for the dog's training to make him sit too long as it is to release him the instant the bird is down.

Your first session should end when the dog has remained steady twice. Then both you and the bird boy play and fuss with him. Put him up and plan to do it all again tomorrow. If the session was particularly rough, you might want to work shorter periods twice a day. But no matter what family crisis comes up, don't miss a single day with this exercise until "he's got it, by George, he's got it!"

Steadying, Step 2

Whether in a shore blind, a duck boat, or on line at a field trial, rarely does the hunter or handler remain motionless lest he disturb his dog before sending the animal for the retrieve. But this is just how some people train when it comes to steadying. They freeze, they don't even breathe for fear they will make a motion which might be misinterpreted by the dog and cause him to break. A steady dog is a dog who stays put because he is told to. A steady dog is one who clearly understands that a change of position or an unexpected movement by his handler does not constitute an exception to the "Stay!" command. Stay means stay, whether the handler is scratching a mosquito bite, swinging his 12-gauge, or turning his body to the right or left. Particularly in the beginning when teaching inexperienced dogs to mark, the quieter the handler remains the better, for there are enough distractions in life without giving the dog a few on your own. But as we said earlier, the well-adjusted retriever should be steady enough to mark in clear conscience without coming apart at the seams if his handler should suddenly stumble or trip; the most successful handler and the safest hunter is the one who knows the dog won't take off until he is directed to do so.

Let's get one thing straight, however: there never was a perfectly steady dog! Frankly, I wouldn't give you a nickel for a dog who cared so little about retrieving that he never ever forgot himself, though I admit I'd just as soon he didn't do it when my entry fee money was at stake. Just don't get the idea that once a dog is trained to "Stay!" he will do so until death do you part. Remember, you have instinct and desire fighting obedience training. The point I'm trying to make is that you must be pretty darned sure of your dog if your training is to be worthwhile. And in order to get that sure, it's wise to train under conditions bordering on reality.

Once Step 1 is going well, usually about two to three days, we start Step 2 by setting up the same practice situation we started with, from the handler's nod to the moment the bumper hits the ground. "One-gobble-gobble-two-gobble-gobble," then suddenly lurch forward as if *you* were taking off to do the retrieving. You'll get one of the following reactions and should handle it as directed:

1. The dog will break to the end of the leash. Correct as originally directed; pet at heel; lurch forward again. If that does it, praise, drop leash, and send dog.

2. The dog may stand up and start forward, correcting himself while the leash is still loose. Pat quietly, drop leash, and send.

3. The dog may fly away from you to the side or back up behind you, clearly disturbed by your shenanigans. Quietly call him to heel and press his head against your leg. Scratch his ears and lurch again. Each time you pat him, do so quietly with great reassurance, clearly saying to him, "You are probably right, I am nuts, but I'm not going to hurt you!" As soon as he's over his fright, drop leash and send.

You can vary Step 2 by waving your hands around your head before sending the dog. (Don't wave your sending hand in his face and not expect him to take off; he may be a bright dog but he's not psychic!) Or scuff your feet back and forth, scratch your head with your sending hand, jump up and down once or twice.

If you are training your dog for hunting only, this is the time to introduce the old shotgun. It doesn't do a trial dog any harm either, provided he's a precocious, not easily shook pup. Start by shifting the shotgun in your free hand. Then take your leash and run the snap end through the handle loop and draw it tightly around your waist. Snap it to the dog again and you have both hands free. After prior instructions to the bird boy, when he throws, *you* throw the gun to your shoulder and yell "Bang!" This is where many inexperienced dogs take off if they can, so be prepared; to them, that big stick you've suddenly raised over their heads looks plenty threatening. If this happens, *don't lower the gun!* Hold it up there with your far hand while you guide the dog back into heel position with your sending hand. Now soothe him against your leg. If he didn't see the bumper go down, tell the bird boy to quietly walk out and throw it up again with no sound. As soon as the bird boy has returned to his spot, send the dog. Collect from him with the gun lying across your free arm. Then try it again.

Step 2 is also when you start practicing the "No Bird!" situation that every dog has to learn to take in stride sooner or later. Be careful never to leave the training arena on a "No Bird," for I believe it is bad psychology to send a dog home remembering he didn't retrieve and got praised for it. After two or three retrieves (during which the dog was steady on leash with agitation), by prearranged signal have your bird boy throw in clear sight. The minute the bumper hits, he is to start yelling "No!, No!, No!" loudly. You are to start in a very low, very firm tone of voice, repeating "No! Heel, boy, No!" and *backing off* the line. Do not drag the dog with you like a sack of meal. *Back up,* repeating "No!" and "Heel!" as you pat your leg, keeping the leash absolutely loose to give him every opportunity to make the error so you may correct him. If he does go, let him—repeat "Stay!" when he hits the end of the leash, call him back to heel and keep moving *backwards.* About three feet off the line, turn around and start heeling him back to the car. Instead of putting him in his crate, take him behind the car and play with him, praising him, roughing him up physically. Then heel him back to line and this time, after boggling and agitating, send him. Lots of praise and end of session!

After a few days of positive results with Step 2, you are ready for

Steadying, Step 3

The time has come for you and the dog to graduate from the training leash to the sending line. Snug your line around the wrist of your sending hand, wrap the surplus around, and tuck the end in. Now heel the dog to line with your leash. Before unsnapping the leash from his collar, uncoil your sending line and feed the free end through the free ring of the collar, as we described earlier. Unsnap your leash, letting him see you throw it away. Give your "Stay" command, snap the line once, and stand up straight, holding the end of your sending line in the hand with which you will send the dog to retrieve. If he breaks, correct as if he were on the leash. "Gobble-gobble" and send him by stepping off on the leg nearest him at the same time you throw the hand nearest the dog forward. As you give your "Back!" command, simply open your fist and the line will slide through the collar, releasing the dog without distracting him. When he returns, praise while threading the line through the collar ring again; have him sit at heel and start again.

As early as you can get a dog under control using a sending line without confusing him or taking the fun out of things, the faster you can progress. But going too fast can be the beginning of the end. If you are at all in doubt as to whether or not your dog is emotionally ready for the steadying exercises we have outlined at this point, don't try steadying. There is a wonderful rule you can absolutely depend upon throughout your retriever training when it comes to teaching anything new or difficult. "If in doubt, don't! You can always train tomorrow, but you can't untrain tomorrow!" It doesn't matter if the other dogs in your group are going ahead faster than yours. It's *your* dog's needs we're talking about, not somebody else's. So if that pup is a slow learner, anxious to please but a little bit worried when things don't go absolutely right, take a month longer to play with him. If he's ever going to get over his insecurities, only time and your extended patience will do any good. Chances are that if at four to five months he is still a bit on the sensitive side in reactions to change and correction, you haven't got a field trial dog; on the other hand, I could name you at least three Fld. Champions who were just this way as pups. They never were completely changed, but extra time, extra forgiveness, extra approval, and extra love put them in line for that coveted title.

Helping the Dog to Concentrate

At all times when teaching steadying, keep in mind the importance of not distracting that dog's attention from the fall any more than necessary. We practice moving around on line to give him confidence, not to see how much we can shake him up. Pat at heel, as I said, quietly and soothingly when you first start teaching "Stay!" but try to send him before his head turns away from the bird. This is the worst habit in the world to break. I know there are many authorities who start pups with marking drills by deliberately making the dog look away from his fall and back again. This makes absolutely no sense whatsoever to me. In answer to the question, "Have you tried it?," "No, I have not!" And I don't intend to; it seems to me too stupid a theory to experiment with.

I want my shooting or trial dog to be aware of me on line only because I can help him get what he wants most. He must be under my complete control at all times, but since I'm using a dog because I'm not a gifted marker, I have no intention of confusing his natural ability in this department. Screaming "Stay! Stay!" at a dog to keep him steady, crouching over him as if your shadow will keep him from breaking, snatching at him because you think he's just about to take off for the tall timber—all these methods are guaranteed to make any dog break, *and* he'll have no idea where he's going when he does bust loose!

If, during your steadying drills, he should turn his head, wait quietly and see if he turns back to his fall. If he does, send him immediately. If he doesn't, whisper "Mark!" quietly. If that works, send him immediately. If he still doesn't get it and focuses on you, give your prearranged signal and let the bird boy get his attention. Send him promptly after he locks on the bird again. Then, the next time you throw, send him as soon as the bird hits the ground for a few times and quit for the day. He may be an overly sensitive creech or even stupid, or you are at fault somewhere in your training approach. As I warned you earlier, by no means start pushing at the dog's head with your hands. For a couple of days throw for him as if he were a puppy again, just you and "ho-ho-ho!" Three at a crack, period. Then start again. Dogs take off throughout their retrieving career in the direction their *heads* are pointing. Never mind the rest of the body—it will go wherever the head goes, I assure you. But if a dog is looking east, don't assume he's just resting his eyes and will automatically go west because *you* know that's where he should go. It doesn't work that way. So make sure that furry little noggin is tilted toward the bumper that is down before sending him.

What to Do if the Dog Gets Loose

Sooner or later, of course, that dog is going to have to be steady (for trials especially) sans leash, sans sending line, sans collar. This point of no return will be thoroughly explored later on. While you still have the control of a leash or sending line, it isn't likely that he will get an opportunity to break free—the whole purpose of these restraints is to build positive attitudes. If a dog is never permitted to

Always make sure, before releasing him, that your dog's head is facing down the line you establish with your hand. His head leads his body, and if the head is not exactly placed, the body will not go where it is sent, no matter how hard you pray! *Photo by T. and R. Phillip*

break and get away with it, it will soon occur to him, we dearly hope, that he isn't going to break and get away with it ever, ever! So why keep trying? However, the best laid plans of mice and men oft go awry, and we'd be foolish if we weren't prepared for the worst. After all, sending lines can slip through clumsy fingers, and training leashes, not to mention chain collars, have been known to break.

Throughout steadying practice, in fact throughout all phases of dog training, the basic principle is: "Do it my way and you'll get what you want faster." The reverse side of this ditty is: "If you do it wrong there's nothing in it for you." This is especially important when teaching a dog not to break. If he is to come to understand that when he is steady you will give him his bird, then it follows he must be convinced from the beginning that if he breaks he *won't* get the bird! It's that simple.

It takes only a few minutes with your bird boy to get across to him that, once you have started to steady a dog, he must never get away with retrieving successfully when he is not sent to do so by the handler's command. Therefore, when I go into the field with a dog we have started to teach to stay, and something goes wrong so that the dog gets away from me, my bird boys know that, no matter how they manage it, that dog is never to get his mouth around the bird on which he just broke. If the boy is sitting in a boat and can't beat the dog to the duck by fast paddling, then he is to go overboard. If, on land, it turns out to be a photo finish, he is to throw his entire body on that bumper and lie there until I arrive to take over. Few retriever training precepts are less conditional. Never is he to get a bird he breaks for—I don't care if you have to tackle the dog, submerse yourself in mud, cover yourself with marsh goop, or skin your knees. I'm perfectly willing to drive five miles back to get you a dry change of clothing or to deliver you to an emergency ward where they can treat your turtle bite or take stitches where you slipped on some glass; I'll even give you artificial respiration myself, and if that doesn't work, I'll notify the next of kin and pay for the funeral. But if you are bird-boying for me and value your skin and your future, don't stand there in the field as a successful delinquent comes in with a bird he wasn't sent for and yell, "Sorry about that, couldn't get it in time!" The serious-ness lies in the fact that once that dog has got that bird and is on the way in with it, I can't do a darned thing about it—to the dog, that is. But I have been known to do dreadful things to lazy bird boys!

The older, experienced dog who breaks shot knows better. If you kite out there and he sees you coming, he knows exactly what to expect and why. But a young dog, particularly in the beginning, is too wound up in what he's doing—retrieving—for this lesson to sink in once he's got the bird. He has forgotten he broke by the time he gets that duck or pigeon. All he knows is that he's bringing you something and sud-denly, "Whammo!" "Bammo!" for some strange reason he's getting the tar whaled out of him.

The timeliness of the punishment is crucial. If you can't catch 'em in the act, forget it. If a half-steady dog does get a bumper the bird boy just couldn't cover, meet the dog halfway, take him by his collar with obvious disapproval, and let him see you give the bumper to the bird boy. Then take him back to line by his choke collar, repeating "Stay!" several times during the trip, always snapping your collar to reinforce the seriousness of the command. Then take it again from the top.

Again, the quickest way to lick this training problem is to never let it happen once you start to steady a dog. That's why you throw in plain sight at the start; it's why the extra bumpers are kept in bags, so if the dog doesn't get the bumper he broke for he can't waltz over to where the bird boy was and pick up another.

Now that you've got the dog under control on the sending line and heeling to and from the line on a loose training leash, you've conquered the first of the two most demanding, necessary commands in yard training. The other sticky wicket is teaching to hold.

TEACHING TO HOLD

Steadying a dog is traumatic, but you cannot doubt the excitement of seeing a piece of clay take the shape of a real dog in your hands. Teaching dogs to hold what they are carrying contains none of that excitement. It's a dirty, nasty, unpleasant chore. But as carefully as you bring them along, few indeed are the dogs who sooner or later don't have to learn that "Hold it!" means, loosely translated, "Once you put your mouth around a bird or a bumper, Buster, land or water, the only place you may put it down is in my eager little hand!"

Since, as you may have gathered, I do not approve of nagging at a puppy or a green older dog because I feel that we must develop his enthusiasm before we concentrate on his manners, I never get in much of a swivet if puppies drop their bumpers at my feet. Because I have quick reflexes, I can usually get my hand under it and save the day. But I find it disgusting to shoot with a dog that litters the riverbanks with semi-retrieved game I am expected to track down and pick up. And if you are going to run field trial dogs, there are enough unexpected problems without having to wonder whether you are going to be quick enough to catch that slippery pheasant before it hits the toe of your boot!

Also, experience has proved to me that to ignore the dropping of game too long can usually cause other problems, which form a long chain of interrelated disobediences. Attacking this problem too harshly and/or too soon can spell disaster in many dogs; to ignore it, hoping it will "go away," is just plain foolish.

Unpleasant as it is, it can be 90 per cent solved in three or four days if you put your mind to it. Just make sure, as we have warned with other corrections, that your dog is emotionally ready for this kind of correction. Under five months, forget it, unless you have a veritable Einstein. But when the dog is dashing out and back with zeal, handling everything you can throw at him, but leaving bumpers all over the field, he is out of control. Your lack of control over him is holding him back, and the longer you wait the worse the sessions are going to be.

Don't overlook the fact that, like human babies, puppies too have teething problems. If you start with a wee one who has ordinarily been holding well and suddenly starts mouthing and dropping things, check his mouth—gently now! If his gums are swollen or perhaps you can see a tooth flapping, lay off your retrieving for a few days. Hand

him a nice big knuckle bone he can chew if he wants to and give
him a chance to grow a little.

The Difference Between Holding and Taking

Now, I am aware that some trainers and several books advocate
teaching all retrievers to take on command, whether or not they retrieve
naturally. I can see no sense in this. If the dog is already breaking
his neck to get out and retrieve (i.e., pick it up, take it when it falls),
I see no need to subject him to more force work, particularly when
it comes to something he is already doing. When I first started training
retrievers professionally, I did force-train or force-break three or four
gun dogs for people. These were dogs that did not retrieve naturally.
They would run out into the field if you threw something, and after
making sure it wasn't a T-bone steak or a squeaky toy, dash merrily
off to pursue other interests. Because I didn't know any better, I taught
these dogs to "Take it" on command, and I sent them home retrieving
because they knew darned well I'd make them follow through if they
weren't so inclined. Trouble was, in the first place, that as carefully
as I went into this with their owners, very few would descend with
unbottled wrath at the first refusal. It didn't take the dog long to figure
this out. Secondly, while some of these "wunderhunds" held together
while the water was calm and the sun was shining, they simply didn't
care to get sloppy, wet birds if the weather was unpleasant or the
cover difficult. They didn't have the natural desire which makes it almost
impossible for real retrievers *not* to retrieve.

After these artificially trained dogs began to fall apart, I changed
my mind about force training. If a dog didn't retrieve naturally, I suggested the owner either take the animal somewhere else or let me find
him a dog that could be depended on in all situations. It simply doesn't
pay off for trainer, owner, or dog in the vast majority of cases.

I have force-trained pointer and setter breeds and some flushing spaniels to retrieve *after* these dogs have been given a season of doing their
particular thing—finding birds. If the dog doesn't retrieve naturally
as some bird dogs do, force training to "take" is the only answer and
these dogs catch on quickly. Because the retrieving part is only a follow-
up to their actual jobs, they rarely backslide.

But a naturally retrieving retriever, in my humble opinion, should
be left alone. Why put in his head the notion that he has a choice?
However, forcing him to "hold" what he is carrying until *you* want
him to release it is essential with most gun or field trial dogs. So let's
get on with it.

Since this is an obedience-type, disciplinary exercise, it's out of the
field and into the garage or some secluded place again, just you and

the dog, with chain collar, six-foot leash, and training bumper. *There will be no more retrieving at all* until you know the dog will hold that bumper while sitting, lying, standing, and walking beside you, behind you, from water and on land. So don't start this exercise unless you mean to finish it, unless you are capable of following through no matter how rough things get. Half-trained in this instance can ruin a dog.

Step One

Have the dog sit with his collar on properly and his leash falling loose to the floor across his right shoulder. Now stand behind him with your feet spread so that the back of his head, if pulled up, will rest against your pelvis. Step on your leash with your right foot so that while it remains loose, the dog cannot get away by running forward; he can't back up because you are behind him. Assuming you are right-handed, tuck the bumper under your right arm. Now open the dog's mouth by pulling up with one hand over the top of his muzzle just behind his canine teeth and pulling down with the other hand on his lower jaw just behind his incisors (the fang-like teeth on the bottom). Once his jaws are apart, prop his mouth open with your left hand and pop the bumper into it with your right. Don't ram it in—roll it in just behind the fang-like teeth near the end of the upper and lower jaw, about midway into his mouth. Now here is the first important part: *Do not hold, or try to hold, the bumper in his mouth; repeat, do not try to keep him from dropping it by surrounding his muzzle with your hands.* Simply pop it in, tap him firmly under the chin with a brisk swat of your hand, and repeat very calmly, very firmly, "Hold it! Hold it!" emphasizing your vowel sounds. Now get your hands off the dog's head and away from his mouth and start patting him on the chest. Know what will happen? He'll drop it, spit it out! And that's just what we want him to do right now, because in order to learn this bitter lesson, you have to let him make the error so you can correct him, otherwise he will never grasp the difference between right and wrong.

Very deliberately and very promptly take his muzzle in one hand and swat him *hard* across the side of the muzzle, repeating "No, Hold it!" Now pick up the bumper quick and get it in place again—don't ram it home, just matter-of-factly place it as you did the first time. You will immediately notice that it is much harder to open his mouth following that slap. Again, that's just what we want. The tighter he clenches his jaws, the harder he'll hold that bumper when you do get it in position. Don't be of faint heart. Pry those jaws apart any way you can manage it and wedge the bumper in place. *Again, get your hands away!* Tap under the chin and repeat, "Hold it!" Then start scratching the dog's shoulder or side or anywhere on the animal away from his face. Watch him like a hawk. If he lowers his head one inch, tap under the chin again and repeat command. Always follow the tap with "Good boy, good boy." After the count of one-gobble-two-gobble during which, with your hands completely away from his mouth, he has sat still and made no attempt to spit the bumper, take hold of the end of the bumper and command, "Out!" and take it from him. Put the bumper on the ground and let the dog bounce around a few minutes and jump up on you. Now heel to another part of your training area and try it again.

One word of caution: you don't rip the bumper roughly *out of* his mouth any more than you cram it roughly *into* his mouth. The dog isn't going to open his mouth when you say "Out!" (or "Give!" or anything else you want to say), either. He'll simply slacken his hold enough so that you can take it with your hand. Don't stand there and hold it like a ninny, waiting for him to yawn so you can see his molars. The minute you put your hand on the bumper, take it. Then praise the dog.

This first session should end only when you can give the dog the bumper and stand up straight behind him, then lean over and pat his shoulder, then stand up straight again before you reach over and take it from him. If the job is proving more complex than you suspected at the outset, chances are you are to blame in two departments:

1. In spite of what I have been repeating, you are probably still trying to keep him from dropping it; your hands are probably still hovering around or swarming all over the dog's muzzle, and dogs hate this. *Knock it off!*

2. In spite of what I have been repeating, you are probably so worried you'll hurt the dog or break his spirit that you haven't really cracked him yet. If you don't get it over with now, my friend, you're just liable to ruin him for good. *Get with it!*

Sometimes this first session is a shoo-in, but don't get too big for your britches. Sometimes it's a battle royal, but don't get all shook up. Stay with it until you have made that important first point: that he is to hang on to that bumper until you tell him to give it up, or the results are not going to please either one of you. You will stay with Step One until he has "compromised" and done things your way. If you *do* get this step licked right off the bat, the rest of it will go smoothly and quickly and very painlessly. Until you do get it licked, nobody is going anywhere!

Step Two

Once you're absolutely sure about Step One, it's time to get moving around the dog. Start behind him as usual. Now move away so the dog is at heel on whatever side you're working him. Take your bumper. Give him his bumper while he is at heel. "Hold it!" Tell him to "Stay!" and move to the end of your leash, making sure you don't tangle that leash around the bumper. Return without wasting much time. Praise at heel, *then* "Out!" and take bumper. Praise.

Increase the length of your stays at the end of the leash. Stand beside him and wave your hands around. Run past him on either side, fast, always giving the dog a few minutes of bouncing recess at the end of each successful completion.

In preparation for getting him to walk with his bumper, have him stand while holding his bumper. This is accomplished by pushing down toward the ground on the back of the top of the dog's head while tickling his tummy way back by his hind leg. Watch that head, for when the head is lowered at all, as you may have noted by now, the bumper is liable to be dropped. Correct and leave the dog standing while you stroke his back. Release and praise. The next time have him stand first, then give him the bumper, then out.

Step Three

Step Three is to get the dog moving while holding his bumper. First pop his bumper into his mouth and give your holding command. Then, before moving one single step, slide the collar around his neck so the leash is located at the top of his neck. Either use a short traffic leash or wad up your training leash so nothing dangles or could come in contact with the bumper to encourage the dog to drop it; for the same reason, be careful as you move not to jar the bumper with your leg.

Give the heel command and start walking. Do so very carefully to begin with, cooing a lot of encouragement as you amble about. Give your "Sit!" command carefully and watch for a dropped bumper at this point—changes in pace or position throw green dogs learning to hold things. Do a lot of heels and sits, and pat the dog a lot in a jollying manner. Try a very careful come-fore (see the obedience section) watching where that lead goes when you extend it, and having the dog go directly to heel. Take the bumper and praise. In all steps, avoid overdoing the sessions.

Step Four

Now move into the field. If you can't count on the dog yet for long stays, put your helper to work. Give the dog his bumper with "Hold it!" and leave him, for instance, on one side of a thick stretch of cover, with the assistant holding him. Now call him with voice and whistle and have him come to heel. If he drops, race right out, replace the bumper in his mouth and lead him back to where you started. Repeat until perfect, and don't hesitate to encourage the dog as he's coming toward you. Pick different areas to work, looking in particular for places where a change in or a certain type of cover might encourage the dog to drop his bird. If at all possible, call him across a very shallow stream, which will be an excellent dress rehearsal for the most dangerous point for "Hold it!" training, which is—you guessed it—coming out of the water.

If you have had no problems with this exercise so far, you can count on them in the water. The most likely place you'll run into trouble is six feet before the dog gets to shore and six feet inland from the water's edge. To be very sure, plan on his dropping his bumper anywhere between the spot you leave him and your side! Leave the dog at a sit-stay chest-deep in water, with or without a helper. Give him the bumper and leave him. Stand on the shore. Call him and, when he's about two steps from you, start backing up and keep going until you are well up on the land. Should the dog stop to shake, don't rush at him and start screaming—you will make him drop! Simply repeat your "Hold it!" in a firmer but positive voice throughout the shaking, then encourage him by whistle and voice to come to heel. If he does drop, correct promptly, of course, shaking or no shaking.

Spend quite a bit of time on the out-of-the-water bit, as this is an exercise that will spare you much grief and save you many dollars in entry fees if you are trialing a dog; if you are hunting, it will save you apoplexy time and time again.

Remember, finally, each time he drops, *there is no excuse;* no matter how unfair it is to the dog, he must *always* hold. Start making exceptions—"Oh, he had an awful hold on the bird!" or "Oh, he stepped on the wing!"—and you'll be worse off than when you started. Gradually, as he goes along with the learning process, he will get confidence in himself through your consistent correction. When he drops anything—"No! (swat) Hold it!"; then, "That's a good boy!" (pat-pat-pat); then "Sit!" (and hold it while you pat and praise); and finally, "Out!" (pat-pat-pat).

When introducing new things, such as pigeons after bumpers, or ducks after pheasants, it is mighty handy to have a dog into whose mouth you can pop *anything* and who won't be disturbed by being asked to carry it around. It makes the transition from land birds to bumpers to waterfowl so much easier.

Delivery from in Front

In teaching any artificial command, the first thing to get across is the supremacy of the handler; things have simply got to be done his way or else. However, after the dog is proficient in holding, there is no earthly reason why he shouldn't deliver his birds as he is coming in instead of going to heel first. Many handlers prefer this approach delivery, but most will agree that how you do it depends upon the dog's needs, his temperament, and his intelligence. After all, the whole purpose of your being out there with him is to help him do his work as efficiently as possible. If I am working with a really high-strung dog that tends to vibrate and could easily start mouthing birds as he is settling himself into the heel position, then I generally take the bird as he gets to my leg and tell him to heel. Usually, using this system, you can count on a dog having shaken when he came out of water so that when he settles at heel all the incidentals are off his mind and he's ready for whatever may come next. If, however, he has a tendency to want to throw the bird at you on the fly, so to speak, and dash out into the field to see if anything else is cooking, you're better off to have him come in and sit or stand at heel before delivering. Play it by ear; the system that makes the most sense and hurries things along more smoothly for you and your dog is the one to choose and stick with.

DOUBLES

Getting Ready

The time when you practice serious obedience and yard work is the time to lay a foundation of prior planning for the coming double retrieve. When you reach the point where the dog will heel to and from the line and deliver to hand at heel or in front, it is time to progress further. There is a definite rhythm to handling a retriever. If you get the dog used to handling his single retrieves in a manner that will prepare him for any number of multiple marks, you will find you have spent your time well and will never regret it, I assure you.

Therefore, every time a dog delivers his bird, be it in front or at heel, never consider the test over until he is sitting at heel facing the field. Don't simply take the bumper from the dog and leave the line. The rhythm is (from in front or standing at heel): give, heel, sit. He is now in position for bird two or three, and if he learns to always finish a single in this manner, he will do so automatically on the first bird of a double and be ready for No. 2 bird without unnecessary delay. If he delivers sitting at heel, let him sit there a moment after you have taken the bird and look again at the field. Then it's "Good boy!" and heel back to the car.

This very small "gimmick" has saved me many hours of yard work with older dogs on complicated marking tests. There is still one more little "secret" you can handle with your yard-training obedience. That is moving the dog around on line. Sounds simple, doesn't it? Well, when an excited dog is facing in one direction and you want him to face another, there is nothing *less* simple on the face of the earth! If you practice doing this without distractions, when the real situation raises its ugly head at least you will feel more comfortable about insisting you be obeyed.

With the dog at heel and your leash wadded so that it is fairly short for easier corrections, turn to your right and tell him to heel, patting your left leg (if he's working on your left). Don't walk to your right; just turn in that direction and insist he do likewise. If he doesn't adjust himself so that he is sitting squarely by your leg facing the direction you are facing, snap that leash sharply and repeat your "heel" command, patting your leg.

Now turn to your left so the dog is sitting almost across you. Give the heel command and snap back on your leash, patting your leg. Don't move from your new position until you have directed the dog to exactly where he belongs. If he is stubborn, try bringing your right knee up and to the left, bumping him back sharply.

Keep changing your position on line in as many ways as you can think of, insisting that the dog adapt to each change and never forgetting to praise once the correct position at heel has been reached.

Where to Start

Just as most beginners fail to realize the importance of the single by oversimplifying it, so they tend to dread the double. They make it so complicated and confusing that the poor dog soon agrees with his handler.

If you repeat quietly, over and over, "The double is just two birds, the double is just two birds," before starting to train on double retrieves, it does a great deal for one's inner peace; as a result, the dog won't get unnecessarily upset either. Now, remember, "A double is just two birds!"

There is no point in starting a dog on doubles if you cannot control him on singles. By that I mean, if you cannot hold him (as in the case of a very young puppy) or if he will not stay beside you on a sending line (if he is old or advanced enough) to permit himself to witness the fact that two birds have fallen, you cannot expect to do doubles. Way back when we were discussing long singles, you may remember I suggested sending a very young dog back over the route of a repeated long single without seeing a bird fall; I also suggested the "Baby Blind" exercise of planting a bumper close enough so that when he delivered his long single he would see it and take right off for it—all this was in preparation for the double.

I like to start my dogs on short-line work and "baby blinds" when they are very small; the minute they have grasped the idea that it is OK to go on command, whether they actually saw anything fall or not, and provided they are controllable either while being held or on a sending line, I start doubles.

What Is the Purpose?

Granted, "A double is just two birds." But why? This is a question every beginner asks. The purpose of a double is to test a dog's memory. After he picks up that first bird, does he (a) remember there is a second, and does he (b) remember where that second bird is? Memory. Intelligence. These are what we are measuring when we give a dog any marking test involving multiple birds.

The double retrieve is handled in reverse most of the time. While there may be an occasion in hunting or a test in a trial requiring that birds be picked up in a different order, the trainer is wise to insist from the beginning that the last bird dropped is the first bird retrieved. Sometimes in trials, careless or very tricky setting up of doubles (or triples) makes it common sense to let the dog pick his own birds— that is, the order in which he will bring them in. But to permit this in early training is a mistake. It is essential that the dog never lose sight of the fact that his handler controls his work in the field; it is equally important that the handler know just what he can expect from his dog in a given situation. If the dog is allowed to do his thing the way he wants, there is no order or pattern to his work. The handler's control is compromised. He is not only at a complete loss to anticipate the dog's needs, but never knows what will happen when the dog takes off. The reason we insist upon the dog's picking up the last bird down first is really quite obvious and sensible: the last bird down is the one his mind and his eyes are full of. It's the last thing he saw. Unless he missed his mark and never saw that second bird, he is self-committed. So why confuse him? Send him for that bird. By the time he returns with it, his mind is clear, his desires are fulfilled, and he is fresh and ready to concentrate on the next retrieve.

Switching

"Switching" is a very misunderstood term. In the standing recommendations of the retriever advisory committee it is clearly defined as follows: "Switching birds implies that a dog gives up in his hunt after a search, leaves 'the area' and goes for another bird, or when he drops a bird he is retrieving and goes for another." The key words here are "the area" of a fall. In other words, let us suppose a dog has a bird down in the water to his right and one in some corn stubble on his left. His handler sends him for the left bird, but after running out a few yards the dog makes a wide arc and picks up the right bird first. *This is not a switch!* If, however, the dog had gone to where the bird landed in the corn stubble, had hunted unsuccessfully for some time, and then clearly said, "Oh, to hell with it!" and taken off for the water bird which he subsequently retrieved, *this would be a switch.*

When you begin to train on doubles you will have little trouble with switching if, at the outset, you keep your two falls spread wide apart. No matter how well trained in the back yard, most dogs starting doubles have a great yen to scoop up No. 1, which is really just a diversion bird, and then take off for No. 2, often referred to as the "money" bird or the "memory" bird, without pausing to "pass go." So in addition to keeping No. 1 and No. 2 birds spread apart, set up your early tests so that in order to get No. 2 the dog must come almost through you, the handler, first. You are even farther ahead of the game if you train by using the corner of a building as your starting place, or even the end of a long fence line. If the dog never learns it is possible to switch, he will probably not attempt it. If he does make an effort in this direction, regardless of age or experience, break it up then and there and most decisively. If using a bird boy, instruct him, in case of a definite commitment to switch, to remove or fall on that "money" bird, so there is nothing for the dog to pick up when he gets to the forbidden area. If working alone, it is very simple, as we said, to set up tests that eliminate even the most remote possibility of switching.

Starting Puppies on Doubles Alone

In warm weather, I favor starting puppies who are secure in the water by giving them one bird (the diversion) on land and the memory bird in the water. The chief advantage here is that the second bumper is easily seen riding high on the water, and you establish a positive reaction to going a second time; you also get over the hurdle of a "mixed bag" double (i.e., one on land and one in water), which seems to throw dogs until they have trained for it. (Remember that at trials there is usually also a change of game involved in this kind of a double.)

Lay in a pocketful of stones. Now, holding the puppy as you were told earlier, heave your first bumper out into the water with a moderate, well-modulated "Bang!" and, not throwing it too far, make sure he sees it. Then pick him up and turn him around so his back is to the water. Start swinging that second bumper around wildly, yelling all sorts of exciting things and holding the pup against you until he is just busting to get that second bumper. Let it fly at the same time you release the puppy, so that its momentum carries the puppy after it. Now cast a quick look over your shoulder to allow for drifting, and position yourself between the puppy and the water bird. The minute the pup picks up the land bird, call him with much noise and enthusiasm and watch like a hawk any intention to get by you. Never mind delivery or anything else. Collect the puppy and swing him around so he is facing the water, give him his "Back!" and let 'er rip. The moment his feet hit the bottom on his return, scoop up that second bumper and, swinging it wildly over your head, run away until the puppy catches you. Congratulations—you have just done your first double!

If the pup is a little confused, as has been known to happen, don't hesitate. Yell to attract his attention and then chuck one of those stones with a big splash next to the bumper. And *don't* be discouraged. Try it again, placing the memory bird a little nearer the bank.

There are dogs that simply never learn to remember a second fall, but I believe they are in a minority. And while some dogs always manage multiple marks better than other dogs, most dogs can be taught to handle a double if you are patient and if, in the beginning, you keep it very, very simple.

Doubles for the Older Dog or the Precocious Puppy

If your dog is working on a sending line, the procedure is very similar. You can do it yourself, if need be, but soon after the initial doubles, get to work with a bird boy. Sometimes, he throws the memory bird, and sometimes you reverse it. Just remember to make it impossible for the dog to miss at the start (one good way is to make the money bird the short bird) and to keep those falls wide apart. Whenever possible, use the corner of a building or a fence as a divider whenever you are working alone and both birds are going to be land birds.

When teaching doubles with a bird boy, first throw *your* bumper short and off to one side, with a very moderate "Bang!" Then have the bird boy make much to-do in waving and screaming prior to letting his bumper go, and make sure you release the dog while the bumper is in the air, which helps keep the dog's mind on the bird he is going for. Never mind that he'll probably beat it to the ground. One thing at a time, remember, and right now we're teaching doubles.

Have the dog sitting at heel on his sending line and let the bird boy do the work in drawing his attention to the second fall—don't push or shove at his head or try to force him around. We went over this "No-No!" in teaching singles, but it is even more important when training on two birds.

One of the most natural things for a dog to try, once he's far enough along to be using a sending line, is to spit that first bird at you and then take off for the second on his own. Nagging him into sitting just "so" and waiting until you are ready is as foolish as trying to hold him bodily from going after something he knows damned well is waiting for him. The first thing you can do to help him is to remember to be facing the money bird when he comes in with No. 1. The second thing is to restrain him only as long as necessary for him to collect himself without distracting him from that second bird. To help you in this, fasten your sending line to his collar just as you fastened it to your wrist. (We are going to assume this dog works from your left; translate all directions otherwise.) Then, when he comes in with No. 1 bird, take hold of the line, which means you don't have to snatch at the dog. If he sits to deliver, have him sit just as if this were a single; no matter in what manner, collect bird. Now take No. 1 bumper, or bird, in your right hand and tuck it behind your back just below your shoulder blade. *Never* take your eyes off the dog, as you must know exactly what he's got on his mind. If he's standing there riveted on that money bird, send him! If he seems a bit confused, have him wait until the dawn comes up and he remembers. If he is throwing his head, talk quietly to him, "Mark! Mark!"

The source of most "Double Trouble" is twofold:

1. Trying to send the dog too soon for the second bird, afraid he'll forget.

2. Holding No. 1 bird carelessly in front of you so that the dog literally runs into it as he crosses on the way to No. 2.

There is an exercise which will help both dog and handler to get over these pitfalls.

Put your bird boy armed with six bumpers directly opposite you in low cover where all bumpers are easily visible. Have him throw two birds, one way to your right, one way to your left. Send the dog for the last bird down. Turn toward the other bird. Collect No. 1 and send for No. 2. As soon as he takes off for No. 2, have your bird boy replace No. 1 bird the dog just delivered. Turn your back on No. 2 and face the replacement bird. As soon as you send him for this, have No. 2 replaced, and so on, until all bumpers are picked up.

The progression here is either

1. Deliver, to heel, wait and back, deliver, to heel, wait and back.

or

2. Deliver at heel, wait and back, deliver at heel, wait and back.

Whatever way you choose to work, do this over and over again, in sets of six (which works out to three in each direction), until you and the dog could do it blindfolded. This exercise is marvelous for teaching *you* to maintain control of your dog and letting you know he *is* under control. It's marvelous for the *dog* because he learns to rely on the same system time after time after time. It becomes a habit with him to do it right.

Practice this exercise on the land and on the water until both you and the dog know it by heart.

Approaching and Position on Line

Just as soon as you get the dog used to two birds, start concentrating on how you yourself approach doubles. The way you bring a dog to line, in training as well as in trials, has a great deal to do with how he ultimately handles that double. That brief hike between the waiting blind and the line can often do you in or get you through.

For instance, if you are faced with a long, difficult-to-see flier on your right and a very short flier on your left with guns standing out in the field like sore thumbs, heel your dog to line from the left side of the line, crossing in front of the judges and aiming the dog squarely at that long bird. He'll see the diversion guns all too soon; if you let him, he could easily freeze on them and miss the other fall completely. If, on the other hand, your long bird is easily in sight with guns very much in evidence on a thrown bird but the short bird is thrown dead in heavy cover and the guns aren't very obvious, show the dog both guns when you get to the line, but set him up so he's facing more to the short bird than to the long. When you have an equidistant, equally obvious flier and a dead bird for a double, show him the guns on the dead bird but face him more toward the flier. You never know where those little dears will go! Wind has a lot to do with how you set a dog up for a double; his personality has a lot to do with how you bring him to line.

The old rule was always to face the long bird, but it won't take the rankest novice long to figure out that that doesn't always pay off! Study the test before you run; try to figure out why the other dogs are failing or succeeding. Don't tell the judges you are "ready" until you have that dog positioned in a manner you feel will best assist him to complete the test.

Variations

While it is vital to practice doubles in your training, be extremely cautious not to train *only* on two birds. Go back periodically to your long singles. Even if you are getting ready for a working certificate where your double is your most challenging test, you'll rue the day you heard the word if you work exclusively on two birds. It doesn't take a dog long to realize there is more than one bird in life, and the first thing you know, his single marking is suddenly gone because as soon as one bird lands in the field he starts flipping his head in search of a second.

One of the best ways I know to teach doubles is to use two singles. For instance, have your bird boy throw a long single to his right and let the dog retrieve it. Now have him throw one to his left and let the dog retrieve it. Then, put them together as a double. I'm sure that by now you can see how we are using repetition to build confidence in both the dog and the handler.

It is also important to vary doubles so the dog doesn't get used to always having the long bird on the left and the short bird on the right, or vice versa. Some of these variations are:

ON LAND OR WATER

1. Two birds, equally long, one on either side of the bird boy.
2. Money bird to the left, long, No. 2 to the right, short.
3. Money bird to the left, short, No. 2 to the right, long.
4. Money bird to the right thrown by you, short, No. 2 longer, thrown by bird boy straight out in front of the dog.
5. Two birds, equally short, one on either side of the bird boy.
6. In very advanced training, narrower angles between birds.

Then mix your land and water falls as I explained earlier. If the dog shows any sign of catching on slowly to doubles, of being a bit hesitant on his money bird, go back to singles for a day or two. Then start again on doubles, low cover, beginning with two singles turned into a double.

You may remember we warned you earlier about learning to use the wind. Doubles call for a healthy respect for the wind and the damage it can do when a thoughtless trainer sets up a double in such a manner that on the way to No. 1 bird, the dog winds No. 2 bird. Be careful with the wind when training on more than one bird!

Setting up your own tests is one thing, but before you take off for your first trial or working certificate, spend some time running tests somebody *else* has set up. It makes a lot of difference in controlling your nervousness.

Be very careful as you go along, in the beginning especially, not to make your diversion bird so difficult that the dog *is* encouraged to give up and go for the memory bird; or, that he takes so long to find No. 1 that he's totally forgotten No. 2. If you are at all in doubt that the inexperienced dog has remembered the second bird, *don't send him!* Treat No. 1 bird as a single, take the dog off line, have No. 2 bird picked up and start again. Positive impressions! Confidence! These are the keystones to success.

It is also important, I feel, to mix your birds when running doubles— water birds on the water and land birds on the land isn't always the way the cookie crumbles. Many years ago I remember competing in sanction trials during which we used nothing but live and dead ducks. Talk about dogs getting confused! And now that we've brought up the subject of birds, let's talk about our feathered friends at length.

ABOUT BIRDS

There is, understandably, a great deal of static concerning the cruelty of retrievers to birds. It emanates from people who don't know what they are talking about—but I say "understandably," for it is difficult for an inexperienced person to imagine a great big dog carrying a little pigeon so gently that his feathers are barely mussed. And of course it is true that birds are shot and killed at trials, not for the amusement of trial people, as certain neurotic types will tell you, but in the interests of:

1. Educating the dogs in the correct handling of game.
2. Giving the dogs experience on the type of birds they may be expected to retrieve during their lifetimes as working dogs.

All field trials are dedicated to simulating as nearly as possible actual hunting conditions. To do this we need to use birds. I would draw your attention to the two rule books, or bibles, of the retriever world: one states, "Humane handling and care of game at a trial should be rigidly practiced"; the other, "A dog should be eliminated for hard mouth or badly damaging game."

Attitudes and Rules

I am often asked how I can justify the killing of birds so that dogs may retrieve them, or the use of live, shackled game during training.

I happen to believe in hunting birds. I know that if we never shot another duck or pheasant in this world we would soon be overrun with a population of feathered friends which were not in the best condition. Overbreeding would produce weakened specimens; the healthy ones wouldn't have a chance because the world, today, couldn't provide proper feeding areas or the right types of feed. Breeding areas would be overrun, and the young that did survive would not be strong enough to fend for themselves long enough to produce other healthy birds.

Now, then, if I am going to hunt birds, then I feel I should kill only those I can eat. A waste of game of any type is a crime in my book. Also, letting wounded birds drift or crawl off to die a slow, agonizing death does nothing for my morale. So if I go out hunting and wing a duck, I want my dog to be able to bring that cripple back to me so I may put him out of his misery humanely, and so that his death contributes food for my table. That's how I justify the use of birds.

In Canada, due to the intervention of humane societies throughout that country, the handling and use of game are rigidly supervised. If shackled ducks are thrown on the water, they are wrapped heavily with masking tape not only to make all falls uniform but to protect the birds from being bruised by stumps or stones as they fall, and, of course, from being ruffled by the dog that retrieves them. This is all well and good. I do not approve, however, of the practice and manner of putting to death, in the name of kindness, those birds with perhaps only a broken wing or a twisted leg: the examining humane society officer who stands on line at the trials in certain areas of Canada places them in a wooden box attached to the exhaust pipe of his car. This is a stupid and criminal waste. Ducks heal beautifully if given a chance, and I can see nothing humane in smothering something to death because it isn't perfect. As I said earlier, all birds used on land at Canadian trials are killed prior to the trial by a method which at least retains their entire bodily form and makes them much easier for the dogs to handle.

In the United States, licensed trials require that in a specified number of tests the guns must shoot to kill, on land and water. Most sanctioned trials give your dog the opportunity to work on "hot" (freshly killed) birds on land and shackled ducks on the water. It is very wise to practice using all three kinds of birds before reporting for a trial or a working certificate test, or showing up in the duck blind or shooting field.

Variety Is Essential

Do not be lulled into believing that one type of feathers will suffice in training for all kinds of birds. A dog who picks up frozen ducks until the skies fall down may be expected to turn up his nose at his first freshly killed Mallard. Some dogs do very well adapting to pheasants and ducks, but have to be really convinced that the lowly pigeon in any state is worthy of his notice. (Chesapeakes particularly quite often display a haughty disdain for pigeons.) A live shackled duck on the water is one thing; a loose duck on land with only his wings shackled is quite another. Loosely shackled ducks which can swim enough to teach a dog the mysteries of outwitting crippled game should certainly be used to prepare for trials or hunting.

Hunting dogs need experience on all sorts of birds. Doves, for instance, the moment they are killed seem to lose entirely all scent. Even experienced retrievers will trip and stumble over doves unless one is thrown for them several times before setting off on a dove hunt. Chukar partridge, which have been used in trials a few times (and threw a great many dogs!) are easy for a dog to find and their feathers are easily handled by young dogs, but their take-off can startle an experienced human, so be careful introducing pups to partridge hunting. Ditto quail. Pheasants, as we said earlier, are "soapy" birds, which a dog cannot carry by the feathers alone as he can often carry ducks. And a crippled pheasant runs like a deer and fights very effectively with his sharp spurs; again, be careful of starting green dogs on a crippled pheasant. The same holds true for a crippled goose. Nothing is much stronger or nastier than a wounded honker, and I've seen green dogs really set back by sending a boy to do a man's job. Geese are hard enough to handle stone dead. Many seasoned duck dogs will turn their noses up at the so-called "fish ducks" which smell fishy because of their piscatorial diet. Brant are good birds to give a dog early training preparatory for goose shooting, as they are a smaller edition of the goose. Jump-shooting rail birds in the swamps is exciting and excellent for pepping-up bored dogs. But again, whenever possible, make sure the dog knows what he is going after before cutting him loose in a strange situation. After a season or two, of course, he won't need such priming.

Humane Handling of Live Game

Ducks and pigeons can be used live over and over again if proper care is given to their tying, handling, and carrying, and if caution is exercised to make sure they are not used too often during one session. Pheasants are hysterical birds and their nervous systems do not make it feasible for them to be used shackled. I have seen more than one shackled pheasant curl up his spurs and die out of sheer fright as the dog approached him.

In the spring and fall, birds kept purely for training purposes must be handled with consideration, as their feathers do not contain the oil that wild birds' feathers have, and they are most susceptible to cold water. In cold weather always rotate your shackled game quickly and religiously—use twelve ducks on one test, for instance, and then have twelve more ready so that the first twelve can be unshackled and returned to a crate out of the wind and weather. Keep your birds sheltered, with grain ready for them when not being used.

In the very hot summer, make sure the birds are not left tied for long periods without water. Rotating, again, makes common sense both for the birds' welfare and your pocketbook. In between work sessions, ducks in summer should be kept in the shade, with water available for drinking at all times.

These weather warnings apply equally to pigeons and ducks, which, incidentally, can be crated together.

In proper shackling lies one of the keys to continued reuse of live game. Do not tie birds' legs so tightly that you cut off circulation either in wings or legs. And remember that all birds' legs are very fragile; don't handle game by the legs, which will snap easily; carry all birds by the wings up close to the body—and by the wings themselves, not by the shackle.

Shackling

String should never be used when shackling game—nor should twine or anything that cuts. Pipe cleaners are strong and do an excellent job. They are also easily removed. Electric tape is popular. I am partial to strips of old sheeting, which are soft and strong. When tying, be sure to make three knots. You will find that bored ducks waiting their turn to work will untie each other! Always have a knife at your belt when using game, so that in case of emergency a bird may be unshackled quickly.

As we warned earlier, always take a bird count going out to work, and a bird count when you are through training.

Tying birds goes easier with two people, one holding, the other shackling. However, it can be managed solo, and here's how to handle a duck (pigeons are done the same way). Clamp the duck between your legs with a strip of sheeting in your mouth. Now slide the sheeting under the wings way up close to the body; wrap it around the wings twice and knot three times. It is not necessary to pull it as tight as you can—simply tight enough so the bend of each wing is adjacent to the other. Now take another shackle in your mouth and turn the duck upside down between your legs. Hold the body with your legs as you pull both his feet out, *gently,* so they are straight from the body. Loop the sheeting twice around the legs and knot three times. Now put him in his crate or burlap bag.

Containing Shackled Birds

Incorrectly used, burlap bags can become death chambers, for prolonged carrying of a lot of birds in one bag will cause many of them to suffocate. When using bags, put not more than six ducks or ten pigeons in one bag. While shackling and loading the birds, leave the bag flat on the ground and slide the birds in as they are tied, so they are all lying on the bottom of the bag covered by the top. Only when ready to move immediately into the field should you carry the bag by the mouth. When you get to the field, lay the bag flat again and shake it until the birds are all lying flat on the ground. In the extreme heat of some summer days, it is wise to empty the birds out of the bag and then cover them with the entire bag; the ground is cooler and there is more ventilation.

Incidentally, when carrying unshackled birds in bags, the same rules apply. When you put the bag down in the field, make sure the open end is tied or your foot is on it firmly before shaking the birds to separate them.

When taking a shackled bird from a dog in a trial, hold it firmly and do not under any circumstances throw it down on the ground. If you want to get it out of your way (in a double, for instance), tuck it up behind your back until the dog has gone for his second bird. Then turn quietly and hand it to the bird boy behind you on the line, or the line marshal or the judge—whatever has been previously established as desirable. In an effort to be helpful, lots of bird boys and marshals tend to reach for the bird the moment you get it, and dogs have been known to be hopelessly distracted. When you come up on line, state clearly that you will give the birds your dog retrieves to whomever is elected to take them from you, and that you do not wish hands reaching for them otherwise.

In training, make certain to put down, gently, on the ground, about three feet behind you, all birds as soon as they are delivered. Teach your dog from the word go that birds behind you, live or dead, are not to be touched. This will save you endless correction and nuisance in the shooting blind.

Keeping Birds for Training

It's easy to maintain a few ducks and pigeons in a wire crate for training purposes. They may be fed cracked corn, stale bread, and greens you might otherwise throw away. One dishpan full of water will allow your ducks to bathe, but you'll find you have to change the water frequently. Attach small water cups up higher for the pigeons, and broomsticks run through kennel wire make fine perches. Using an empty kennel for a bird run is dandy as long as you don't kennel a dog next to it without separating dog and birds by a solid barrier.

Finally, the use of dead or live game should be carefully regulated with green dogs lest they decide they like feathers so well they reject bumpers. Too many birds too soon can take the edge off a dog or make him extraordinarily hyper, depending upon his personality. I like to use birds with young retrievers about three times a week, no more. I usually yell "Bang!" with bumpers and save my training pistols and shotguns for live game—for obvious reasons.

Use of Dead Game

In introducing dogs to game, dead birds are your best bet, and you can usually beg, borrow, buy or "liberate" them from trial clubs after events. Pick the least mutilated you can find—ducks, pigeons, and pheasants. Lay them out so that their wings are folded flat against their sides, their feet pointing toward their tails. Now wrap them in plastic and freeze them solid. They can be used over and over again if handled in this way. I have found that small pups or hesitant older dogs do quite well when introduced to pigeons which are still solid from freezing but not too cold to handle. While they are still quite rigid is the time to use them for "Hold it!" training.

You can beg birds from hunting acquaintances. And as you drive along the highways every now and then you'll see a pheasant or a pigeon that tangled with twentieth-century traffic and lost.

Dead game is eminently easier to keep and handle than live, so most people use dead birds for most of their training. But let me repeat again a word to the wise: before trialing or shooting or going for a working certificate, be sure to practice on the other kinds, too!

Women and Birds

There seems to be something about birds, live or dead, frozen or shot, that turns off an awful lot of ladies. They love retriever training and are excellent handlers or trainers, but some of them just can't *bear* to touch those birds!

I have always regarded this as nonsense. But, since I am unreasonably afraid of snakes, I can hardly pooh-pooh other people's idiosyncrasies. For years in teaching retriever clinics I doggedly insisted the gals handle their own game. This proved universally unsuccessful, for those who were really in terror would close their eyes, clench their teeth, and grab at the last minute; not only did they often miss, but their hours of "Hold it!" training went by the boards. Finally I capitulated and agreed there had to be some form of compromise.

We have found that, in the summer months, rubber gloves such as those used for household chores do a splendid job. Not only do the ladies relax more with their bird handling, but the nonskid gloves help them hang on better too. In the winter, slip plain cotton glove liners on, then a pair of rubber gloves one size larger than you need over those. The combination is warm, and the first lady to drop her bird is a rotten egg!

FINISHING THINGS OFF

From puppy training to yard training, from sending line to check line, from canvas bumpers to Canvasbacks, from singles to doubles on water and land, from Sit-Stay to Stay Put to Get Back—we're just about at the point where you can start polishing up your act to get ready for shooting, field trials, or bringing home that working certificate. From this point on, you'll learn nothing new, only variations on an old theme. Where you go with your knowledge is up to you.

Those of you who are primarily interested in a shooting dog will be split into two camps: some of you will want that dog steady to shot or else; some of you want the dog to bust out of the blind and get back with the bird the fastest way possible.

The field trialer will have to insist that his dog not run the bank; the working certificate trainee won't have to be quite so fussy about such niceties; and the hunter usually doesn't give a darn—fast out, fast back again is the watchword.

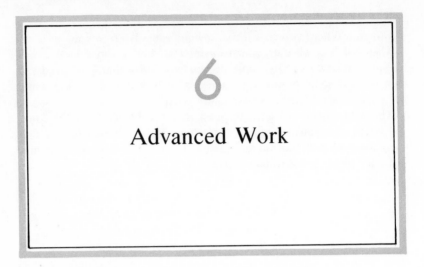

6

Advanced Work

THE BASEBALL DIAMOND SYSTEM

As noted earlier, this book is not going to delve into the intricacies of grown-up blind retrieves and hand signals. But I have not mentioned the common exercise of training for field work by using the baseball-diamond system, because I find most novices just can't wait to try it. Once they do, they can't wait to see if it really works in the field; and as I've said before and will repeat, introducing hand signals too early is a peachy way to rob a dog of his desire to mark.

However, while it is true that dogs have to be allowed to develop their noses and the confidence to hunt on their own, it is equally true that there are hunting situations where the only way to get a dog to a bird is to handle him because it is impossible for the dog to see where a bird has fallen. It doesn't hurt the gun dog, the field trial youngster, or the working certificate trainee to learn his directions from a distance, provided his handler is smart enough to keep handling in the back yard only and out of the field until the dog is ready for this kind of serious work. If you are going to trial your dog as a Derby in sanctioned or licensed trials, then lay off handling him to marks until he is almost through his second year, when he will move into qualifying stakes, which include tests designed to start seeing how the high-school kid will handle to blinds in strange situations. Every once in a while there comes along a dog—I've known exactly two in my lifetime—who is brilliant enough to be winning or placing in Open All-Age Stakes at the same time he is tabulating scores to make him high-pointed Derby dog of the year. There is a small possibility that you have one of these dogs—but the possibility is *so* small it isn't worth mentioning. Remember the rule we gave earlier: You can always retrain tommorow, but you can't always untrain!

In a trial situation or a working certificate setup, you may be unfortunate enough to be faced with the decision of trying to handle a dog to a fall he has obviously not seen or has completely forgotten and by so doing either secure that working certificate or capture a J.A.M. Out there alone on line it's up to you whether, at that moment, it is more important to stick to your training or to win recognition. You're damned if you do and damned if you don't. Of course, if the dog refuses the whistle, you're out anyway!

Let's face it, handling is very important to all retrievers. Also, let's face one more thing—all marking and nothing else makes Blackie a dull dog. So we're going to give you the rules for playing baseball with your retriever. It can be stimulating, fun exercise for you both. It is certainly a further means to your control of the dog, and of gaining the dog's increased respect for the ingenuity of his handler. If it goes wrong through misuse, my friend, the blame rests squarely on your shoulders.

Many people recognize that there are three directions you can send a dog from a distance: right, left, and further back into the field or water. The fourth direction, come in nearer, is all too often ignored and is one of the reasons we warned you earlier never to use your whistle to call your dog to you for correction. How many, times have I seen a dog a few feet from a bird refuse a come-in whistle because he clearly said to himself, "Oh God, now what have I done wrong?" We're going to train your dog to handle *four* directions from the very beginning. You will need three pieces of equipment we haven't mentioned earlier, because I didn't want you to think about handling until now. These are called (by me) handling boards, and constitute an aid in encouraging green dogs to relate hand signals to direction of the signals.

Take eight pieces of board of any kind measuring roughly twelve inches by twelve inches. Paint them flat white. Now hinge four pairs together at the top so they will fold flat for carrying and will stand up when spread at the bottom. They will be set up at first, second, and third base of your theoretical baseball diamond, and just in front of home plate. Your dog will work from the pitcher's mound, which will be located on a straight line between first and third base, and directly opposite second base and home plate, where you will be standing.

The dog wears his choke collar and is on a six-foot training leash. Get under way by taking the dog out to the pitcher's mound. Using voice and whistle, have him sit and tell him to stay. Now, being very sure he is watching you, make a big "thing" out of walking to your right and placing the bumper beside the handling board at first base, where he can clearly see it lying there by the marker.

Walk back to the dog, pick up the leash and face him at the end of it. Since from the beginning of teaching any dog to handle we want to associate the sound of the whistle signaling him to stop with the fact that he will be given a direction to the bird by his handler, we are going to preface every direction we give with the whistle command to sit (or stop). So, standing there facing the dog with your right hand extended stiffly toward the bumper and held no higher than your shoulder, give a short, loud blast of the whistle. The moment he looks in your direction, snap your wrist and point toward that bumper and take several steps in that direction at the same time you command "Over!" The minute the dog starts out, drop the leash; if he hesitates, jerk the leash in the direction of the fall. Keep pointing and walking until he takes off. Then much praise and much approval.

The key phrase in the directions given above is "the moment he looks at you." It seems almost impossible to convince novice handlers starting hand signals that if the dog isn't looking he can't see the direction you are indicating. That's why we have you working so close to the dog to begin with—so he is very aware of you. If the dog is swinging his head from side to side or if he is riveted on the bumper and refuses to look at you, move in closer and talk to him, calling his name. The main reason he is on leash is to prevent him from taking off without your command. This is a very important moment in your handling training; *don't cheat yourself or the dog!*

Everyone trains differently, but I believe that if a dog spins around and gives you a three-second look-see and you flip him a quick wave of your hand, you are liable to miss each other completely. This is why I want my dogs to turn around on a whistle command and stand or sit; when they do so they will see me standing like a scarecrow in the field indicating which direction he will ultimately go, *but not until I have told him to do so!* In my opinion, this gives me the power of telling the dog twice what he is to do without giving a double command. Start this way on your diamond, and I guarantee your dog will take direction quietly and well.

Repeat your sending of the dog for that right bird until he gets the hang of it. But as you stand like a right-armed scarecrow in front of him, use your leash to make sure he doesn't take off until you move in the direction of the bird. Then drop your leash and let him fly.

Another confusing thing amateurs tend to do is emphasize the direction they want the dog to take so forcibly that *both* hands go out at the same time, one to the right, one to the left—it's a wonder more dogs aren't cross-eyed! On your right "Over!" keep that left hand holding the leash folded across your tummy or hooked in your belt. On the left "Over!" tuck the right hand out of sight.

When giving directions to a retriever from a distance, make sure you are clearly outlined and that you keep your spare hand against your body to make your directions as clear as possible.

The command for "Back!" on a baseball diamond can be particularly confusing if you are not scrupulously careful with your arms. Many of our Canadian friends use both hands high over the head to indicate further back to a dog on a blind. I favor one hand only, using that hand nearest the direction of the bird. But one hand or two, you *must* give that "Back!" with your arm or arms *straight up,* as if you were reaching for a trapeze bar directly over your cranium. Do not bend forward as if to point to the distant spot you want the dog to reach, because (remember the dog's eye view of marking?) the dog, at a distance, cannot see such an arm movement, hidden as it is against your body. Reach for the sky, pretend someone has just held you up. And if you are using only one hand, remember to hide the other against your body.

The "Come in!" command is indicated by making a backward pulling motion near your leg with the hand nearest the fall (one only, remember!).

Teach only one direction at a time, adding new directions carefully to avoid confusion. Stay on leash until you are certain the dog is not going to take off before you command him to do so, and always, *always* preface every direction with the stop or sit whistle. When the dog is commanded "Back!" he is to go to second base; right "Over!" he goes to first base; left "Over!" to third base; and "Come In!" means he will approach a bumper placed between you at home plate and the dog on the pitcher's mound.

USING HANDLING BOARDS

SECOND BASE

THIRD BASE

PITCHER'S MOUND
(where the dog is positioned)

FIRST BASE

HOME PLATE
(where the handler is positioned)

There are many variations you can dream up to keep this exercise challenging and to increase your control of the dog. Move into the field as soon as he's letter-perfect in the back yard, and take along your sending boards. Use them until he's taking straight, true casts, then fold them up for the next dog, but be ready to use them at any sign of indecision.

Set up a diamond on water using a submerged shooting stool if necessary, so he can watch you and take your directions. When you get him swimming you'll have to give your directions more quickly, as a dog can tread water only so long!

Mix up a land-and-water diamond, give "Overs!" through ditches and backs across roads. Put a bumper out to his left and let him see you do so; now place a second bumper directly in front of him about two steps from your feet as you stand about eight feet away from him. Hit the stop whistle and make him go left. Plant a bumper to your right and a "no bird" beside him on the other side. Force him right. Put a bumper on either side of him as he sits at pitcher's mound and make him go back for a bumper you have put at second base. Put him beyond pitcher's mound and call him in to the mound, stop him, then send. Keep your leash on until you have won these arguments. Winning them now will speed you on your way at trials or in the duck blind faster than you can imagine.

To give your dog confidence in long water casts, lead him on a right or left "Over!" with small stones always about ten or twelve feet ahead of him. After three or four stones, pitch the bumper or bird in the same line.

FINAL STEADYING EXERCISES

Steadying, as I said earlier, depends upon your personal needs. If the dog is going to run in trials he has to be steady; he gets no extra points for steadiness at working certificate trials, and if you take a chance and he breaks, he may miss his marks and fail. But all retrievers should be steady enough to sit still for bumpers and for birds. We'll give you some steadying exercises for trial dogs, and the rest of you can use just as much of them as you deem necessary. Remember, now, these are final steadying exercises. They are *not* for puppies or older dogs starting out. They are to be used as a last step when the dog is at the very least reliable and secure at heel on a sending line.

The Walk Up is a marking and control test that dogs can expect after getting out of Derby stakes. However, it is an excellent training exercise for steadying. You will need a bird boy, half a dozen bumpers, dog, chain collar, and six-foot training leash. Station the bird boy out in a field of low cover. You start much further back than you intend to retrieve. Give the command "Heel!" and start walking toward the bird boy. When you nod your head he is to start yelling like a banshee and throw a bumper high and away from him, either side. The minute the bird goes up, give the command to sit and stay. Jiggle your legs to try and get the dog to break. If unsuccessful, count to three, gobbling, and send dog.

Start again and have the boy throw two bumpers, one at a time, very near each other—it doesn't make any difference which one is picked up, as they are close together, but we don't want to encourage switching areas. Insist the dog remain steady. Work up to four bumpers in one tight little pile. Now start over—remembering to caution the bird boy about scooping up that bumper if the dog breaks! Give your leash a healthy snap and command, "Stay!" Remove leash and collar, putting them on the ground. Start off with directions to throw *one* bird. This exercise does as much for your confidence as it does for the dog's control. That should be it for the day. At each session start on leash and then gradually work up to the four falls off leash.

This same exercise is excellent on dead and shackled game, and it can be quite effective for steadying on the water.

HONORING

Honoring is another excellent way to steady and is a training "must." Working certificate dogs don't honor, but they can benefit from this training as much as gun and trial dogs can.

As we explained in our glossary of terms, honoring means that after a dog has worked a certain test, he must sit on line without physical or vocal restraint and watch a second dog do the same test. The minute your dog is old enough and experienced enough to be working on a sending line, it is always a good idea to make him honor at least a single each time he has finished his last retrieve. In the beginning, do so behind the line (so he won't disturb the other dog in training) and use your leash, not the sending line, so that if he breaks he may be corrected.

An excellent steadying exercise is to work two dogs together, each with his own handler. One bird boy stands behind the dogs who are at heel a few feet from the water's edge. Agree in advance which dog is to go for the first bird. Then give the command to stay and signal the bird boy to pitch a bumper smack over the dogs' heads, splashing it down about twelve feet in front of them with much screaming and yelling. Try to make them break as we instructed you earlier, leashes loose enough to be touching the ground. Send the first dog. The minute he connects with the bumper, heel your dog off line and around, patting and praising, until dog No. 1 has delivered. Now back to line and it's the other dog's turn to work.

Alternate this test, also, with dead and live game. In the final stages, set one dog on the shore, on leash to begin with, and have a shackled duck thrown near him. Then send another dog from behind him, unexpectedly.

Getting off leash is hard; throwing away that sending line is traumatic. Removing all restraint is positively earth-shattering the first time it occurs. It is also liable to leave you with egg on your face, and since it is almost impossible to stop a committed young dog, here is the place to trot out that air pistol.

Remember how we held our hands across the tummy when we first started steadying on leash? Well, this is a good position to assume while honoring or working a dog until it comes time to send him; and to get him used to your negative body position, hold that air pistol

The honoring dog, on the right, sits quietly without vocal or physical restraint on the part of his handler, watching the working dog. This is the highest form of control work. The honoring dog is supposed to be fully aware of everything going on in case the working dog fails to complete the job. In an actual hunting situation, he would then be pressed into use.

Three alert, controlled retrievers wait their turn to work as a fourth hits the water with enthusiasm. This "multiple honoring" exercise is to be attempted only in advanced stages of training. Too much of such control work too early can confuse a puppy and take a lot of his enthusiasm away forever.

in just the same position. Your leash and collar are off now, remember. If the dog breaks, snap off a few shots as soon as he is away from your side. He will probably "Kiiiiyiiii!" Quickly repeat heel and stay commands again. When the dog is in position, praise and then send him. Run the test again. Rarely is it necessary to sting him a second time in one training session, though it may be necessary to repeat the correction during later sessions.

The beauty of the air pistol is twofold, The dog doesn't resent you, and having once been stung, will often stop at a distance if you only fire into the air. The little "ping!" instills powerful memories!

SERIOUS LINING AND HAPPINESS BLINDS

The lining work we started with baby puppies should never be ignored. Using a just-run marking test to teach lining is a fine idea. Setting out with one dog and three bumpers, leave the bumpers, with the dog's knowledge, in a pile while you retire to various distances and send the dog. This is a simple exercise with much value. You could, for instance, throw three bumpers close together into the center of a pond. Now, as you walk around the pond with the dog, stop and pick up those bumpers, each time sending from a different distance and angle. Once you have planted the bumpers for a few days with the dog's knowledge, go out and plant them in exactly the same places before bringing the dog into the picture. Start closer until you're sure he's as sharp as you think he is.

Flipping out the hand nearest your dog on a mark is not what we mean by giving a line. This action is a quick indication of the direction of the retrieve, giving an added boost to your vocal "Back!" The *hand*, here, *re-emphasizes the dog's forward motion* and then is returned to the side.

In lining, the *dog follows the line of the hand.* Now, in order for the animal to realize the direction you are indicating he should take, he must be literally able to sight along your finger or hand lying alongside his muzzle, between you and him, and extending forward of his muzzle a short distance. Many things are invented by handlers to make it clear to the dog that he is about to negotiate a blind retrieve as opposed to a mark, and to get him jazzed up so he'll start off strong. One system is to hover over the dog repeating "Dead Bird, Dead Bird!" That seems to make sense to dogs trained that way. Others seesaw that hand out and back, out and back, until, when they finally send the dog, he is exceedingly eager. Whatever method makes sense to you, fine; invent something of your own. I like my dogs, when being lined, to come up into a standing position from the sit so they are really ready to run. I whisper anything exciting I can think of and keep cocking my hand at the distant point I'm aiming for until I think I have the dog's complete and absolute confidence and attention. When you send on a blind, follow through smoothly, not down toward the ground, but out toward that distant place in the field and up as the dog leaves the area of your hand.

Once a dog is steady to shot and as absolutely obedient as a retriever ever gets, you can expect him to sit still while you stick that hand out to launch him as straight as possible. Until then, it's good to use your sending line attached to his collar and held across your stomach in your free hand so he doesn't go too soon, necessitating your calling him back. I think it's quite obvious that a dog called back repeatedly will soon decide there isn't much future in trying to go.

Happiness blinds are the best way in the world to teach lining, get distance, and build confidence. Again we're working in a unit of threes, and we need a well-schooled bird boy completely hidden about seventy yards straight out. Remember that the success of this test lies in not having to open your mouth to the bird boy. He must be perfectly clear about what you want him to do.

Face the dog directly at the hidden bird boy and fasten your sending line through his collar. Now stick your lining hand—the one nearest the dog—out in front of the dog and tell him "Watch it, now—what's coming?" in an excited whisper. Keep that hand next to his eye, your fingers a bit beyond the end of his nose, When you think he's really with you, keep whispering but nod your head. At this signal the bird boy will start hollering "Bang! Bang! Bang!" The dog will come up on his toes at that sound, mentally and physically. Send him toward the noise with a positive "Back!," dropping the sending line. Just before he arrives at "Hernando's Hideaway," have Hernando throw the bumper in a straight line between himself and the dog. Hernando is to stay hidden at all costs!

As the dog is returning, get back a few more yards to lengthen the next line. This second time, since the dog has already been the route once, we're not going to have anybody make any noises. Just line him up carefully and send him on his way. Make sure your bird boy understands that the moment the dog looks unsure, he is to throw high. Otherwise, he's to wait until the dog is almost on him before throwing a bird for him in the place the first bird landed. As the dog returns to you, the bird boy is to replace the bumper without the dog catching him in the act. You, of course, have backed up even further. The last happiness blind is cold turkey: no bangs, no thrown bumpers. But he's been there twice now, and the first two should see him through. The bird boy should be ready with a spare, emergency bang if the dog starts to slow down or veer off his line. This is one of the most effective exercises known in the lining department.

The success of any blind retrieve depends largely on the line the dog is given. So take plenty of time to direct his attention in the *exact* direction you wish him to go. He must be physically positioned so that his body follows his head in a direct line to the fall. *Photo by T. and R. Phillip*

He cannot be expected to follow the line of your hand or arm unless that hand, or arm, leads him a bit. It's like sighting down a gun barrel for the dog. It takes time and practice to know just the exact moment to kick him off, the precise moment when his concentration on that desired line is as exact as yours. *Photo by T. and R. Phillip*

At the exact moment of take-off you "know" whether or not the two of you hit it just right. But a stylish, purposeful take-off is half the job done. The more decision with which a dog goes out on a blind, the further his clarity of mind will carry him. As his mind and body move forward, so should the handler's. *Photo by T. and R. Phillip*

In order not to jeopardize that good, positive cast, the handler should follow through with body, mind, hand, and arm. Now your job is to keep your eyes glued to the dog to make sure he keeps going and to watch like a hawk for signs that he is running out of confidence. But again, that send-off on a blind is the most important part of the whole retrieve. *Photo by T. and R. Phillip*

FINAL TIPS

No matter what you plan to do with your dog, train for that specific occupation under as nearly actual conditions as you can find.

Field trial and working certificate dogs run in series. So as soon as the dog gets into the swing of it, train in series. Run him in one test, then put him up; run him in another test, then put him up. Exercise him between every single series, training or for real, and when you first get to the trial and when you are through for the day.

If your dog is going to be your hunting companion, then take him often to your blind to train him, if you have a blind of your own. Working him there when it's unbrushed makes it easier for him during the season when it's brushed up proper. If you aren't this fancy, find a place along a riverbank or beside a pond where you can pull down some old tree limbs or dead branches and make yourself a little natural blind for him to get used to. Because you'll use decoys and guns more than at trials, train that way.

There are times, incidentally, when you are required to shoot over your own dog at trials (never during working certificates). You are supposed to make an honest effort to get the bird, but you are always backed up with two qualified field trial guns. Therefore, particularly with very inexperienced dogs, the thing to do is to shoot (pull the trigger) when you hear the bird go up and never take your eyes off that dog. But as soon as the dog knows about such things, you can, if you like, knock down your own birds. Incidentally, ammo and a gun are always provided in these instances, but you may use your own equipment.

Hunters should always have a few stones in their pockets to help young dogs get through their first few tricky retrieves. And in starting a hunting dog, don't take him out all day, every day—work up to it gradually.

While you are not allowed to throw anything to help a dog at a trial or a working certificate test, once the dog is obviously lost you are not under judgment any longer, so a judiciously placed stone is very much in order for young dogs. In licensed and sanctioned derbies and working certificate stakes, both judges and bird boys usually stand ready to do anything within reason to make sure a dog doesn't quit without a bird. Don't be too proud to ask for help—it could save you weeks of back-up training. Just don't expect the trial to come to a screeching halt while you and your dog spend a half hour littering the working area with falls from birds he refuses to pick up.

If you wind up with a field champion you have trained yourself, you deserve the highest praise for your dedication and your perseverance. If you can manage only a working certificate, you should be no less proud than the hunter whose table is groaning under the game his dog has put there.

No matter "wither thou goest," just remember to let that good working dog know you are proud of his accomplishments; and see to it, that when he's lying in his kennel at night, the tales he spins for the other dogs tell of his pride in you.

With time, patience, and a little elbow grease you can make a passable retriever out of just about any dog. But it takes a real dog to make his man or woman into a handler; still, it has been known to happen!

7

At the Field Trials

GETTING THERE

Instructions for getting to dog shows seem simple when compared to those for seeking out field trials. It's one thing to pull into downtown Cleveland and ask a pedestrian, "Where is the Municipal Auditorium?" It is quite another to studiously follow the retriever club's home-drawn map directing you to "the junctions of Route 76 and Rural Route 11 near the Sweet Valley Interchange of Interstate 92 and Clifton Pike, where field trial signs will begin," only to look up and discover that at 5 A.M. you are at a dead end facing what appears to be the eleventh hole of a private golf course. There is no one to ask except a sleepy cow in a pasture off to your left.

Allow yourself plenty of time for such crises, and even more time to get from the perimeter of the trial grounds to the exact pond or corn field where the trial is being conducted at the moment. In the case of game refuges which often host trials, the information that the event is going to be held at Bombay Hook only refers to the sign at the gate. It could take you a half hour *more* of driving to get where your stake is being run!

I must confess, all joking aside, that compared to dog shows, working certificate meets, and obedience trials, clubs hosting sanctioned and licensed trials are far and away the most efficient about signs and directions. The vast majority of the time, the field trial committee changes arrows diligently whenever the field moves to a new hilltop or pasture, and many clubs leave behind at tricky places a forlorn but beloved person who parks in a conspicuous spot ready to give all sorts of intelligent information.

Canadian licensed trials are sponsored by the world's most considerate, helpful people. If you arrive the night before, generally one room in the motel designated as Field Trial Headquarters is open all night. There is always coffee, sometimes more interesting beverages, sandwiches—and all sorts of directions and other information. I like to think it's a congenital trait, this attitude of the Canadians that they are glad, repeat, glad you came to their trial!

Of course, nothing's perfect and there are clubs on both sides of the border which hold their trials at the same place year after year. After a while it occurs to some of the more casual members, "Lord, by now everyone knows where Pine Orchard is!" This is very true in the case of the regulars who turn up at all retriever events; it is a wee bit tough on the newcomer who is coming to Pine Orchard for the first time and, for some weird reason, wasn't born knowing that all you have to do is go to Jake's red barn and turn left!

Last-minute arrivals mean frayed nerves and, with entry fees and the price of gas climbing steadily, it doesn't make sense to spend these monies foolishly. "Oh, Cynthia, what in the world do you want to leave so early for? You known they've got to finish the Derby before they start Open and they've got fifty-two Derby dogs!" Such advice comes under the heading of Famous Last Words. I was once a trial marshal when, out of thirty starters in the Open stake, exactly six were called back for the second series. Just think what *that* did to those running in the stake to follow!

FIELD TRIALS ARE DIFFERENT

Those of you who are used to dog shows will find that field trials are very different! Instead of sitting at a dog show inside a stuffy building trading opinions on what blankety-blank judge was bought by what so-and-so exhibitor, you can elect to attend a field trial where you huddle together in all extremes of temperature, early and late, wet and dry, up to your ankles in mud or your elbows in burdocks, and trade opinions on what blankety-blank trainer ruined what so-and-so dog. Rather than worrying whether shows are better than trials, or trials are more honestly run than shows, why not just admit we're all a little nuts and let it go at that?

WHEN YOU ARRIVE

Once you arrive at the trial, find the Field Trial Chairman, the Trial Secretary, or the Chief Marshal. Sometimes these people wear buttons.

Otherwise, look for short nails and a glazed eye! If they are all occupied, try for a member of the Field Trial Committee or any one who looks as if he or she had done this before. Try to get a copy of your field trial catalogue, which is free, some sort of idea of how long it is going to be before your stake is called, and if it is going to take place in this or a distant area.

You will run in the order you are listed in the catalogue, and the number opposite your name will be your number for the day. You are wise to repeat your number to the judges each time you go up on line, for absentees can make things confusing. You may be asked to run out of order or without much warning if someone has to run another dog in a separate stake, or is being called back for a rerun, or if a dog ahead of you breaks. So be prepared.

After you locate the trial and the area, have your catalogue, and have determined the other information you need, drive off again far away from where dogs are running and exercise your dog. Water him if necessary and make sure he moves his bowels and urinates. Do any refresher work you think necessary. Then return to the trial grounds. I suggest you park your car containing your dog well down the road from the line. It will mean more walking for you, but it will also mean a quieter, less-excited animal when it comes time to run.

It might be a good idea here to advise you that field trial traffic, as a rule, moves as a unit. On the little country roads that lead to most trial areas, there isn't room for cars to pass or turn around; also, in wet weather, tearing up dirt roads by too much unnecessary driving bogs down any trial and annoys landowners. Following each test, the Marshal will inform everyone whether the field is moving or staying put. If the former is true, you will be told to follow, for example, single file behind the bird truck. These instructions are meant to be obeyed and are strictly enforced. He who careens through the middle of a test scattering dogs and handlers right and left is apt to find himself in a heap of trouble! At the very least, the resulting confrontation could be horribly embarrassing.

ETIQUETTE

To save yourself embarrassment of any kind (who needs it?), here is a list of *don'ts* which should serve to keep you out of hot water:

1. Don't exercise your dog in a field adjacent to the one in which dogs are running, in case they might need that field to hold a test. If in doubt, ask.

2. Don't let somebody talk you into "one little drink" to calm your nerves. You're liable to wind up trading in your wits for no butterflies!

3. Don't slam car doors, talk loudly, blow whistles, or rustle papers near where dogs are running.

4. Don't leave motors running where exhaust fumes could creep into somebody else's car.

5. Trial people are very ecologically minded—don't litter unless you want to be rudely called to task for your sloppiness.

6. Never stand up straight to watch a handling test if you are directly behind the handler; for the dog's clarity, his handler must be the only silhouette on the horizon.

7. Don't clap for a dog until he is entirely through his work and off the line.

8. Don't try to pet dogs coming from or going to the line; don't ever offer them a tidbit.

9. Don't waylay a handler coming from or going to the line with a dog; if you have a question, follow him until the dog is put away and then ask him if he has time to talk to you now or later.

10. If you should hear the frantic call "Loose Dog!" and it goes streaking by you toward the line, by all means tackle it if you can and hang on. If, however, a dog picks up a bird and for some strange reason comes to you with it instead of to his handler, freeze. Don't look at the dog, reach for the bird, or make a movement. Try not to breathe!

11. Small children, uncontrollable kiddies of any age, and family pets have no place at field trials. There is live ammunition going off and a great deal of nervous strain all around; either leave these beloved appendages at home or stay there yourself if you can't bear to be parted from them.

PROCEDURES

Field trials are run in series. After the completion of each series, or test, the line Marshal will take the "call backs" from the judges and announce them clearly several times for everyone to hear. After the last series—a stake can run anywhere from two to seven series, depending upon a lot of things!—the Marshal will announce, "The Derby Stake is now over." As soon as the judges have made their decisions, the result of that stake will be announced, usually starting from the bottom and working up, although this is not always the case.

If there is to be a formal dinner presentation of awards, the results will be announced on the spot, but ribbons and trophies will be handed out after the cold coffee and hot ice cream.

Judges (see your rule books for their qualifications as they change from country to country and stake to stake) have in their minds a theoretical perfect score of ten. Some judges score, on a double for instance, ten for each bird; some score five. Before each dog runs, the judge draws a quick line sketch of the test. As each dog is running he follows its progress with his pencil as he watches it with his eyes. In case of dispute, a judge can show you his sheets to help clarify the situation. If you don't understand why you were dropped or failed to place, ask politely immediately after the stake before the sheets are scrapped.

In case you have a justifiable grievance, ask the Field Trial Committee to rule on it. They will know how to handle it and advise you.

Weather can make things just as rough for retrievers as it does for show dogs and obedience competitors. Deadly hot weather can kill, as we explained earlier, and dogs running hard and long, swimming, climbing, and jumping in high temperatures need extra consideration.

Park in the shade, leave doors and windows open. (People who keep trial or working certificate dogs loose in cars are beyond me; again, get, borrow, buy, or make a crate!) Cool water should be available before and after running, but not in large quantities. Ice cubes make good substitutes. I never use bedding for retrievers in the summer; they don't want it because it makes them warmer. Use any of the tricks we suggested in our dog show section for protecting dogs from the heat.

In the fall and winter, cold, wet dogs are a problem. Keeping the car heater running sometimes helps, but never run your motor near another car, or in your own car with the tailgate down. Exhaust fumes ruin noses and kill dogs. In the winter I always carry a burlap bag full of fresh dry straw, hay, or cedar bedding. I set out with the dogs dry and snug and make no attempt to change them during the trial; it may be damp, but their body heat warms the moisture in the bedding. But when I get to the motel or before I start home, while the dogs are getting a last run after having been fed, I clean out my crates, removing all wet straw or whatnot, and replace with dry. Then and only then will my own personal inner genii let me sleep! And dream of the happy day just past or, perchance, happier ones to come.

At Last

Write a book! Write a book! Write a book! I've been hearing that for years and years. "Write a book, for gosh sakes!" people scolded at handling classes. "You really ought to write a book, Martha!" they insisted at obedience clinics. "Hey, somebody ought to write a book about this—why don't you?" my retrieverites kept at me.

Maybe they were right. So I started scribbling. It was not to be a short-term project! There were always dogs to wash or birds to tie or jumps to paint. Shows had to be attended, obedience matches and sanctions had to be judged, picnic trials needed organizing. I made notes on the backs of field trial programs and dog show catalogues. I wrote memos to myself and lost them. I misplaced clippings I saved and found others. I wrote down field trial ideas in the pouring rain with my pen and pad inside a plastic baggie for protection. When I dried out the paper, I couldn't read what I'd written for mildew! I used a tape recorder for a while, but the batteries were always running down at the wrong minute. I decided I'd never get it done; worse yet, everyone else was finishing books and publishing them. Very discouraging.

"When will the book be finished?" asked those hardy souls who believed fervently enough to keep me going. "Next spring," I replied, "next summer, next fall, soon, soon—" Excuses. I never thought, really, that I would get it done. Not in this lifetime, anyway.

And all of a sudden on a gray afternoon in Woodstock, New York, here I sit eying rather suspiciously, and a little bit weepily, a ragged tower of yellow and white typing paper, stuck together with Scotch tape and paper clips. It looks very much as if I have, indeed, written a book.

Between this awesome moment and the publication, my book will be pruned, blue-penciled, clarified, smoothed, and indexed. But in these raggedy pages right now is everything I know about dog shows and show dogs, obedience titles and obedience dogs, field trial retrievers and gun dogs. Certainly I don't know all there is to know by a long shot. But every single sliver of what I do know is finally down in black and white.

I give it to you, my doggy friends, to help you, guide you, teach you, comfort you, amuse you, hold you down, and give you incentive. Sometimes as I attacked the typewriter keys, I laughed with the good memories until the tears ran down my face; sometimes other kinds of tears splattered over the pages.

My way isn't the only way, but I believe honestly it is a good way. Whatever knowledge I possess I share here with you—my fellow professionals, amateurs I have met along the way, clients, friends, enemies, good judges, bad judges, and my competition, without all of whom I would have learned absolutely nothing.

I hope it will help you to dislike mediocre dogs a little less, to value good dogs more, and to recognize the difference.

I would like to think that when you have gained some particularly useful bit of knowledge you would feel an obligation to pass it on, as I always have felt, and as others apparently have in helping me, keeping the chain intact. Sometimes it is difficult to remember that we would all remain beginners forever if someone didn't hold out a hand to steady us in rough cover, or offer a boost up when the chips were down.

In particular, I would wish for you my greatest blessings—the privilege of a comforting paw, the cheer of a wagging tail. May you at least once know the disappointment of that awful moment when a good dog lets you down; it will prepare you, in part, for the once or twice in life when a dog you didn't have much faith in went "all the way."

Now I think I shall go for a walk with Kimmy, Casey, Rasputin, and Prune. Because they are dogs, I can weep as much as I want. Humbling in the extreme, isn't it, that those I love so much are least impressed that I have, finally,

Written my book!

The author "takes five" with her own gun dog and brood bitch, Quick-step's Kim Again, W. C. This photo was taken when Kim was seven years old. The age of the handler is immaterial! *Photos by T. R. Phillip*

Index